The Complete Book of Drawing People

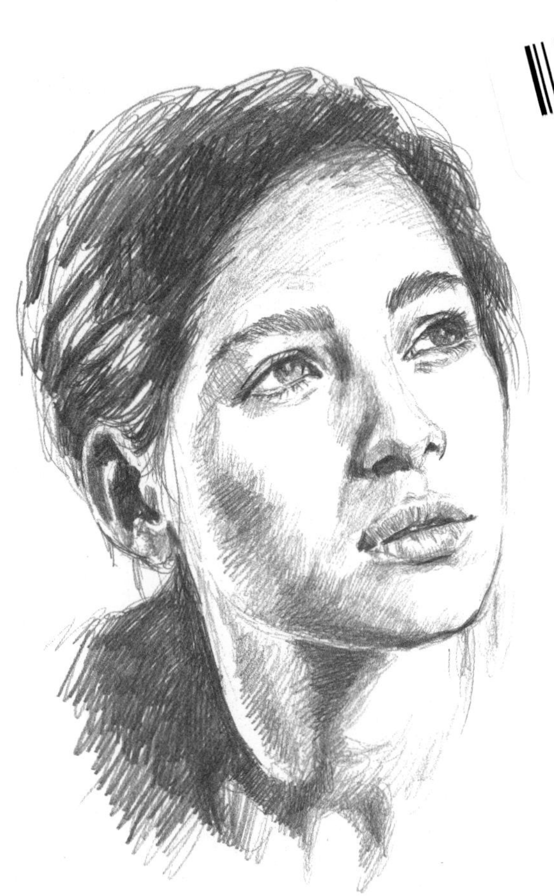

The Complete Book of Drawing People

BARRINGTON BARBER

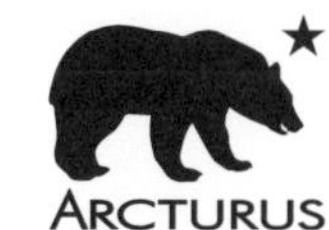

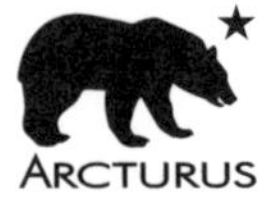

This edition published in 2019 by Arcturus Publishing Limited
26/27 Bickels Yard, 151–153 Bermondsey Street,
London SE1 3HA

ISBN: 978-1-78950-576-4
AD006649UK

Printed in China

CONTENTS

Introduction

Drawing people is both the most satisfying and the hardest subject for artists. The huge variety of people to draw and the potential to introduce an emotional element into our work makes humans fascinating subjects. However, because of our close connection with other people, it's easier not only to follow our preconceptions rather than relying on observation, but also then to realize we have got things wrong. Drawing people may be a challenge, but I have found in many years of teaching that anyone can learn to draw anything competently, with the combination of a certain amount of hard work and the desire to achieve success.

The aim of this book is to explore all the practices necessary to achieve a good level of drawing people. The first chapters are intended to ease you into the subject and build your confidence, while the following chapters will explore both portraiture and figure drawing in greater depth. Portraiture is a form of art that's fascinating for both artist and viewer. Catching someone's physical likeness is a particular skill and managing to convey something of the sitter's character as well marks out a great portrait from a merely good one. Don't be deterred if at first your portraits don't look very much like your subjects, since this field is one of the most difficult for drawing. Keep at it, and with practice and hard work you should eventually be able to produce good likenesses of your sitters.

The human figure is one of the most interesting, most subtle and most taxing of subjects to draw. There are many approaches to this field of drawing, and we will progress from simple sketches of clothed figures to studying the bone structure, musculature and the unclothed human form. The hardest thing to show accurately is movement, and I have dedicated a chapter to capturing the range of human movements, from body language and gestures to running and sports.

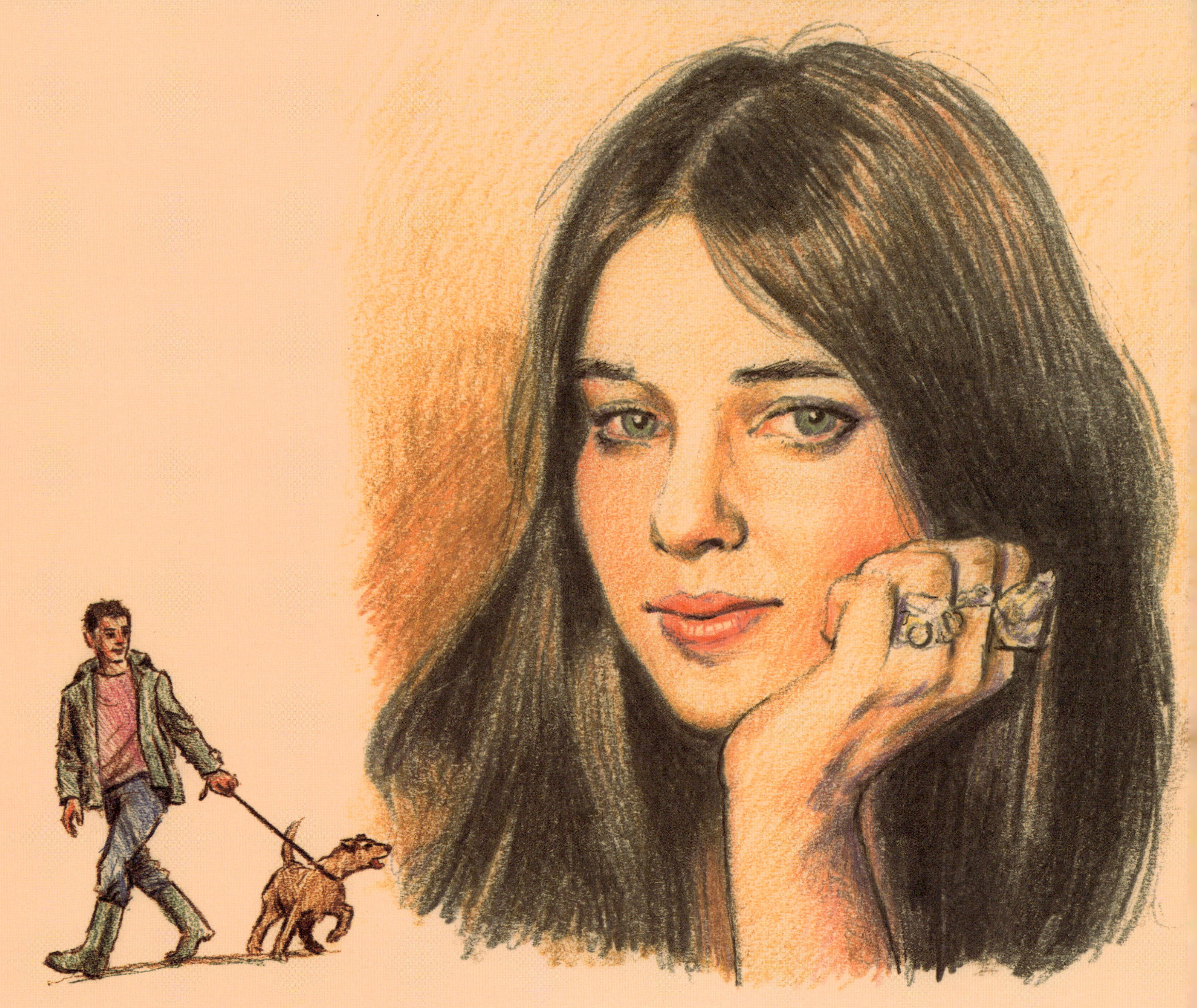

Drawing Materials

The first thing to consider before you start drawing is your choice of materials. There are many possibilities and good specialist art shops will be able to supply you with all sorts of materials and advice. However, here are some of the basics to start with.

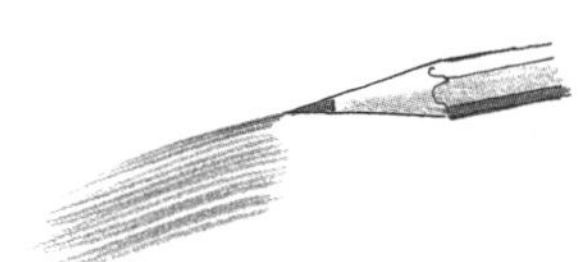

Pencils, graphite and charcoal

Good pencils are an absolute necessity, and you will need several grades of blackness or softness. You will find a B (soft) pencil to be your basic drawing instrument, and I would suggest a 2B, 4B, and a 6B for all your normal drawing requirements. Then a propelling or clutch pencil will be useful for any fine drawing that you do, because the lead maintains a consistently thin line. A 0.5mm or 0.3mm does very well.

Another useful tool is a graphite stick, which is a thick length of graphite that can be sharpened to a point. The edge of the point can also be used for making thicker, more textured, marks.

An historic drawing medium is, of course, charcoal, which is basically a length of carbonized willow twig. This will give you marvellous smoky texture, as well as dark heavy lines and thin grey ones. It is also very easy to smudge, which helps you to produce areas of tone quickly.

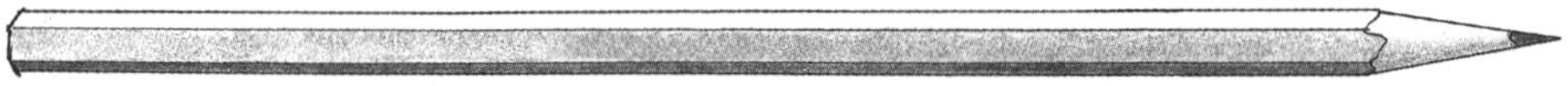

B (soft) pencil

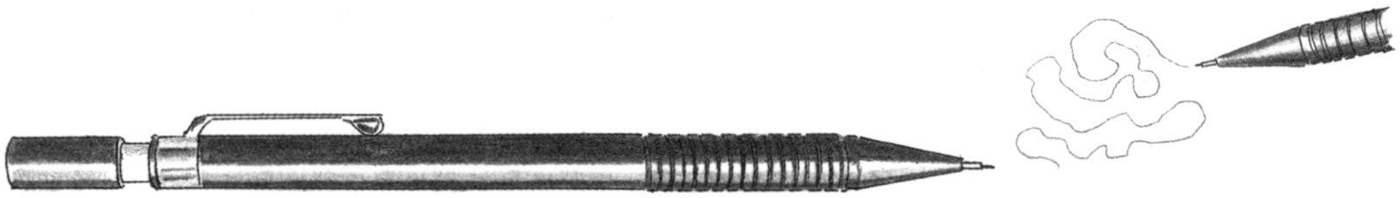

propelling or clutch pencil

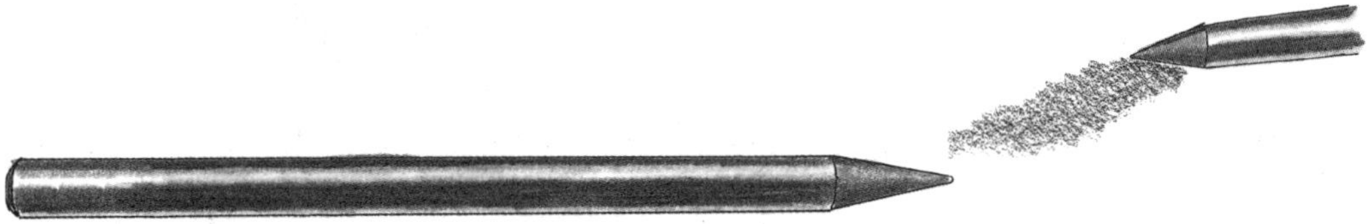

graphite stick

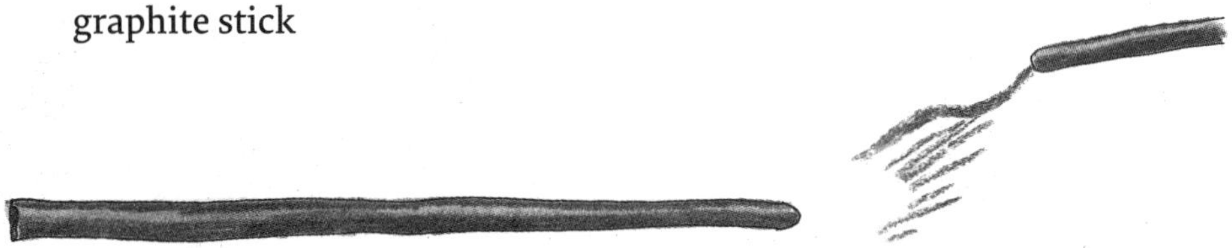

charcoal

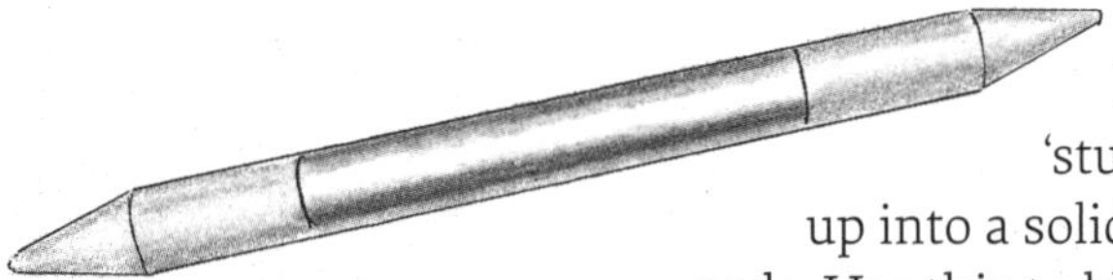

stump

Now for an instrument called a 'stump', which is just paper rolled up into a solid stump and sharpened at both ends. Use this to blend tones in a drawing – it produces very gradual changes of tone quite easily.

Pen and ink

Next, take a look at the various pens available for ink drawing, a satisfying medium for many artists. There is the ordinary 'dip and push' pen, which requires liquid ink and can produce lines both of great delicacy and boldness just by varying the pressure on the nib. With this you will need a bottle of Indian ink, perhaps waterproof, or a bottle of liquid watercolour.

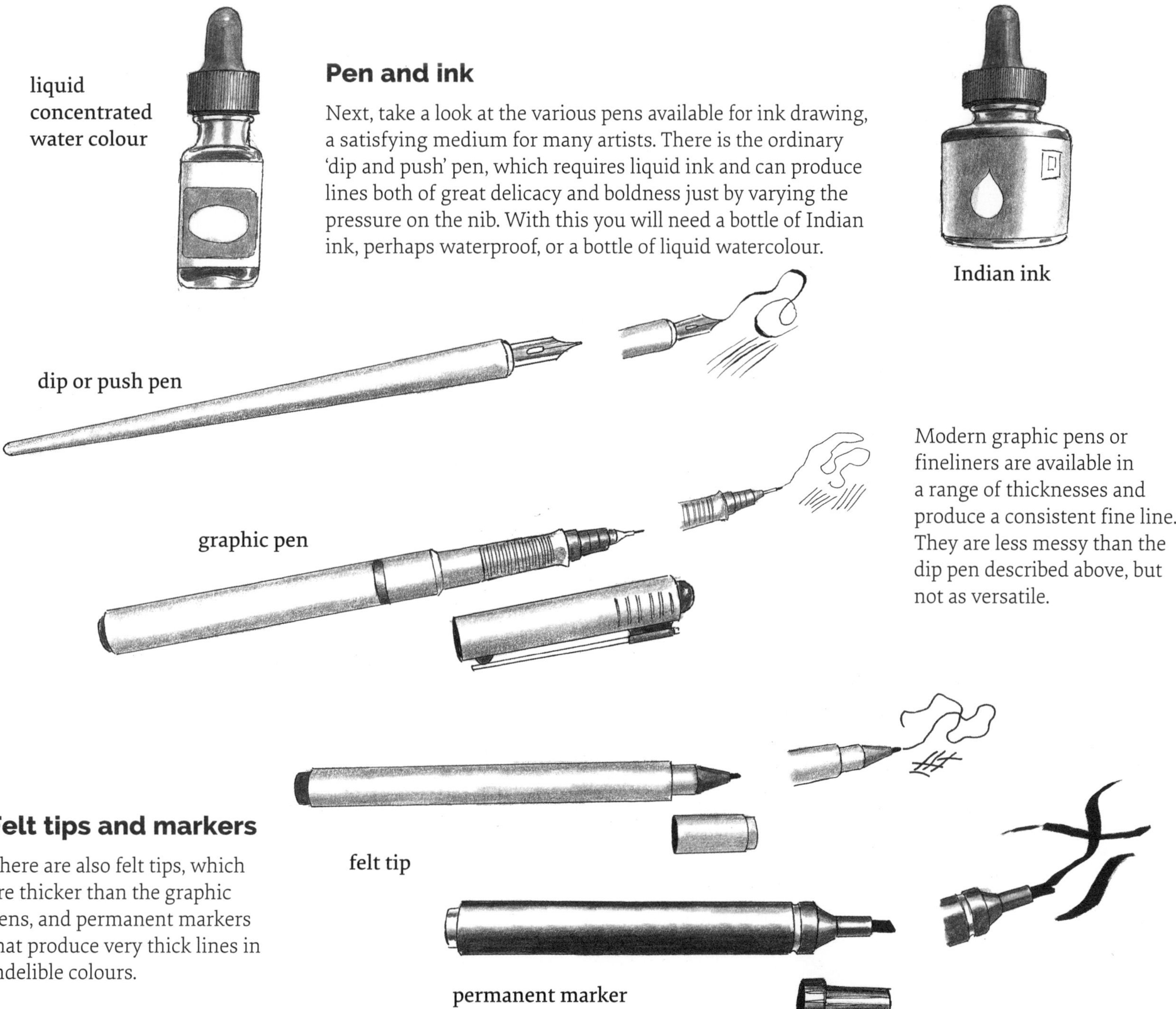

Modern graphic pens or fineliners are available in a range of thicknesses and produce a consistent fine line. They are less messy than the dip pen described above, but not as versatile.

Felt tips and markers

There are also felt tips, which are thicker than the graphic pens, and permanent markers that produce very thick lines in indelible colours.

Brushes

If you wish to work in brush and wash, you will need a couple of brushes of different thicknesses; I find that Nos 2 and 8 are the most useful. The best brushes are sable hair, but some nylon brushes are quite adequate. Use your brushes with a liquid watercolour as shown on page 9.

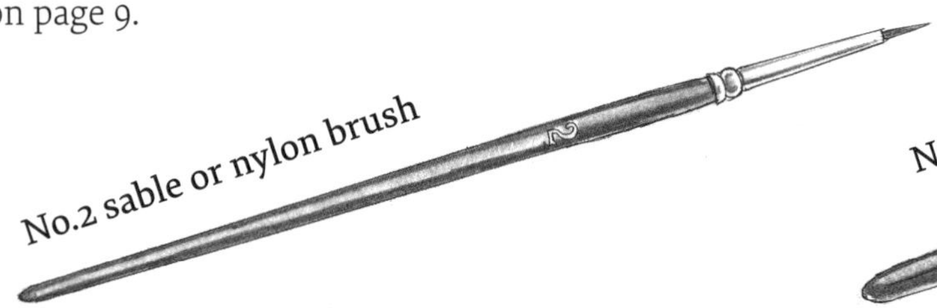

No.2 sable or nylon brush

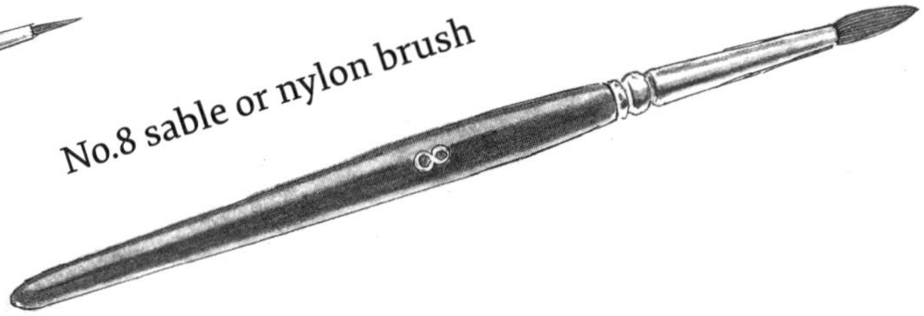

No.8 sable or nylon brush

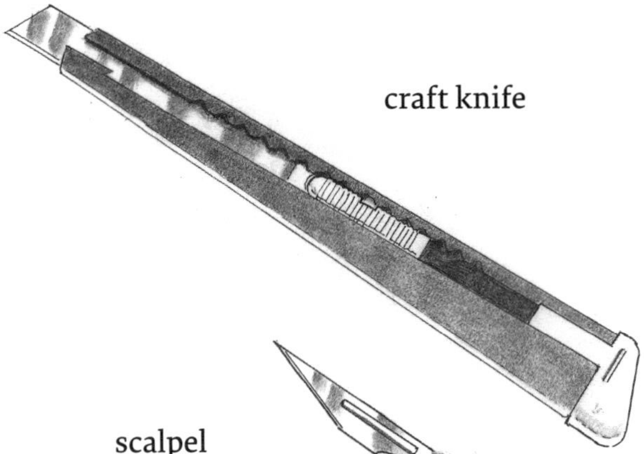

Erasers

When using pencil you will almost certainly want to get rid of some of the lines you have drawn. There are many types of eraser, but a good solid one (of rubber or plastic) and a kneadable eraser (known as a 'putty rubber') are both worth having. The putty rubber is a very efficient tool, useful for very black drawings; used with a dabbing motion, it lifts and removes marks leaving no residue on the paper.

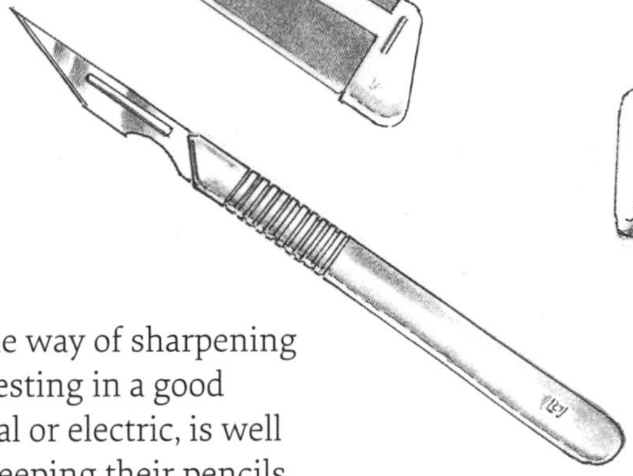

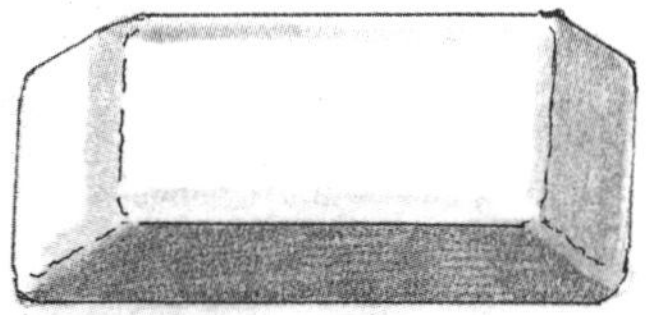

craft knife

scalpel

soft rubber eraser

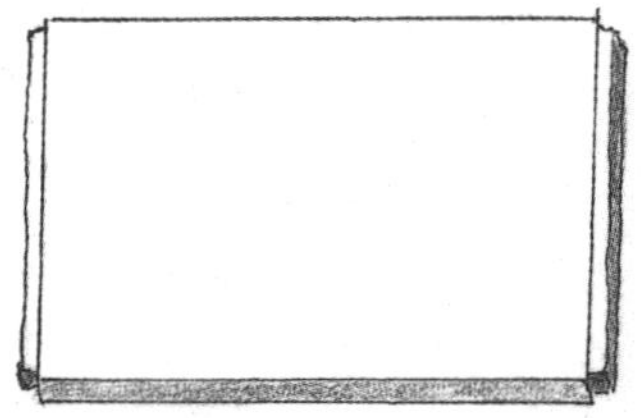

putty or kneadable eraser

Sharpeners

Don't forget you will need some way of sharpening your pencils frequently, so investing in a good pencil-sharpener, either manual or electric, is well worth it. Many artists prefer keeping their pencils sharp with a craft knife or a scalpel. Of the two, a craft knife is safer, although a scalpel is sharper.

Working in Colour

Throughout this book I have shown examples drawn in colour and, as you will see, colour can add an extra dimension to your work. If you enjoy working in colour, experiment with some of the options shown here.

Felt tip pens and illuminators

These pens allow thicker, more solid areas of colour to be put on quickly and are useful for larger drawings.

Coloured pencils

Don't concern yourself too much with the brand, although some are better than others. Go for as many variations in colour as you can find. Thinner pencils can be of superior quality but that is not always the case. Try them out and make your own judgement. Watercolour pencils are similar to ordinary coloured pencils but you can use a brush with water to spread their colour over larger areas. There are several brands available.

Fineline graphic pens

These pens are good for drawing and behave similarly to a coloured pencil but with a more intense colour value.

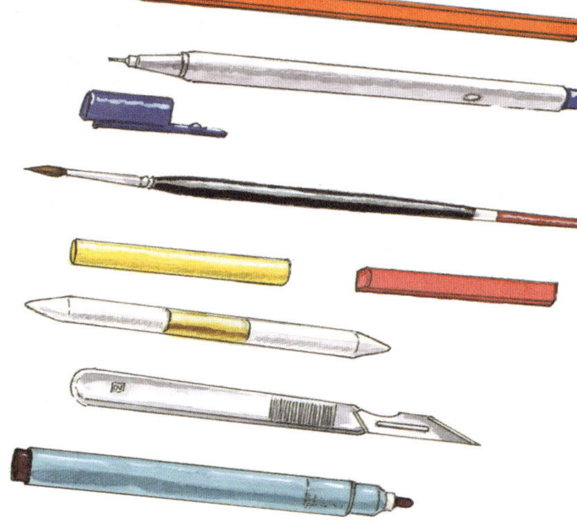

Soft pastels

These come in a wide range of colours and are very useful if you want to spread or smudge your marks. However they are very expensive and tend to get used up quickly.

Hard pastels

Also known as conté crayons, these are essentially the same material as the soft ones but bound together in a compressed form. Hard pastels are square in section whereas the soft ones are round. They last longer and are easier to manipulate. The range of colours is again enormous.

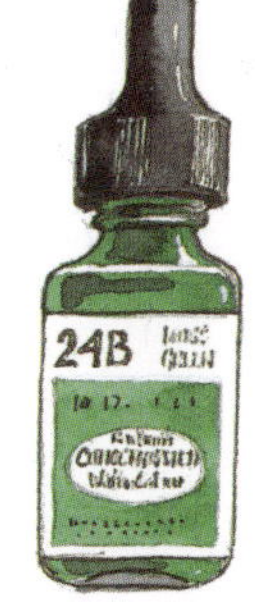

Liquid watercolour (concentrated)

These colours are just like ink but may be diluted with water. They can be used with a pen or a brush.

Watercolour box

Watercolours are easiest to use from a box but they can be bought in small tubes as well.

Chapter One

PROPORTIONS AND FIRST DRAWINGS OF THE FIGURE

The first chapter of this book serves as an introduction to drawing the human figure. We start by looking at the basic proportions and the obvious differences between male and female, child and adult. Then we will look at how to draw clothed figures quite simply, capturing the main shapes and sketching in a minimum of detail. The aim here is familiarize yourself with the subject, learning to gauge the correct proportions of figures in a range of situations. Observation of the human form is the key to increasing your drawing skill. You will need the cooperation of your family and friends, but you will find that most people are happy to oblige. You will also find that a good supply of photographs can be very useful. While the best drawings are done only from life, using photographs, especially if you have taken them yourself, is very helpful.

Following these first drawings, we will focus on the hands, arms and legs, which are the parts of the body you are most likely to see unclothed in a day-to-day setting. Drawing your own hand is an exercise that artists have always engaged in to test their powers of observation. The hand is a remarkably complex living structure and, while you may be very familiar with its appearance, translating it on to paper is a challenge for every artist and never a wasted exercise.

Finally we will combine the aspects of proportion, posture, clothing and limbs into a straightforward step-by-step drawing of a figure on a beach.

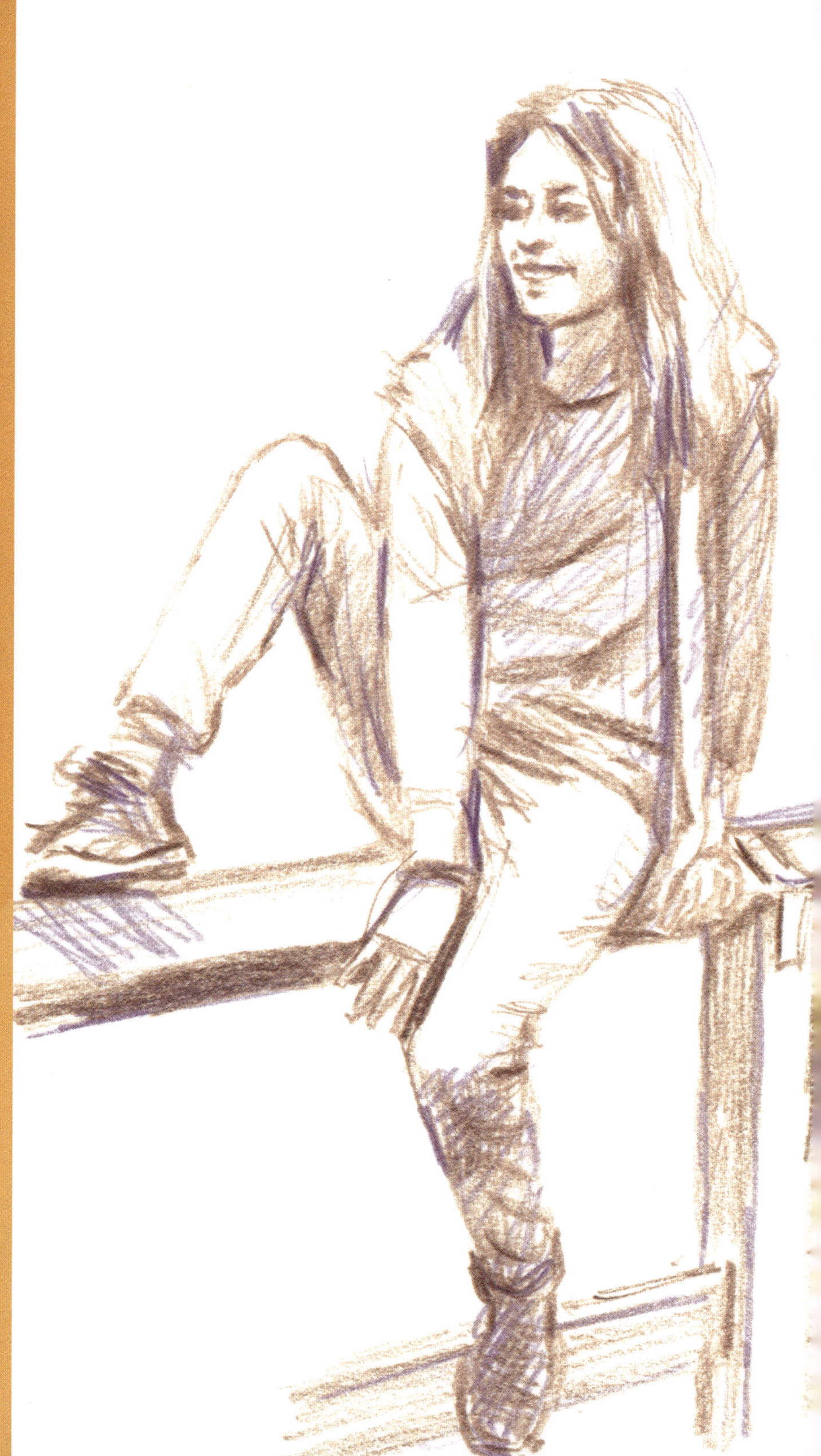

Proportions of the Figure

Before you leap into your first figure drawing, pause to study the proportions of the human figure. These are not the precise proportions of every individual but represent an average.

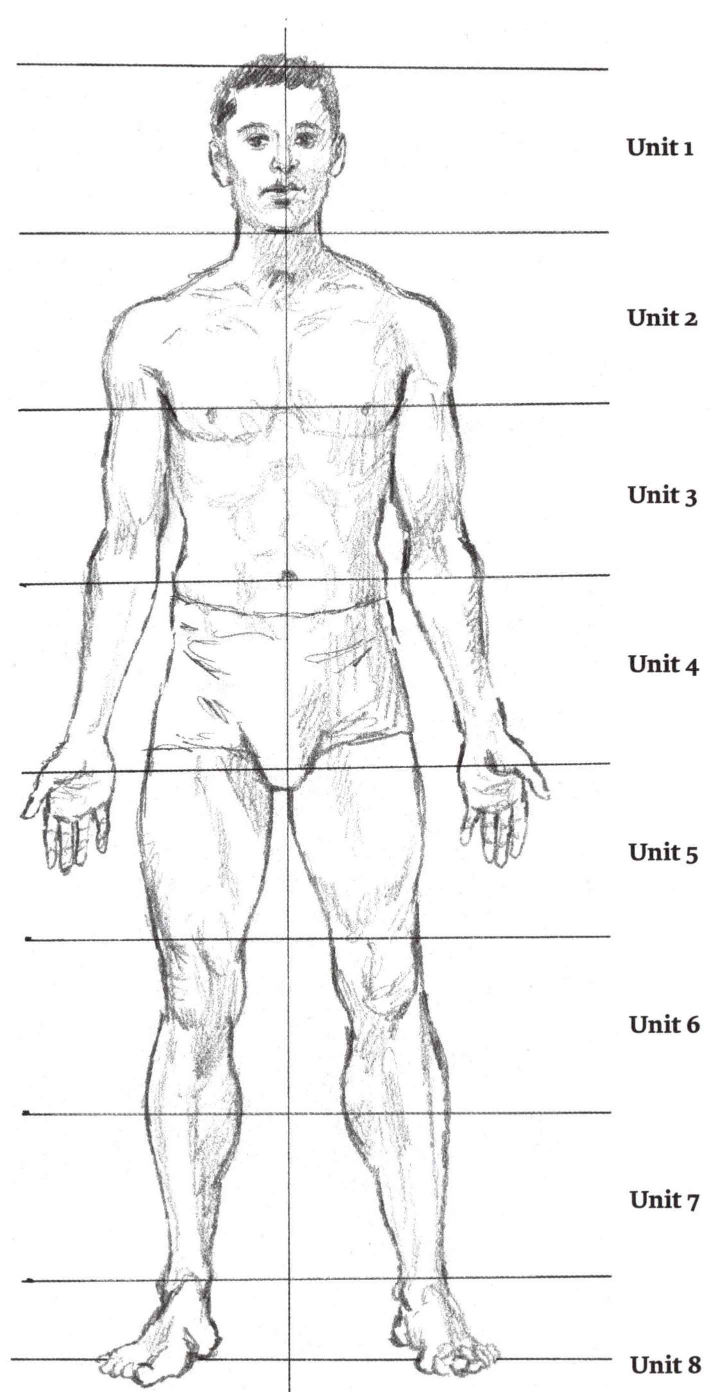

Viewed from the front, the height of the average adult – male or female – is approximately seven-and-a-half to eight times the length of their own head, measured from top to bottom. Women are generally smaller-boned than men but the ratio of head to overall height remains the same.

Notice how the halfway mark of the human figure is the lower end of the torso and the top of the legs. The second unit down is the level of the nipples on the chest, and the navel is three units down.

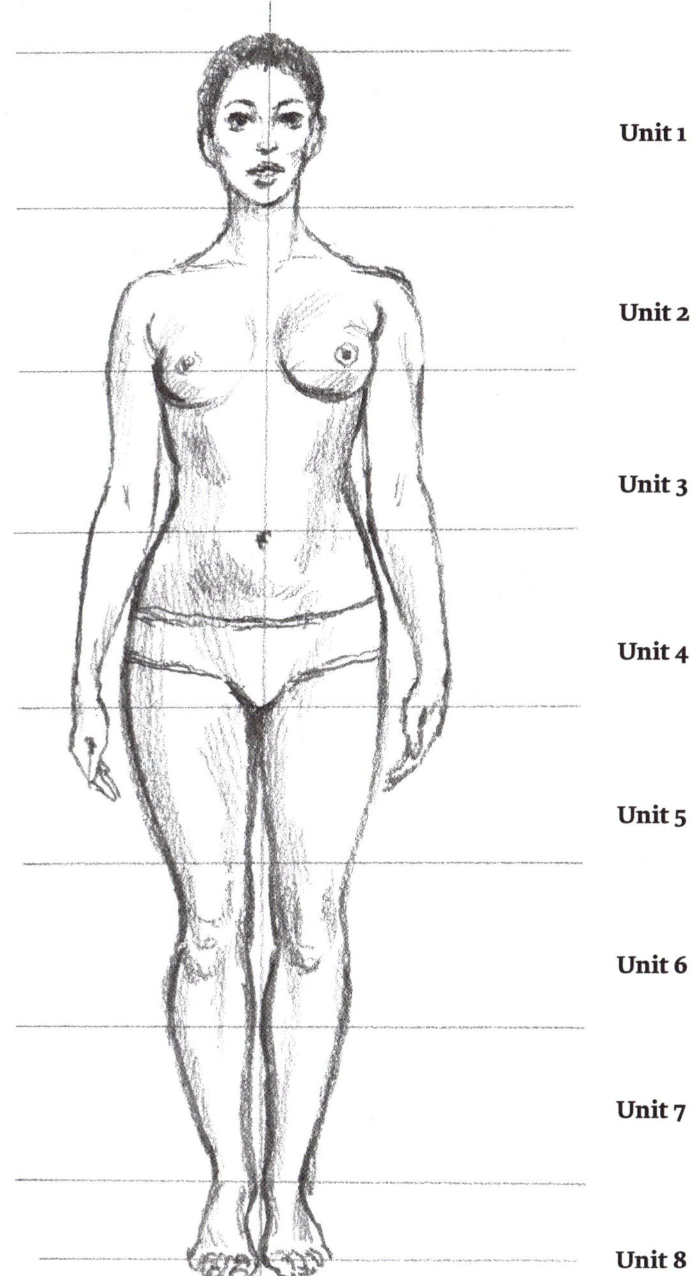

Note how the figures shown here are the same height; in reality the female is probably shorter than the male but the proportion of head to height remains the same. The differences between the sexes are fairly minimal. The male figure is usually heavier in build, the skeleton often being significantly more solid than the female's. The female form also has a layer of subcutaneous fat that the male form lacks, so that she usually looks softer and rounder than her male counterpart. There are occasional exceptions to these rules, but these diagrams are a good starting point.

Individual Proportions

The greatest difference between adult bodies tends to be in the amount of flesh spread over the skeletal frame. While the proportion of head to height may be the same, the relative width of the body can be vastly different. This may be a result of lifestyle choices such as diet and exercise or of the individual's metabolism.

A broad appearance may be caused by muscle rather than fat, but the distribution and appearance of the bulk will be very different.

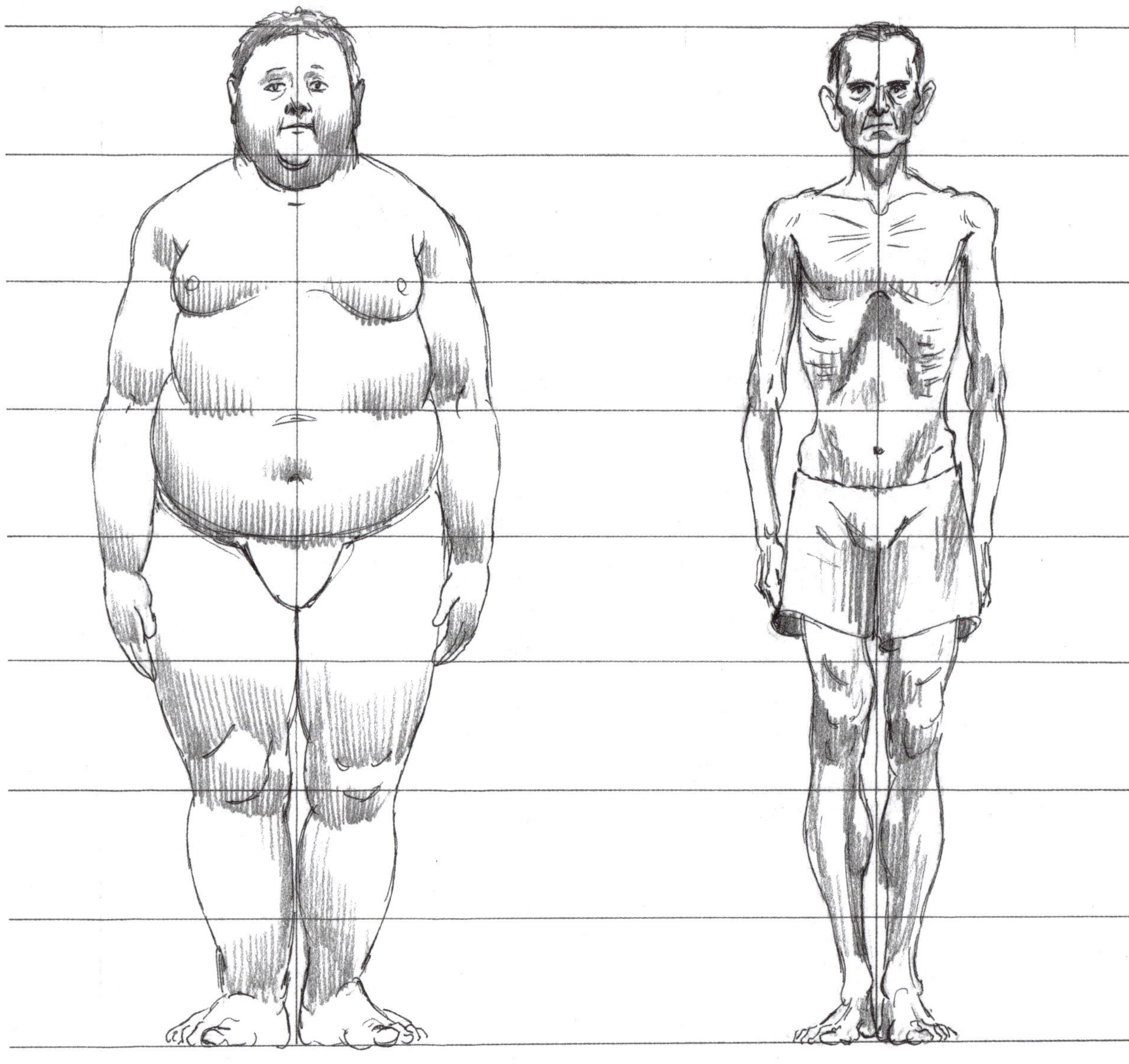

Most extra fat gathers around the central area of the body, and the first area to increase in width is usually the waist. The upper parts of the legs and arms are often thicker and there tends to be extra bulk around the neck and chest.

At the other extreme, when someone is below normal weight, the human frame is reduced to a very meagre stringy-looking shape. The width of the torso and limbs is dictated only by the bone structure.

Proportions of Children

The proportions of children's bodies change very rapidly and because children grow at very different speeds what is true of one child at a certain age may not always be so true of another. Consequently, the drawings here can only give an average guide to children's changes in proportion as they get older.

The thickness of children's limbs varies enormously but often the most obvious difference between a child, an adolescent and an adult is that the limbs and body become more slender as part of the growing process. In some types of figure there is a tendency towards puppy fat which makes a youngster look softer and rounder.

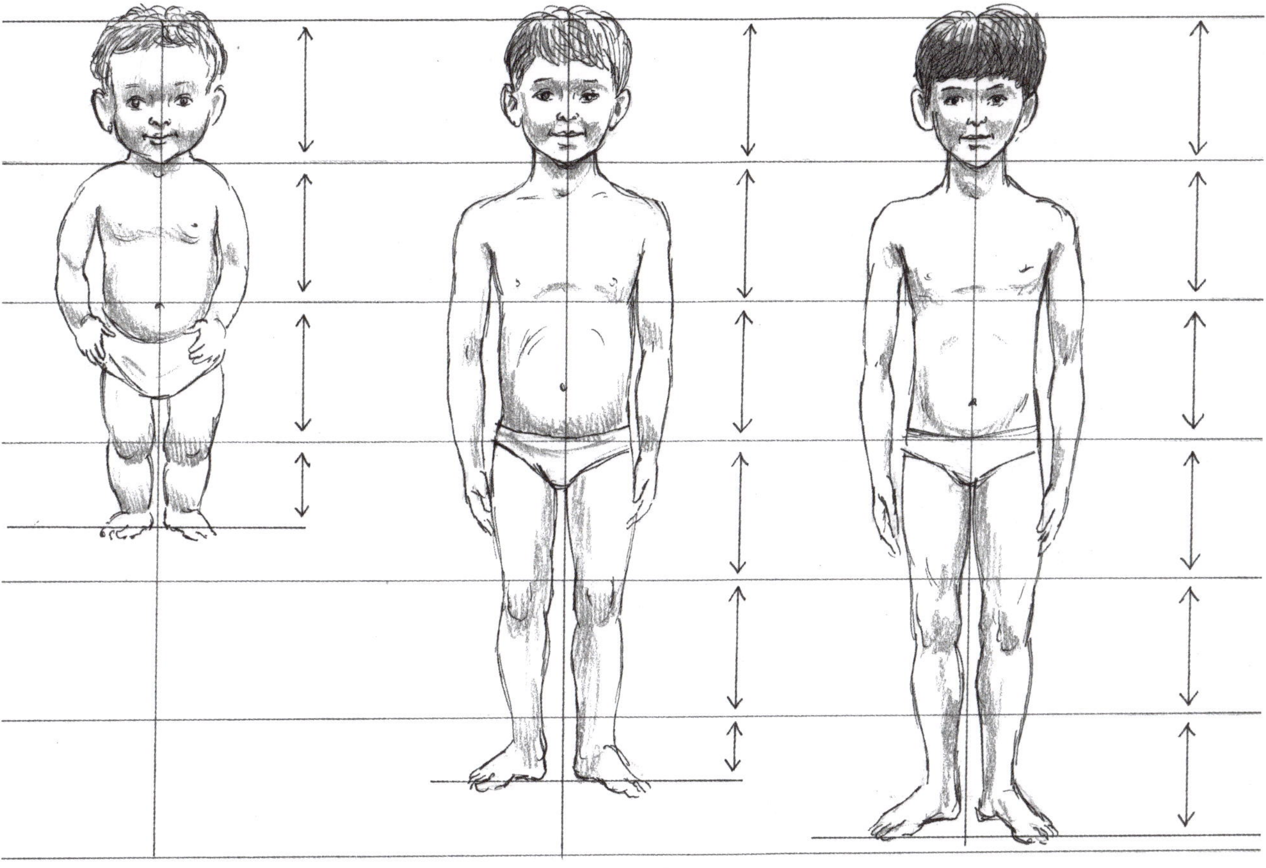

At the beginning of life the head is much larger in proportion to the rest of the body than it will be later. On the left I have drawn a child of about 18 months old, giving the sort of proportion you might find in a child of average growth. The height is only three and a half times the length of the head, which means that the proportions of the arms and legs are much smaller in comparison to those of an adult.

At the age of about six or seven, a child's height is a little over five times the length of the head, though again this is a bit variable. At about 12 years, the proportion is about six times the head size. Notice how in the younger children the halfway point in the height of the body is much closer to the navel, but this gradually lowers until it reaches the adult proportion at the pubic edge of the pelvis where the legs divide.

Drawing Simple Figures

For your first drawings of figures, keep things simple. Start by making a rough outline of the main shapes of your figure, then sketch in a little more detail but don't spend more than a few minutes on each drawing. You will find that a good supply of photographs can be very useful for practising a range of figures.

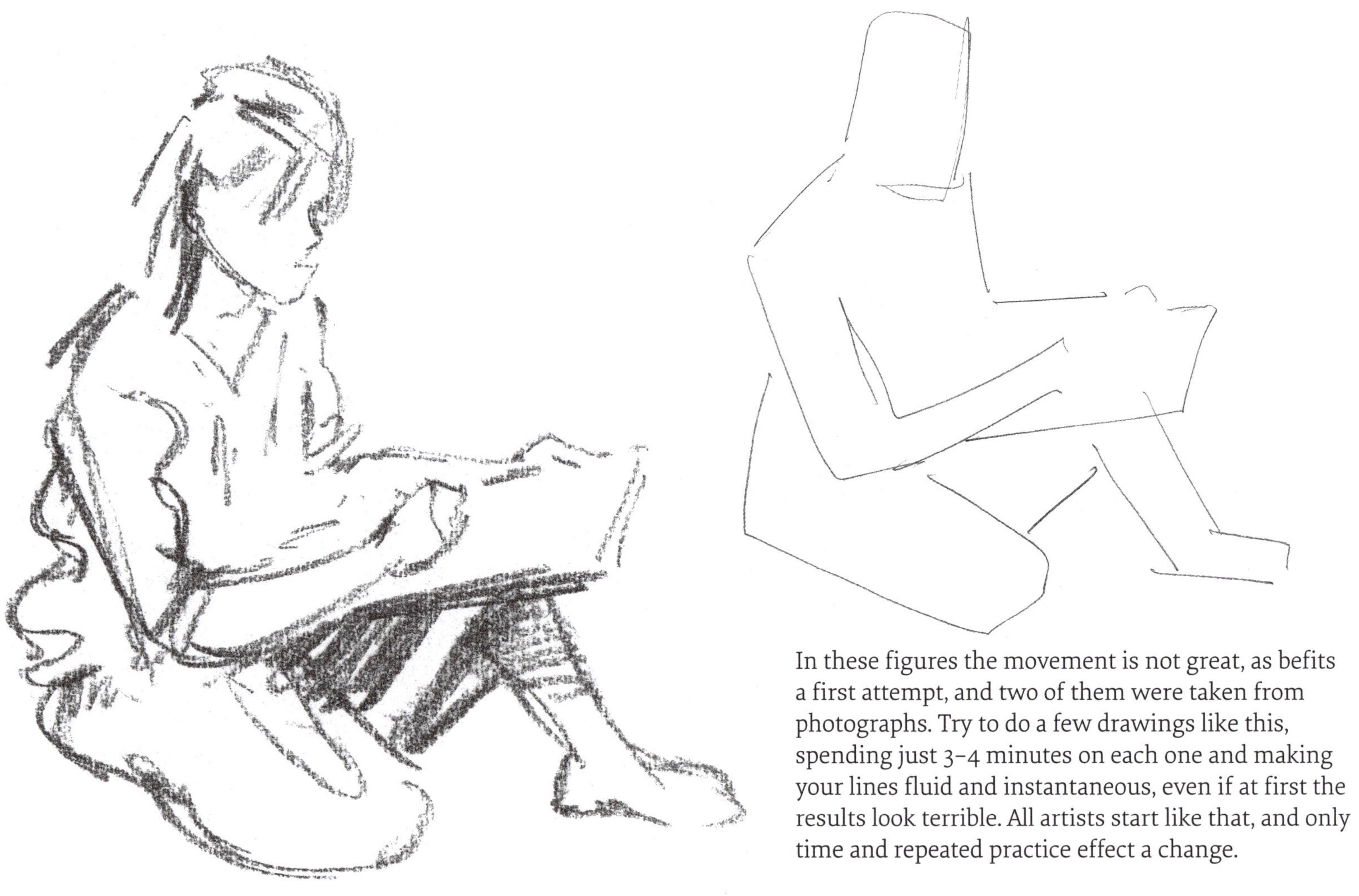

In these figures the movement is not great, as befits a first attempt, and two of them were taken from photographs. Try to do a few drawings like this, spending just 3–4 minutes on each one and making your lines fluid and instantaneous, even if at first the results look terrible. All artists start like that, and only time and repeated practice effect a change.

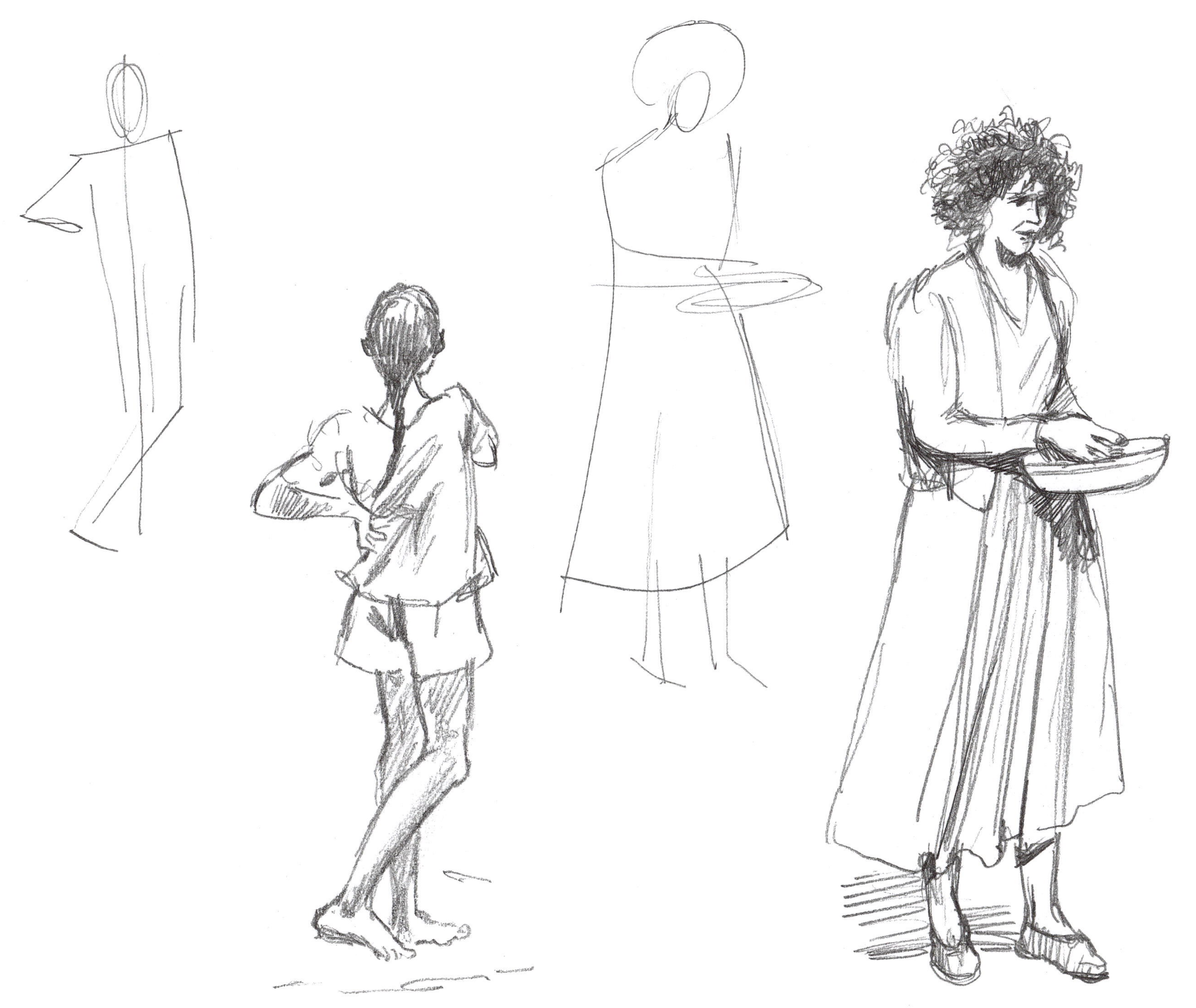

Seated and standing

Continue to practise very simple figures, perhaps asking a member of your family to pose for a few minutes while you sketch. Here I have shown one standing figure and one seated, sketched in brown and blue pastel. Again, start by denoting the overall shapes, trying to capture the feel of each pose. Then firm up your outlines and add a little detail to the clothing. For the seated figure, observe carefully how one leg crosses over the other, with the top leg obscuring the thigh of the lower leg.

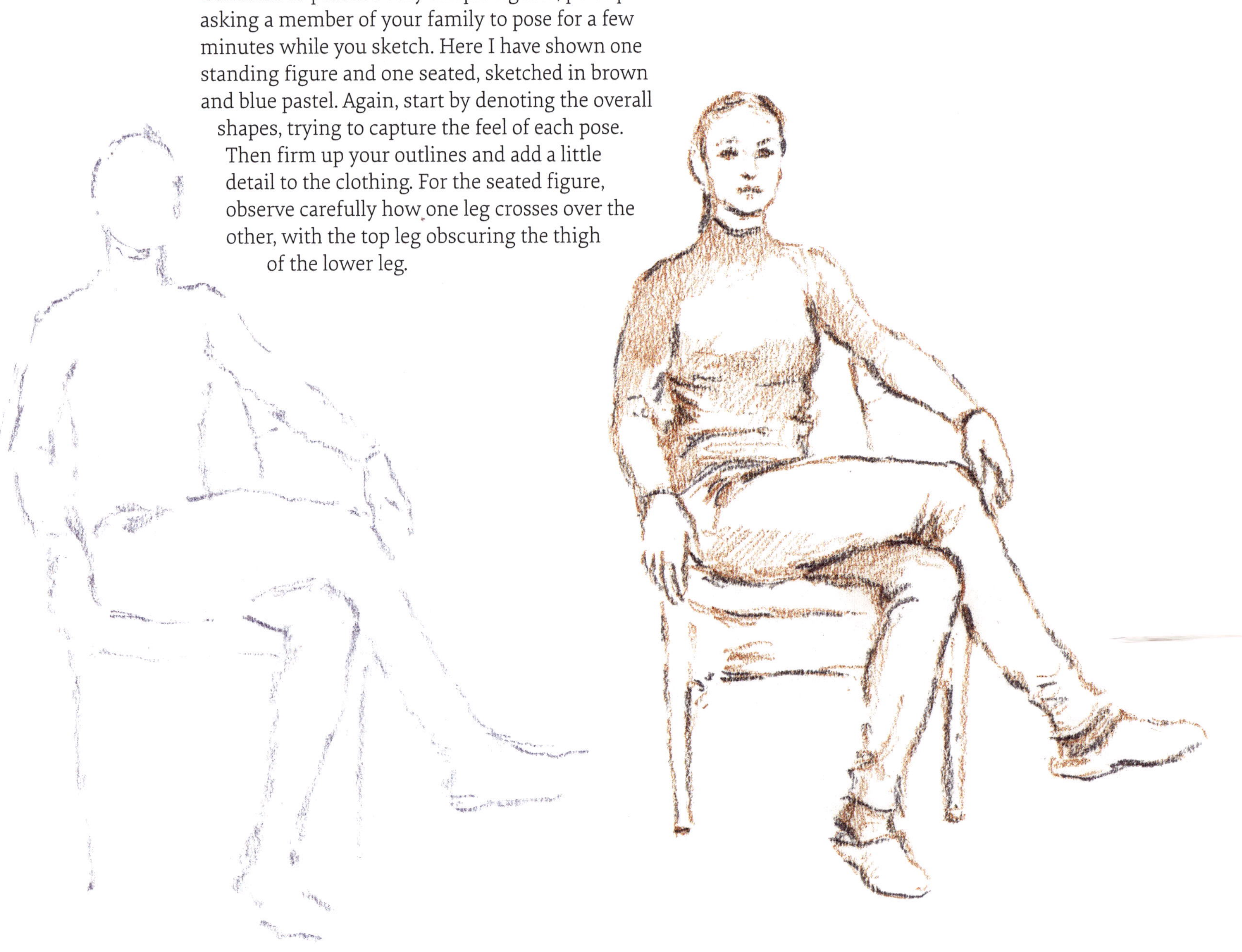

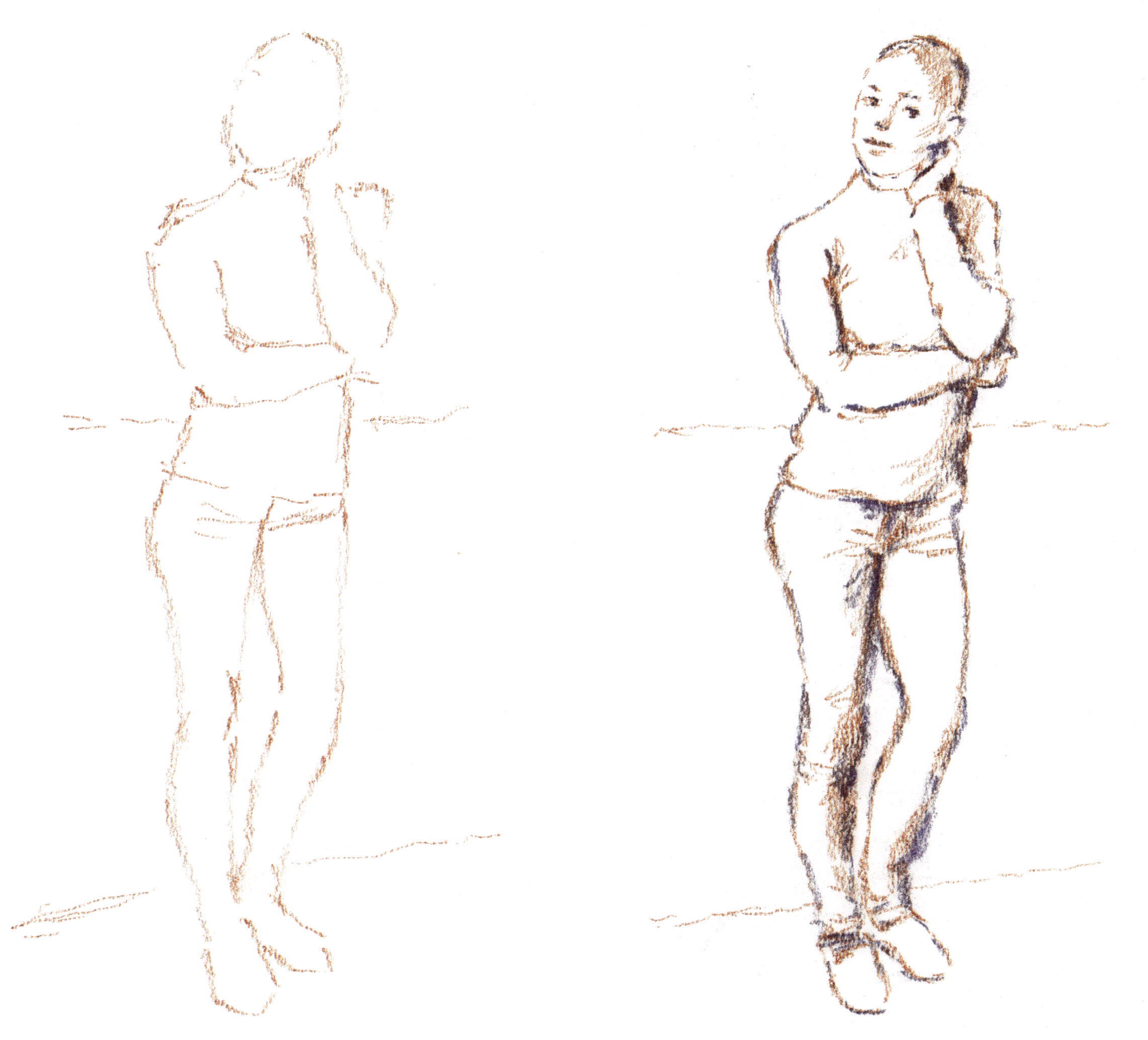

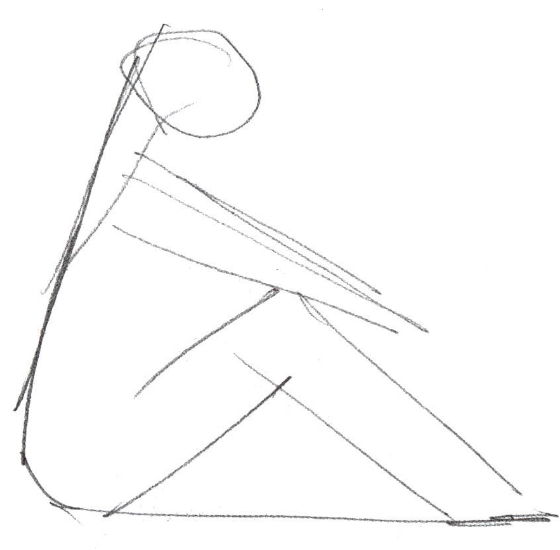

Blocking in figures

The next four drawings show slightly more compact poses, and I have blocked in the main shape so as to concentrate on the solidity of the shapes. There is no detail at all in these drawings – even the features are mere dashes of pencil to indicate their position rather than their shape. Make your own drawings of figures in more varied positions than you have tried so far.

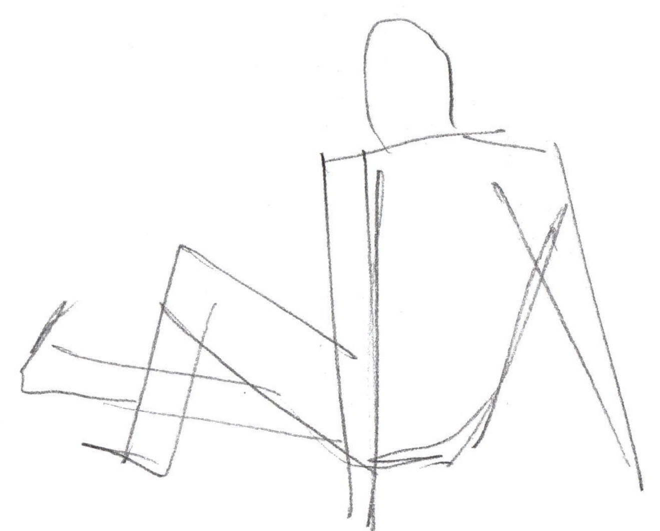

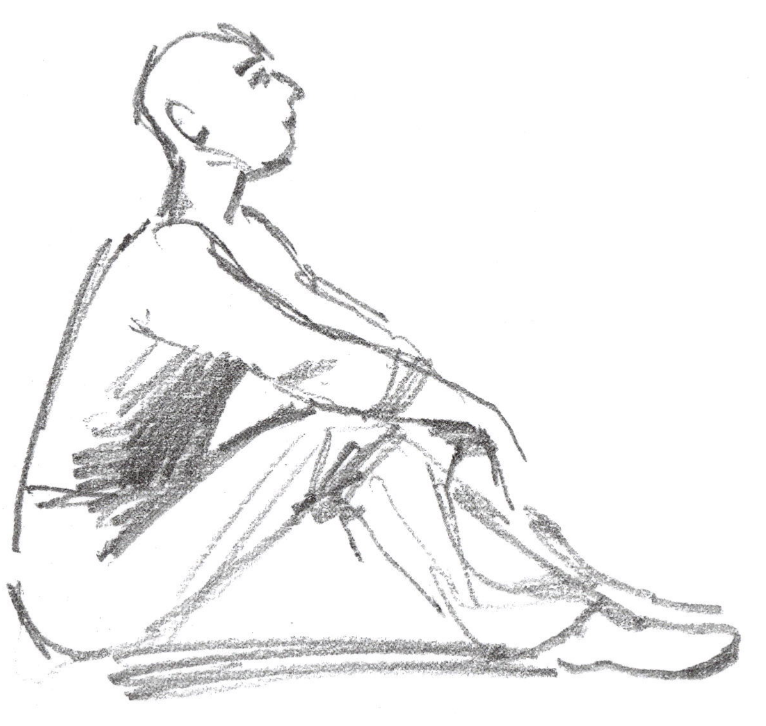

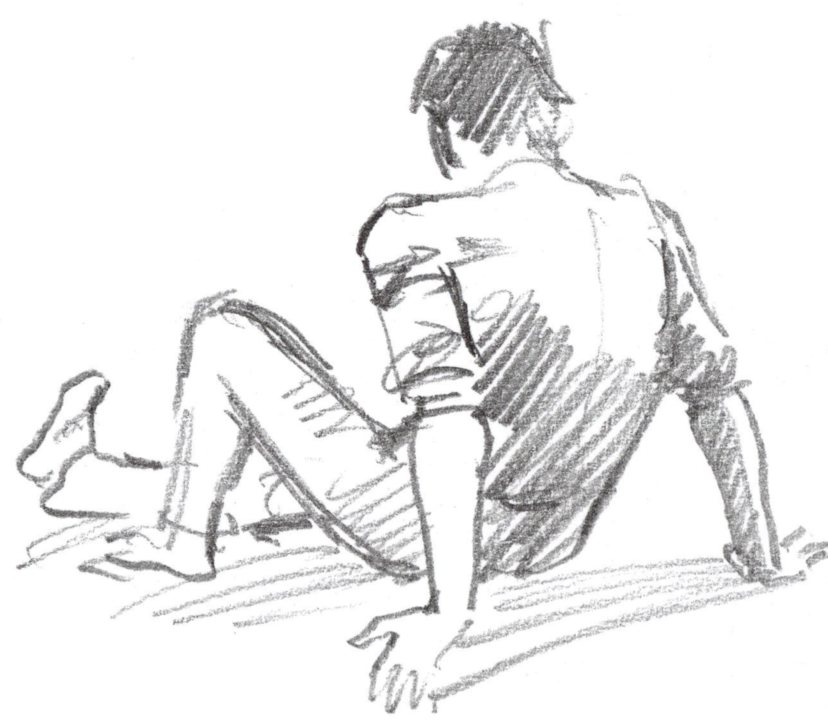

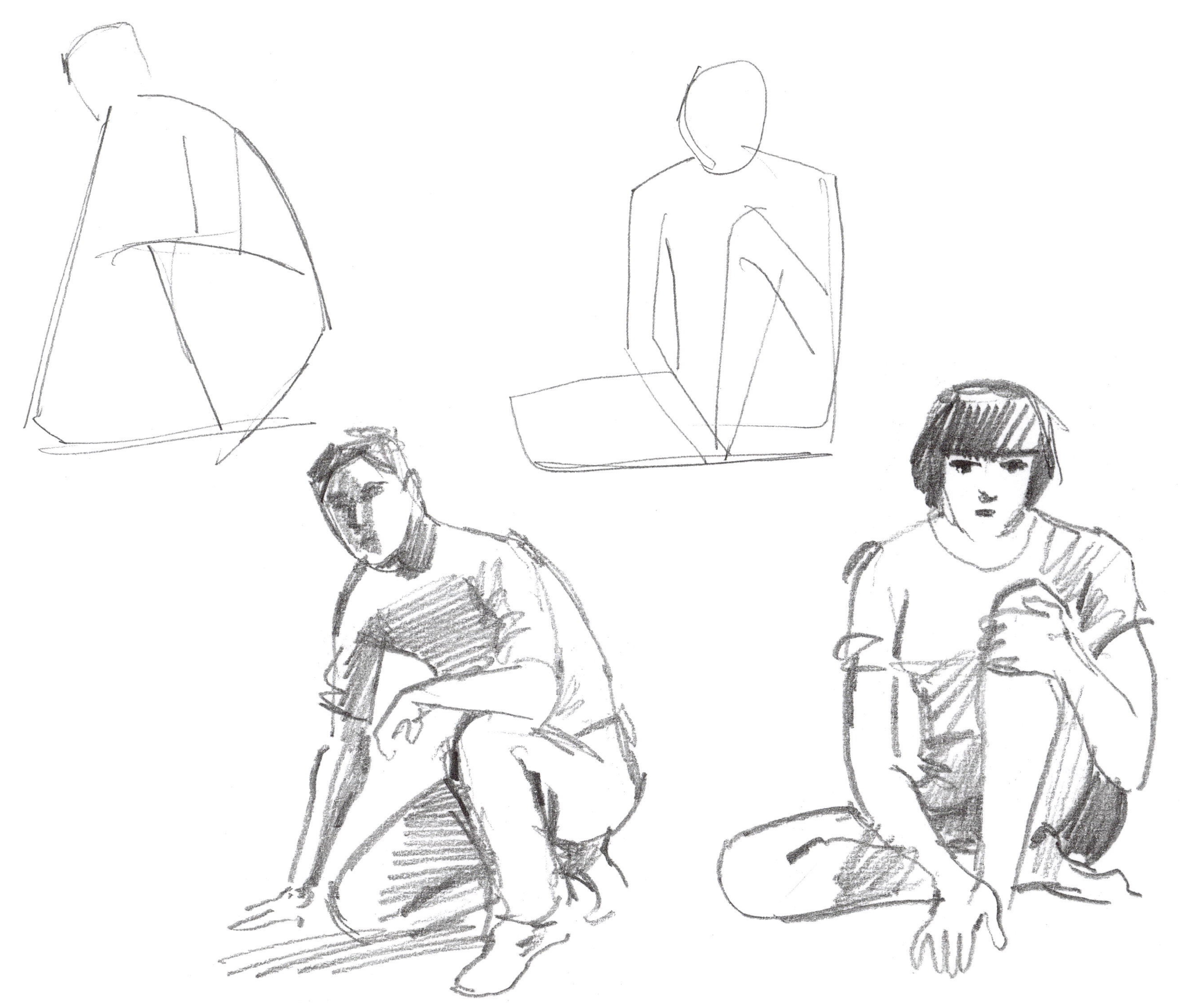

A Figure in Steps

In this exercise, try to take your figure drawing a bit further, adding some more detail. I chose to use a couple of different colours in my example, which adds some interest to the overall result.

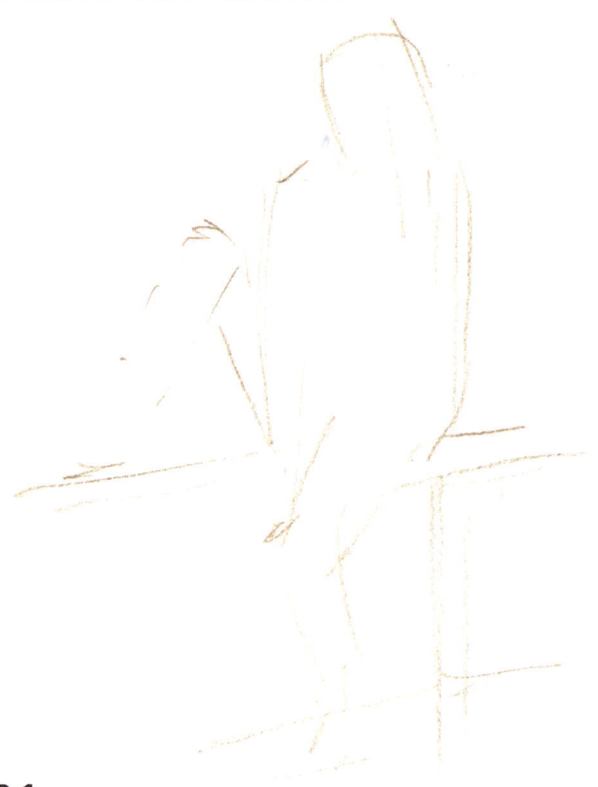

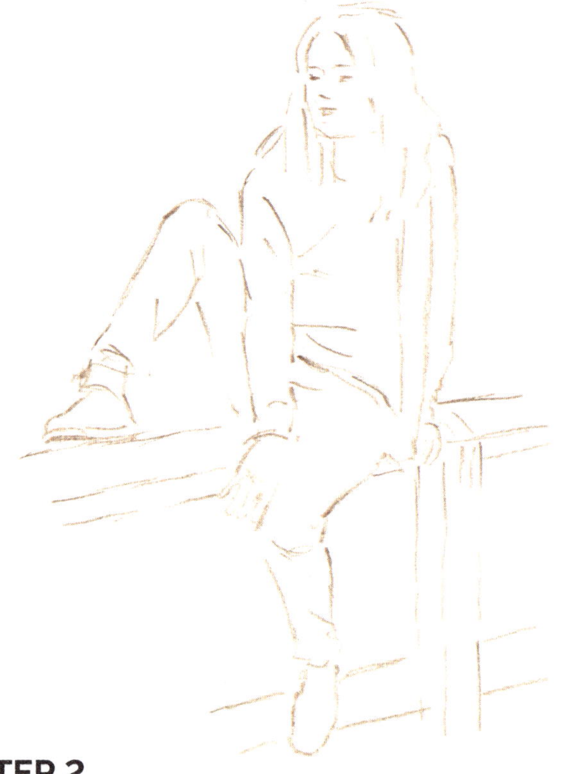

STEP 1

The first stage is to sketch the very basic shapes of the head, torso and limbs, in the simplest geometric way. Use a brown coloured pencil to do this, but don't draw too heavily. This young woman is sitting on a fence, balancing; the pose gives an upright body and head, with one foot up on the top of the fence and the other on the lower rung. Her upper leg makes a triangle shape and the lower leg is slightly bent.

STEP 2

The second stage is to draw the figure in a bit more detail so that it starts to gain some volume. Draw in the shapes of the hair and face, adding simple marks to denote the features. Fill out the shape of the jacket hanging over the torso and arms and define the legs and feet. Note the positions of the hands as they keep her poised on top of the fence.

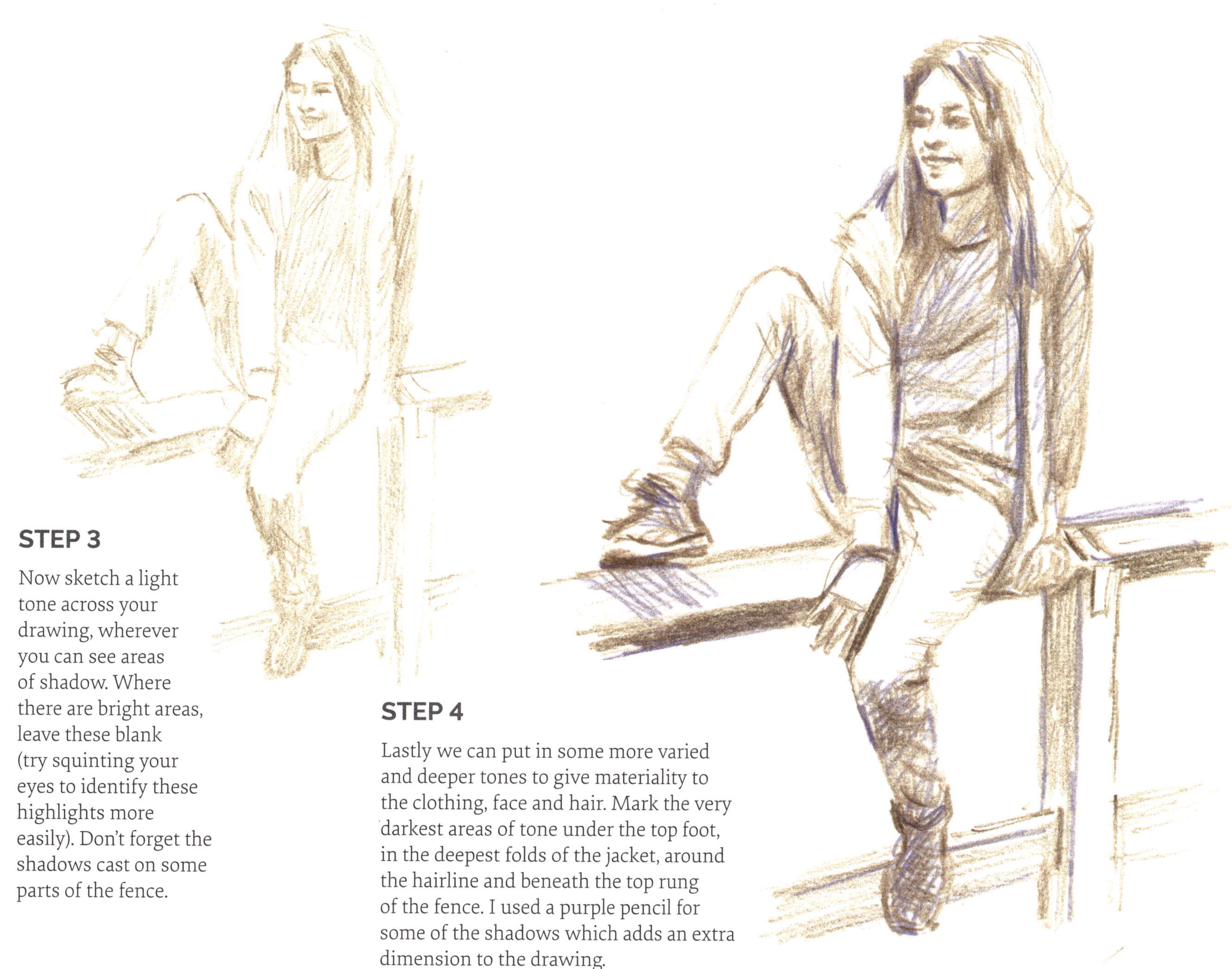

STEP 3

Now sketch a light tone across your drawing, wherever you can see areas of shadow. Where there are bright areas, leave these blank (try squinting your eyes to identify these highlights more easily). Don't forget the shadows cast on some parts of the fence.

STEP 4

Lastly we can put in some more varied and deeper tones to give materiality to the clothing, face and hair. Mark the very darkest areas of tone under the top foot, in the deepest folds of the jacket, around the hairline and beneath the top rung of the fence. I used a purple pencil for some of the shadows which adds an extra dimension to the drawing.

Expressive Figures

Here we look at some people in poses that are more expressive. The four figures on this spread are not even shown in full, because my interest is in the gesticulating hands. These might be easier for you to draw from photographs that have frozen the moment.

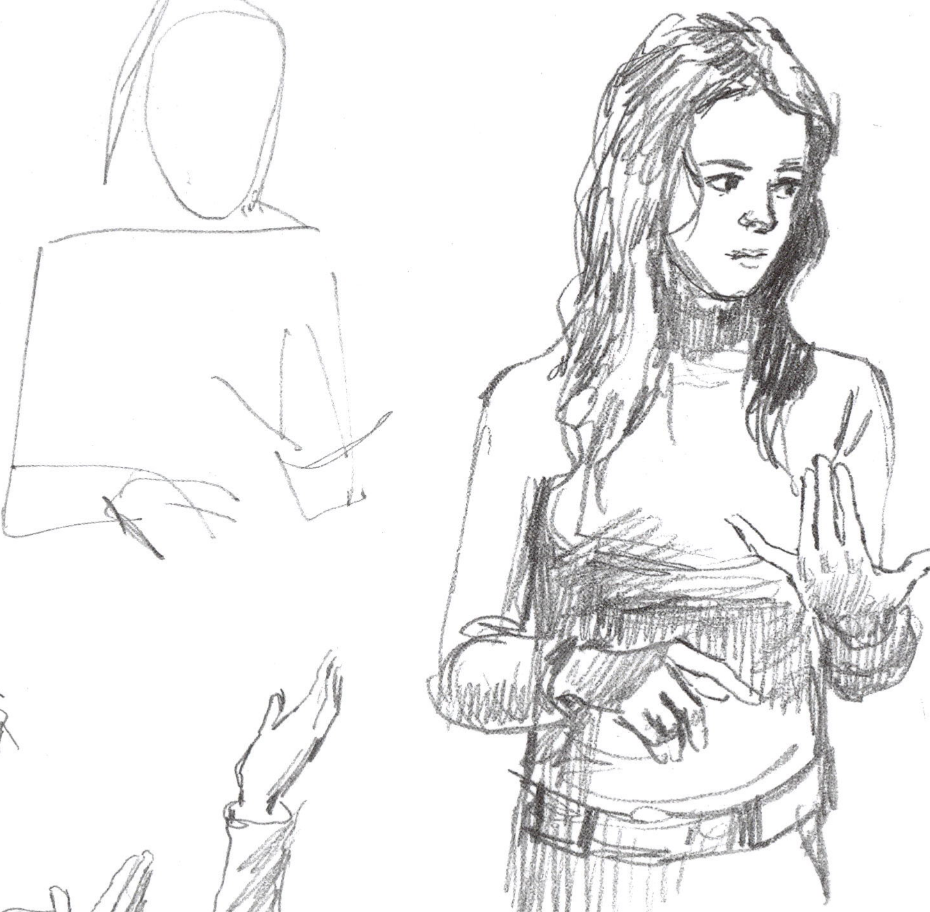

Block these in to start with, paying particular attention to the position of the hands. One woman looks as if she is ticking off points on her fingers, one man is gesturing to draw attention to something, the other woman is in the process of combing her hair and the last man is sitting down to draw something ... perhaps you!

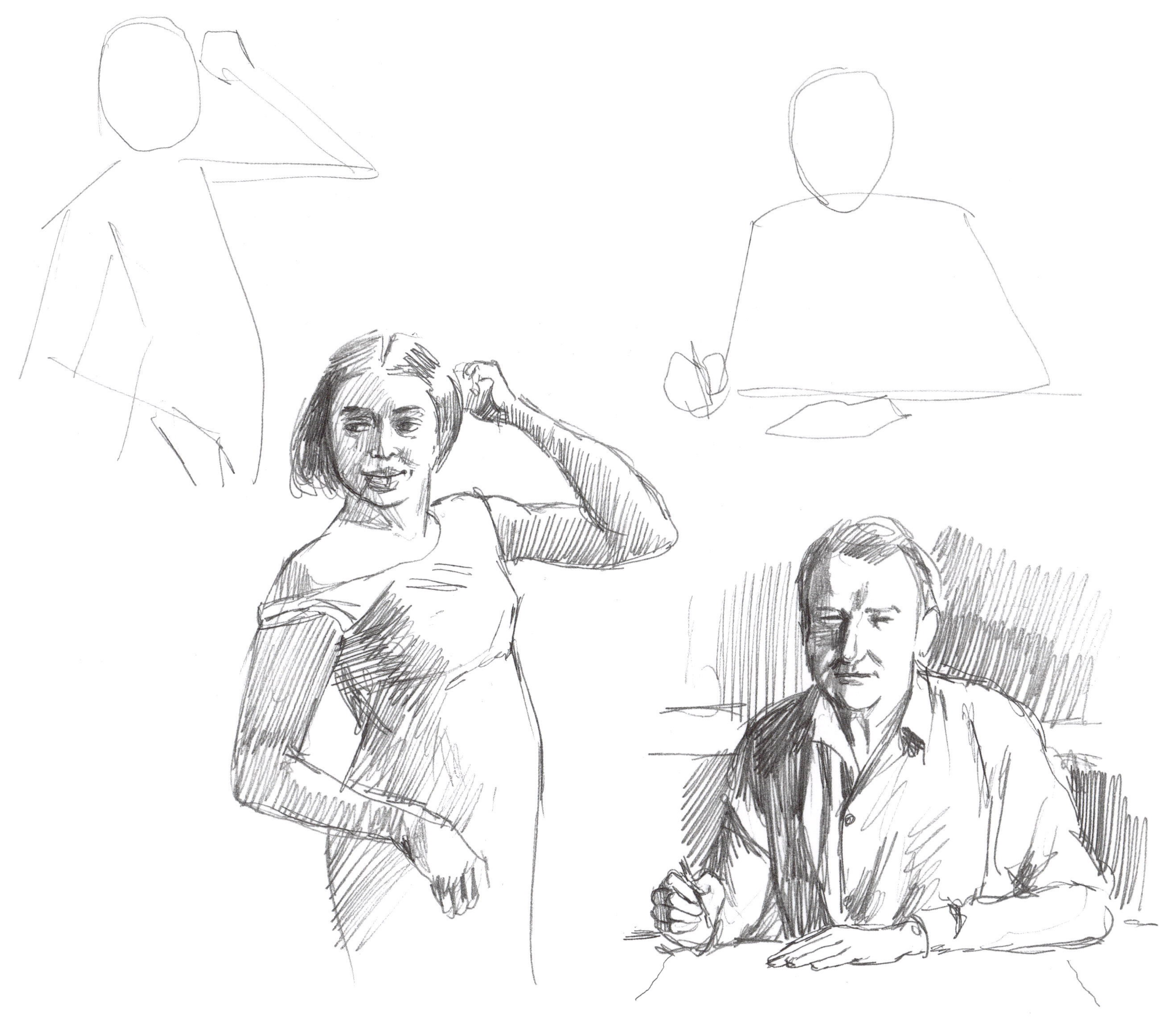

Foreshortened Figures

The next drawings look at figures which are lying and sitting in such a way that some of their limbs are foreshortened, making your task more difficult. You will have to look carefully at how the proportions of the limbs differ from how they would appear if the same figures were standing up.

Here, the first girl sits with her legs folded under her, supporting herself with her hands. Her feet and knees project forwards from her trunk and are shown proportionately larger.

The woman lying down holding her knees creates the problem of working out the proportion of both the arms and legs because of the angle we see them from.

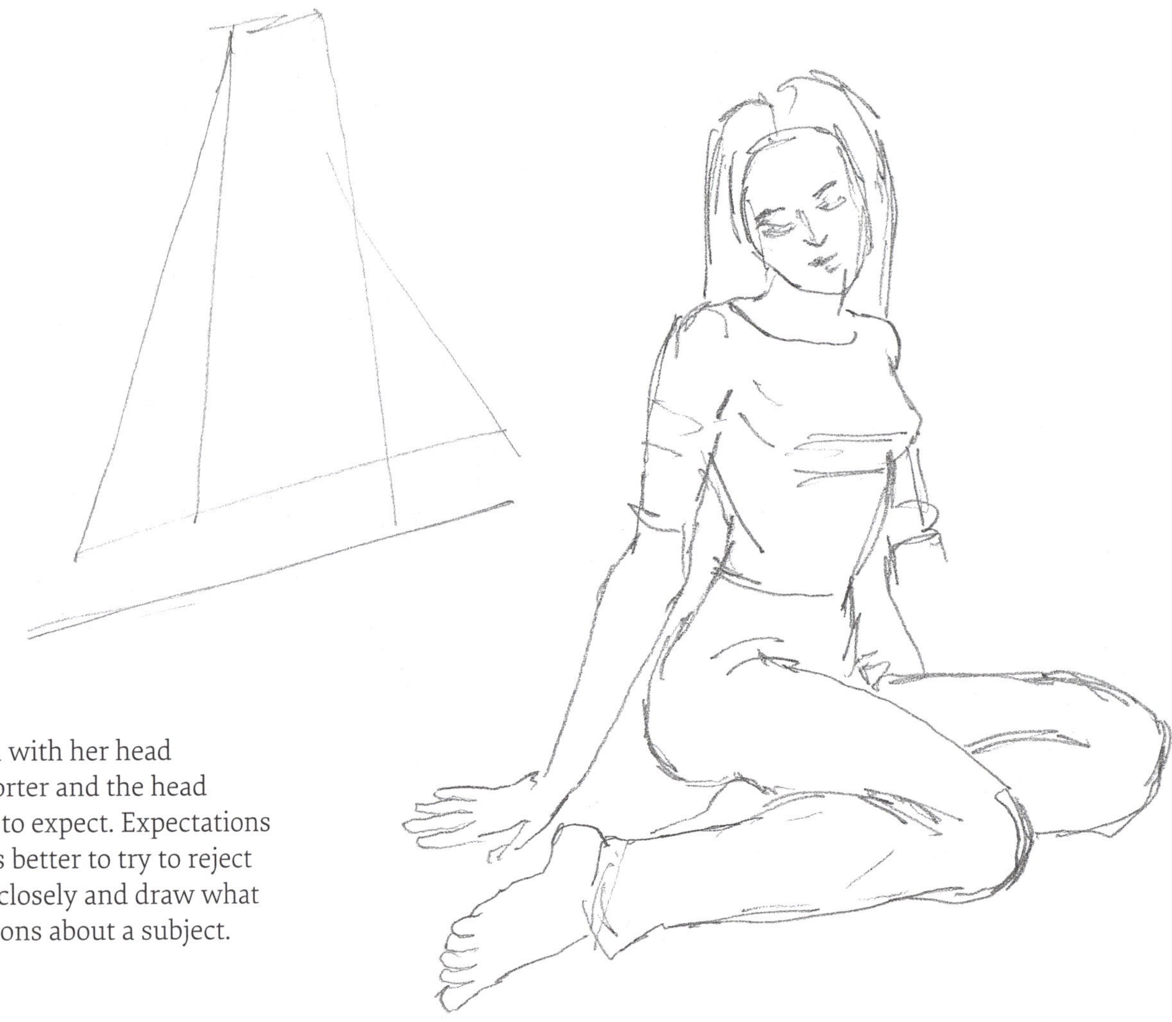

In the case of the woman lying down with her head towards us, the legs appear much shorter and the head correspondingly larger than we tend to expect. Expectations are always a distraction in art, and it's better to try to reject them. Instead, remember to observe closely and draw what you can really see, not your assumptions about a subject.

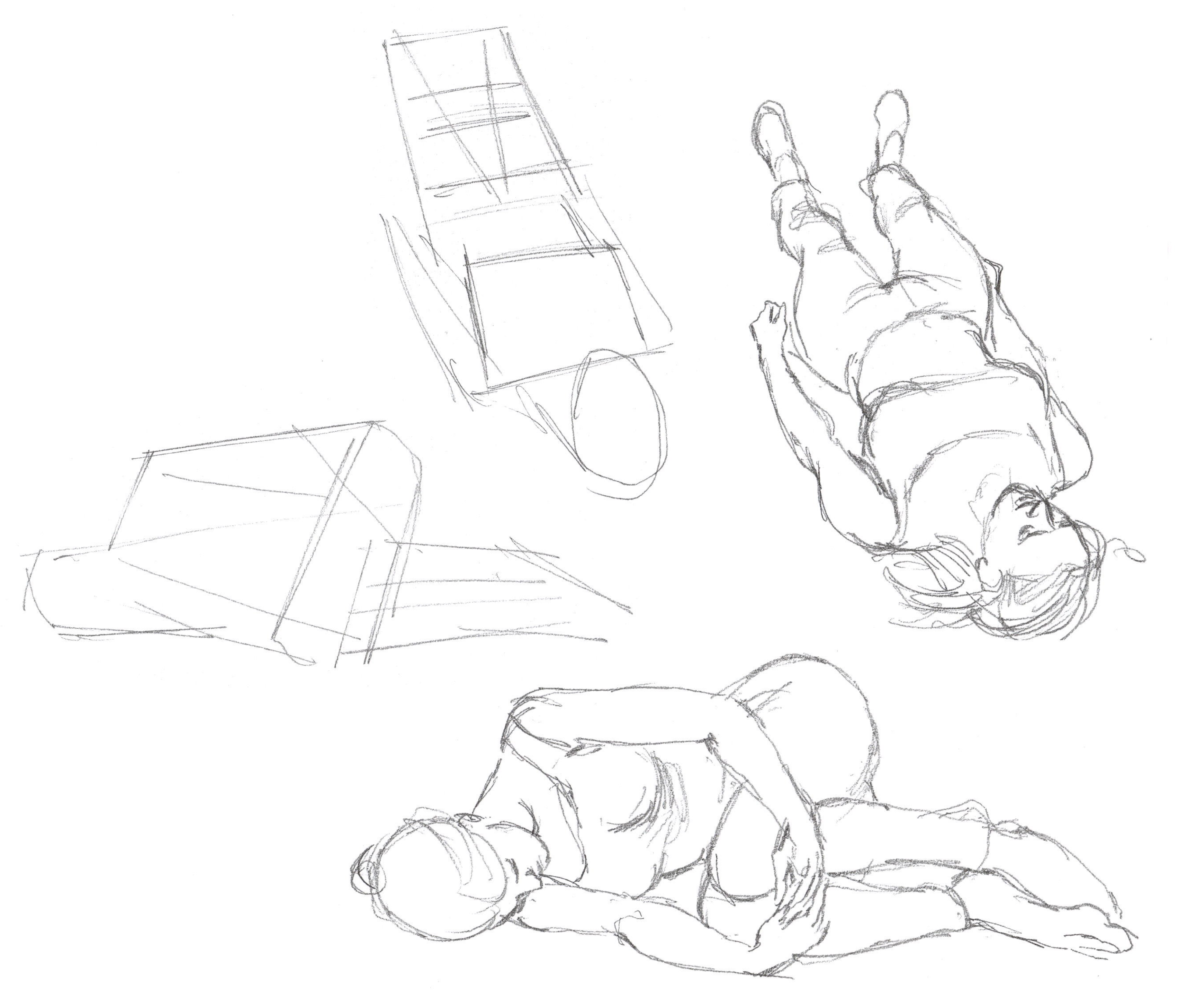

Here are three male figures in poses where the foreshortening of the limbs needs to be noticed as you draw them. When you ask your friends or family to pose for you, make sure that sometimes they sit with their limbs advancing or receding to create this opportunity for you to draw in perspective.

The first figure, sitting on a stool, is relatively straightforward where the legs are concerned, but the folded arms pose a foreshortening problem.

The second man is seen almost from above, so that the arm he is resting on half disappears, and the lower part of the bent leg is almost hidden from our sight.

The last figure of a kneeling man poses problems both with the arms and the legs, so observe them carefully if you try this pose. These drawings are all more useful if done from real people posing for you, but if you can't get enough patient models, use photographs – but take them yourself. As before, don't forget to block the pose in before you try to put in all the details.

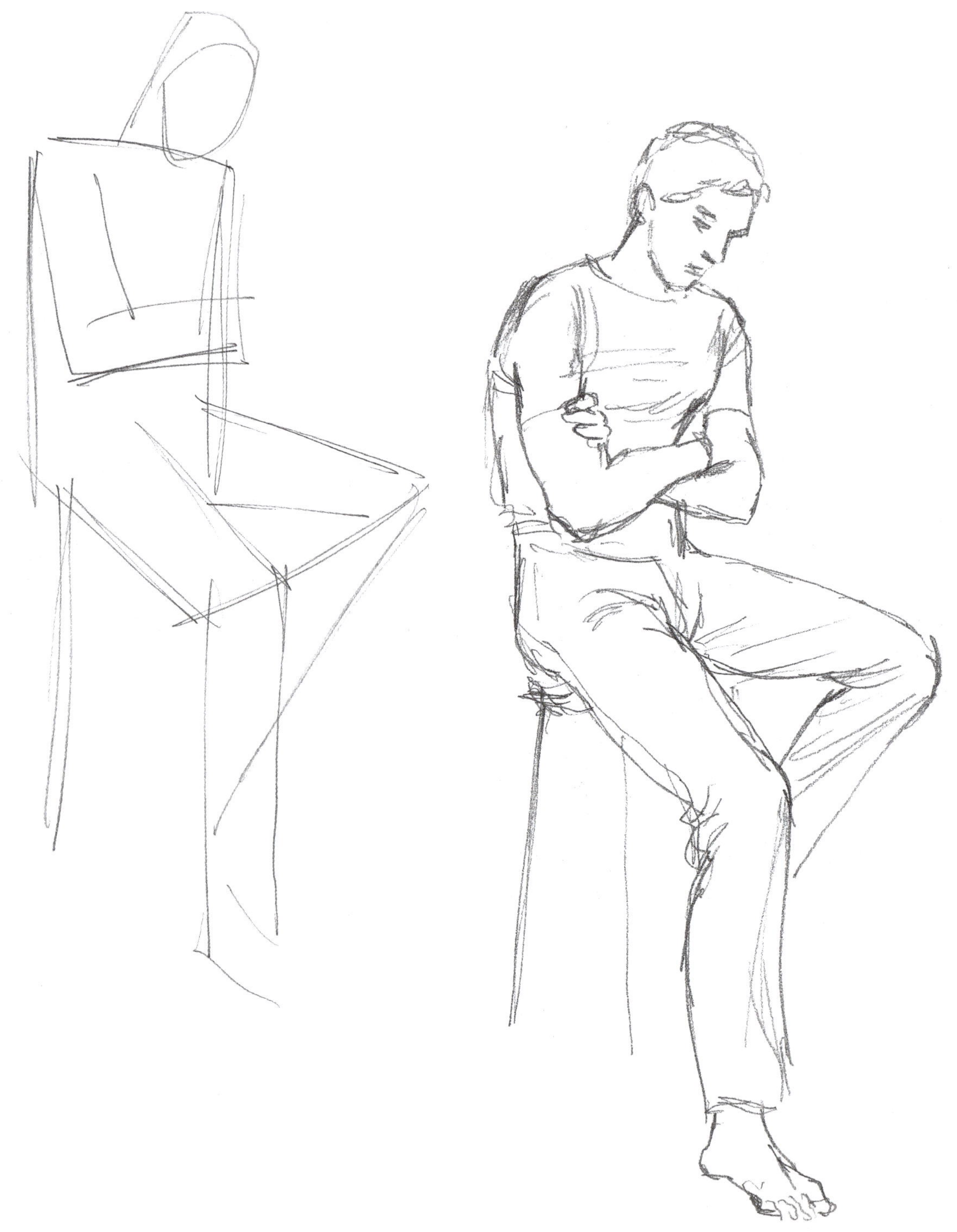

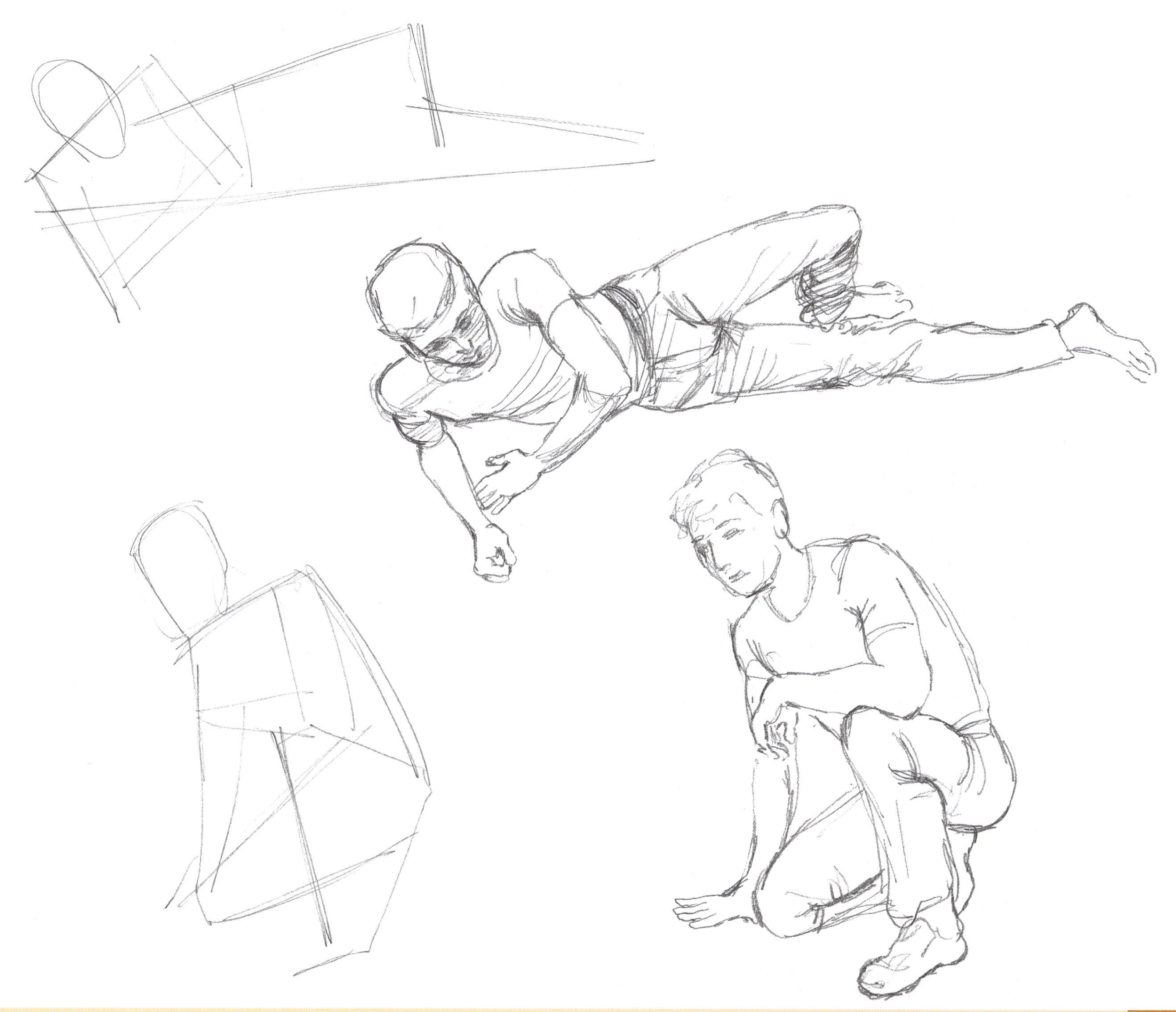

Drawing Your Own Hand

This exercise starts with the simple task of drawing around the outline of your own hand. Just place your hand flat on the paper and then carefully draw all around the shape, making sure that the pencil point does not get too far away from, or too much under, the edge of your hand.

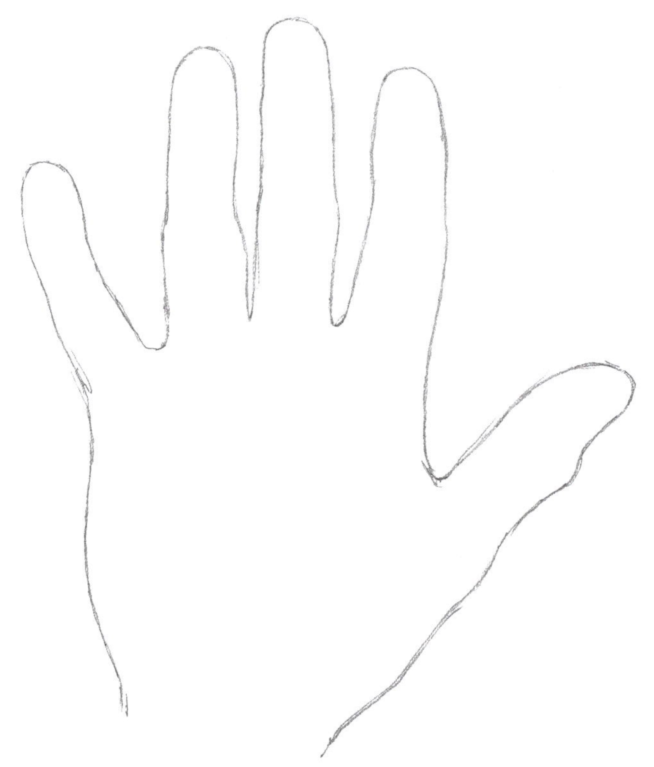

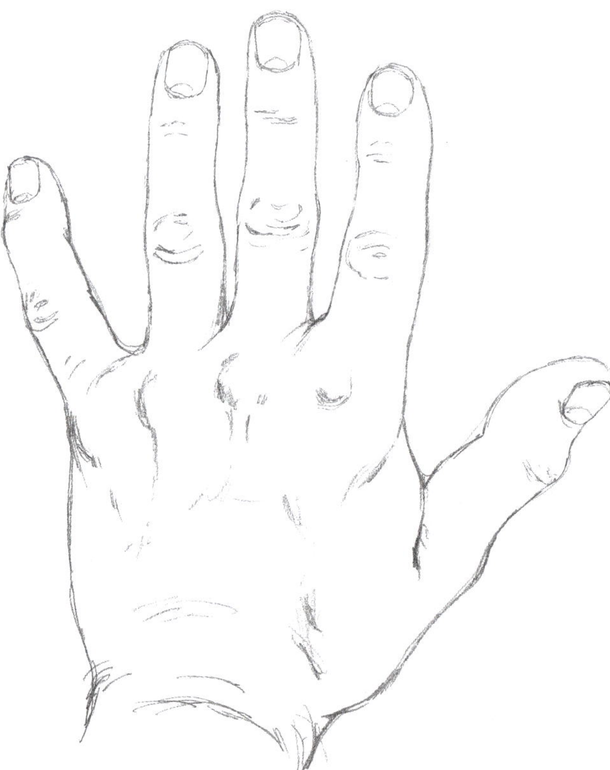

Lift your hand carefully off the paper, keeping it flat and in the same position as before, then draw in all the wrinkles, bumps and hollows that you can see in the simplest way possible, and of course the fingernails too. You will have a fairly good representation of your own hand, matching it for size and shape. Now have a go at drawing it in the same position but without tracing around the edge of it. Does the second drawing look as good as the first one?

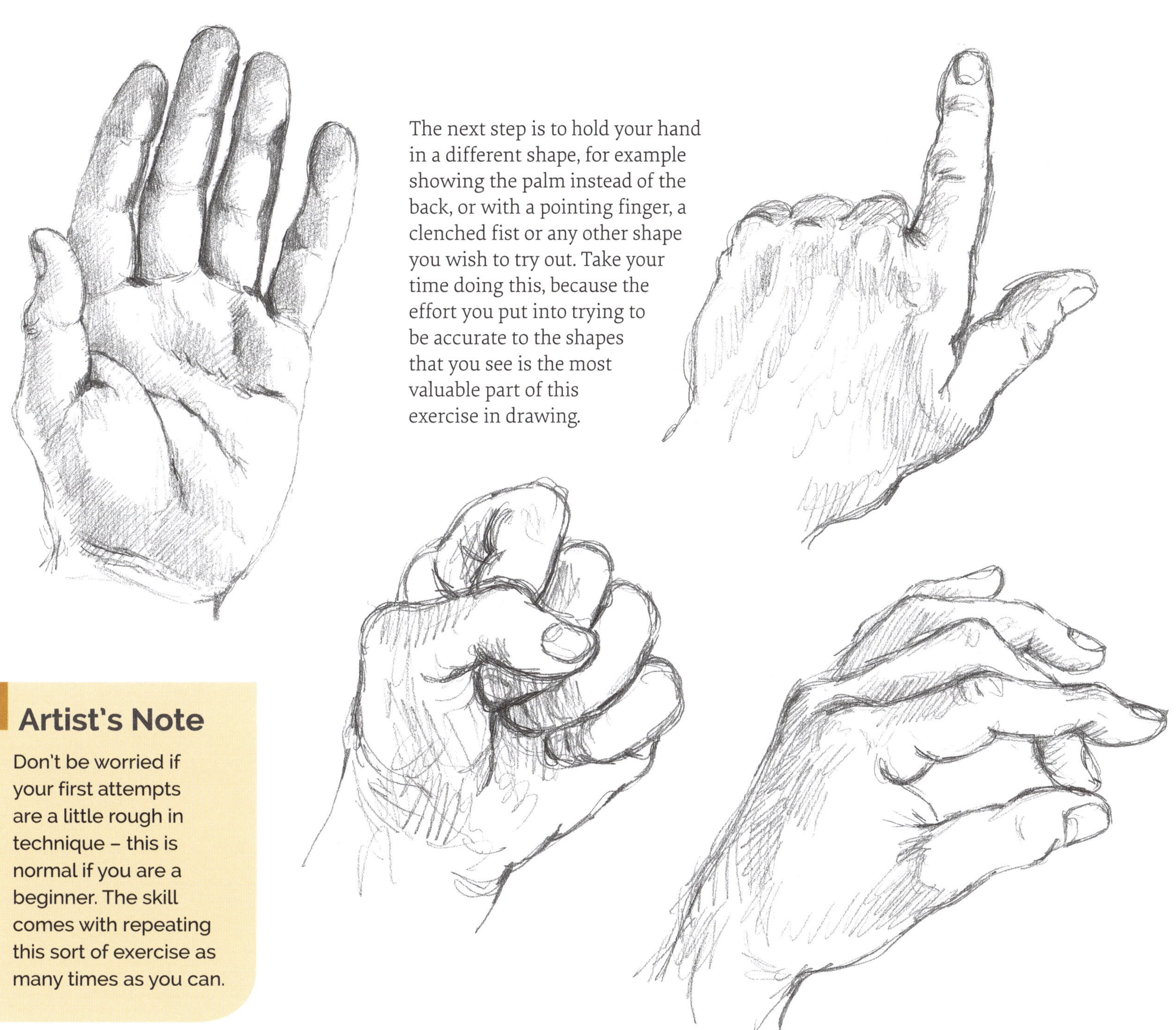

The next step is to hold your hand in a different shape, for example showing the palm instead of the back, or with a pointing finger, a clenched fist or any other shape you wish to try out. Take your time doing this, because the effort you put into trying to be accurate to the shapes that you see is the most valuable part of this exercise in drawing.

Artist's Note

Don't be worried if your first attempts are a little rough in technique – this is normal if you are a beginner. The skill comes with repeating this sort of exercise as many times as you can.

Arms and Hands

Apart from the head and neck, the arms and hands are the parts of the body that are most likely to be visible when you are drawing people. For this reason it is well worth familiarizing yourself with their forms.

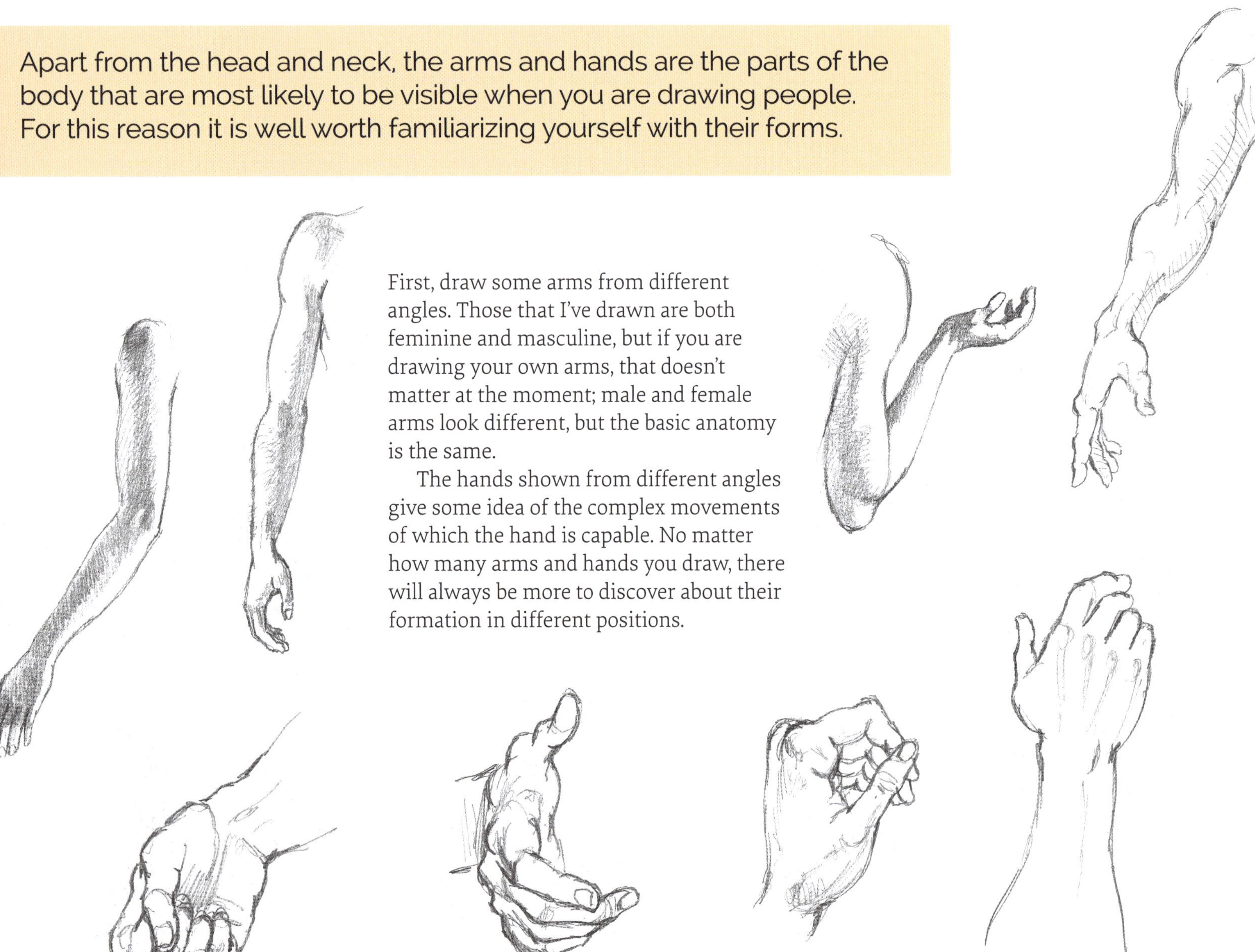

First, draw some arms from different angles. Those that I've drawn are both feminine and masculine, but if you are drawing your own arms, that doesn't matter at the moment; male and female arms look different, but the basic anatomy is the same.

The hands shown from different angles give some idea of the complex movements of which the hand is capable. No matter how many arms and hands you draw, there will always be more to discover about their formation in different positions.

To draw arms effectively, you need to look at them from every angle. Remember, the arm is larger in section nearer the body and thinner further away, towards the extremities. The only time this appears not to be so is through foreshortening, when a thinner section, such as the wrist, can seem as thick as the bicep, due to the effect of perspective.

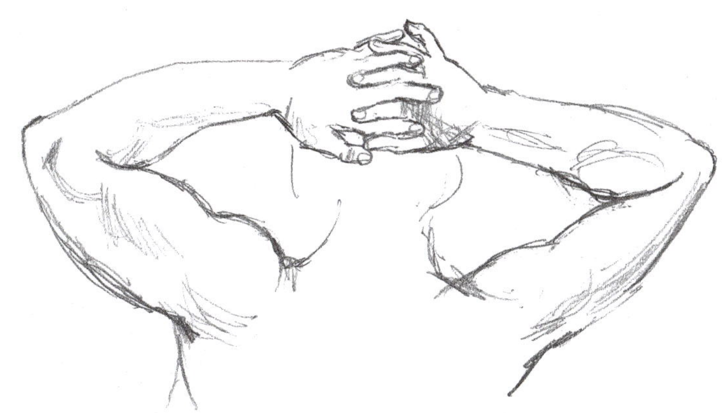

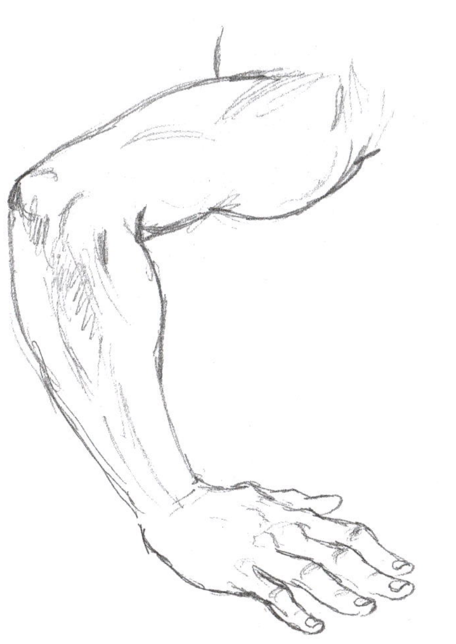

For these colour studies I used conté pencils, which give a soft quality to drawing, well suited to skin. Whereas the two studies at the top are quite loosely drawn, the crossed arms show a more precise technique using carefully modulated brown and dark blue tones to give a smoother effect.

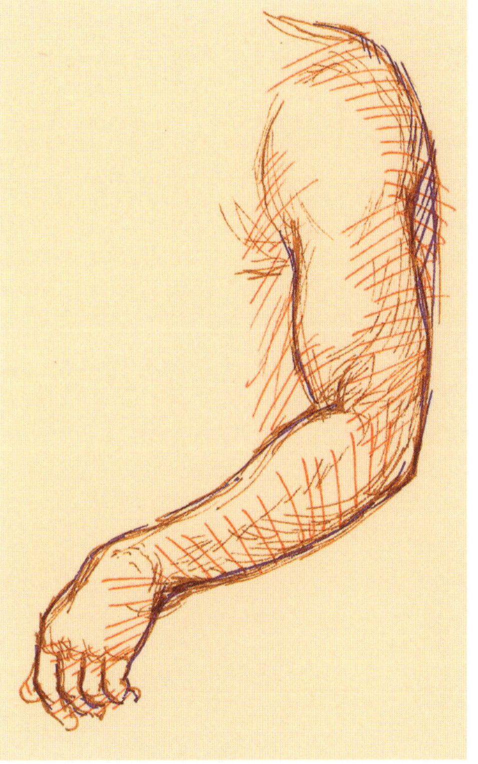

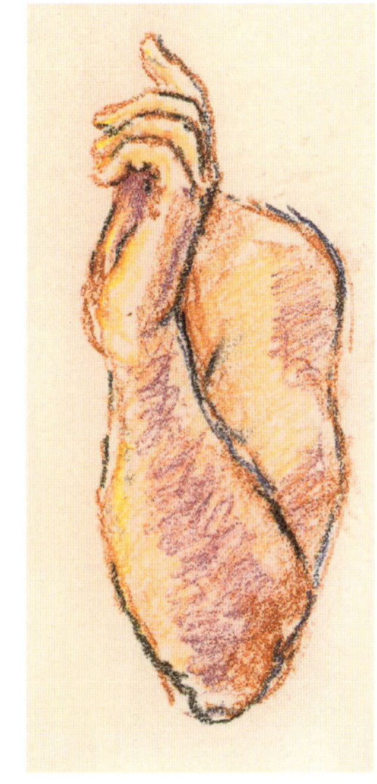

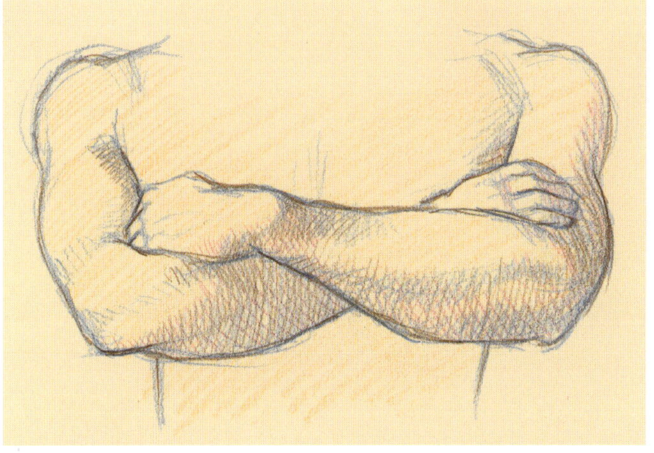

Legs and Feet

To draw the legs and feet, you can use your own seen in a mirror or ask people to pose for you. You will need to show the difference between female and male legs, which is evident in the softer, rounder forms of the former and the harder lines of the latter. However, the difference may not be so obvious on the legs of a female athlete compared to the legs of a sedentary male. The hardest part is to get the proportion between the upper and lower leg correct, and the drawings of the knee and ankle joints.

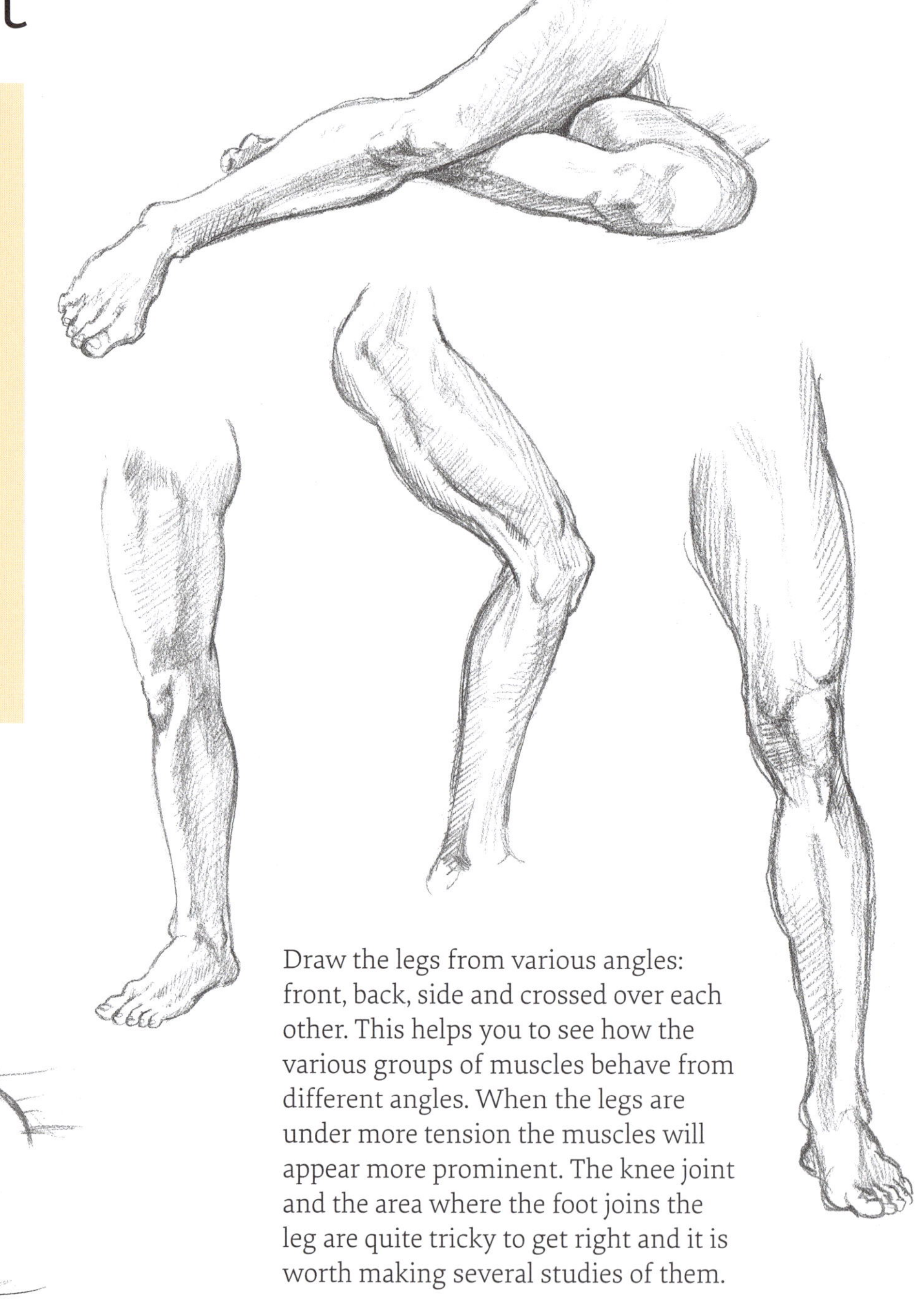

Draw the legs from various angles: front, back, side and crossed over each other. This helps you to see how the various groups of muscles behave from different angles. When the legs are under more tension the muscles will appear more prominent. The knee joint and the area where the foot joins the leg are quite tricky to get right and it is worth making several studies of them.

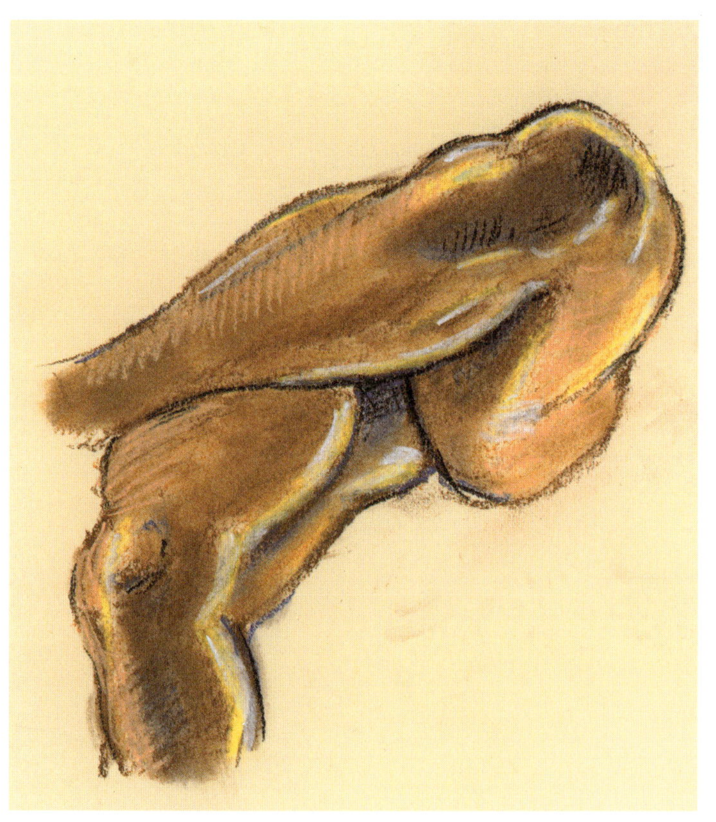

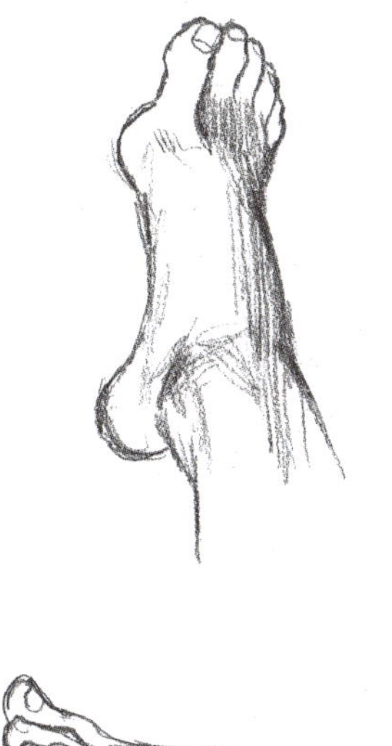

Feet are not too difficult in themselves, being less flexible than hands, but the difficult angles are drawing them from directly in front or from the rear.

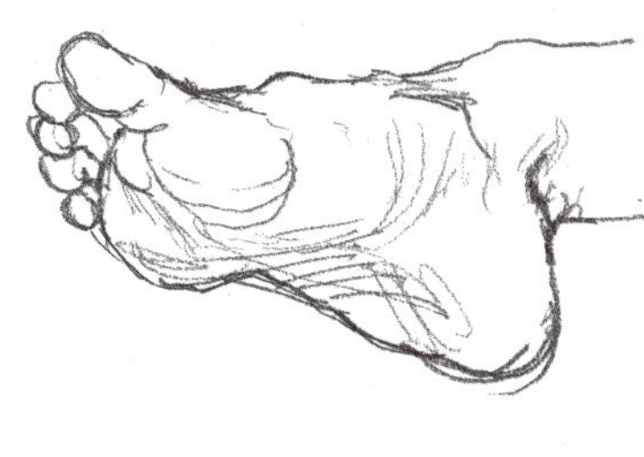

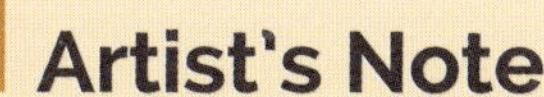

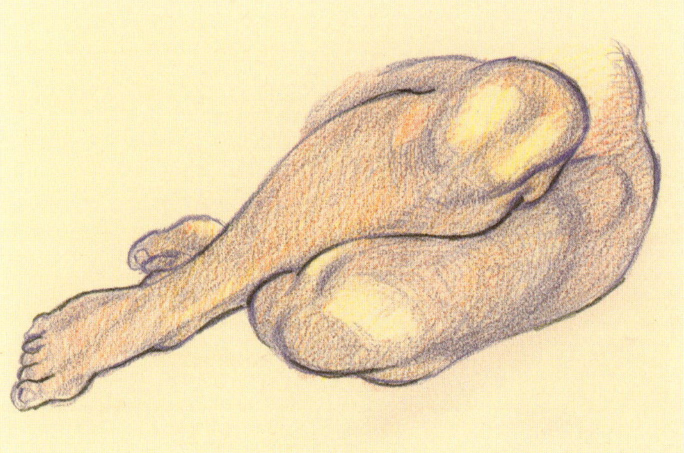

In these two colour studies of folded legs I have taken the drawing a step further. In the drawing of male legs (top) I used a black chalk outline in combination with soft colour pastels, smudging the pigment in places to give the smooth effect of muscles under skin. The female legs were drawn in coloured pencil, with a strong outline to denote the unusual shapes produced in this view.

Artist's Note

Drawing the parts of the human body is never a waste of your artistic time. It will teach you more about drawing than any other kind of drawing that you can think of. It is at one and the same time the most difficult and the most satisfying exercise and will help you to become an efficient draughtsman quicker than any other kind of work.

Putting It All Together

In the final exercise in this chapter, we'll bring together what we have learned about the figure so far and apply it to a realistic subject in a simple setting. My example is of a young woman sitting on the beach on a windy day, with shorts and a hooded top. She is looking ahead while she holds her phone in her hand, as seems usual.

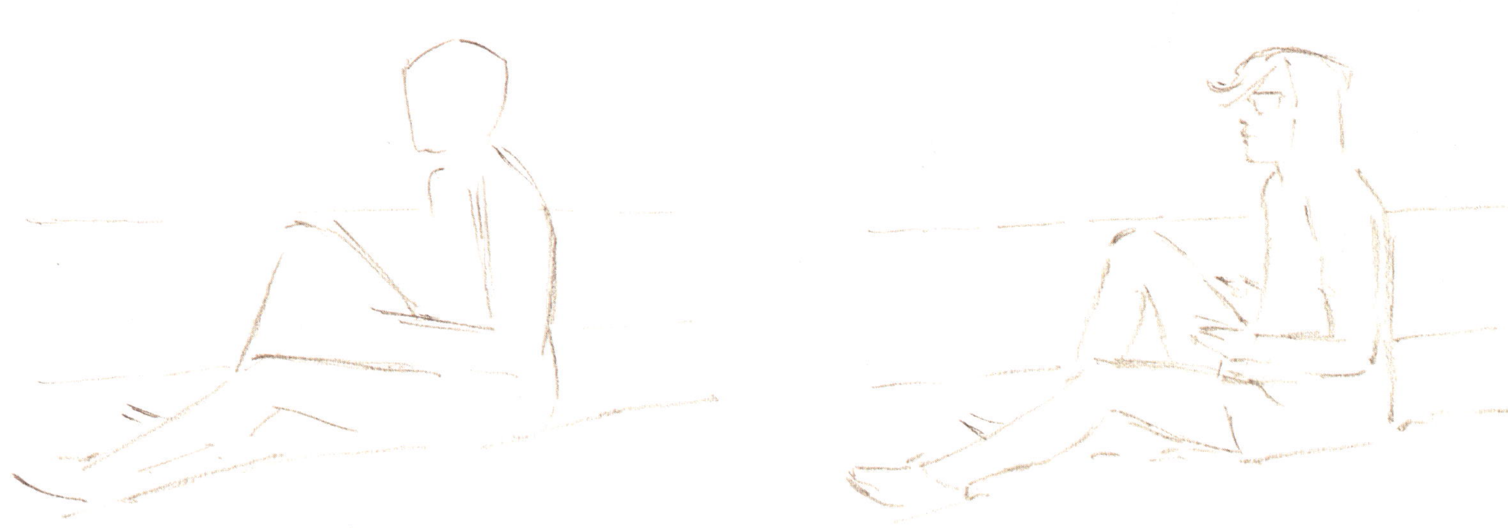

STEP 1

As before, start by sketching in the main shapes of the figure to get the right proportion and position of the limbs. I have a used a dark brown pastel crayon.

STEP 2

Now start to draw the full shape of the figure and the background. First carefully outline the main shapes of head, torso, arms and legs. This drawing needs to be as accurate as you can make it, because it is the basis of everything that you draw from now on. While the forms of the girl's legs are clearly visible, the arms and even parts of the neck and head are obscured by her clothing. Try to get the dimensions and angles correct nevertheless, or your drawing will not be convincing. Sketch in the line of the horizon of the sea behind her and the sloping shape of the beach that she is sitting on.

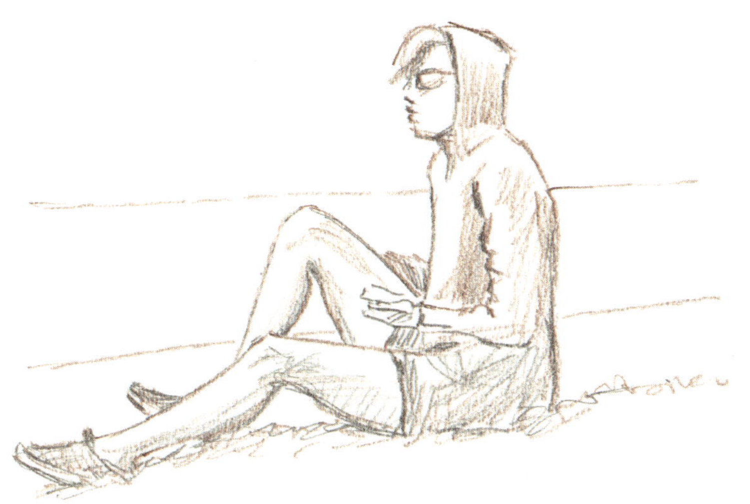

STEP 3

The next stage is to begin lightly putting in the tone or shading in all but the brightest areas. Squinting your eyes will help you to identify these highlights. Do not apply tone too heavily yet; you want an all over tone to start with as this makes it easier to balance the tones in the final stage. Don't forget the shadow that the figure casts on the beach below and behind her.

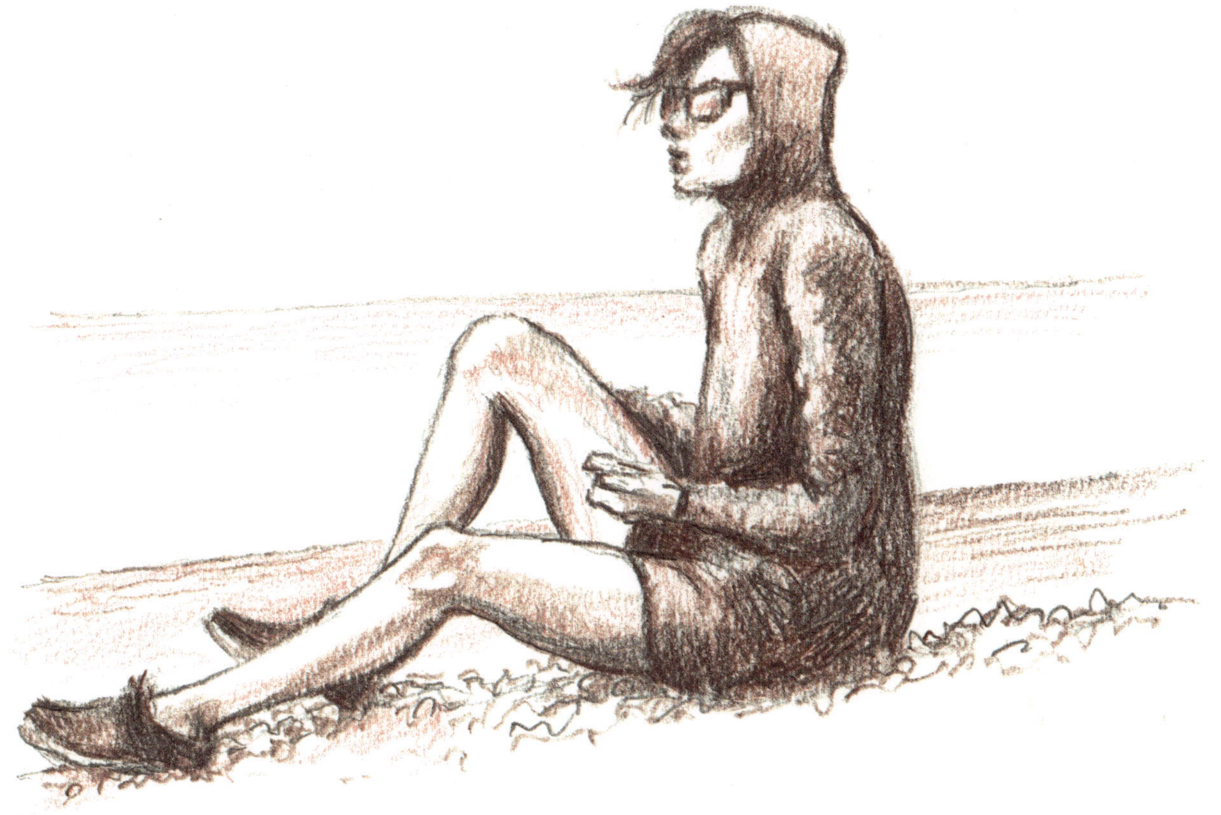

STEP 4

Now build up the darker tones to give volume to your figure. If you are following my colour scheme, use a warm, reddish brown to add tone, before putting in darker tones of the dark brown that you started with. For the very darkest bits a touch of a dark blue will help to give more intensity.

Chapter Two

PROPORTIONS AND FIRST DRAWINGS OF THE HEAD

One thing that beginners often fail to realize when starting out on a portrait is that understanding the whole head is the key to getting a good result. Unless the artist has a thorough knowledge of the proportions and structure of the head, a portrait can look like a face lacking the foundation of a properly constructed skull. We start this chapter by looking at the proportions of the head and how it appears from different angles. Then I will set out two methods for drawing the head accurately: one using carefully observed outline shapes and the other by measuring the placement of the features within the shape of the whole head. Both of these are valid starting points for a portrait.

Close study of all the facial features will further inform your drawing. The eyes are paramount, because they are what makes a person recognizable to us. The mouth and nose are next. The pecking order of the rest depends on the characteristics of your subject. What we will show is the normal formation of these features, but bear in mind that the features of individuals do vary quite dramatically sometimes.

Finally, we will consider just some of the variations you will come across when drawing the head, from the effects of ageing to the myriad range of expressions that we can make using the muscles of the face.

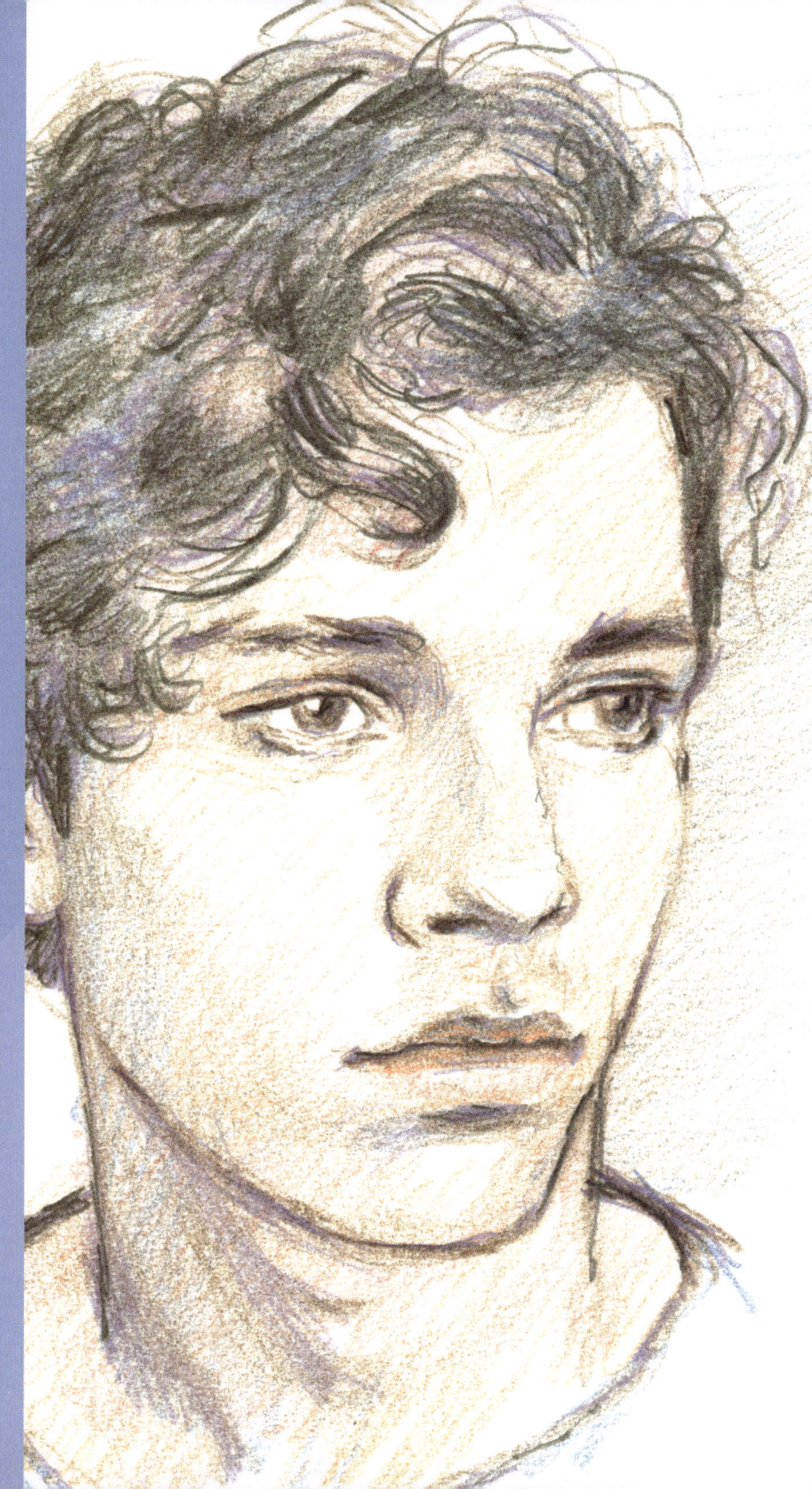

Proportions of the Head

The head proportions shown here are broadly true of adult humans of any race or culture. If this is the first time you have studied these measurements you may find some of them a little surprising; for example the eyes are not situated in the top half of the face, but exactly half way down the head.

Profile view

This view of the head can be seen proportionately as a square which encompasses the whole head. When this square is divided across the diagonal, it can be seen immediately that the mass of the hair area is in the top part of the diagonal and takes up almost all the space, except for the ears.

When the square is divided in half horizontally it's also clear that the eyes are halfway down the length of the head. Where the horizontal halfway line meets the diagonal halfway line is the centre of the square. The ears appear to be at this centre point, but just behind the vertical centre line.

A line level with the eyebrow also marks the top edge of the ear. The bottom edge of the ear is level with the end of the nose, which is halfway between the eyebrow and the chin. The bottom edge of the lower lip is about halfway between the end of the nose and the chin.

While these measurements aren't exact, they are fairly accurate and will hold good for most people's heads.

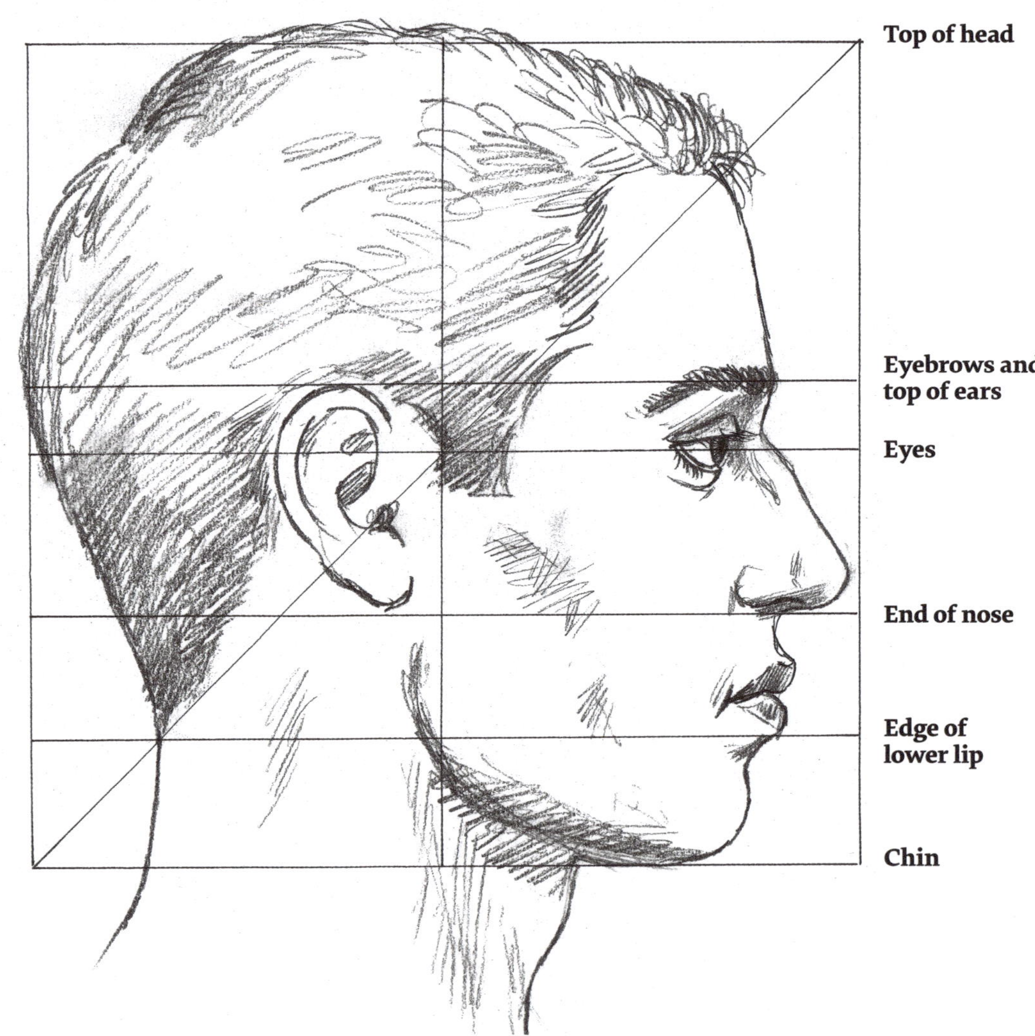

Front view

From the front, as long as the head isn't tilted, it is about one and a half times as long as it is wide. The widest part is just above the ears.

As in the side view, the eyes are halfway down the length of the head and the end of the nose is halfway between the eyebrows and the chin; the bottom edge of the lip is about halfway between the end of the nose and the chin.

The space between the eyes is the same as the length of the eye. The width of the mouth is such that the corners appear to be the same distance apart as the pupils of the eyes, when looking straight ahead.

These are very simple measurements and might not be quite accurate on some heads, but as a rule you can rely on them – artists have been doing so for many centuries.

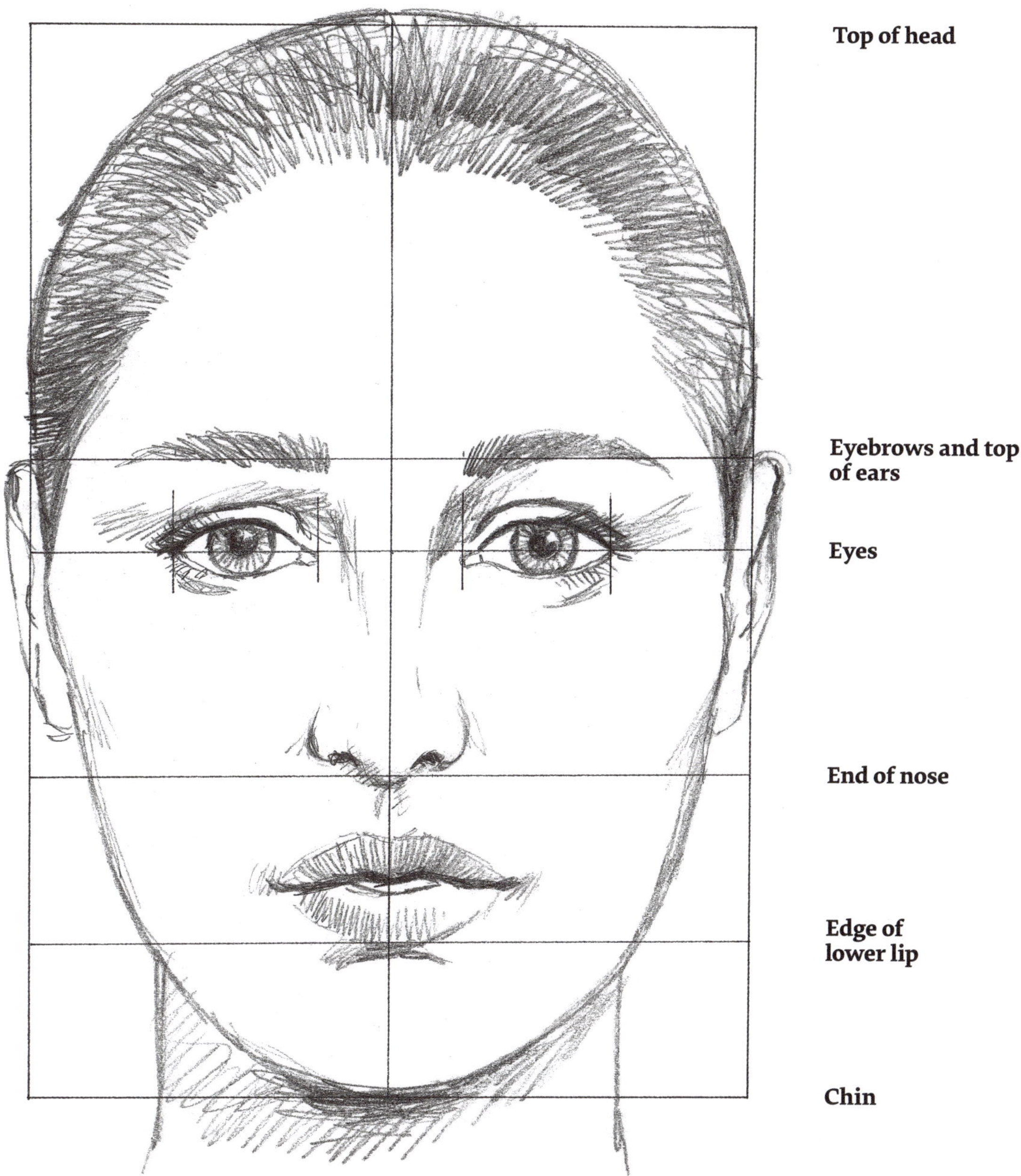

Children's heads

There are significant proportional differences between the heads of children and adults which the artist has to bear in mind when undertaking a portrait; I have the listed the main ones below. The features, too, change with growth. In adults the eyes are closer together and are set halfway down the head. Nose, cheekbones and jaw become more clearly defined and more angular as we mature.

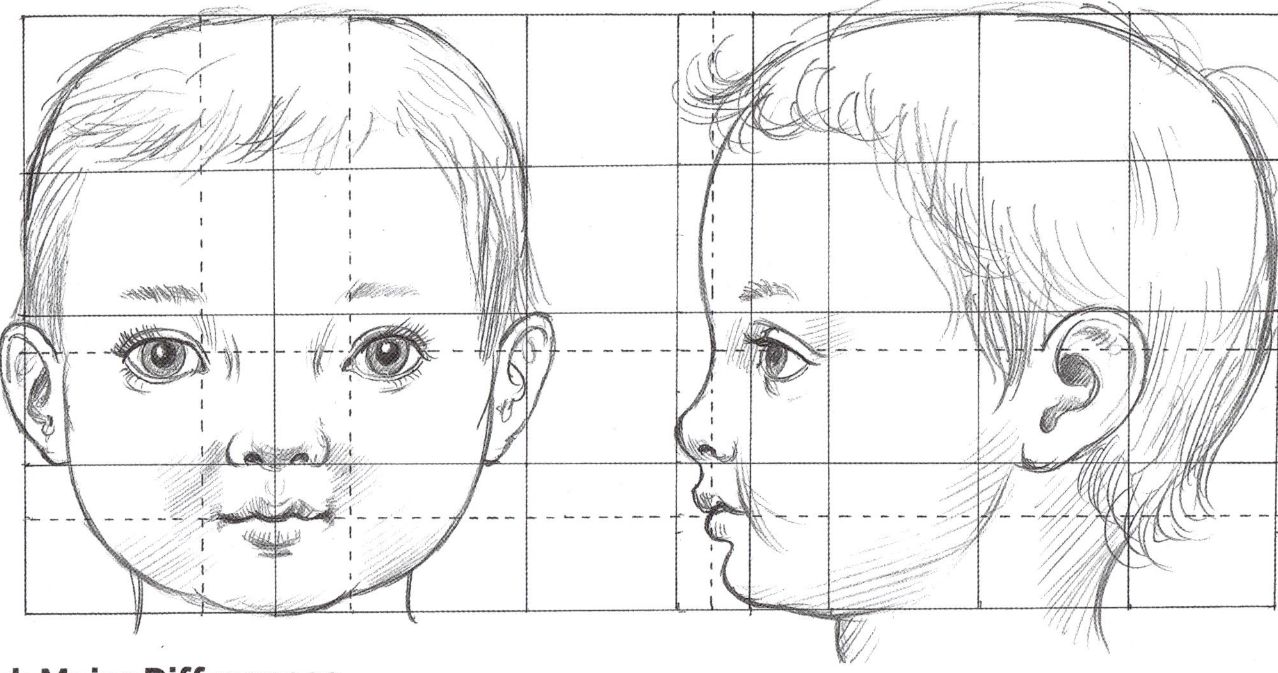

The Head: Major Differences

- In relation to its body, a child's head is much larger; this will be evident even if you can only see the head and shoulders. A child's head is much smaller than an adult's, but the proportion of head to body is such that the head appears larger.
- The cranium or upper part of the child's skull is much larger in proportion to the rest of the face. This gradually alters as the child grows and reaches adult proportions.
- The child's eyes appear much larger in the head than an adult's, whereas the mouth and nose often appear smaller. The eyes also appear to be wider apart. The nose is usually short with nostrils facing outward so that it appears upturned.
- The jawbones and teeth are much smaller in proportion to the rest of the head, again because they are still not fully developed. The rule with the adult – that places the eyes halfway down the head – does not work with a child, where the eyes appear much lower down.
- With very young children, the forehead is high and wide, the ears and eyes very large, the nose small and upturned, the cheeks full and round and the mouth and jaw very small. Also there are no lines to speak of on the face.
- The hair is finer, even if luxuriant, and so tends to show the head shape much more clearly.

The Head from Different Angles

Studying the overall structure of the head from various angles gives us a thorough understanding of the appearance of our subject and is key to getting a good likeness. Notice how, as the head turns, the look of each feature changes, sometimes quite dramatically.

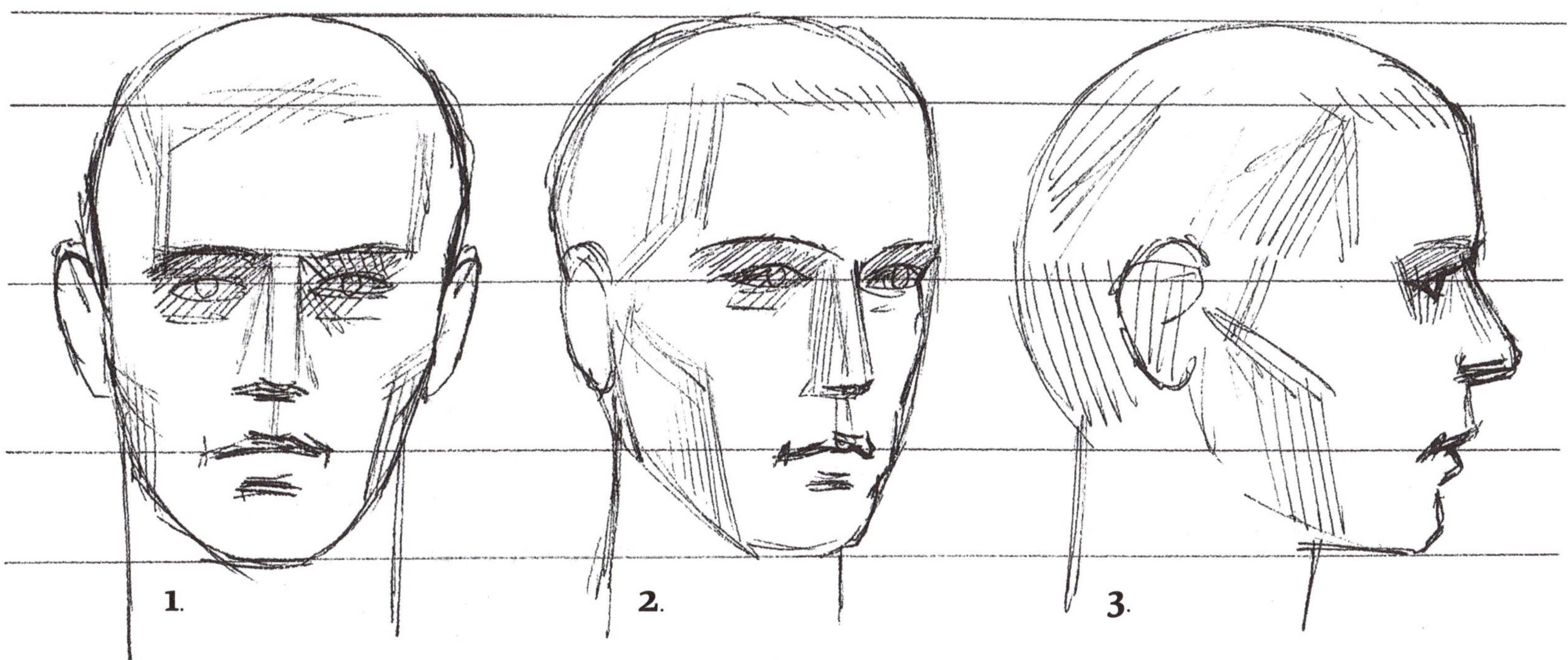

The head is often observed turning from full face towards a profile view. Looking at the full face (1), both eyes are the same shape, the mouth is fully displayed, and the nose is indicated chiefly by the nostrils. As shown in our diagram, when the head turns, the features remain the same distance apart and stay in the same relationship horizontally.

However, as the head rotates away to a three-quarter view (2), we begin to see the shape of the nose becoming more evident, while the far side of the mouth compresses into a shorter line, and the eye farthest from our view appears smaller than the nearer one.

Continuing towards the profile or side view (3), the nose becomes more and more prominent, while one eye disappears completely. Only half of the mouth can now be seen and – given the perspective – this is quite short in length. Notice how the shape of the head also changes from a rather narrow shape – longer than it is broad – to quite a square one, where width and length are almost the same. We can also see the shape of the ear, which at full face was hardly noticeable.

Next, we shall look at the head in another sequence that opens with the full face, but this time the head will be lifted backwards with the chin tilting up, until very little of the face is seen from below.

Note at the beginning that the front view goes from the top of the head to the tip of the chin, and the facial features are all clearly visible.

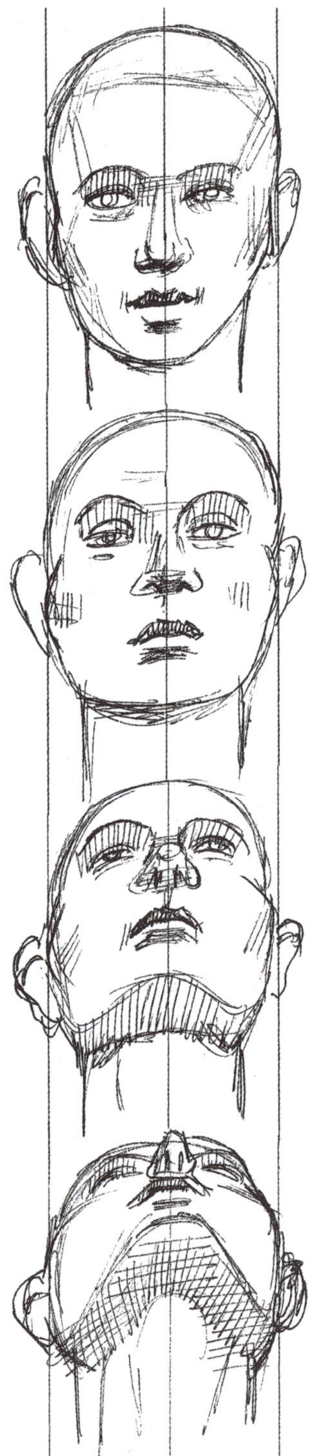

Now, as we tilt the head backwards, we see less of the forehead and start to reveal the underside of the jaw and the nose. The end of the nose now seems to be about halfway down the head instead of three-quarters, as it was in the first diagram. The eyes appear narrower and the top of the head is invisible.

One more tilt of the head shows an even larger area underneath the jaw, and the mouth seems to curve downwards. The underside of the nose, with both nostrils very clearly visible, starts to look as though it is positioned between the eyes, which are even more narrowed now. The forehead is reduced to a small crescent shape and the cheekbones stand out more sharply. The ears, meanwhile, are descending to a position level with the chin, and the neck is very prominent.

One further tilt lifts the chin so high that we can now see its complete shape; and the nose, mouth and eyebrows are all so close together that they can hardly be seen. This angle of the head is unfamiliar to us, and is only usually seen when someone is lying down and we are looking up towards their head.

Note how the head looks vastly different from this angle, appearing as a much shorter, compacted shape.

These examples show variations on viewing the head from slightly unusual angles, and you can see how they all suggest different expressions of the body's movement. Although the models for these drawings were not trying to express any particular feelings, the very fact of the movement of the head lends a certain element of drama to the drawings. This is because we don't usually move our heads without meaning something, and the inclination of the head one way or another looks as though something is meant by the action.

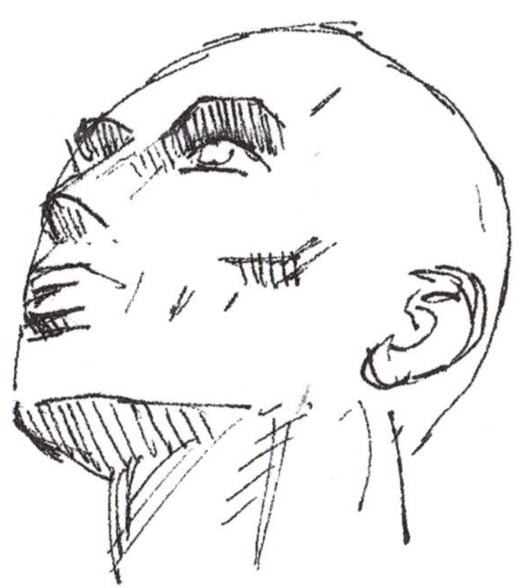

Leaning back seen from below

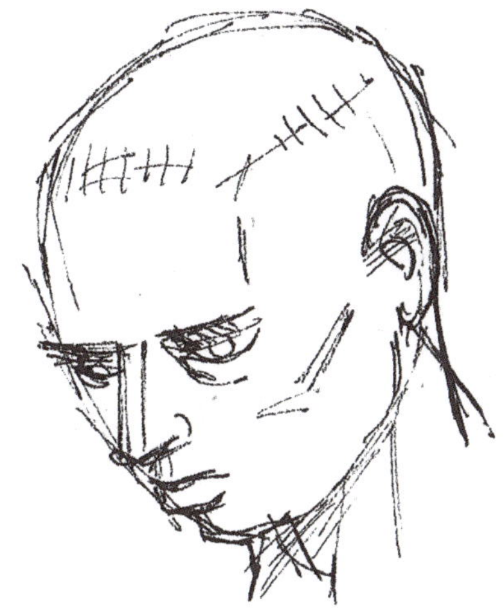

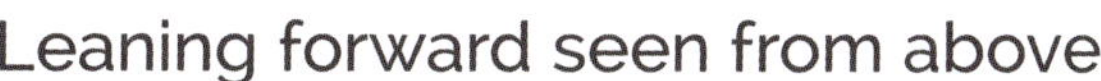

Leaning forward seen from above

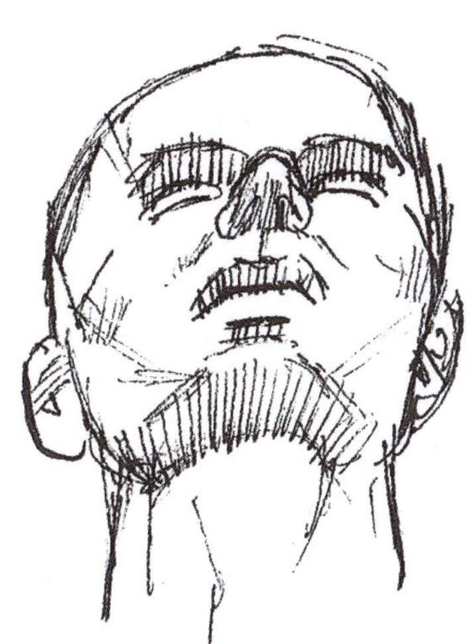

Leaning back seen from below

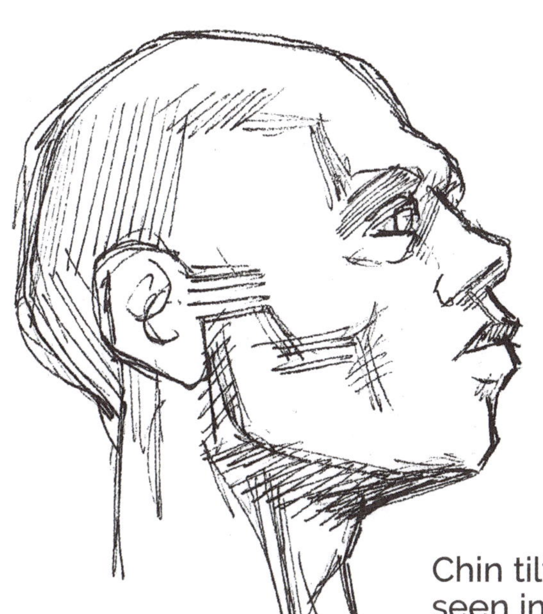

Chin tilted up seen in profile

Three-quarter view, head tilted towards viewer

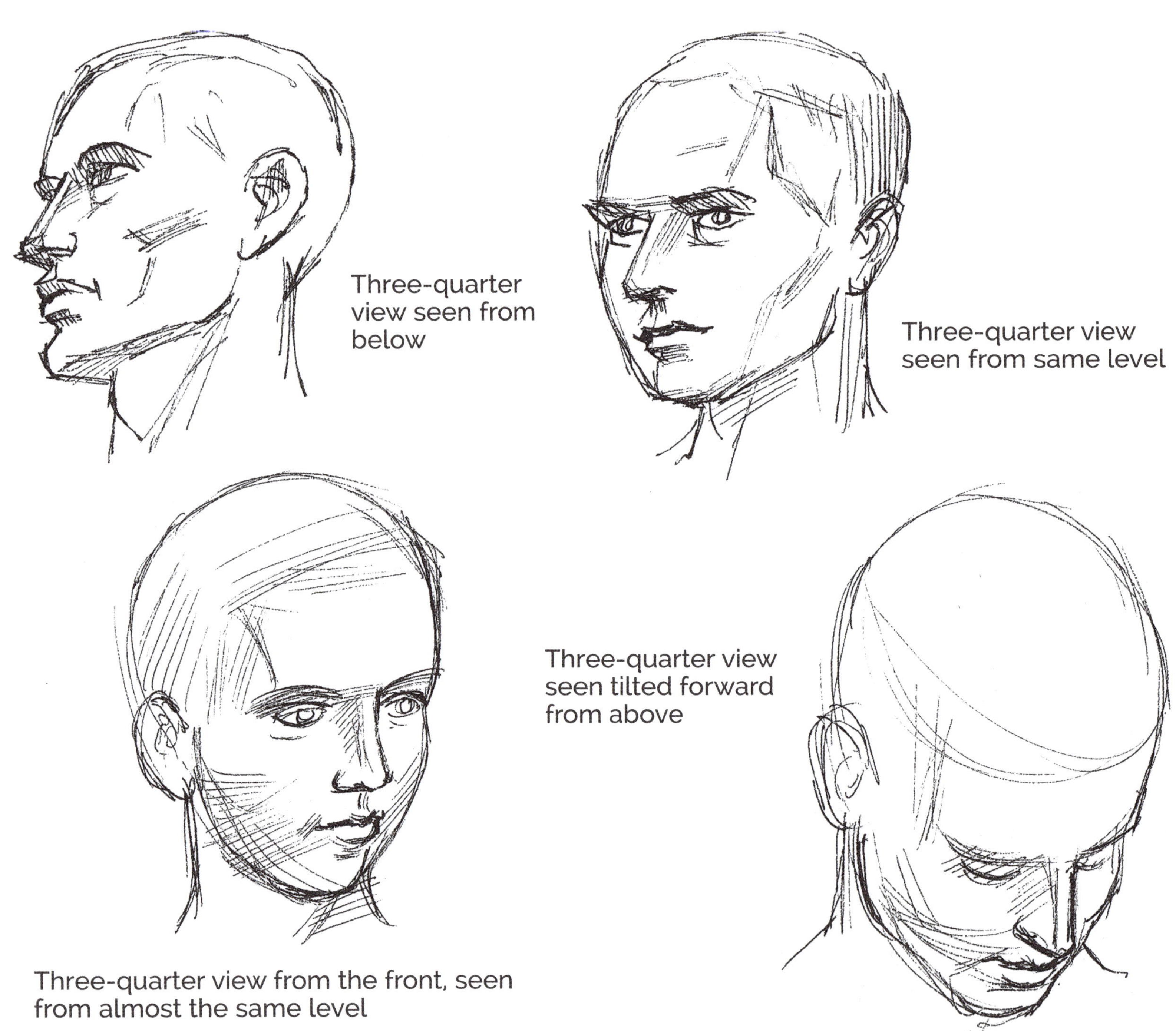

Three-quarter view seen from below

Three-quarter view seen from same level

Three-quarter view seen tilted forward from above

Three-quarter view from the front, seen from almost the same level

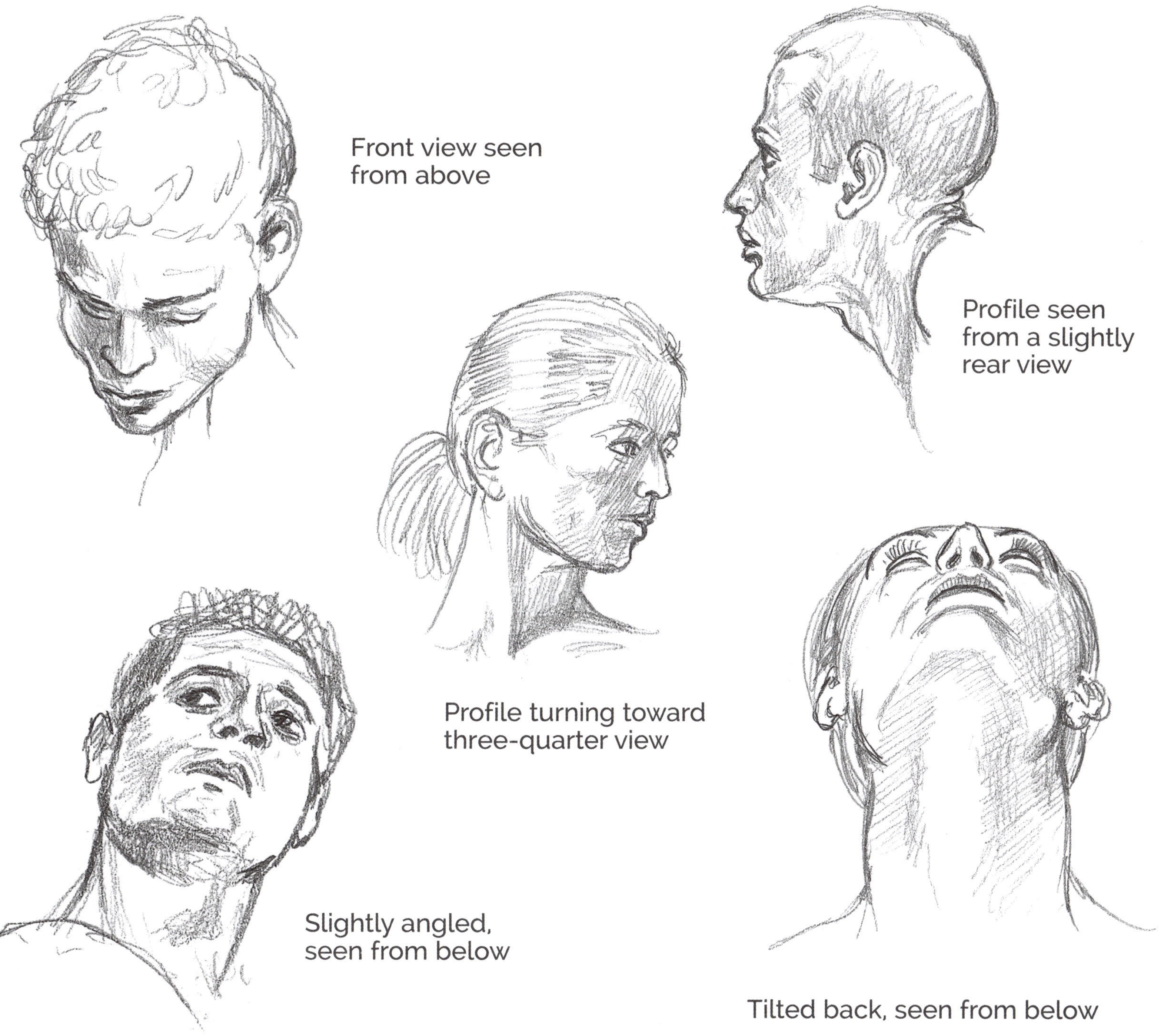

Front view seen from above

Profile seen from a slightly rear view

Profile turning toward three-quarter view

Slightly angled, seen from below

Tilted back, seen from below

Drawing the Head: Basic Method

Here I have shown a classic three-quarter view of the head, drawn in five steps. Starting with the basic shapes and areas of the head, you can then add in the subtle individual shapes and marks that will make your drawing a realistic representation of a particular person. You can use this technique as the basis for a portrait.

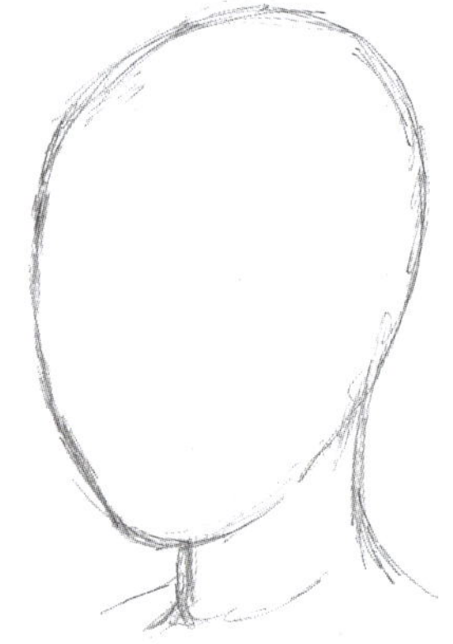

STEP 1

First ascertain the overall shape of the head or skull and the way it sits on the neck. It may be very rounded, long and thin or square and solid. Whatever its shape you need to define it clearly and accurately at the outset, as this will make everything else easier later on.

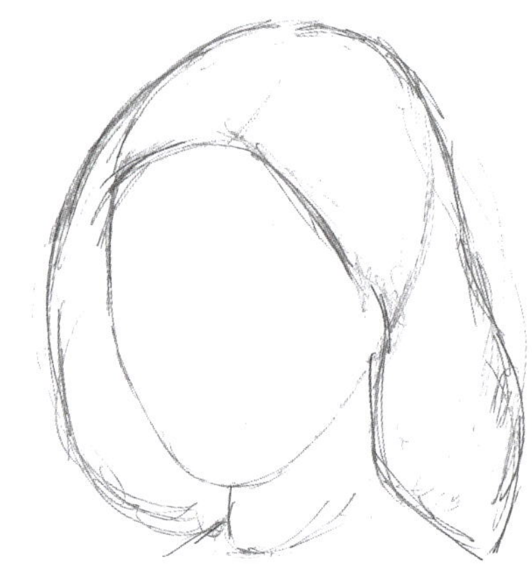

STEP 2

Decide how the hair covers the head and how much there is in relation to the whole head. Draw the basic shape and don't concern yourself with details at this stage.

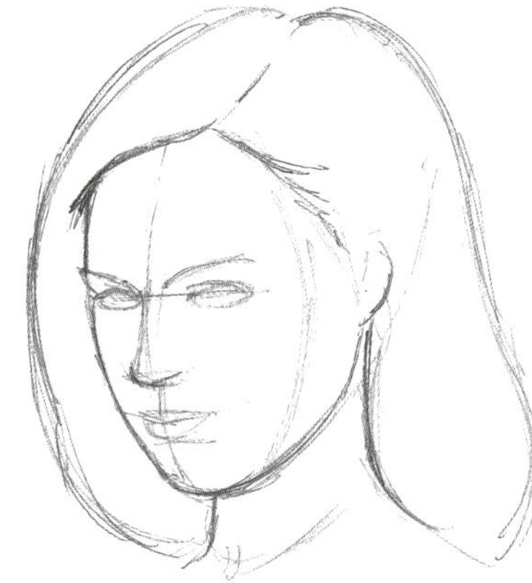

STEP 3

Now ascertain the basic shape and position of the features, starting with the eyes. Get the level and size correct and their general shape, including the eyebrows.

The nose is next, its shape (whether upturned, straight, aquiline, broad or narrow), its tilt and the amount it projects from the main surface of the face.

Now look at the mouth, gauging its width and thickness, and ensuring that you place it correctly in relation to the chin.

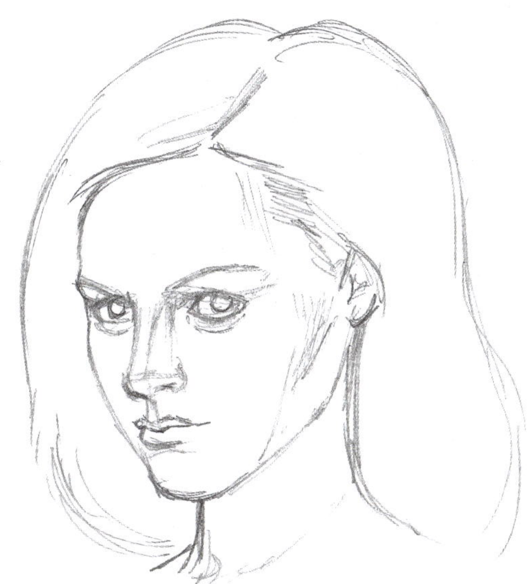

STEP 4

The form of the face is shown by the tonal qualities of the shadows on the head. Just outline the form of these shadows and concentrate on capturing the general area correctly.

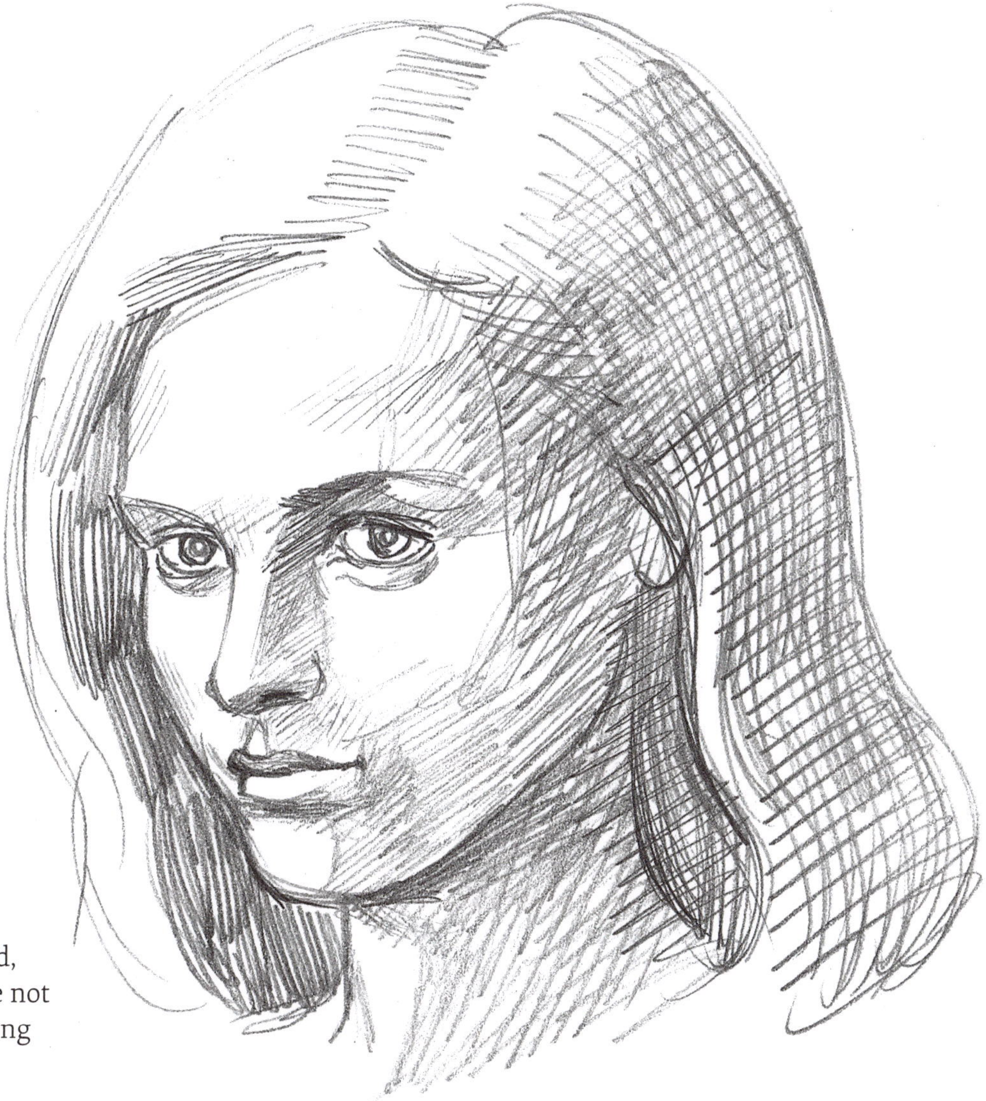

STEP 5

Work in the tonal values over the whole head, noting which areas are darker and which are not so dark, emphasizing the former and softening the latter.

Drawing the Head: Alternative Method

In this exercise we take our drawing of the head a step further, using some subtle shading to model the features. You may experiment with using some colour as I have, or stick to graphite pencil for your shading.

STEP 1

This method of measuring the head uses the proportions shown on pages 42–3. It is very helpful if you are not too sure about judging proportions.

- Remember that when the head is level, the eyes are halfway down its length. Mark in the top of the head and the bottom of the chin, and make a mark halfway between them. Then sketch in the shape of the eyes, remembering that the space between each eye is the same length as the eye itself.
- Then mark in the nose end about halfway between the eye line and the chin line.
- The bottom of the ear is roughly level with the nostril and the top of the ear is level with the eyebrow just above the eye.
- Now mark in the mouth line which is slightly closer to the end of the nose than the chin.
- The hairline is roughly halfway between the top of the head and the eyeline (though hairlines can vary considerably).

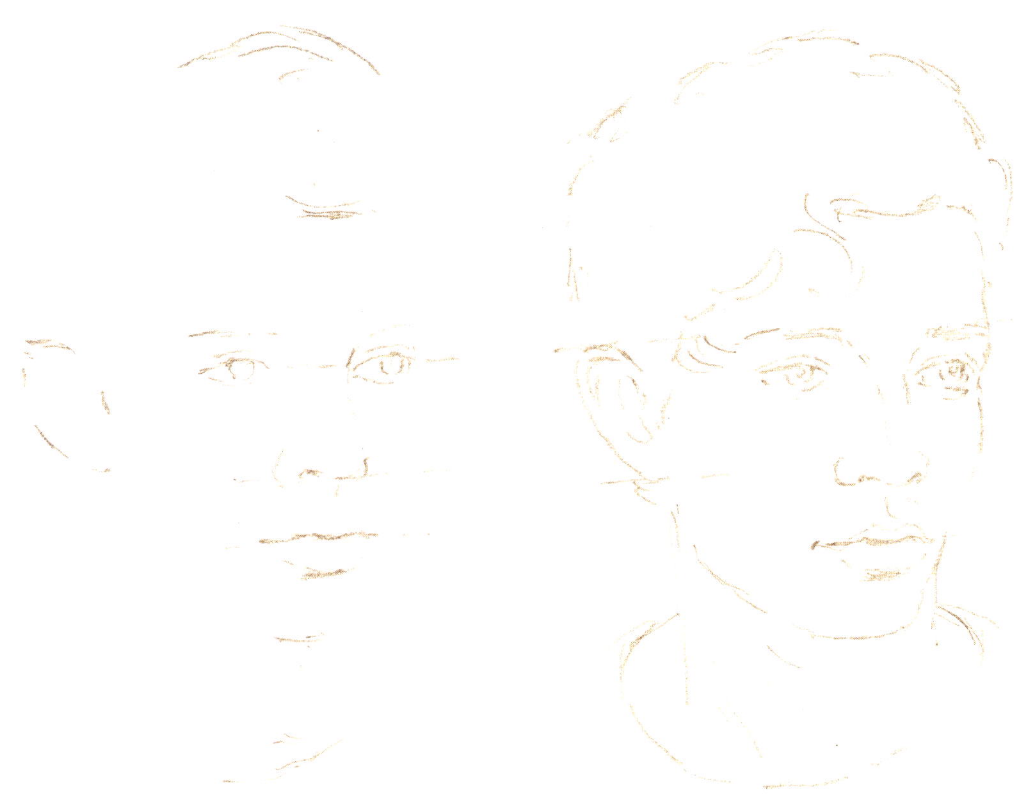

STEP 2

With all these marks made you can now attempt a simple line drawing of the main shape of the head and position of the neck. Try to get the shapes of the eyes, the nose and the mouth as accurate as possible, because this is how we all recognize a face. The position, shape and thickness of the eyebrows are also very characteristic. The ears and hairline, while not quite so fundamental, can help to achieve a likeness.

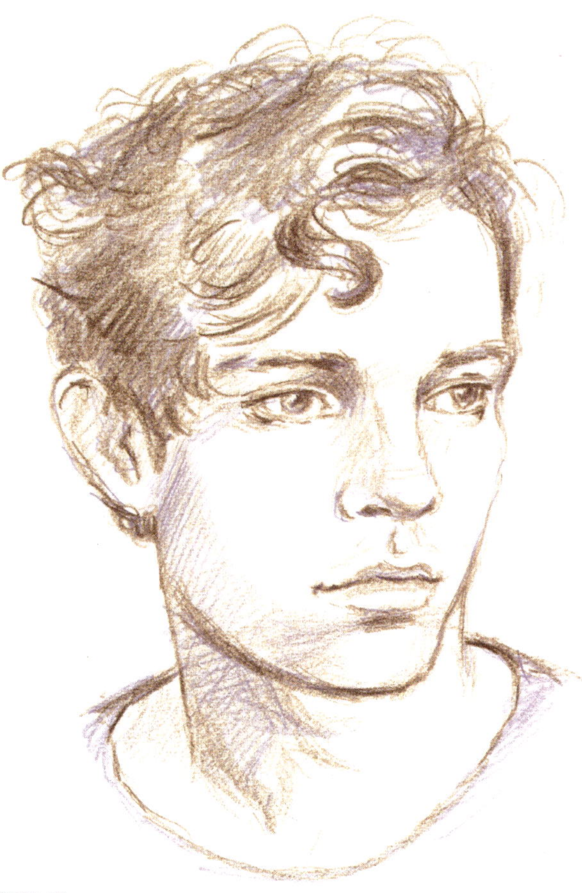

STEP 3

Now you can erase your guidelines and start to shade the face and the hair carefully but still in a very light tone. Apart from the darker area of the hair, there is more shading in the lower part of the face, especially around the jawline. Note the upper lip looks darker than the lower lip, but there is a shadow under the lower lip. Add a bit of tone under the eyebrows, particularly in the inside corner between the eye and the nose. Darken the pupils and iris of the eyes but leave a little bit of paper showing for the highlight near the pupil.

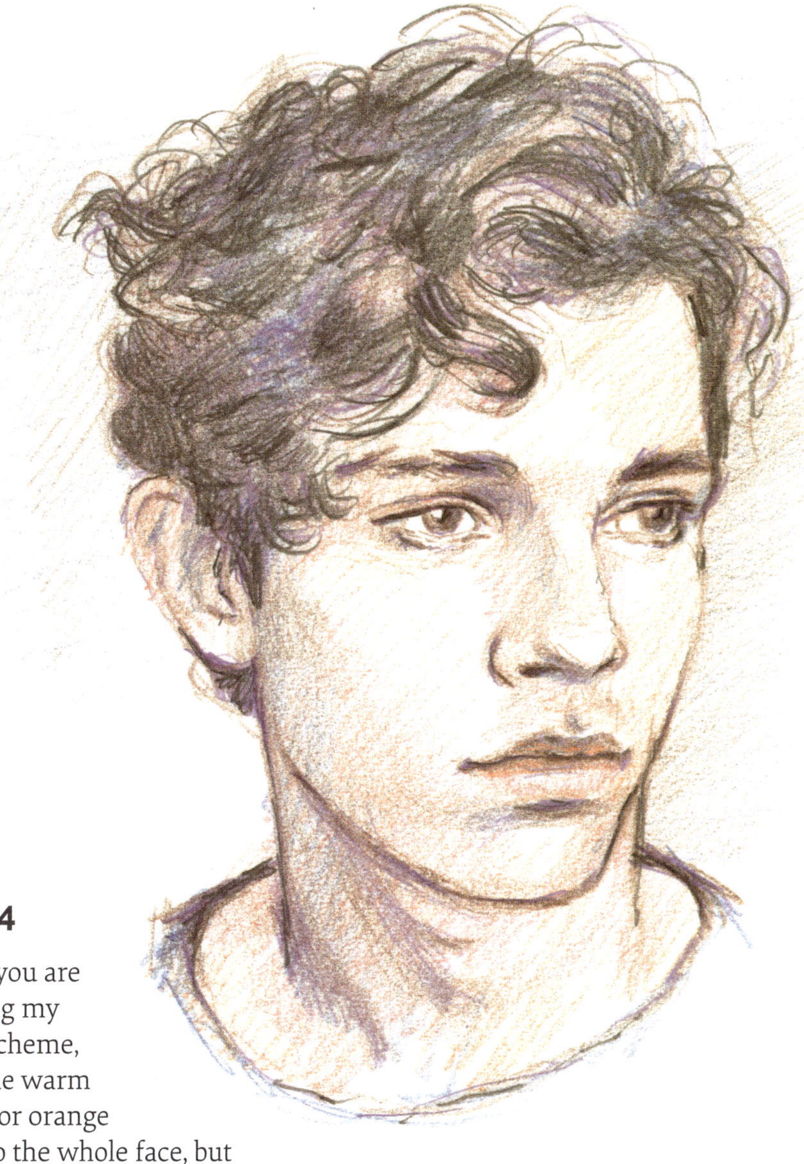

STEP 4

Now, if you are following my colour scheme, add some warm pinkish or orange colour to the whole face, but very lightly. It must not be very noticeable. Then darken all the shaded parts of the head. Half close your eyes as you look at the person and it will be more obvious where the darker parts are. The hair can be worked on with even, darker tones and so can the pupils of the eyes, the eyebrows, the nostrils, the line where the mouth opens and around the edges of the jawline, neck and forehead.

Drawing Facial Features

The variety to be found in the features of the face is astounding, and this variety is what helps us to identify others. Each individual has a unique combination of features that, once we know them, we are programmed to recognize. When it comes to drawing you need to go beyond recognition and study the features of your sitter in depth.

Eyes

The most significant part of the face that we recognize are the eyes, so we will start there. You can begin by drawing only one eye, but it's probably a good idea to draw both together so that the relationship of the two eyes to each other is observed.

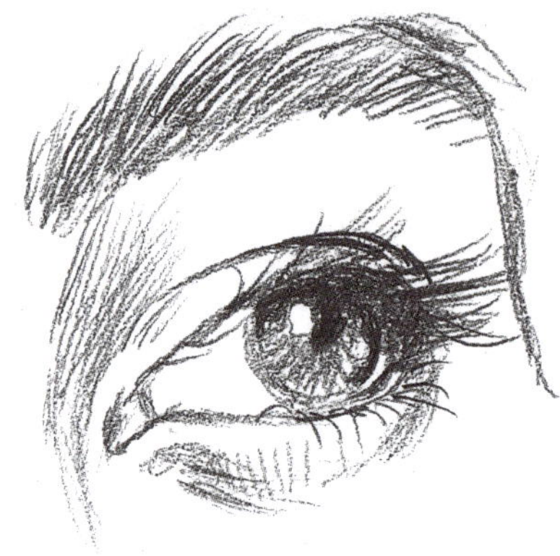

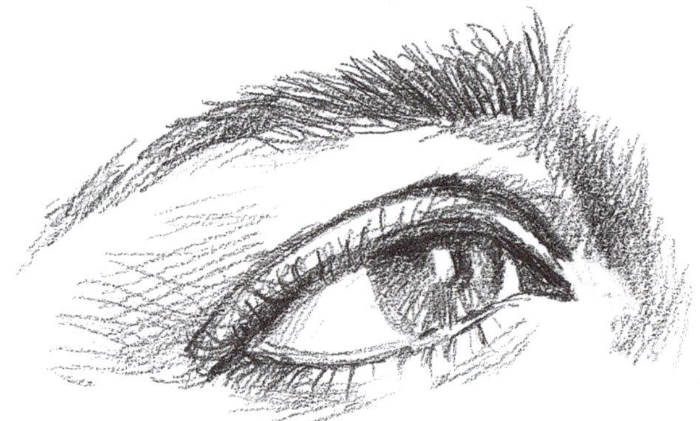

My first drawing is of the eyes of a young woman who is looking to one side. Notice how the inner shape of the corner of the eye is different to that of the outer corner and how the eyes are set slightly around the curve of the head. Draw the eyebrows as well so that the space between the eyes can be judged more easily. This girl's eyes are looking up towards the light, so they are not open wide – the iris (the coloured part of the eye) is covered slightly by the upper lid and is touching, if not slightly under, the lower lid, something that is often not observed by beginners.

Now try drawing one eye, taking note of every detail of its shape and construction. I have drawn a diagram of the eye as well to emphasize its form. Note that the inner corner has the tear duct hollow, while the outer corner is simpler. The thickness of the eyelid can be seen on both the upper and lower lid, and they curve over the eyeball; the iris and the pupil curve too. The pupil will of course enlarge or diminish according to how much light is shining on the eye.

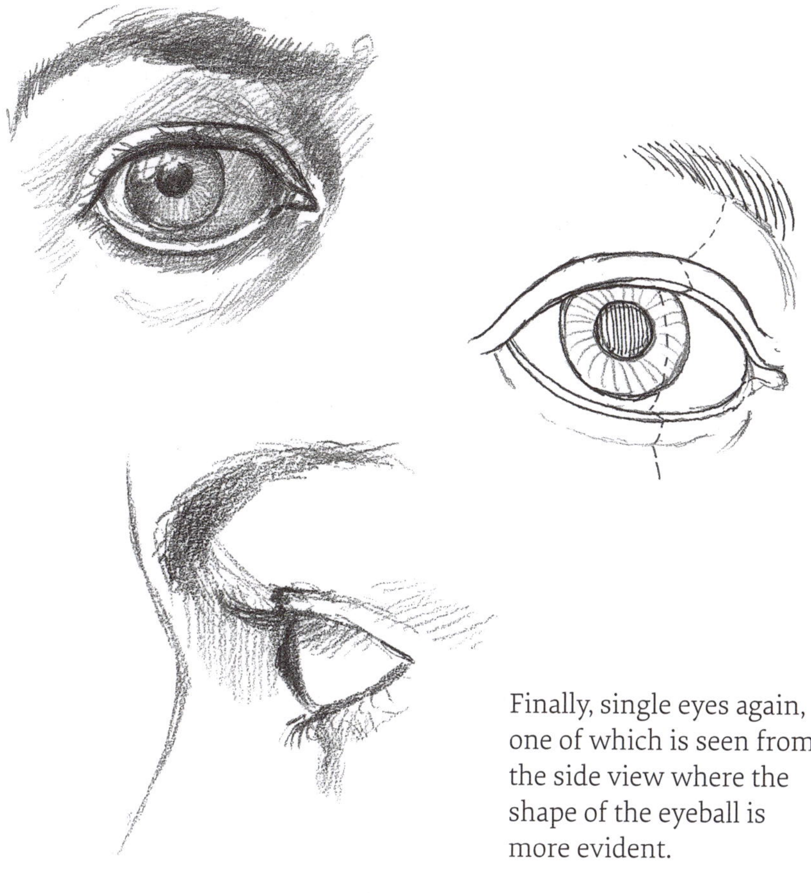

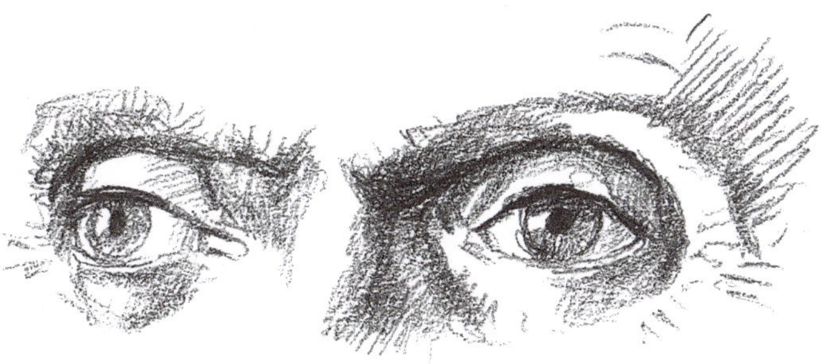

Now go back to drawing a pair of eyes, only this time try someone of a different age. I have shown the eyes of two older men (above and below). Notice the wrinkles and pouches in the skin around the eyes, and the texture and shapes of the eyebrows. While all eyes are a bit different, the main form is always the same; younger eyes are just a bit simpler in form, without all the marks of time.

Finally, single eyes again, one of which is seen from the side view where the shape of the eyeball is more evident.

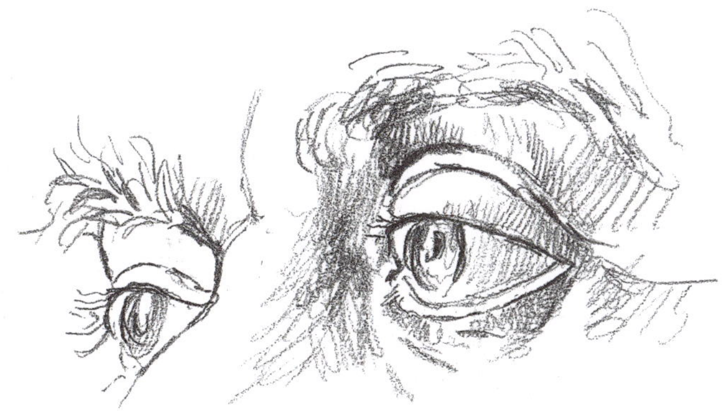

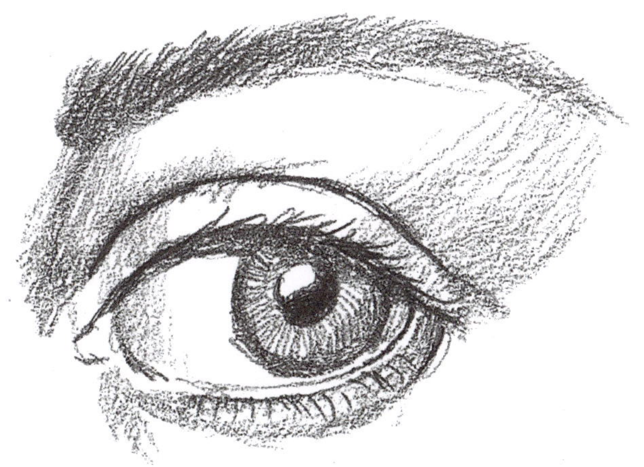

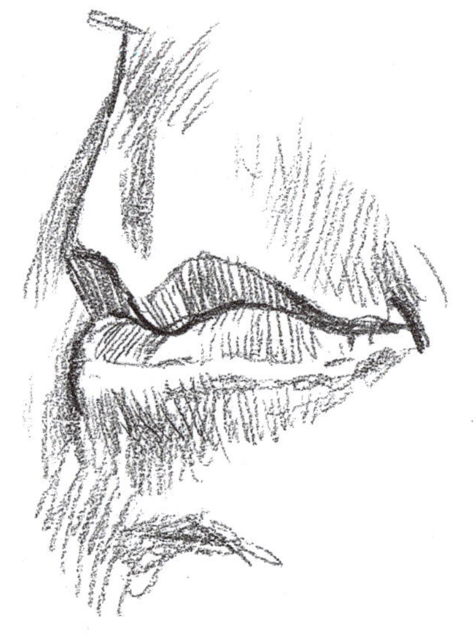

Mouths

Mouths are the next most recognizable part of the human face, except in the case of someone with a really dramatic nose. Draw mouths both shut and slightly open to understand the formation of the lips; the lower lip is often thicker than the upper one, but this is not invariably the case.

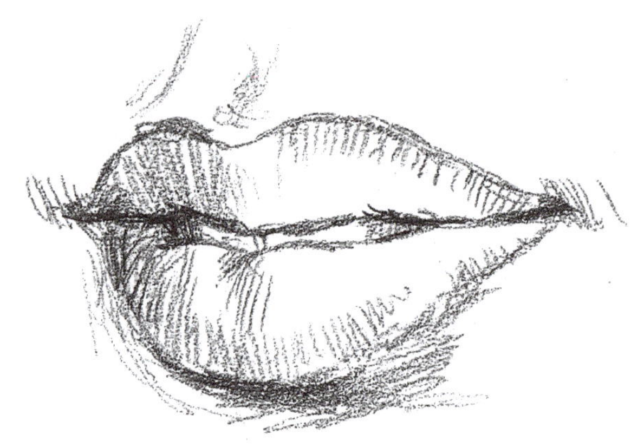

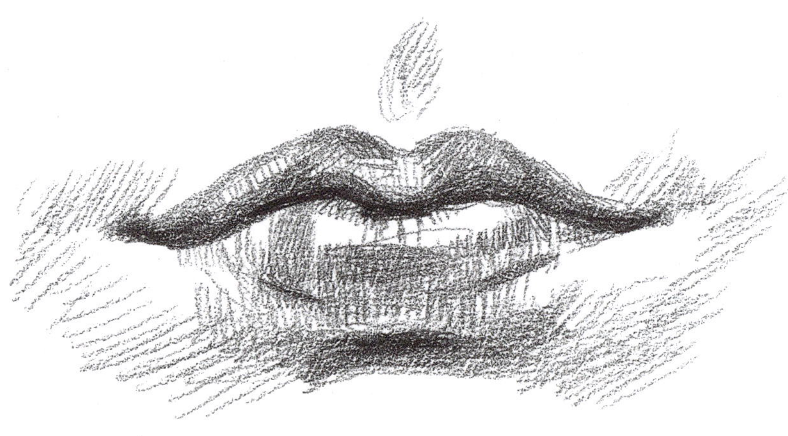

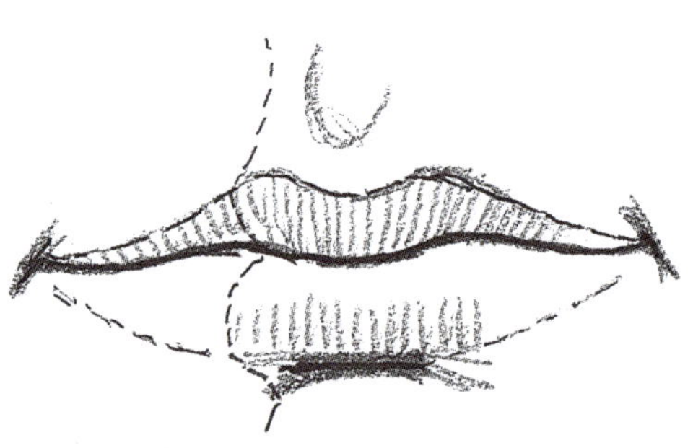

The typical Cupid's bow shape of the upper lip is often more sharply defined than the lower lip. When you draw the mouth, don't draw the colour of the lips, just their form, otherwise it will look as though all your people have strong lipstick on. The diagram on the left shows how the curves of the lip work as an overall shape.

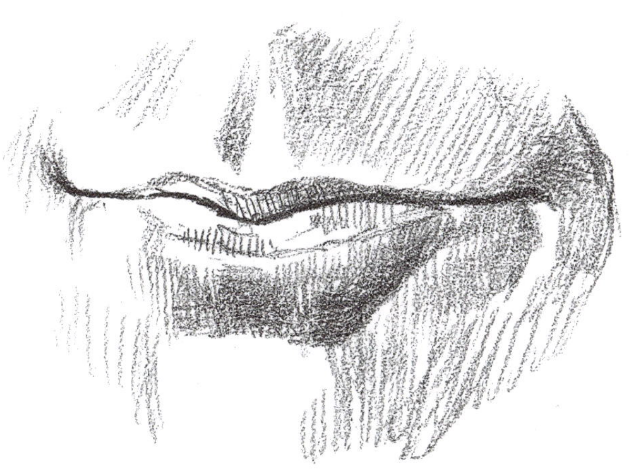

The strongest line on the mouth is where the lips meet, not their outer edge.

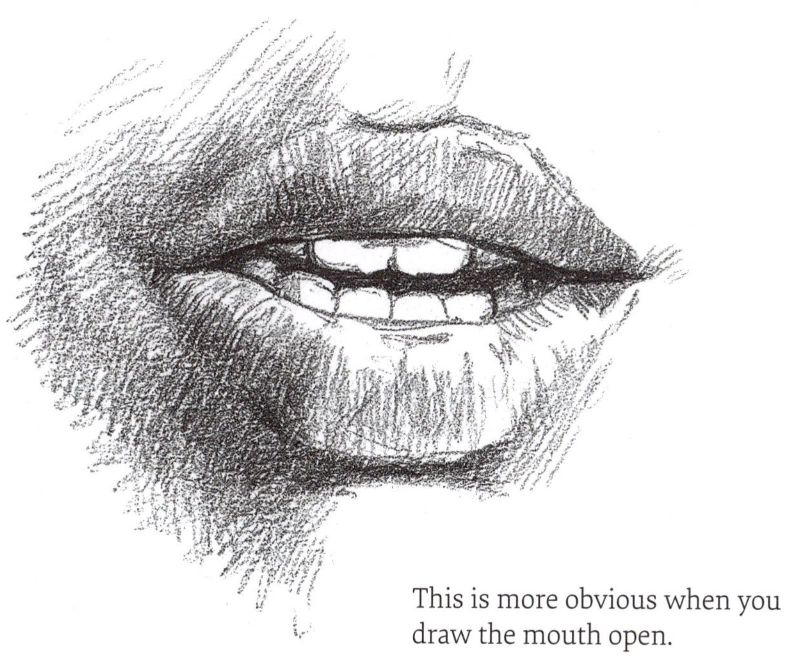

This is more obvious when you draw the mouth open.

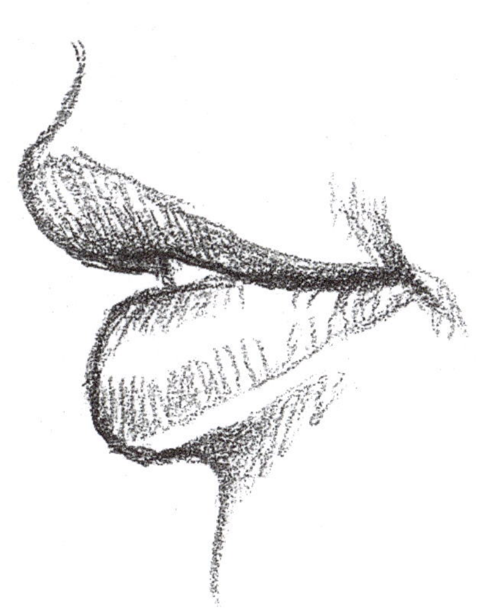

Don't forget to draw the mouth from the side as well, and notice whether the lower lip protrudes less or more than the upper lip.

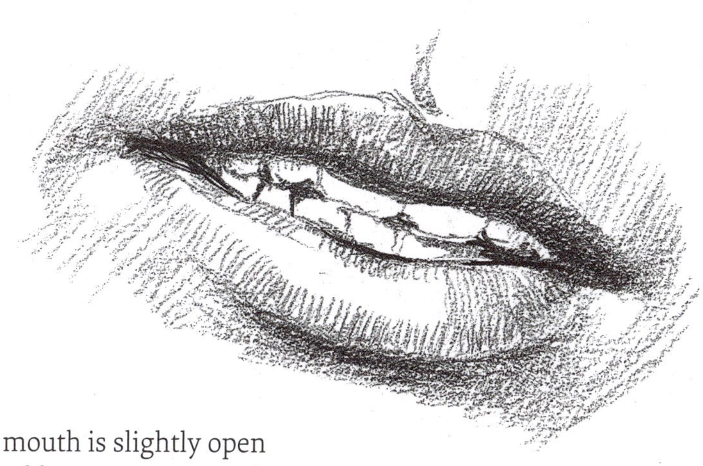

When the mouth is slightly open you will be able to see some teeth. Leave plenty of untouched paper here or they will look very grubby.

Noses

There is a lot of variation in noses, and they often form a very characterful part of the face. They are not at all hard to draw in profile, but quite tricky full-face.

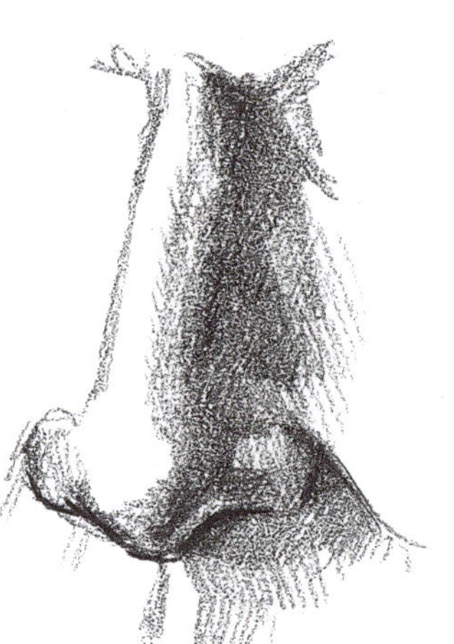

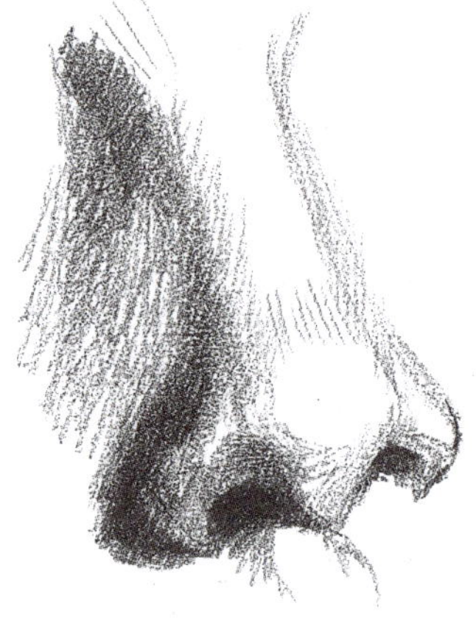

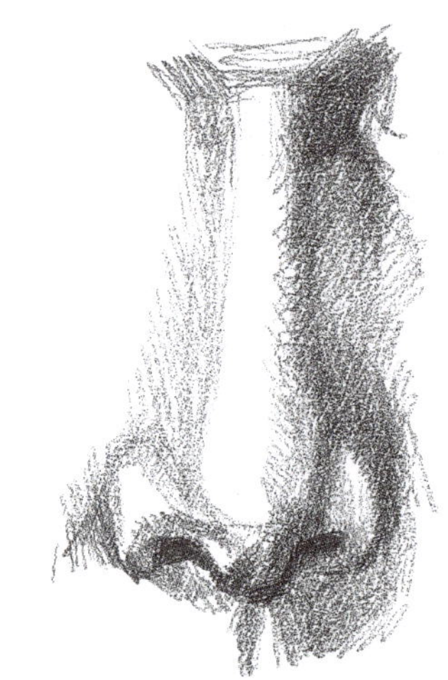

It's easiest to describe the shape from the front when there is a strong light coming from one side to cast a shadow.

If the light is more even, be careful not to overemphasize the tonal values on the nose unless it is a very strong one.

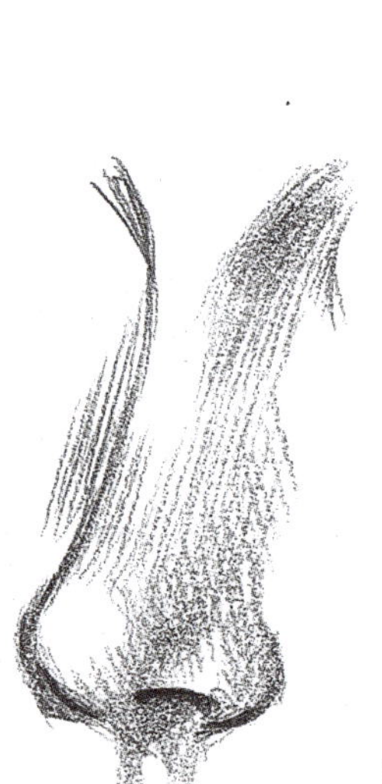

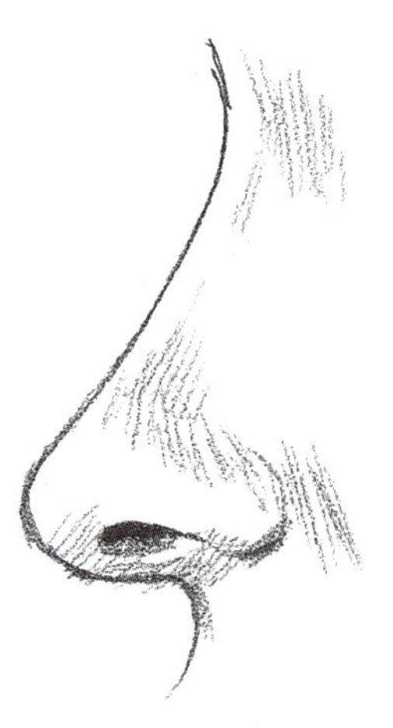

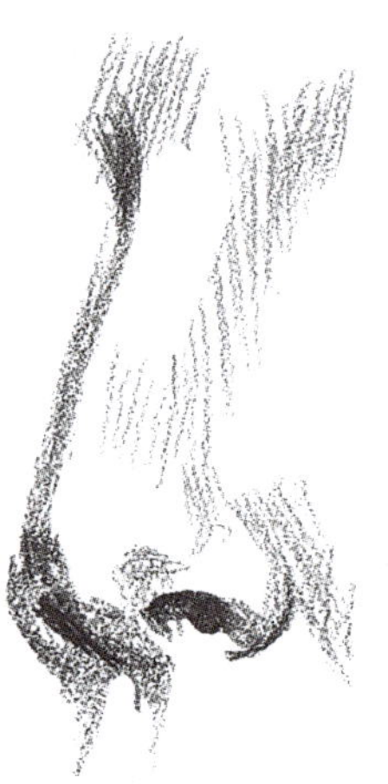

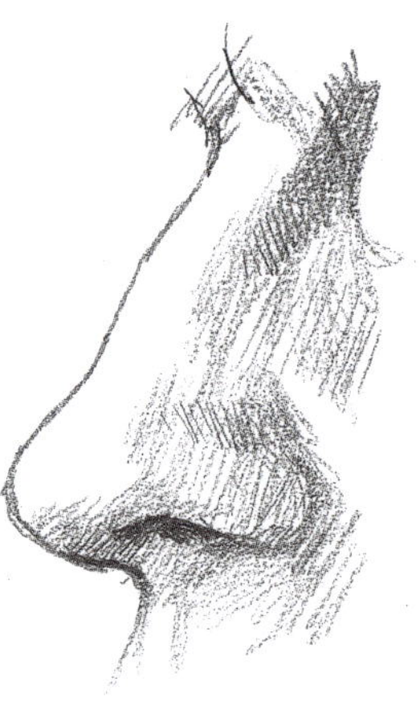

Most noses come in three or four types: the snub or retroussé nose, the straight nose, the strong, curved nose or the broken nose. The straight nose is probably the most difficult to draw because of the lack of bumps or indentations. Most beginners tend to make their subject's nose too long or too short, so observe it carefully in relation to the rest of the face.

Ears

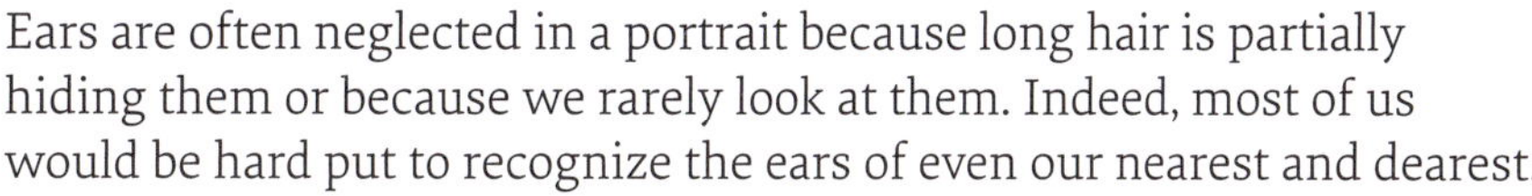

Ears are often neglected in a portrait because long hair is partially hiding them or because we rarely look at them. Indeed, most of us would be hard put to recognize the ears of even our nearest and dearest.

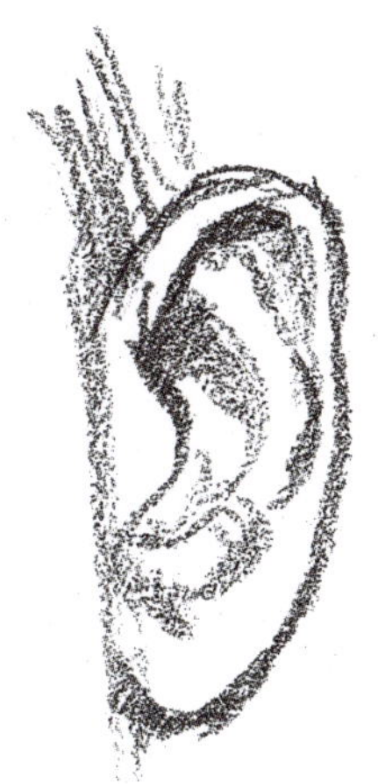

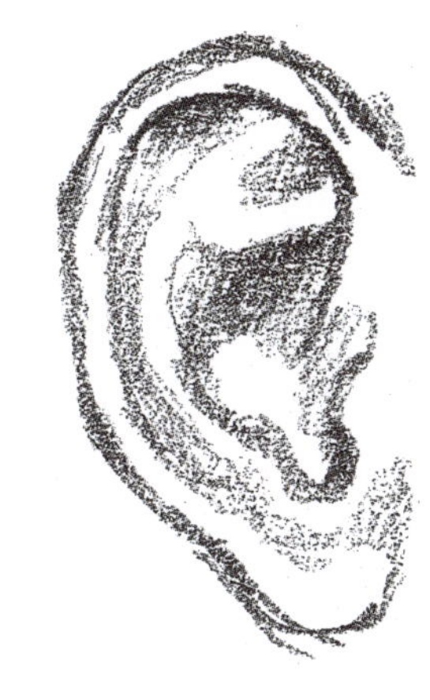

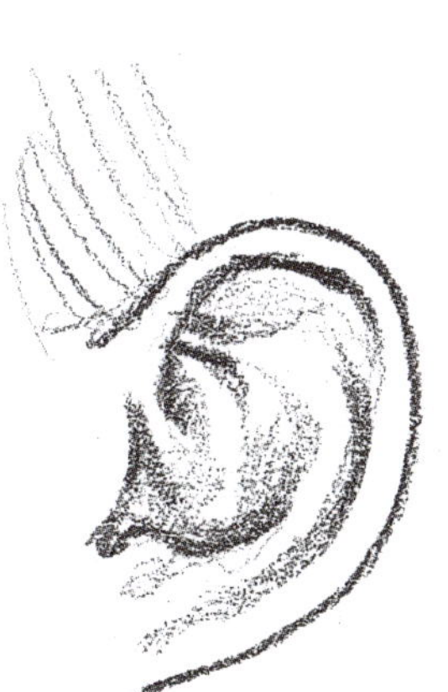

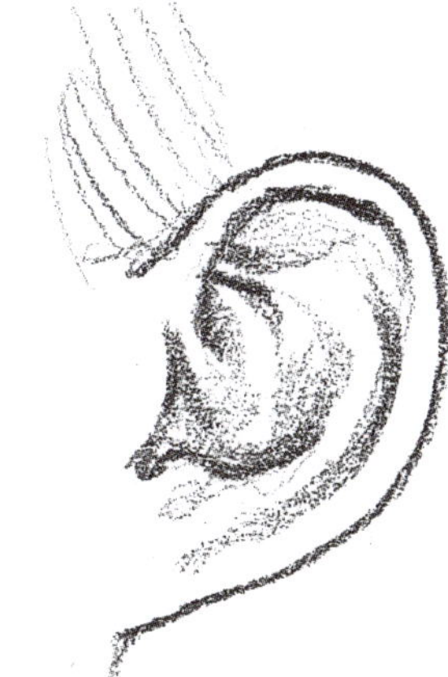

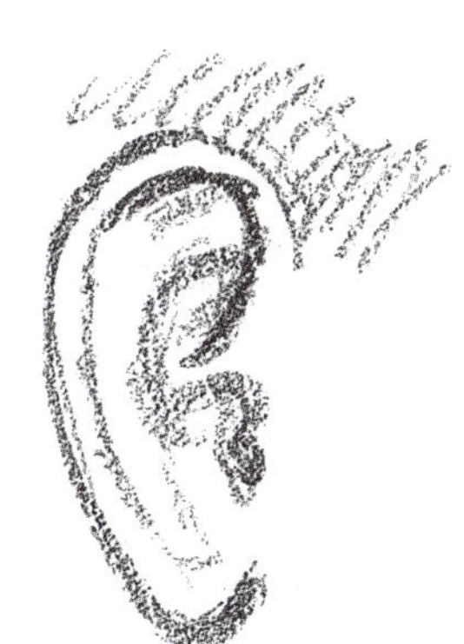

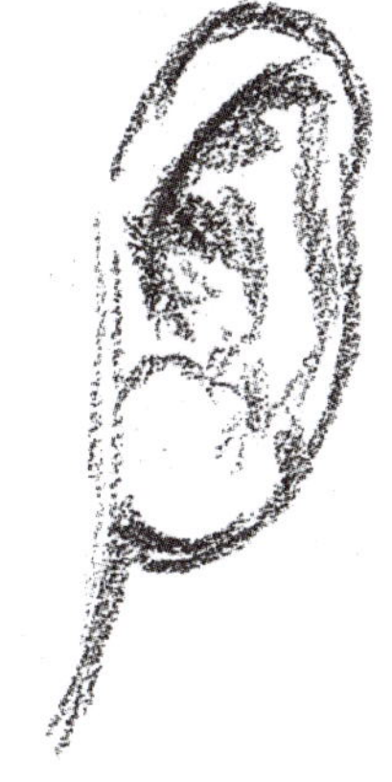

Here are a few examples of different ears and you should have a go at several, because they do have various shapes. The construction is basically the same, but the details differ. Draw some ears from the side and then from the front as well to get some idea of how they look.

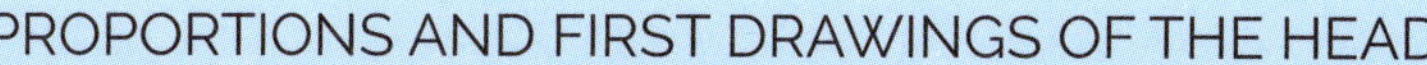

Hair

There is a lot of interesting variation in hair, particularly if it is long. The main overall difference is between curly and straight hair, the former being the most difficult to draw correctly. Notice how the hair forms in lumps and hanks – you don't have to draw every strand.

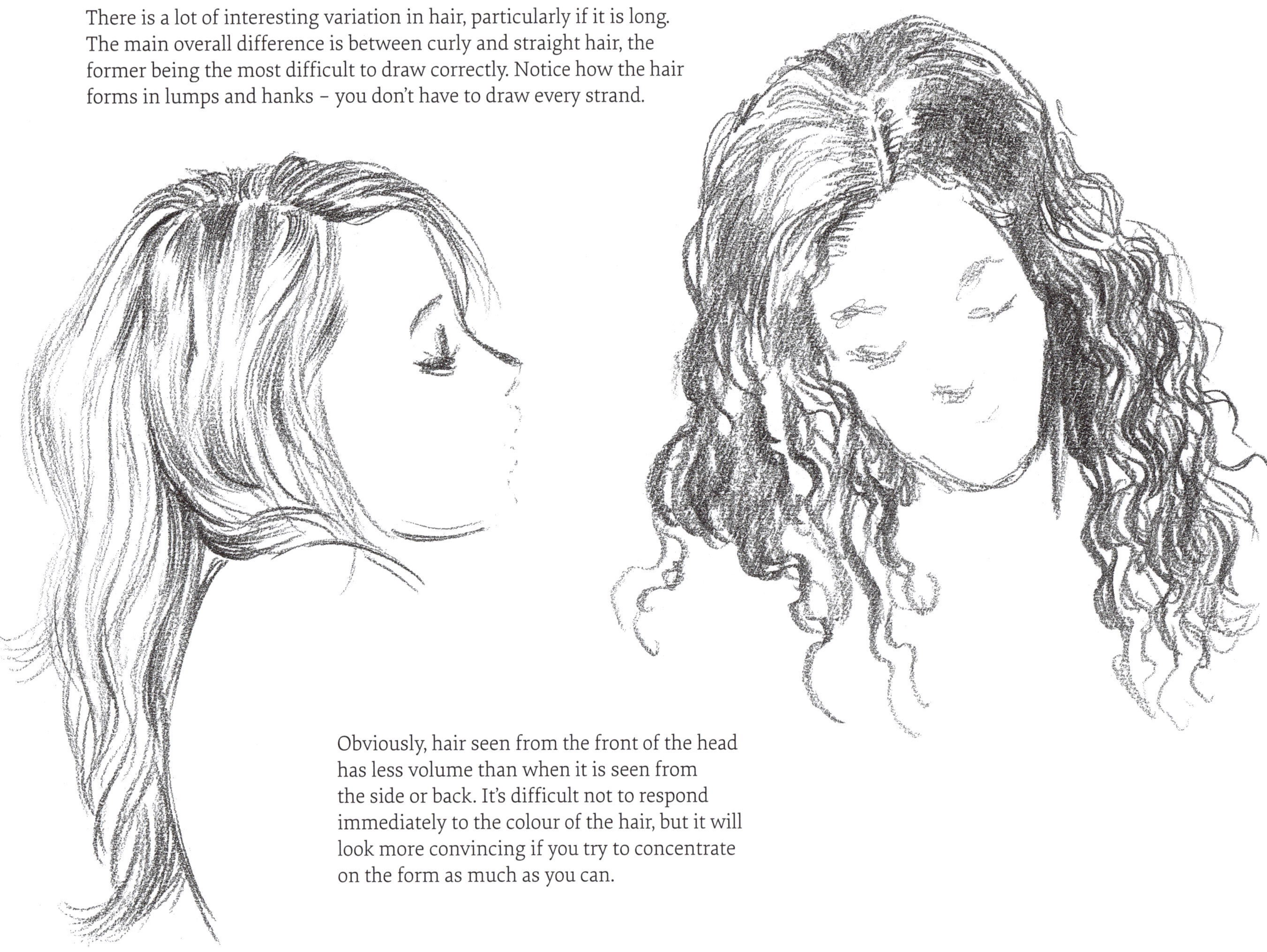

Obviously, hair seen from the front of the head has less volume than when it is seen from the side or back. It's difficult not to respond immediately to the colour of the hair, but it will look more convincing if you try to concentrate on the form as much as you can.

Now you've seen how varied the human face can appear, finish this section by drawing a simple profile view, putting in only the outline of the top of the head, the forehead, the nose, the lips and the chin, with just the main shape of the eyes, eyebrows and hair.

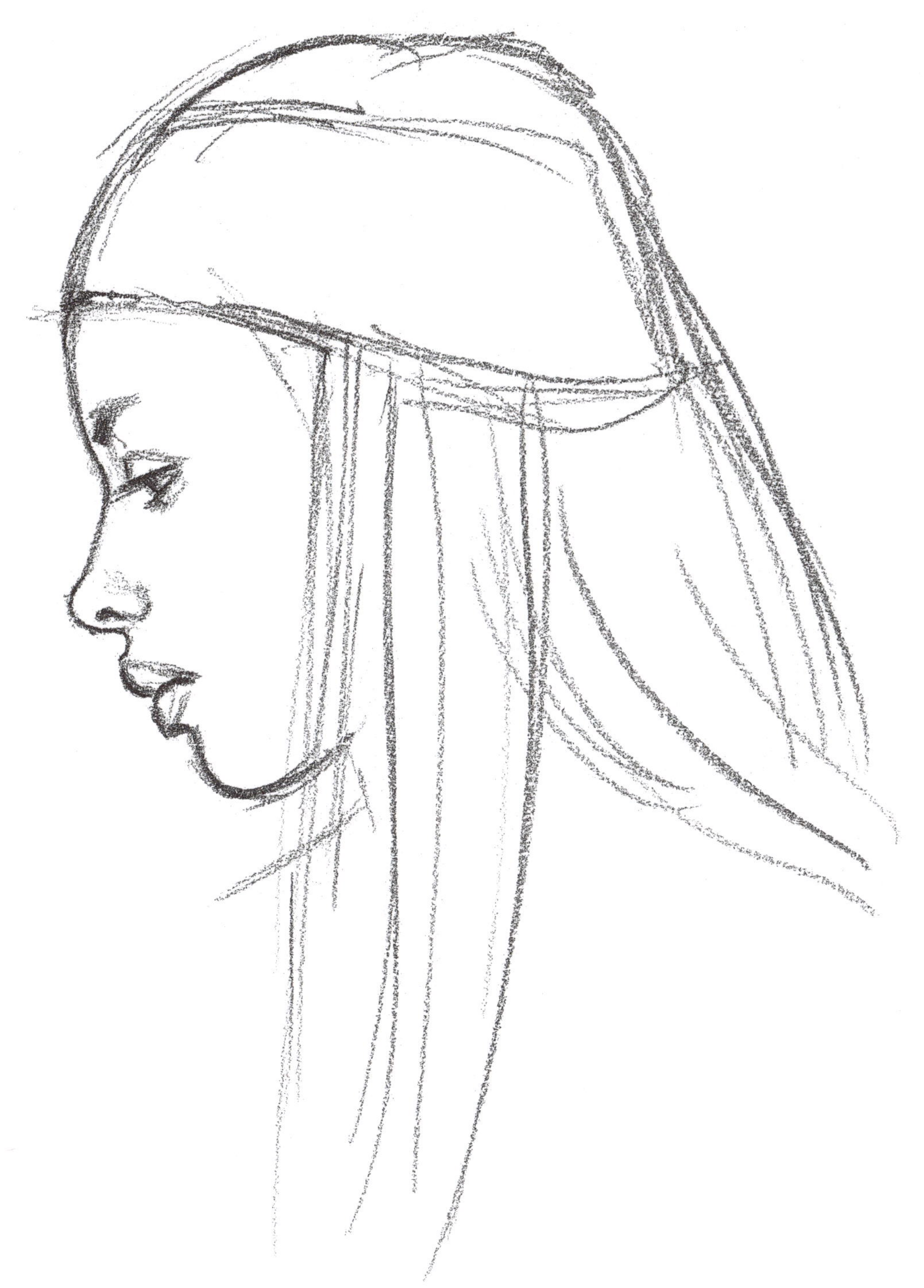

Artist's Note

Hair can radically change a sitter's appearance as well as bring a lot of drama and interest to a portrait. We will look at hair in more detail on pages 226–9.

The Effects of Age

The age of your sitter is perhaps the most fundamental thing that you need to convey in your drawing. In youth, the face has a clarity and charm that are surprisingly difficult to capture. With age, experience of the world begins to tell and the character of your sitter becomes evident in the habitual lines on their face.

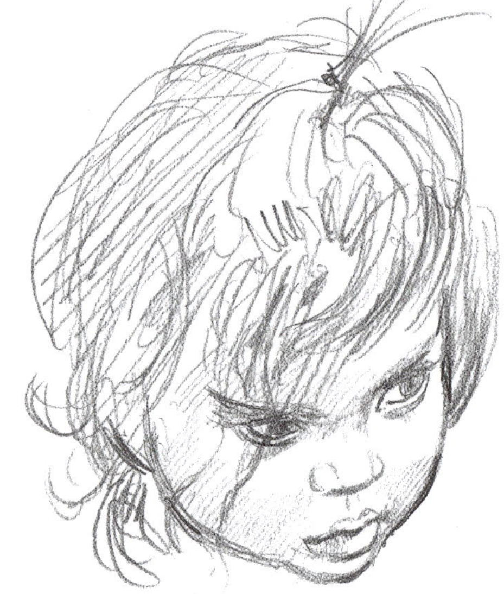

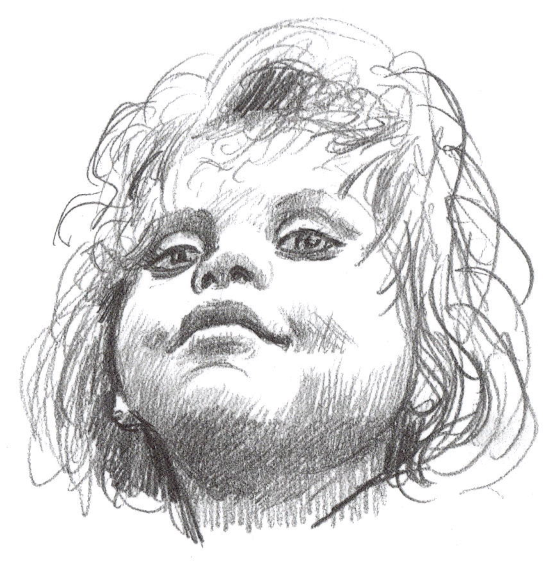

As we saw on page 44, children's heads don't match the proportions of an adult head. The greatest difference is the size of the cranium in relation to the lower jaw, but also the eyes are more widely spaced than in an adult and the cheeks are usually rounder. All the features fit into a much smaller space, and of course there are hardly any lines on the face.

The drawings above show a little girl of four or five years of age, viewed from above and below. She has the soft rounded cheeks and small snub nose which are fairly typical of the age group.

The little boy is a bit older but doesn't have a fully grown jaw yet, and his eyes and ears look much larger in relation to his nose and mouth than they would in an adult.

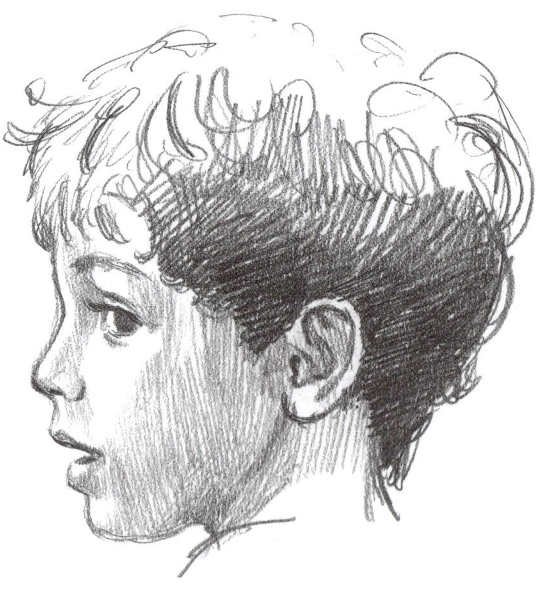

Here are drawings of a young woman at her peak and one of an old man – my youngest daughter and myself. See the difference in the quality of the hair, on the one soft and shiny, the other white and sparse. Then look at the surface of the skin. Although my daughter is grinning widely she has very few lines on her face and her eyes are very clear. My own skin is furrowed with lines of all kinds, especially around the eyes and on the forehead. The cheeks look more hollow and the mouth is defined only by its edge. I appear to be staring intently; that's because I am of course drawing myself in a mirror.

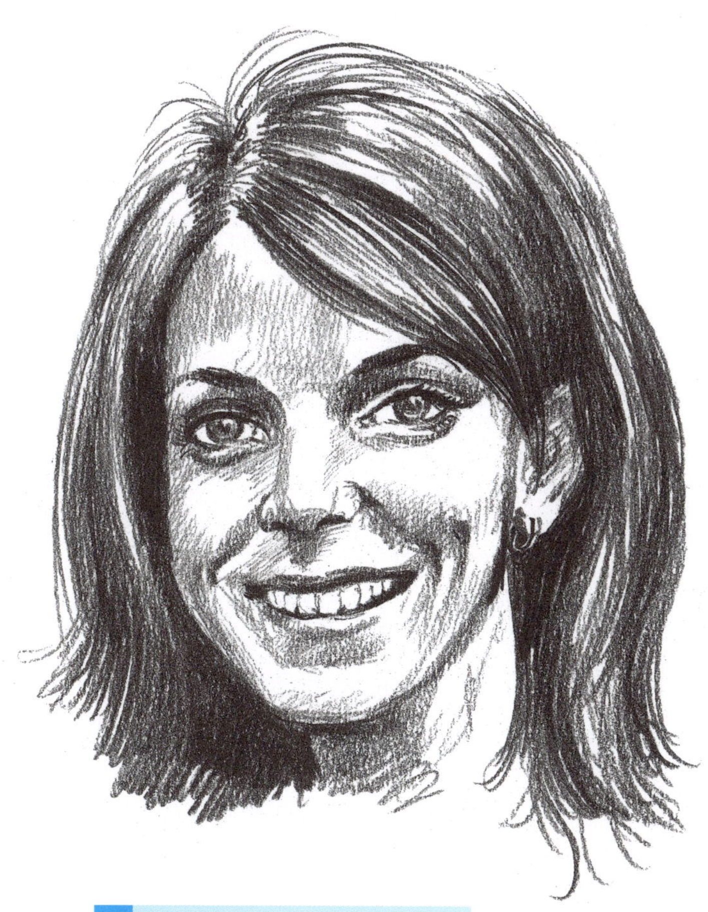

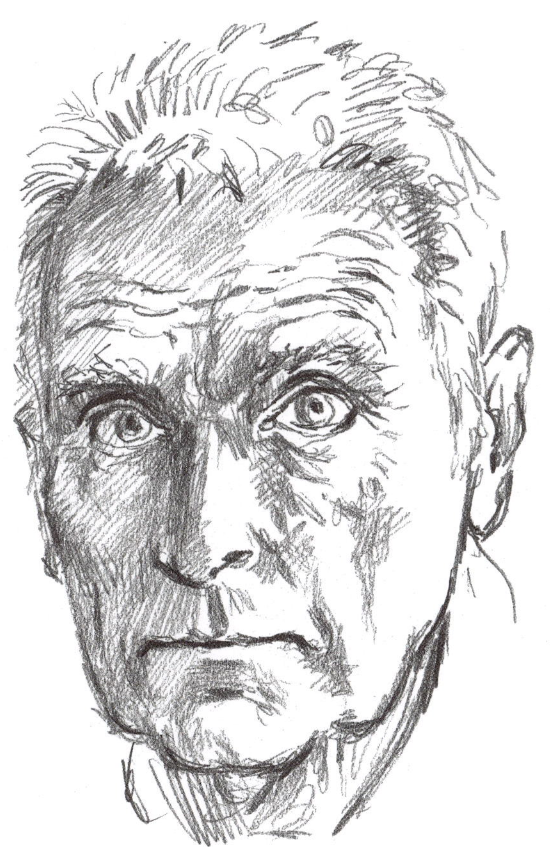

Artist's Note

Be careful not to overdo the characterful lines of your sitter's face as you risk making them look older than they would like. Making people look younger is not normally a problem because most of us have an image of ourselves as younger than we are in reality.

Faces and Expressions

The most interesting thing about a face is the way that it changes expression so easily and rapidly. We all watch these changes quite carefully in other people because they give the best clues to what our friends and relations are thinking about, and maybe about us. Here are a few of the most obvious facial expressions together with some suggestions for drawing them easily.

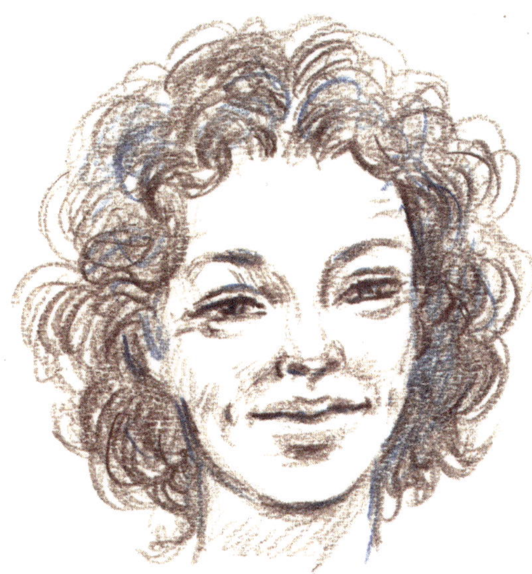

The smile

First, that most charming of all expressions, the smile: this is not quite so easy to draw as you might imagine, because it is quite a subtle image. If you make the mouth and eyes too exaggerated, the whole thing looks rather manic. So, it is important to show restraint in your drawing, marking the corners of the mouth very slightly curved, and the eyes only narrowed a little.

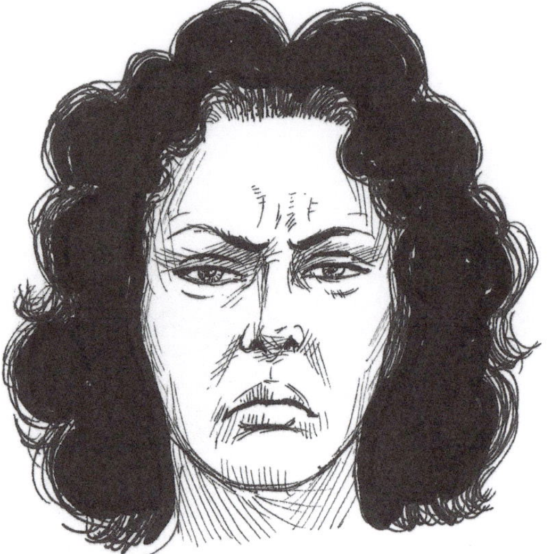

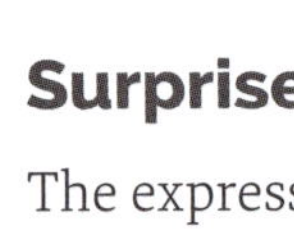

Surprise

The expression of surprise, however, is one where you can go over the top to good effect. Open the eyes so that the iris is not touching either the lower or the upper lids. Open the mouth into a fairly rounded shape and put some small lines above the eyebrows, which should be well arched. Some stress shadows around the jaw and nostrils will help portray the general air of astonishment too.

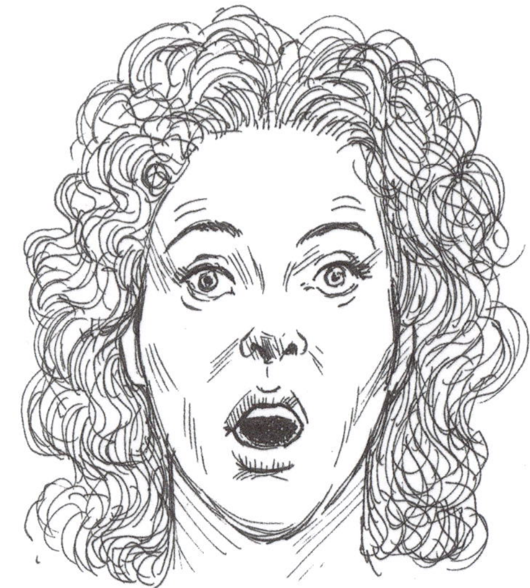

Anger

Anger is a good expression to depict because you can really let yourself go on the down-turning of the mouth and the knitting of the brows. The eyes may be narrowed, as in this picture, or opened wider to give a more ferocious aspect. Frown lines in the middle of the brow, and lines from the corner of the nostrils and under the mouth, all help to make the face look suitably lowering.

Laughter

Laughter can also look a bit mad, if you overdo it, but the key feature is the widely stretched mouth with an upturn at the corners. The eyes should be almost closed and there should be creases around the mouth and nostrils. Make sure that the cheeks are rounded and perhaps add dimples either side of the mouth.

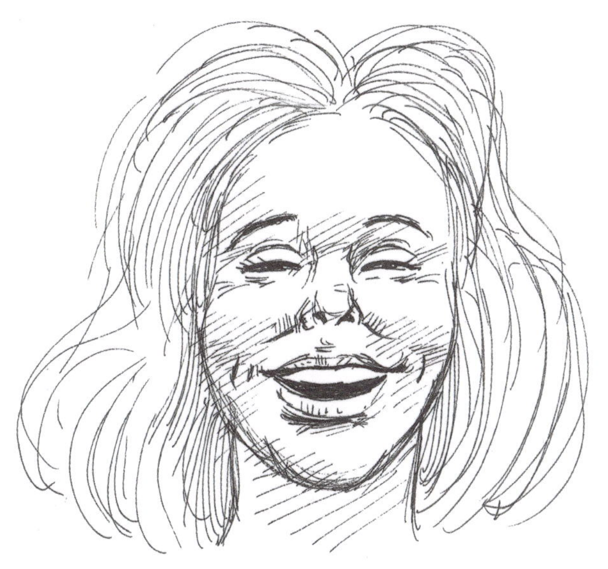

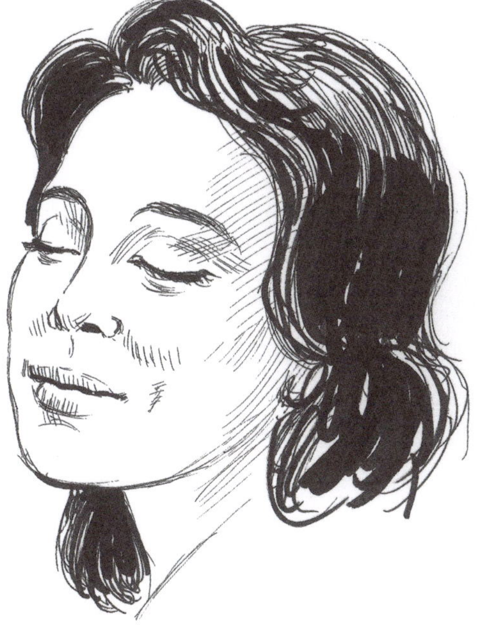

Fear

Fear is a difficult one because it is all too easy to make it look ludicrous. Make sure that the whites of the eyes show all around the irises. The eyes are wide open and the eyebrows are arched as high as they will go, with lines on the forehead above them. Shadows under the eyes also help. The mouth is open but turned down, with lines around it and the nostrils.

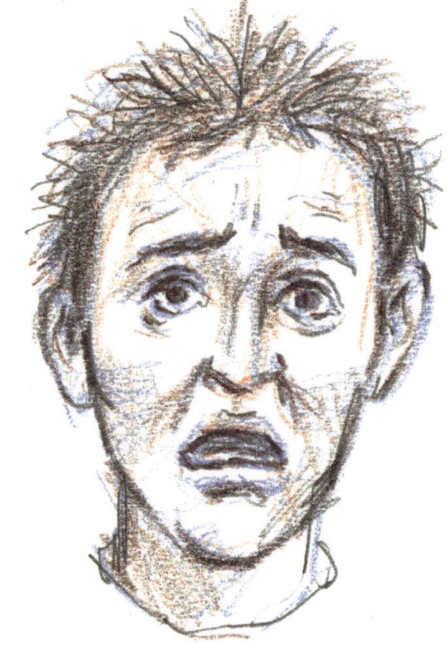

Satisfaction

Satisfaction is a rather more subtle expression, and closed eyes that still look relaxed are a good sign. The mouth should be very gently smiling, nothing too exaggerated. The head held to one side completes the picture.

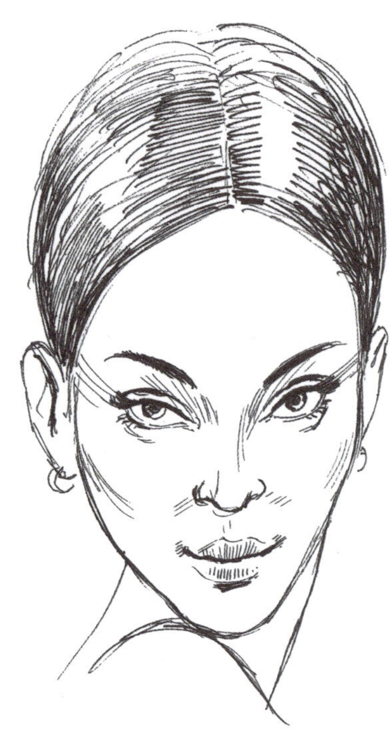

Suspicion

Suspicion is often shown with a sidelong glance and a defensive tilt to the head. The mouth might be open but there should be no hint of a smile or a grim look. The eyebrows could be arched a little to indicate doubt.

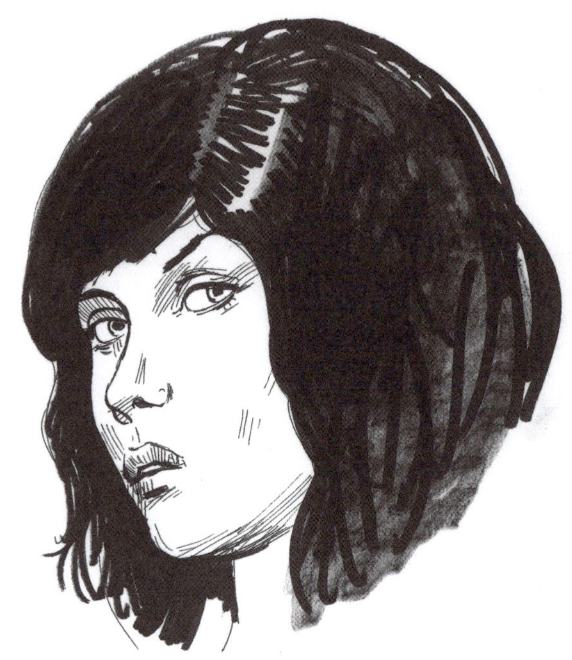

Come hither

The 'come hither' expression is not too difficult. The first thing is to tilt the chin down slightly. Then the eyes look more cat-like, especially with the lids lowered a little over the eyes. The mouth should have a mild smile that suggests that there is more to come and the gaze should be directed straight at you.

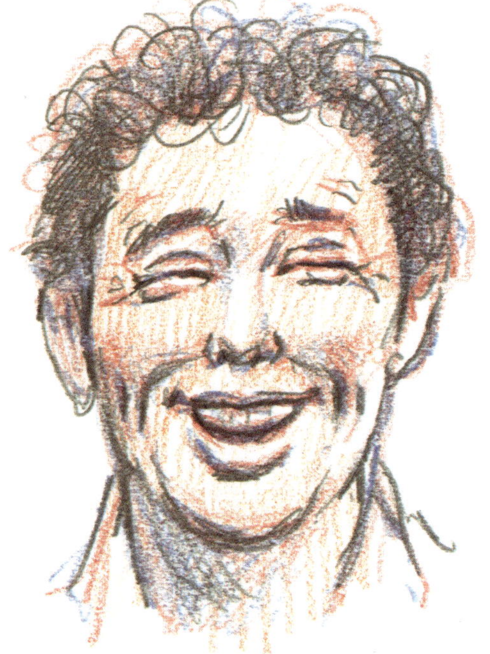

Delight

Delight is a nice one and not too difficult. The mouth is perhaps open and curves upwards. The eyes are open too and looking at something that causes the feeling of delight. Probably the teeth should be on show and the eyes curved a little in laughter lines. But everything on the face should look relaxed and open.

Dislike

Dislike is rather like a milder form of anger, but with none of anger's force and not too many lines involved. The face should be a bit blank, but the brows should be knitted a little, and the mouth turned down. The eyes should be open but staring rather directly.

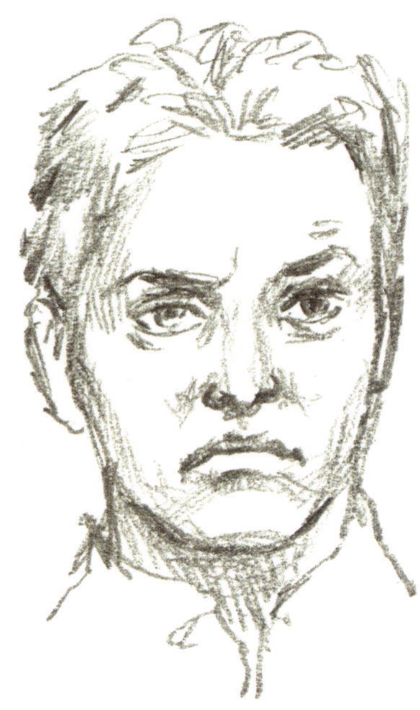

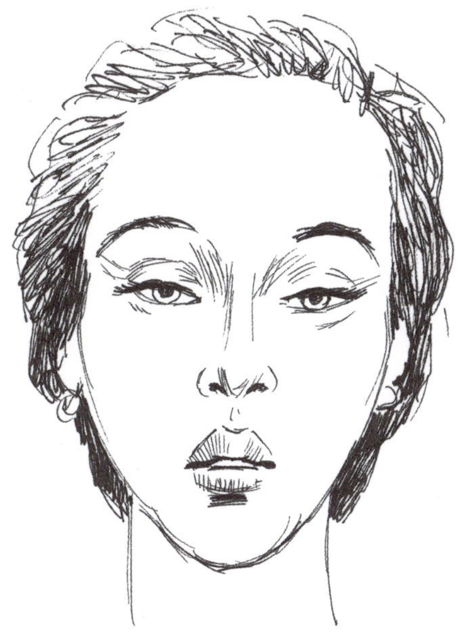

Haughtiness

A haughty expression means that the face looks as though it finds what it observes rather distasteful. Draw nothing too extreme, but arched eyebrows and narrowed eyes will help. The mouth can be open or shut but should appear downward-curving rather than upward-curving.

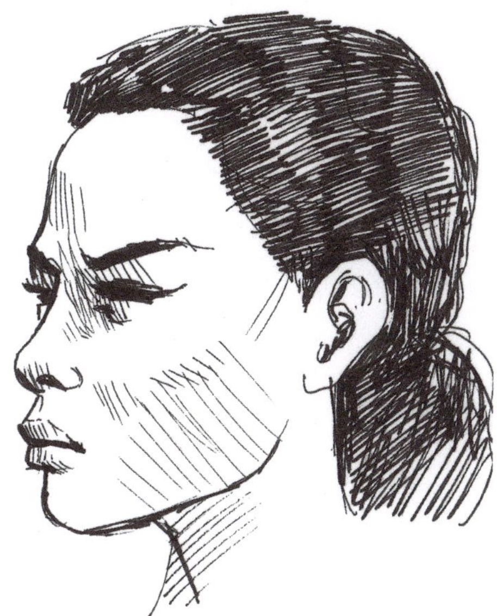

Indignation

Indignation is like anger but not so pronounced. The eyes can be narrowed and the mouth pushed forward a bit. No hint of humour should show on the face, and there should be few if any lines on it.

This is just a selection of expressions that you might like to try drawing – there are many more that you may observe for yourself.

Chapter Three

PORTRAITS

The human face is often the most attractive subject for an artist. In a way, producing a good portrait of another human being proves to yourself how well you're progressing; it's the hardest area in which your skills will be tested, because everyone can see at once whether you have obtained a resemblance to the individual or not.

However, that isn't the be all and end all of a portrait – it's also meant to be a work of art, not just an accurate record of someone's features. In this chapter you'll be learning about portraits in a way that will enable you to capture likenesses of your friends and family as well as producing pictures that stand up as art in their own right.

Arranging the setting for a portrait requires some thought – you will need to consider not just the character of the sitter but also the way that they are lit and posed. This can give vastly different effects to the style of the portrait and make it much more interesting, both for the sitter and the artist.

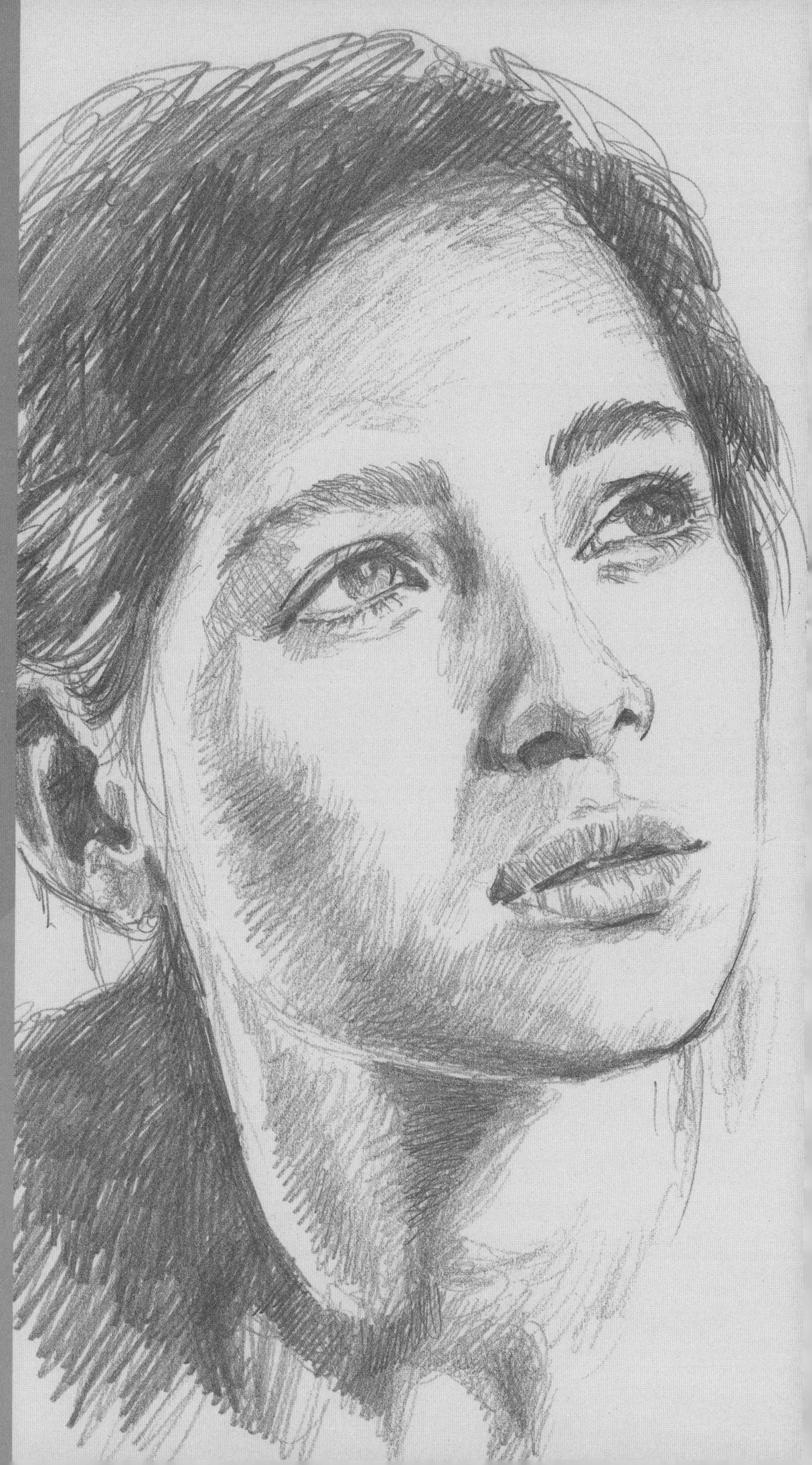

Portraits: Different Approaches

While a portrait should resemble the sitter in some way, that doesn't mean it must be time-consuming and full of detail. On these pages we shall consider several examples of portraits that approach the subject in different ways before embarking on a short portrait project.

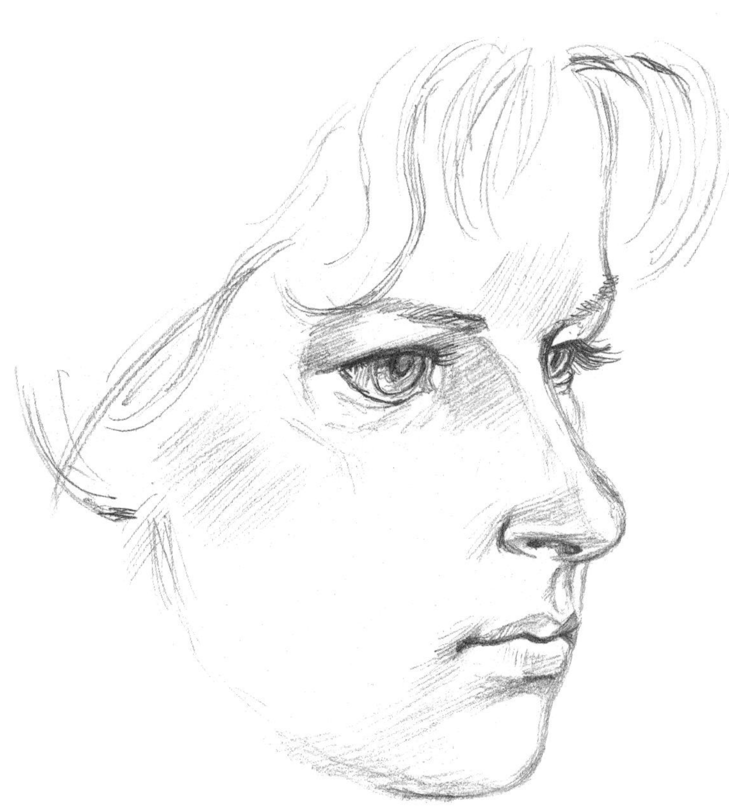

The first one is of a girl who was busy drawing in one of the classes I used to teach. There wasn't enough time to get much in, so I concentrated on the eyes, nose and mouth and merely sketched in the chin, forehead and hair.

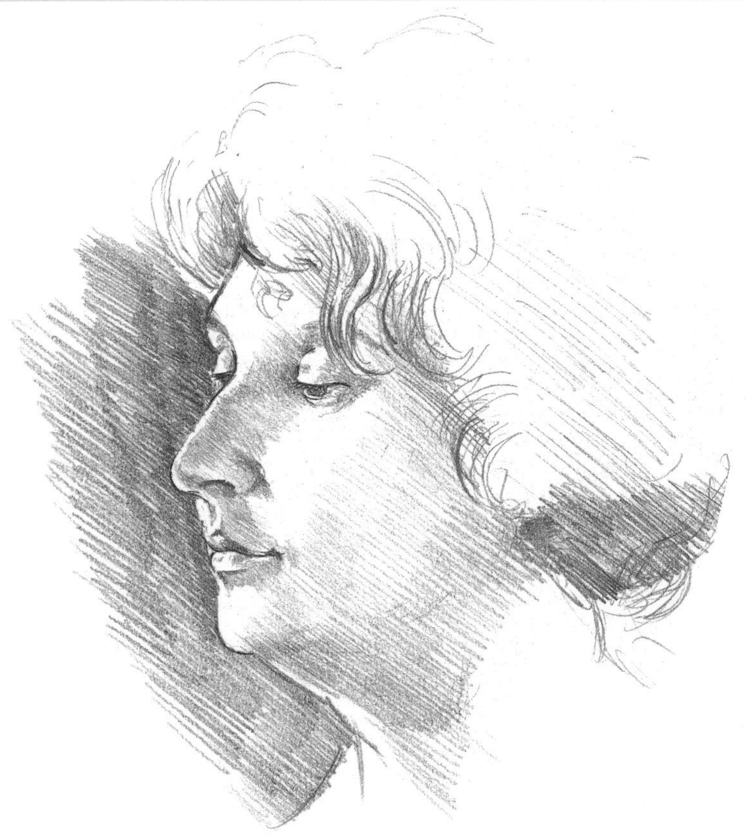

The next subject was unable to sit for long, so once again I drew the main features of the face and just indicated the rest of the head. Notice how the background tone that shows up the profile clearly is just as important as the face itself.

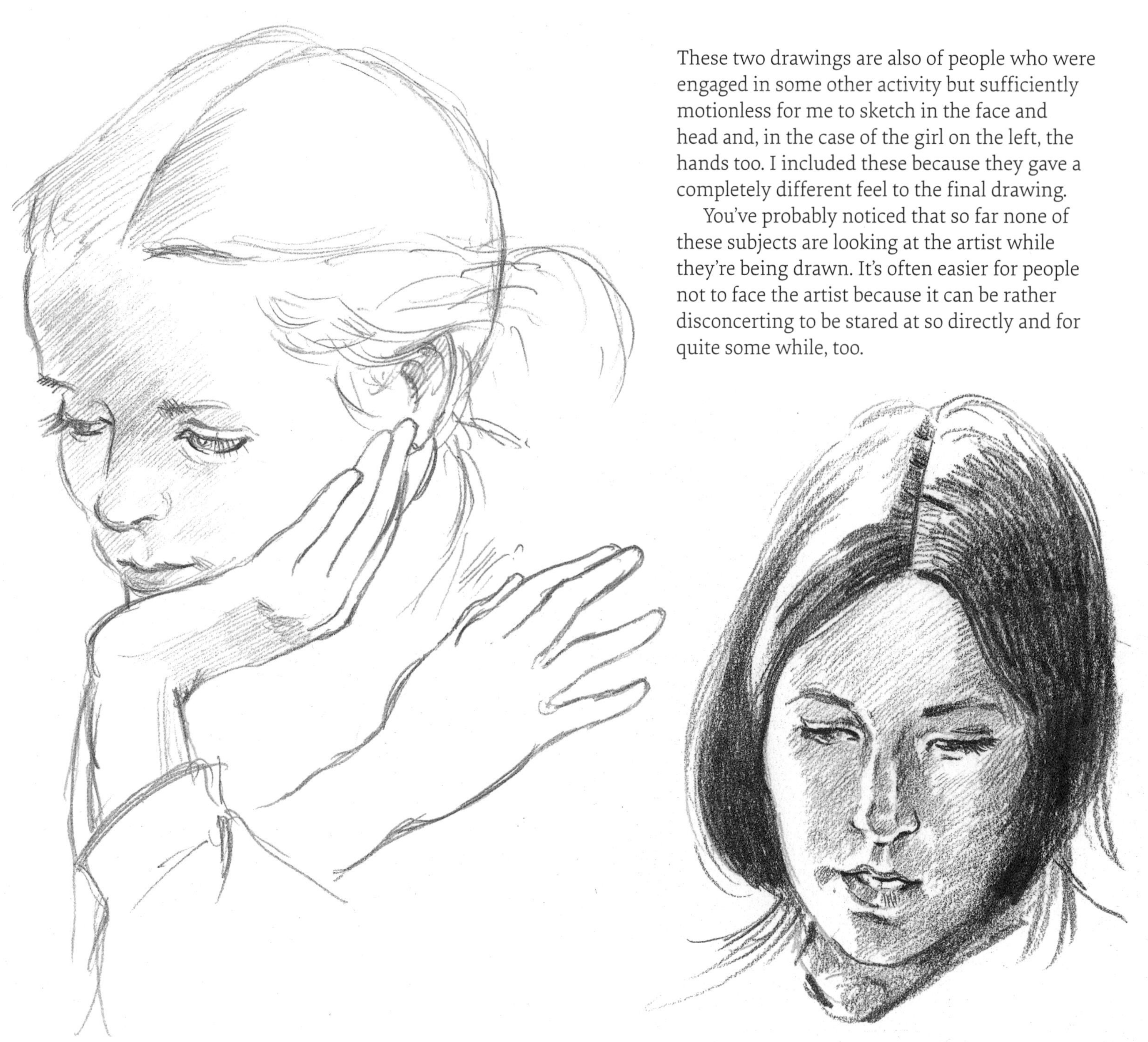

These two drawings are also of people who were engaged in some other activity but sufficiently motionless for me to sketch in the face and head and, in the case of the girl on the left, the hands too. I included these because they gave a completely different feel to the final drawing.

You've probably noticed that so far none of these subjects are looking at the artist while they're being drawn. It's often easier for people not to face the artist because it can be rather disconcerting to be stared at so directly and for quite some while, too.

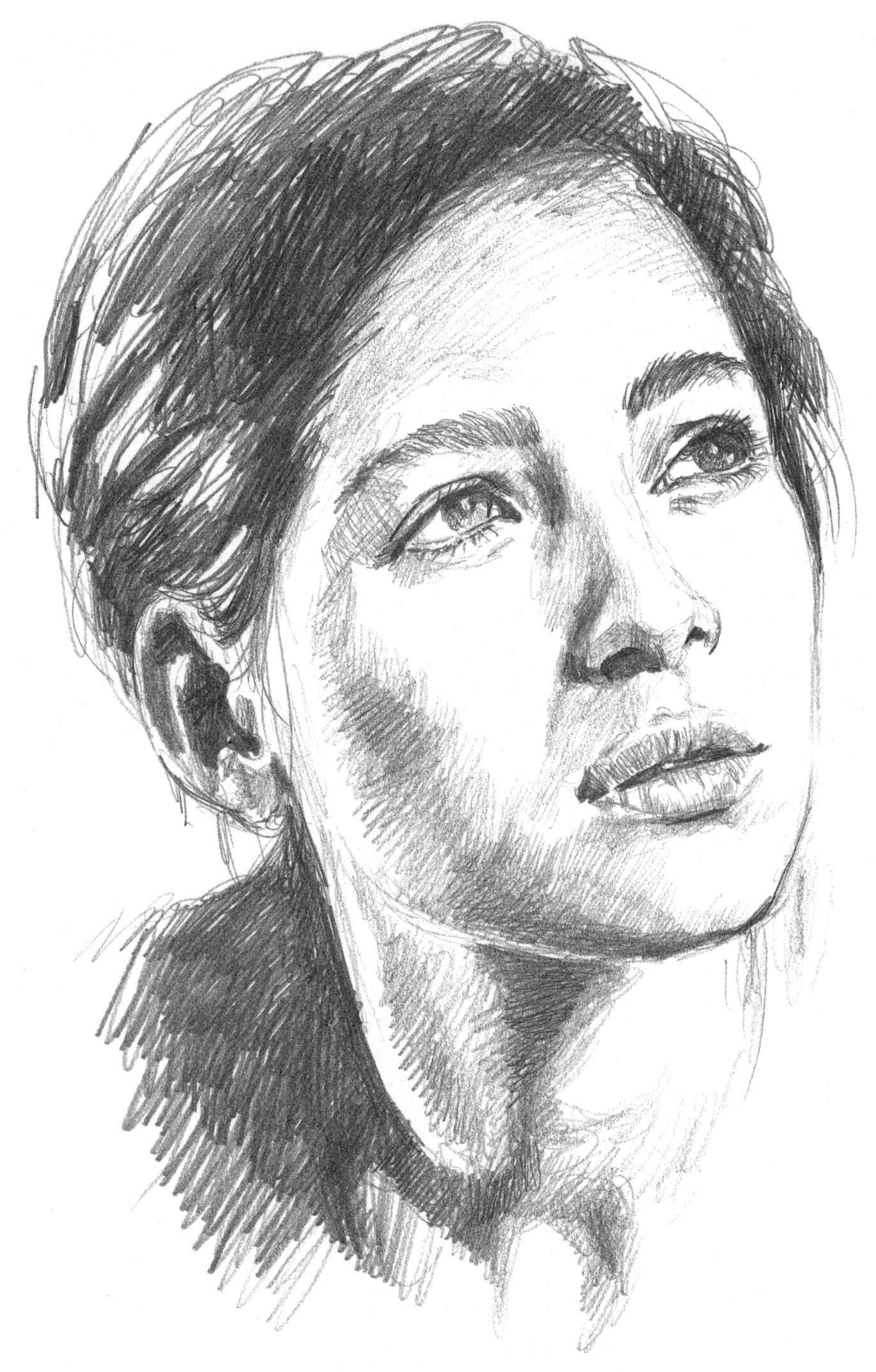

The next drawing is of a girl looking upwards, which tilts the head slightly back and makes the main shape different. There is much indirect light, which creates an interesting reflected edge to the darker side of the face.

This portrait is a complete profile view of a man's head, with a strong dark background behind the face and a lighter one behind the back of the head. Profile views were very popular in the early Renaissance period in Italy, and you might find it quite a good way to start drawing, as it seems easier to catch the exact shape of the face and head. However, it won't be the view that most people like to see in a portrait.

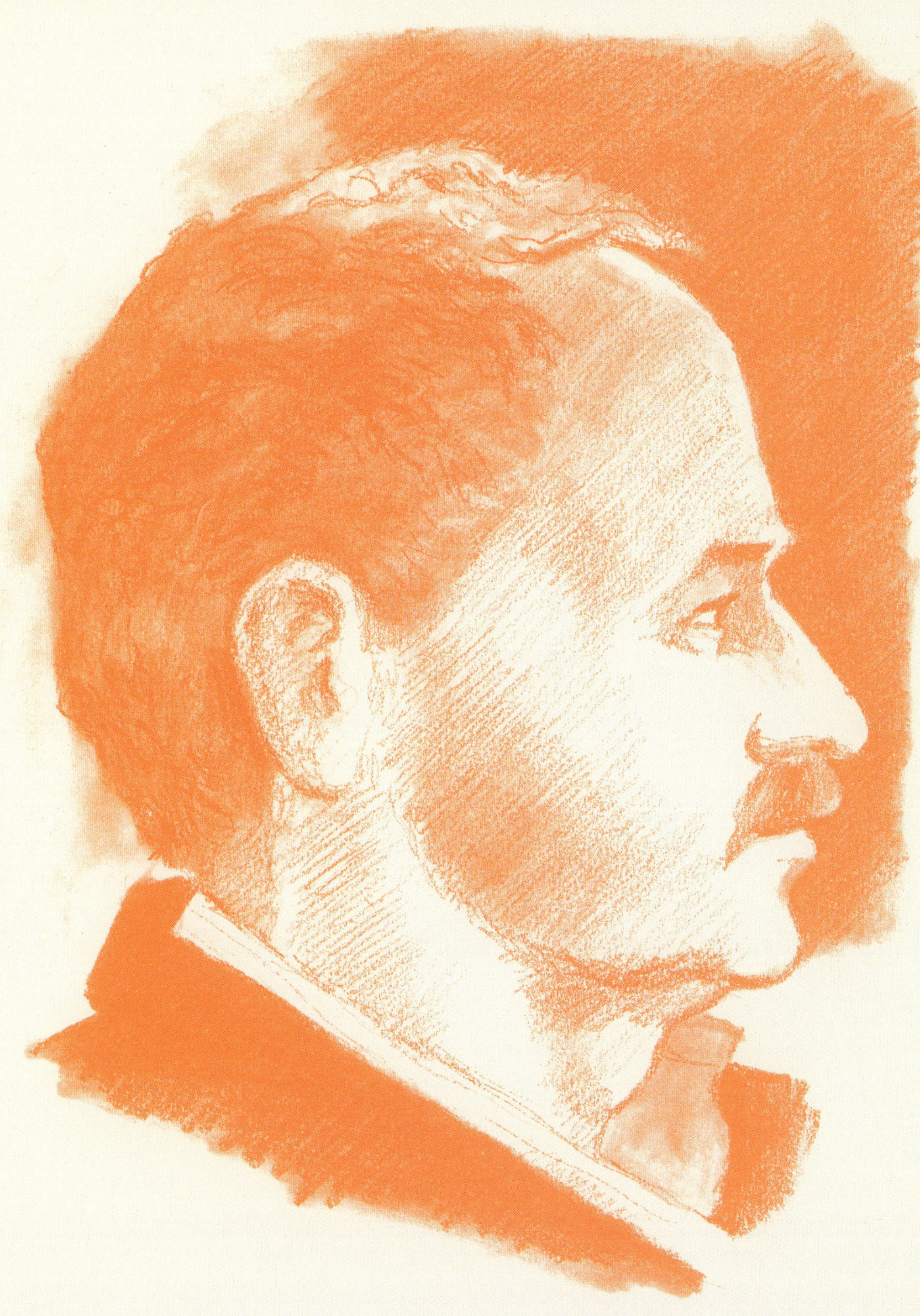

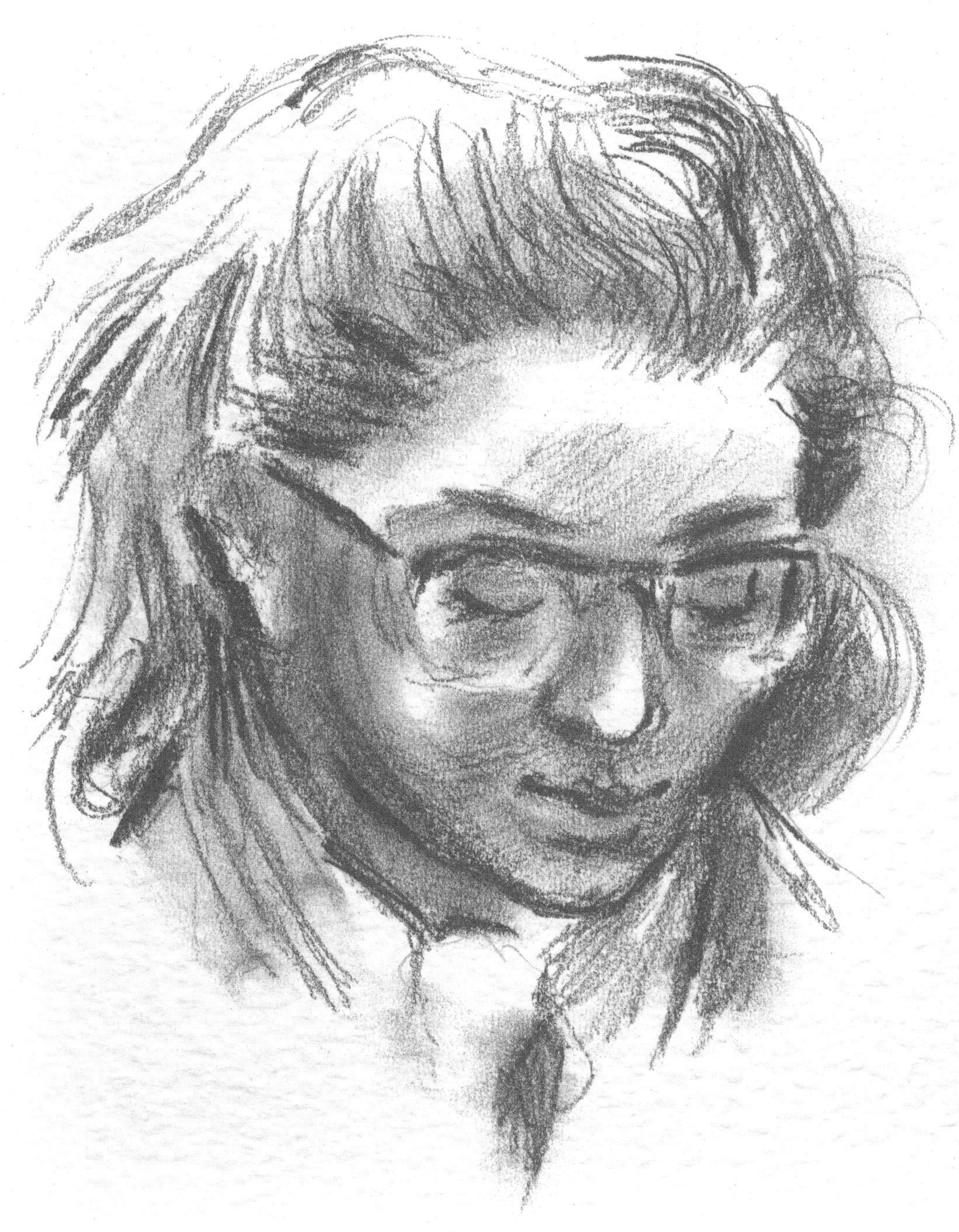

This time the model is looking downwards, and the significant thing here is the spectacles. These are often omitted from portraits as they can act as a sort of disguise to the face. Of course, if your model always wears spectacles, removing them will result in a portrait that looks less like the person that everyone is familiar with. Notice how much shadow there is on the lower half of the face, because the model's head is inclined.

The next two drawings are both of people looking directly towards the artist, and of course this is often the best way to draw someone because it's how they are most recognizable. This man is looking almost challengingly towards the artist, and you can see that he isn't afraid to meet someone's eye.

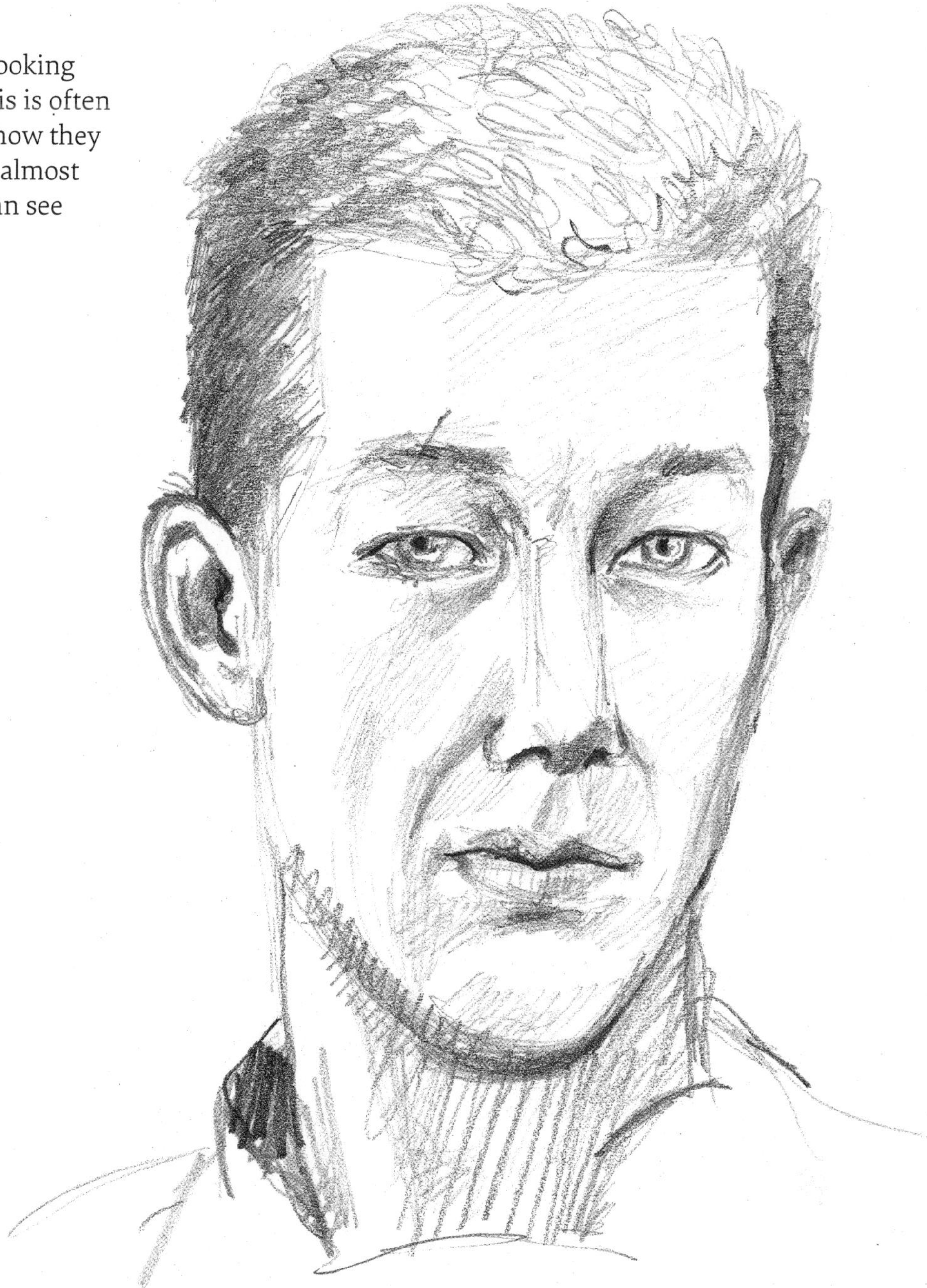

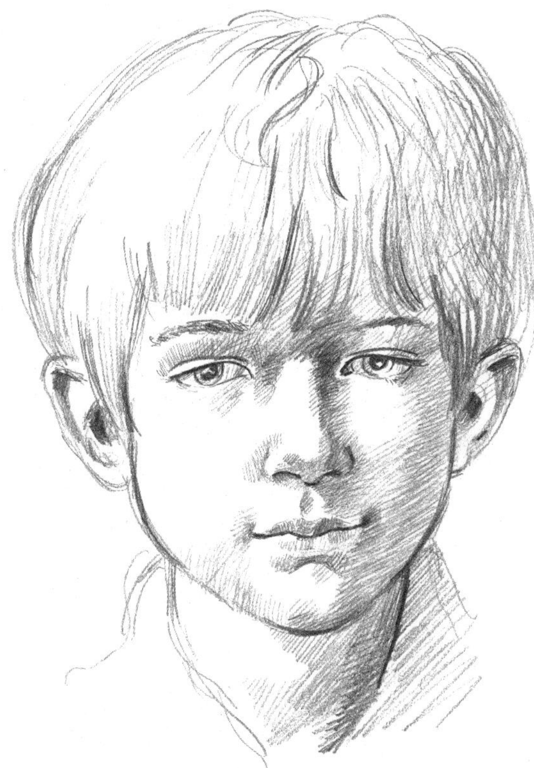

This young boy is my eldest son, drawn when he was quite young. He found it difficult to keep still long enough for me to draw much detail, but we just about managed it. It's noticeable that he didn't look directly at me as I was drawing his eyes.

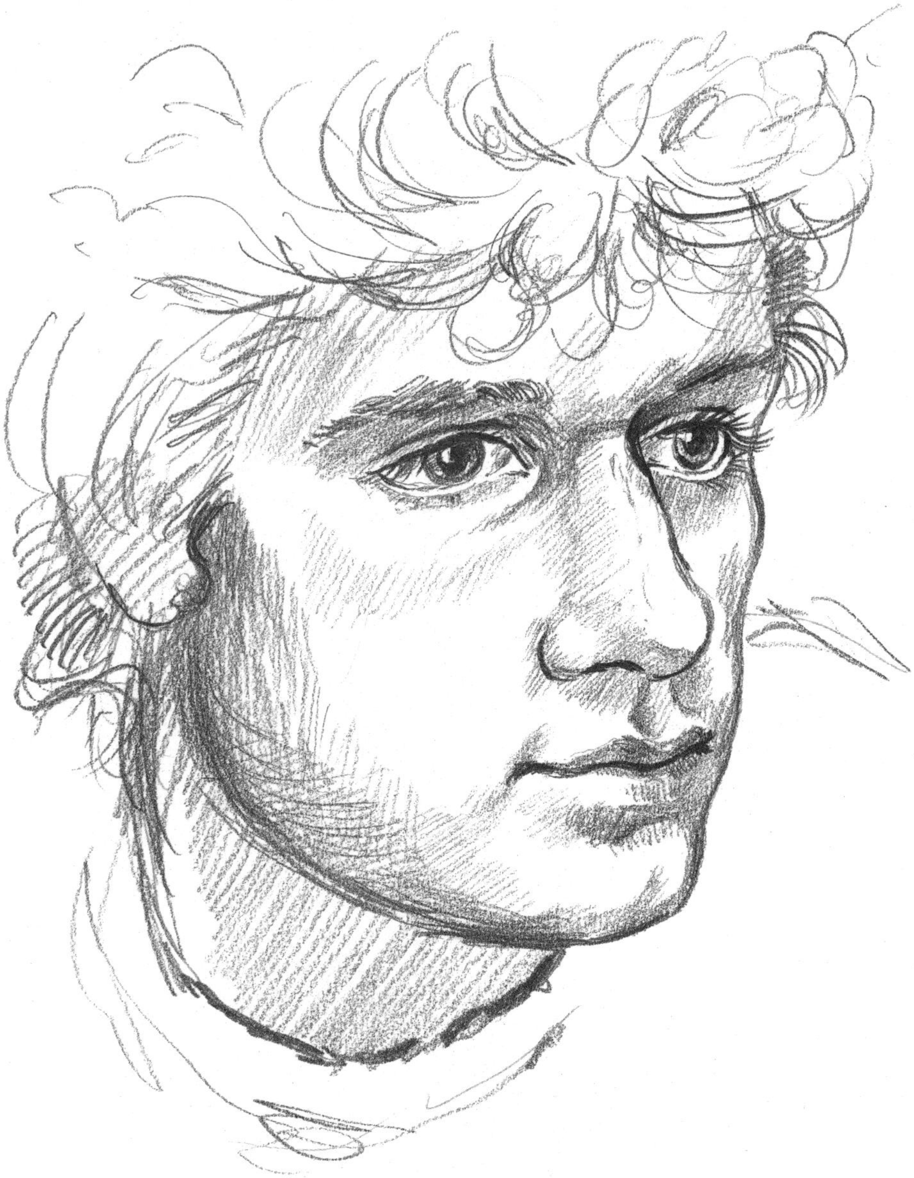

Here's my son when he was a lot older, seen in the three-quarter view that most portraits are drawn from. This is because the shape of the eyes, mouth and nose can all be seen clearly. As you can see, he didn't stay long enough for me to draw the rest of the head.

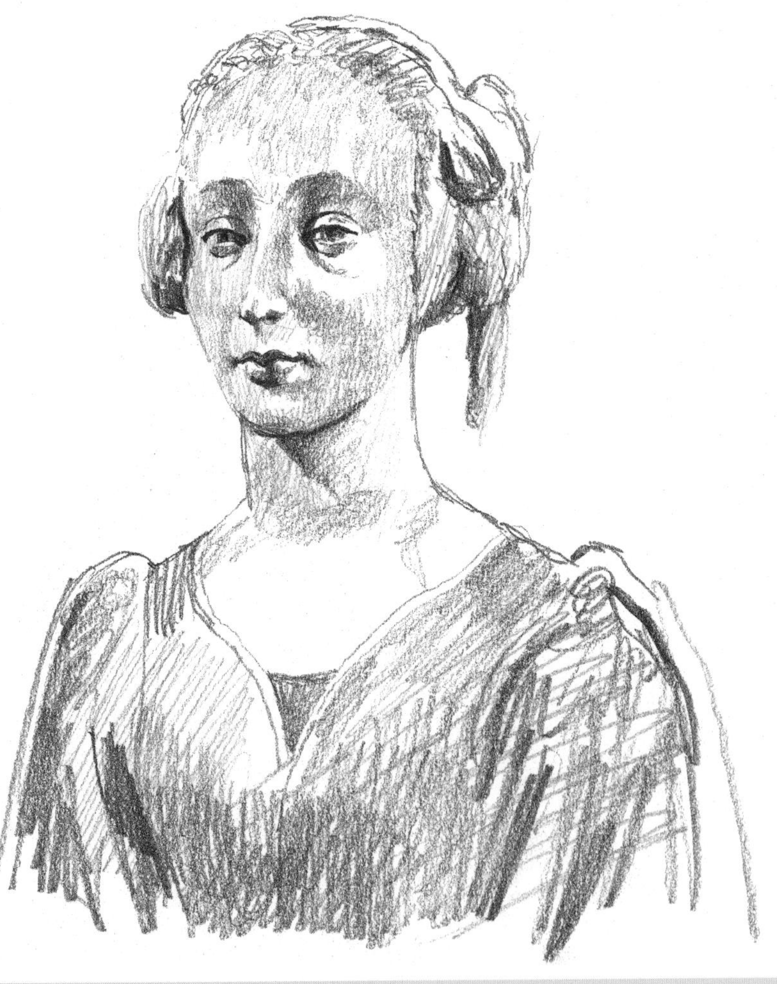

Next is another classic three-quarter view, but this time as a head and shoulders portrait. This immediately gives a new effect to the drawing, bringing in the beginning of the body, a style much used in the Renaissance period. The drawing is taken from a carved and painted portrait, probably by the sculptor Pietro Torrigiano (1472–1528).

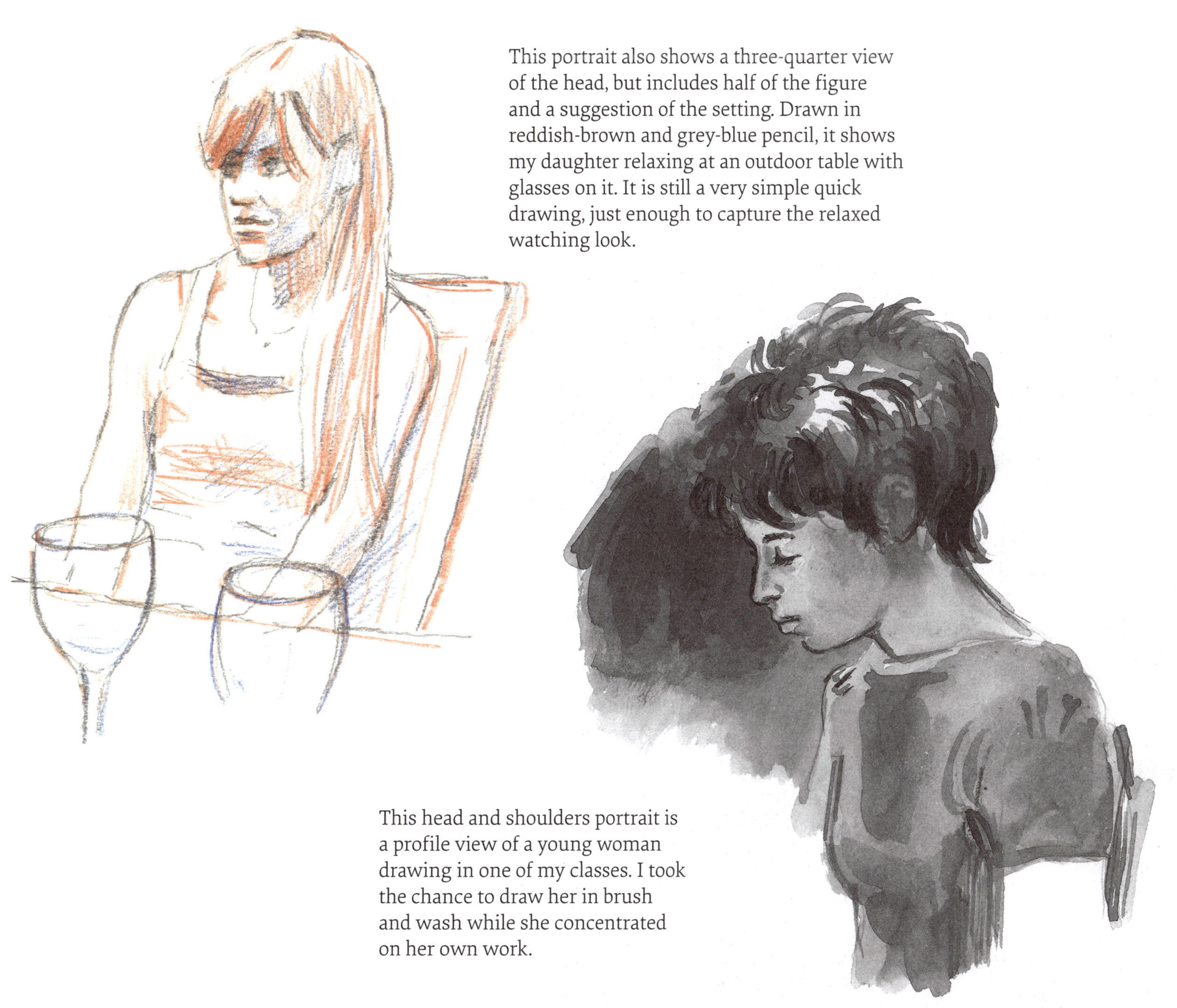

This portrait also shows a three-quarter view of the head, but includes half of the figure and a suggestion of the setting. Drawn in reddish-brown and grey-blue pencil, it shows my daughter relaxing at an outdoor table with glasses on it. It is still a very simple quick drawing, just enough to capture the relaxed watching look.

This head and shoulders portrait is a profile view of a young woman drawing in one of my classes. I took the chance to draw her in brush and wash while she concentrated on her own work.

The next three drawings are full-length portraits, which are great fun to do but can take a bit longer than just the head or head and shoulders. Here extra interest comes from the way in which people use their body to express their character or mood. Sometimes you may even find that body language contrasts with the messages in the facial expression.

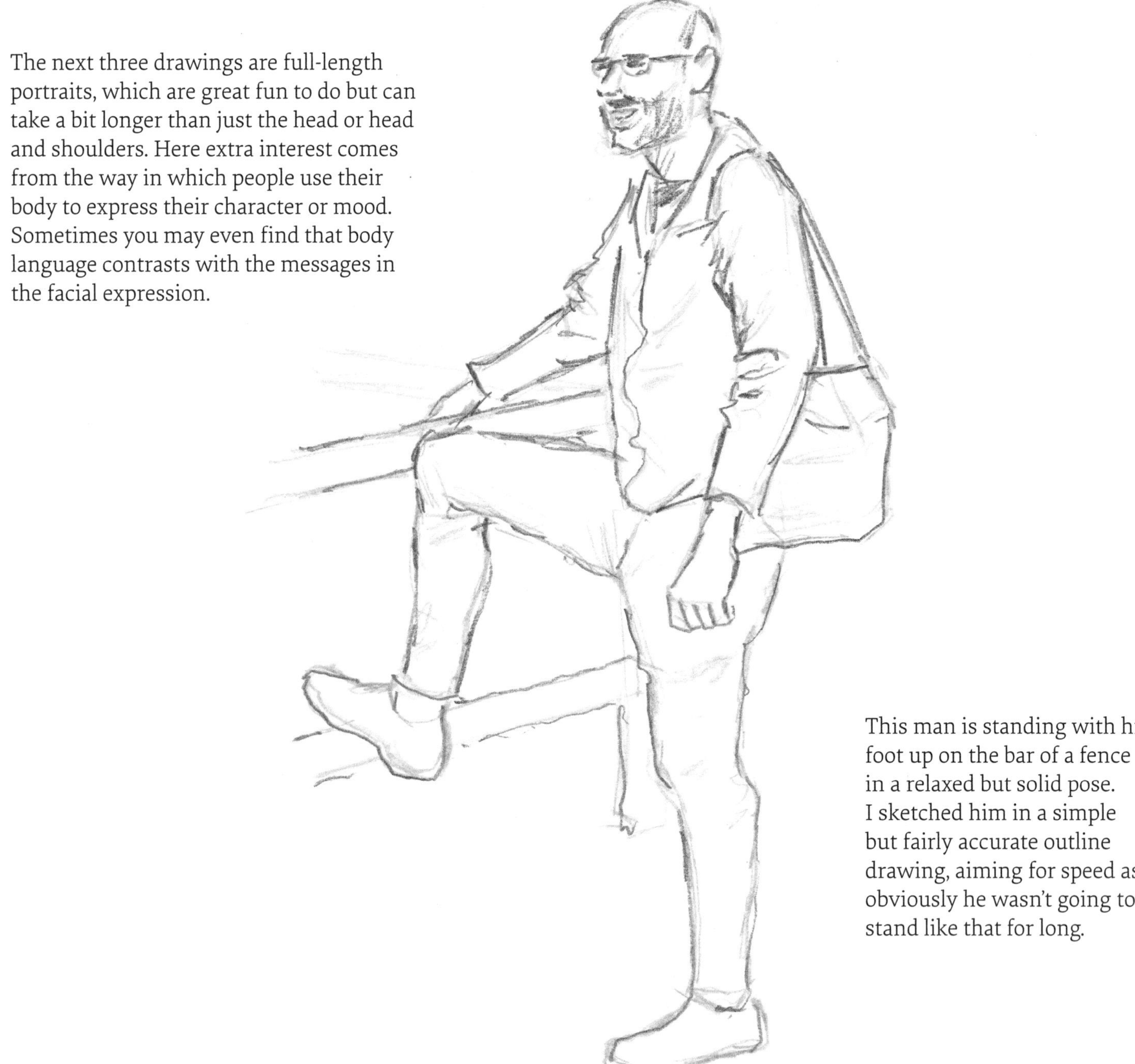

This man is standing with his foot up on the bar of a fence in a relaxed but solid pose. I sketched him in a simple but fairly accurate outline drawing, aiming for speed as obviously he wasn't going to stand like that for long.

Here is another drawing of a young woman on a skate board, about to flip it. The drawing captures the slightly awkward angles of the arms and legs in the balancing position. Showing your subject engaged in an activity is a good way to record their interests and their character, though it can add an extra layer of difficulty to your portrait.

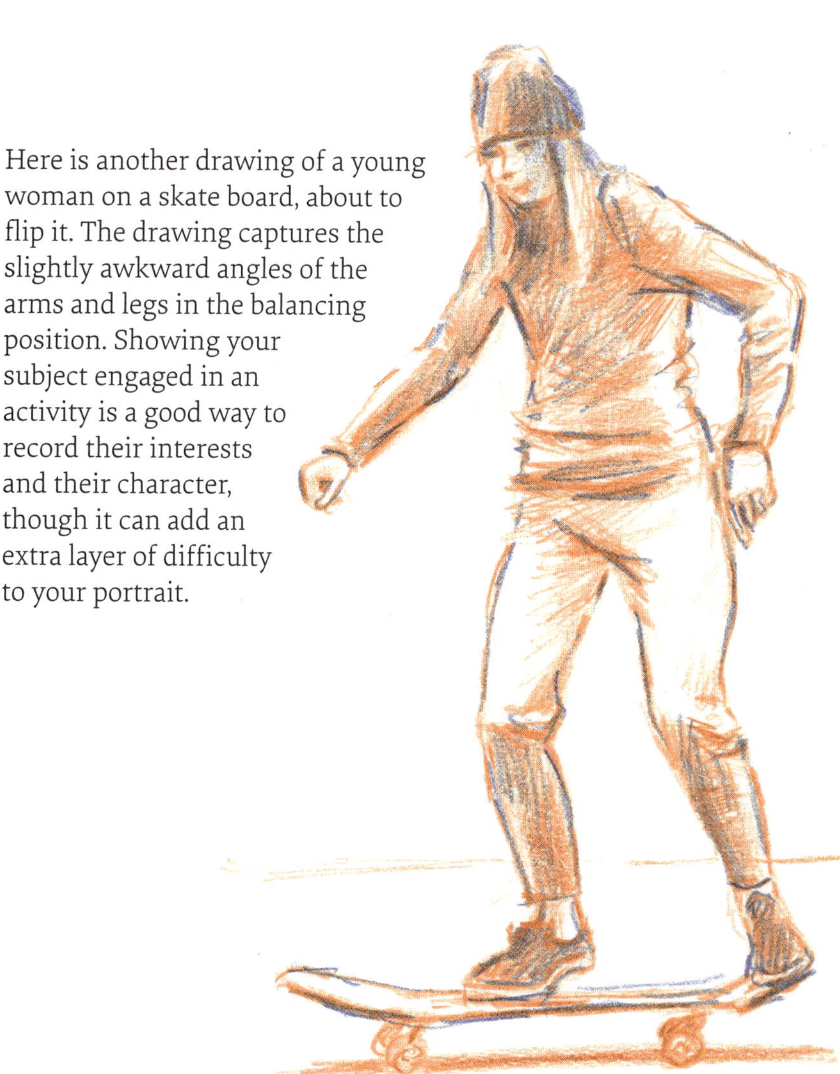

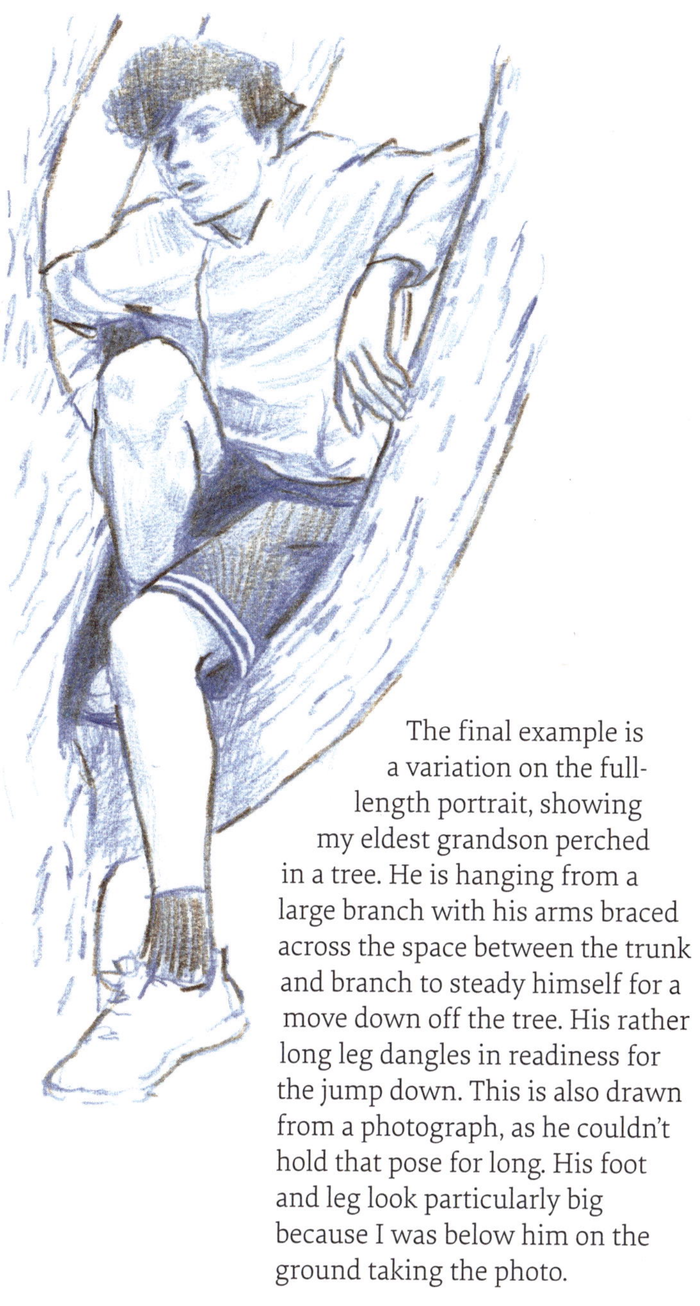

The final example is a variation on the full-length portrait, showing my eldest grandson perched in a tree. He is hanging from a large branch with his arms braced across the space between the trunk and branch to steady himself for a move down off the tree. His rather long leg dangles in readiness for the jump down. This is also drawn from a photograph, as he couldn't hold that pose for long. His foot and leg look particularly big because I was below him on the ground taking the photo.

Lighting the Head

Before you start to draw a portrait, consider the lighting around your subject as it can alter their appearance quite substantially. Look at these examples which show what happens when you light a face deliberately in order to draw it.

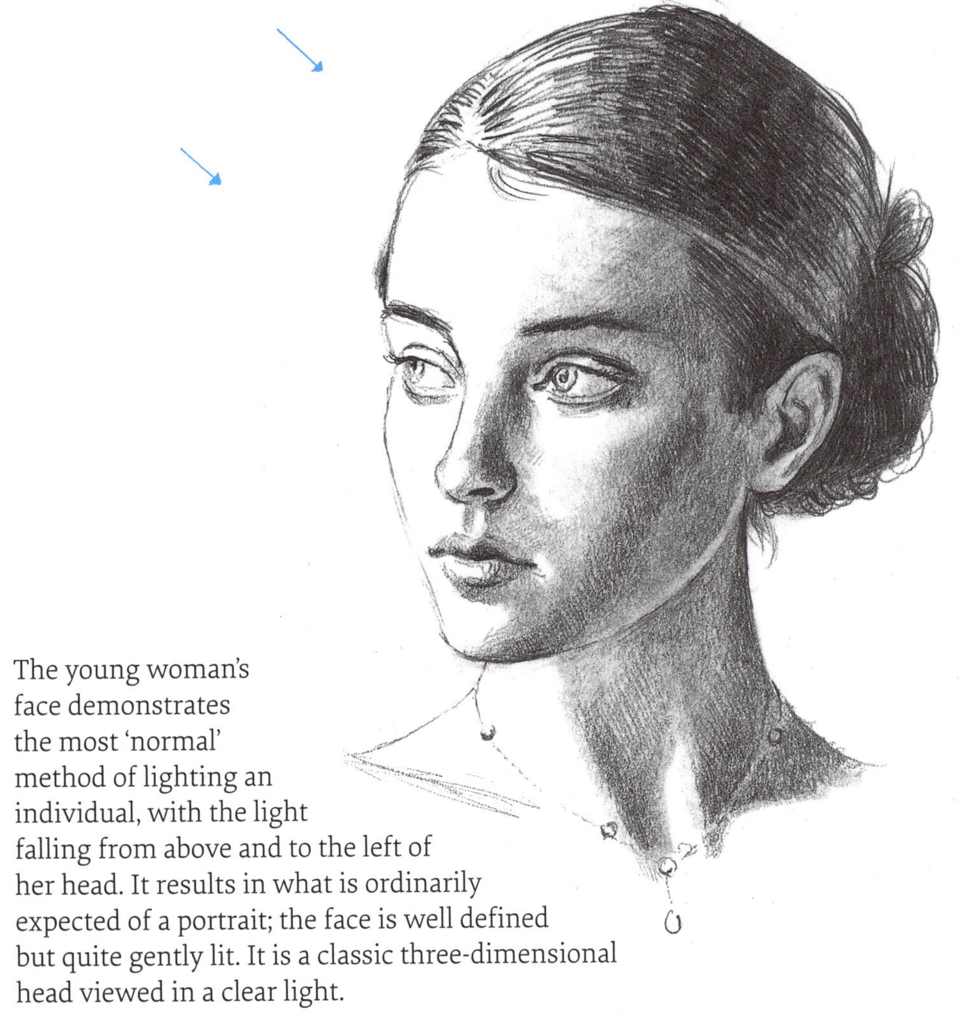

The young woman's face demonstrates the most 'normal' method of lighting an individual, with the light falling from above and to the left of her head. It results in what is ordinarily expected of a portrait; the face is well defined but quite gently lit. It is a classic three-dimensional head viewed in a clear light.

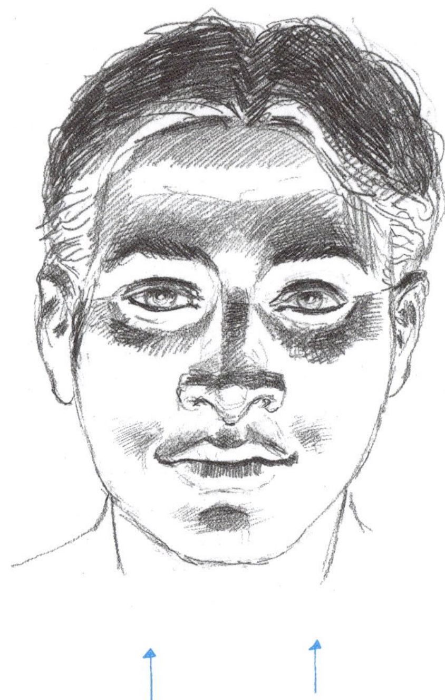

The second head shows what happens if you reverse everything. 'Uplighting' is the familiar method of showing a 'sinister' face, with which everyone is familiar from horror films. The light emphasizes the cheekbones below the eyes, the nose is shown with the bridge and upper nostrils darkened, the top of the head is in shadow and the lower jaw is lit up. It looks scary because it subverts all our expectations of a normal, friendly human face.

The next two pictures show the difference between the effects of daylight and of artificial light.

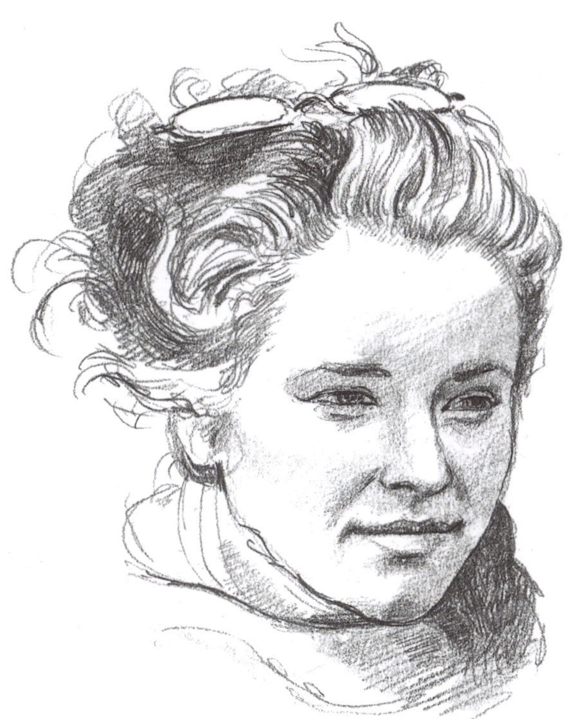

The daylight example comes from a picture taken outside in the sunshine. The sunlight in this case is very diffuse and gives a fairly even distribution of light, with subtle shadows on the side of the head that is facing away from the sun.

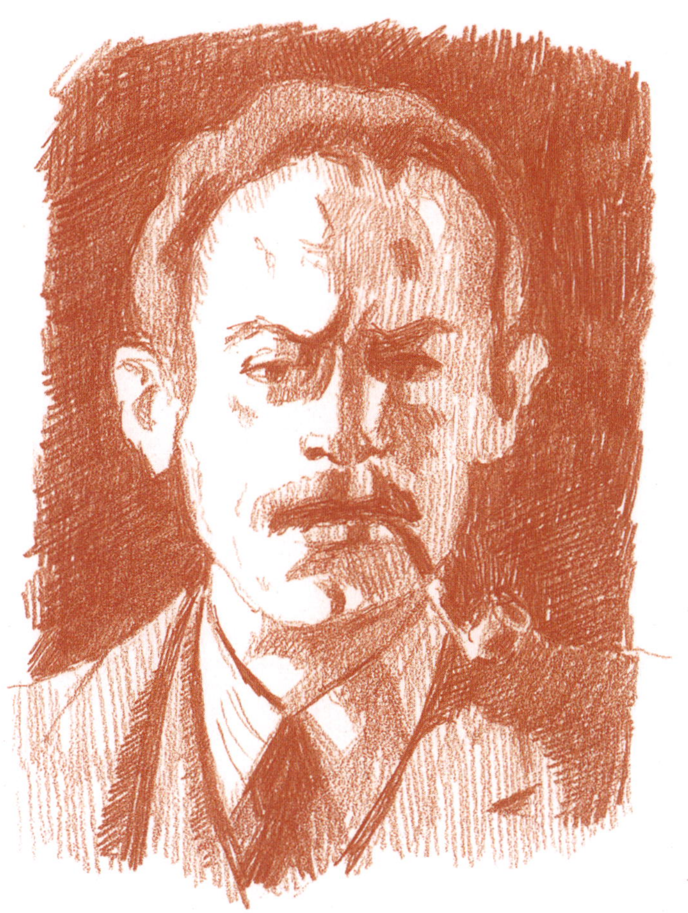

The second example shows a strong directional light that could only come from an artificial source, delivering some strongly illuminated portions and deeper shadows on the other side. However, there is a certain amount of reflected light on the shadowy side, which is probably due to the light bouncing off other surfaces in the room. The dark background is a useful device for making the head more prominent.

And so, as you can see, the lighting in a picture can be chosen just as much as any other part of the drawing.

A Portrait Project

This exercise entails quite a bit of drawing and you will learn a lot about your model's appearance by spending a whole session drawing and redrawing him or her from as many different angles as you think would be useful.

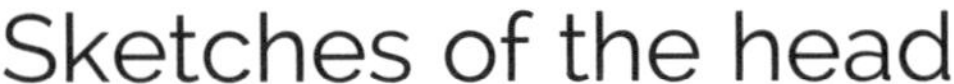

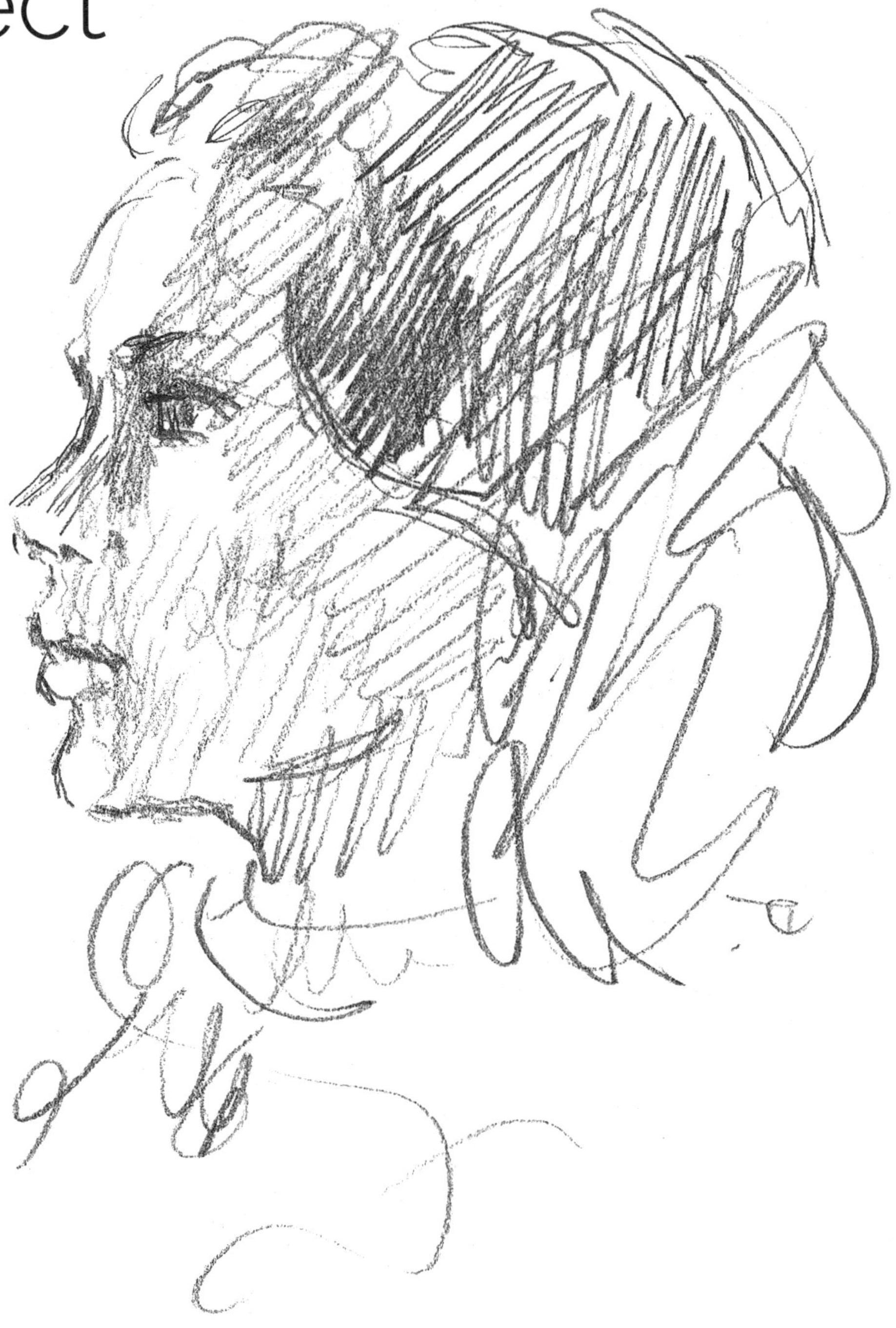

Sketches of the head

I chose as my sitter my eldest daughter, who has sat for me often, like all of my family. Not only that, she is an accomplished artist herself, so she knows the problems of drawing from life. This sympathy with your endeavours is useful, as models do get bored with sitting still for too long.

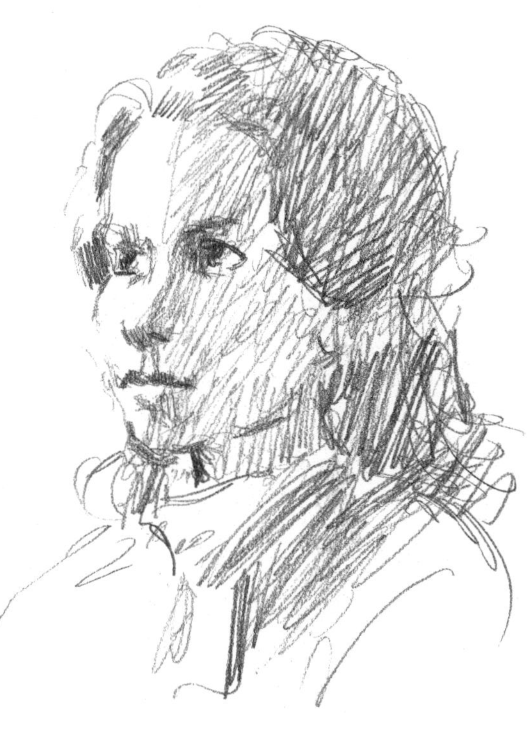

I worked my way round my sitter's head by drawing her first from the side or profile view, then from a more three-quarters view and finally full face. I now had a good idea as to the physiognomy of her face.

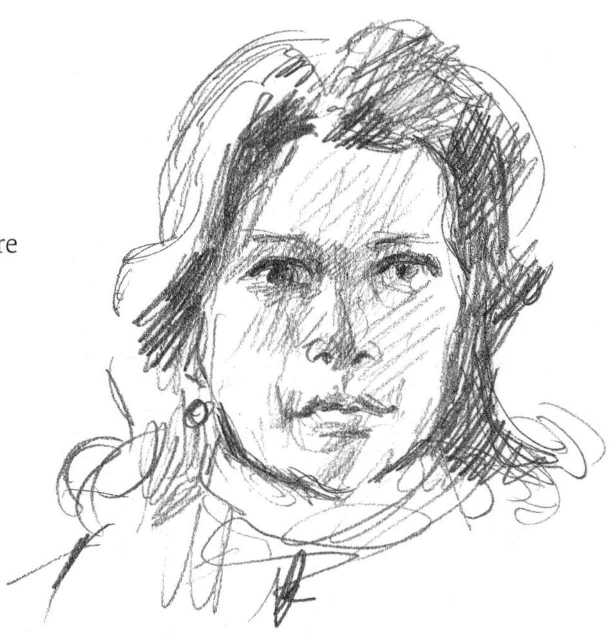

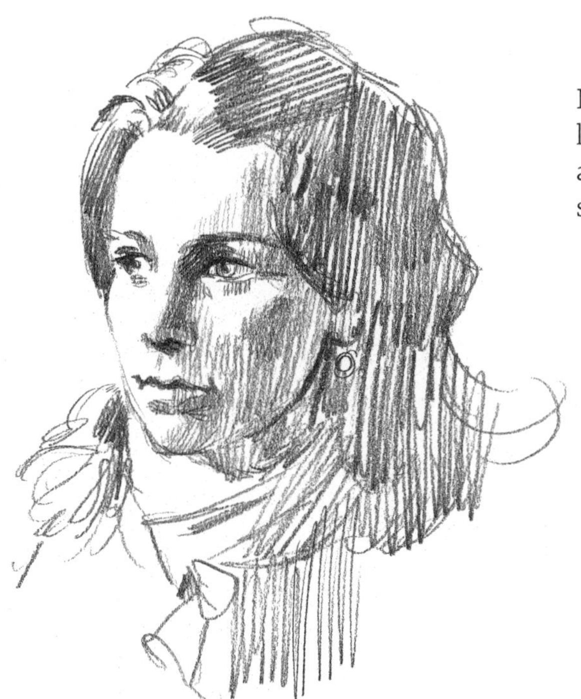

Next I took more account of the lighting, drawing her full-face and three-quarter face, both with strong light cast from the left.

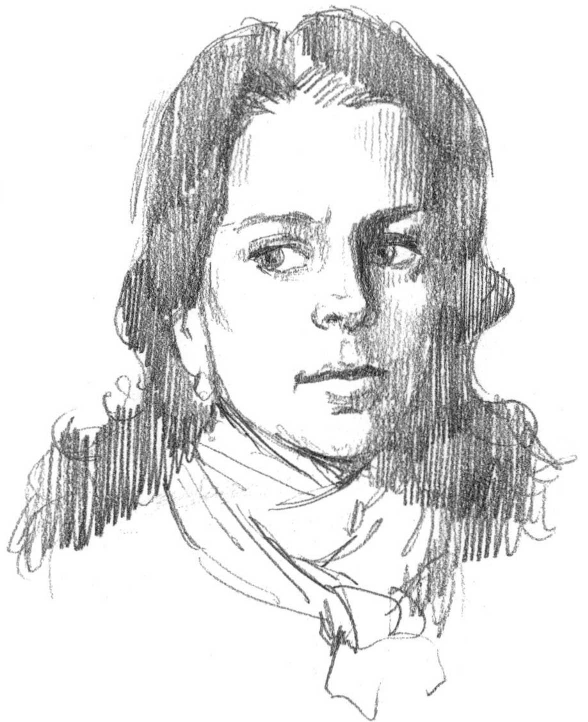

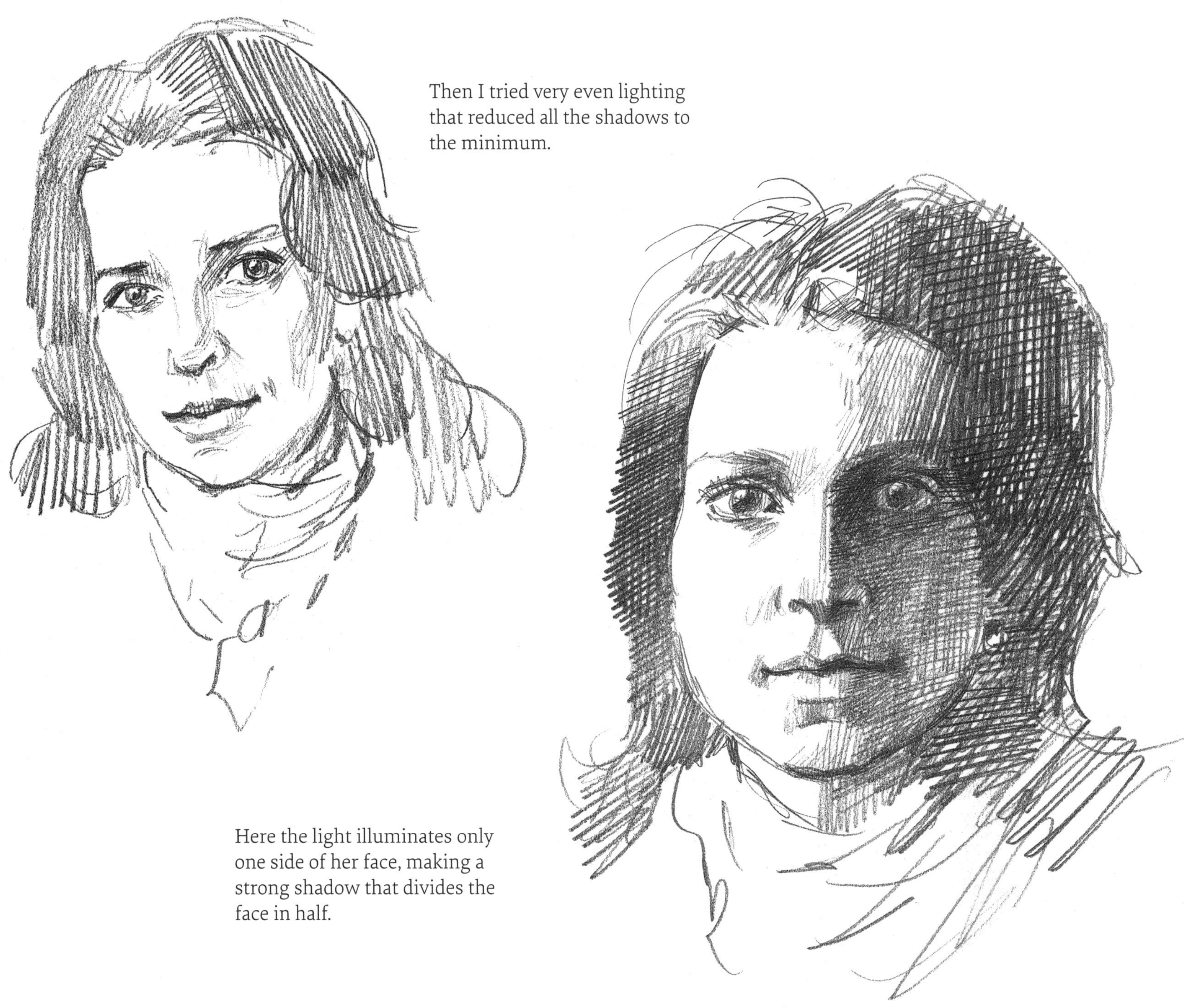

Then I tried very even lighting that reduced all the shadows to the minimum.

Here the light illuminates only one side of her face, making a strong shadow that divides the face in half.

Sketching different poses

Now you need to spend some time drawing the sitter full or three-quarter length in order to decide how much of the pose you might want to draw.

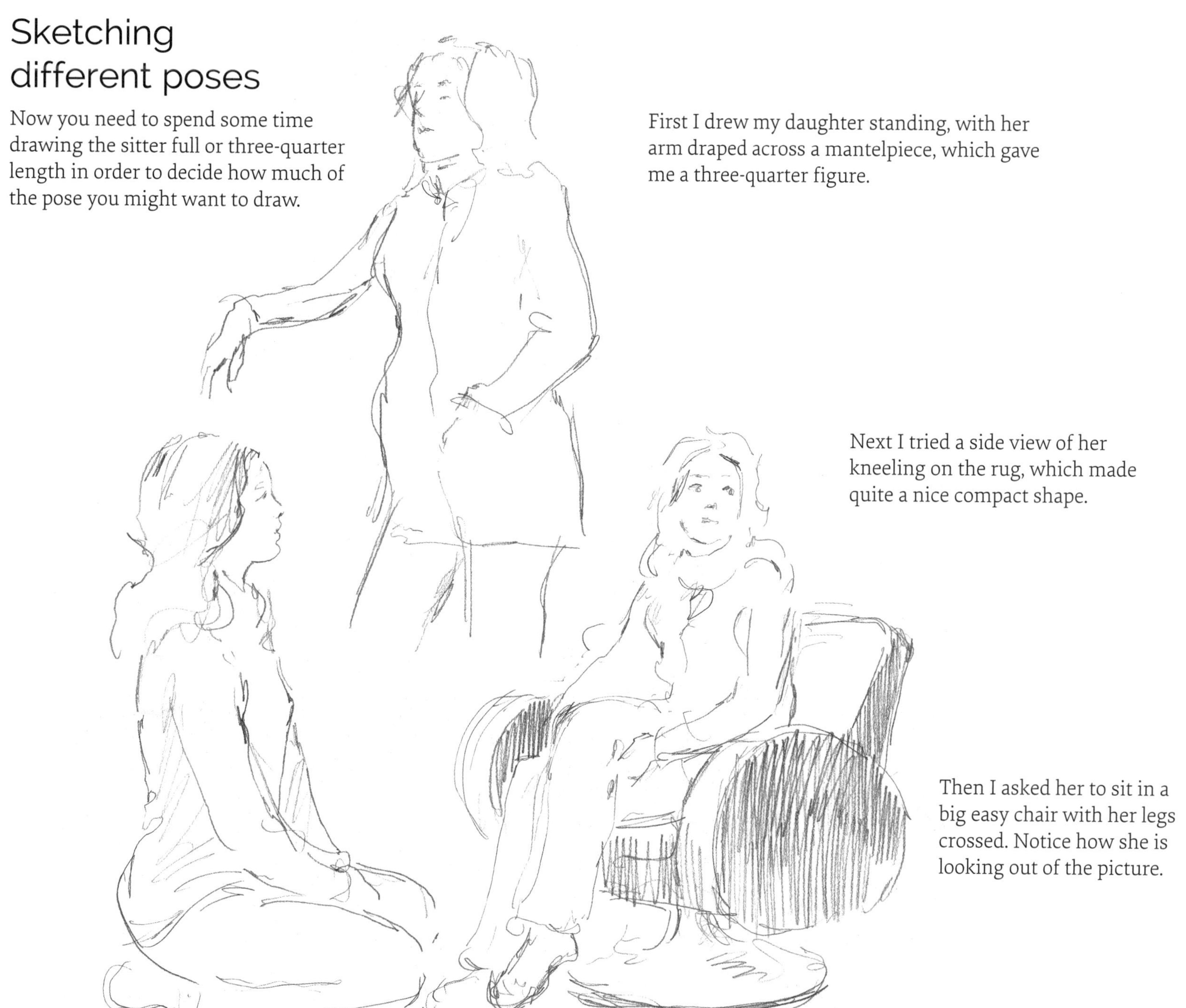

First I drew my daughter standing, with her arm draped across a mantelpiece, which gave me a three-quarter figure.

Next I tried a side view of her kneeling on the rug, which made quite a nice compact shape.

Then I asked her to sit in a big easy chair with her legs crossed. Notice how she is looking out of the picture.

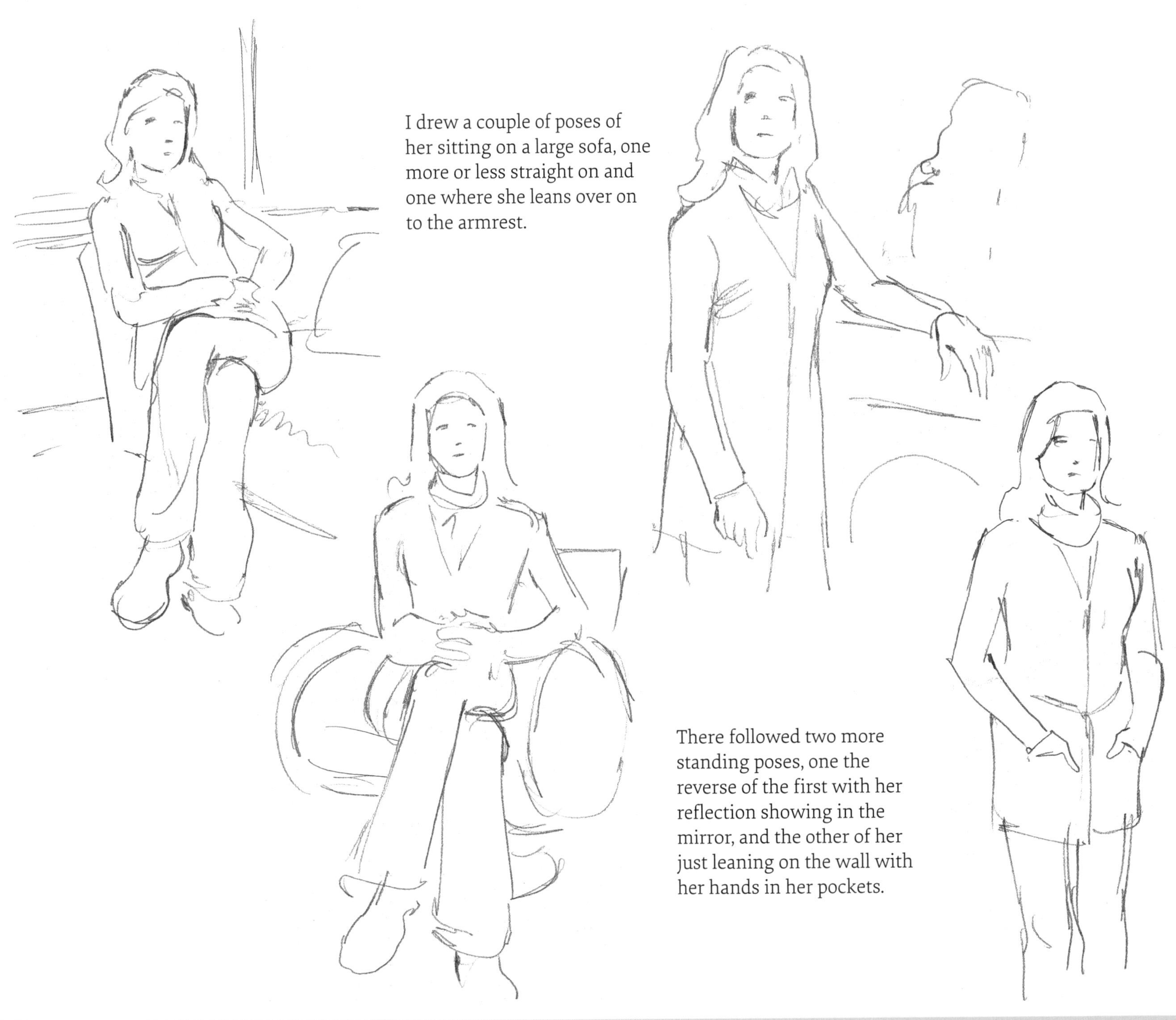

I drew a couple of poses of her sitting on a large sofa, one more or less straight on and one where she leans over on to the armrest.

There followed two more standing poses, one the reverse of the first with her reflection showing in the mirror, and the other of her just leaning on the wall with her hands in her pockets.

Two more variations on seated poses came next. Notice how all these drawings are much less detailed than the face drawings, because here I was just looking for a pose and I wasn't worried about whether the face was accurate; the position was everything.

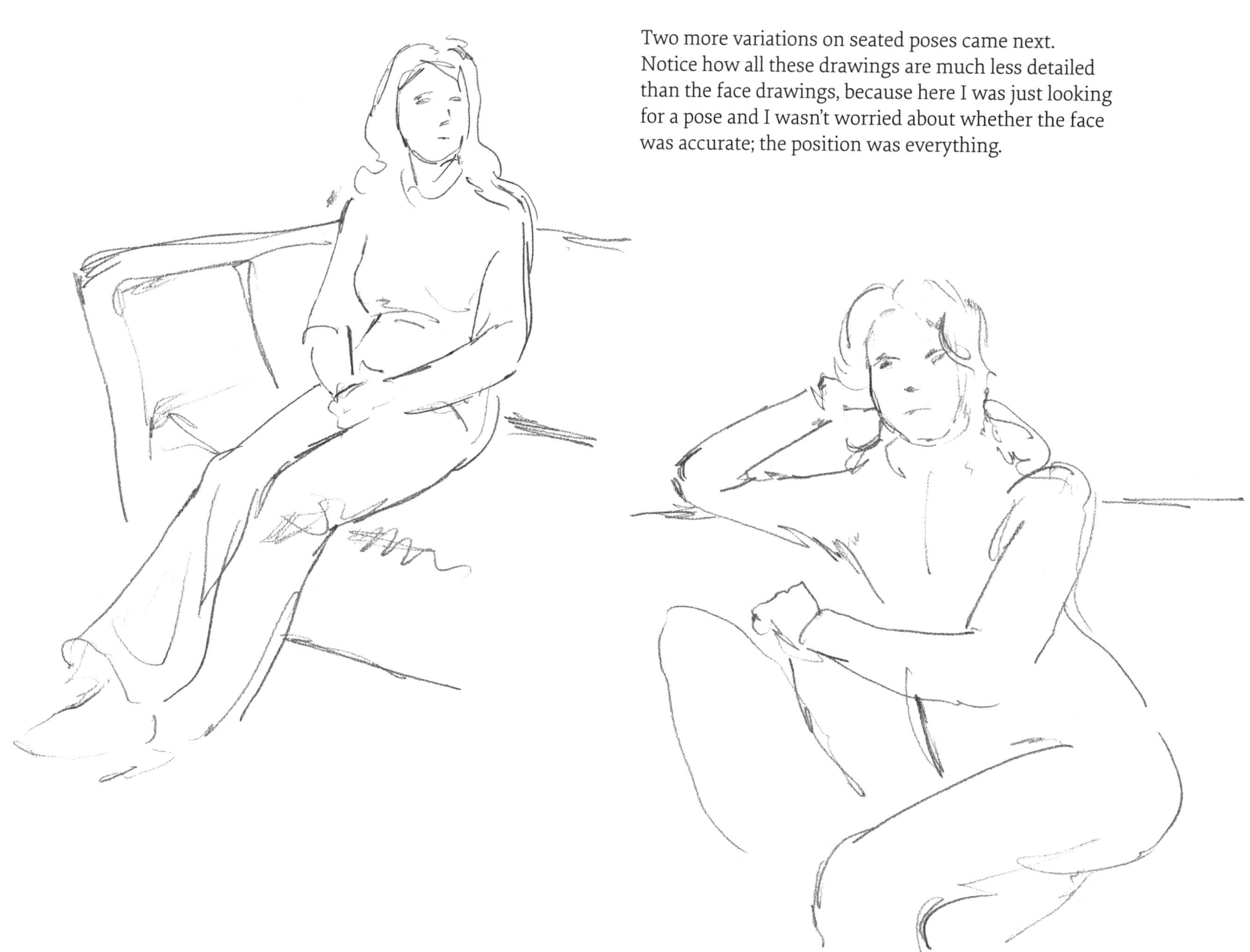

Drawing the features in detail

Once you've decided upon the pose you need to turn your attention to the details of the sitter's face, taking each of the features and making detailed drawings of them.

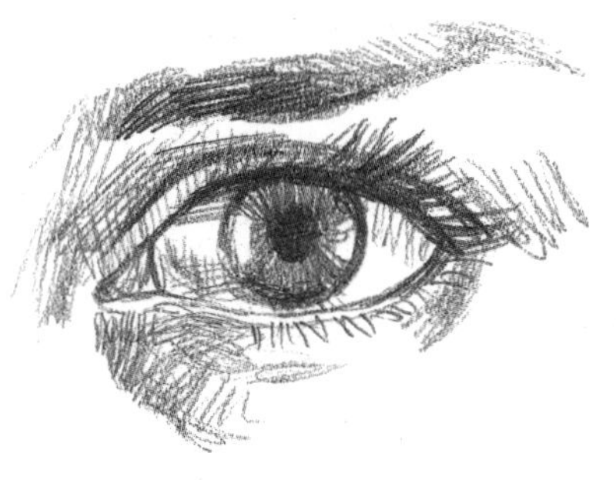

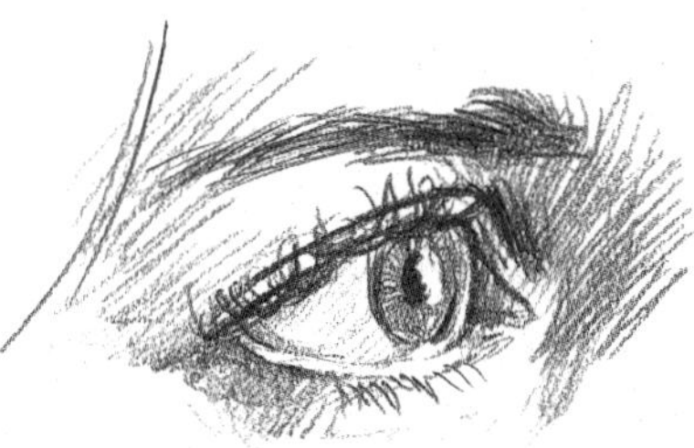

I started by drawing just one eye. This is a difficult thing to do, as the model will find your concentrated stare a little daunting. However, it's also very revealing as to how carefully you have observed the eye. Having drawn my daughter's eye directly facing me, I then drew it from a slight angle so that I got a side view of it. I did this with both eyes, then drew them as a pair to see how they looked together, as well as the space between them.

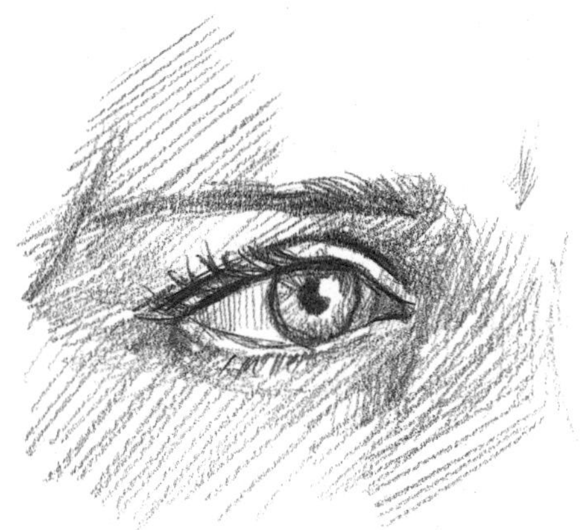

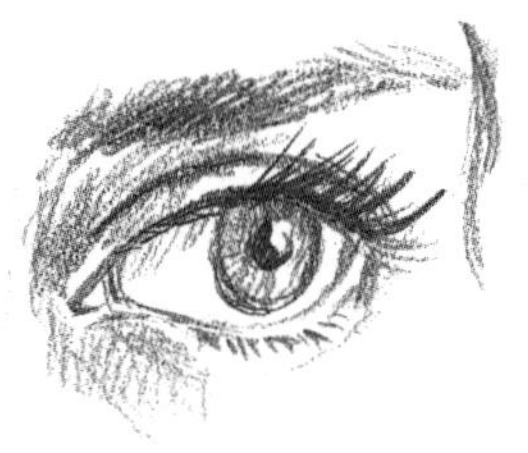

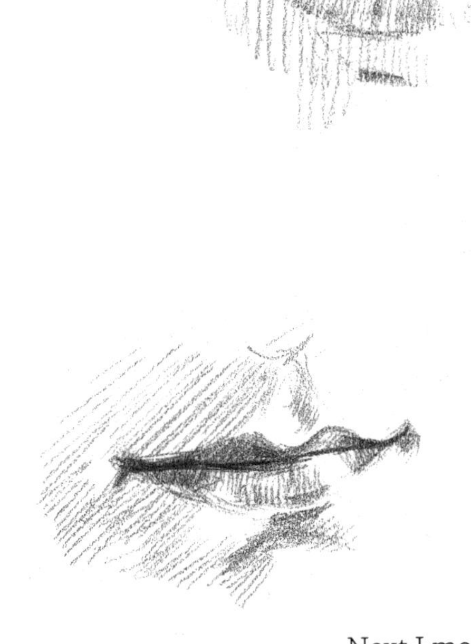

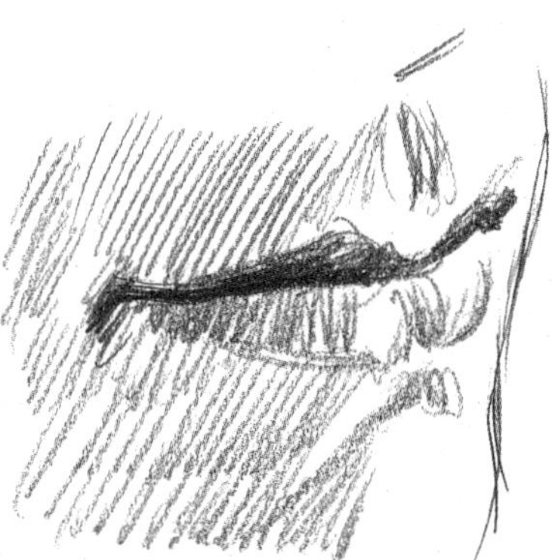

Next I moved on to the mouth and drew it two or three times, exploring the front, side and three-quarter view.

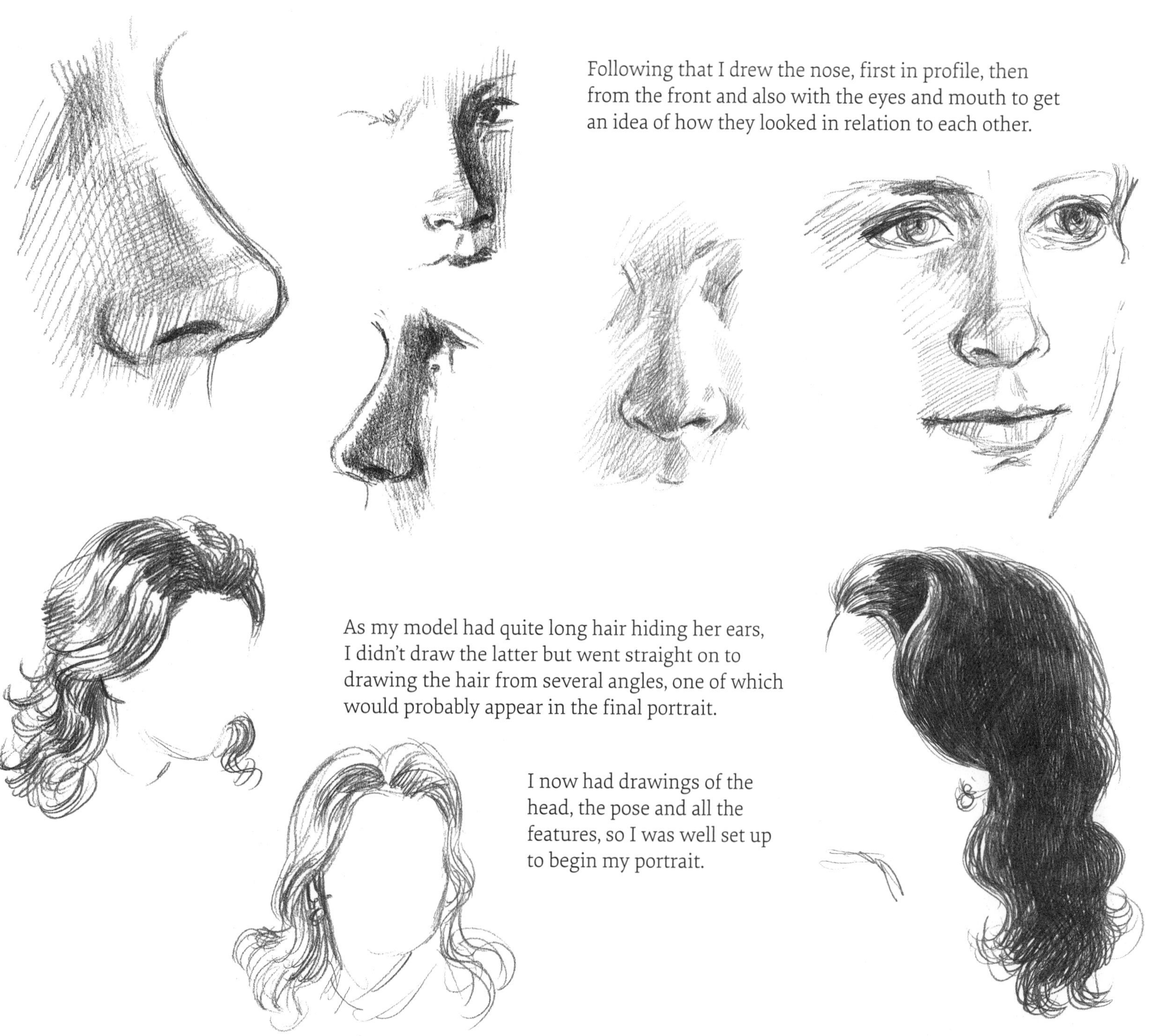

Following that I drew the nose, first in profile, then from the front and also with the eyes and mouth to get an idea of how they looked in relation to each other.

As my model had quite long hair hiding her ears, I didn't draw the latter but went straight on to drawing the hair from several angles, one of which would probably appear in the final portrait.

I now had drawings of the head, the pose and all the features, so I was well set up to begin my portrait.

Choose your composition

With my drawings gathered together and my model refreshed and ready to sit for me again, I first had to choose the pose and then draw it up in as simple a way as possible but with all the information I needed to proceed to the finished portrait. I decided to place her on a large sofa, legs stretched out and hands in her lap, with her head slightly turned to look directly at me. The light was all derived from the large window to the left and so half of her face was in soft shadow.

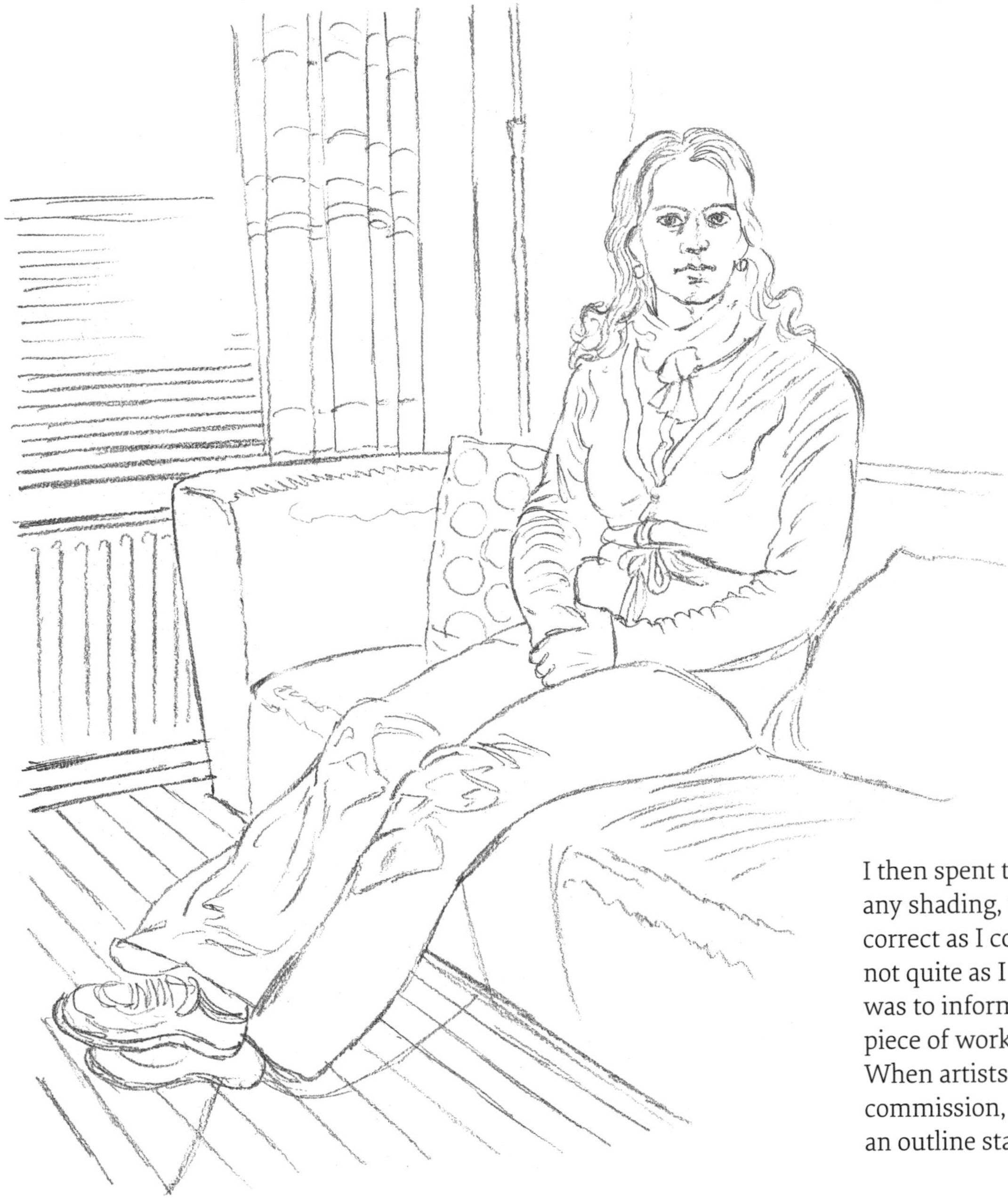

I then spent time drawing her in some detail, but without any shading, to create my cartoon. I tried to make it as correct as I could, but it didn't yet matter if the drawing was not quite as I wanted it because the purpose of the cartoon was to inform me as to what I needed to do to make the final piece of work the best possible portrait that I could manage. When artists in traditional ateliers were painting a large commission, they often drew up the whole thing full-size in an outline state from which to produce their final painting.

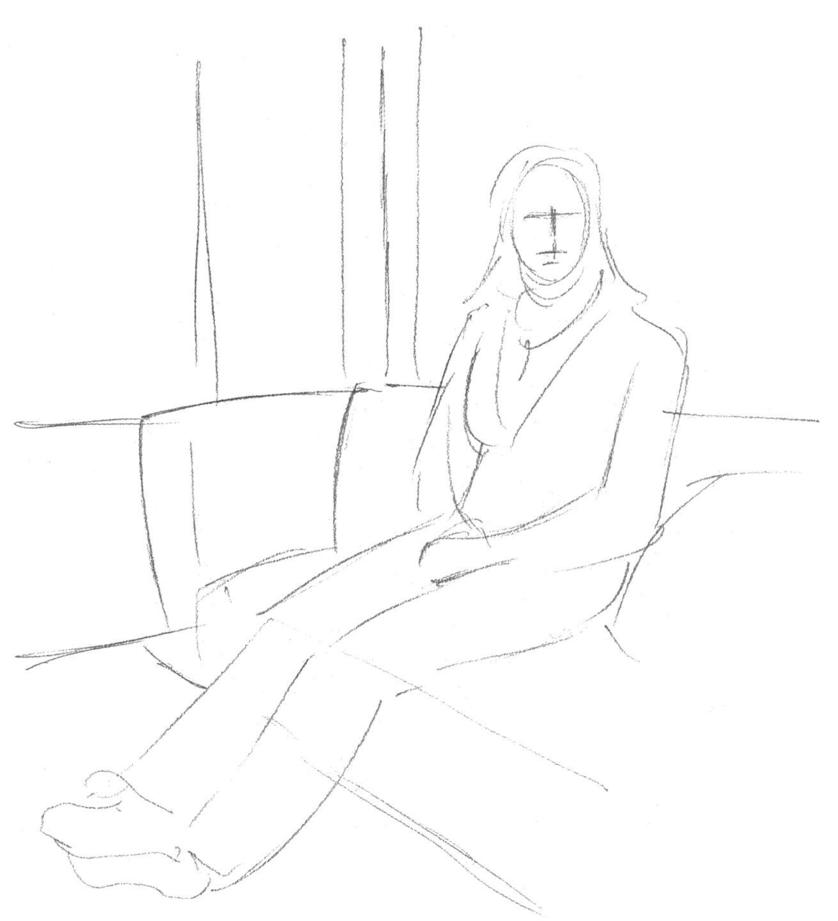

STEP 1

First I drew up a quick sketch that told me where everything would be placed. This almost exactly echoed the shape of my cartoon, which I had in front of me.

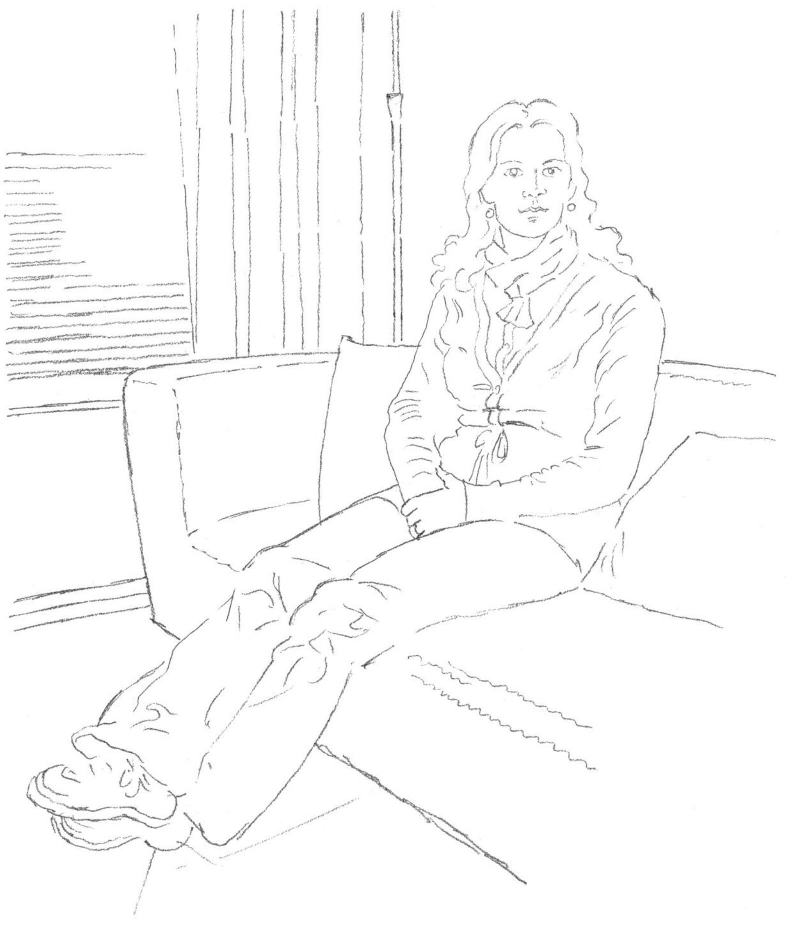

STEP 2

Then, still using my cartoon as a guide, I drew up a careful outline drawing of the whole figure and the background setting in some detail. This was the last stage at which I could introduce any changes if they were necessary.

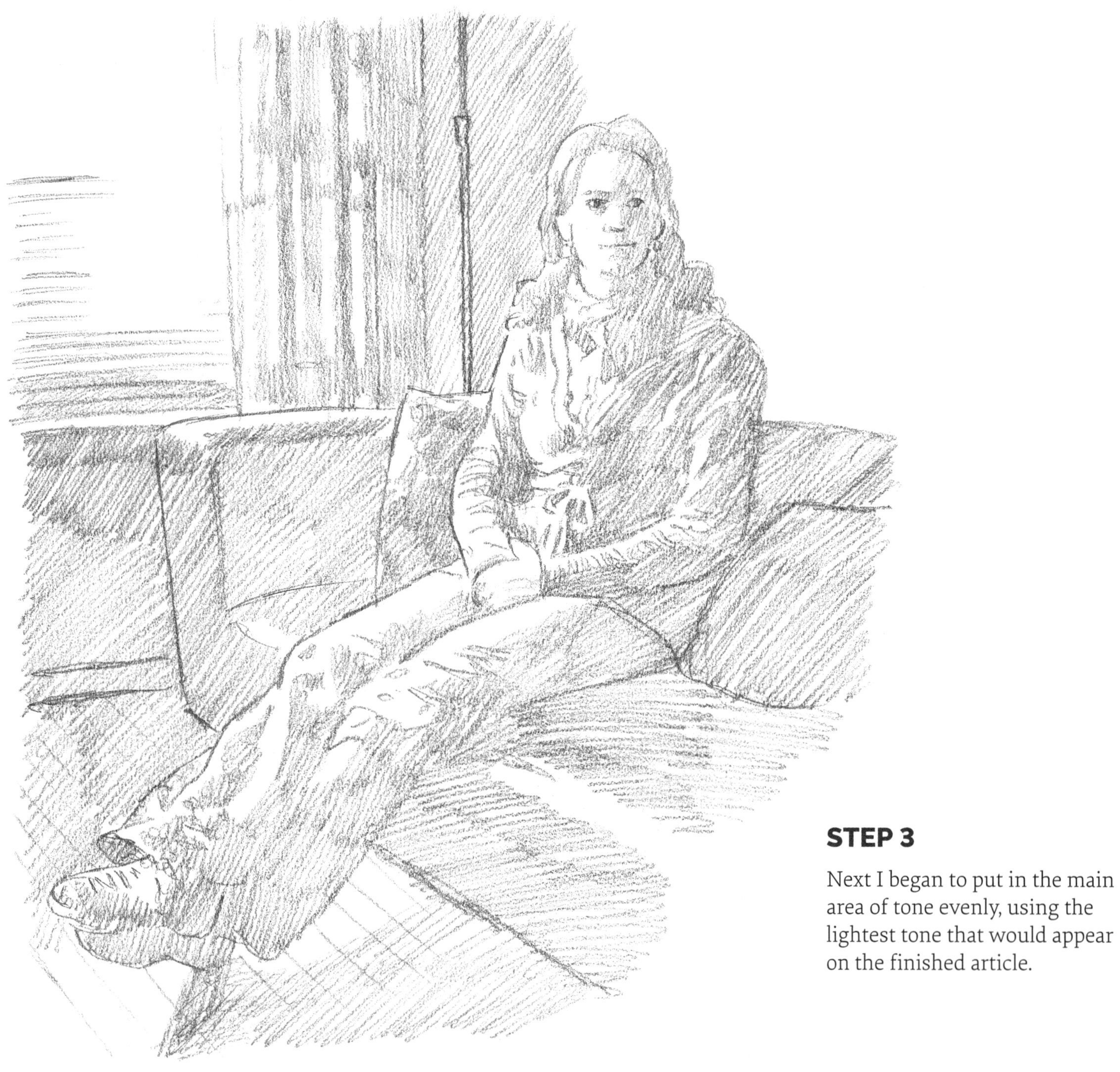

STEP 3

Next I began to put in the main area of tone evenly, using the lightest tone that would appear on the finished article.

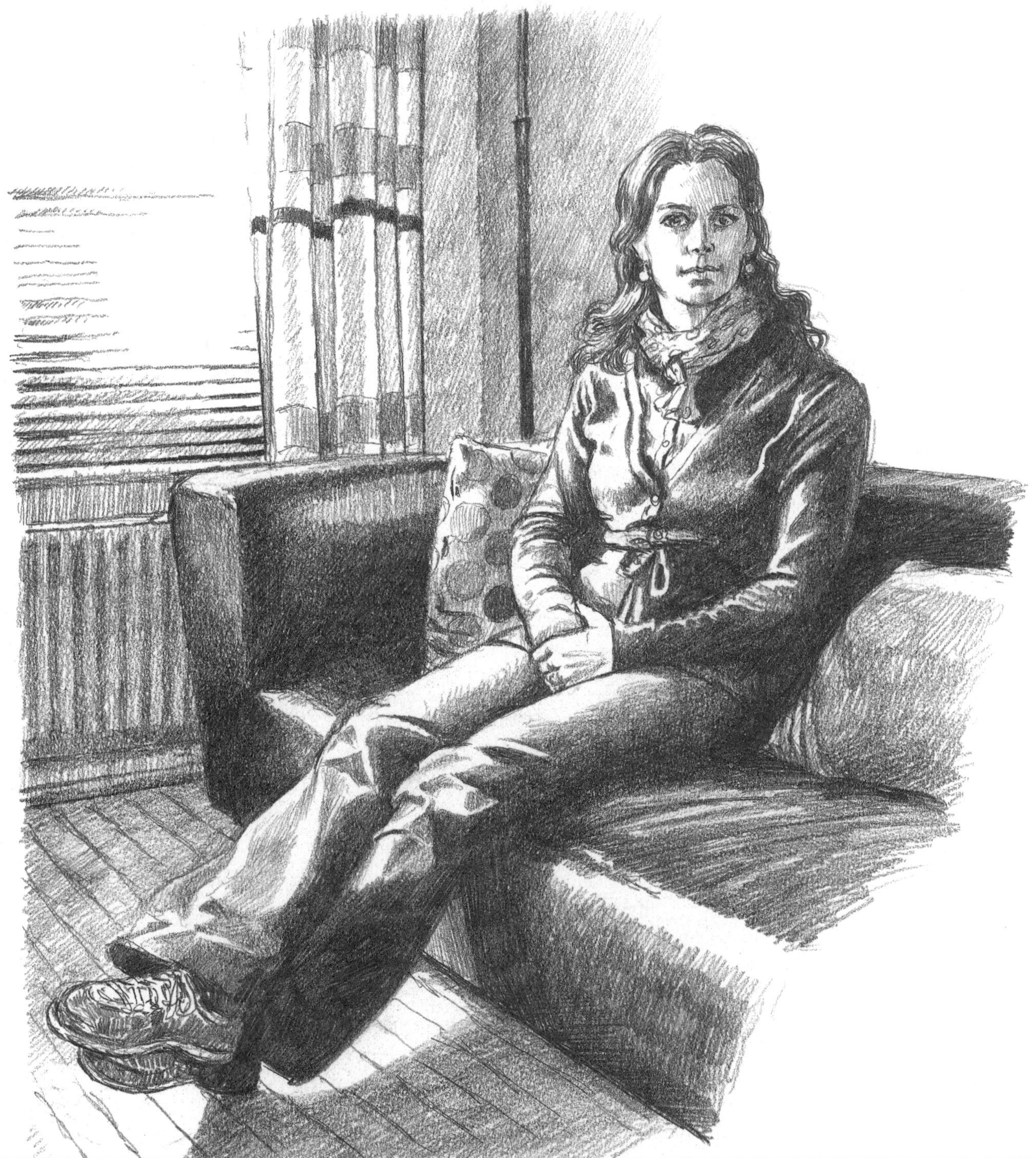

STEP 4

I could now build up all the different tones until I had produced a convincing three-dimensional portrait that looked like my sitter. This may have struck you as quite a long process, but if you take all this trouble to make your own portrait the chances are that not only will the sitter be pleased with the result, so will you.

A Colour Portrait in Steps

For this portrait, the aim is to get closer to your subject and to focus on how to use colour in your drawing. My sitter was looking directly at me, resting her chin on her hand, which lends a relaxed and intimate feel to the portrait. Drawing her hand also allowed me to show her collection of large rings, which add interest and hint at her individuality.

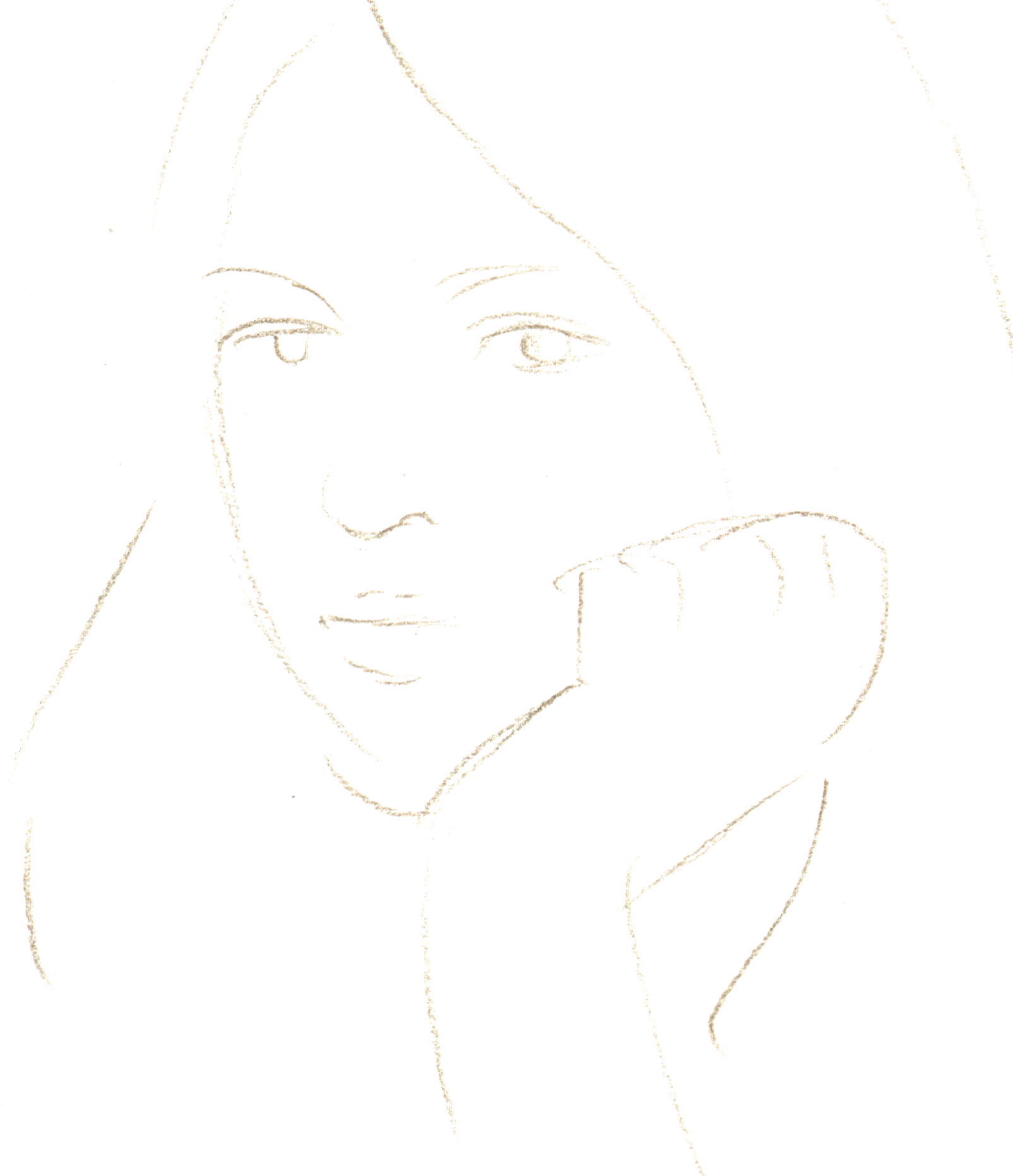

STEP 1

As usual, start with a careful but simplified drawing of the main shapes of the face, hair and hand. Try to gauge the size and distance between the features accurately, using the measuring methods shown on page 52 if necessary.

STEP 2

The next stage is to draw all the features in detail, correcting any mistakes as you go. This stage is the most challenging and may take the longest, as it is when you will get your likeness down on paper. Look carefully at the shapes of the eyes, noting how the farther eye differs in shape from the nearer one and the eyelids cover the tops of the irises. The far nostril is hidden, and a slight upward curve of the mouth can be seen on the near side. The shapes of the wrist and hand are also important in this composition, so take time to get them right.

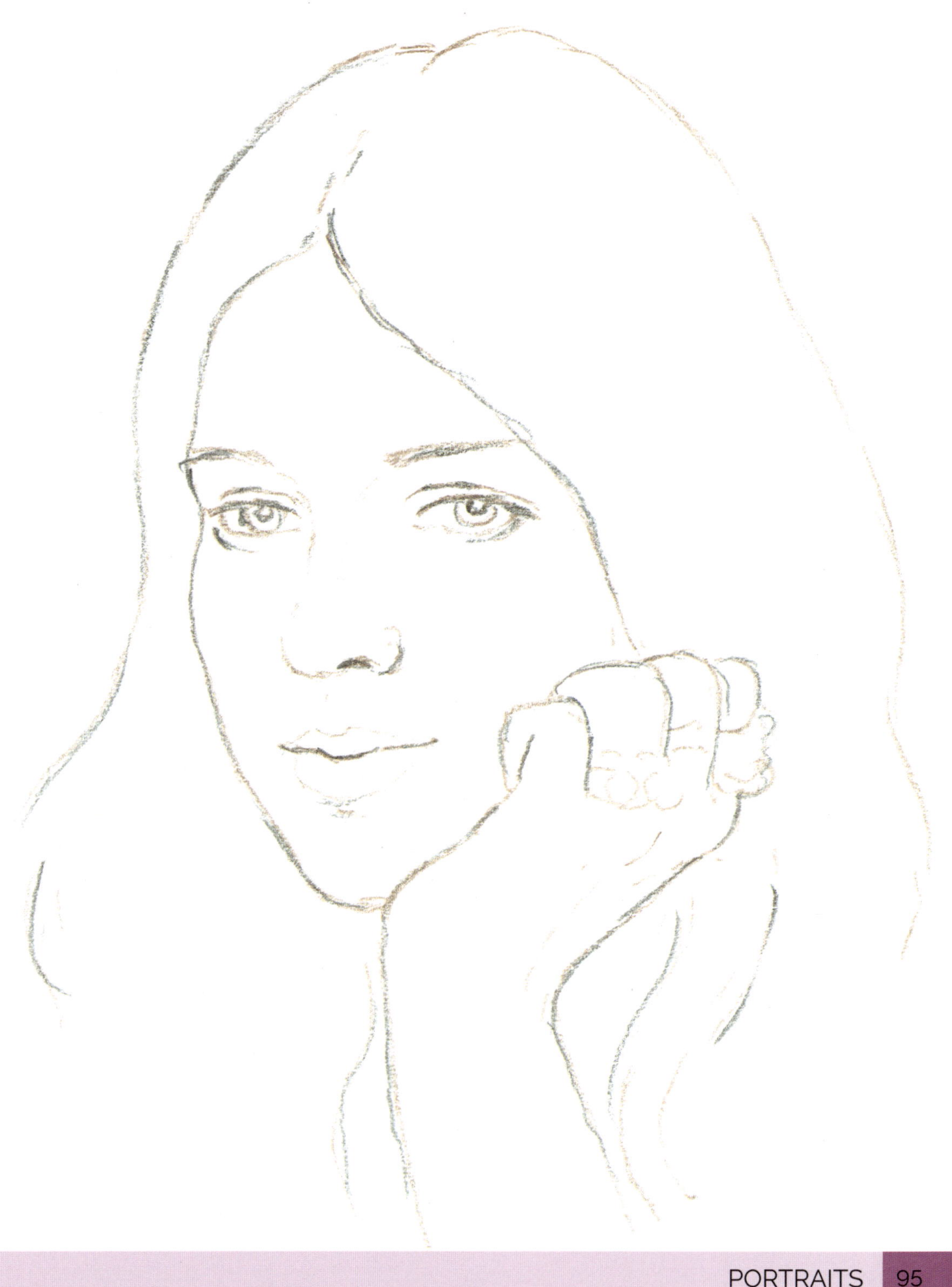

STEP 3

In this step the colour becomes significant. First of all make sure all the tonal areas are put in with coloured strokes, not too heavily, in order to build up the main areas of colour. I used brown and black for the hair, pink, red and pale brown for the skin areas, plus a touch of background colour (burnt sienna) and some blue for the eyes. Keep the colour light and general at this stage.

Artist's Note

When it comes to tonal values in a portrait, you may well find that the colour of the human face is not always uniform. If a person has quite dramatic changes of colour in their facial features, you could be tempted to put them in very strongly. However, this would reduce the structural composition, turning it into a caricature of the real person. In order to avoid this, grade your colour gradually from one part of the face to the next and the result will look more natural.

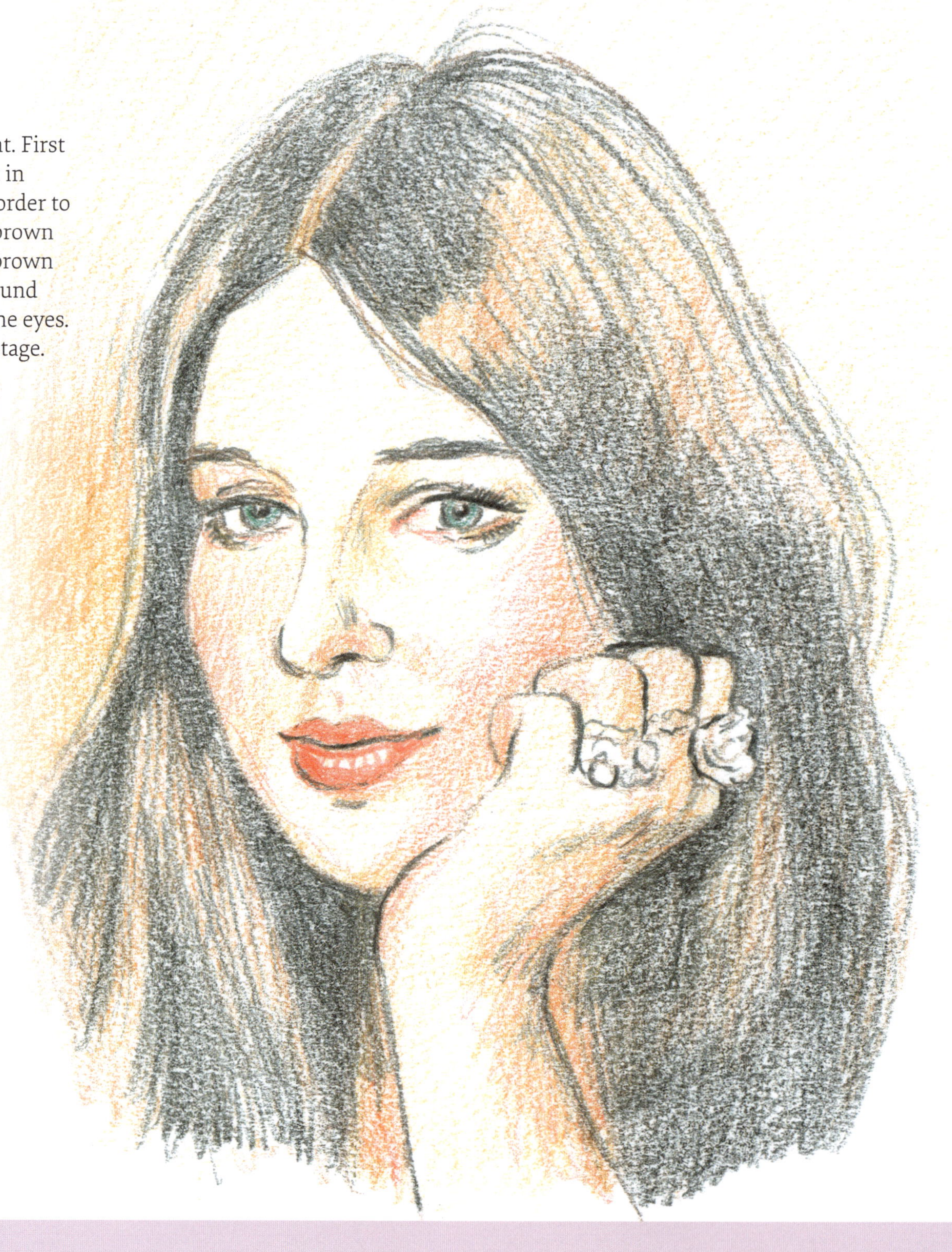

STEP 4

In this last step you will need to really increase the strength and solidity of the colours. The hair demands a lot of dark areas, sometimes solid black. A little touch of this black tone will strengthen the eyebrows, lashes and pupils of the eyes, as well as the darker shadows around the edges of the nostrils, mouth, wrist, hand and fingers. The warm pink and brown colours can add more depth to the face, mouth, hand and arm. Also increase the background colour strength. Once the depth and strength of colour is established, carefully touch in any small marks to increase the intensity of the eyes, features and hand. When you are satisfied with the look of your portrait, stop and enjoy your efforts.

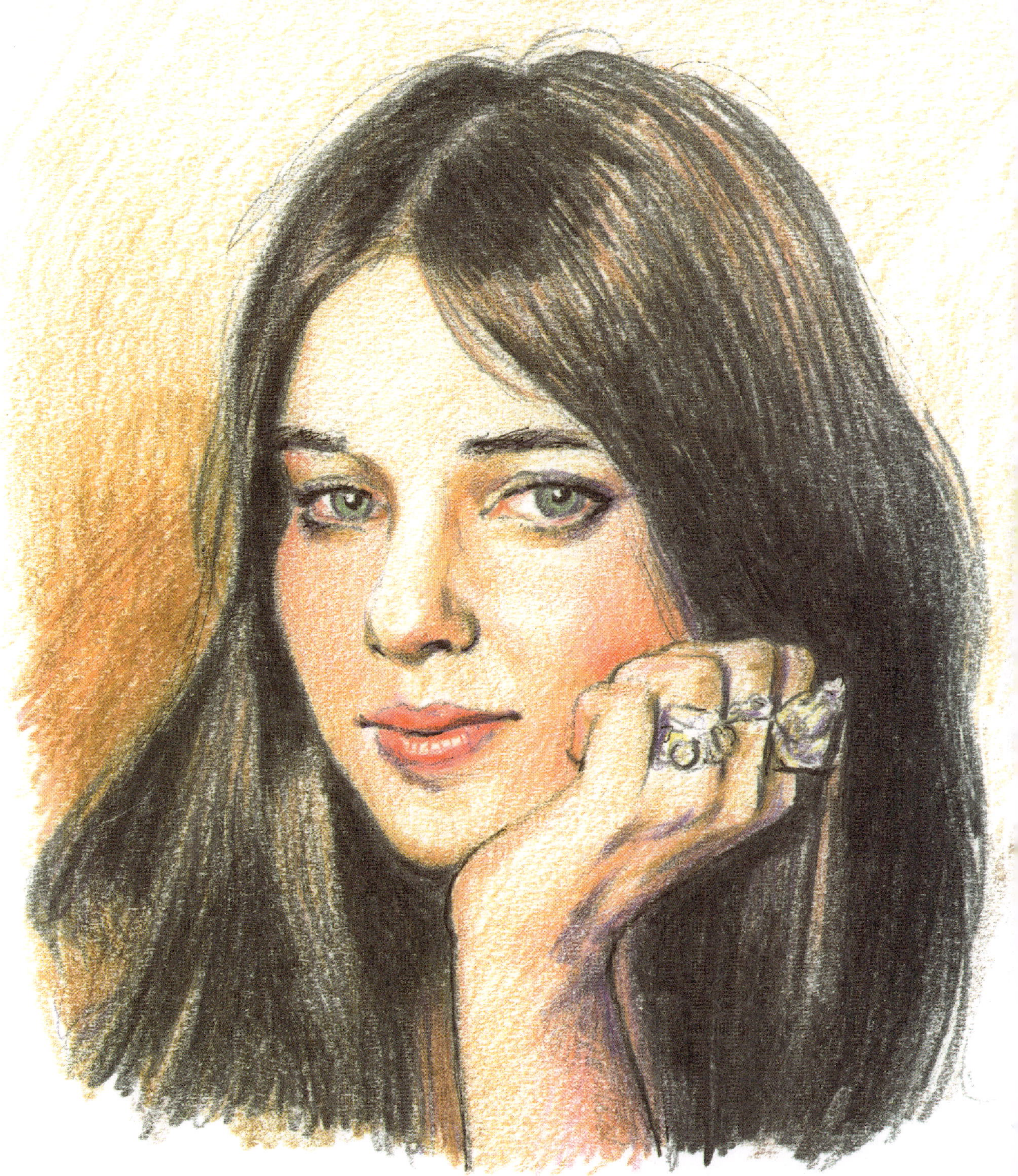

Portraiture by Master Artists

The examples on these pages show how portrait styles have changed over time. The artists of the Renaissance introduced a new realism to their work, looking hard at their subjects to put down recognizable images of individual faces. However by the time of the Impressionists in the 19th century, many artists wanted to make more intimate images in a looser style.

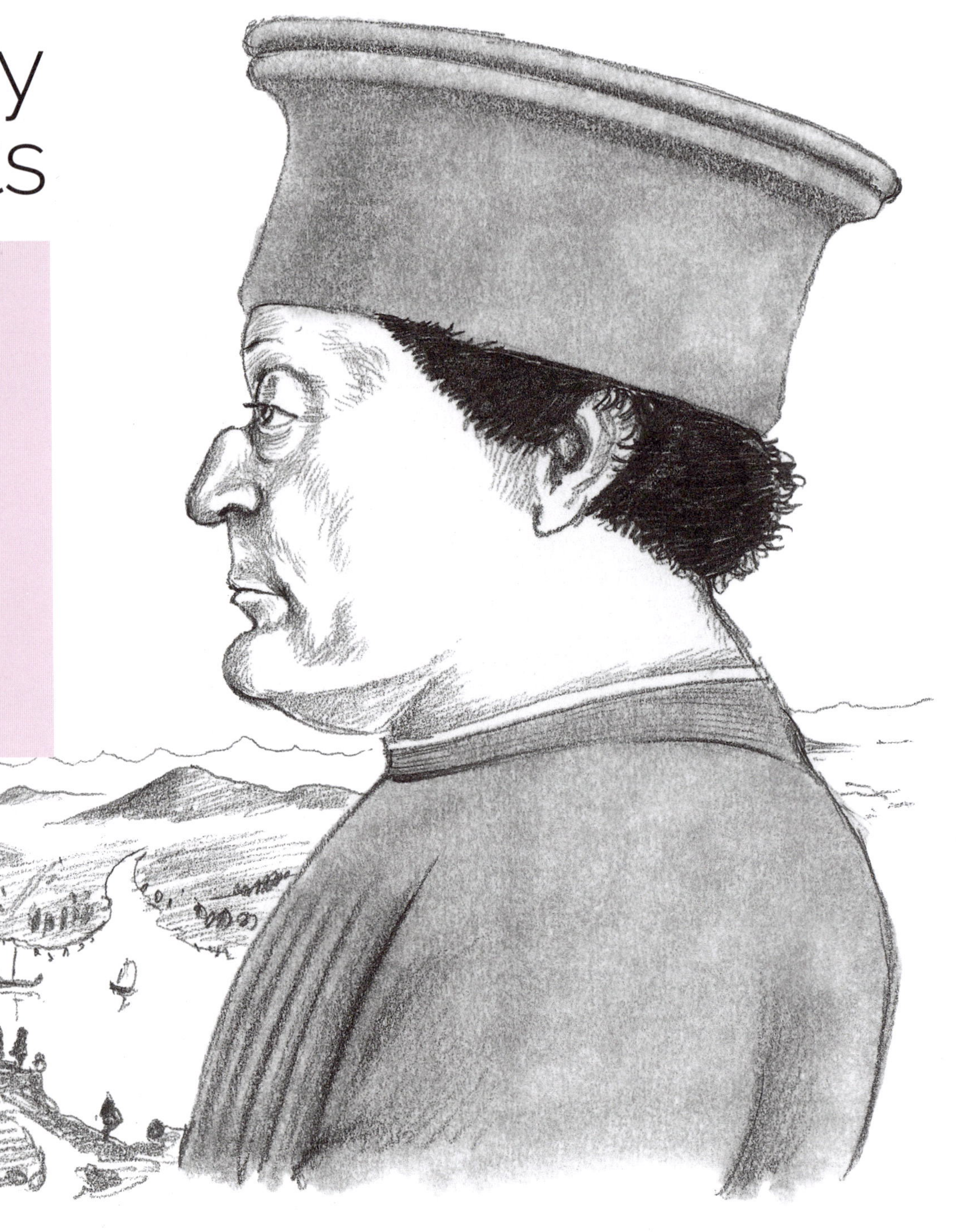

The first portrait is by Piero della Francesca (1415/20–1492) and features the distinctive profile of the Duke of Urbino, Federico da Montefeltro. This learned statesman, patron of the arts, and 'condottiere' – leader of mercenary soldiers – would only allow the left side of his face to be portrayed because of a disfiguring wound on the other side. But from other contemporary paintings and medallions, we recognize that this was indeed a true likeness of the Duke.

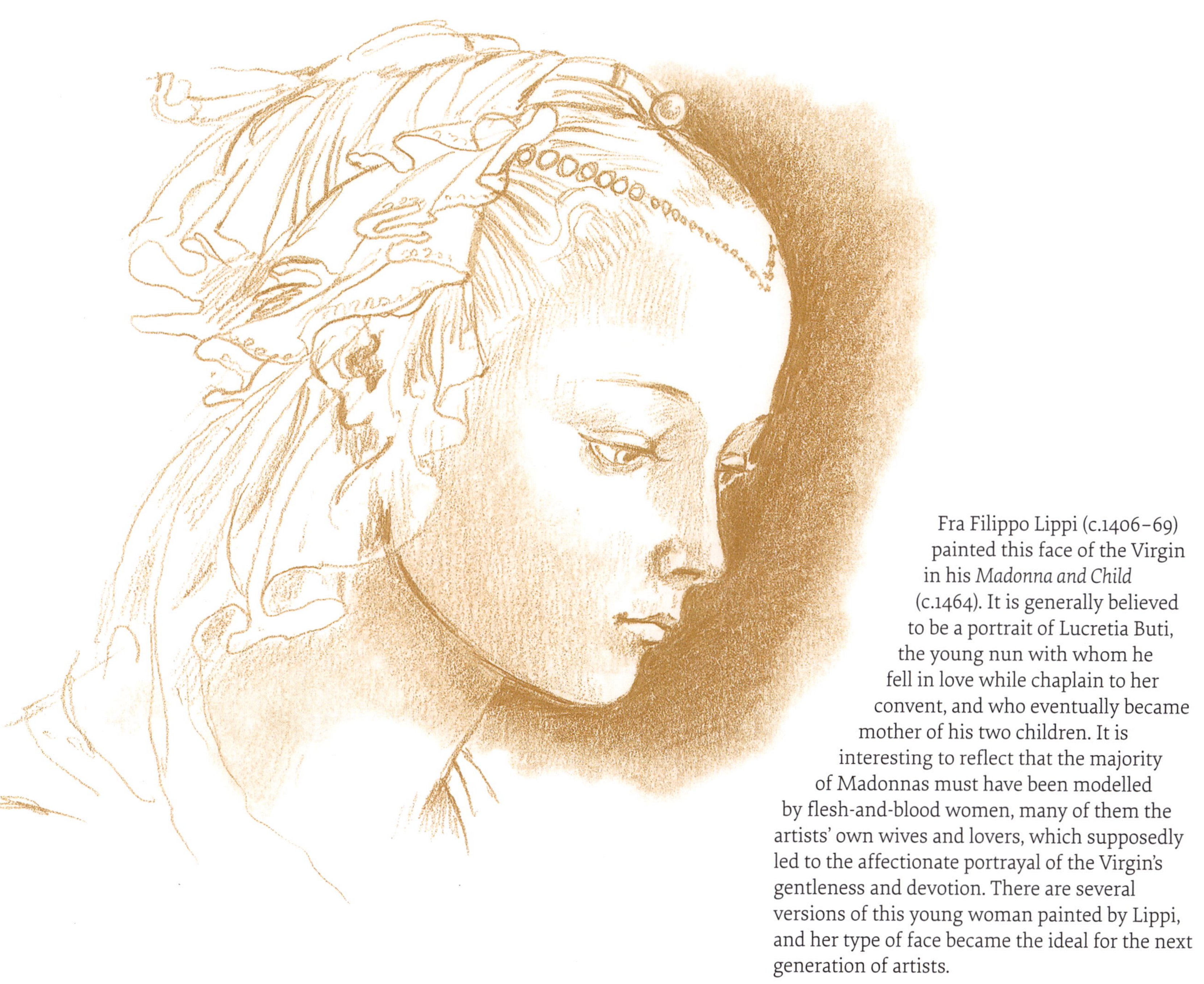

Fra Filippo Lippi (c.1406–69) painted this face of the Virgin in his *Madonna and Child* (c.1464). It is generally believed to be a portrait of Lucretia Buti, the young nun with whom he fell in love while chaplain to her convent, and who eventually became mother of his two children. It is interesting to reflect that the majority of Madonnas must have been modelled by flesh-and-blood women, many of them the artists' own wives and lovers, which supposedly led to the affectionate portrayal of the Virgin's gentleness and devotion. There are several versions of this young woman painted by Lippi, and her type of face became the ideal for the next generation of artists.

The next two drawings are after portraits by Mary Cassatt (1844–1926), the American painter who was an habitué of the Impressionist circle in 19th-century Paris. The first is quite an early example of her work, and you can see the traditional qualities of earlier portrait styles showing strongly. However, her ability sings out in this face, which has some quality of a Goya. She has kept the picture very simple and direct.

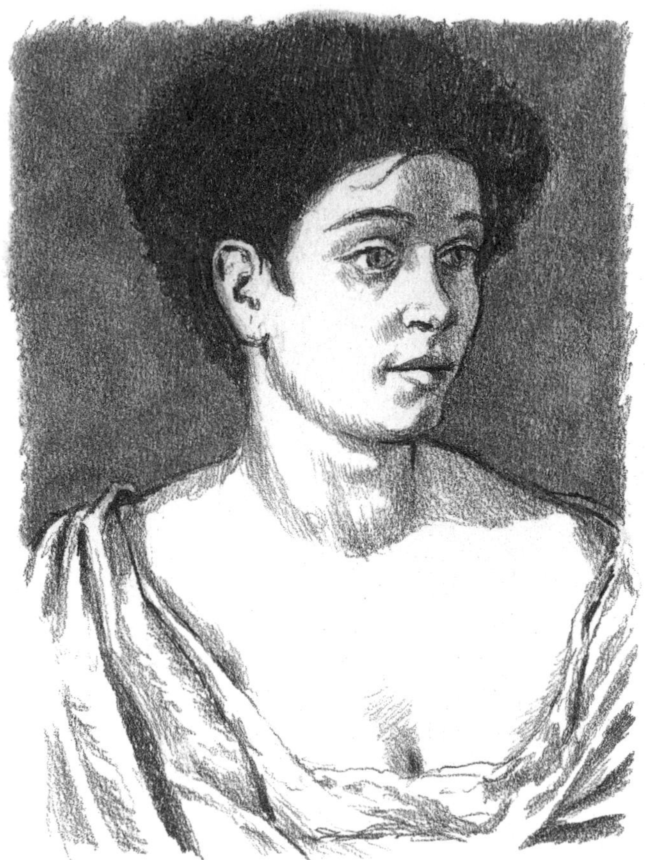

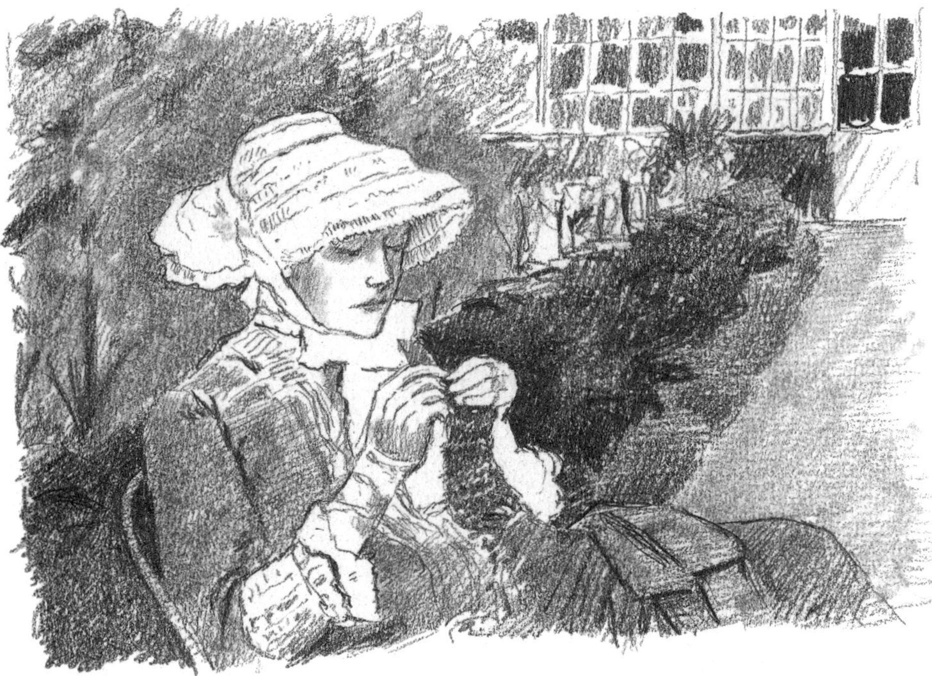

In the second portrait, Cassatt has now become much more the Impressionist, in that the whole scene, including the background, makes a pattern of shapes with no obvious focal point. She has caught the daylight feel of the garden location, the figure of the woman being very much part of the scene.

This example is based on a portrait of Miss Cicely Alexander by American artist James McNeill Whistler (1834–1903). The young girl is in an elegant standing pose, wearing a rather frothy party dress and holding a broad hat. While Whistler's original painting is in oil paints of muted colours, I transposed it into watercolour, using the medium to capture the delicate subject and her flouncy dress. I first flicked in the outline of the figure with a small brush and then, with a large brush, I washed in the entire background in the same colour. When all that had dried, I put in the other colours, leaving large white areas for the dress and being careful to avoid too much contrast.

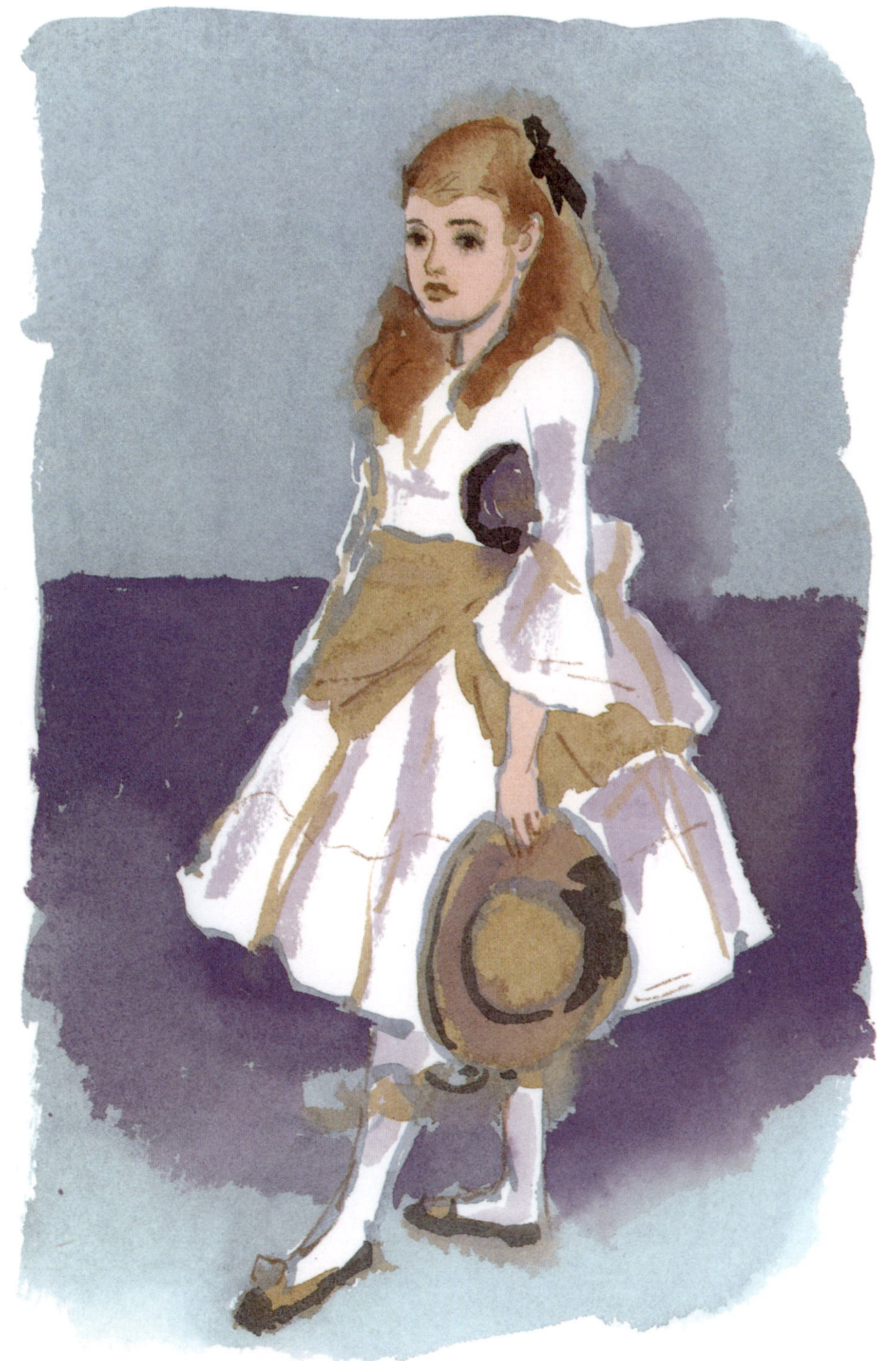

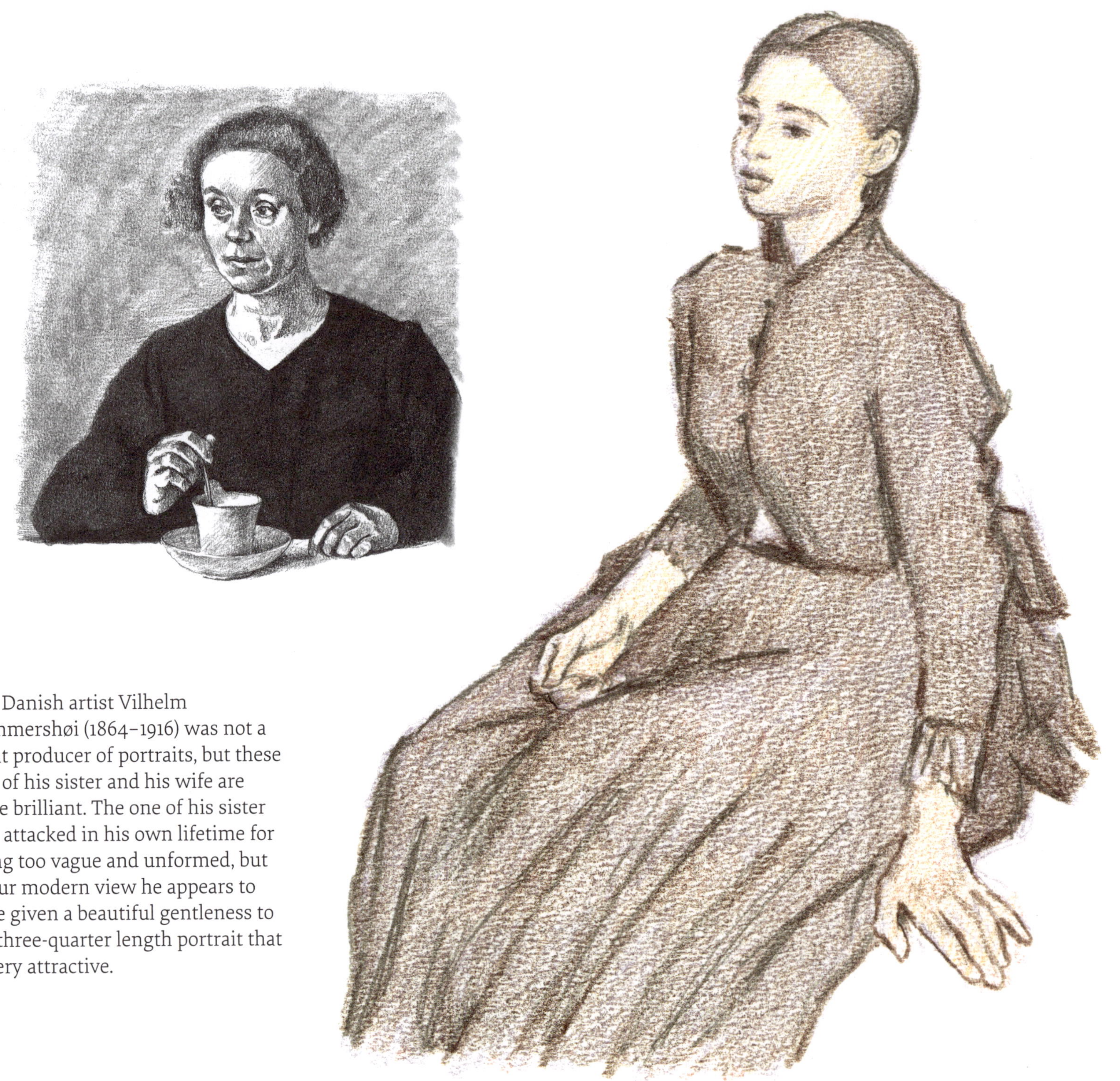

The Danish artist Vilhelm Hammershøi (1864–1916) was not a great producer of portraits, but these two of his sister and his wife are quite brilliant. The one of his sister was attacked in his own lifetime for being too vague and unformed, but to our modern view he appears to have given a beautiful gentleness to his three-quarter length portrait that is very attractive.

Drawn after Amadeo Modigliani (1884–1920), this portrait is called *The Little Peasant* (*c.*1918). The painting is highly stylized, as was Modigliani's habit. In the original oil painting the colour is quite thinly painted with a clearly brush-marked technique, except for the face, which is more smoothly painted. The features and form are kept to their minimum shapes although there is enough in the curves of the clothing to make the figure look solid. This example shows that you do not always have to be totally accurate in your drawing, as long as the result is believable. I've used coloured pencils in light tones of blue, brown, red, and yellow ochre to get the colours similar to Modigliani's, with the shading indicated by darker tones of grey and black.

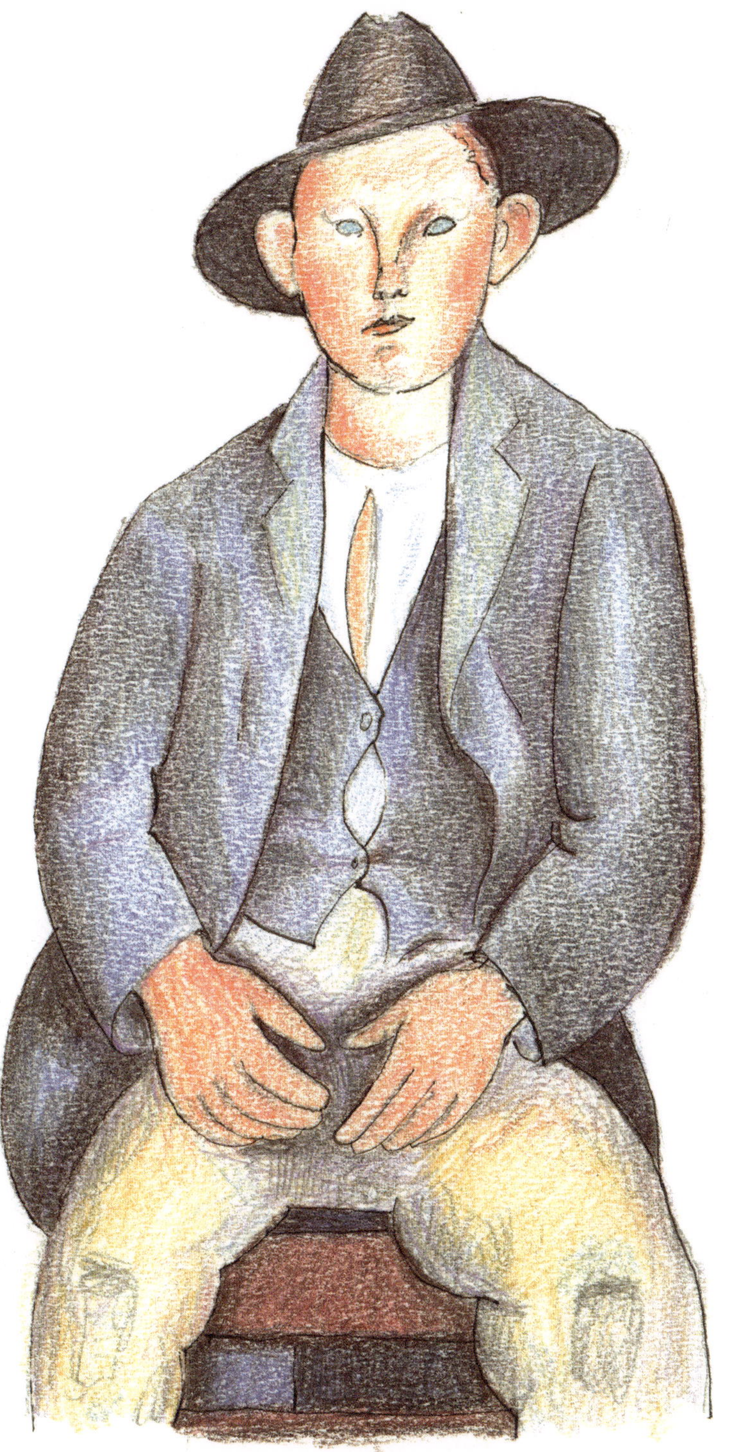

Self-Portraits

Artists are their own easiest models, being always around and willing to sit. What you learn by drawing your own face in various states and at various ages will expand your skills when it comes to drawing others.

The most difficult aspect of self-portraiture is being able to look at yourself in a mirror and still be able to draw and look at your drawing frequently. What usually happens is that your head gradually moves out of position, unless you have some way of making sure it always comes back to the same position. The easiest way to do this is to make a mark on the mirror, just a dot or tiny cross with felt-tip pen, with which you can align your head. You might ensure the mark falls between the centre of your eyes, corner of an eye or your mouth, whichever is easiest.

You can only show yourself in one mirror in a few positions because of the need to keep looking at your reflection. Inevitably, the position of the head is limited to full-face or three-quarters left or three-quarters right of full face. In these positions you can still see yourself in the mirror without too much strain. Some artists have tried looking down at their mirrored face and others have tried looking upwards at it but these approaches are fairly rare.

If you want to see yourself more objectively you will have to use two mirrors, one reflecting the image from the other. This way you can get a complete profile view of yourself, although it does make repositioning the head after it has wandered out of position slightly more awkward.

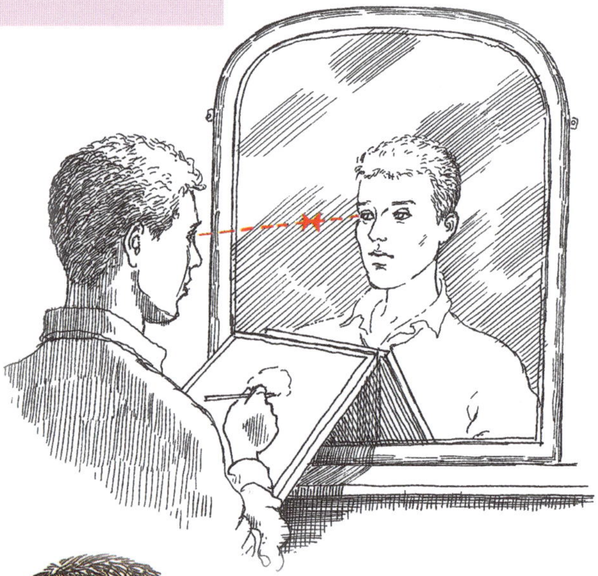

To keep your head in the same position while drawing, use a marker to make a spot on the mirror and line it up with something on your face.

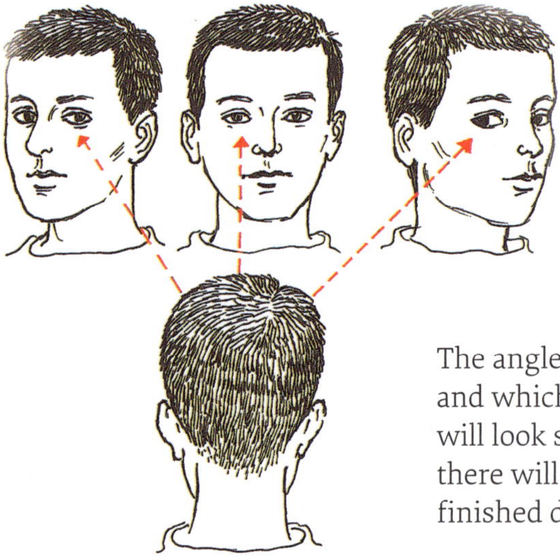

The angles of looking are restricted and whichever way you turn the eyes will look straight at you. This means there will be a similar effect in your finished drawing whatever the angle.

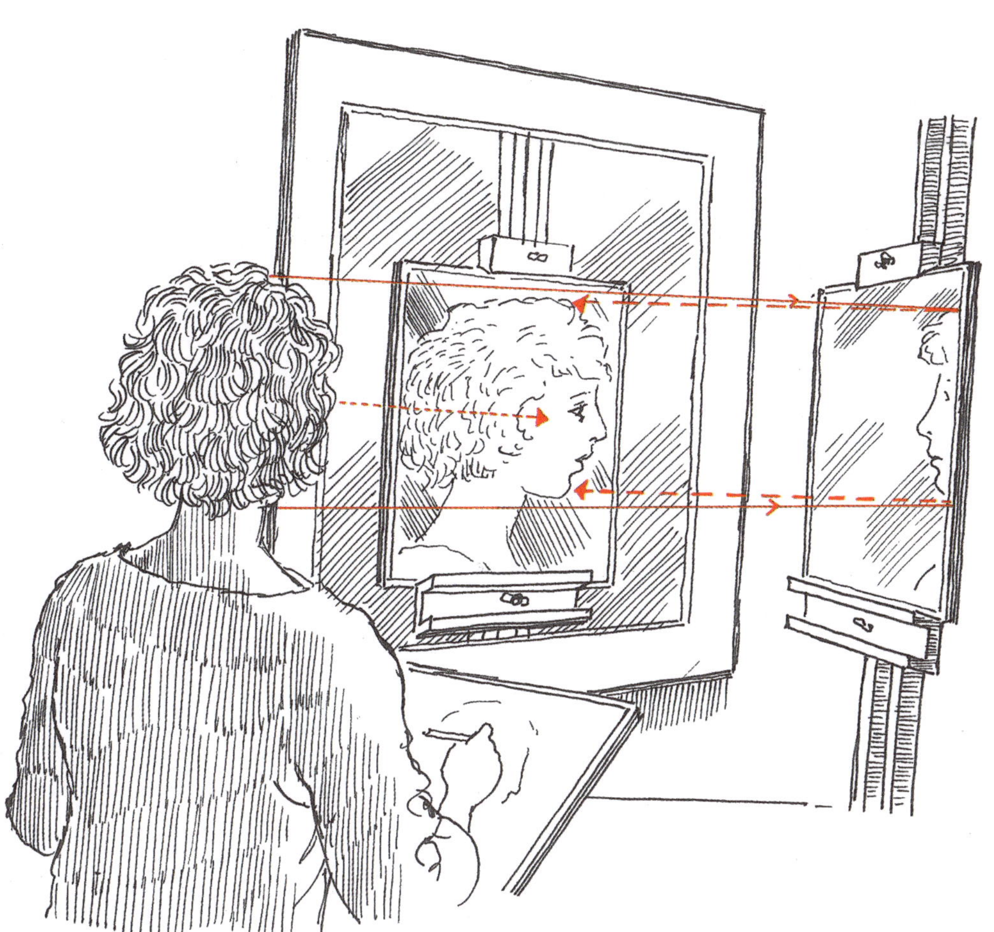

You can use two mirrors in order to draw your own profile image. Rarely do we see ourselves in this perspective, so it can be quite interesting visually.

Although a self-portrait is often just an exercise for the artist to learn how to draw, it can also be useful in pictures of large groups. Many Renaissance artists painted themselves into their large-scale figure compositions, partly because they wanted to include a signature but more importantly because a face shown looking out at the viewer – as in this detail from a Botticelli – helped to draw the viewer into the picture.

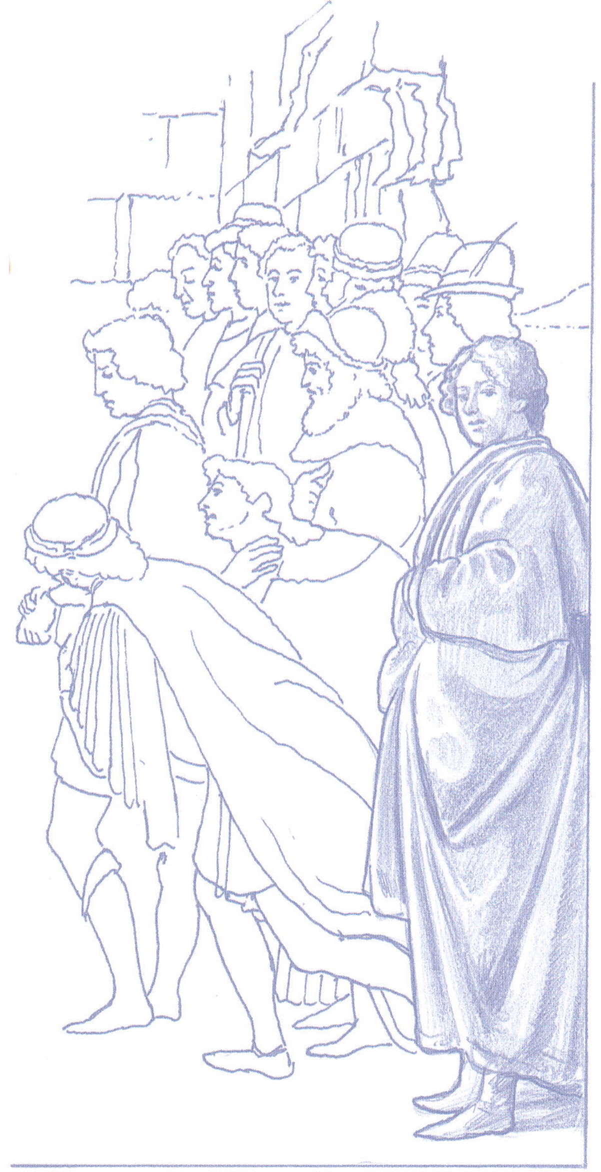

A Self-Portrait in Steps

Here I show the stages of a self-portrait that I attempted while in my garden studio. The light is behind me so that my face is in shadow, and as I was wearing a white shirt at the time there's a big contrast between the area of skin and the area of cotton shirt. The glasses emphasize the stare of the eyes which is endemic in most self-portraits.

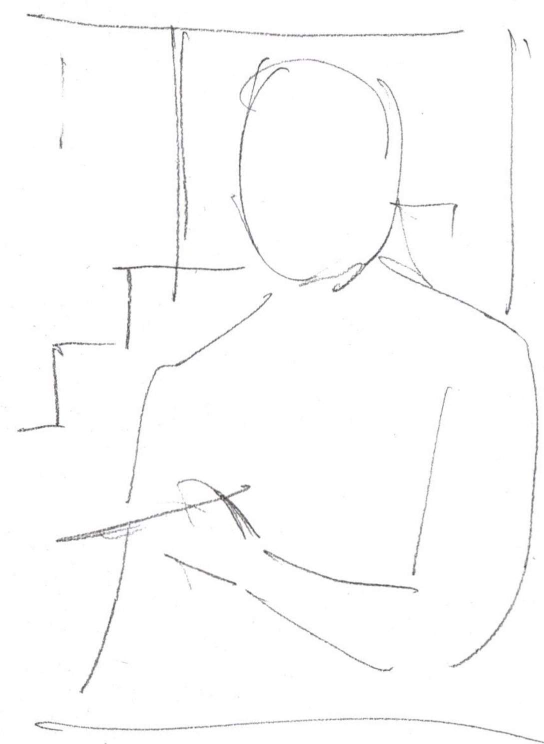

STEP 1

I started by just blocking in a simple shape that gave me the proportions of the head and body. This is well worth doing, because it's easy to lose the proportion when you get into the detail.

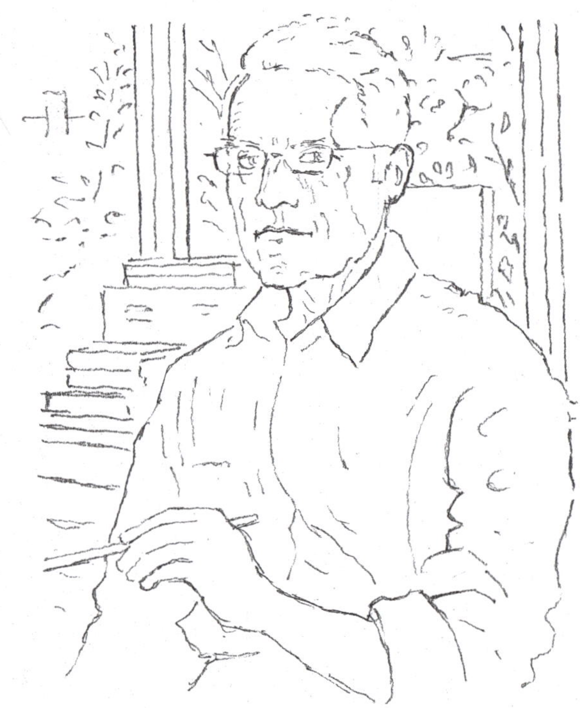

STEP 2

Then I began to describe more carefully an outline of the main shapes and form, which I drew lightly so that I could easily change it if I made a mistake. This is the stage when any erasing is done, so take your time about this part in your own self-portrait. It's worth getting it right now, because later on it will be more difficult.

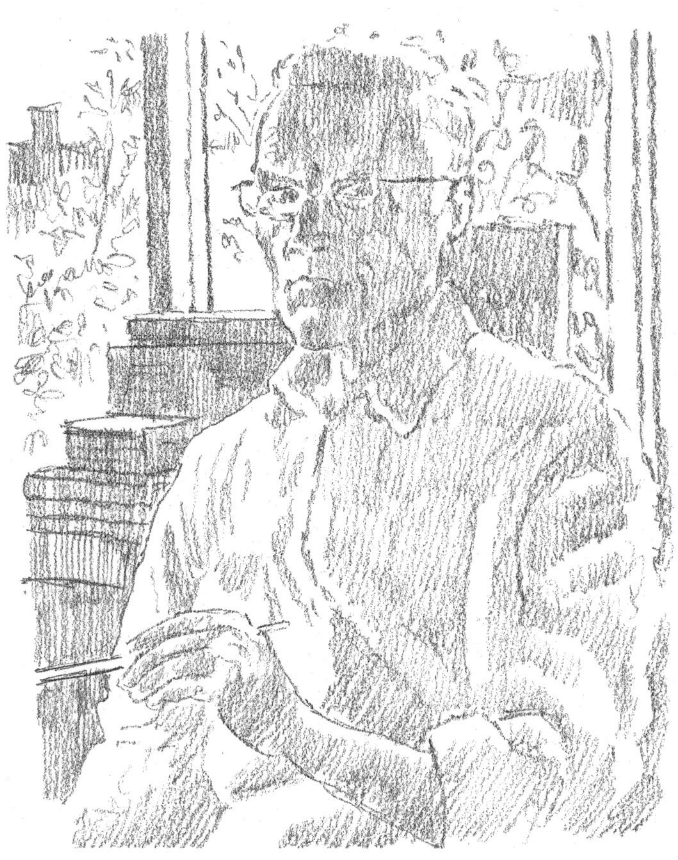

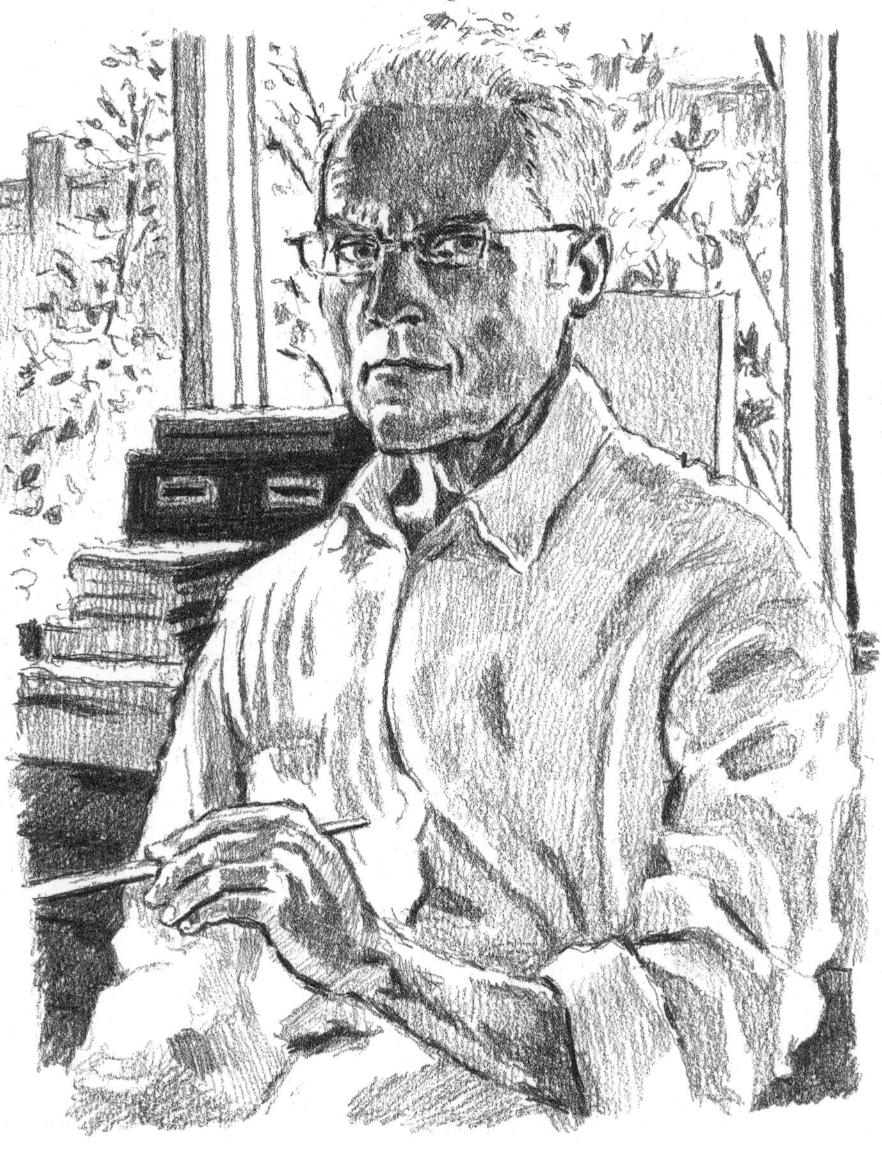

STEP 3

Then I put in the tonal area, keeping the tone the same all over the picture. This is important, because it's easy to get tones wrong if you start putting them in heavily straight away.

STEP 4

The last stage was to build up my tonal values so that the picture started to look properly solid and with the effect of the light falling on the edge of the face and the shirt folds. The tone of the objects just behind my shoulder was useful to bring my figure forward in the picture. This is a very straightforward, naturalistic drawing, unlike some of the examples that you've just seen, but that's my own style – and fortunately it makes for an easier demonstration of how to do a self-portrait.

Chapter Four

ANATOMY AND LIFE DRAWING

All figure drawing benefits from a knowledge of what lies beneath the surface of the skin. In this section I present some anatomical diagrams of the bone structures that support our bodies, and the musculature that informs all of our movements. Learning the names of the bones that make up the human form and how they connect to each other might seem like rather a dry exercise, but they constitute the basic scaffolding that the body is built on and to have some familiarity with this element of the human frame will really help you to understand the figures you draw. When it comes to the muscles, as artists, our primary interest is in the muscles on the surface. When you draw the human body, you cannot see exactly where the muscles start and end. However, if you know something about the configuration, you'll find it makes it easier to indicate the main shape of any muscle more accurately in your drawing.

Once we have studied the anatomy of the various parts of the body, we will then look at how you might approach drawing a nude figure from life. The human body is the most subtle and difficult thing to draw and you will learn more from a few lessons in front of a live model than you ever could drawing from photographs. Even professional artists will attend life drawing classes whenever possible, unless they can afford their own models.

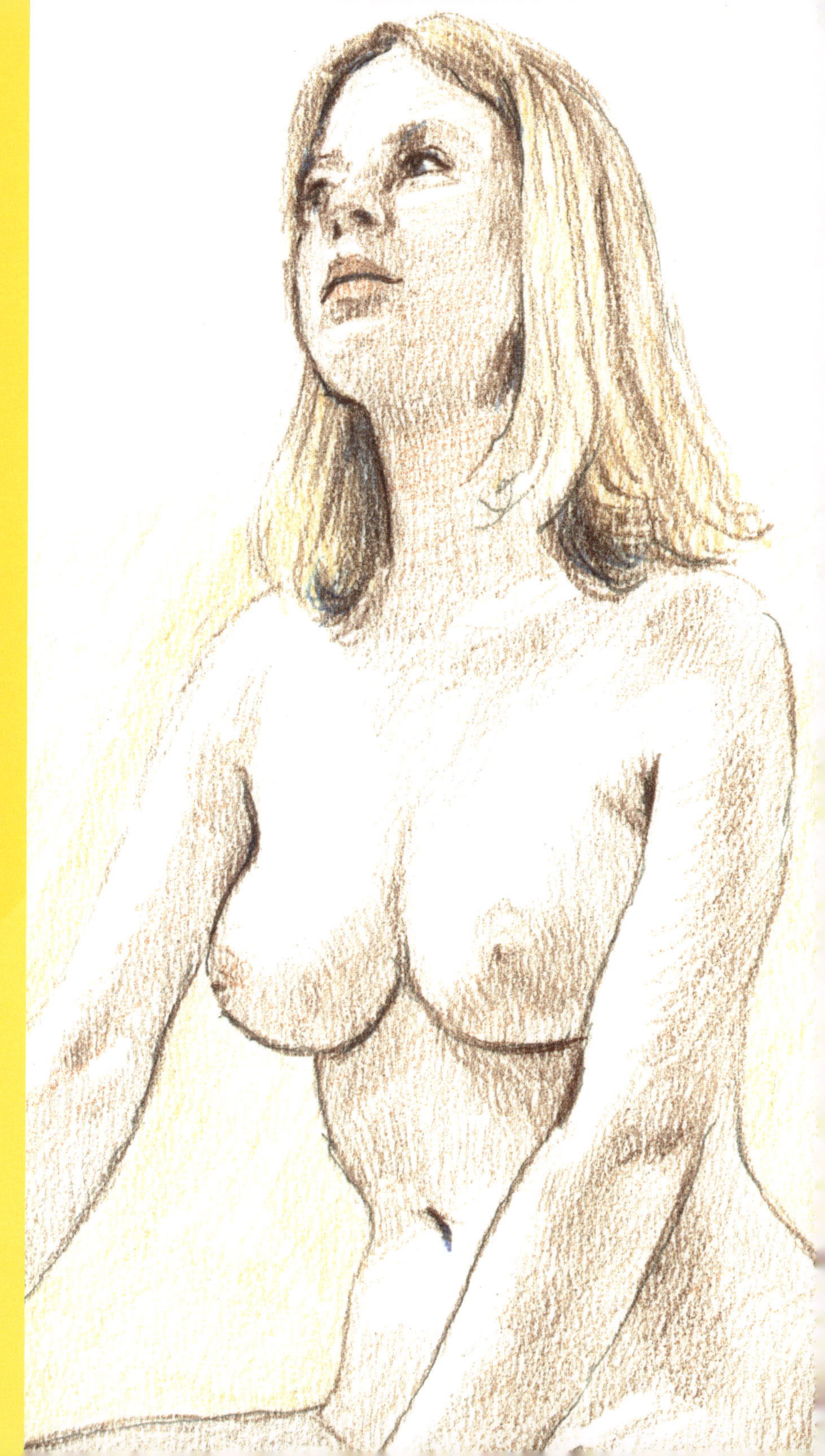

Skeleton of the Head and Torso

Front view

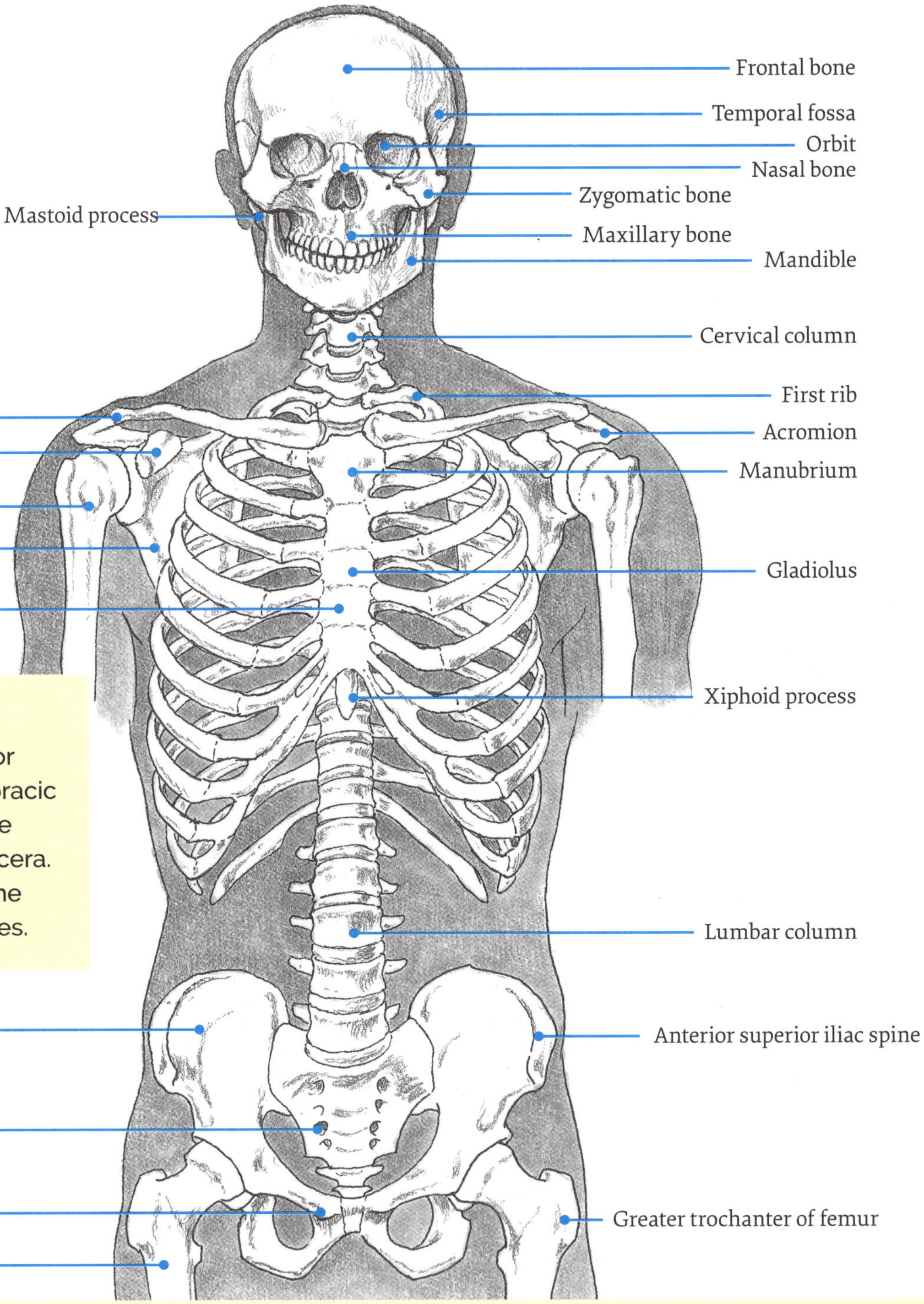

Frontal bone
Temporal fossa
Orbit
Nasal bone
Zygomatic bone
Mastoid process
Maxillary bone
Mandible
Cervical column
First rib
Clavicle
Acromion
Coracoid process
Manubrium
Humerus
Scapula
Gladiolus
Sternum
Xiphoid process
Lumbar column
Ilium (iliac bone)
Anterior superior iliac spine
Sacrum
Pubis
Greater trochanter of femur
Femur

The thorax is the area of the trunk between the neck and the abdomen, including the sternum or breast bone, the 12 ribs or costae and the 12 thoracic vertebrae. These make up the thoracic cage (the ribcage) which protects the heart, lungs and viscera. Below the thorax, the abdomen is made up of the lumbar vertebrae or column and the pelvic bones.

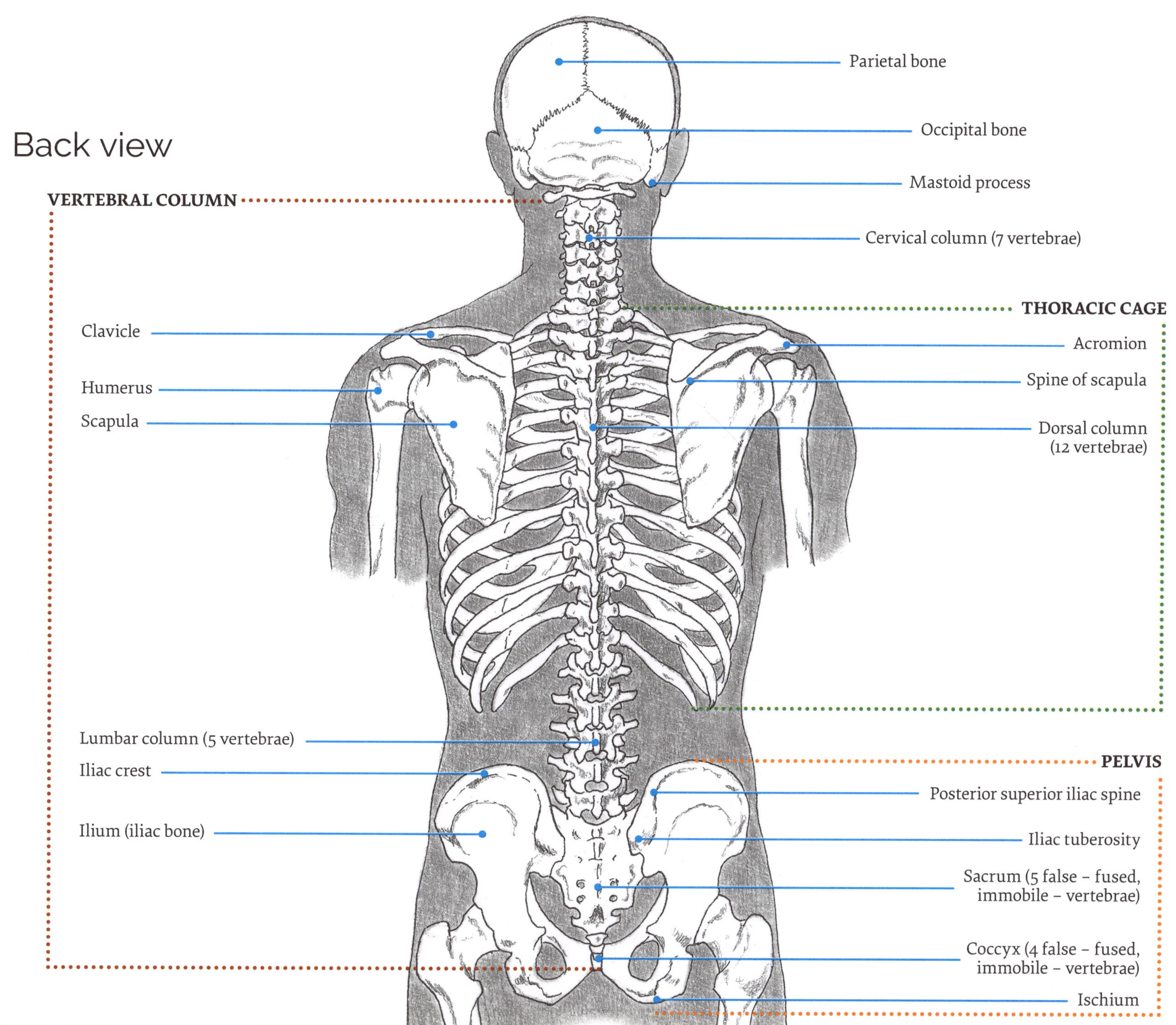
Back view
VERTEBRAL COLUMN
Parietal bone
Occipital bone
Mastoid process
Cervical column (7 vertebrae)
THORACIC CAGE
Clavicle
Acromion
Humerus
Spine of scapula
Scapula
Dorsal column
(12 vertebrae)
Lumbar column (5 vertebrae)
Iliac crest
PELVIS
Posterior superior iliac spine
Ilium (iliac bone)
Iliac tuberosity
Sacrum (5 false – fused,
immobile – vertebrae)
Coccyx (4 false – fused,
immobile – vertebrae)
Ischium

Side view

Parietal bone
Frontal bone
Occipital bone
Zygomatic bone
Mastoid process
Maxillary bone
Mandible
Cervical column
Acromion
Superior angle of scapula
Clavicle
Angle of the sternum
Humerus
Scapula
Inferior angle of scapula
Thoracic cage (ribcage)
Lumbar column
HIP BONE
Ilium
Sacrum
Coccyx
Pubis
Ischium
Femur

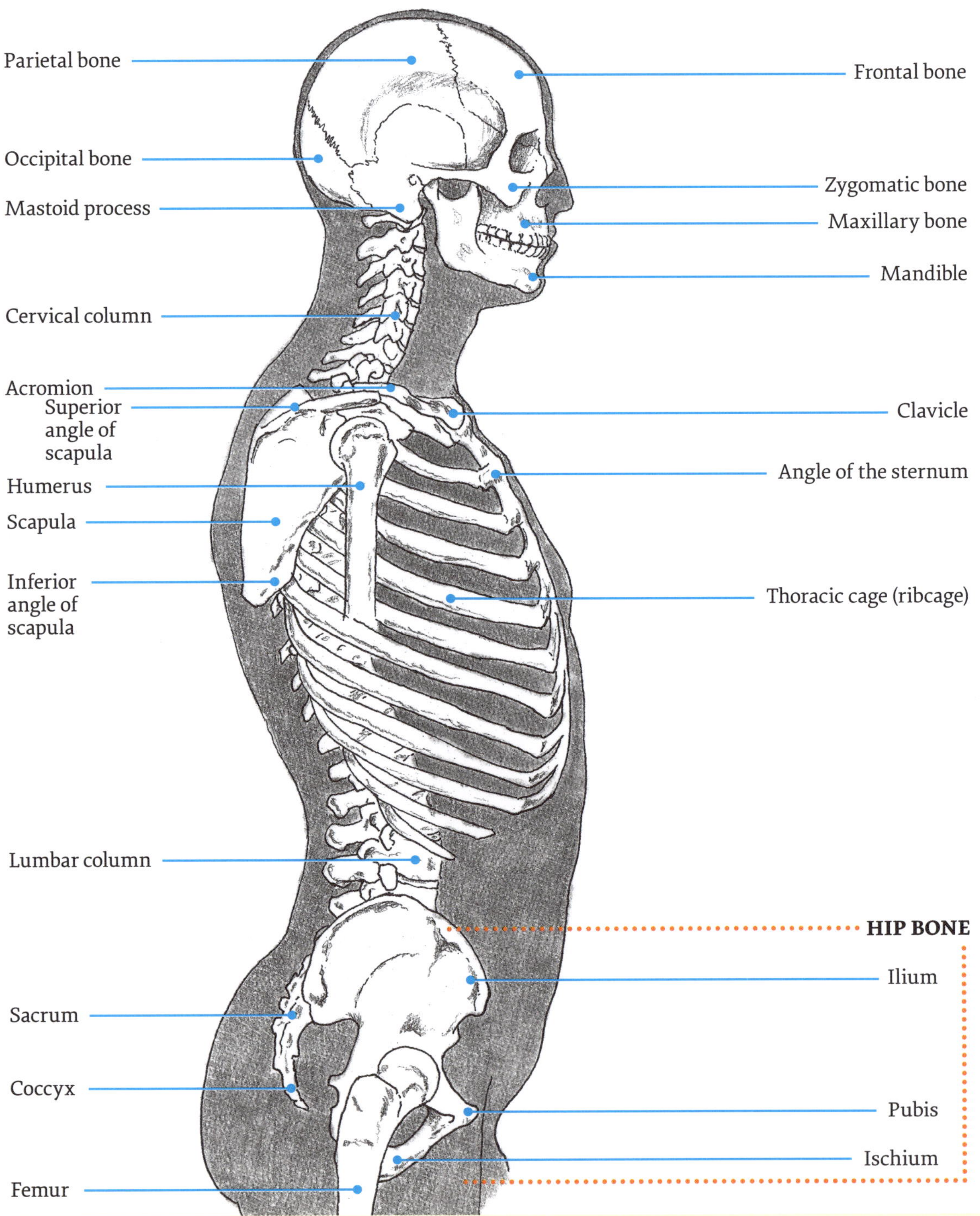

Muscles of the Trunk and Neck

Front view

The muscles of the trunk are in the main quite large and fairly flat in shape. They are layered over the ribcage and pelvis and cover the big joints of the hips and shoulders. There are deeper layers of muscle in the back that sometimes help shape the more superficial muscles.

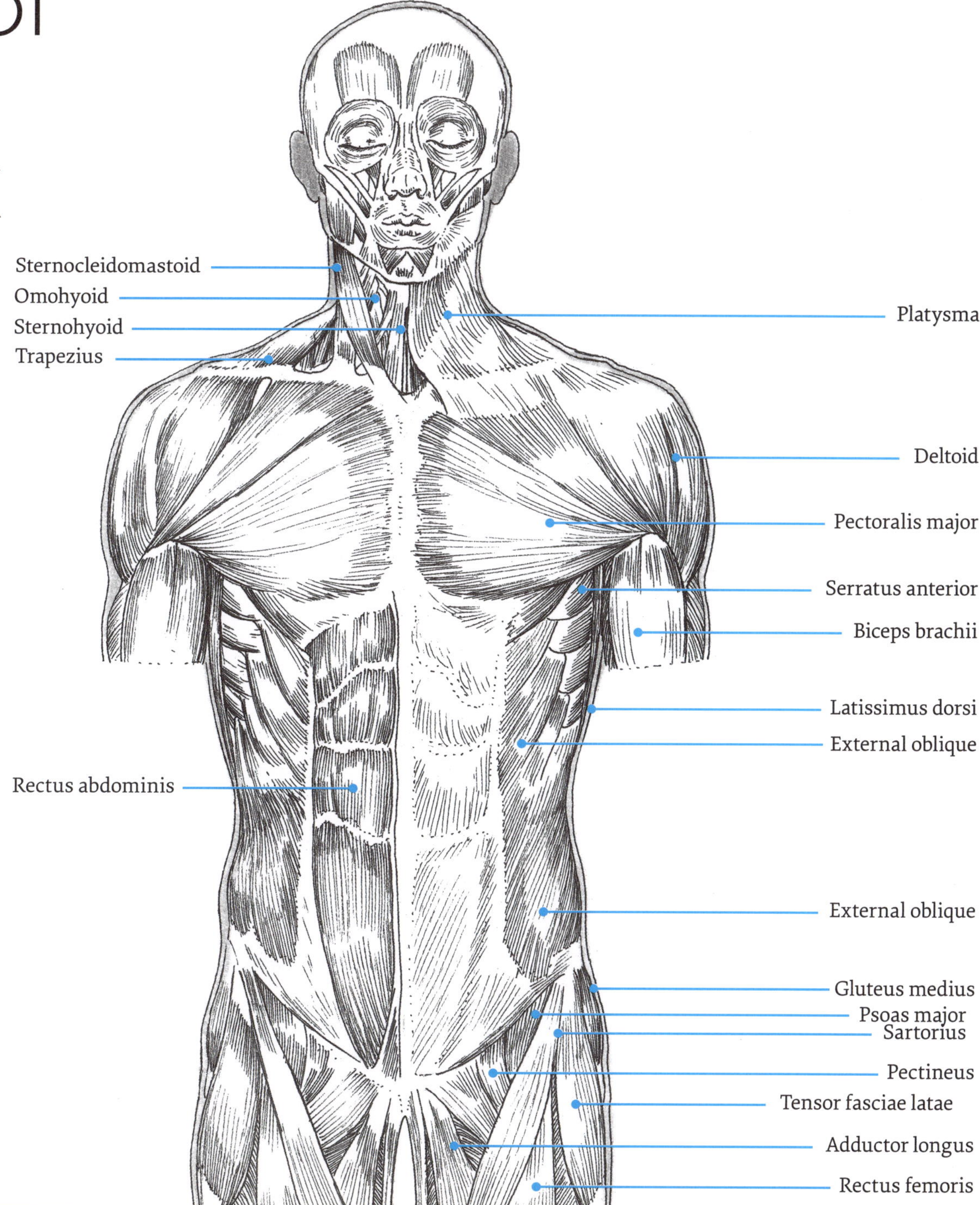

Back view

Trapezius
Splenius capitis
Sternocleidomastoid
Trapezius
Trapezius
(continues)
Deltoid
Infraspinatus
Teres minor
Teres major
Triceps brachii
Latissimus dorsi
Aponeurosis of latissimus dorsi
External oblique
Gluteus medius
Gluteus maximus

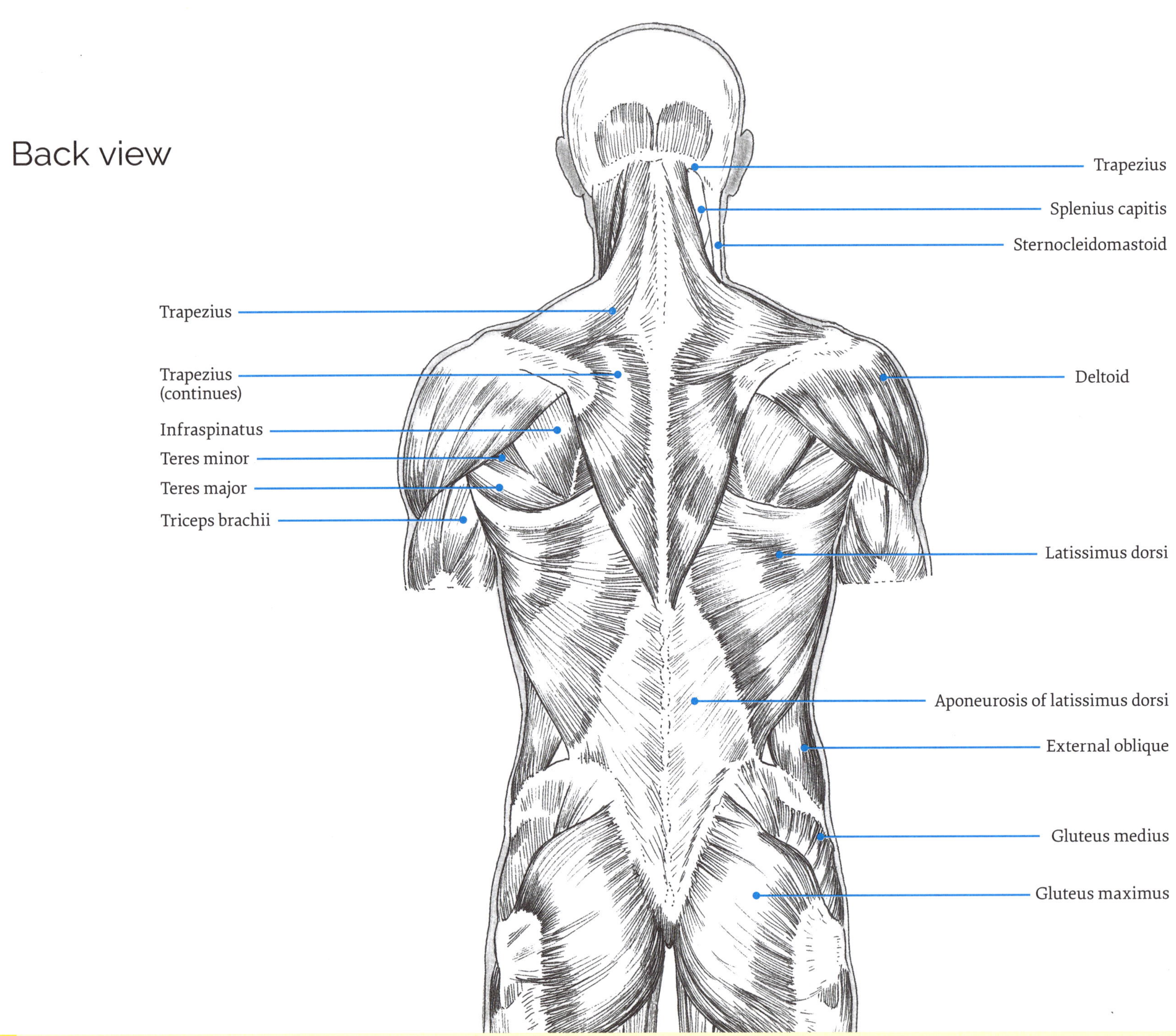

Side view

Semispinalis capitis
Splenius capitis
Sternocleidomastoid
Thyrohyoid
Levator scapulae
Scalenus posterior
Scalenus anterior
Trapezius
Deltoid
Infraspinatus
Teres minor
Teres major
Latissimus dorsi
Gluteus medius
Gluteus maximus
Digastricus (posterior)
Mylohyoid
Omohyoid
Sternohyoid
Omohyoid
Pectoralis major
Serratus anterior
External oblique
Rectus abdominis
External oblique
Sartorius
Tensor fasciae latae
Rectus femoris

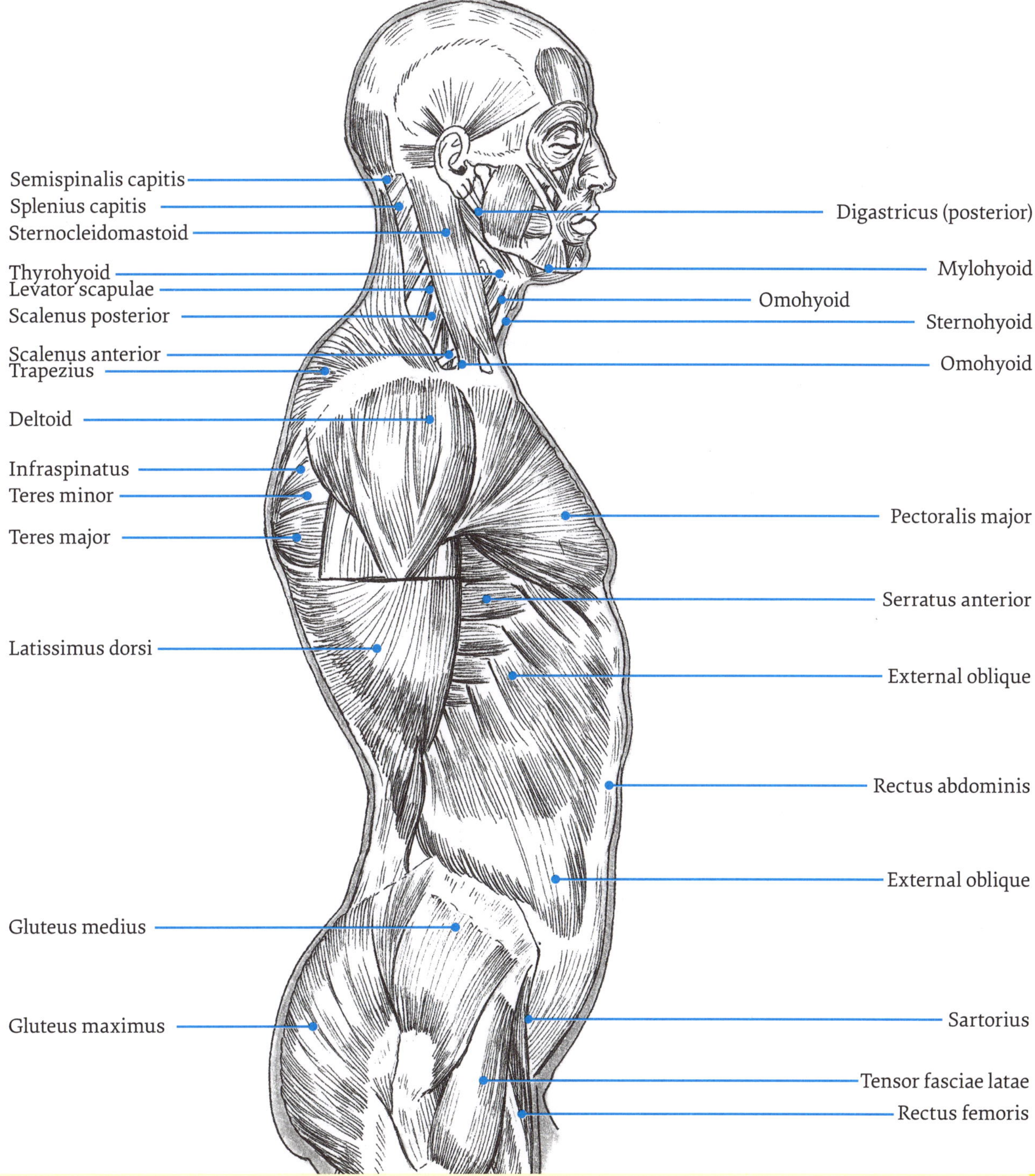

The Skull

The upper part of the skull contains the brain and the organs of sight and hearing. The front and rear parts consist of the thickest bone, where impacts are most likely; the sides of the head are much thinner. There are various openings in the case of the skull, such as the eye sockets, which contain smaller apertures for the passage of the optic nerves to the brain, and the nose and ear holes. The lower part of the skull is the mandible, which houses the lower teeth and is hinged at the sides of the upper skull just below the ears. The first (milk) teeth fall out during childhood and are replaced by much larger adult teeth, which fill out the growing jaw.

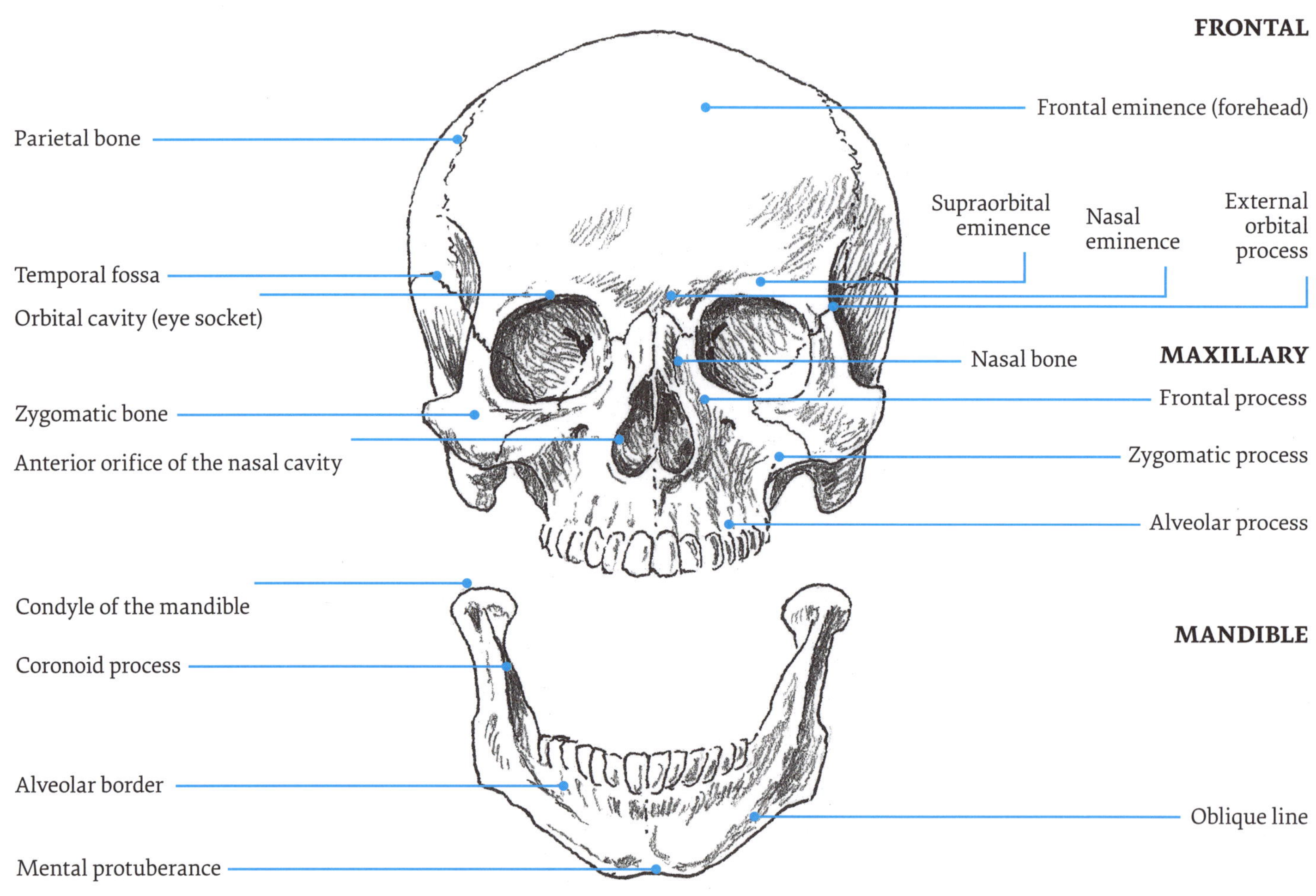

Muscles of the Head

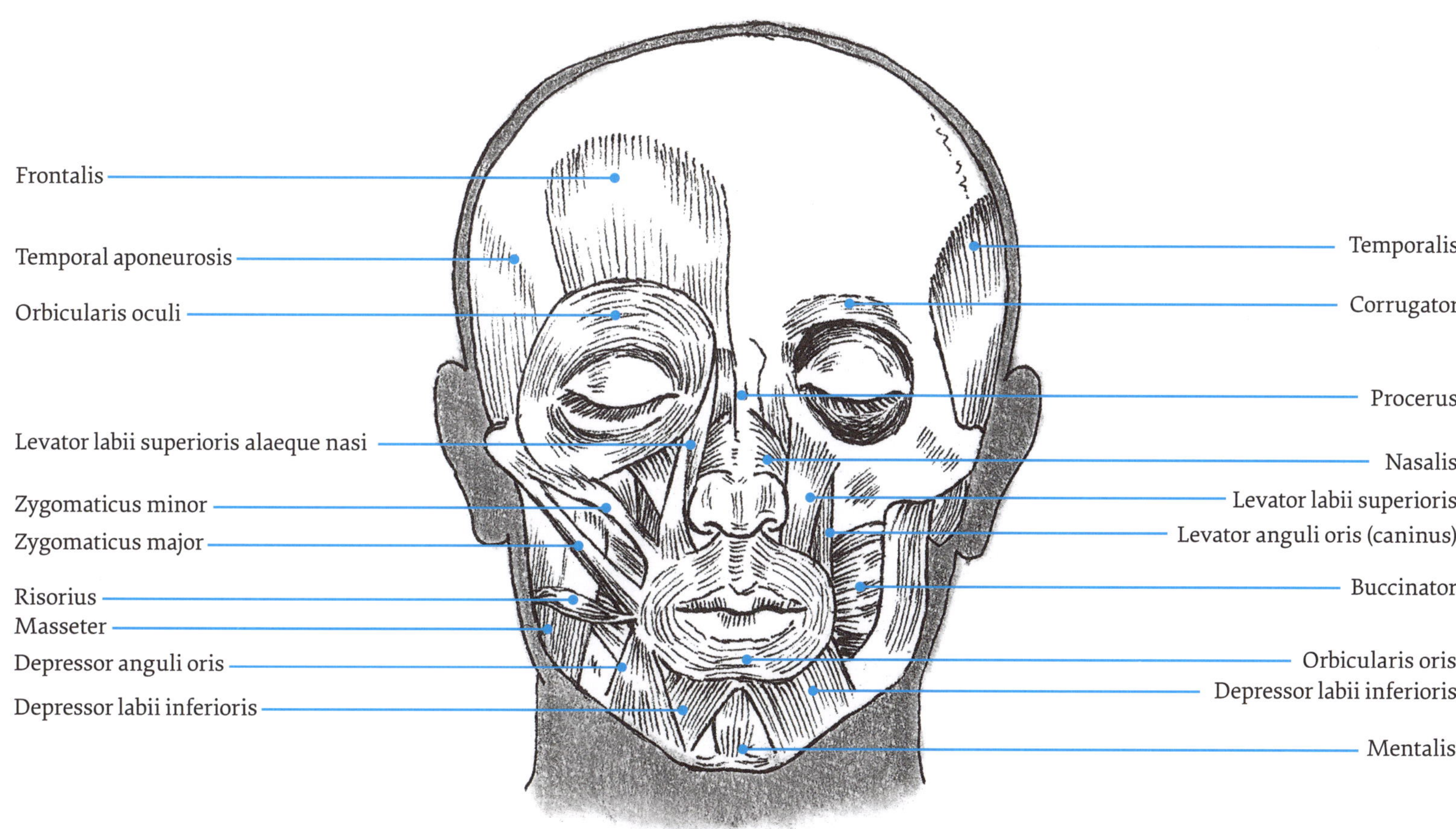

These are the muscles that enable us to eat and drink, and of course they surround our organs of sight, sound, smell and taste. Although they don't have the physical power of the larger muscles of the limbs and trunk, they do play an important part in our lives.

Skeleton of the Arm and Hand

Front view

The bone structure of the arm appears quite straightforward at first glance. However, the areas of the shoulder and the wrist are quite complex and help to allow the many movements of the limb.

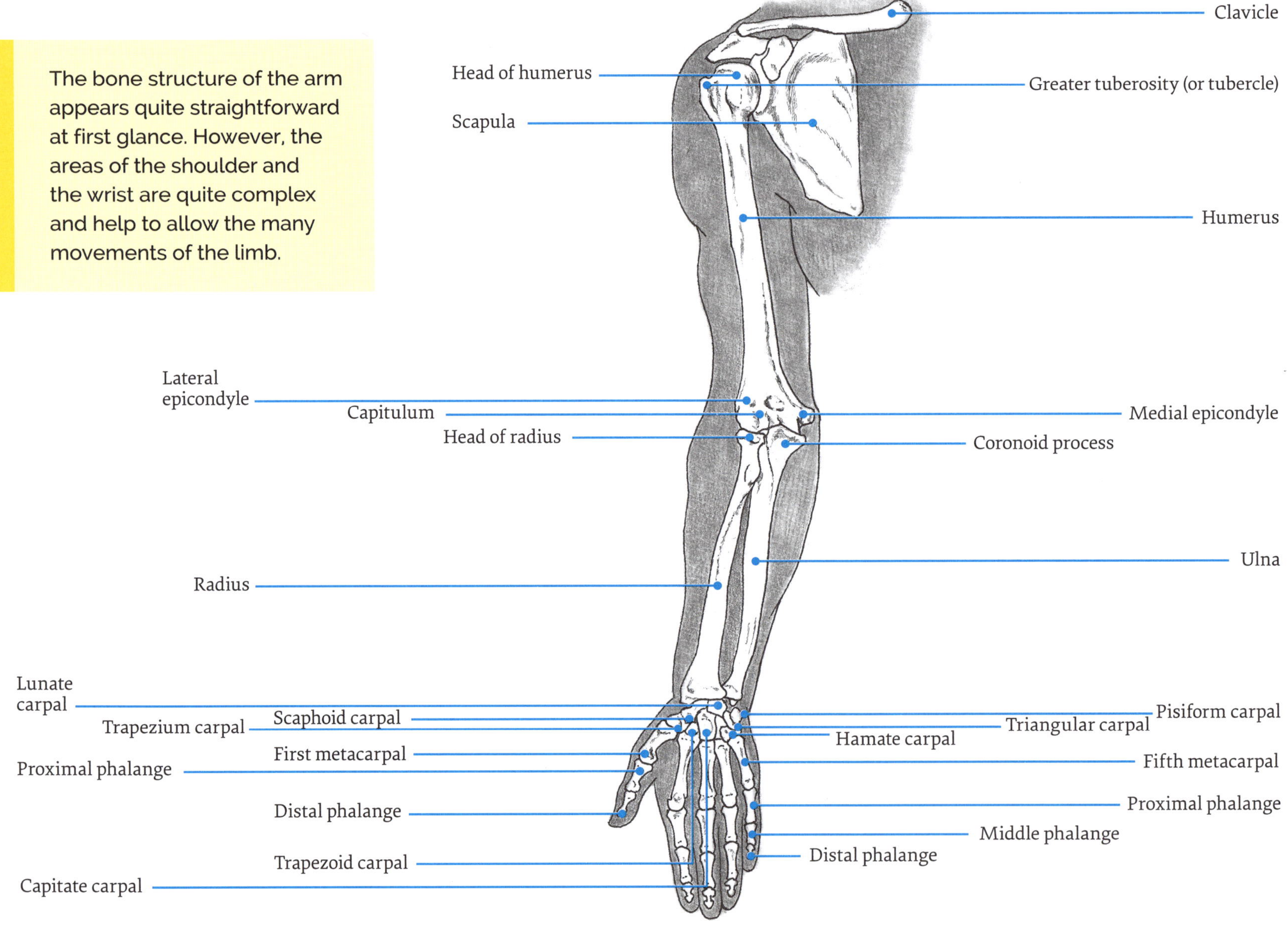

Back view

Clavicle
Head of humerus
Scapula
Humerus
Medial epicondyle
Lateral epicondyle
Olecranon
Head of radius
Ulna
Radius
Styloid process
Scaphoid carpal
Triangular carpal
Pisiform carpal
Trapezium carpal
Hamate carpal
First metacarpal
Fifth metacarpal
Proximal phalange
Proximal phalange
Distal phalange
Middle phalange
Distal phalange
Trapezoid carpal
Lunate carpal
Capitate carpal

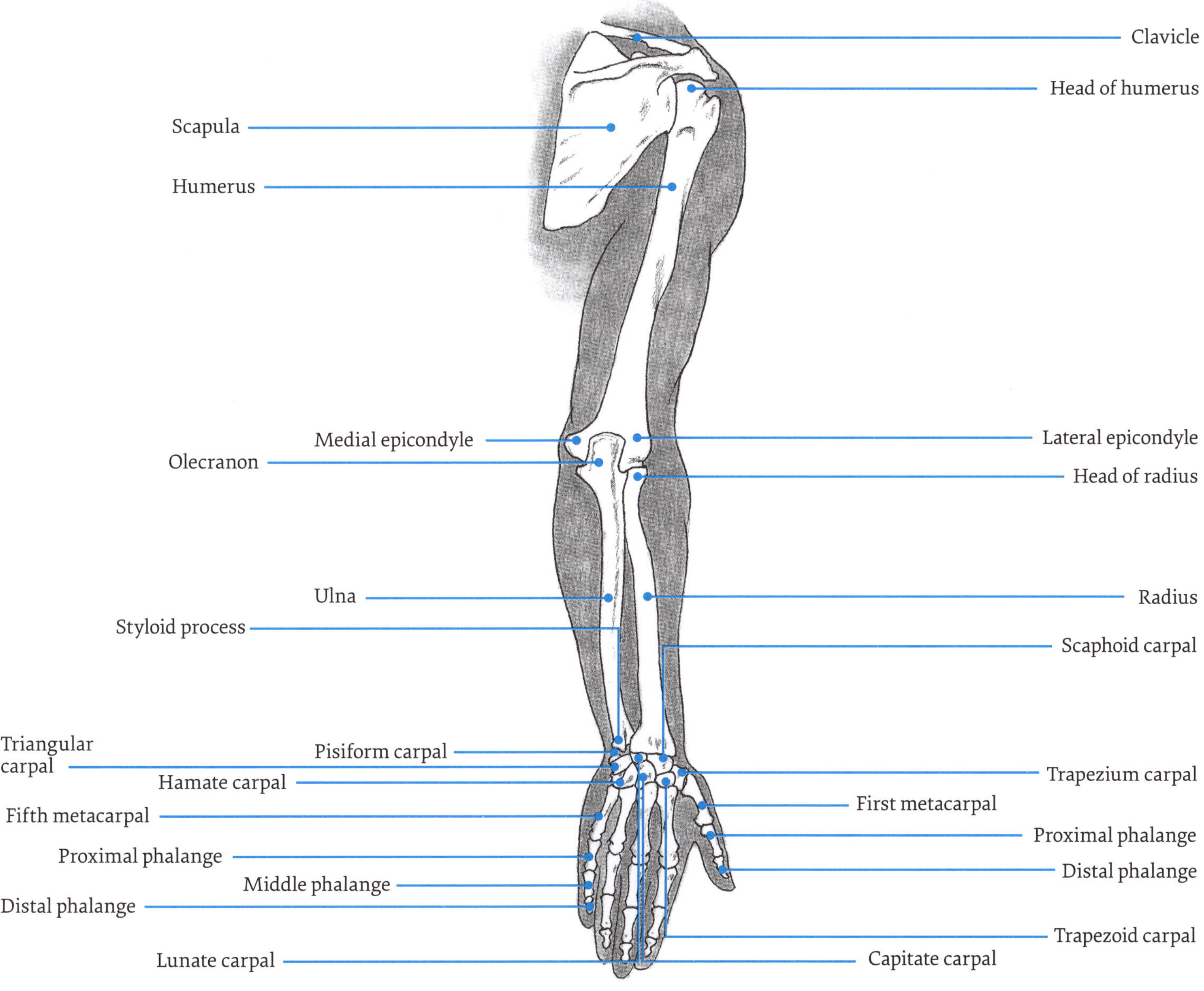

Muscles of the Arm and Hand

Front view

Notice the complexity of the interleaving muscles around the shoulder and elbow, and the long strands of tendons passing through the wrist. The bone structure only appears at the point of the shoulder, the elbow and the wrist, but of course on the hand, the bones of the fingers are more obvious.

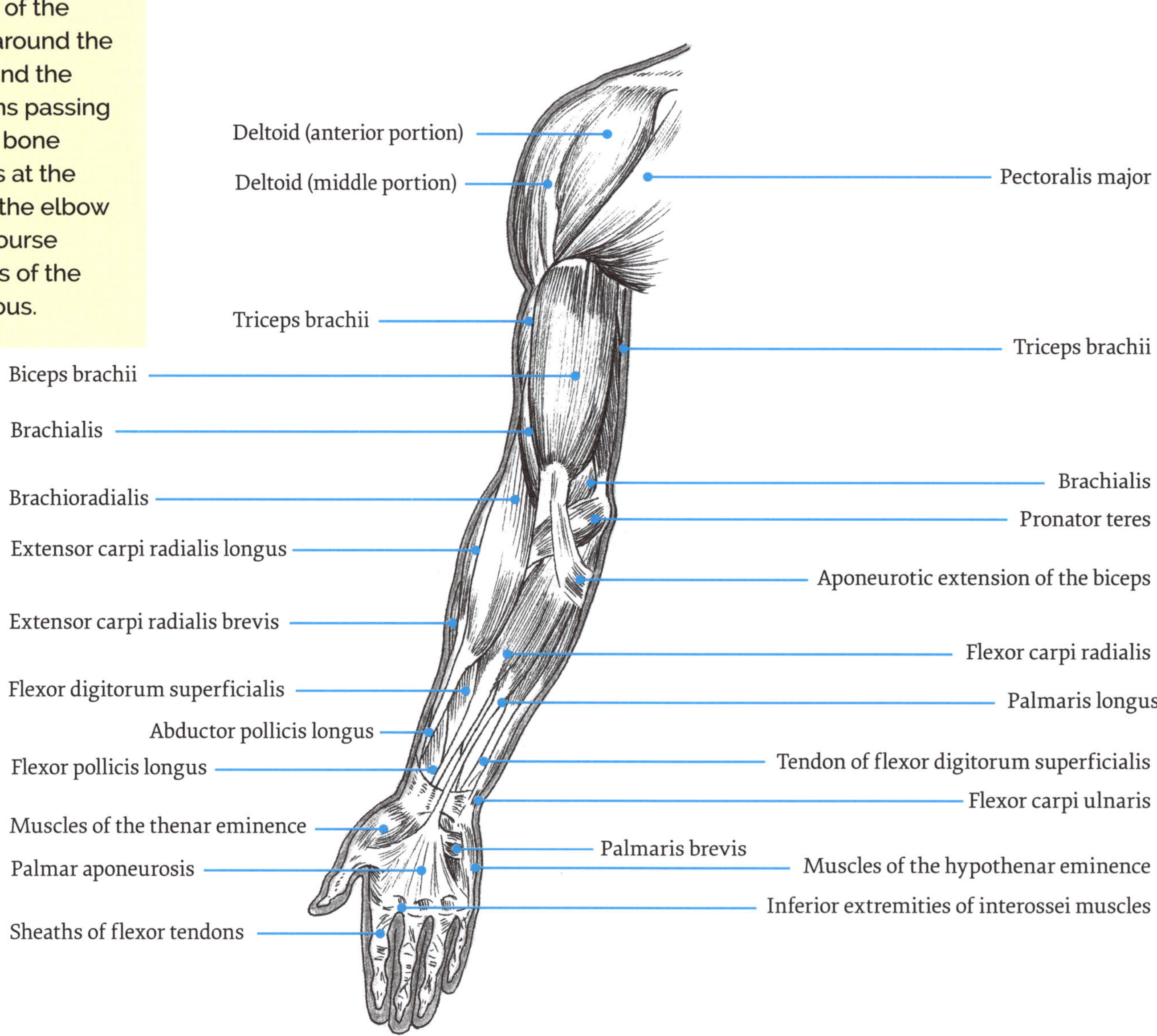

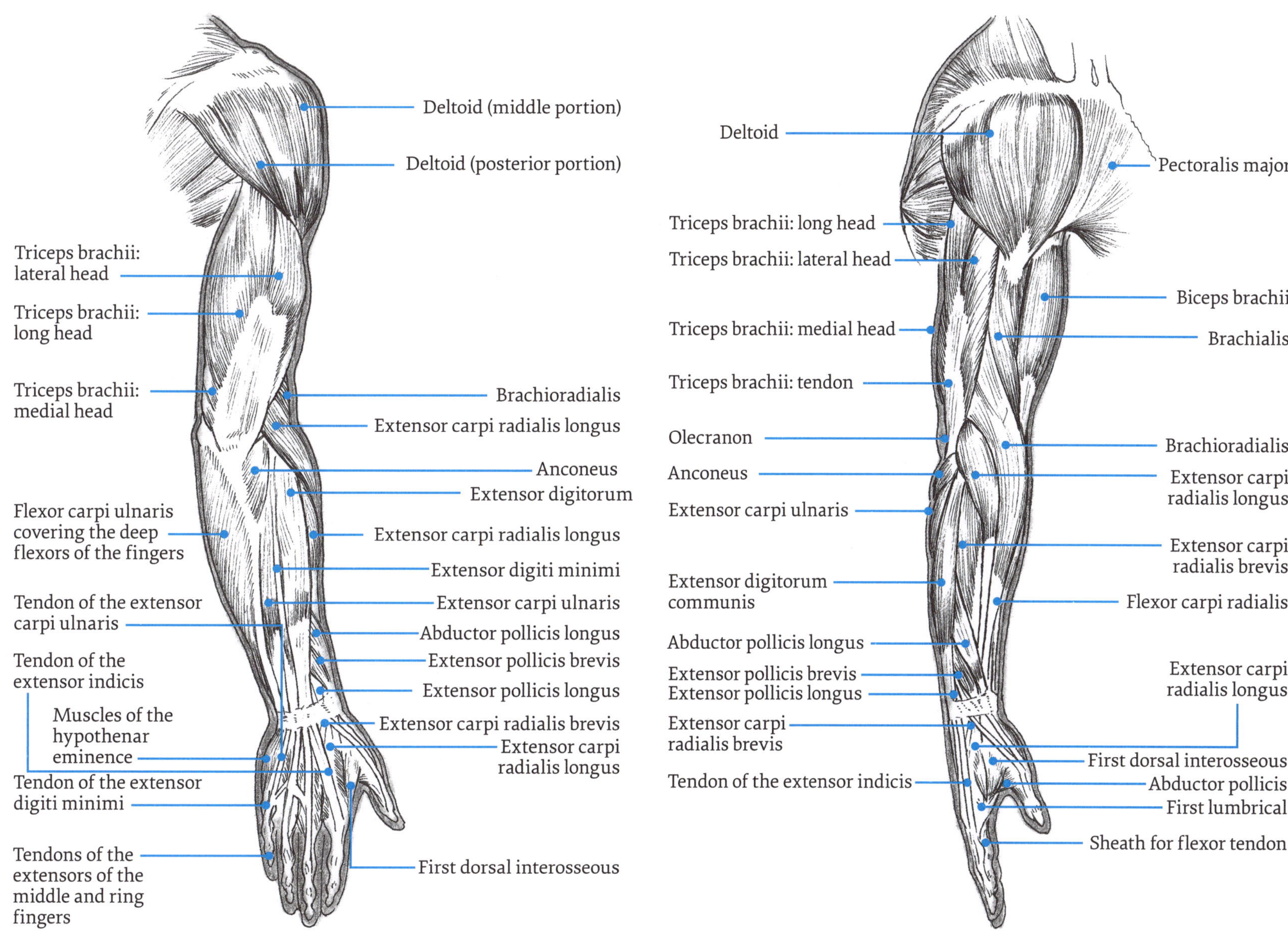
Back view
Deltoid (middle portion)
Deltoid (posterior portion)
Triceps brachii: lateral head
Triceps brachii: long head
Triceps brachii: medial head
Brachioradialis
Extensor carpi radialis longus
Anconeus
Extensor digitorum
Flexor carpi ulnaris covering the deep flexors of the fingers
Extensor carpi radialis longus
Extensor digiti minimi
Extensor carpi ulnaris
Tendon of the extensor carpi ulnaris
Abductor pollicis longus
Extensor pollicis brevis
Tendon of the extensor indicis
Extensor pollicis longus
Muscles of the hypothenar eminence
Extensor carpi radialis brevis
Extensor carpi radialis longus
Tendon of the extensor digiti minimi
Tendons of the extensors of the middle and ring fingers
First dorsal interosseous
Side view
Deltoid
Pectoralis major
Triceps brachii: long head
Triceps brachii: lateral head
Biceps brachii
Triceps brachii: medial head
Brachialis
Triceps brachii: tendon
Olecranon
Brachioradialis
Anconeus
Extensor carpi radialis longus
Extensor carpi ulnaris
Extensor carpi radialis brevis
Extensor digitorum communis
Flexor carpi radialis
Abductor pollicis longus
Extensor pollicis brevis
Extensor pollicis longus
Extensor carpi radialis longus
Extensor carpi radialis brevis
First dorsal interosseous
Tendon of the extensor indicis
Abductor pollicis
First lumbrical
Sheath for flexor tendon

Skeleton of the Leg

Front and Back Views

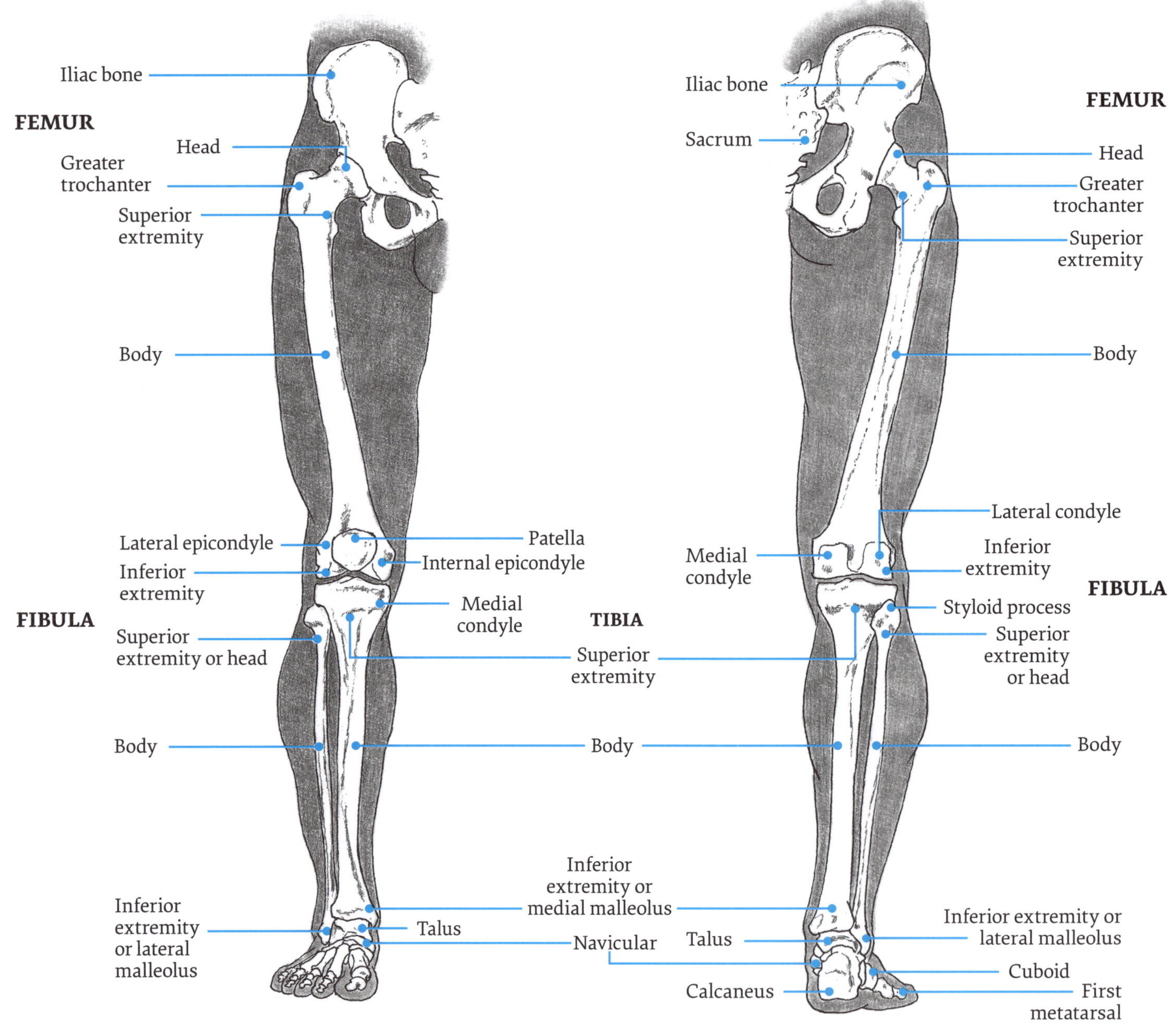

The skeleton of the lower limb is composed of noticeably longer, stronger bones than the upper limb. The femur is the longest and largest bone in the human body and is in the classic shape that we think of when we visualize a bone, comprising a powerful straight shaft and bulbous ends which help join it to the bone structures of the hip and knee.

Side View

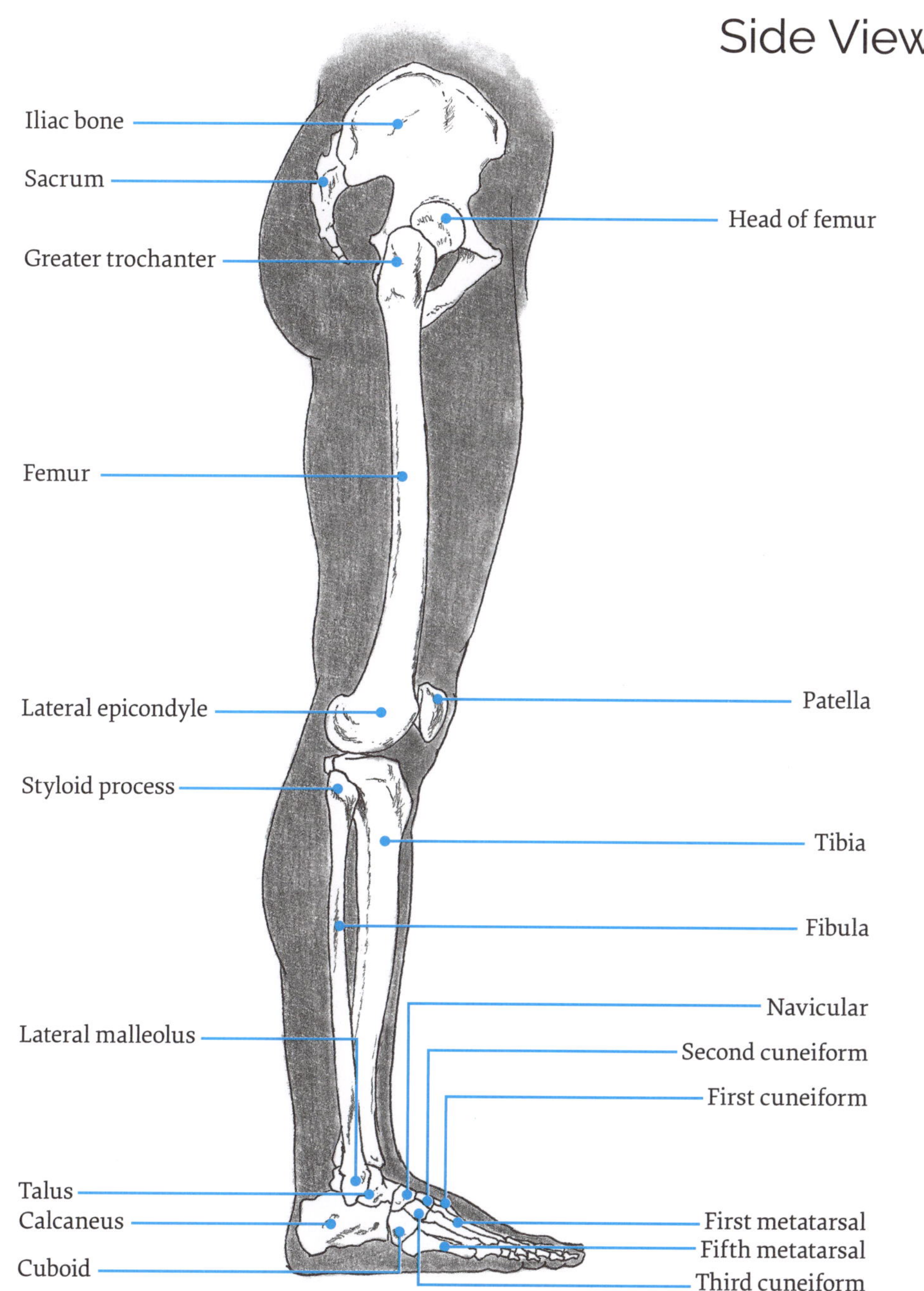

Muscles of the Leg

Front view

Like the upper limbs, the legs are wrapped in long, layered muscles that help to give flexibility. However, because of the increased strength needed to support the rest of the body's weight, the leg muscles tend to be longer and bigger. I have included the band of fascia running down the side of the leg over the muscles (the fascia lata and the iliotibial band) and the band of Richer which holds the muscles in at the front of the thigh.

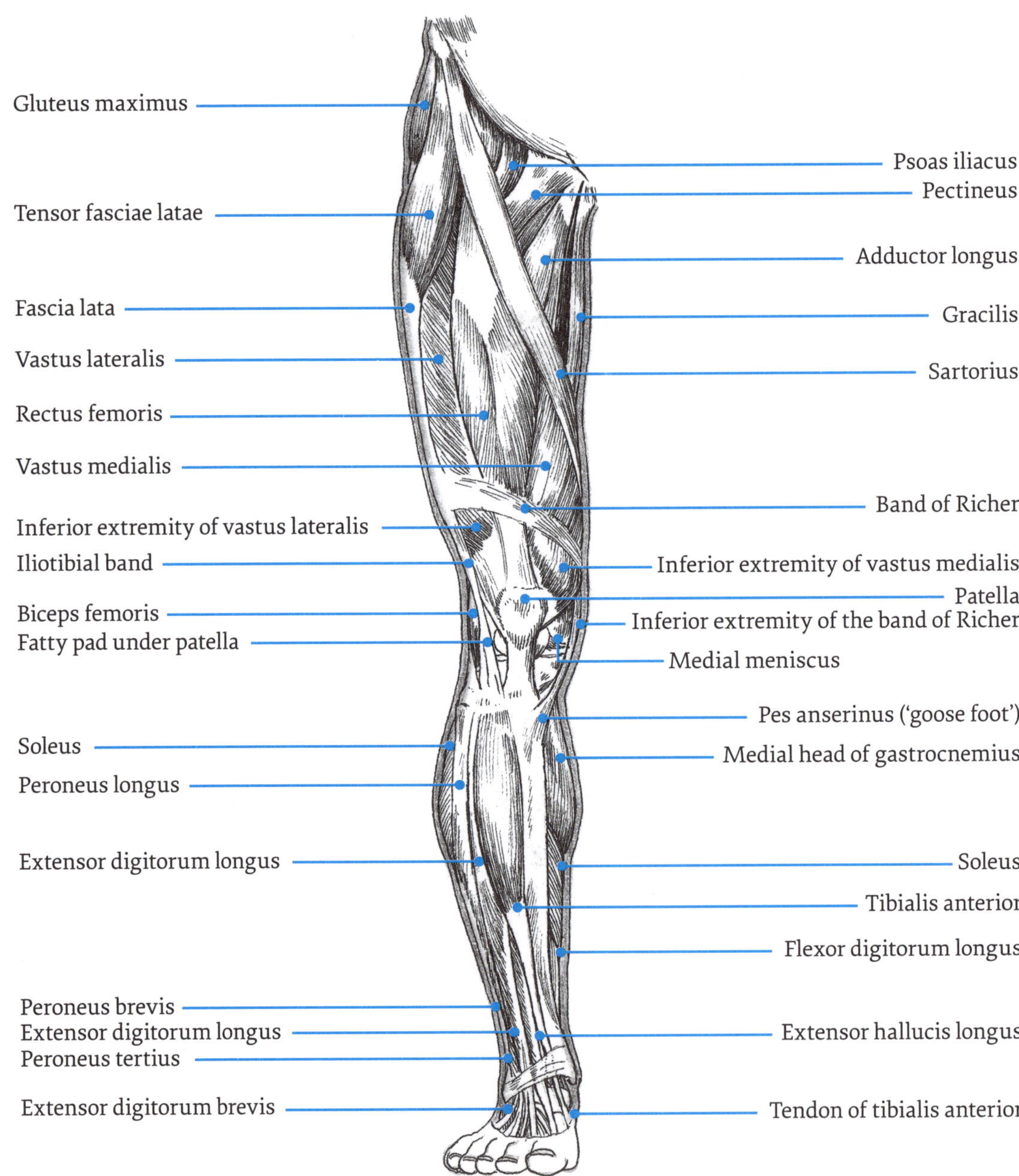

The group of tendons that run down the back of the leg to the knee are collectively known as the hamstrings. These are the tendons of the biceps femoris, the semitendinosus and the semimembranosus.

Back view

Side view external aspect

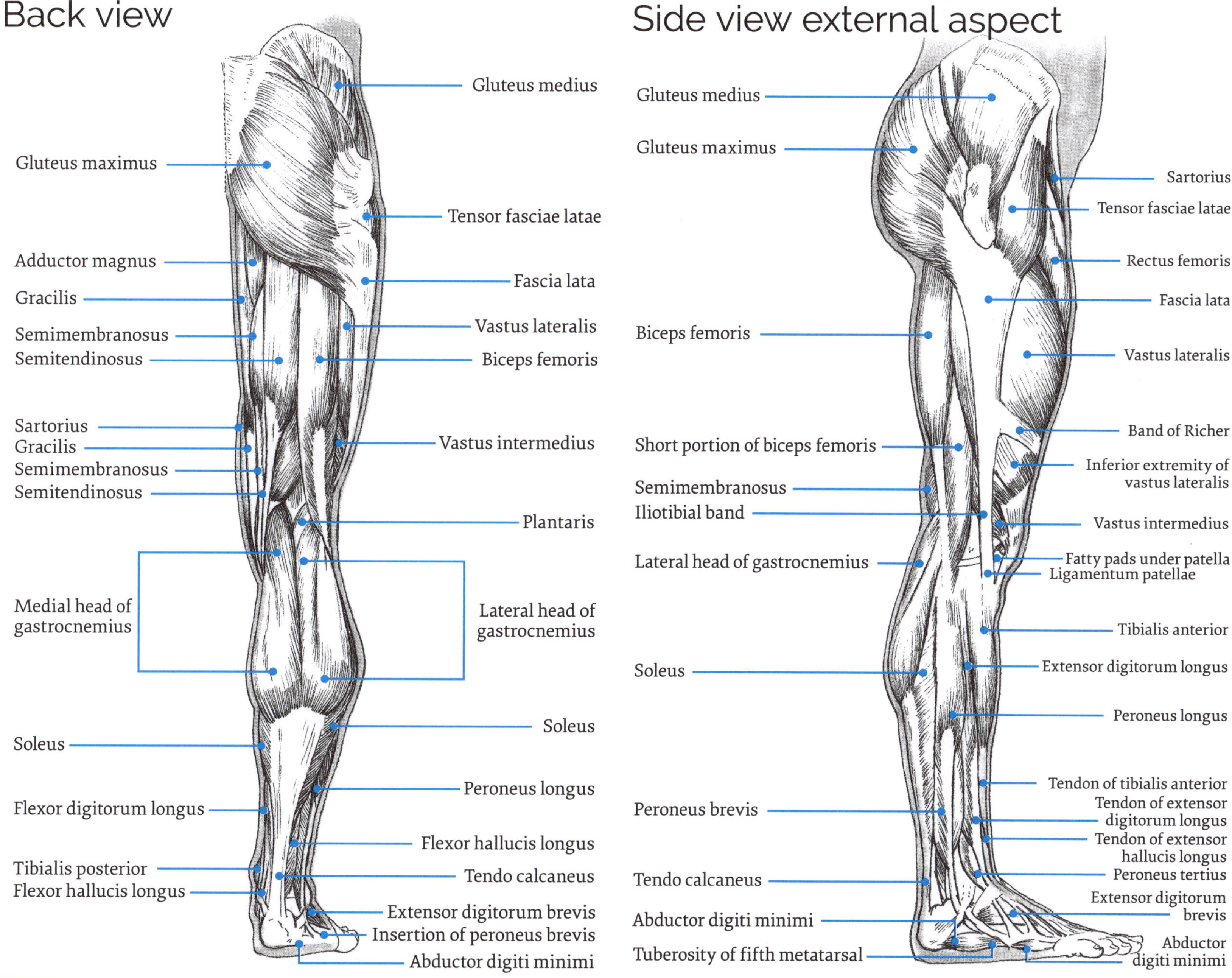

The Nude Figure Showing the Muscles

In these examples after master artists, we identify the muscles and bone structures visible on the surface of the body. This is where your knowledge of anatomy, however basic, can be put to use in your drawings of the human figure.

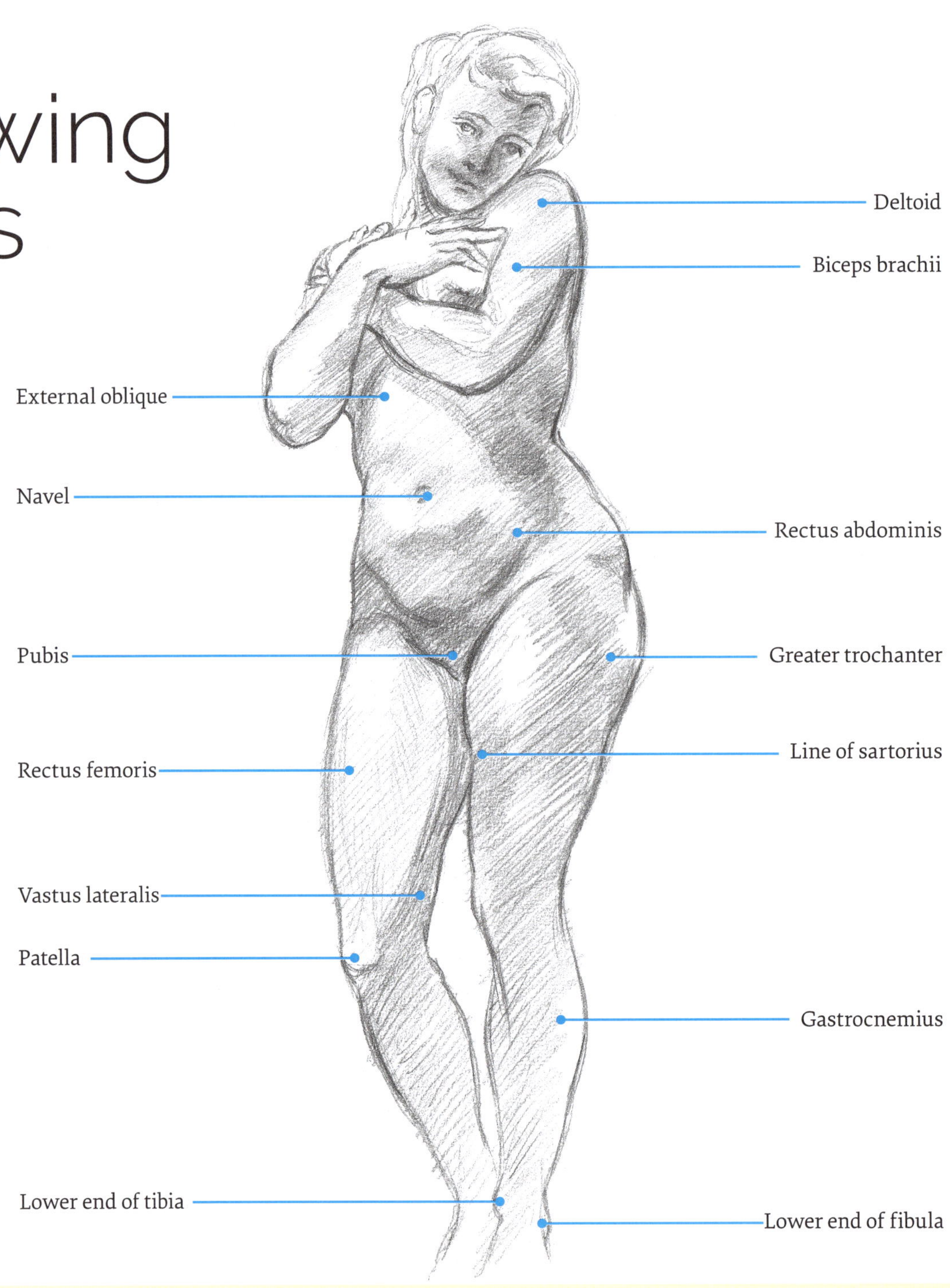

after Camille Corot (1796–1875)

Corot's drawing is interesting to the student of anatomy, because despite primarily showing smooth, flowing forms, it is still possible to see the main shapes of the muscles and bone structure underneath.

after Luca Signorelli (1445–1523)

Signorelli's figure drawing always shows the large muscles very clearly. This study of the back view of a male figure shows how well he understood the muscularity of the human form.

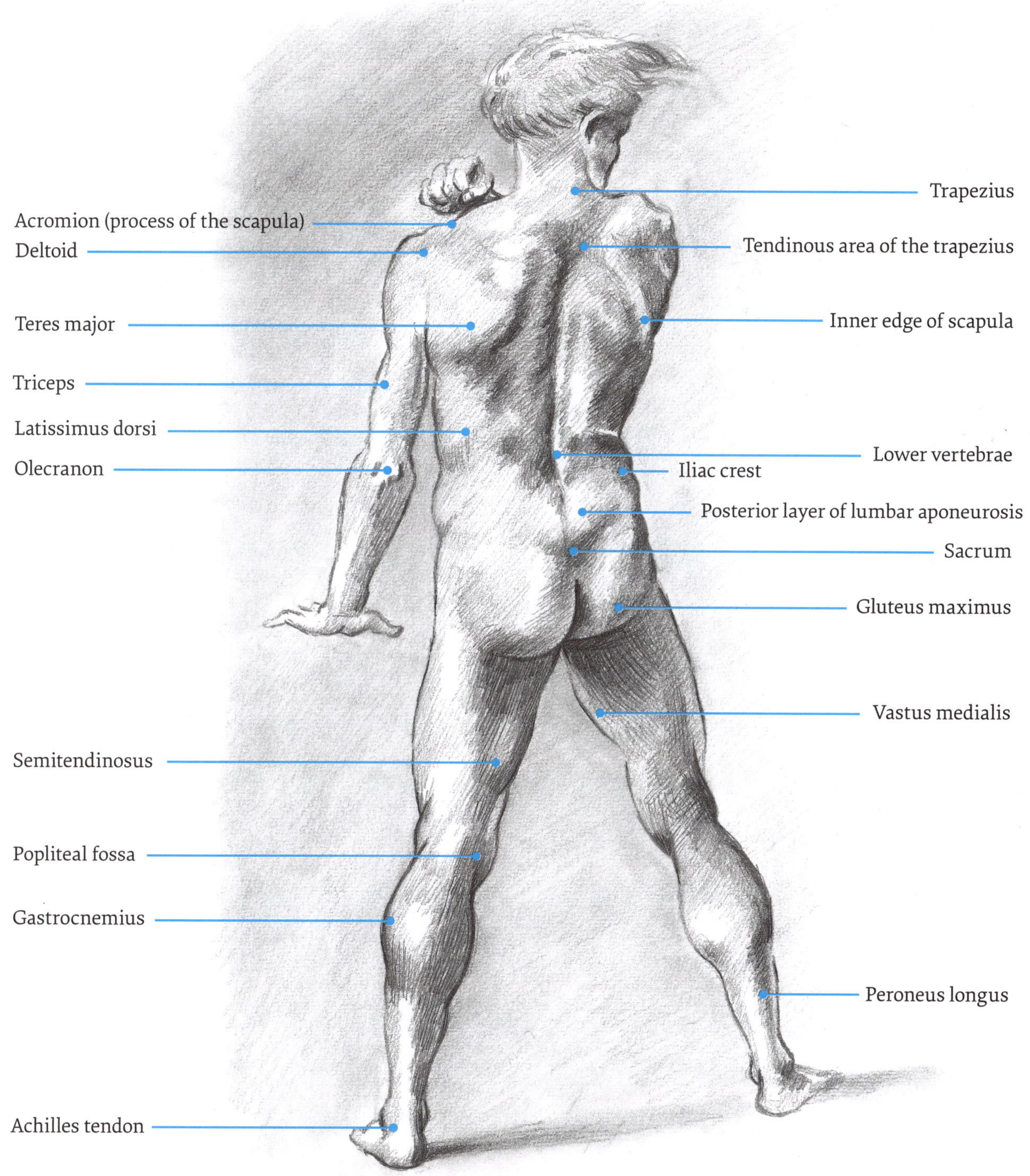

The arms and legs showing the muscles

The studies of masculine arms show the interest that the Renaissance artists had in the careful depiction of the body. These drawings are the equivalent of the best modern photographic work. On the facing page, Michelangelo's dense hatching in ink gives a certain sharpness to the definition of forms, while the female leg after Ingres is drawn in pencil and gives a softer, more subtle effect.

After Federico Barocci (c.1530–1612)

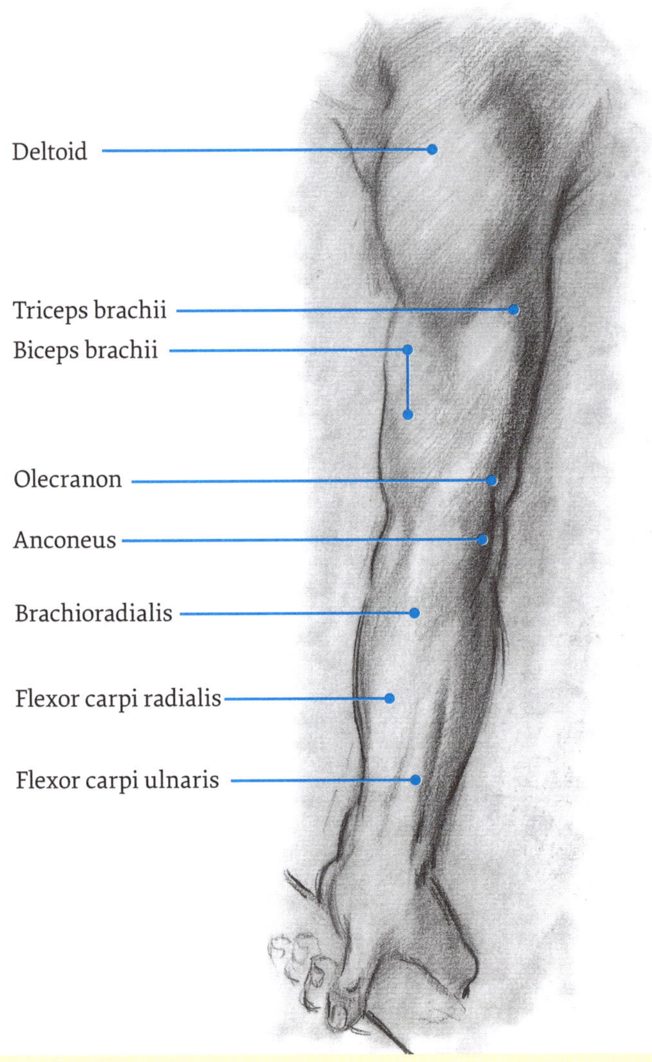

After Raphael Sanzio (1483–1520)

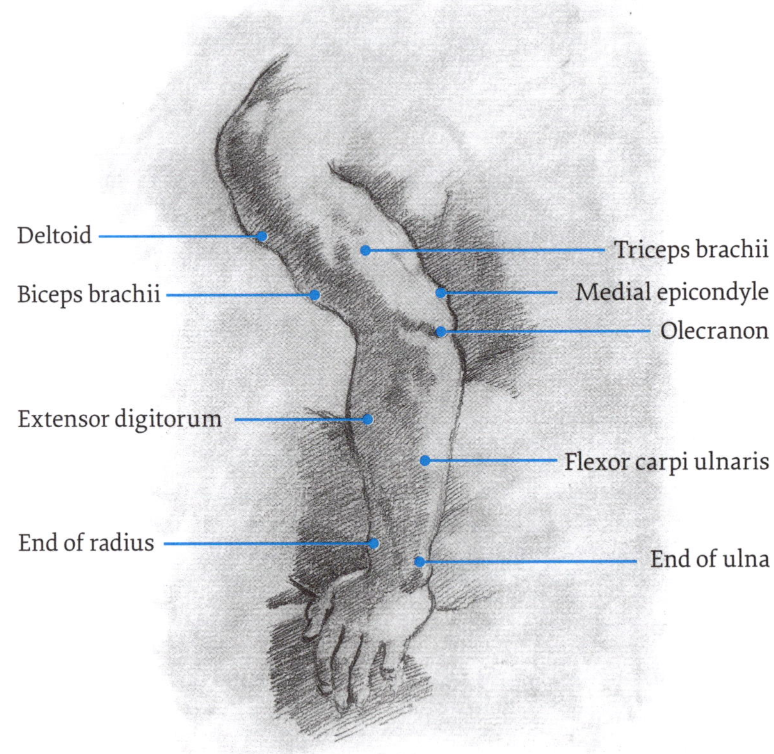

After Michelangelo Buonarroti (1475–1564)

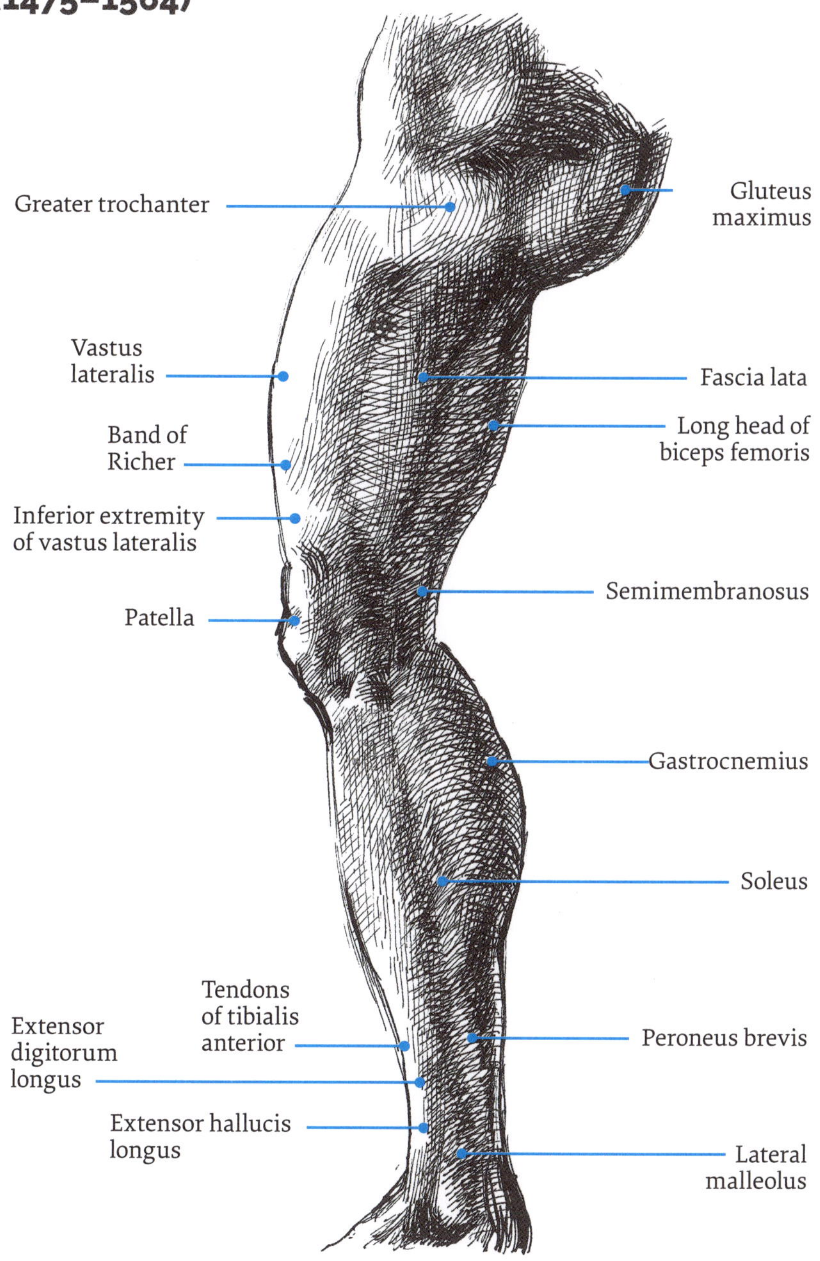

After Jean-Auguste-Dominique Ingres (1780–1867)

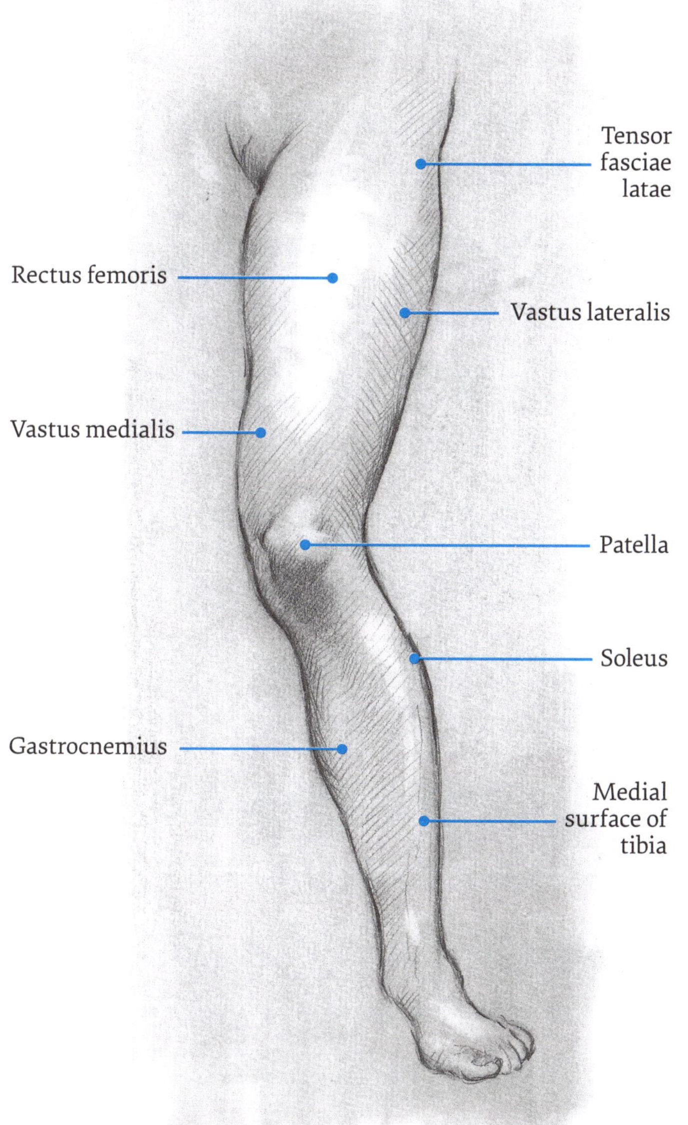

Life Drawing

When it comes to drawing the human figure, you can learn a lot from diagrams and examples but there is no substitute for drawing a model from life. This set of figure studies, all from life models, is to give you some idea of the variety of ways that you can show a figure to convincing effect. They use different techniques, attempting to echo the feeling of the particular pose or model.

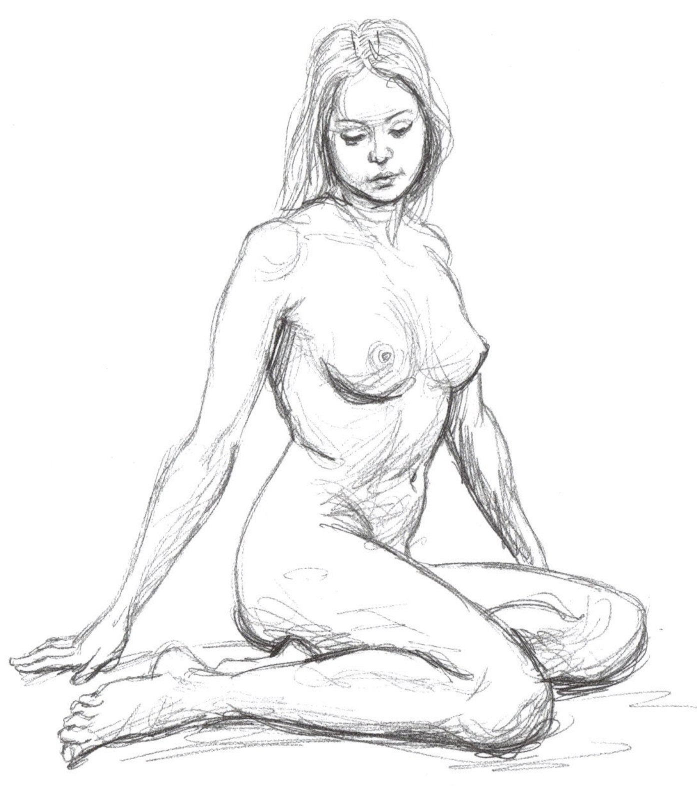

The next drawing is more tentative in one way, but also very definite when the main shape has been detected. The wiry pen line sometimes suggests that an edge has not yet been clearly seen, and at other times is put down so strongly that there is no doubting its position. This results in a certain assurance, because we do actually tend to view things like that, sometimes sure about the image and sometimes uncertain.

The first model is drawn in pencil and the approach has been fairly fluid – meaning that although there are some strong lines, the way they have been repeatedly sketched around, in order to find the best line to describe the model's pose, gives a very soft feel to the edge of the figure.

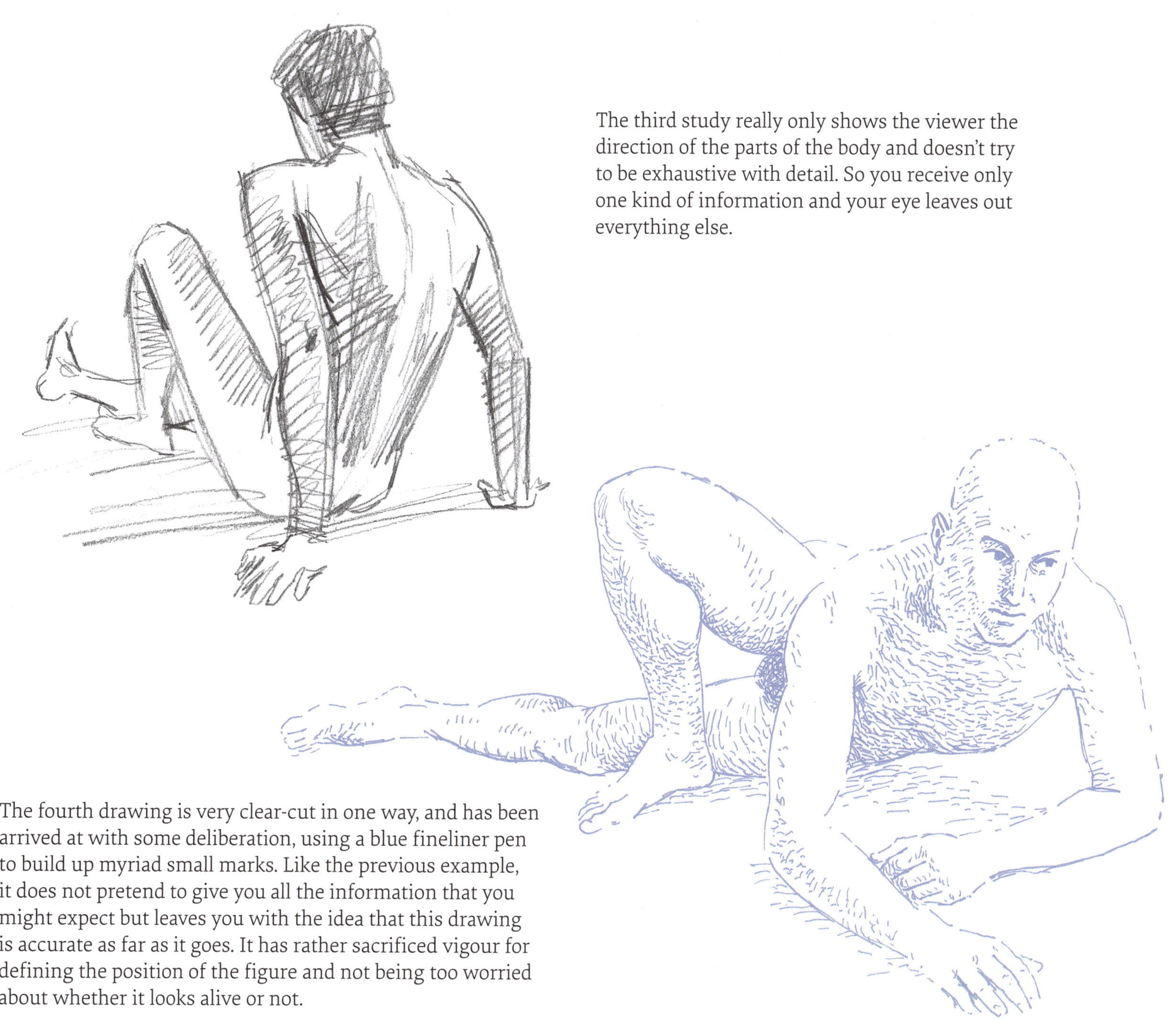

The third study really only shows the viewer the direction of the parts of the body and doesn't try to be exhaustive with detail. So you receive only one kind of information and your eye leaves out everything else.

The fourth drawing is very clear-cut in one way, and has been arrived at with some deliberation, using a blue fineliner pen to build up myriad small marks. Like the previous example, it does not pretend to give you all the information that you might expect but leaves you with the idea that this drawing is accurate as far as it goes. It has rather sacrificed vigour for defining the position of the figure and not being too worried about whether it looks alive or not.

Describing Form

One of the greatest challenges of life drawing is the need to indicate the three-dimensional qualities of the figure, so that the eye is convinced that what it is seeing has mass and volume. There is no fixed methodology for this and artists down the ages have tackled the question in many different ways. Here are just a few of the most obvious.

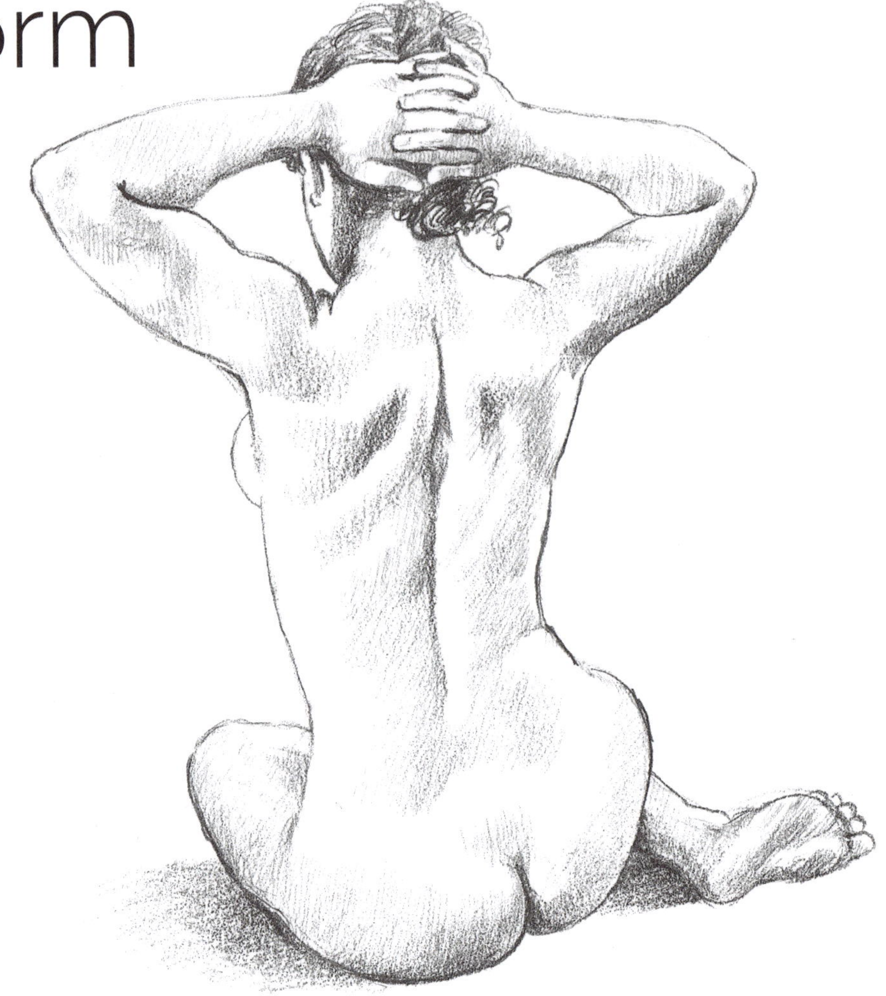

The first example shows the classic method of shading in pencil, which the majority of artists use at some time or another, and it is probably one of the most effective methods of showing solidity. What artists rely upon here is the fact that we cannot see anything without sufficient light both to illuminate one surface and throw another in the shade. Traditionally, the way to illustrate light and shade is to move your pencil across the paper in regular, close-set lines to affect an area of shadow. This has to be done in a fairly controlled way and the better you become at it, the more convincing is the result. Leonardo da Vinci was famous for laying on shadow in this way, using a technique called *sfumato*, meaning that the result was so subtle and soft that the gradation of tone looked almost like smoke. Our example doesn't claim to be as expert as Leonardo's, nevertheless you can see how by very careful progression with the shading, the impression of a solid body with the light falling on it from one side is convincing, and gives roundness to the limbs and torso of the model.

The third one is simplified and rather angular; it works by describing the planes of the body in very clear-cut terms. This method has the tendency to sacrifice subtlety for the conviction of the main shapes and surfaces. It can give a dramatically strong look to a drawing but might well miss out on the detail.

The second example is more drastic and less lifelike but does indicate the solidity of the figure quite clearly. The style is rather like the lines that a chisel makes around a piece of wood that is being carved.

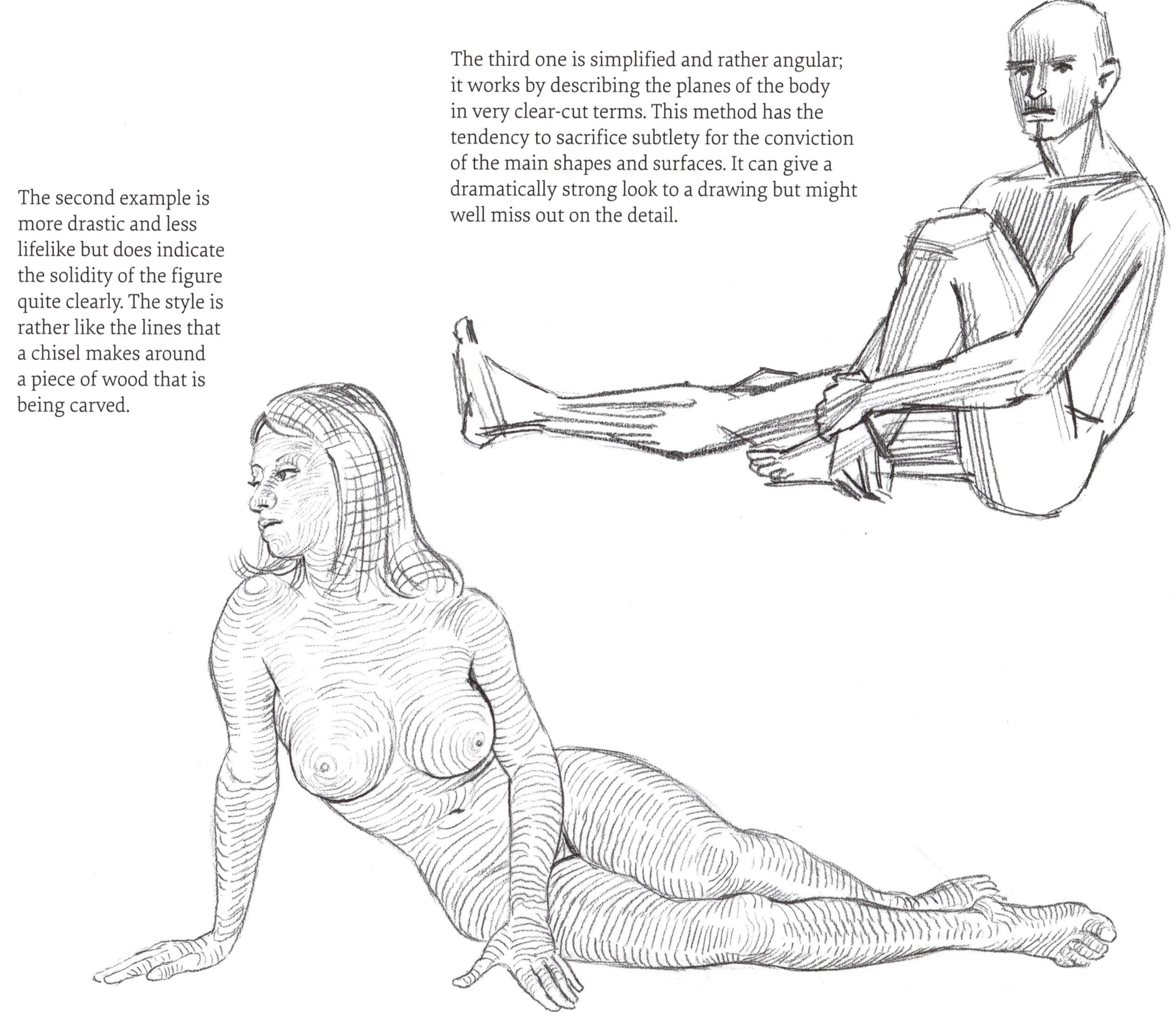

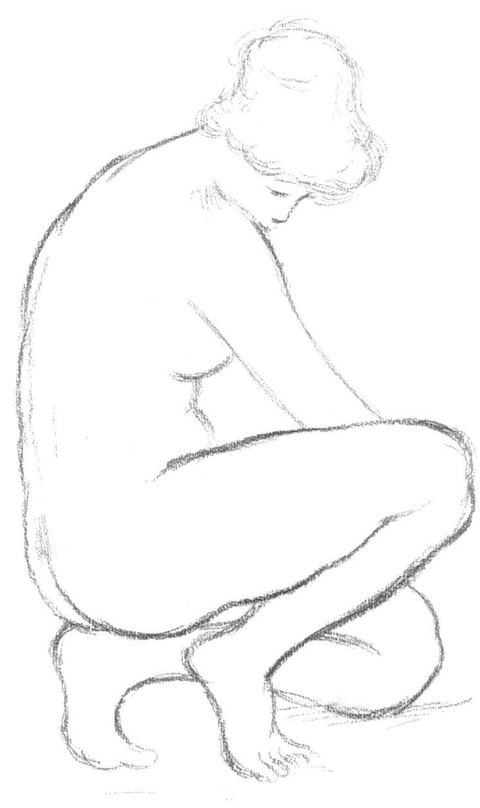

The next method sacrifices everything in an attempt to describe form purely by the outline. A line drawing like this can be most rewarding, because it enables the eye to read into the picture a great deal that is, in fact, only hinted at. In this example after Aristide Maillol (1861–1944), the soft smoky texture of the chalk line gives a feeling of the roundness of the limbs and the soft quality of the flesh.

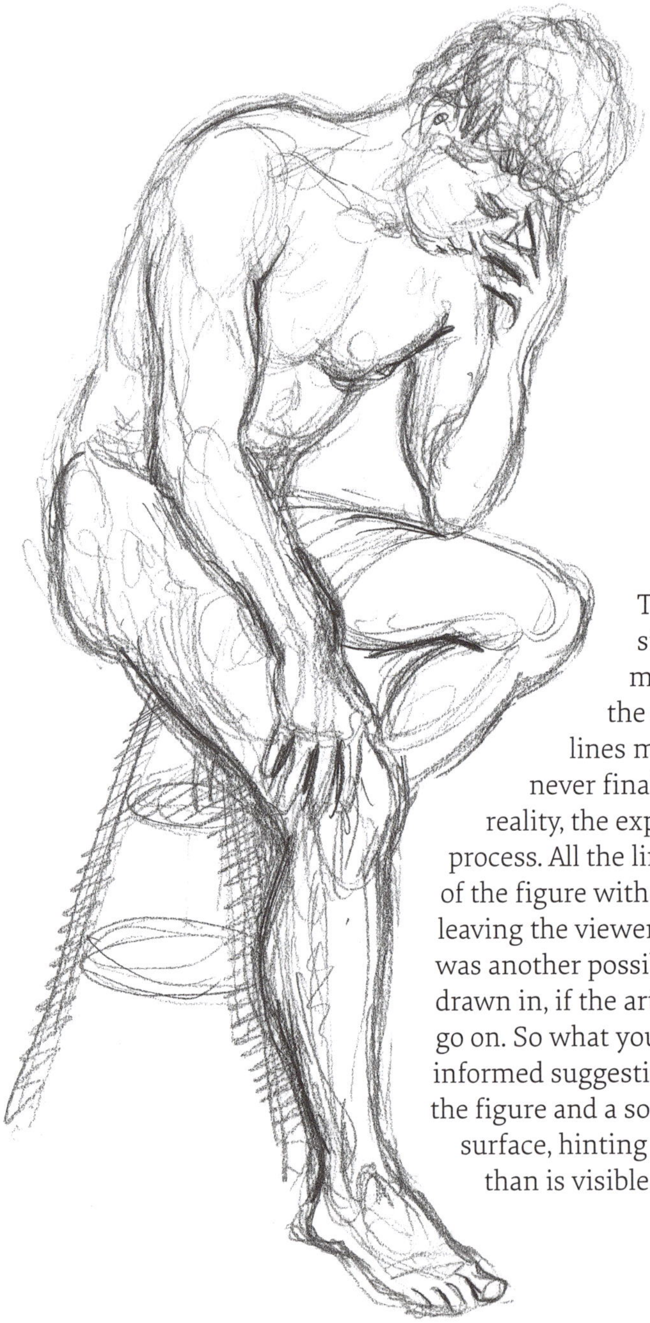

This drawing is somewhat similar in style but is even more of an exploration by the artist of where the final lines might be. This technique never finalizes the image and is, in reality, the expression of an ongoing process. All the lines suggest the limits of the figure without actually defining it, leaving the viewer with the idea that there was another possibility that might have been drawn in, if the artist had had the time to go on. So what you are observing is a well-informed suggestion of the probable shape of the figure and a sort of movement across the surface, hinting at a bit more of the form than is visible.

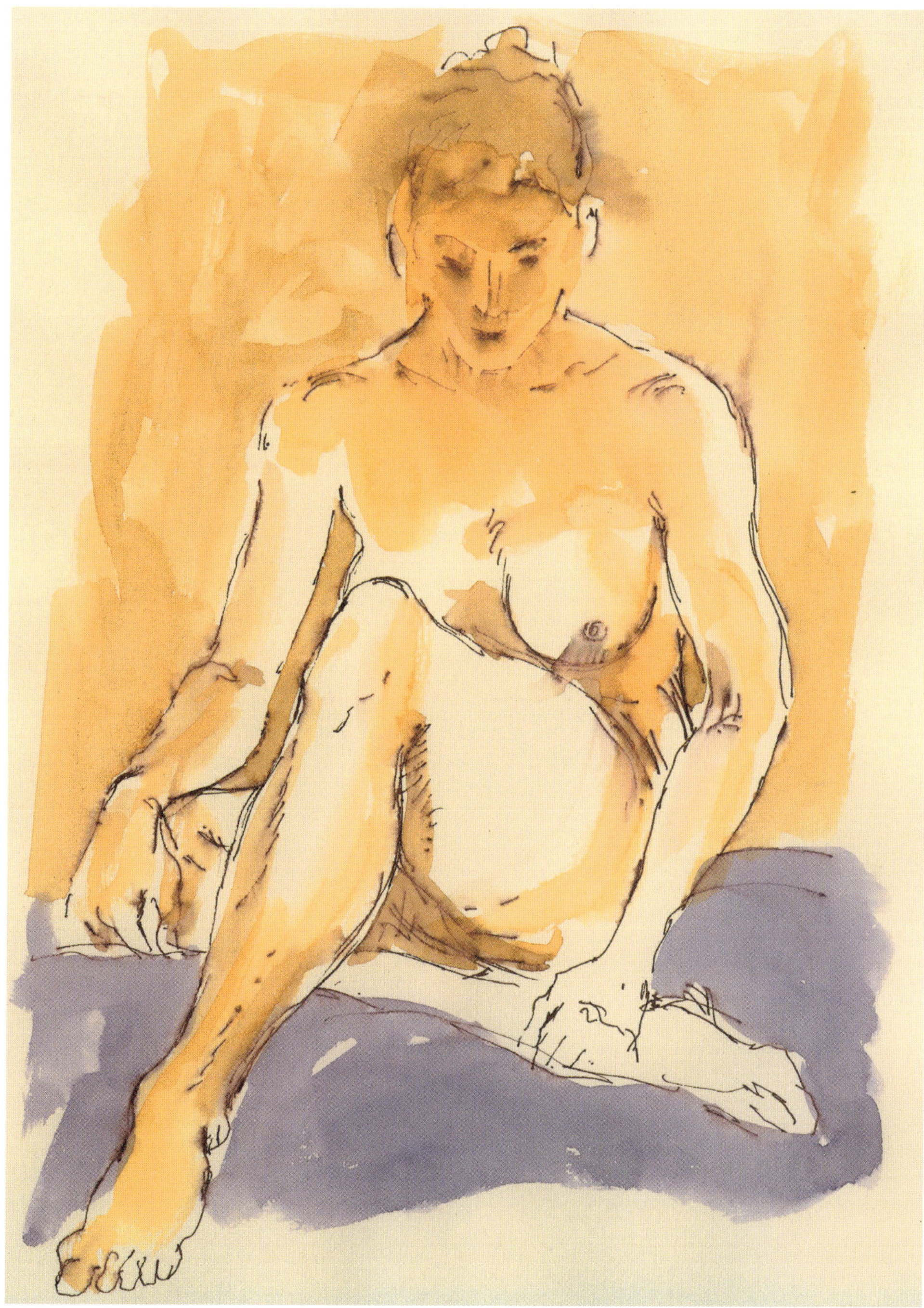

This nude is drawn in pen and ink on cream, almost flesh-coloured paper. I used sparse lines to indicate the outline of the figure and added some colour washes to give a more spatial effect. In the areas where the figure caught the light around the breasts, thigh and lower leg, I left mainly blank paper. Where the tones and shadows were darker I added more colour to the wash. The contrast between a simple line drawing and the addition of washes of colour shows how much even limited colour can achieve.

Working at Speed

Another practice always useful for life drawing is to draw extremely quickly with just a few fluid lines to see how fast the whole figure can be sketched in. This is encouraged by many life class tutors as it teaches students to look for the essential lines of the pose. Practise a dozen or so drawings like these of the model, taking various one- or two-minute poses and putting in the absolute minimum. You should be working so quickly you have no time to correct errors.

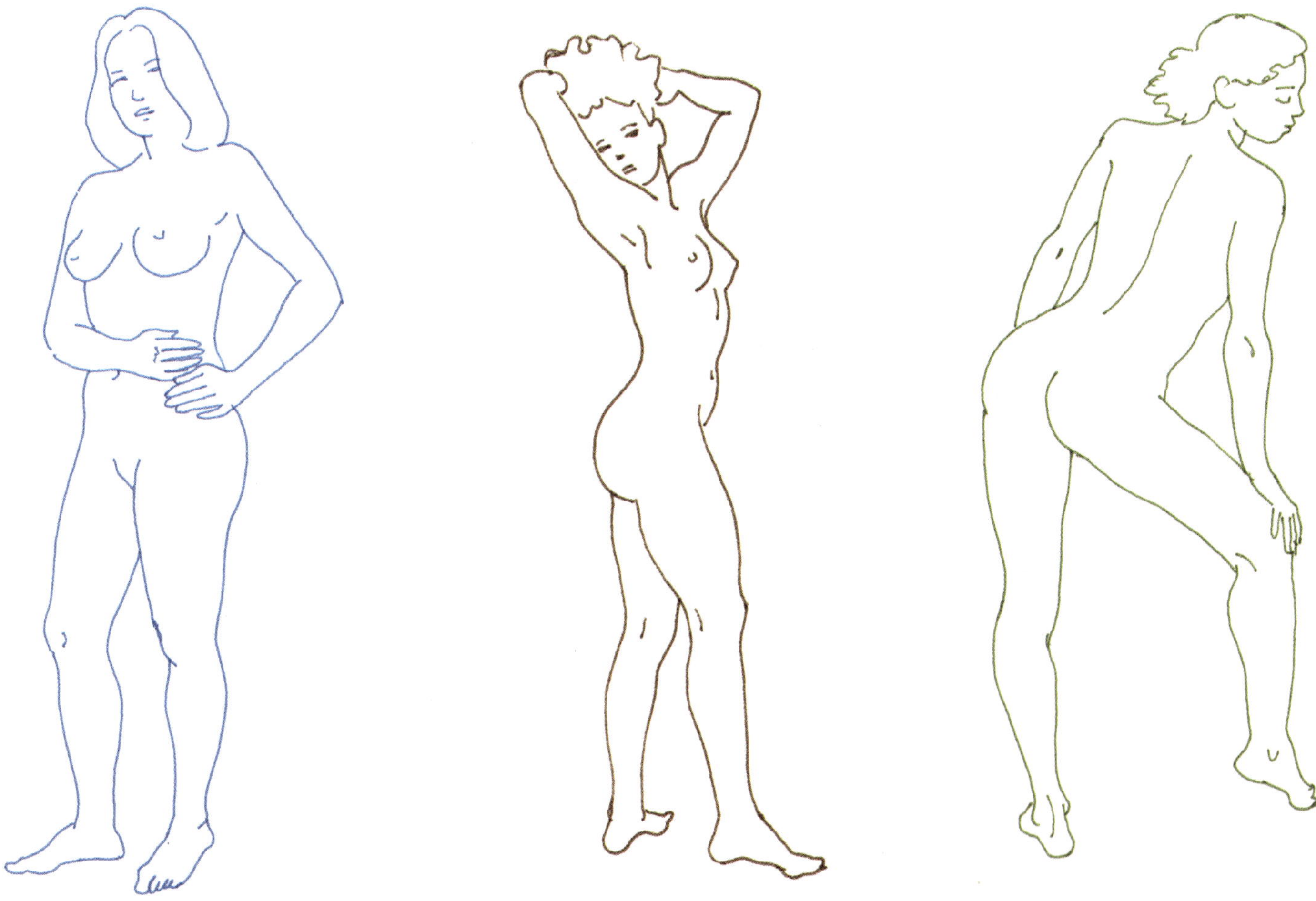

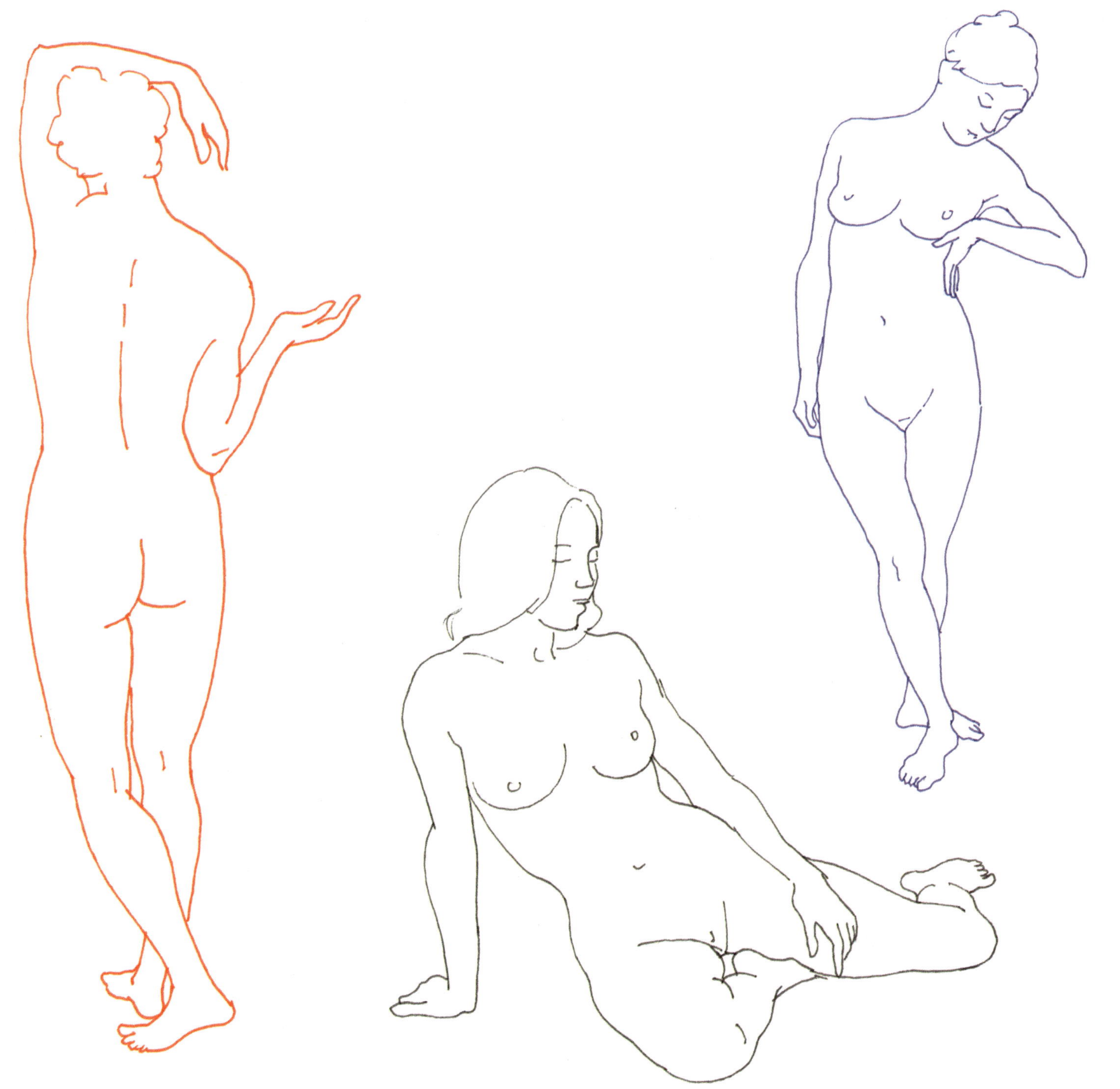

Light and Dark Tones

Here are some examples of figures drawn in colour which demonstrate how to balance out your tonal range. The problem with drawing a figure in colour is the risk that you run of making the final result look too melodramatic. The range of tones on the human body is quite subtle, but they do go from cool or cold colours to warm, rich tones. The sort of light that is used makes a difference – sunlight being so strong that it often washes out contrasts of colour, and artificial light being restricted and therefore changing the natural colour of the body.

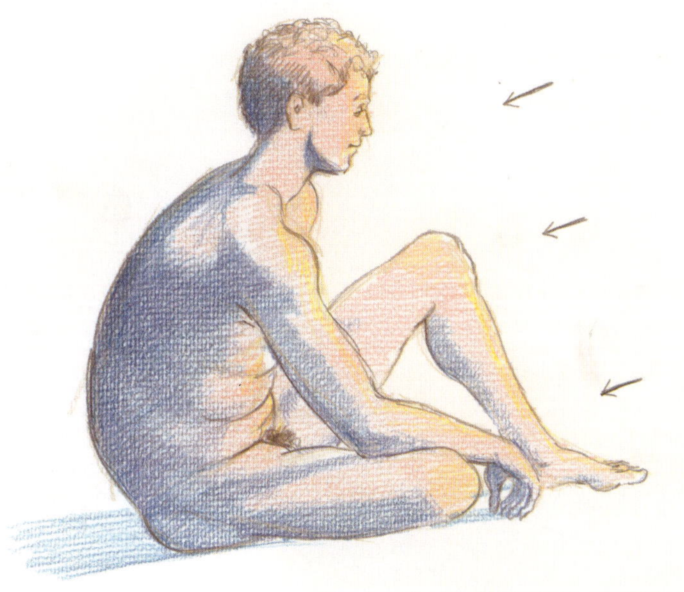

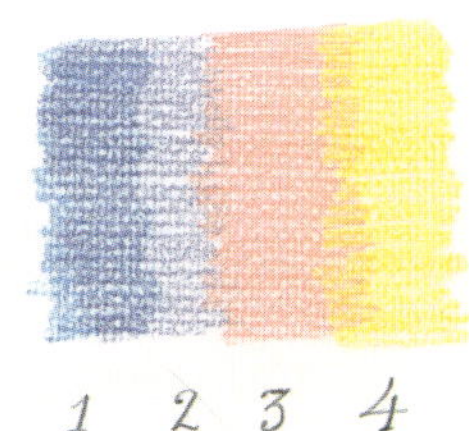

The man is seated, facing the source of light and since he is drawn in coloured pencil, there is no great contrast between the very darkest tone and the very lightest. Note how the shadowed area is mostly in cool blue tones and a warm yellow has been used in the areas where the light is falling on the figure. The numbered patches show the colours used.

Artist's Note

When drawing the human form, the simple understanding of the geometric shapes and the overall tones are far more important than the details. Without this care in the main shapes and colours, the details won't work to your advantage. So, take immense care with the large, main shapes and colours of the body, and then the details will really take off.

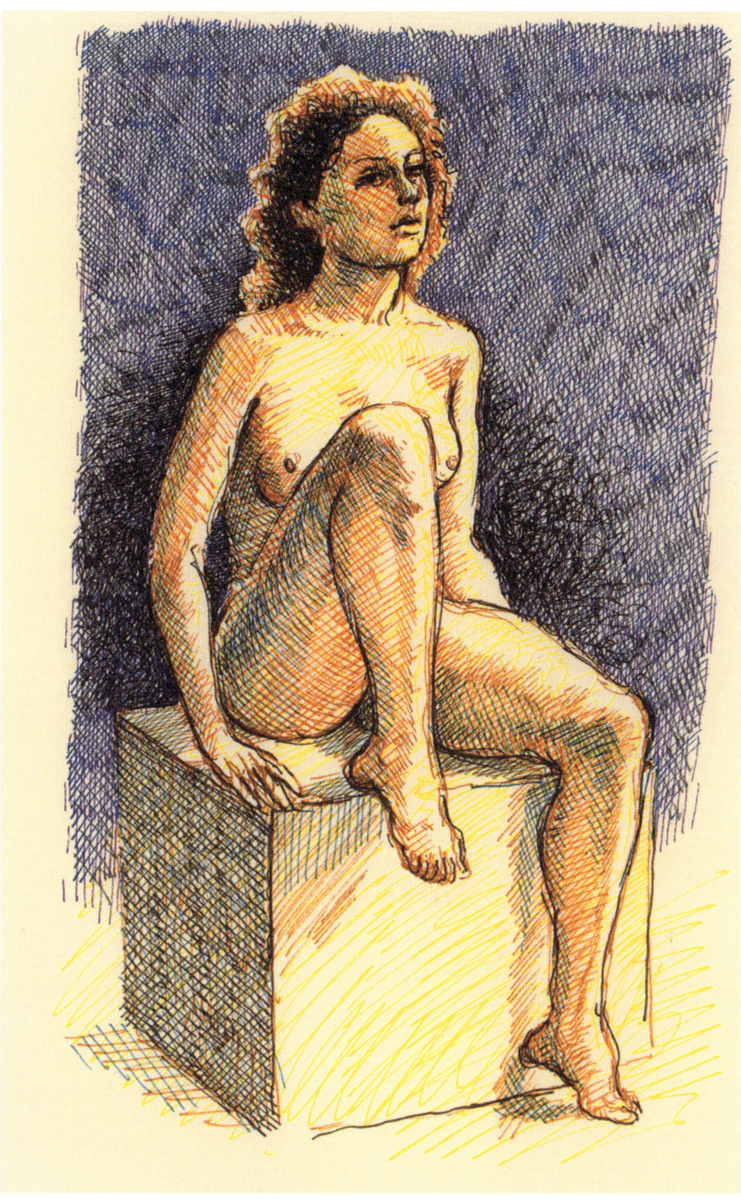

This dark, densely sketched background in deep blues has the effect of throwing the lighter, yellow-toned body forward into relief.

For maximum contrast on the black background, I have used pastels. Note the use of warm and cool colours for the light and dark areas; and to add a touch more warmth to the picture I've put in a rich reddy-purple to prevent the blue from becoming too dominant. When working like this you should do the initial drawing in a single colour first, to establish the overall shape of the figure.

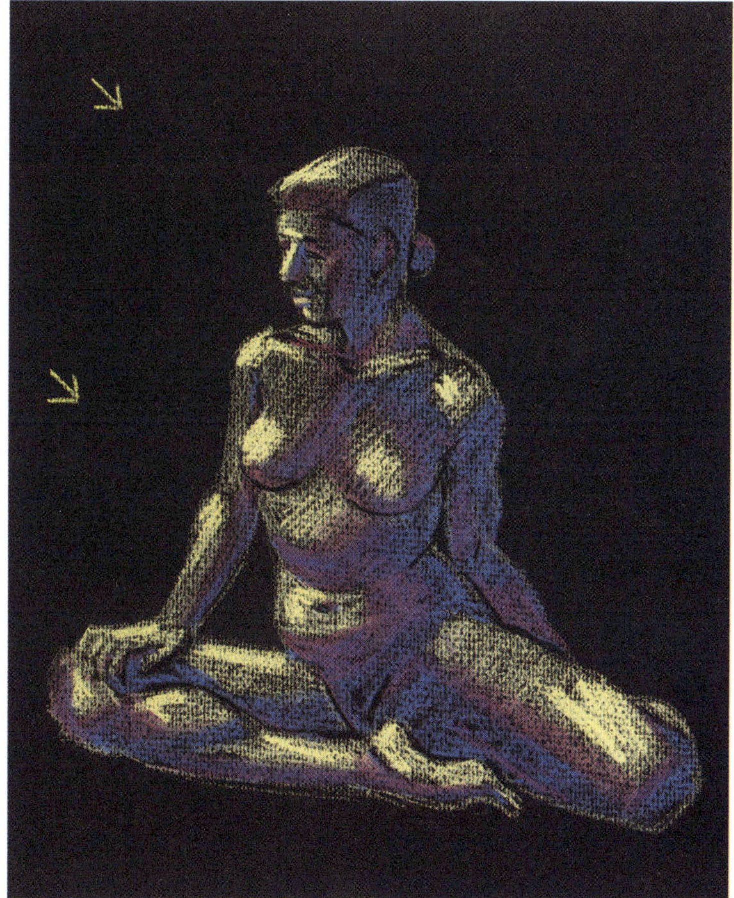

Life Drawing Step by Step

Here is a life drawing of a nude model in a pose that you might well see at a life class. This is a step-by-step approach and shows how I normally proceed with a live model posing for me. I used coloured pencils for this study, starting with a faint ochre line and adding more colour as I developed the figure.

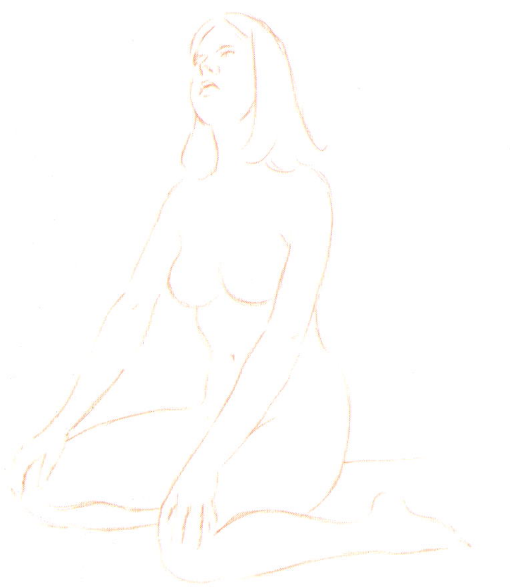

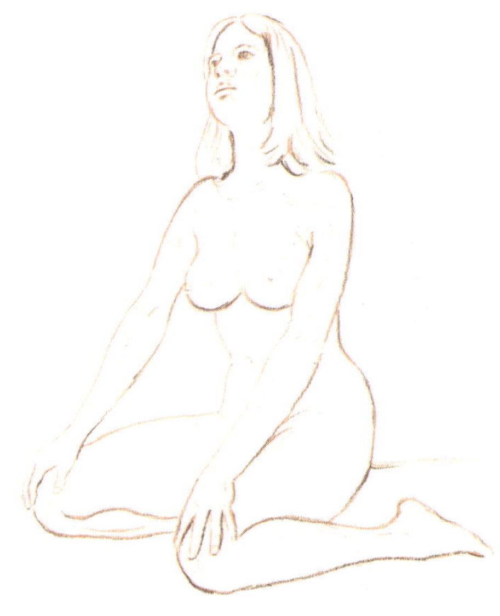

STEP 1

First, make a few swift, light marks, just to give an idea of the proportions and shapes of the main figure. At this stage you only need to get a feel of the overall shape of the whole body in space.

STEP 2

Next, start to define the figure more fully, getting the shapes of the limbs and head and torso as accurate as possible. Keep drawing lightly so that you can correct any mistakes easily. This stage is extremely important to help produce a good drawing.

STEP 3

Now you can start to define the forms with clear edges and darker tones. At this stage I used a much darker brown, and if you are working in pencil you can apply greater pressure for more definite marks. With a lighter tone, I outlined the areas of tonal shading on the body, to guide me at the next stage when tone will be added. Look carefully at your model to get these areas accurate.

STEP 4

Now at last you can begin to build up the tone with careful, light marks to get a good even area of shading which appears to indicate the roundness of the limbs and torso. If you are working in colour you can also put in a touch of a warm fleshy colour for the skin and a bit of yellow ochre for the hair. Note where the darkest parts of the shadows are and increase their density. It also helps to put in the surface the model is sitting on. I used a blue tone for this, to give some basis for the whole figure.

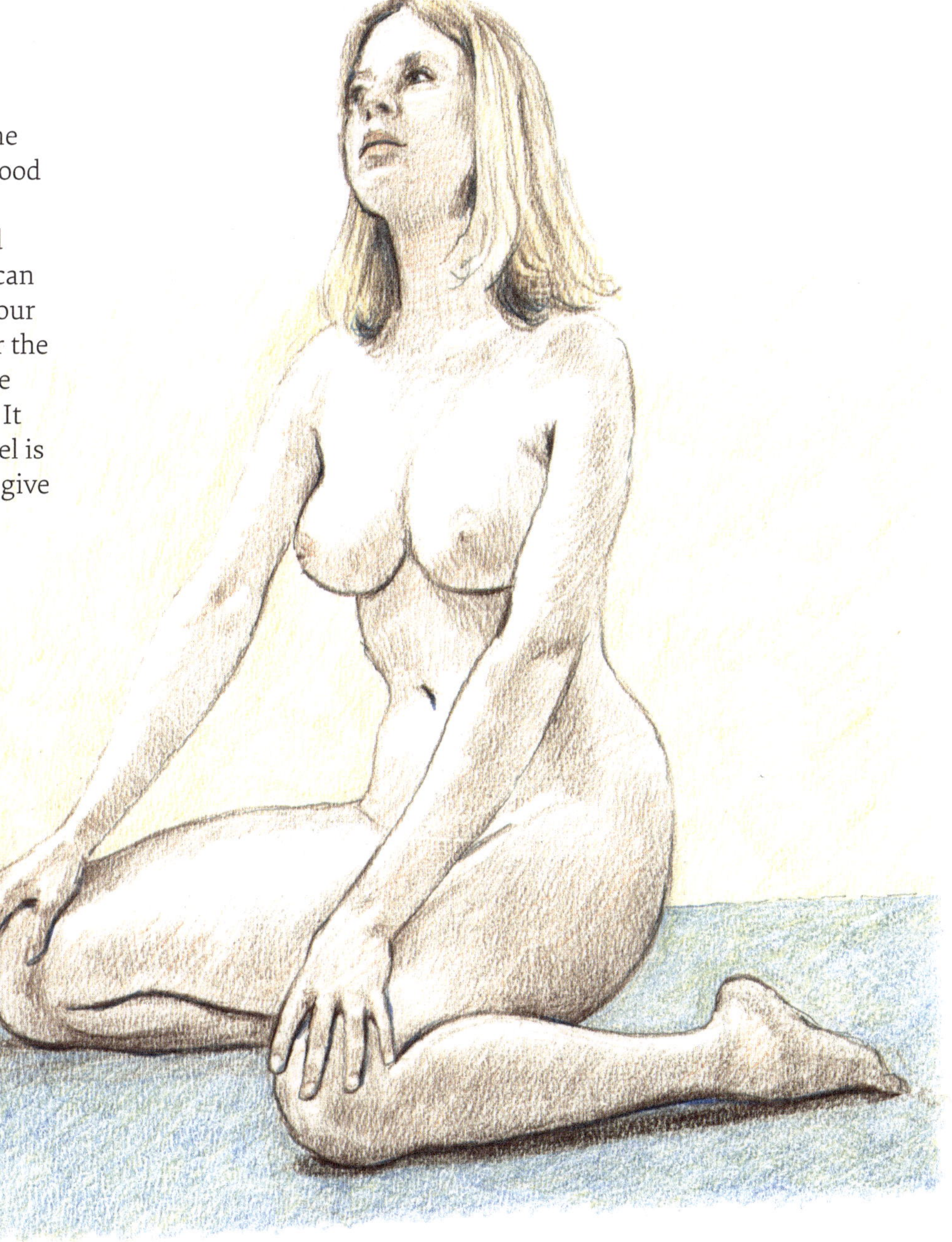

Whatever the shape or pose of your model, by following these steps you should end up with a fairly solid-looking figure.

Examples by Master Artists

To develop an individual style of portraying the human form, you will have to experiment with your style and materials. Here we look at three very different approaches to life drawing taken by three master artists.

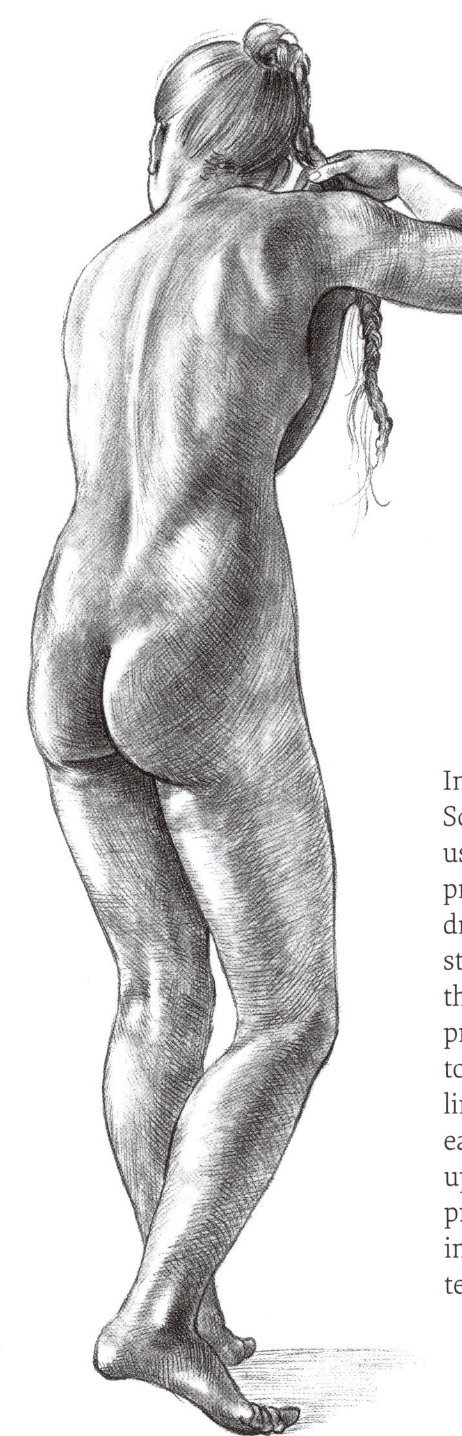

In this example after the German artist Julius Schnorr von Carolsfeld (1794–1872), the pencil is used almost scientifically with the line taking pre-eminence. It is one of the most perfect drawings I've ever seen in this meticulous pencil style. The result is quite stupendous, even though this is just a copy and probably doesn't have the precision of the original. Every line is visible. The tonal shading which follows the contours of the limbs is exquisitely observed. This is not at all easy to do and getting the repeated marks to line up correctly requires great discipline. It is worth practising this kind of drawing because it will increase your skill at manipulating the pencil and test your ability to concentrate.

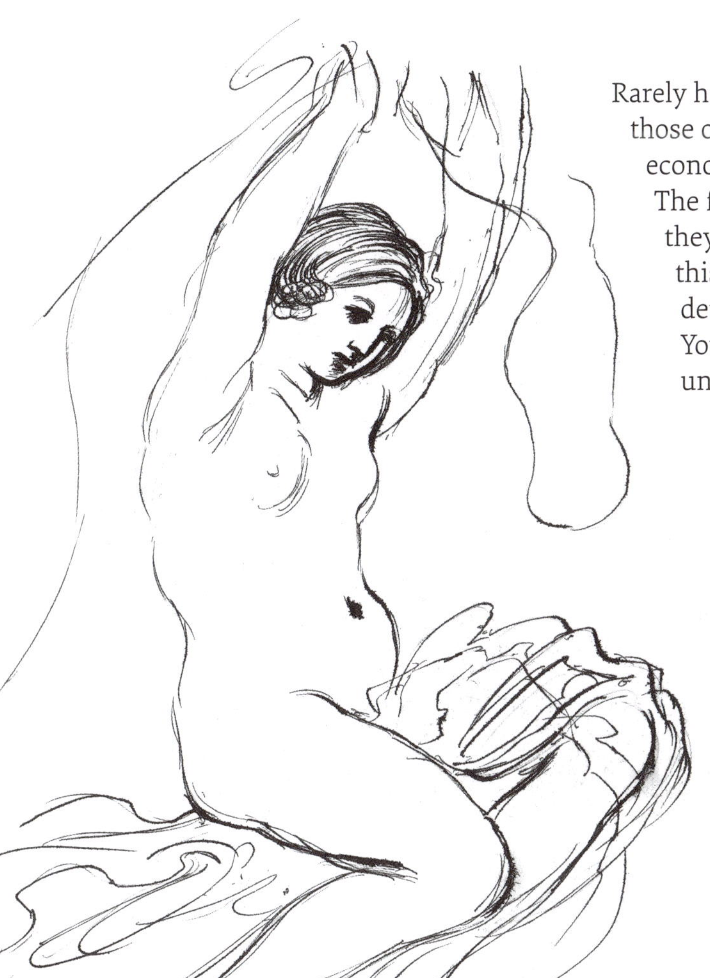

Rarely have I seen such brilliant line drawings in ink of the human figure as those of the painter Guercino (1591–1666). In this example the line is extremely economical and looks as though it has been drawn from life very rapidly. The flowing lines seem to produce the effect of a solid body in space, but they also have a marvellous lyrical quality of their own. Try drawing like this, quickly without worrying about anything except the most significant details, but getting the feel of the subject in as few lines as possible. You will have to draw something directly from life in order to get an understanding of how this technique works.

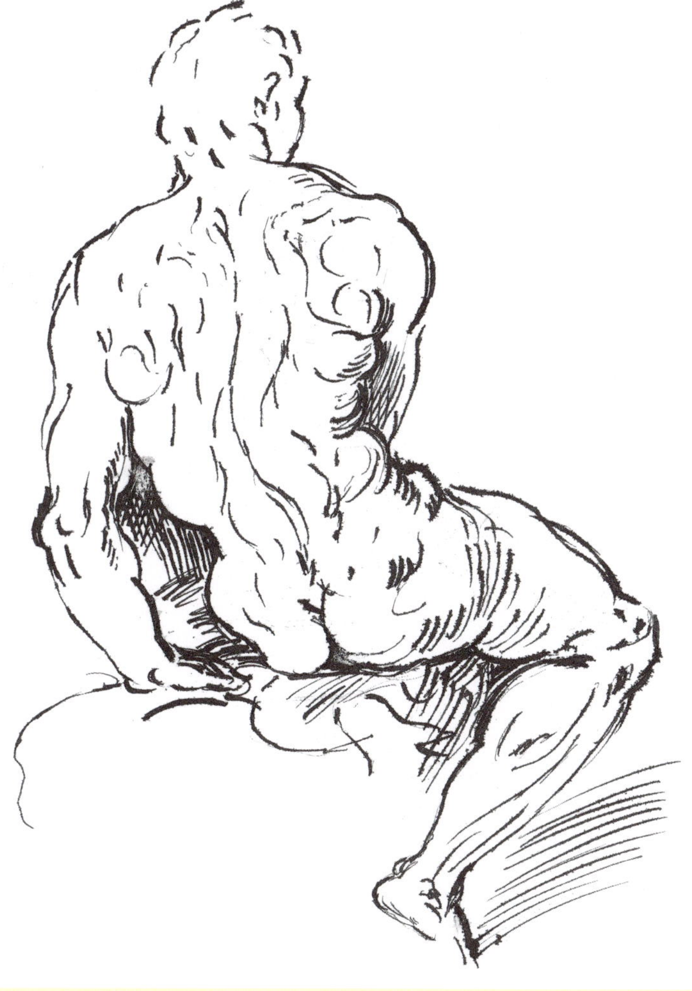

In his masterly original of this drawing in line (and ink), Tintoretto (*c.*1518–94) was careful to get the whole outline of the figure. The curvy interior lines suggest the muscularity of the form. There is not too much detail but just enough to convince the eye of the powerful body; every muscle here appears to ripple under the skin. The barest of shading suggests the form.

Chapter Five

THE FIGURE IN MOVEMENT

Once you have begun to produce drawings that look like convincing pictures of human beings you will soon want to have a go at drawing figures in movement. This is more difficult, but artists are helped a lot these days by photographs which have caught the mobile figure and show us how the movement breaks down into its various parts. Nothing quite takes the place of quick sketches of people moving about, but obviously you need to have a good enough memory to get some sort of reference drawing onto paper immediately after you have seen a fleeting movement. You can then supplement this by looking at photographs of people in similar motion.

It is also helpful to ask someone to model for you, slowly performing the action you want to study. This way you can draw the action at different stages, out of which you can pick a final image. Observation is the key to drawing movement and you have to keep watching people and noticing how their balance changes, how their arms move, how their weight shifts and how their head turns. All these elements give you clues to the movement and if you can capture them in a drawing the figures will look more mobile.

Watching people engaged in sports provides a great opportunity for the artist to observe the moving body. In this section I have chosen the type of sports that clearly show the muscles in action, such as running, jumping, climbing, wrestling and weightlifting.

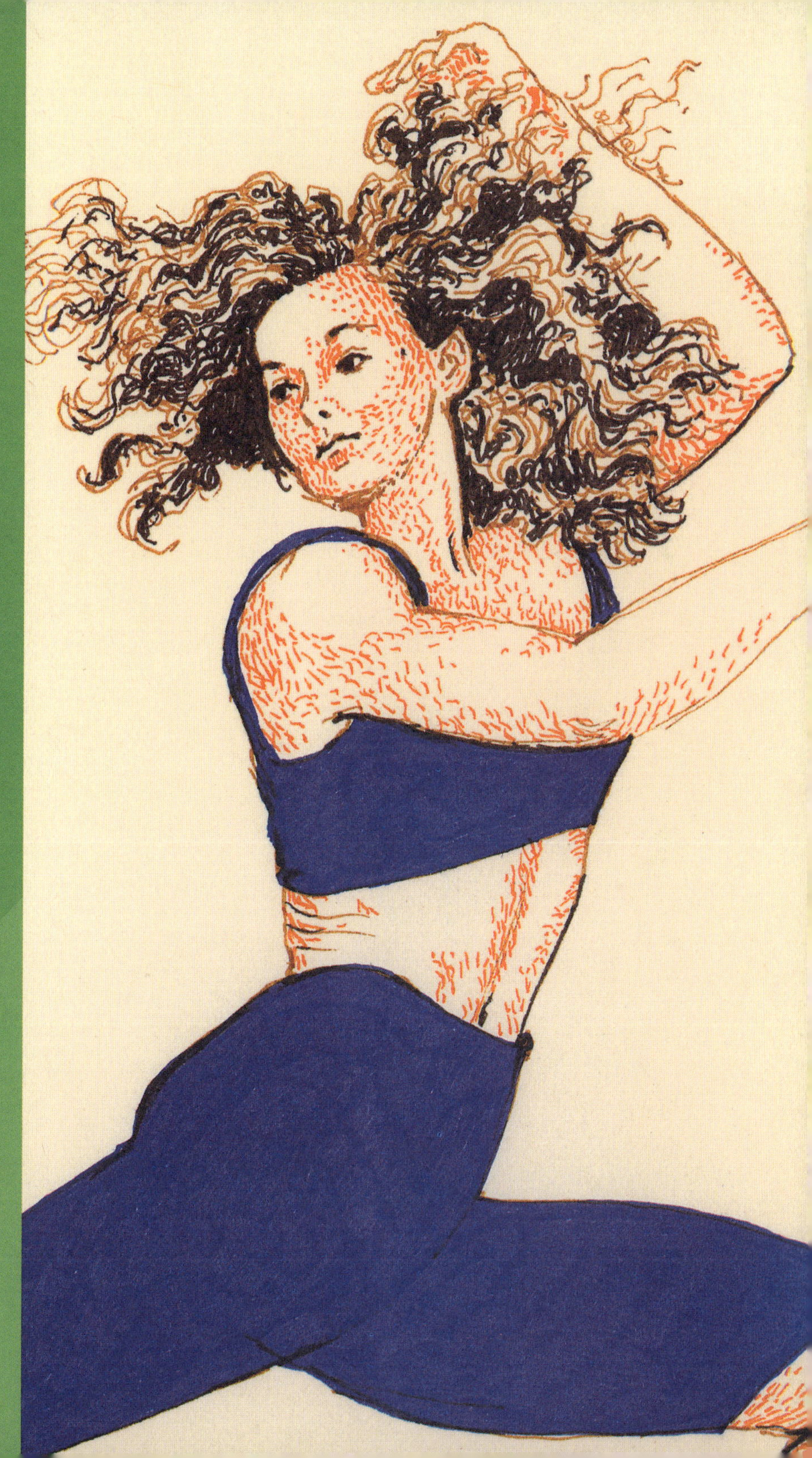

Drawing Movement

Photographs are a great boon to the artist wanting to discover just how the parts of the body relate to each other as the model moves, but they should be used with caution as copying from a photograph can produce sterile results. An artist should be looking not just to make an accurate drawing of lines and shapes but also to express the feeling of the occasion in a way that can be understood by the viewer: look particularly at the styles of depiction chosen here. Study photographs, but stamp your own mark as an artist on your drawings.

Walking and running figures

The figures shown here are quite precisely based on photographs of people walking and running. A photograph gives you one particular moment in the action and because you can draw it with a precise line, given the benefit of a still image from which to copy, the final result tends to look slightly formalized. This produces a certain stiffness in the drawing which you can overcome by more direct experience.

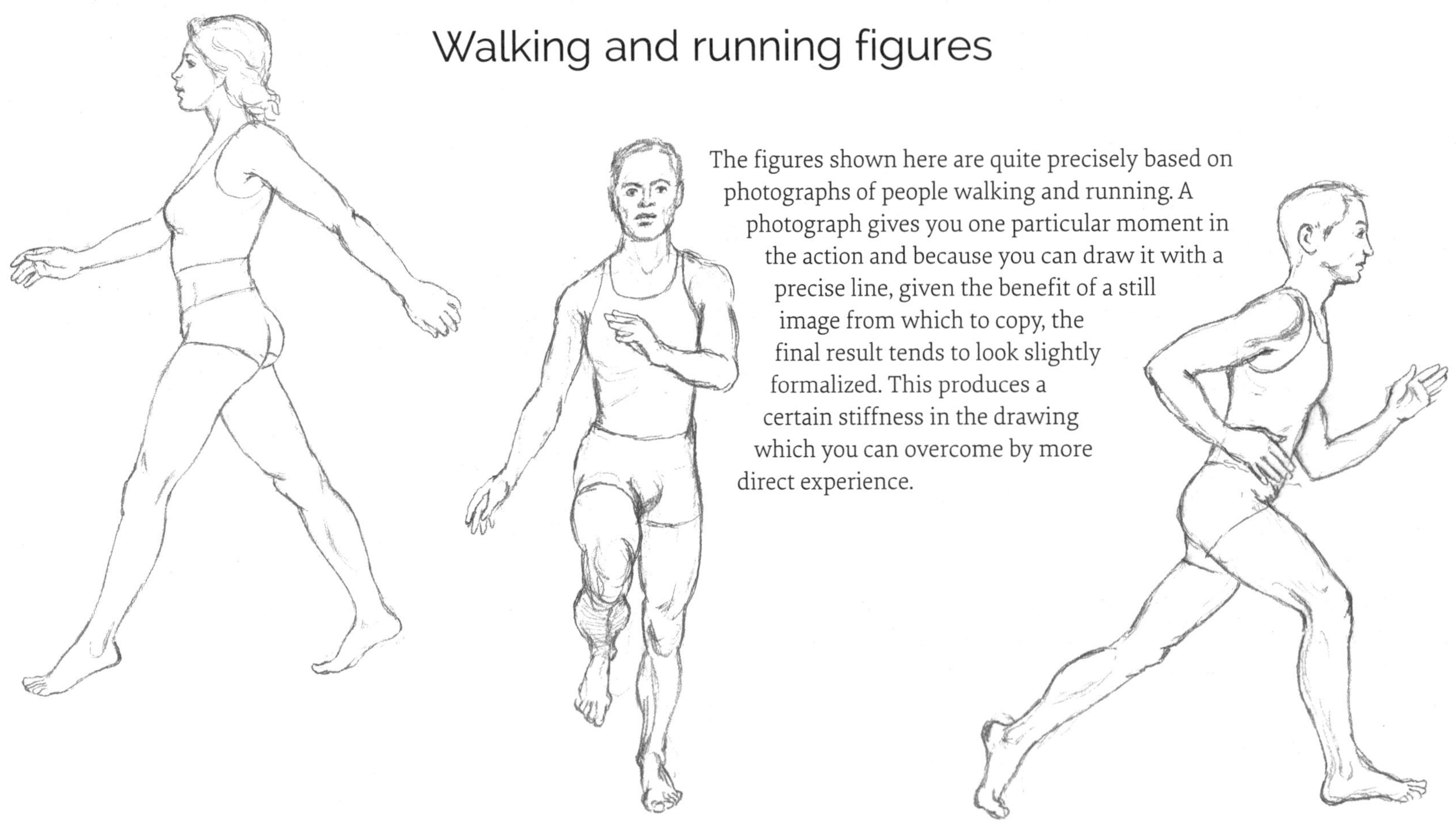

The next three figures, drawn much more loosely without the aid of photographs, give an impression of the movement. The type of line used helps to produce an image which looks as though it is in motion; none of the lines are exact and in some cases there are several lines, which create a blurred effect. Notice how the shoulders and hips work in opposition; the torso is sometimes vertical but is quite often tilted forward or back at different parts of the movement.

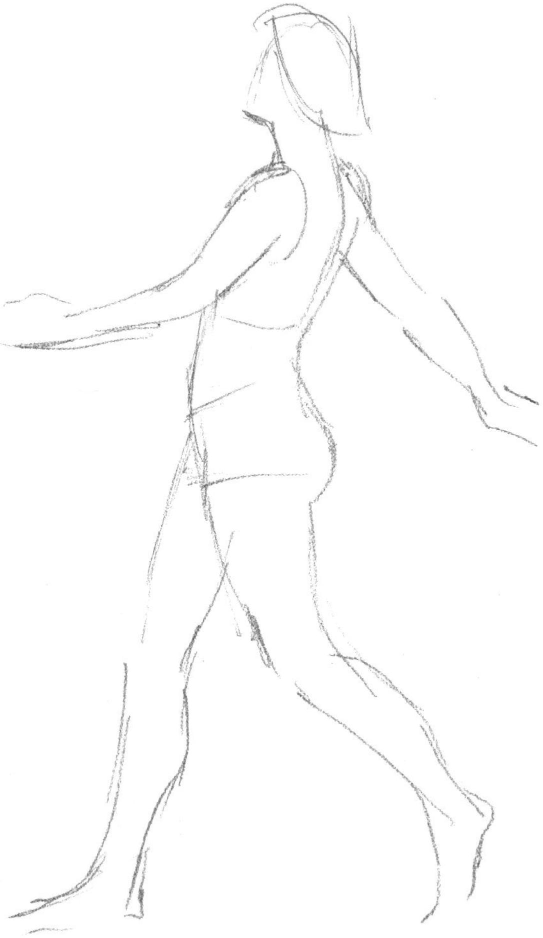

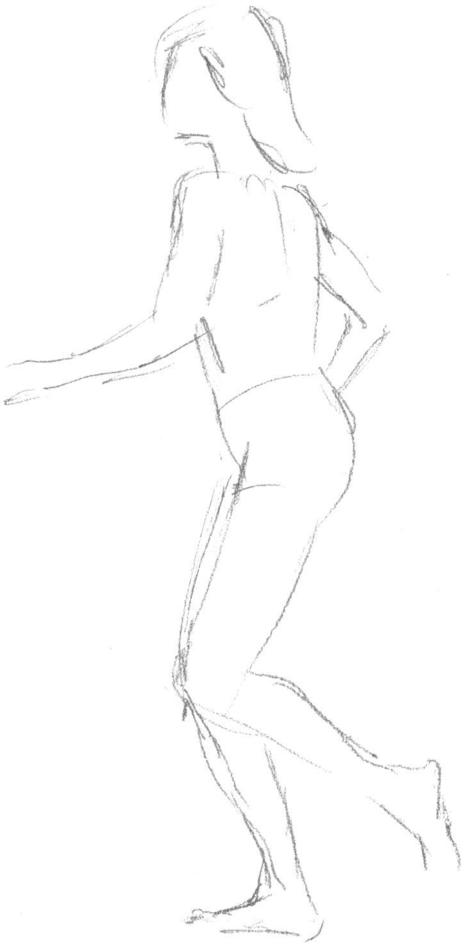

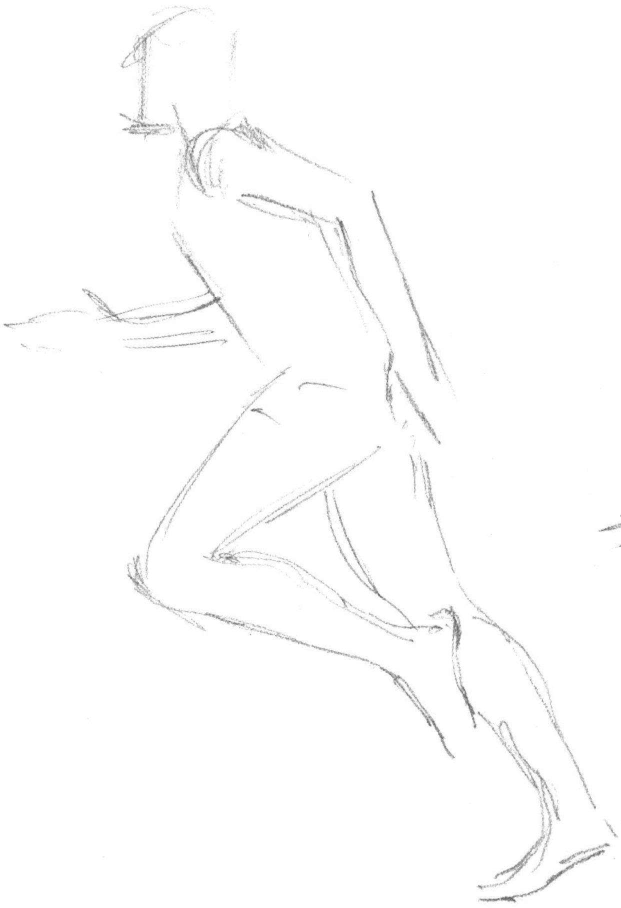

Drawing a figure in motion is not easy but at some time you should take the plunge and have a go at it. Instructing your model to keep repeating the same movement is one approach that works very well. While this performance is going on, you should try to capture each phase of the sequence and sketch it as well as you can. If the movement is repeated often enough, it is possible to keep returning to a certain position and take another look at how to draw it.

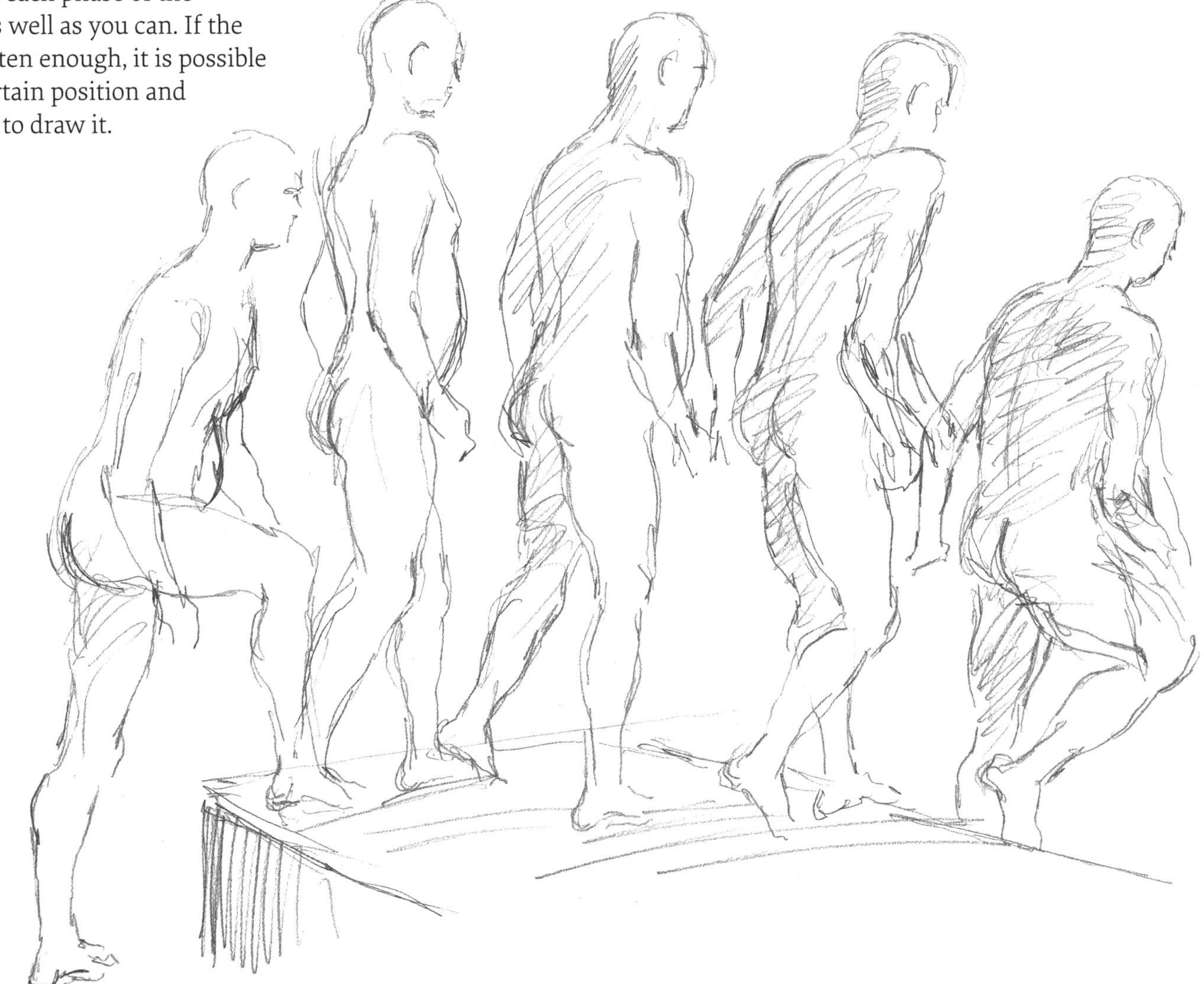

In this example, which is from a life-class session, the model walked across a dais over and over again, trying to keep the action the same each time. You could enlist the help of friends for this, if you were to choose some simple movement to begin with. Even if early attempts don't look too good, persevere with practising whenever you can and you will find that your 'fast drawing' will improve.

Catching the fleeting gesture

Once you have begun experimenting with action drawing, set yourself up in a place where you can view plenty of people walking about and see how many quick sketches you can get down. If that is not so easy for you, try getting a friend to move around slowly and draw as many of their changes of position as you can.

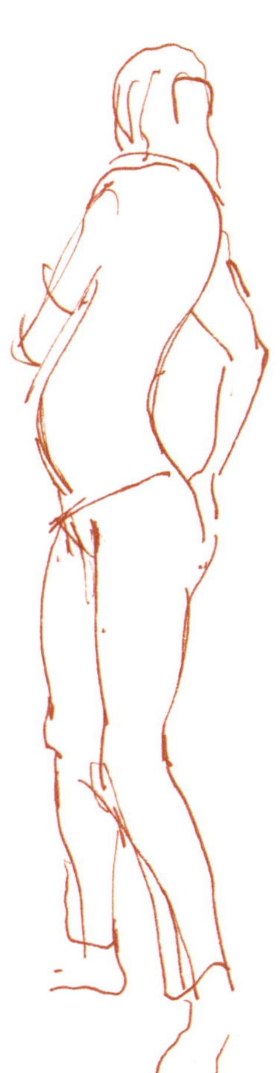

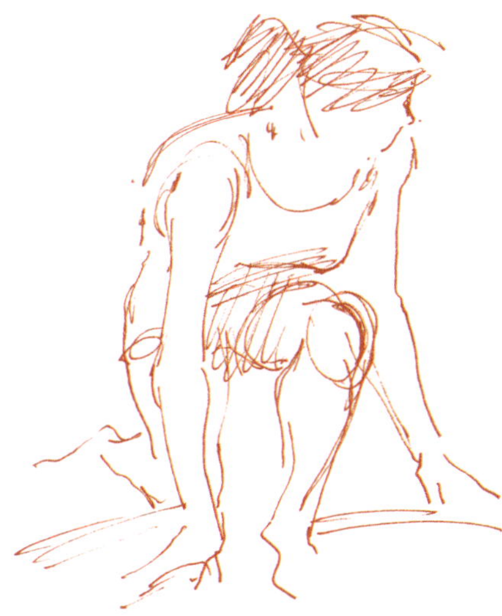

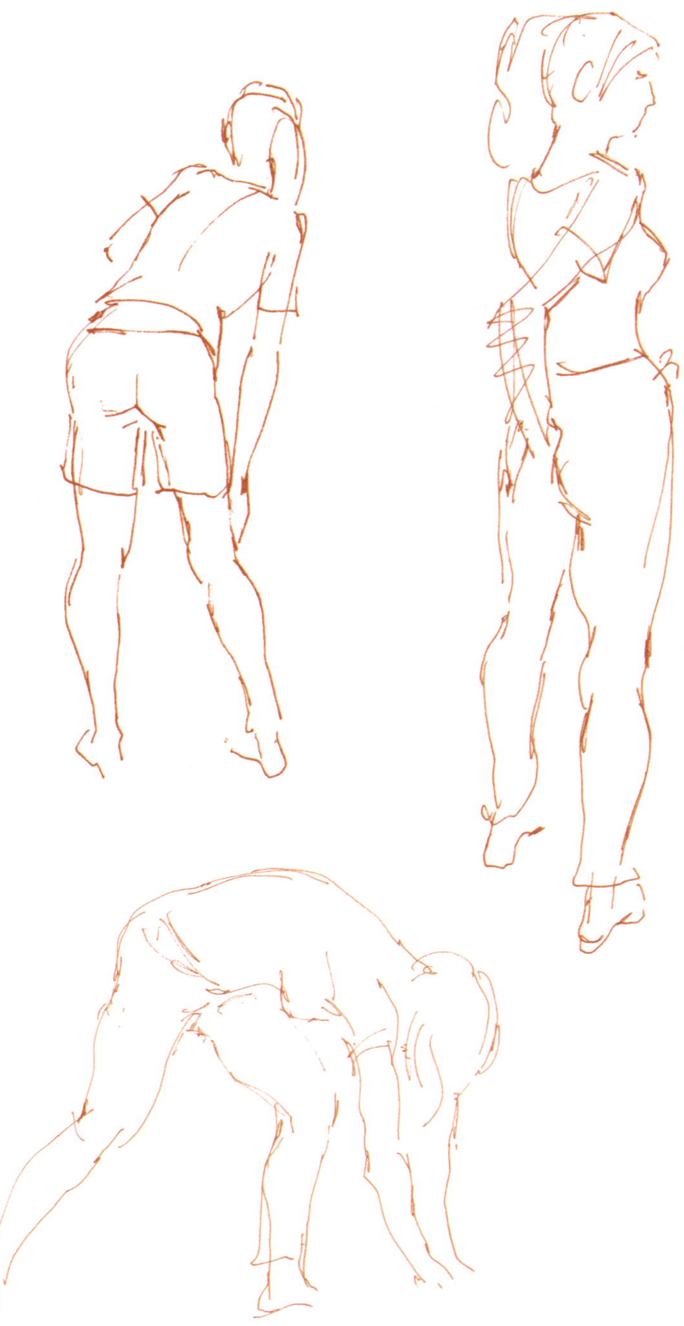

These drawings were all done extremely quickly, with the same model moving around and performing very simple, ordinary movements. Don't struggle to be too accurate, but remember that the more you do this the easier it gets.

Children playing

When it comes to children the variety of movement becomes much more flexible and the shapes they produce have a delightful energy and spontaneity.

The pair of children on the left are out in the garden and the boy is indicating something that has caught his interest. The girl is watching him but isn't about to move to join in his inspection.

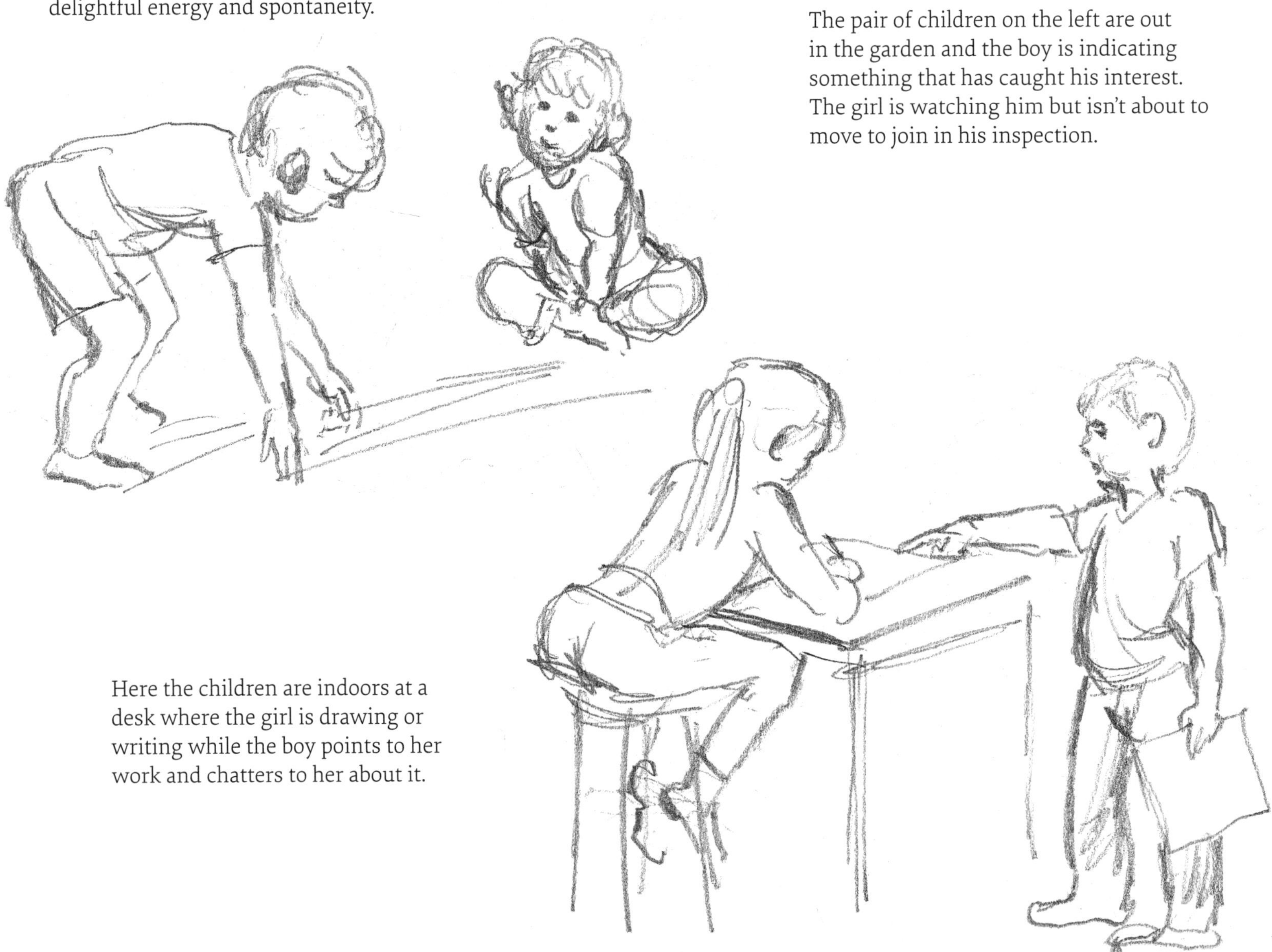

Here the children are indoors at a desk where the girl is drawing or writing while the boy points to her work and chatters to her about it.

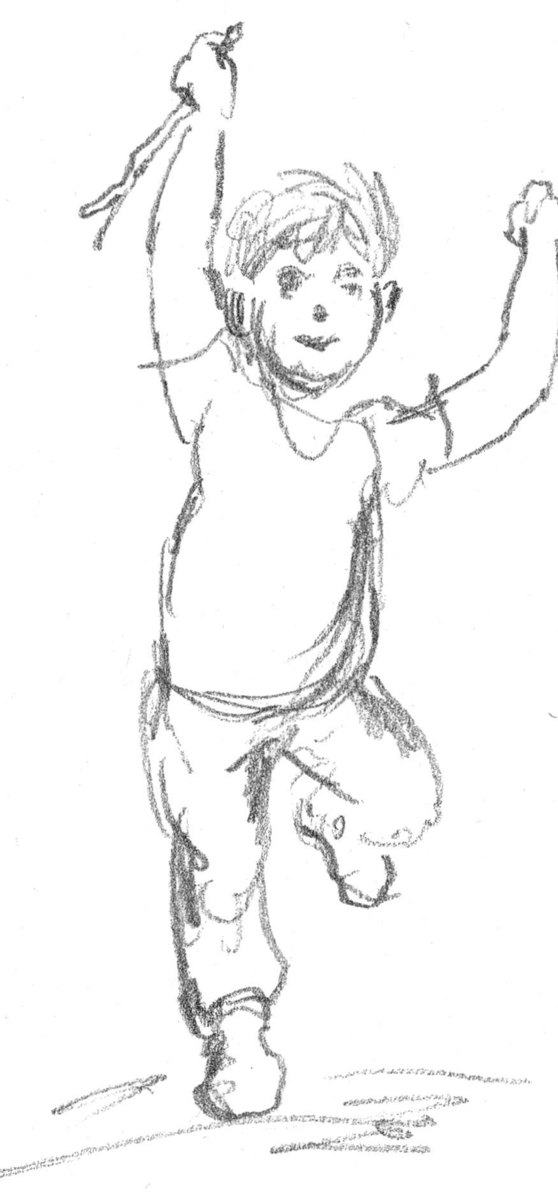

In the last two drawings the children are separate. The boy is running and brandishing a stick, while the girl is engaged in swinging a hoop around her waist. Both of these figures are very mobile and getting an exact sketch of their movements from life would be difficult. Once again the camera can come to the rescue, but do try to draw people in motion sometimes to catch the feeling of the movement rather than copying it frozen by the camera.

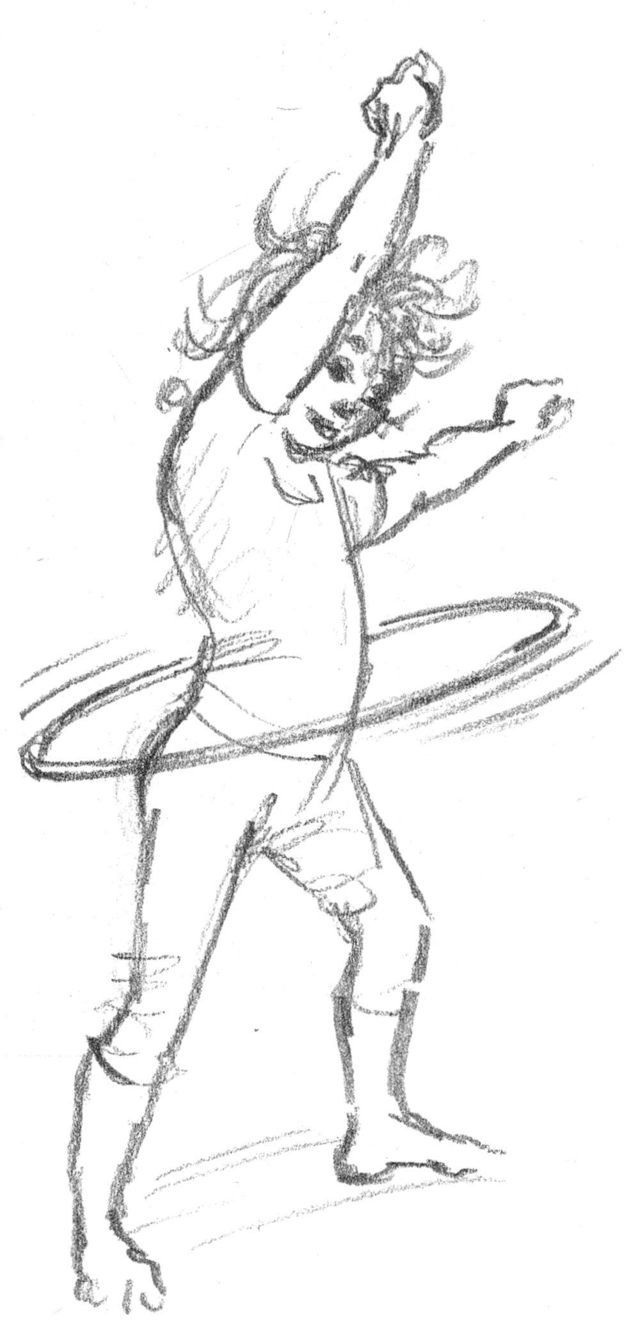

A Walking Figure

Once you have made a few sketches of moving figures, try your hand at a more detailed drawing. I chose a man walking a dog as my subject, to show how the figure when moving can be drawn with some convincing effect. I used pastel pencils, which give a soft slightly fuzzy line, to keep the drawing looking more mobile.

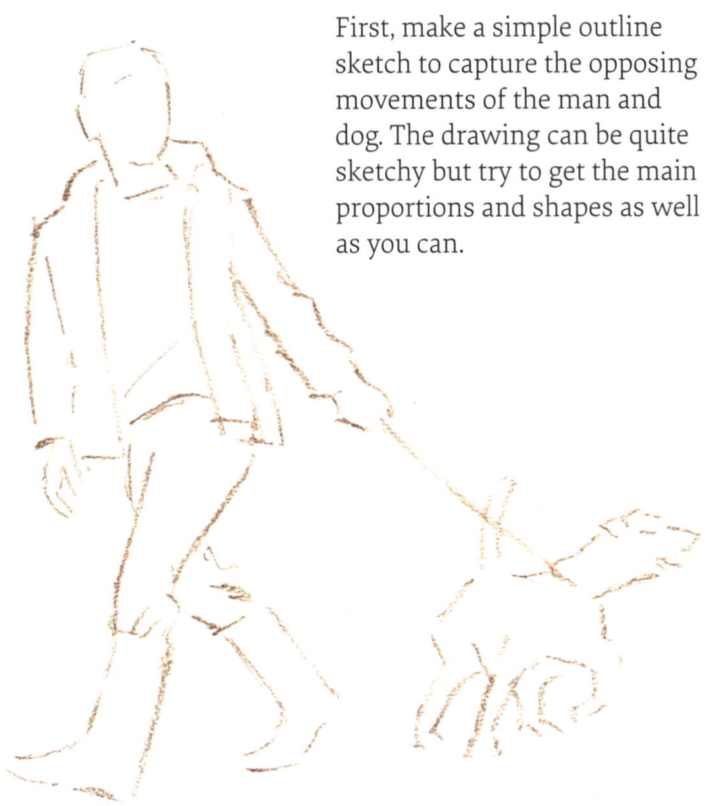

STEP 1

First, make a simple outline sketch to capture the opposing movements of the man and dog. The drawing can be quite sketchy but try to get the main proportions and shapes as well as you can.

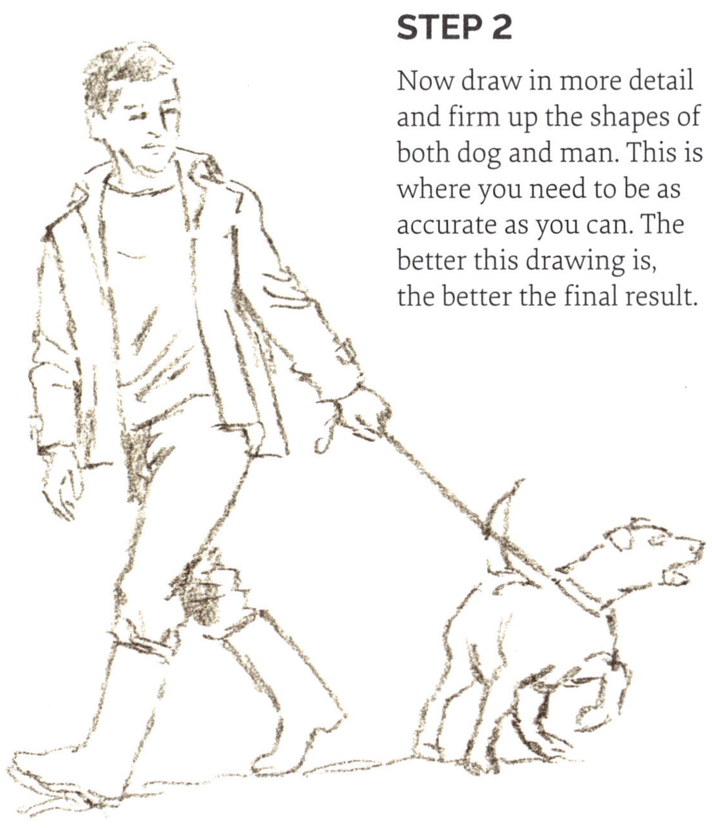

STEP 2

Now draw in more detail and firm up the shapes of both dog and man. This is where you need to be as accurate as you can. The better this drawing is, the better the final result.

Artist's Note

If you are not working in colour, sketch in the main areas of tone in a mid-tone in step 3, leaving white areas for the highlights. In the final step, refine your shading and add more tone to the darkest areas.

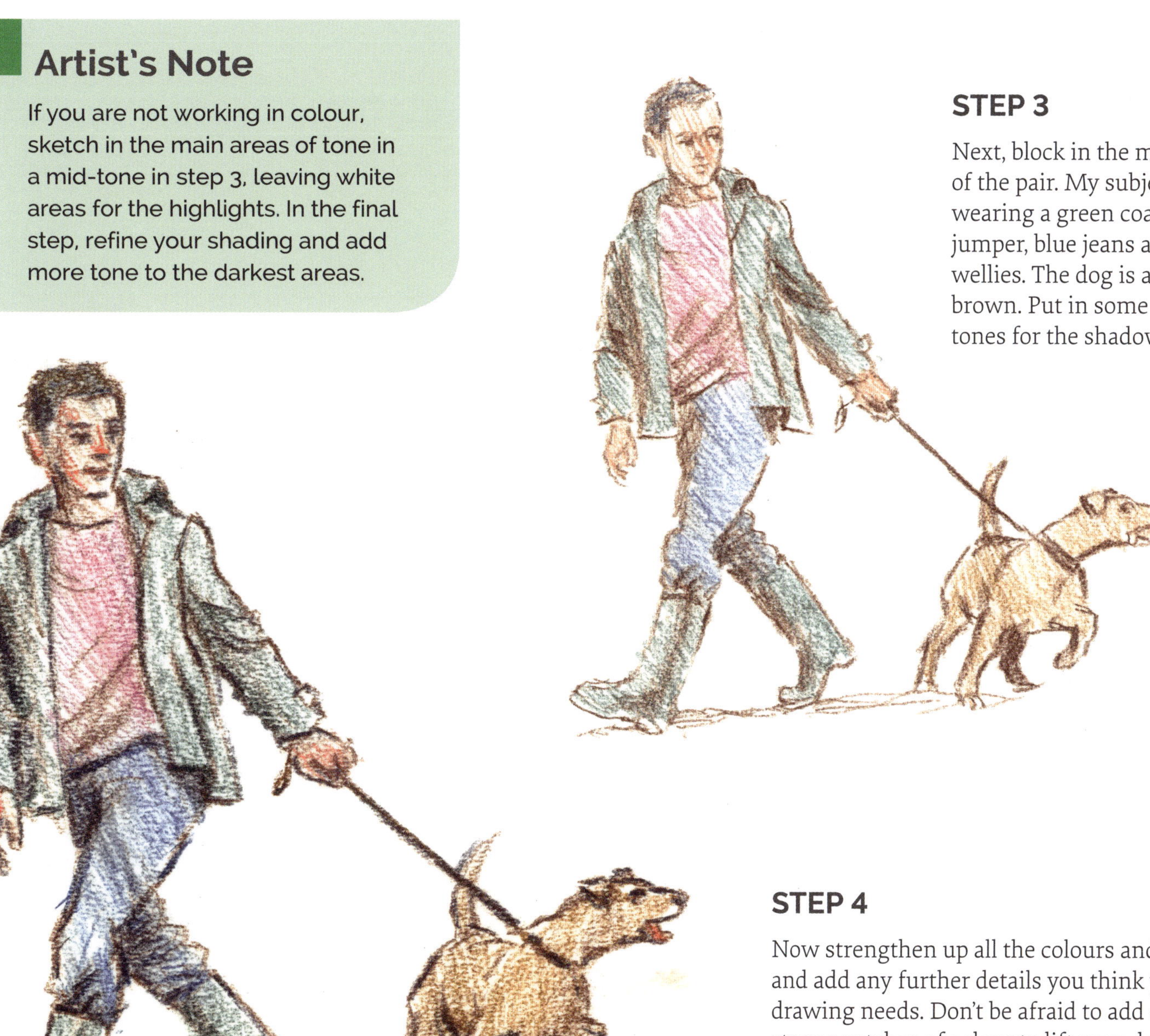

STEP 3

Next, block in the main colours of the pair. My subject was wearing a green coat, a purple jumper, blue jeans and green wellies. The dog is an overall brown. Put in some darker tones for the shadows.

STEP 4

Now strengthen up all the colours and tones and add any further details you think your drawing needs. Don't be afraid to add some strong patches of colour to lift your drawing: I used red pastel on the man's nose to suggest bracing outdoor air and exercise.

Body Language

Even when not walking, running or engaged in sporting activities, people are constantly moving. Often they adopt poses that convey their attitude and emotional state, whether that is slouching in a dejected posture, or gesturing wildly with excitement. If you can capture this body language in your drawings, your subjects will seem more human and believable.

Shortcuts to body language

Here are some stickmen (a graphic shorthand for the human figure) in the sort of positions that the human body might adopt when trying to express certain attitudes.

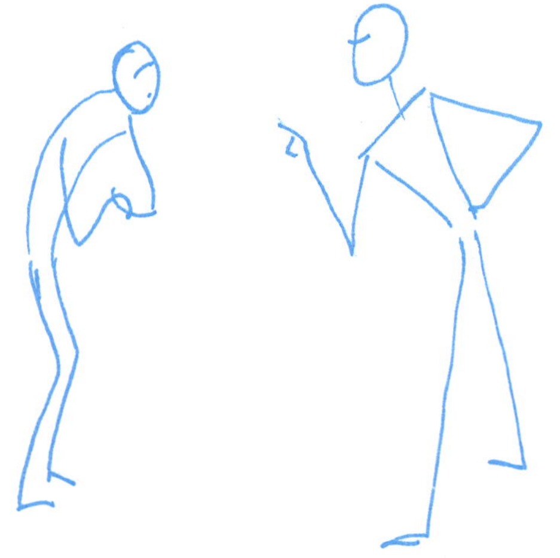

1 The figure on the left suggests humility. The hands are wrung together, the shoulders droop, the face expresses worry. Also, the feet are turned a bit towards each other to give the idea that the figure will not move far.

2 The second figure is quite the opposite, in that it seems to be taking charge of things and laying down the law: hand on hip, the other wagging a finger in disapproval, firm stance on both feet, and a frown on the face.

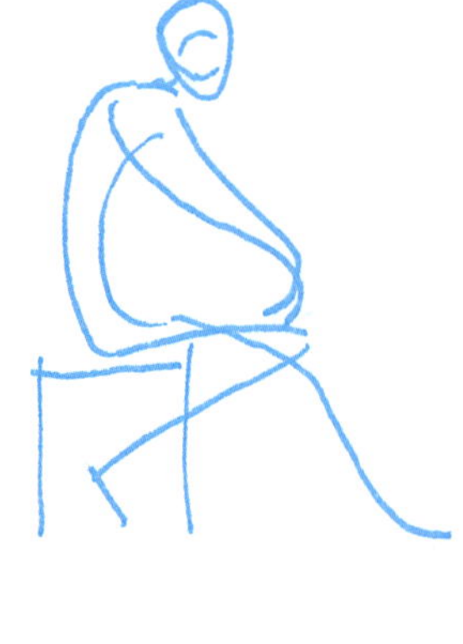

3 This figure could be a bit ambiguous: caught in some form of embarrassment, an uncomfortable gesture of hands poking knees, legs a bit constricted, face apologetic but grinning to get approval. He is probably at a crowded function and feeling out of place.

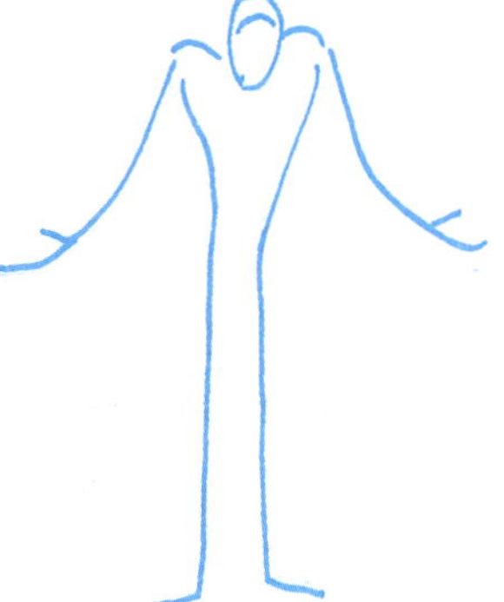

4 The classic pose of disbelief, with the shoulders shrugging and the arms and hands held out in a questioning attitude. A raised brow indicates an expression of surprise.

5 Triumph, demonstrated in the familiar gesture of punching the air, accompanied by a big grin.

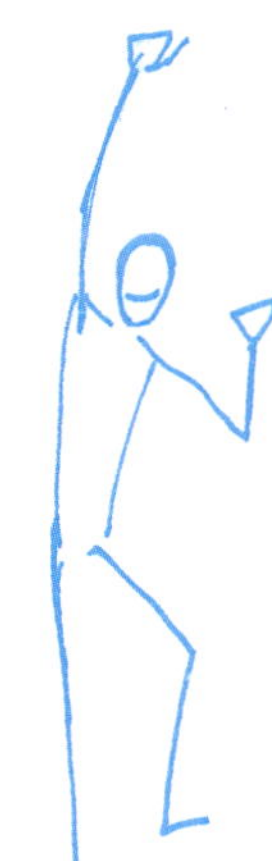

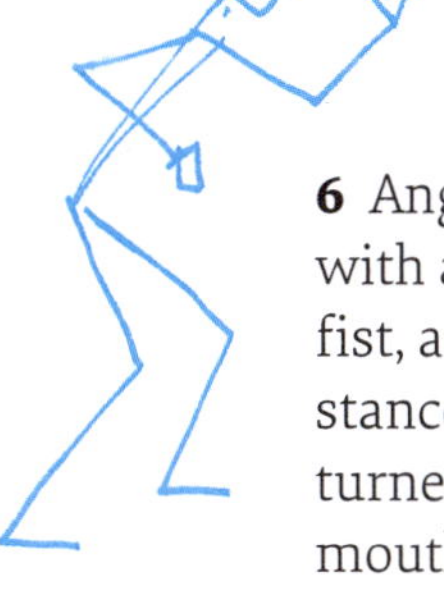

6 Anger shown with a shaken fist, an aggressive stance and down-turned brows and mouth.

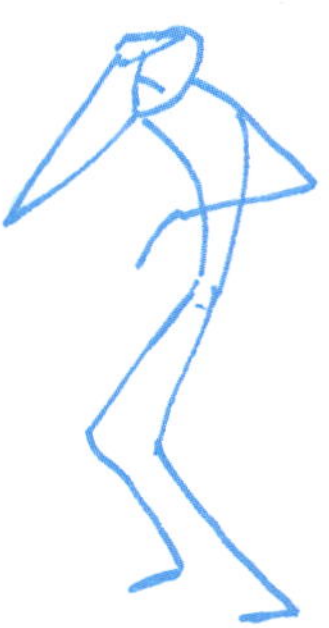

7 Guilt is shown with the hand clapped over the eyes and an apologetic stoop to the whole body.

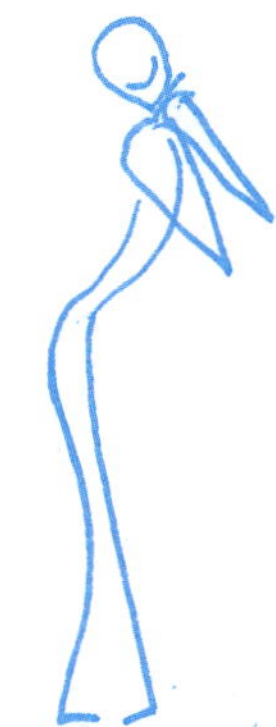

8 Adoration is difficult to show subtly, so I have gone for a cartoon-style exaggeration of hands-to-face, big smile, squirming body and close-together feet.

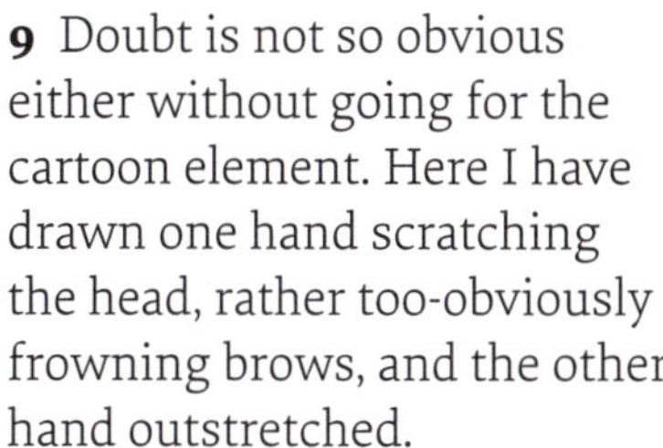

9 Doubt is not so obvious either without going for the cartoon element. Here I have drawn one hand scratching the head, rather too-obviously frowning brows, and the other hand outstretched.

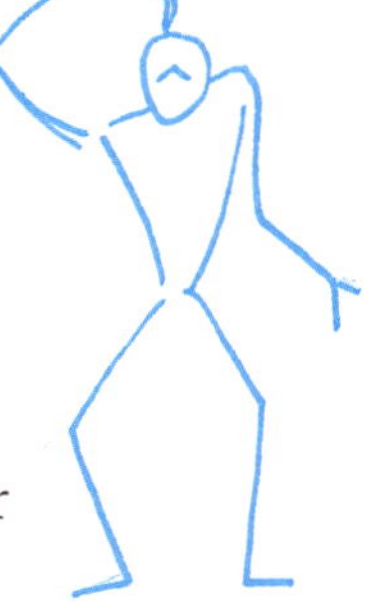

10 Determination shows a fast-moving figure with fists clenched, head pushed forward, chest stuck out. A real 'don't get in my way' attitude.

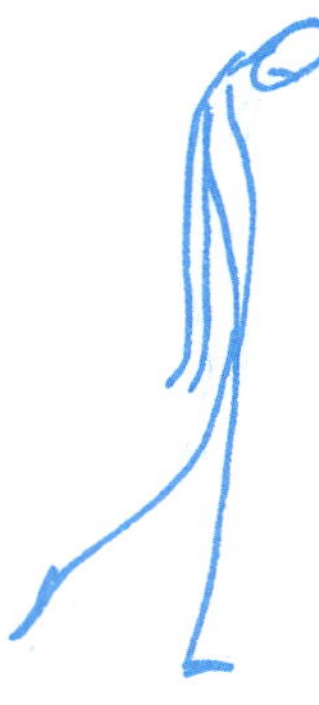

11 The unwilling figure is rather like Shakespeare's reluctant schoolboy, dragging his feet, with arms and head drooping, and a downturned mouth.

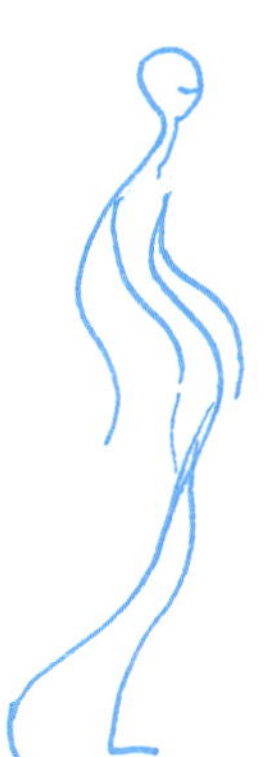

12 This sinuous figure, gliding along with everything smoothly undulating, is someone confident of attracting attention. The smile on the face also gives a clue.

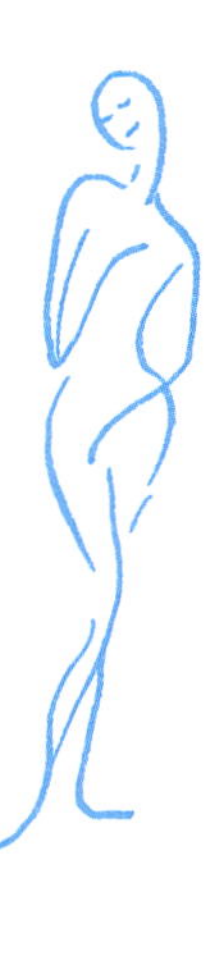

13 This figure has adopted the classical 'contrapposto' pose where the hips and shoulders are counterbalanced. The arms are gesturing to cover the body and are reminiscent of the central figure in Botticelli's *Birth of Venus*. Like the goddess of love and beauty, the figure seems to be responding to adoration.

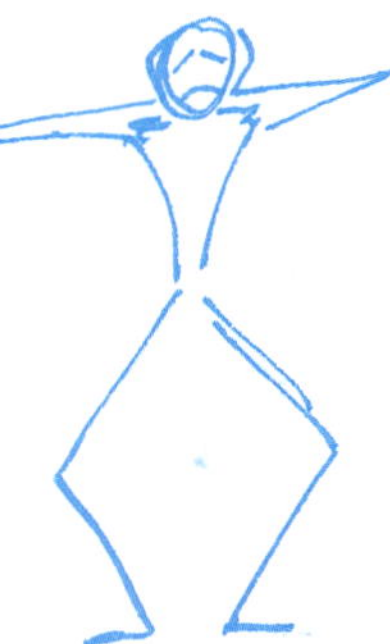

14 Lastly, the figure of distraction with the 'I'm going mad' look: hands holding the head, face showing anguish, and knees bent to brace against shock.

These are just a few of the shapes that our bodies assume to express emotional states, and no doubt you will have fun trying out other expressions of body language in your own figure drawings.

Capturing body language

The next series of figures are more considered examples of how to express something characterful through attitudes and dispositions. I show first four male and then four female forms that give impressions of certain attitudes.

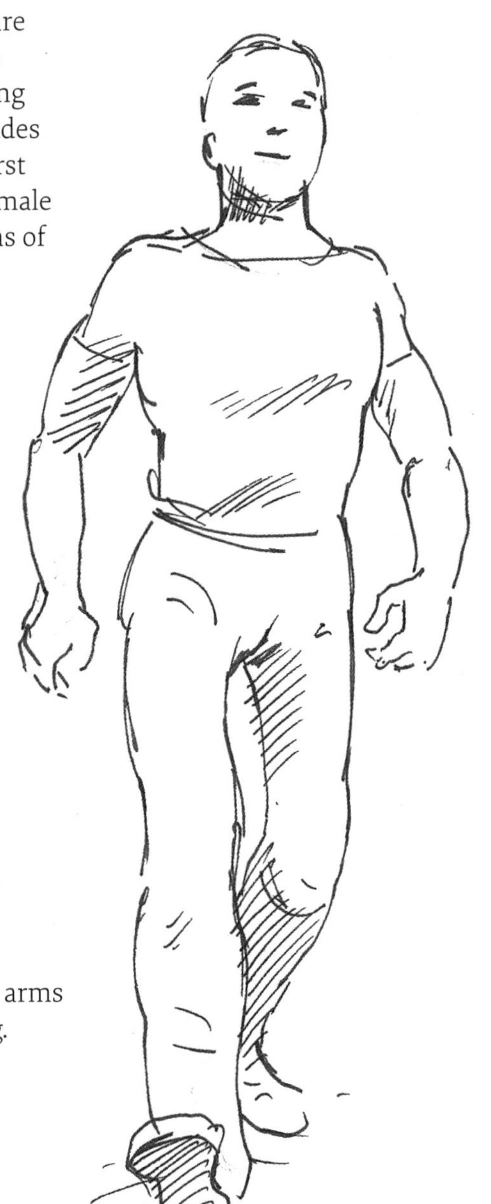

Swagger

Here is the classic cocky swagger usually shown by younger men when they think they have everyone's approval. Upright posture, arms swinging and legs striding.

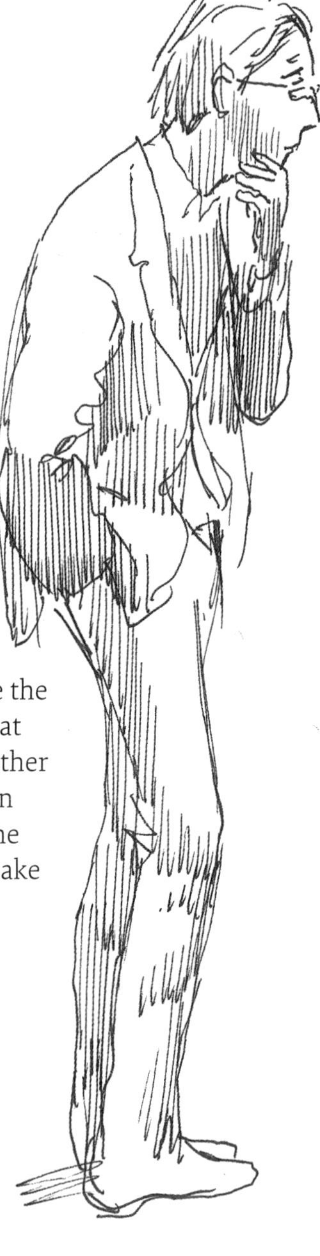

Doubt

Now for the opposite, where the figure looks as if he is in great doubt about something. A rather scholarly stroking of the chin complements the stoop of the shoulders. This chap can't make up his mind at all.

Confidence

The relaxed gesture of someone who thinks that they know all about the topic in question. Possibly a little conceited with it, as well.

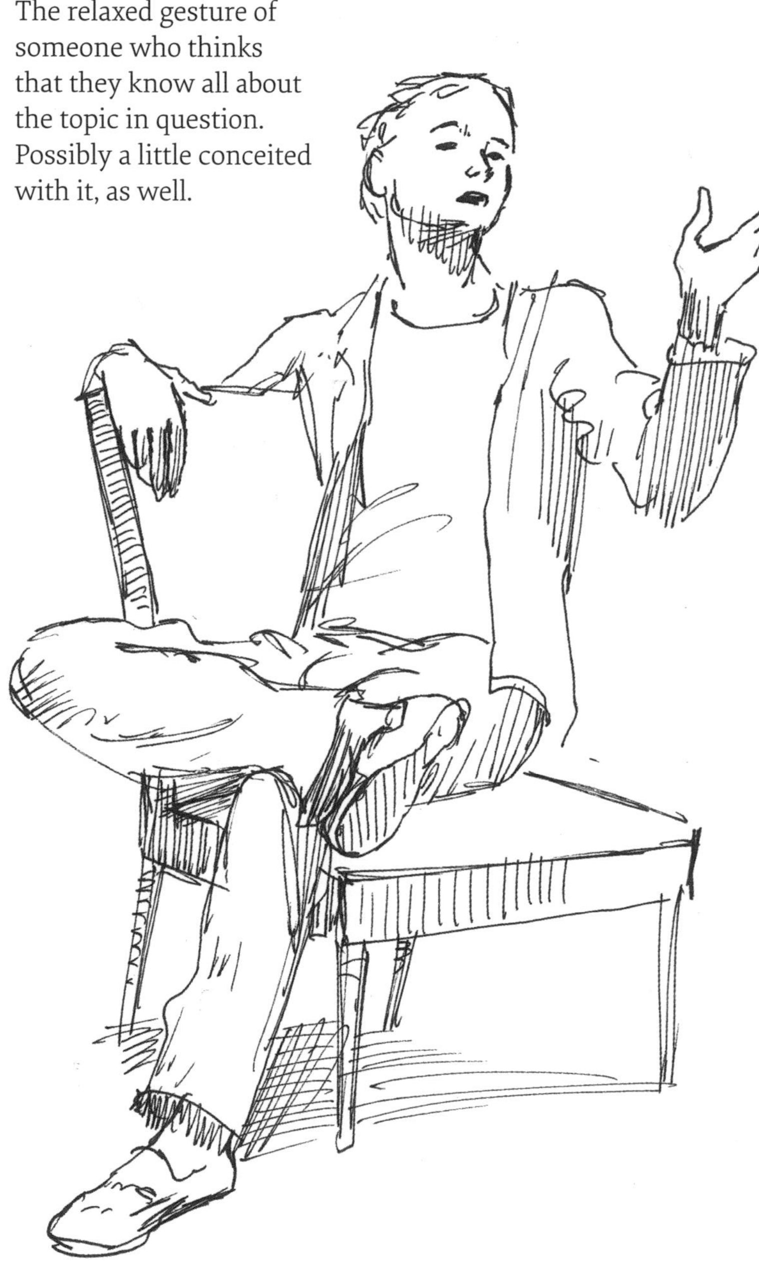

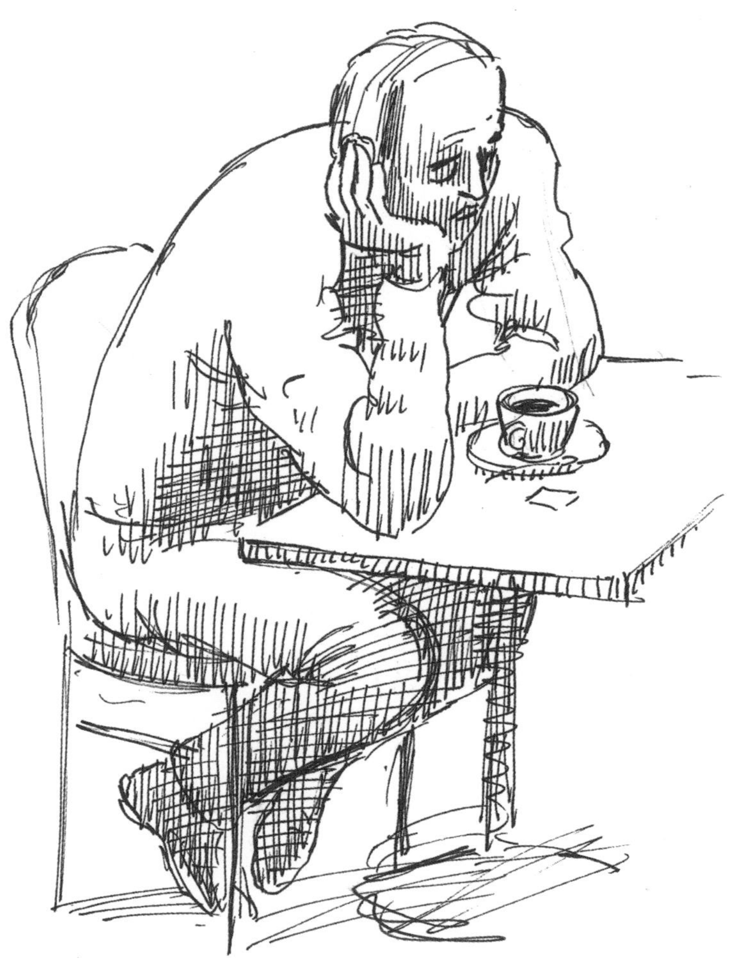

Despair

This poor fellow has obviously been crossed in love or lost his job. Total droop suggests despair rather than just fatigue, the tucked-in feet showing tension.

Assuredness

This young lady looks like a ballet dancer with her out-turned toes, her upright stance, poise and confident appearance.

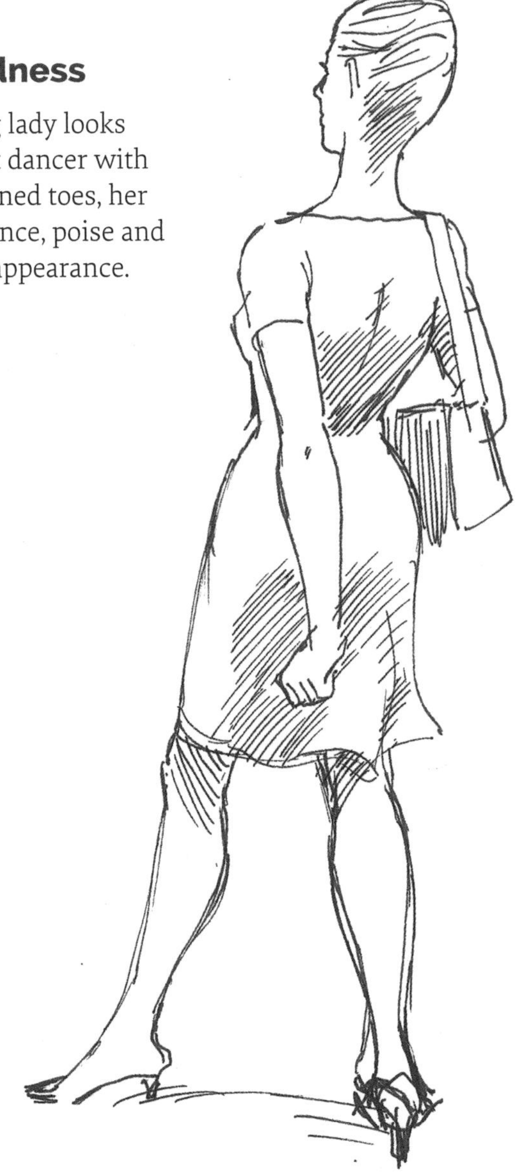

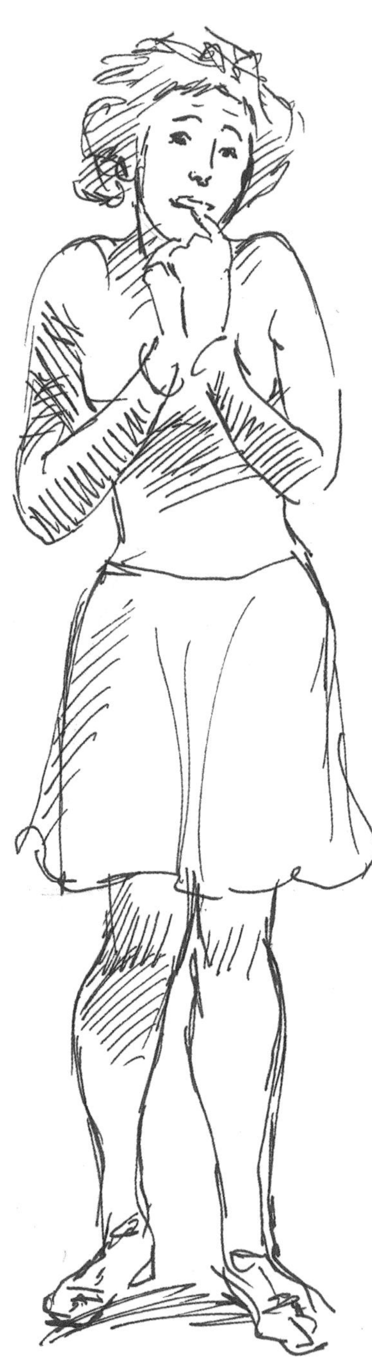

Embarrassment

This figure is reduced to a squirming held-together shape, with hands up to her mouth and anxious eyebrows. Not a happy situation to be in.

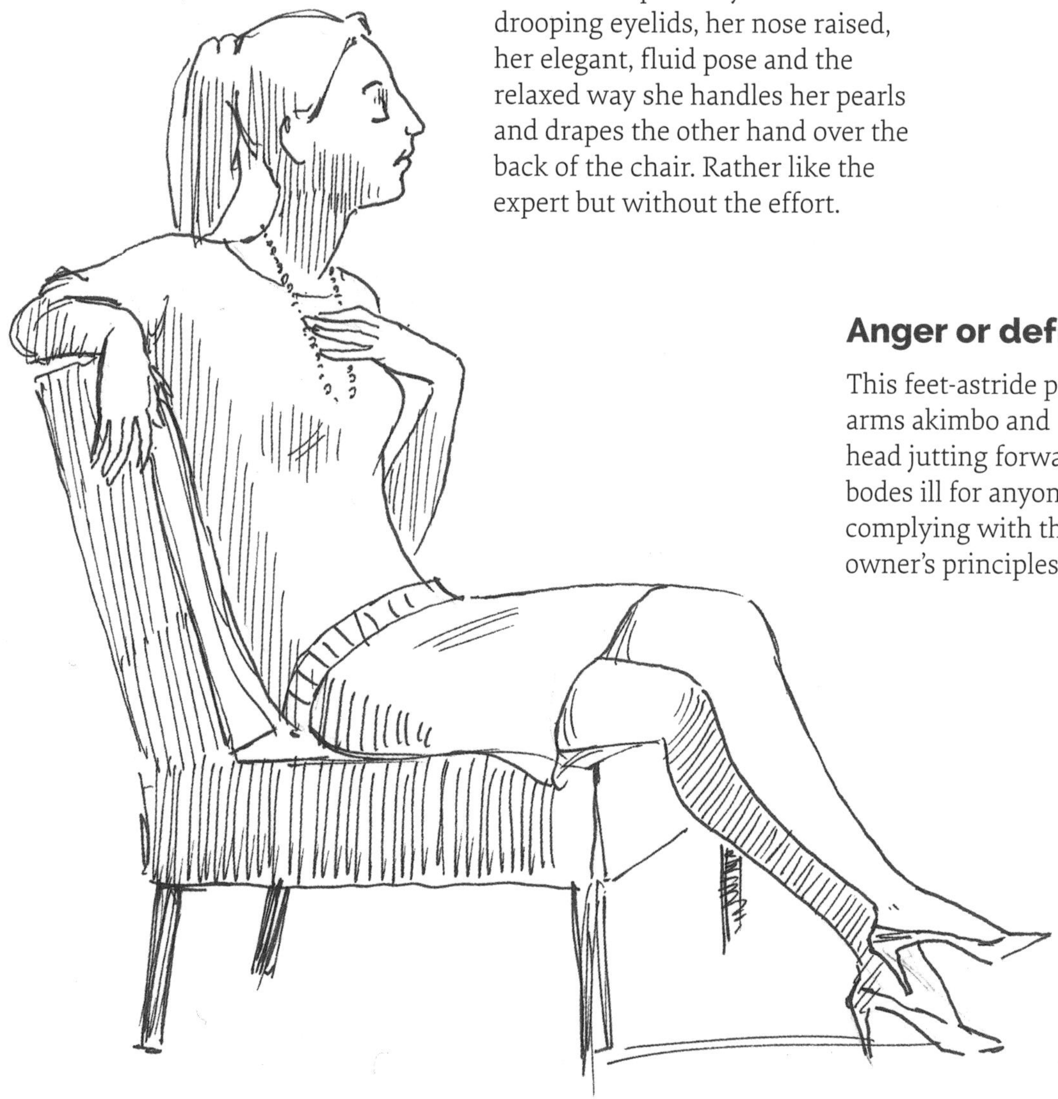

Disdain

The sitting figure evinces effortless superiority with her drooping eyelids, her nose raised, her elegant, fluid pose and the relaxed way she handles her pearls and drapes the other hand over the back of the chair. Rather like the expert but without the effort.

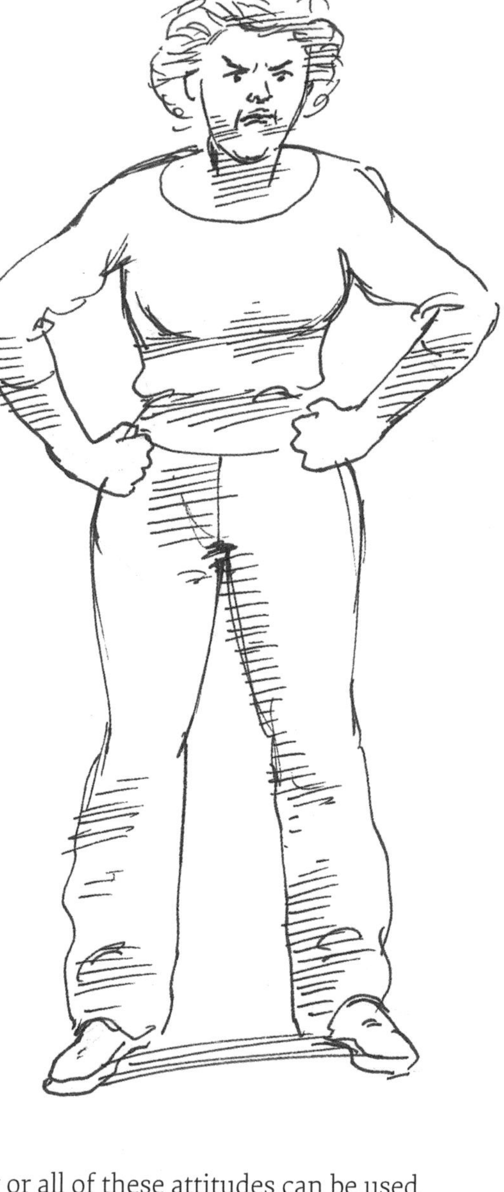

Anger or defiance

This feet-astride position, arms akimbo and head jutting forwards, bodes ill for anyone not complying with the owner's principles.

Any or all of these attitudes can be used in your figure compositions to create activity or tension in the picture or to get a dynamic story across to the viewer.

Sports

Here we look at the whole body engaged in action, through a range of sporting activities. Some of the figures are nude, but generally speaking it is possible to see the shape of the body well enough under clothing. It is very interesting for an artist to watch sportspeople and observe what happens to the musculature as they move.

Climbing

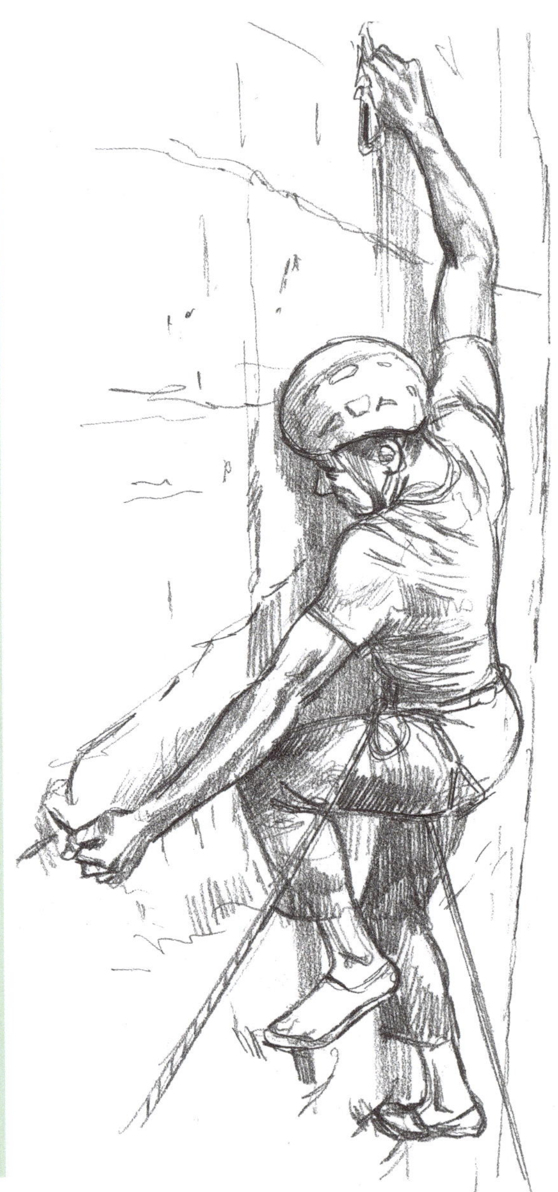

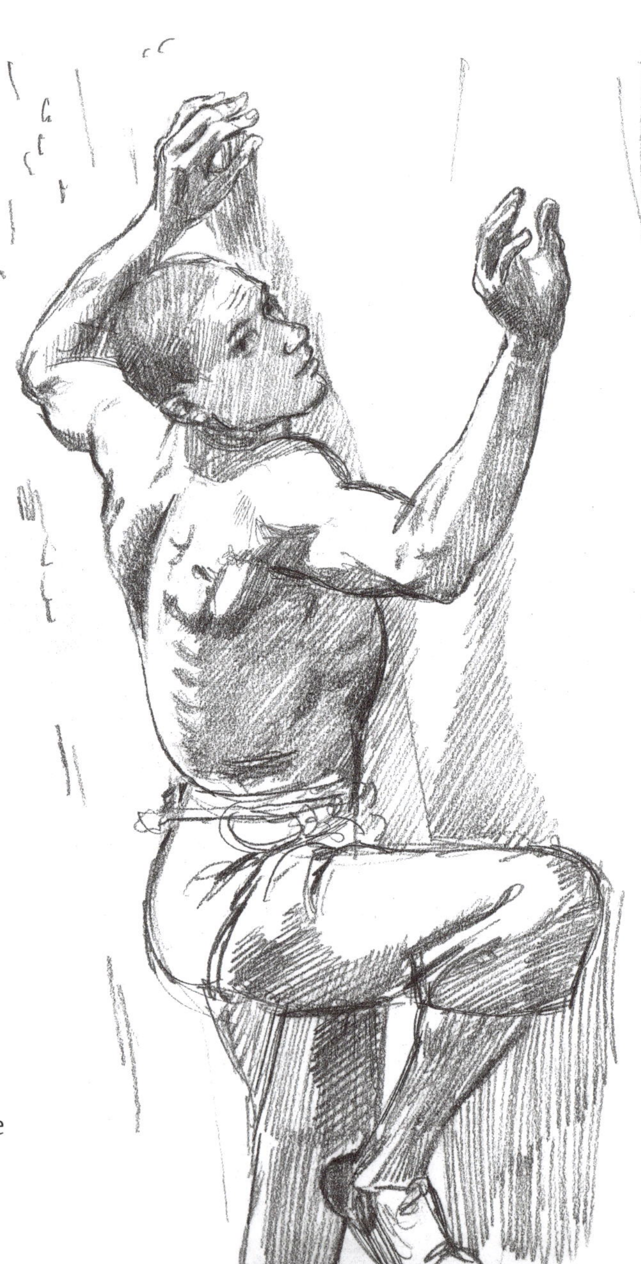

Climbing, one of the more extreme sports, relies on tremendous muscle co-ordination. It is also the sport which calls most upon your sense of balance and the ability to grip well with your hands and feet. Observe the great tension shown in the body when it is clinging to a difficult rock-face; notice the muscles in the arms and back.

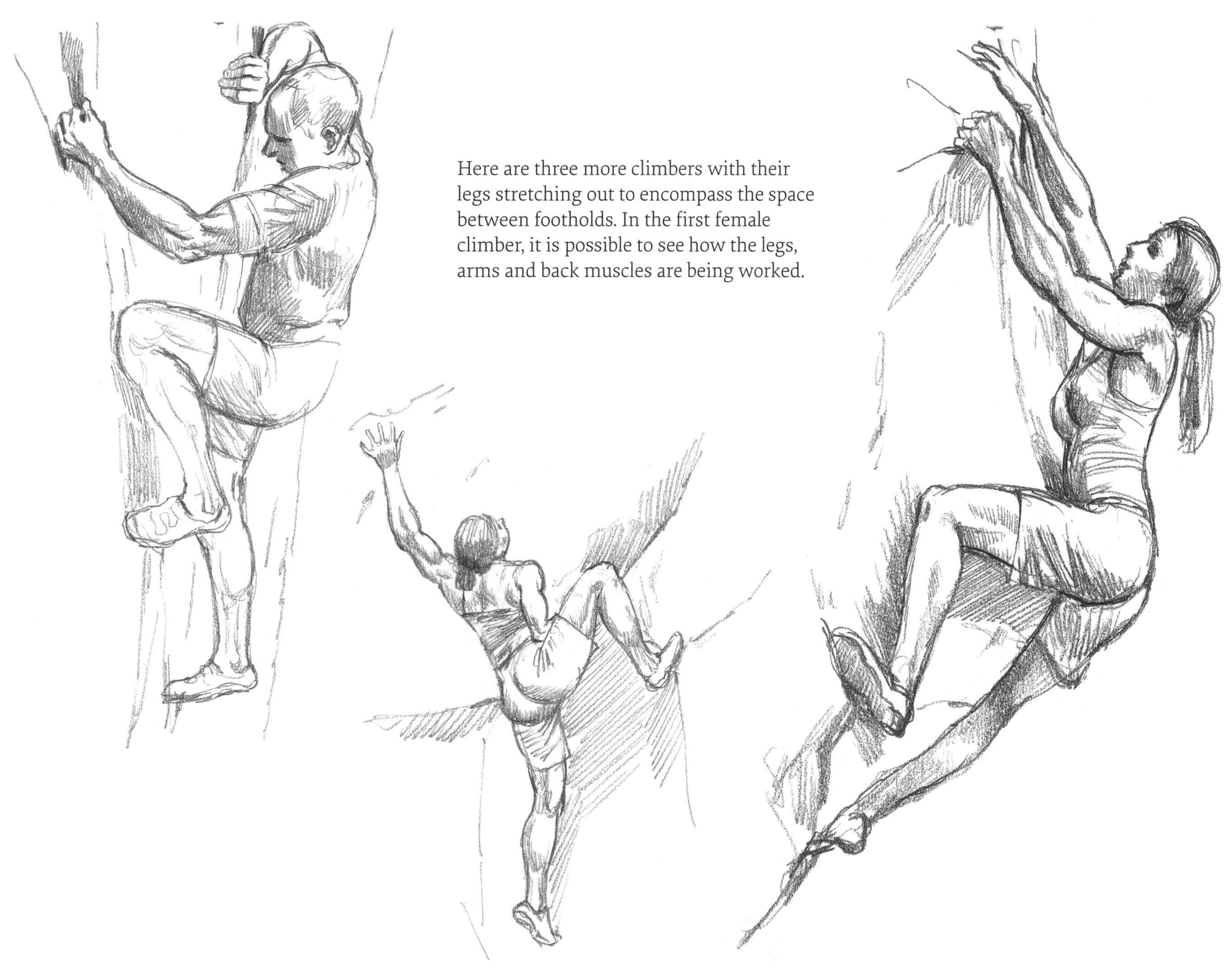

Here are three more climbers with their legs stretching out to encompass the space between footholds. In the first female climber, it is possible to see how the legs, arms and back muscles are being worked.

Football

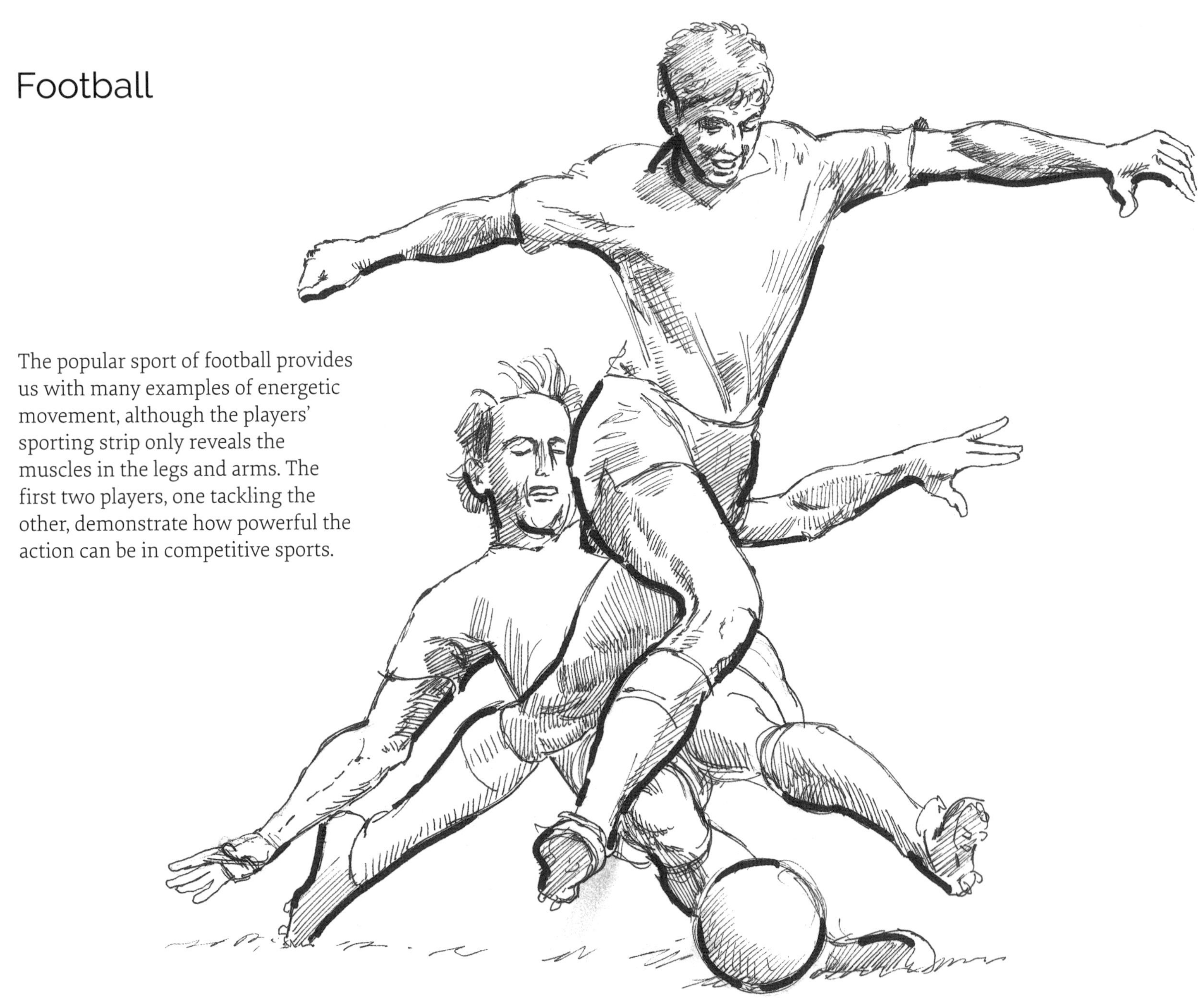

The popular sport of football provides us with many examples of energetic movement, although the players' sporting strip only reveals the muscles in the legs and arms. The first two players, one tackling the other, demonstrate how powerful the action can be in competitive sports.

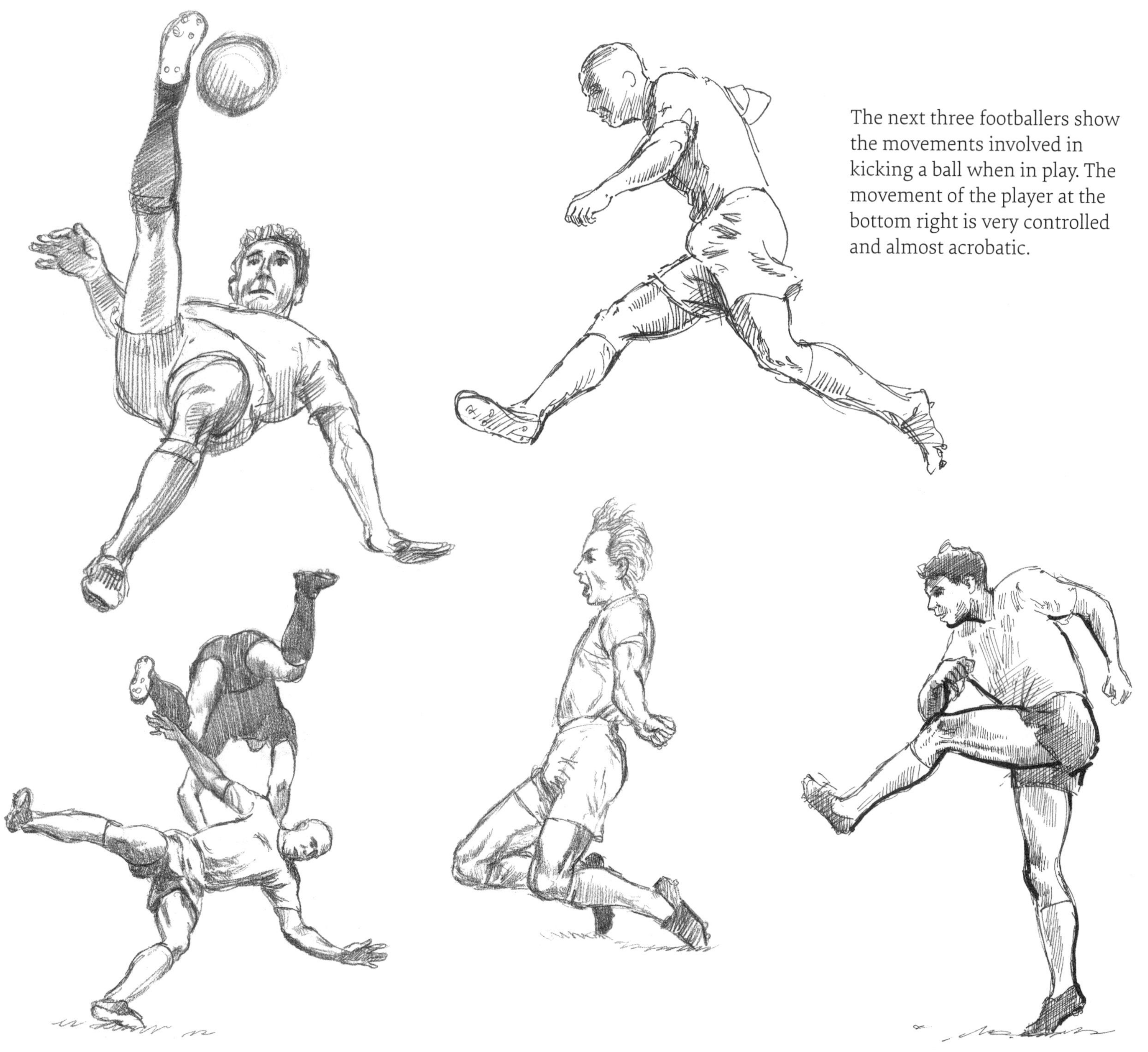

The next three footballers show the movements involved in kicking a ball when in play. The movement of the player at the bottom right is very controlled and almost acrobatic.

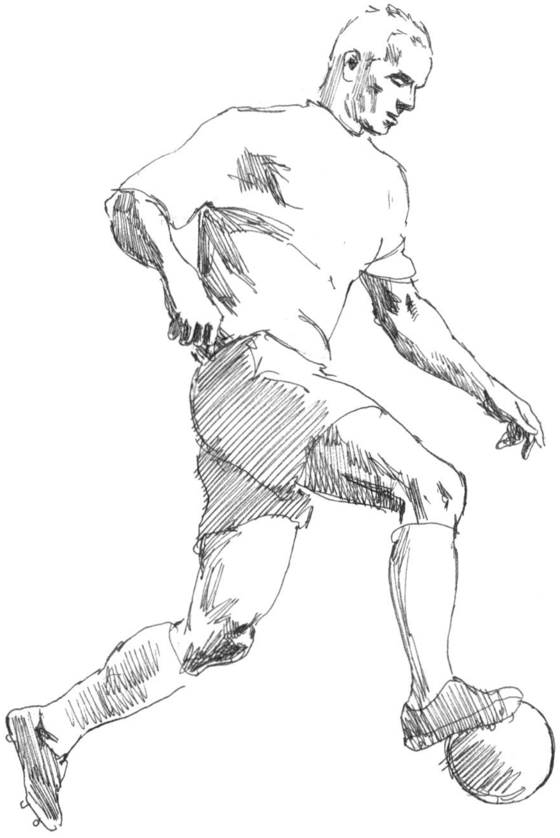

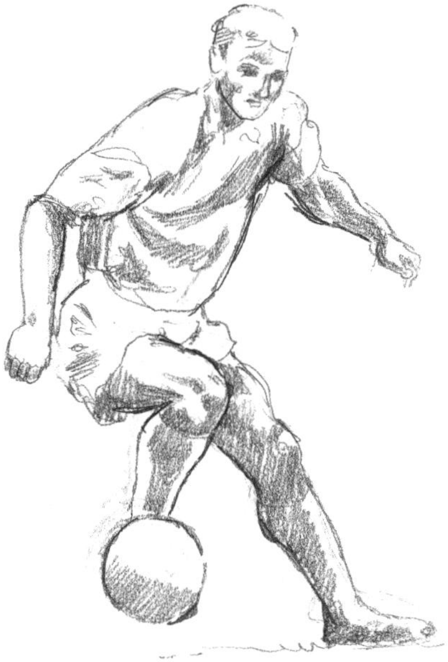

These four pictures show the balance and effort required when moving fast and trying to control a ball with your feet at the same time. Notice how, in every case, the players are using their limbs to keep the body in movement and balanced at the same time.

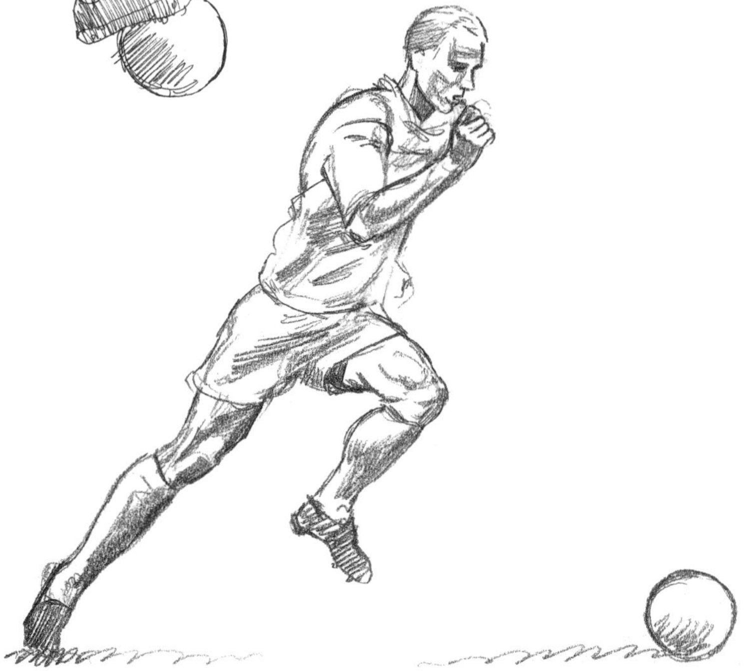

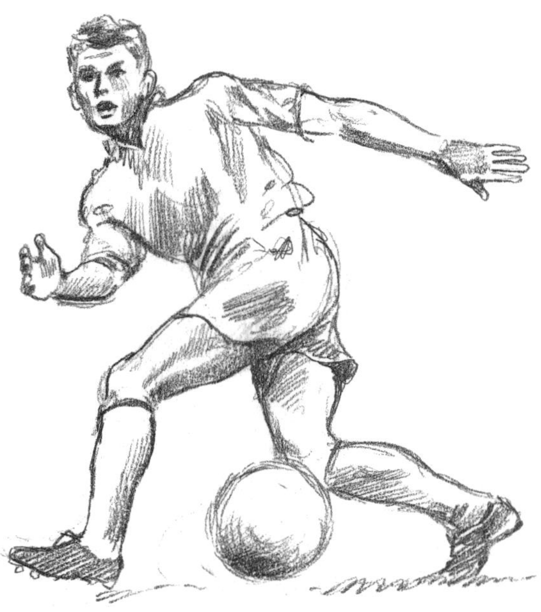

Dancing

The next picture shows a dancer suspended in midair, in the middle of a great leap, and it is obvious enough that this pose could only have been captured by a camera. Clearly the figure is not supported by anything except her own impetus. Note how the coloured hatching on the dancer's skin helps to show the angles of her body and the direction of movement.

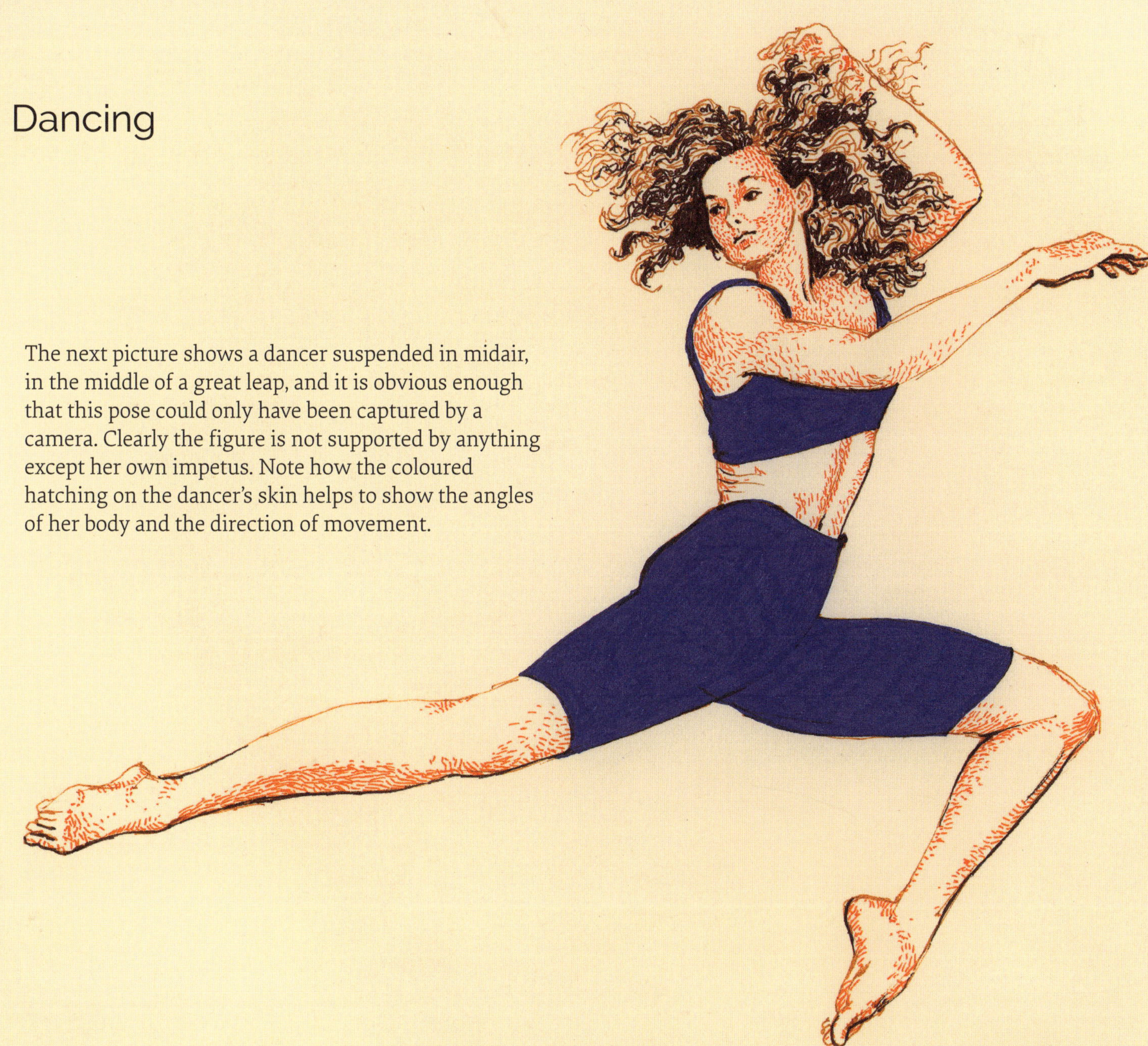

Jumping

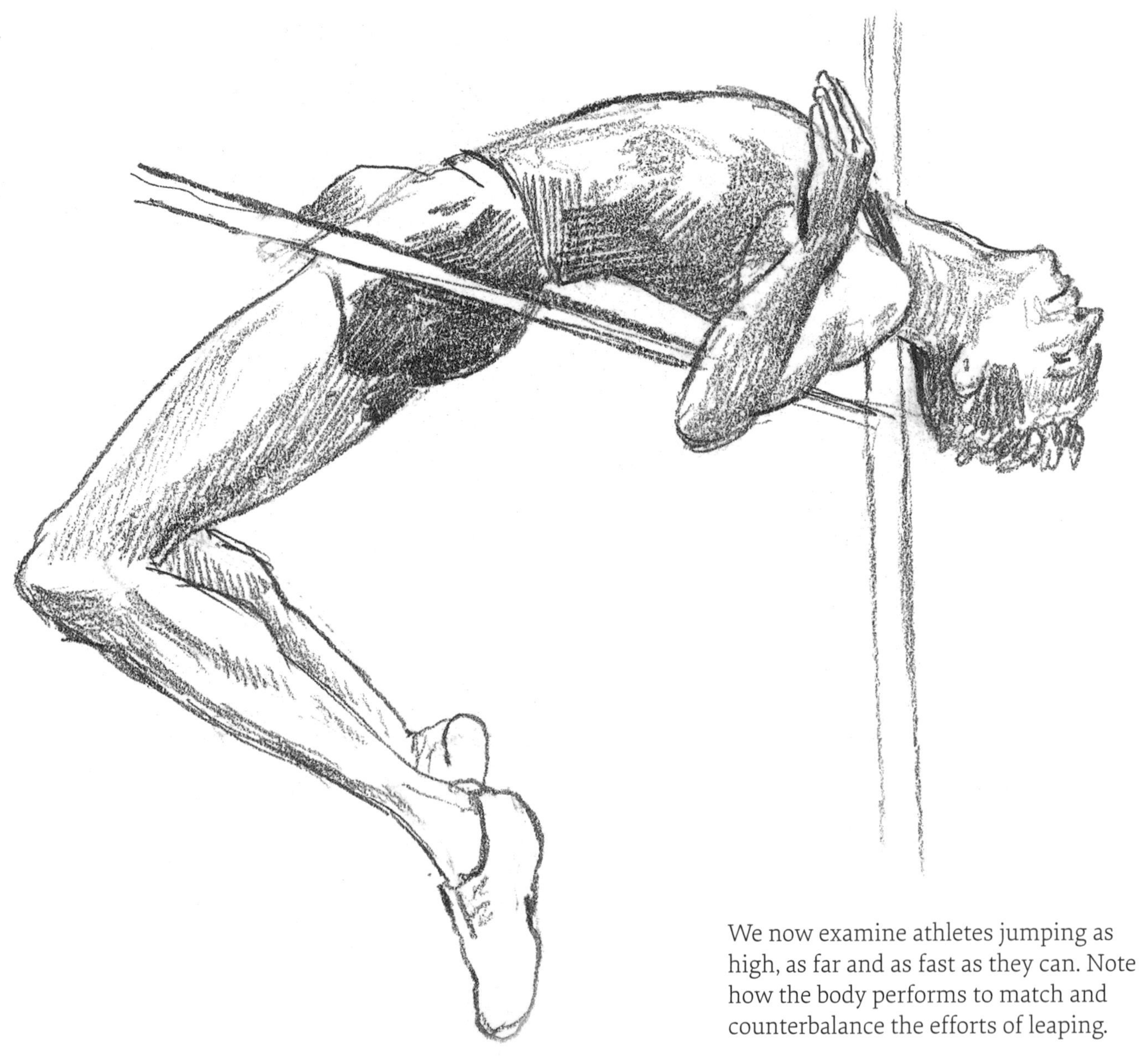

We now examine athletes jumping as high, as far and as fast as they can. Note how the body performs to match and counterbalance the efforts of leaping.

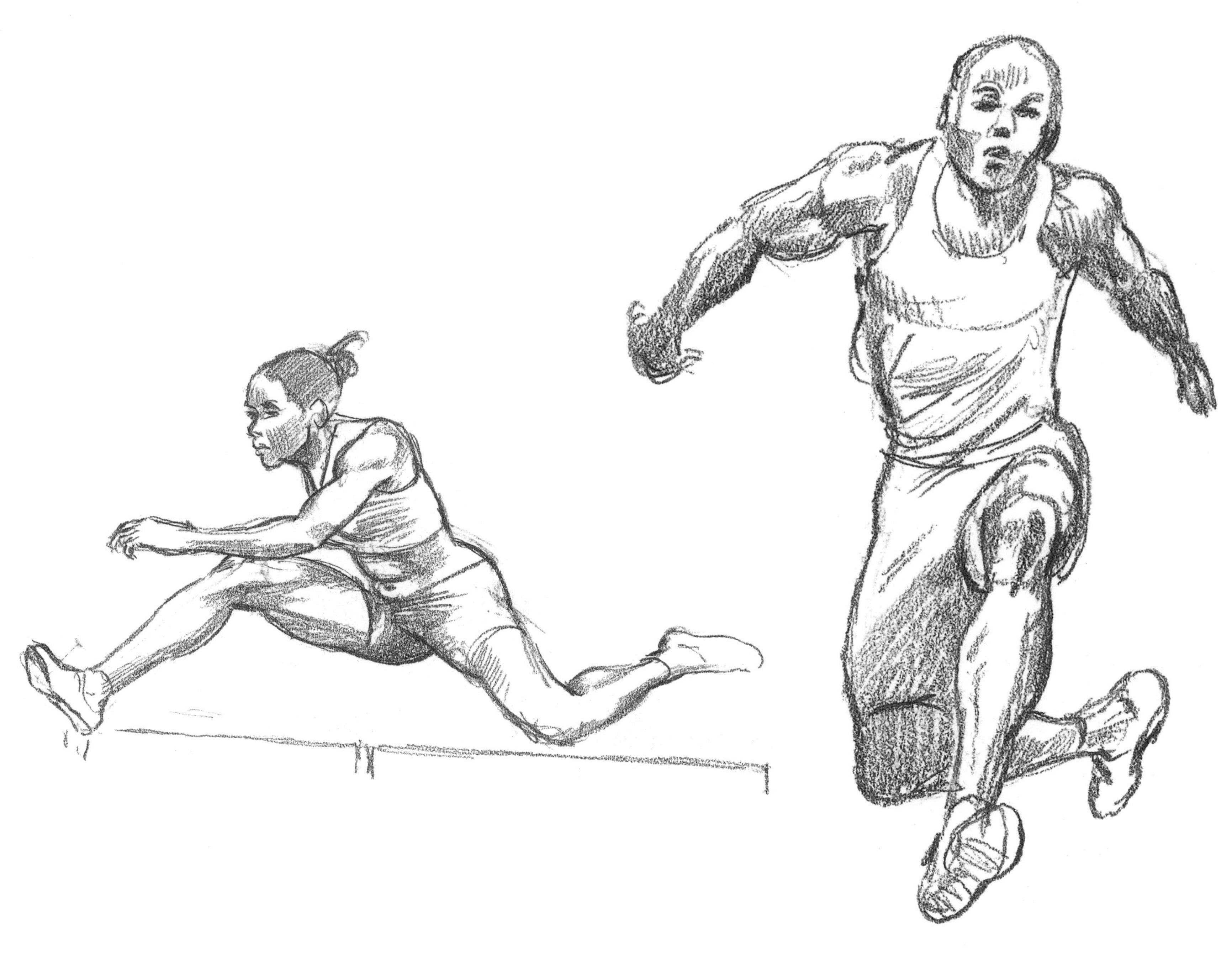

Throwing

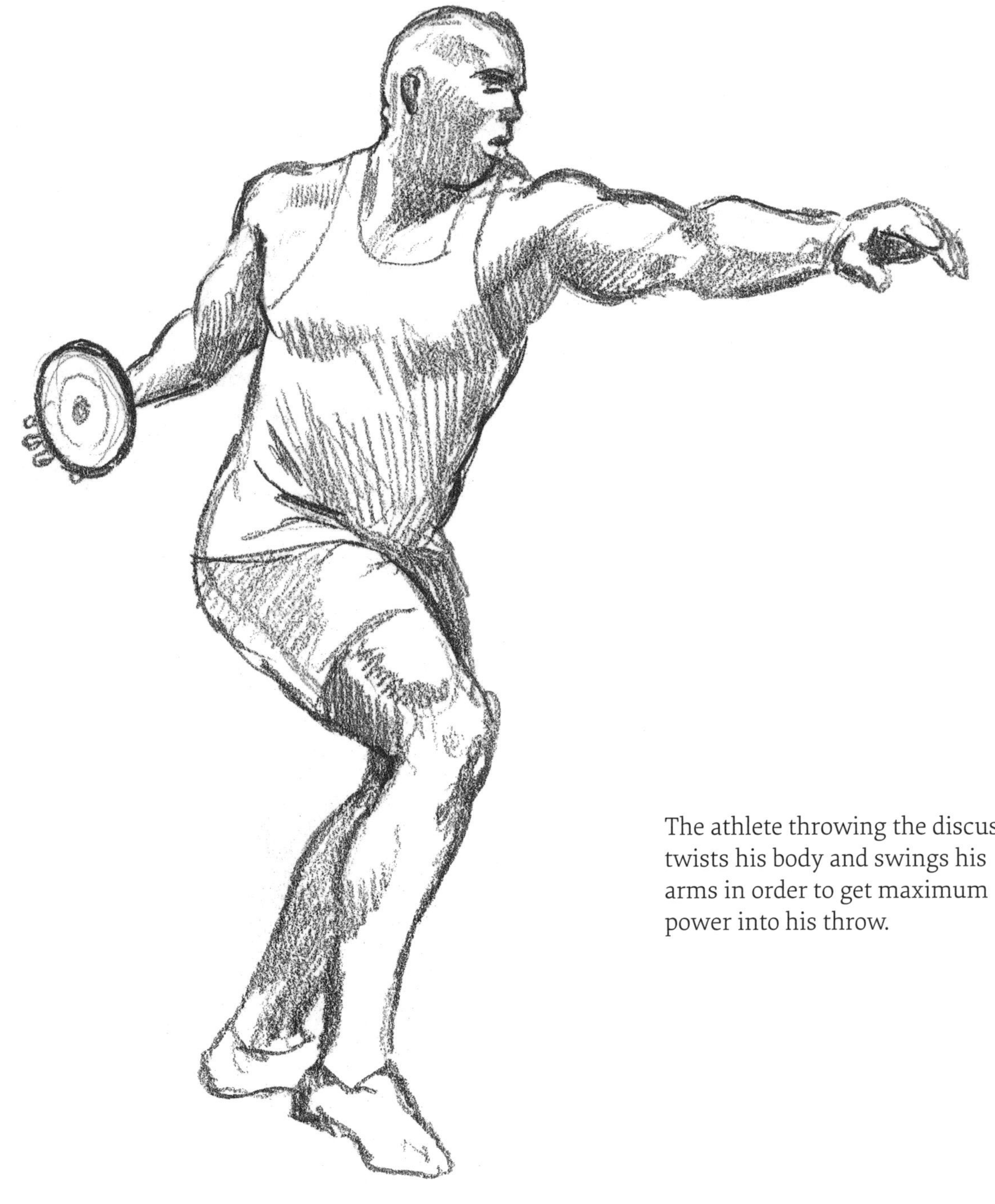

The athlete throwing the discus twists his body and swings his arms in order to get maximum power into his throw.

Running

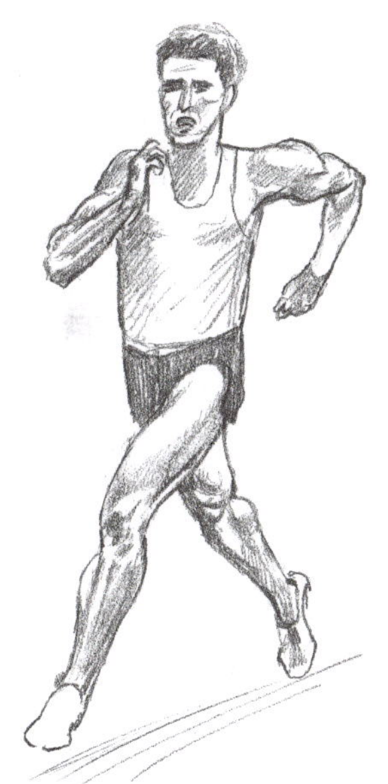

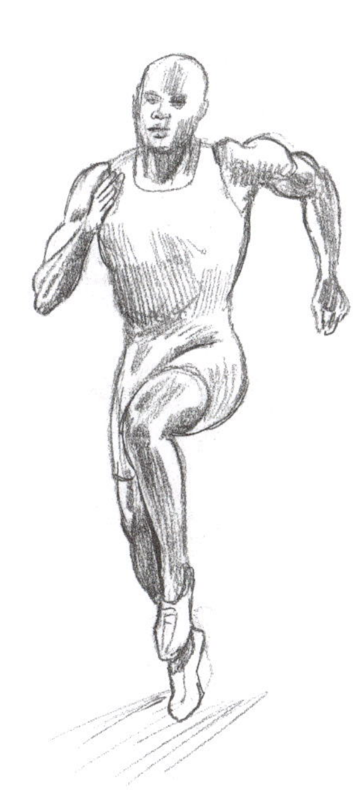

The two runners illustrate the body's efforts to gain speed along a level surface, pumping the arms and legs to keep them moving as fast as possible while remaining balanced and controlled.

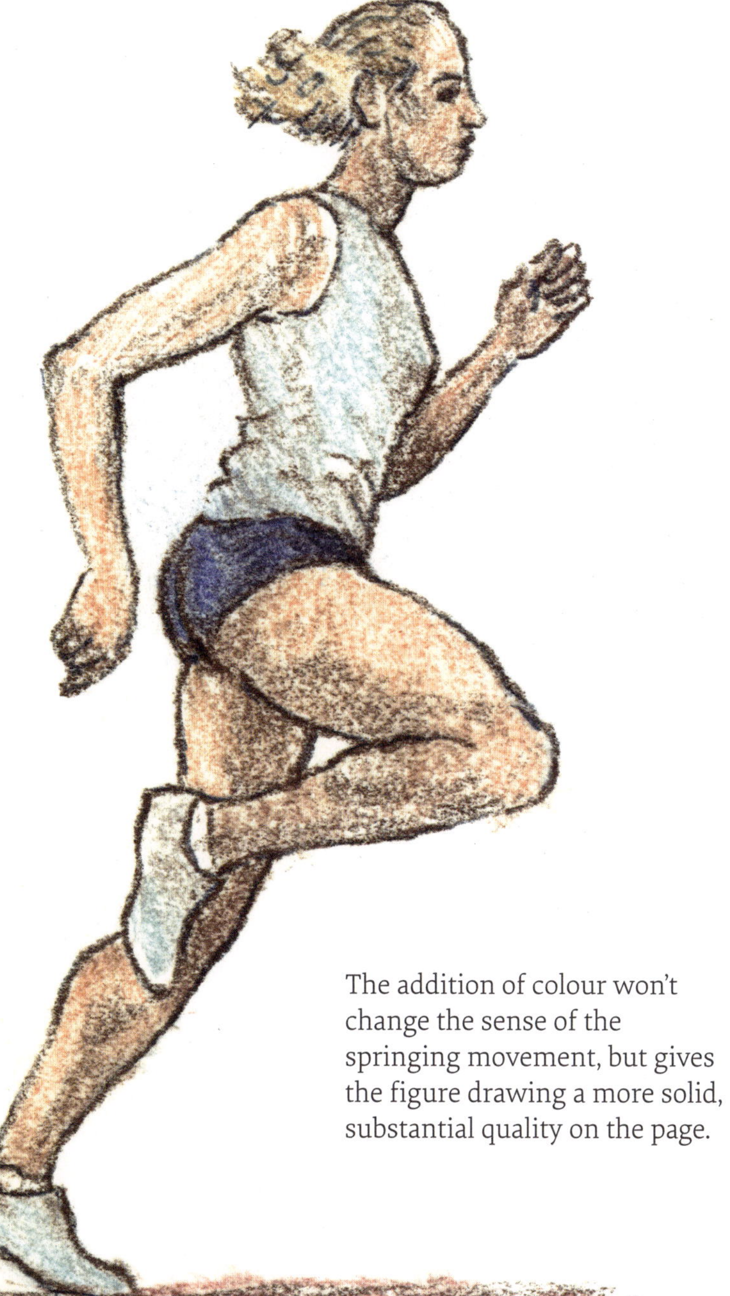

The addition of colour won't change the sense of the springing movement, but gives the figure drawing a more solid, substantial quality on the page.

Wrestling

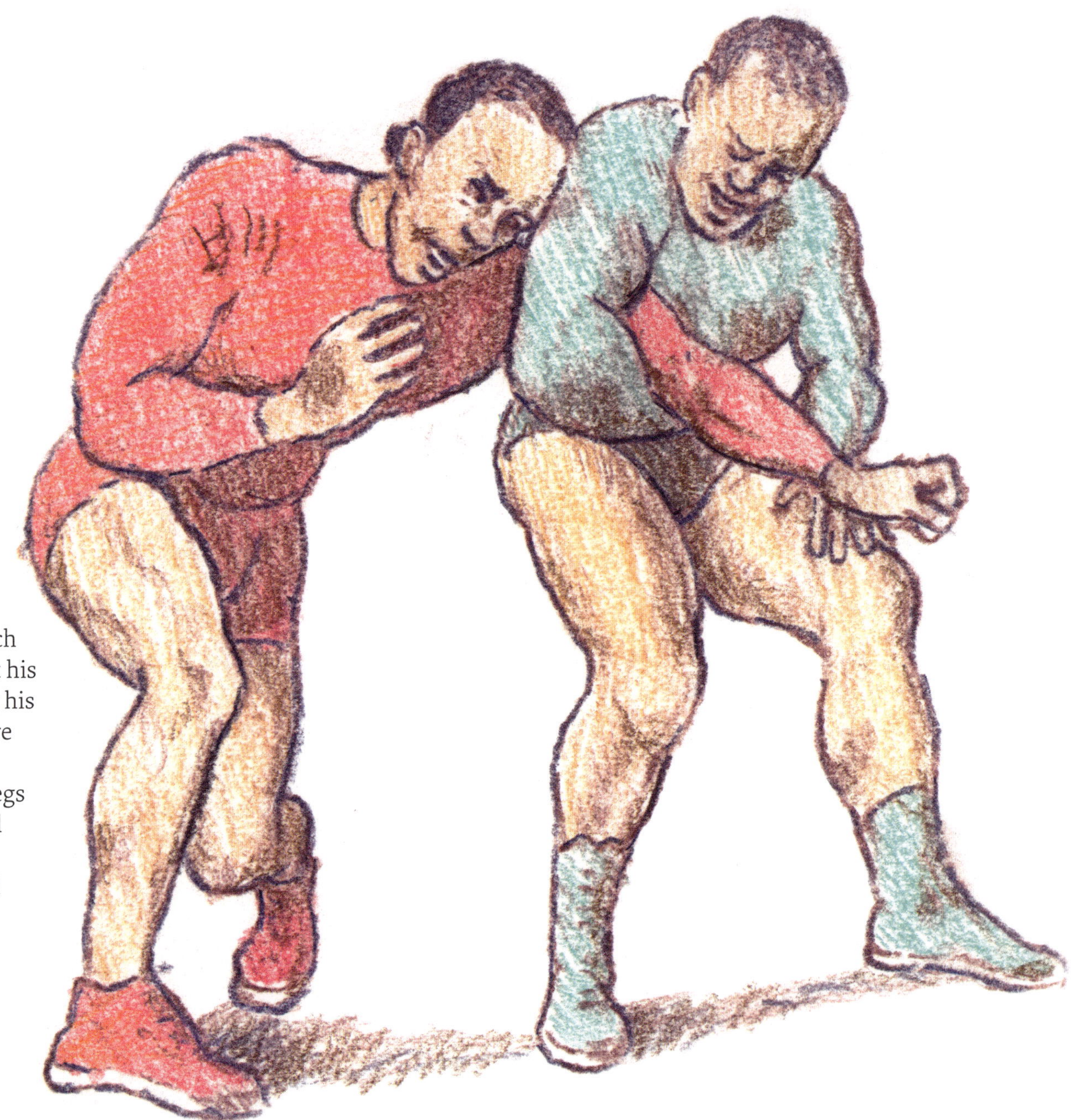

In this wrestling pair, each man is straining to upset his opponent without losing his own balance. In the figure on the left, the strange angles of the wrestler's legs demonstrate the unusual positions the body can adopt in intense physical situations such as this.

Weightlifting

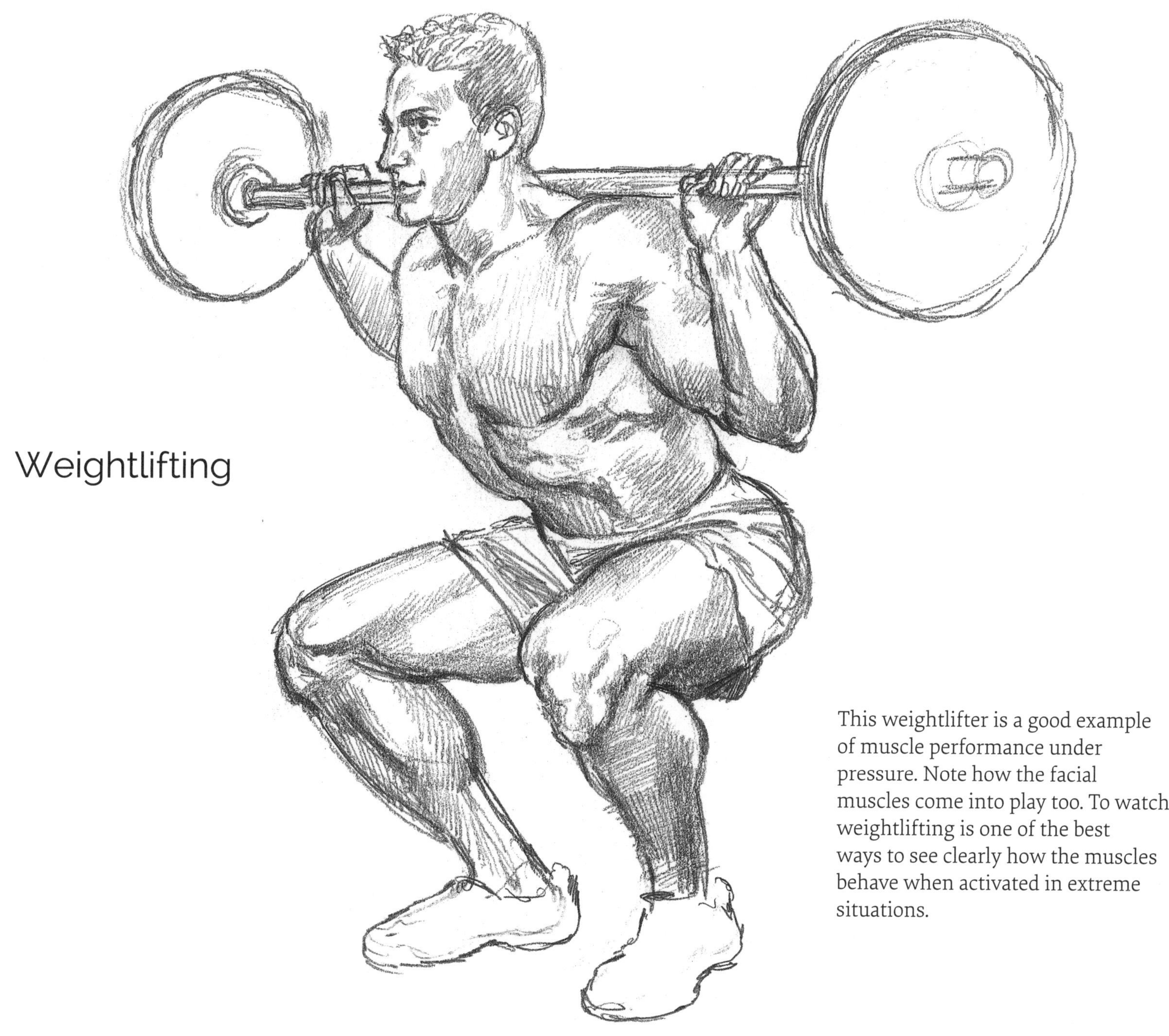

This weightlifter is a good example of muscle performance under pressure. Note how the facial muscles come into play too. To watch weightlifting is one of the best ways to see clearly how the muscles behave when activated in extreme situations.

At a Life Class

The next drawings show some dynamic life class poses. These are poses that the model obviously cannot hold for long, so you have to get down the main shapes of the body before adding detail.

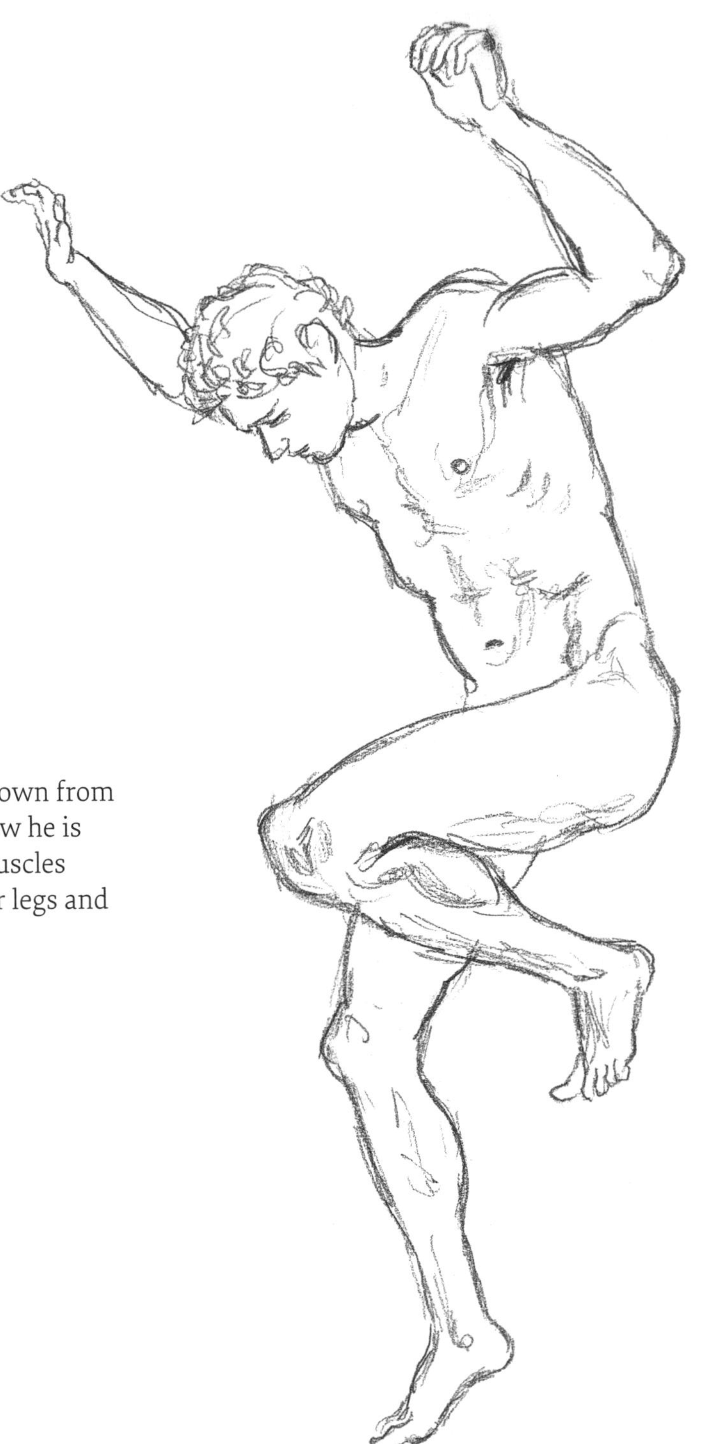

The leaping man is obviously on his way down from a higher level or a very high jump. Note how he is concentrating on his landing place. The muscles most noticeable here are those in the lower legs and along the front and side of the torso.

The woman bending over to touch the floor at her feet is stretching both her leg muscles and those of her back. This kind of detailed cross-hatching can be very effective in giving substance to your figure. It is time-consuming, so this shading was finished after the model had abandoned her pose.

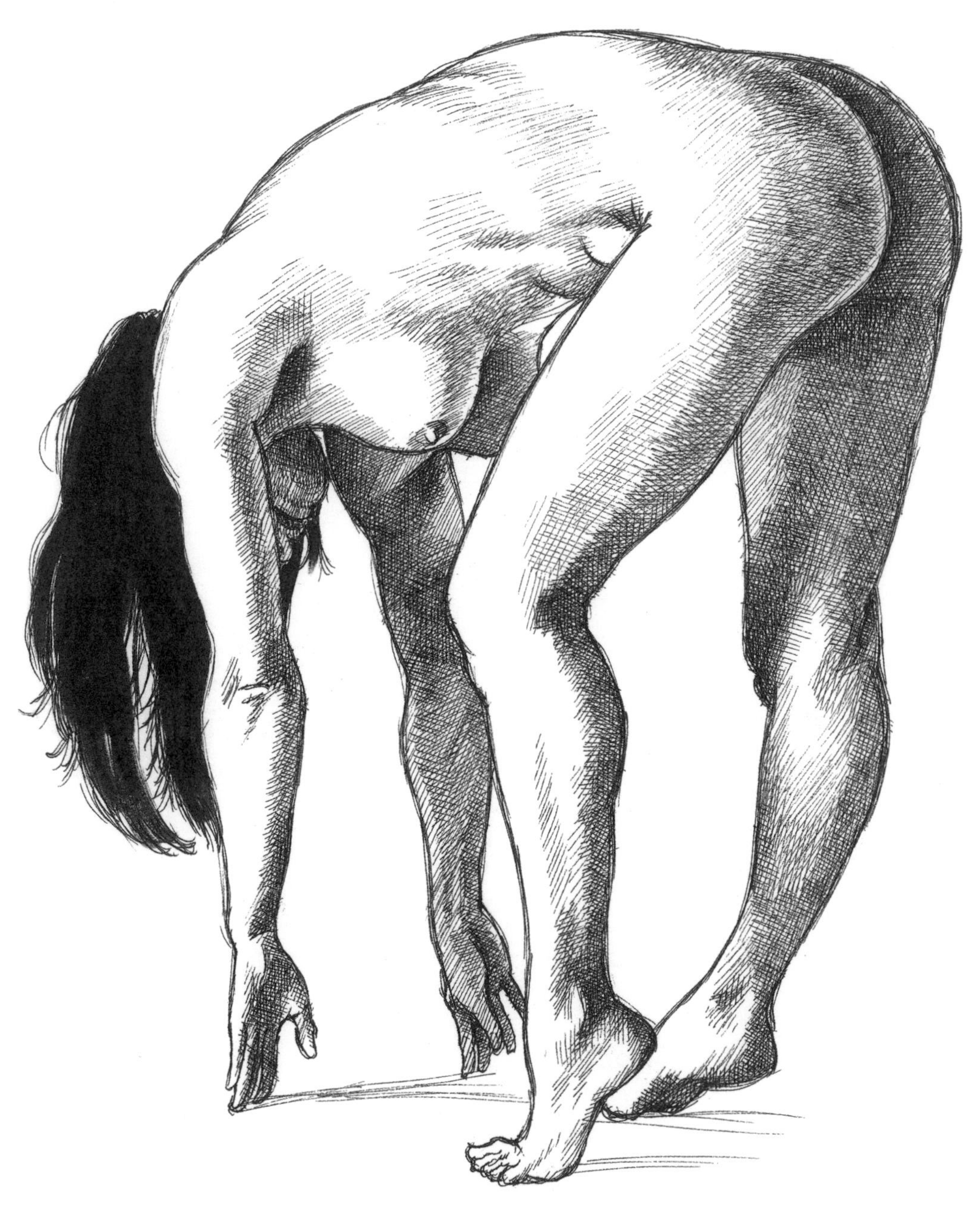

The model sitting cross-legged and stretching her arms above her head is showing very clearly the bony ribcage and her knee joints.

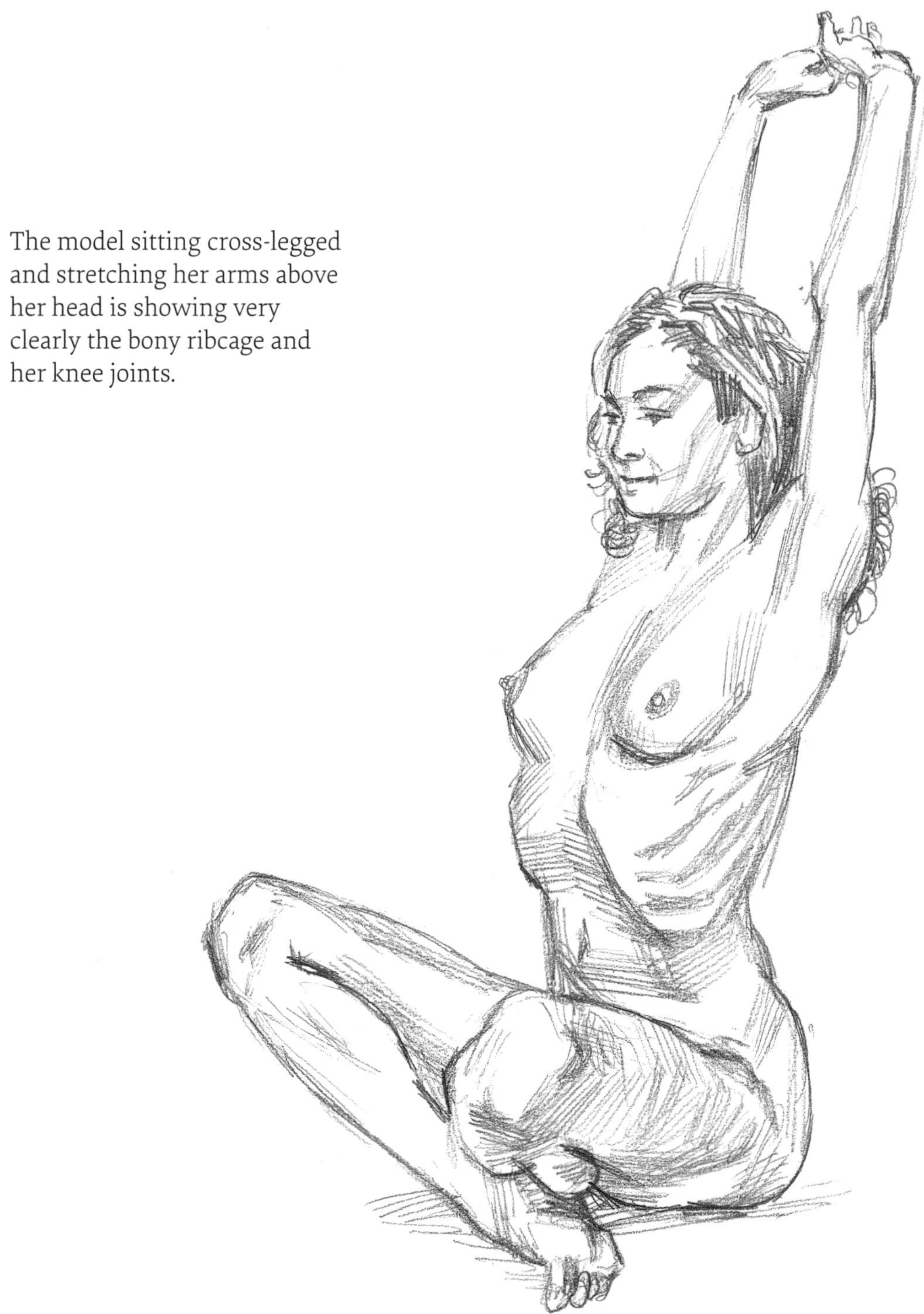

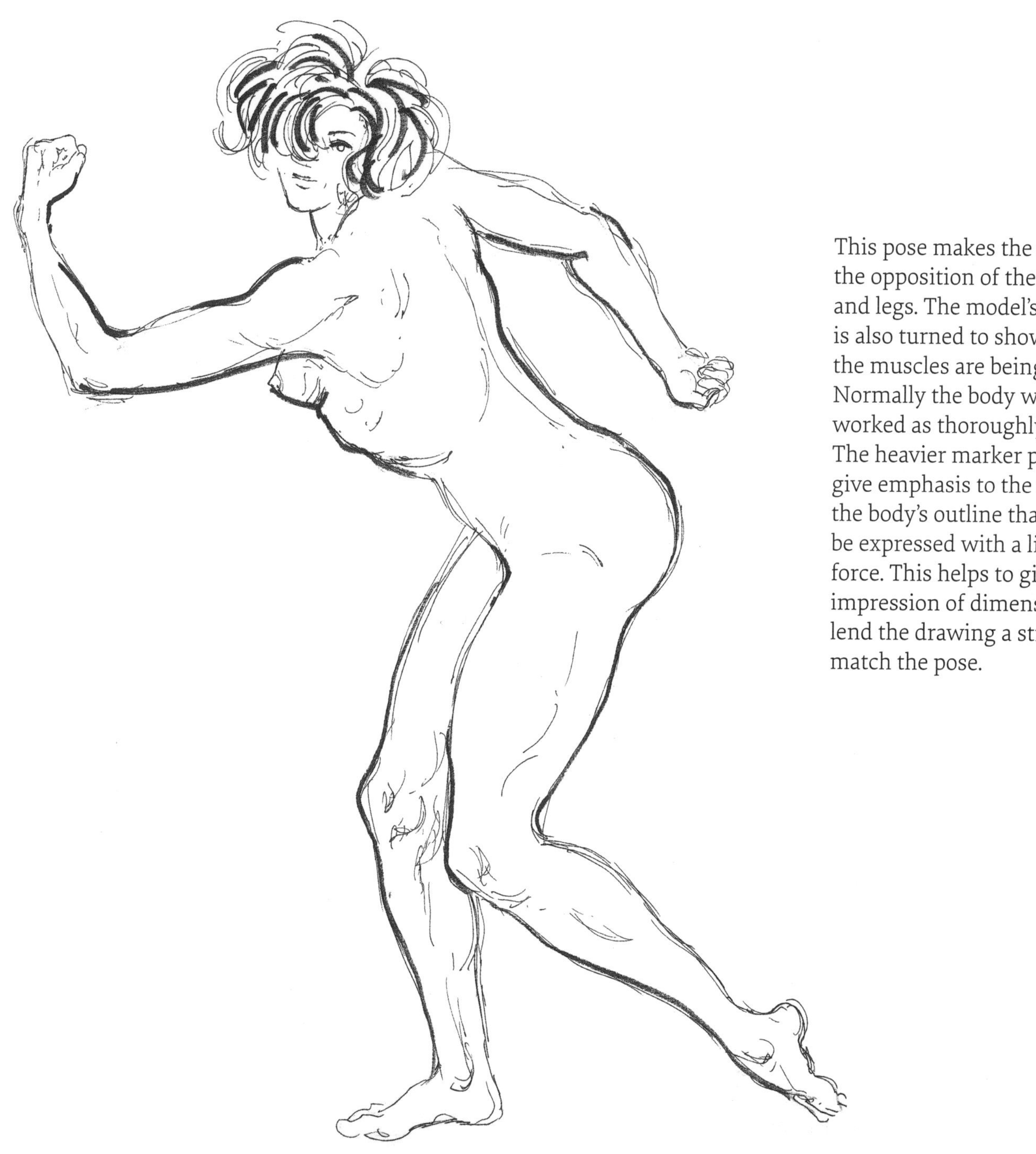

This pose makes the most of the opposition of the arms and legs. The model's torso is also turned to show how the muscles are being used. Normally the body wouldn't be worked as thoroughly as this. The heavier marker pen lines give emphasis to the areas of the body's outline that need to be expressed with a little more force. This helps to give an impression of dimension and lend the drawing a strength to match the pose.

Examples by a Master Artist

In all these drawings after Ingres, the figures show a fluid line which makes them look very mobile. Ingres doesn't define the muscles very sharply, preferring a smoother overall look to his figures. Nevertheless, it is obvious enough which muscles are being indicated in these drawings.

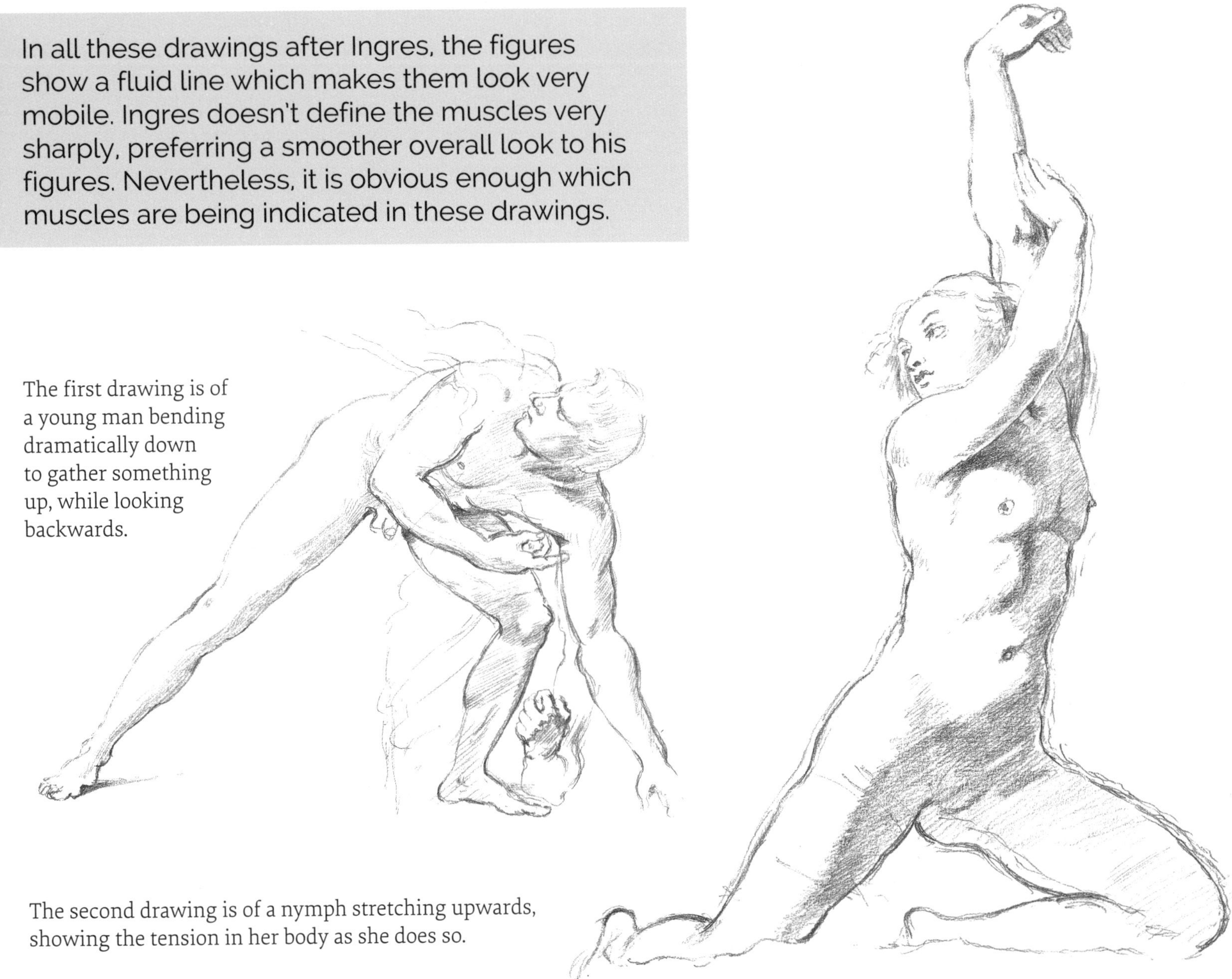

The first drawing is of a young man bending dramatically down to gather something up, while looking backwards.

The second drawing is of a nymph stretching upwards, showing the tension in her body as she does so.

The next drawing shows a man lifting a chair above his shoulder as he walks forward. The arm muscles are particularly obvious.

The final Ingres life study shows a man reaching down to lift something from the ground. The stretching of the legs and arms brings into play all the muscles of the limbs.

As happens in many life drawings by accomplished artists, Ingres has drawn extra definitions of the feet in the standing pose and the stretched arm in the drawing below. These workings help to clarify what is actually happening in a complex part of the pose.

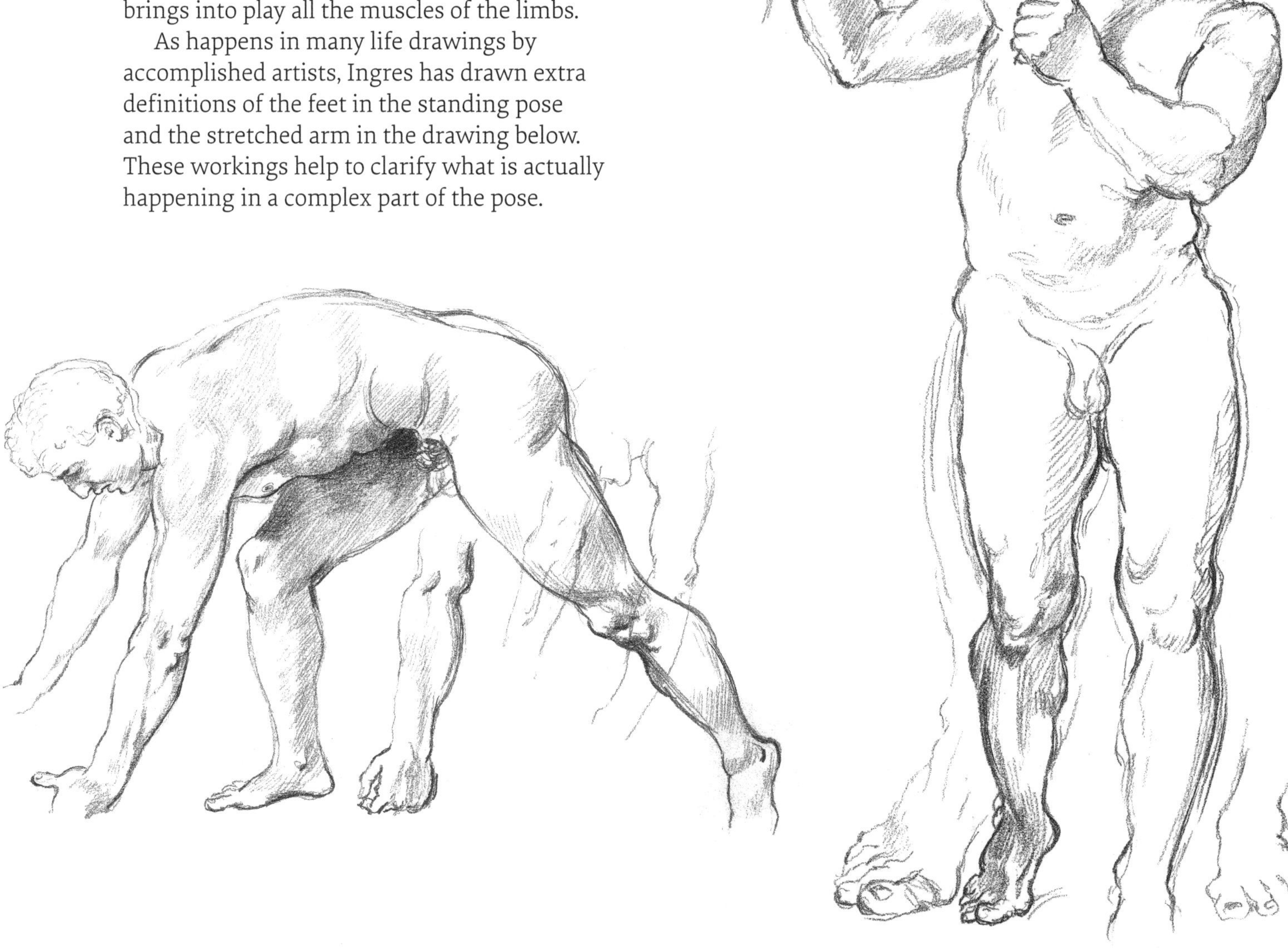

Chapter Six

GROUP PORTRAITS AND FIGURE COMPOSITION

In this section we look at some more challenging ways of presenting your human subjects: in groups. A group portrait differs from any other portrait only in that you have several people present, which of course makes the project more time-consuming. The main thing is to compose the figures and faces of your sitters in an interesting way and to work hard to achieve a resemblance, just as you would with a single portrait.

It's not easy to collect several people together in order to draw them at once, so usually the best bet is to draw them individually and fit them together later on. The point you have to watch here is that they are all the same proportion and relate to each other; you need to make the figures harmonize and form a group, rather than just a disparate set of people. To achieve this you can make the characters in the drawing look towards each other or connect with their body language, which makes the composition much more potent.

Considering the composition of your picture in this way will enhance it greatly. In this section we also look at some examples of how master artists have approached figure composition, showing how their careful division of the frame and placement of figures is crucial in turning an ordinary picture into a piece of art.

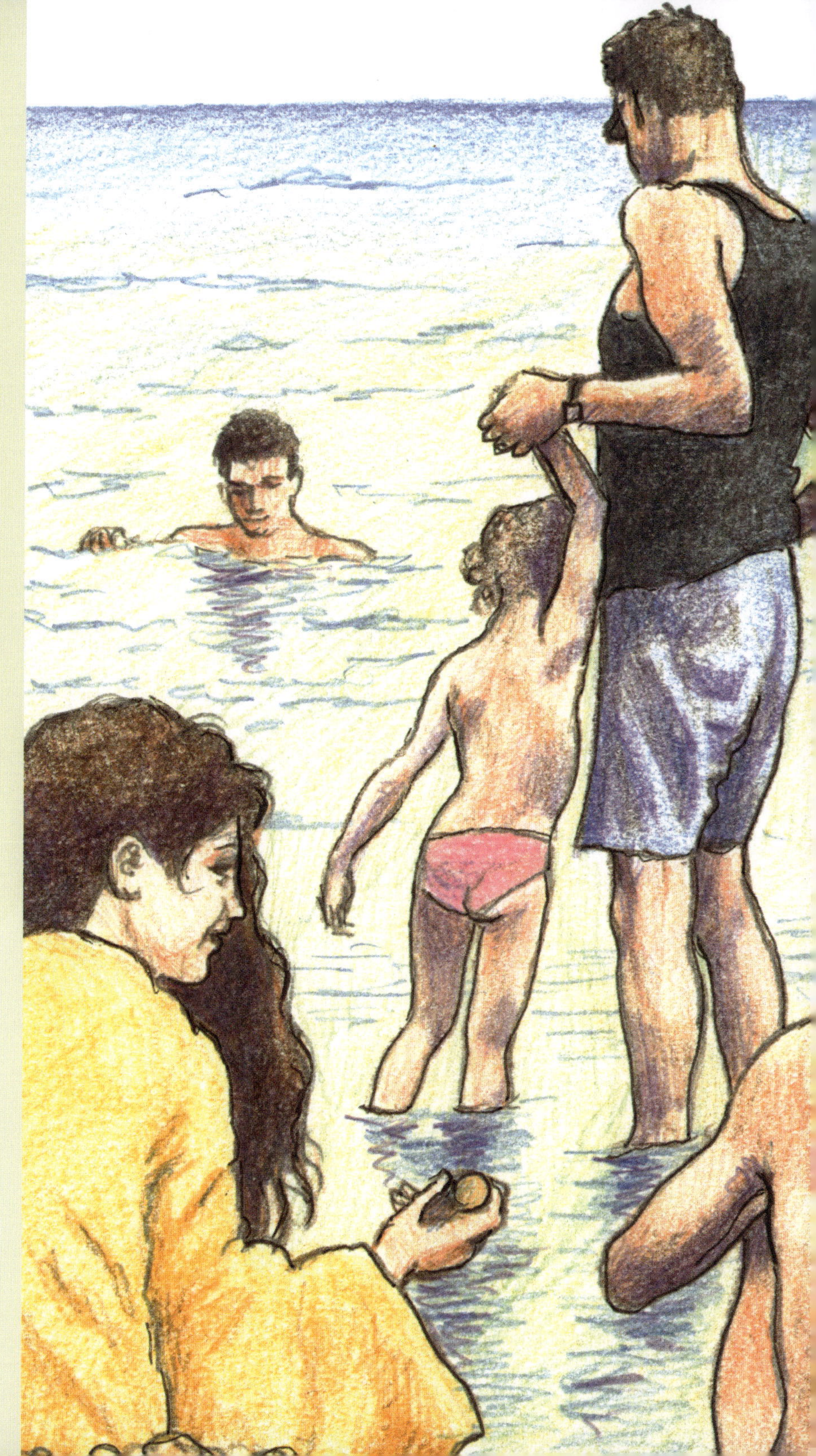

Group Portraits

In a group portrait as with a single portrait, you will need to capture likenesses of the people concerned, as well as deciding on a composition that shows something of their relationships to each other. Here we look at some preparatory steps you can take to help in your endeavour.

Preparing a group portrait

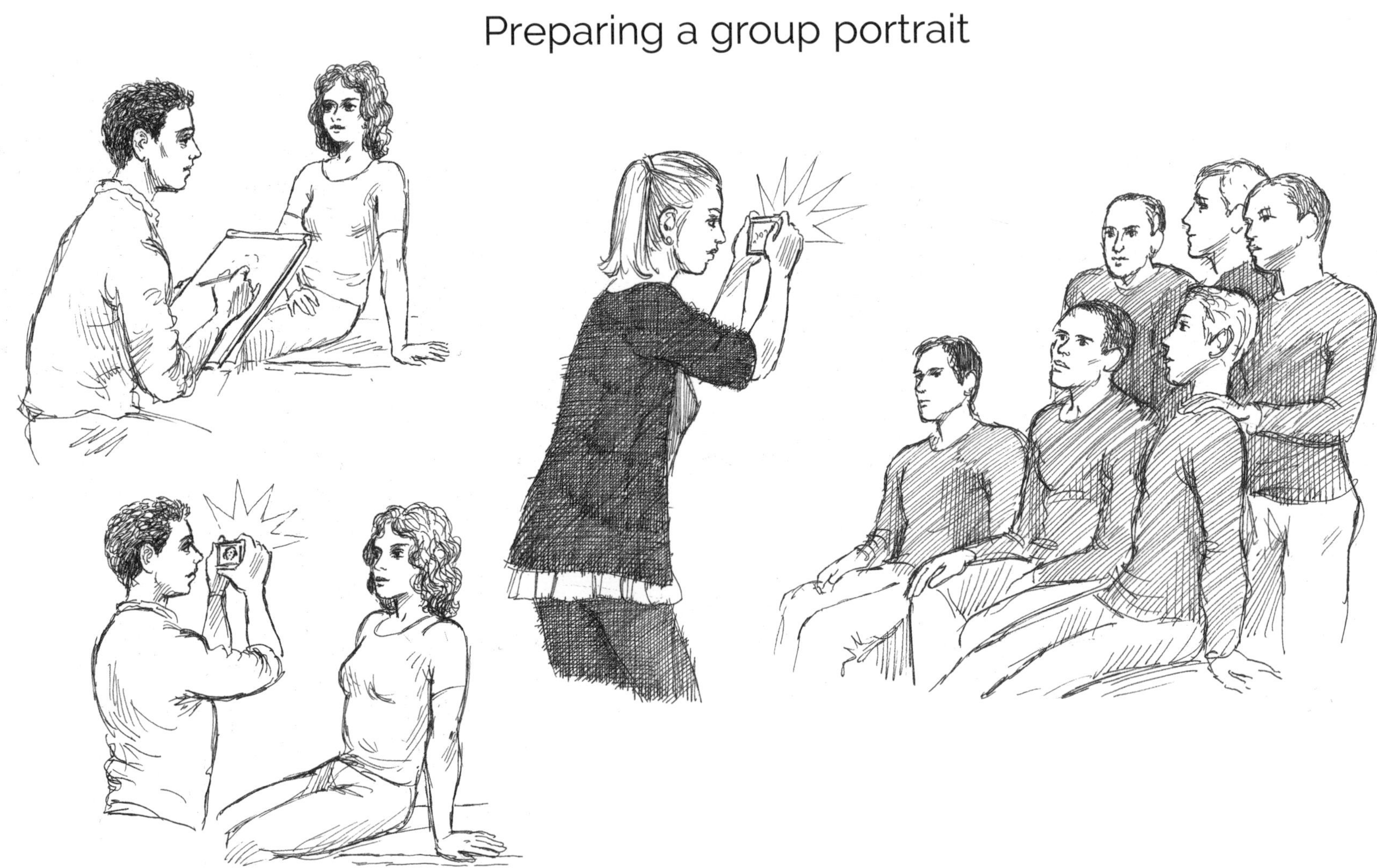

When it comes to drawing a group of people, the task in hand is to make sure that all the faces of the individuals are recognizable enough to satisfy their inspection. It's a good idea to get some photographic reference as well to ensure that you have got all the necessary information, taking shots of each face from different angles and also the whole composition. Draw sketches of each person and the composition to give yourself plenty of reference material that will work as backup if you need to halt the proceedings at any time and return to them later – especially with a large group, who may not all be able to reassemble.

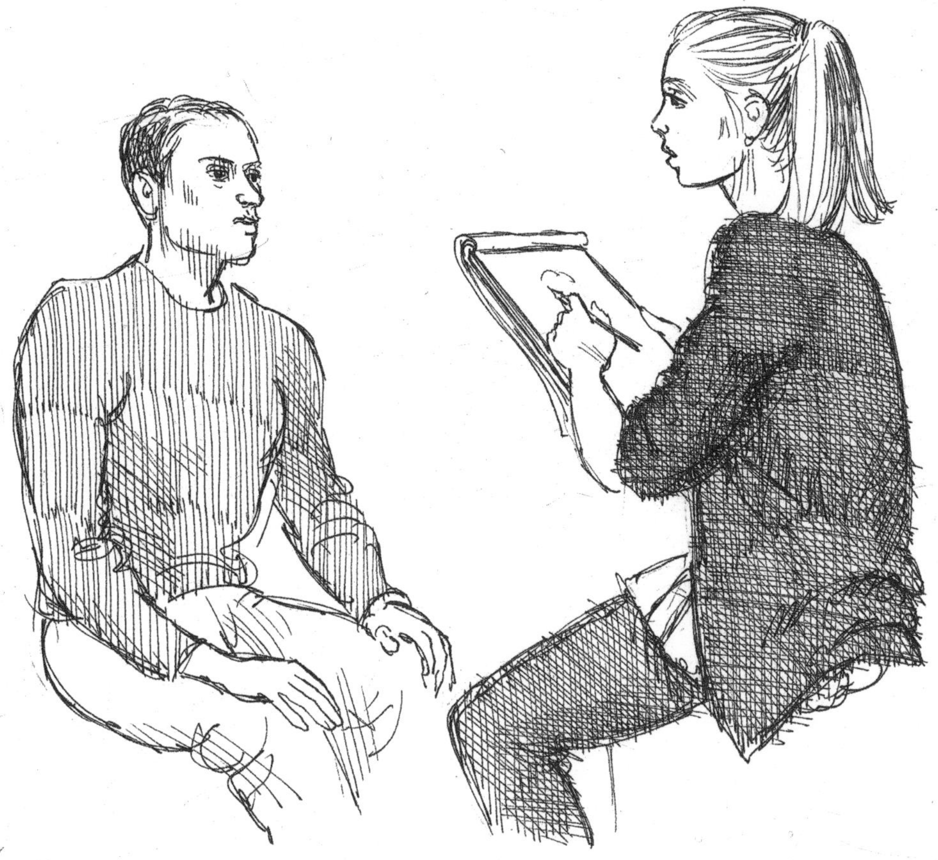

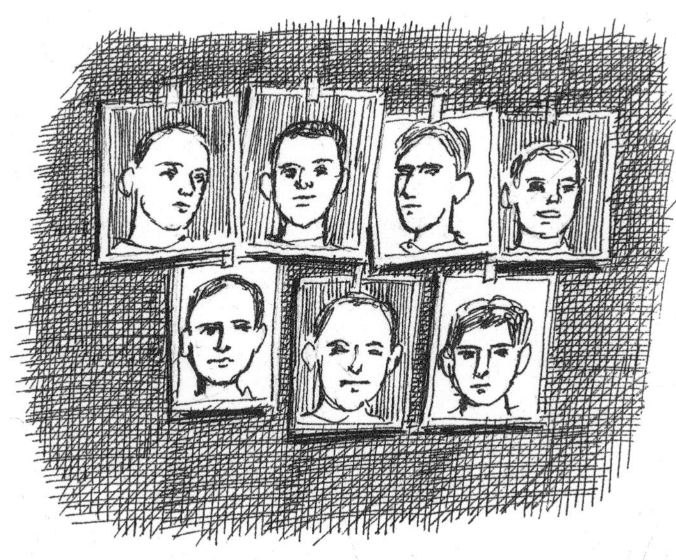

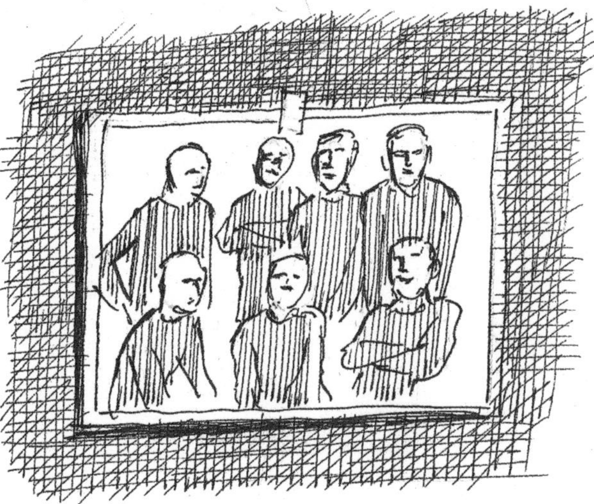

Small groups

In this portrait context, 'group' means anything other than one person, and the group you will most often be asked to draw is just two people, usually with a close relationship with each other.

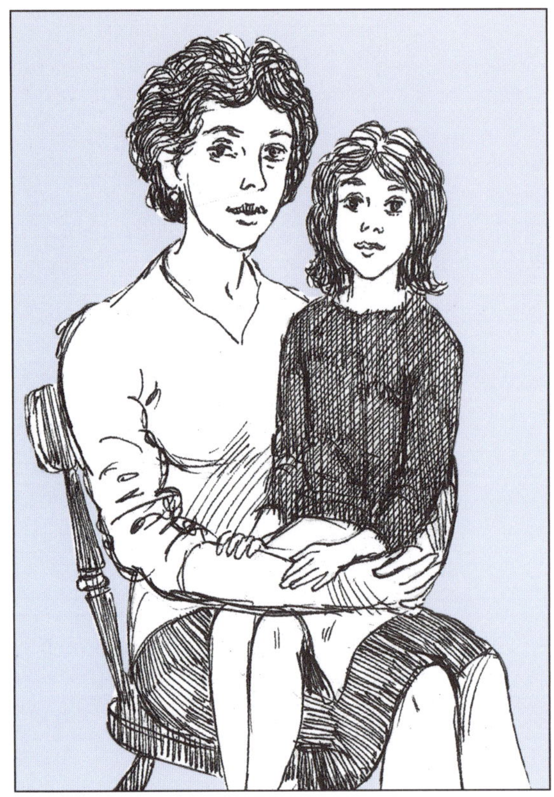

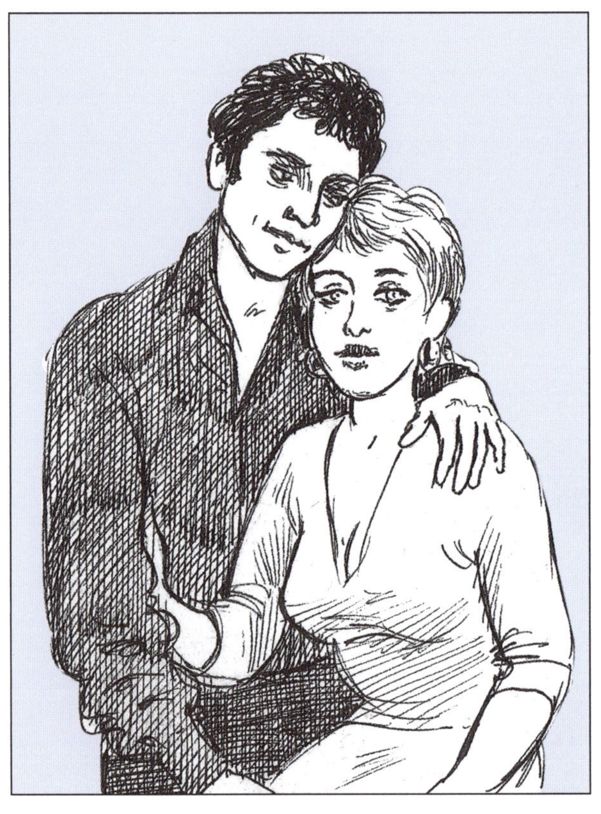

The first example I show here is a mother with her little girl on her lap, which creates a nice tight composition, and as long as the child will stay still for long enough there's no real problem with such a drawing. Obviously, once you've sketched in the main shapes of the two figures you can then draw the child first as quickly as possible, and when he or she wants to move you can then concentrate on the mother. The other thing about this combination of figures is that you only really have to satisfy the mother; the child usually is pleased with any representation that is even slightly human!

The second type of group, probably lovers or a married couple, is a bit more tricky because you will want a close connection between the two people, but they may find it difficult to sit so close as in my example for any length of time. Entwining figures can make a good composition, but depending on your speed of execution, you may find that they have difficulty in holding the intimate pose.

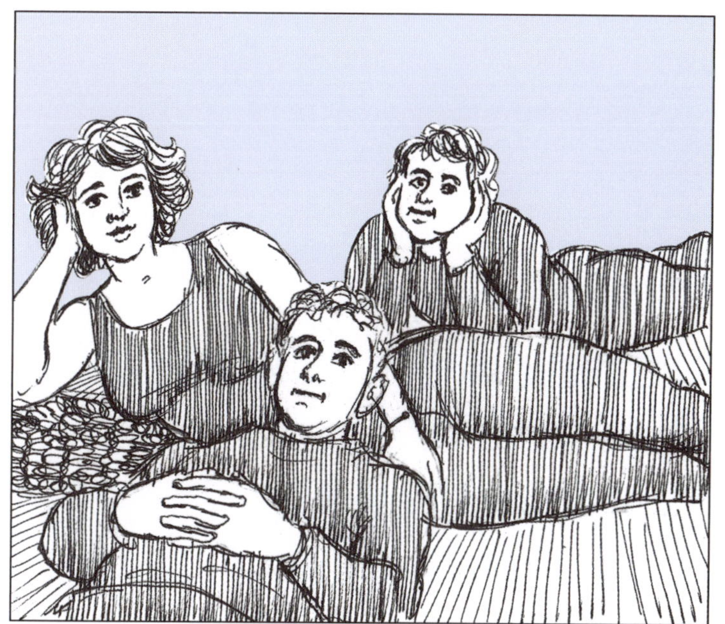

The second trio is two brothers and their sister, arranged in a much less formal composition than those shown so far. This isn't usually difficult with siblings under a certain age because of the sort of relationship they tend to have with each other. They probably won't mind a less conventional pose because they'll treat it as a sort of game.

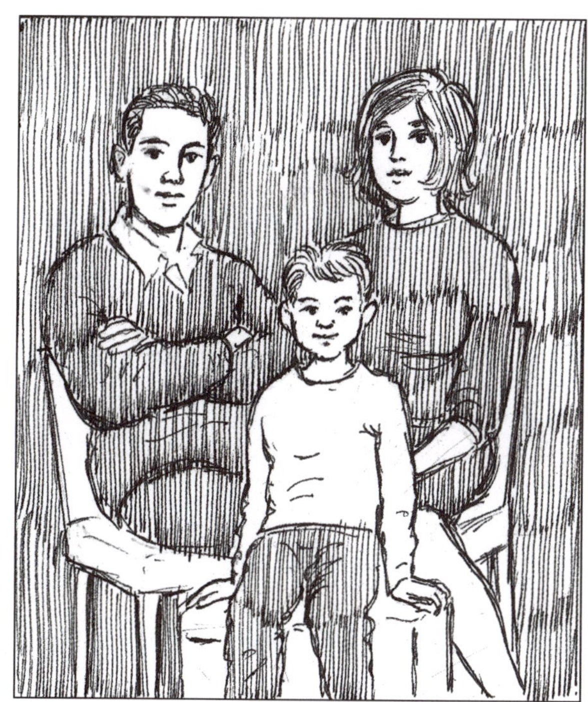

The next group has progressed to three people. The first trio is the obvious one of a couple and their child. The two adults sit next to each other and the child is in the centre of the composition, linking the two larger figures.

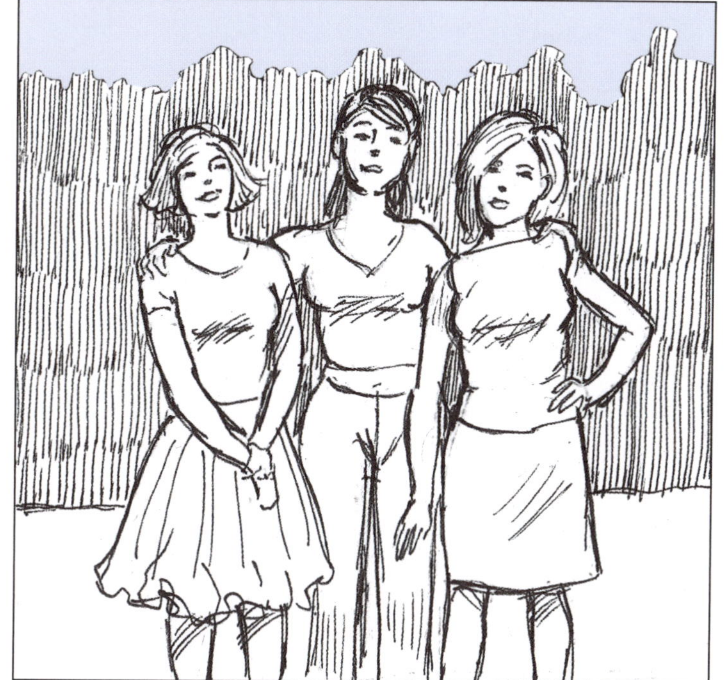

The last of these groups (left) is of three female friends, who are drawn as though interrupted out on a jaunt. Posed against a backdrop of trees, they might have been caught on camera as they were on a day out in the country. Quite often a photograph of the composition is a good idea, supplemented with careful drawings of each person which you can do individually later on.

Larger groups

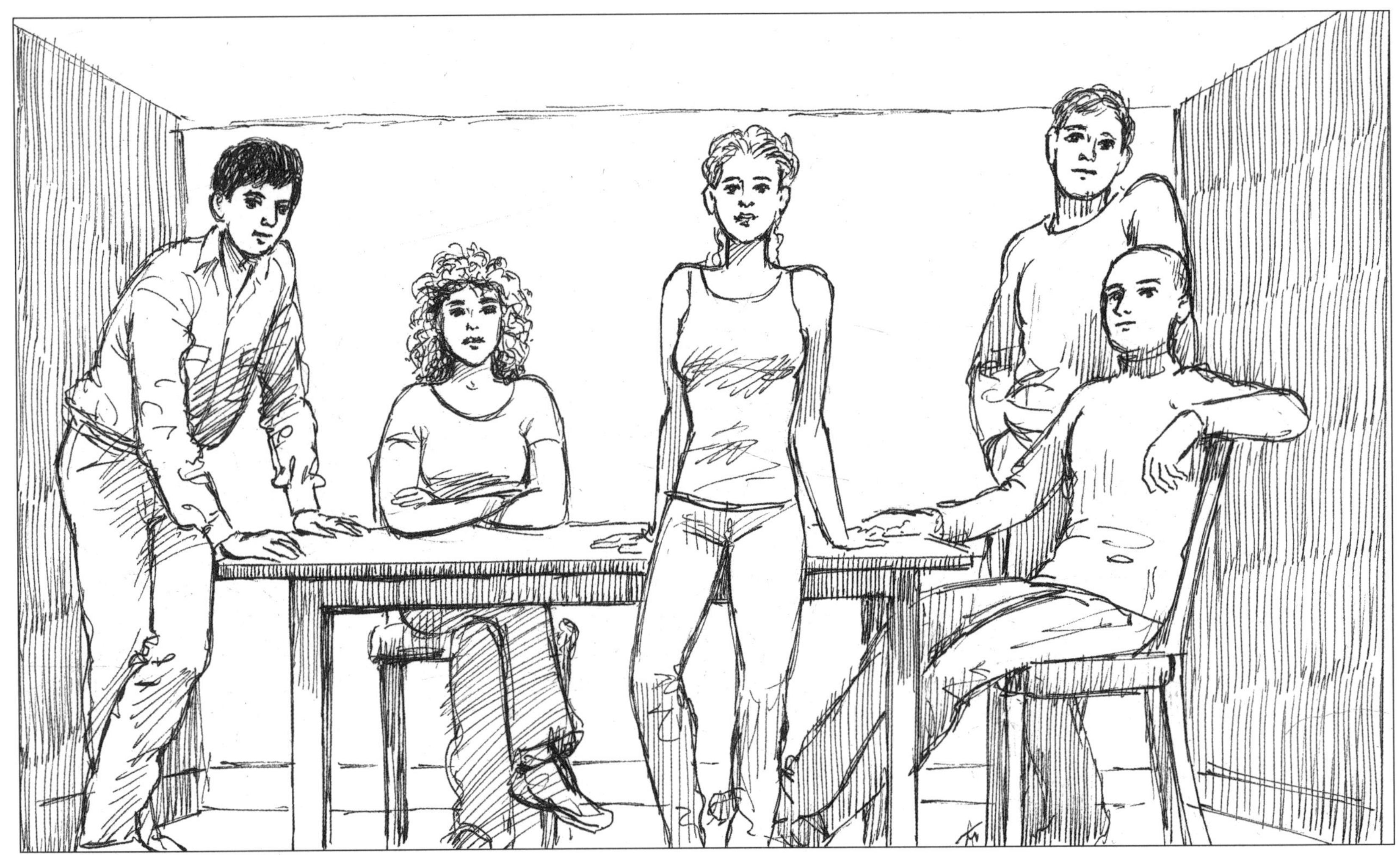

Now we look at a group of five people gathered around a table, which acts as a sort of support structure. With two sitting and three standing you get a certain dynamic in the composition which creates interest. It's also easier to make an interesting group with an uneven rather than even number of people. One of the standing figures is leaning on the back of the chair of the sitting figure at one end while another leans on the table at the opposite end. The central figure also leans back on the table, but being female she is not too bulky for the central role. The two seated figures, male and female, help to create a more horizontal shape to the arrangement.

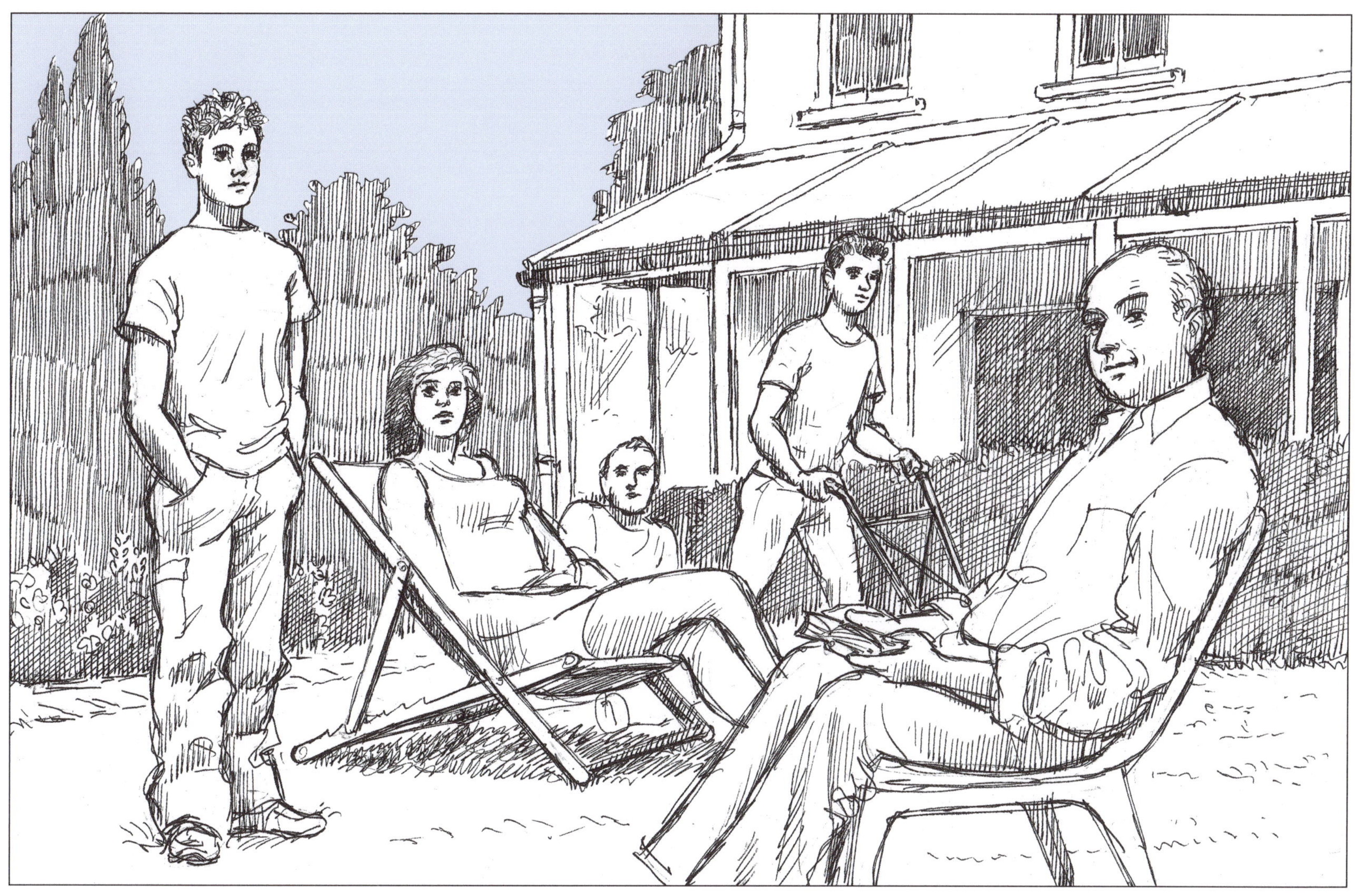

Here's another group of five people, but this time out in the garden, obviously in summer. The arrangement isn't as limited as the interior scene because there's more depth of space in which the figures can be placed. The main thing is to arrange them so that the group looks natural. I have opted for one young man standing with his hands in his pockets to one side of the composition, and an older man on the far side reclining in a deck chair with a book on his lap. These two enclose the others neatly. The other seated figure of a woman is opposed in arrangement to the seated man, their legs overlapping from our viewpoint. In the centre, but much further back, are a young man pushing a lawnmower and another man seated on the grass behind the woman so that only his head and shoulders show. The background of the conservatory, bushes and trees gives more sensation of depth in the composition.

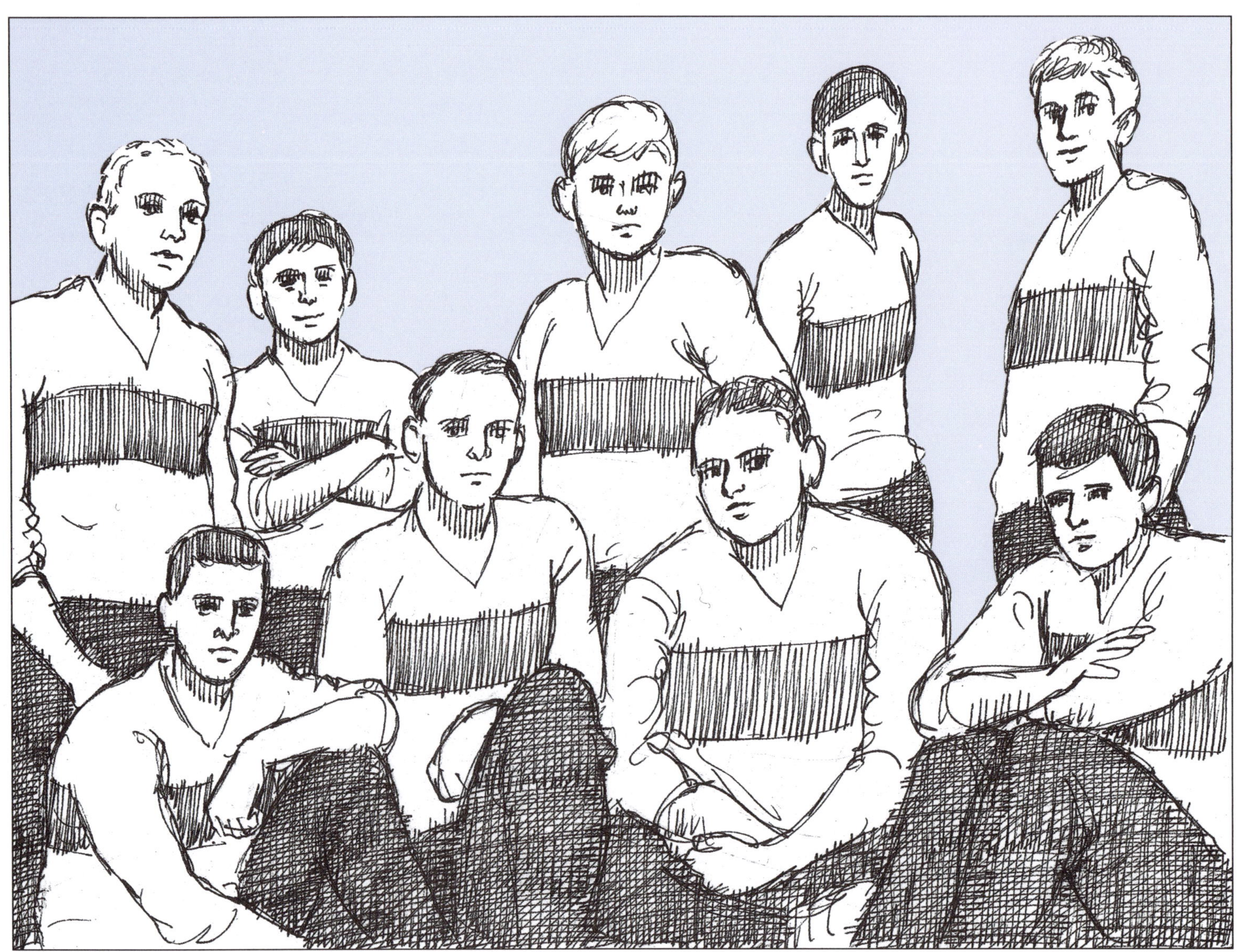

Next we look at an even larger group that's more like a team portrait of the sort that might be commissioned. Here a group of young, athletic-looking men are casually grouped with those in the foreground sitting and the others standing behind them. There's a certain amount of artistic licence here, because the standing men appear to be on ground lower than that on which the others are sitting. This is done in order to bring their respective faces closer together to create a tighter composition. The fact that they are wearing matching sweaters also helps to bind the figures together.

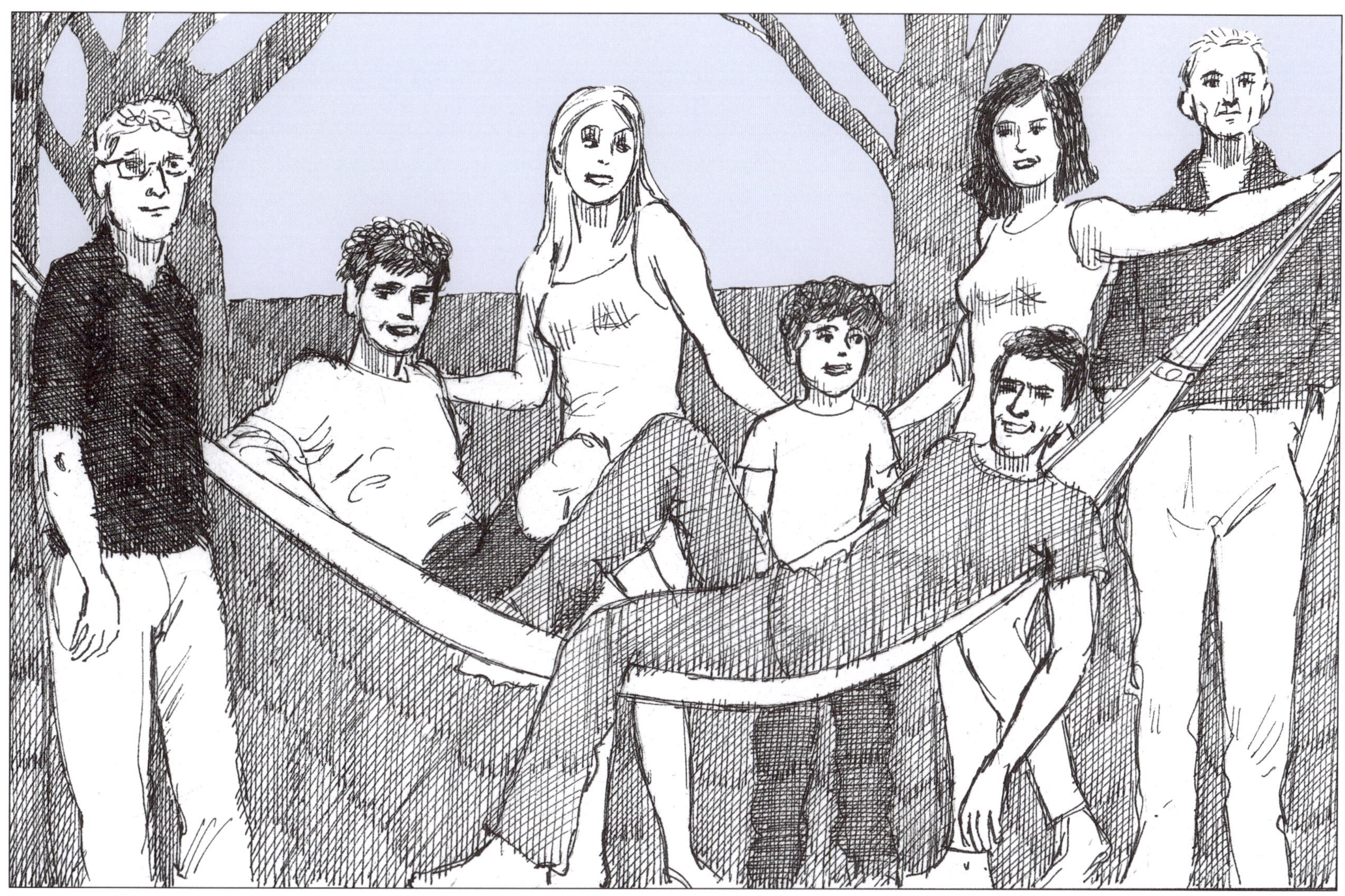

This group is much less formal – it's the sort of gathering that you sometimes find in a family that's getting together for a party in the garden during the summer. The compositional feature is a large hammock on which two of the people are reclining. Arranged around them is the rest of the group. Again the figures at each end are the brackets that hold the arrangement and I've put them in as two men, the older people in the group. Two young men are in the hammock, one closer to the viewer with arms and legs dangling down. The figures behind are two young women and a small boy who add a sort of grace note to the scene. Behind them we can see a fence and a couple of tree trunks, so there is not a great deal of depth. It is almost like a group on a stage.

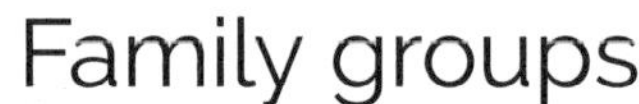

Family groups

An easy way to set about drawing groups of people is to start with your own family – they're usually available, and they might be more amenable to your first experiments than people that you don't know so well. So here's a series of portraits of my own family to give you some examples of how you might go about it.

The first is of my eldest son and grandson, caught in a pose photographically, as the latter wouldn't keep still for any time at all. It's an unusual portrait because a profile view isn't the norm.

The next is of two of my grandchildren, but actually drawn at different times. Needless to say, young people aren't used to sitting for a portrait for any length of time and so it's simpler to draw them apart and then place them together afterwards. You just have to make sure that they appear similar in size.

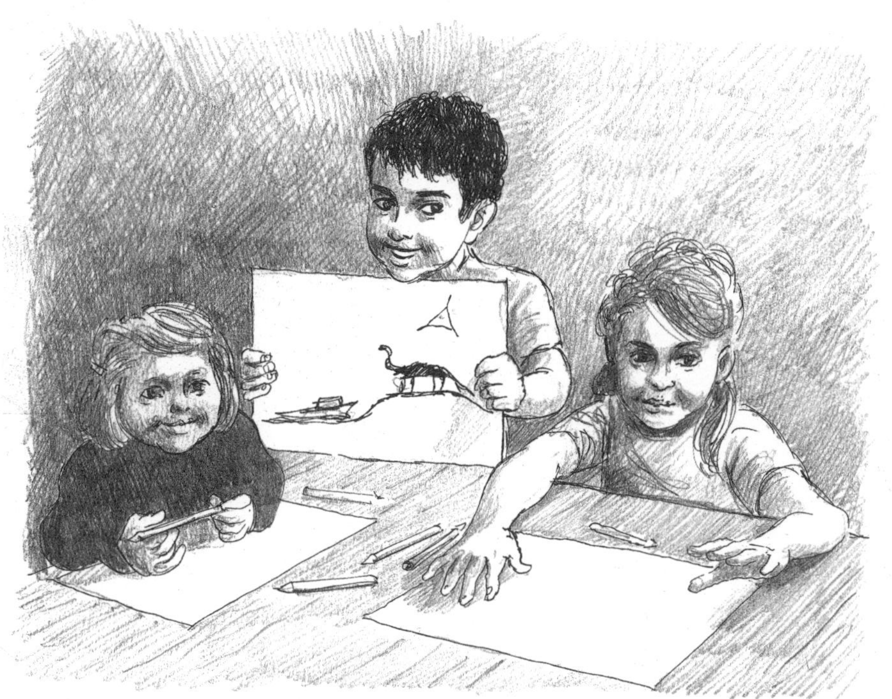

Next comes a pair of trios, one of a grandchild and friends, and the other of myself and my sisters. These are based on photographs because the children were quite animated and the self-portrait needed some reference. Both compositions make use of the fact that the figures are placed quite close together, with the drawing activity of the children and the dark clothing of the older group linking each trio.

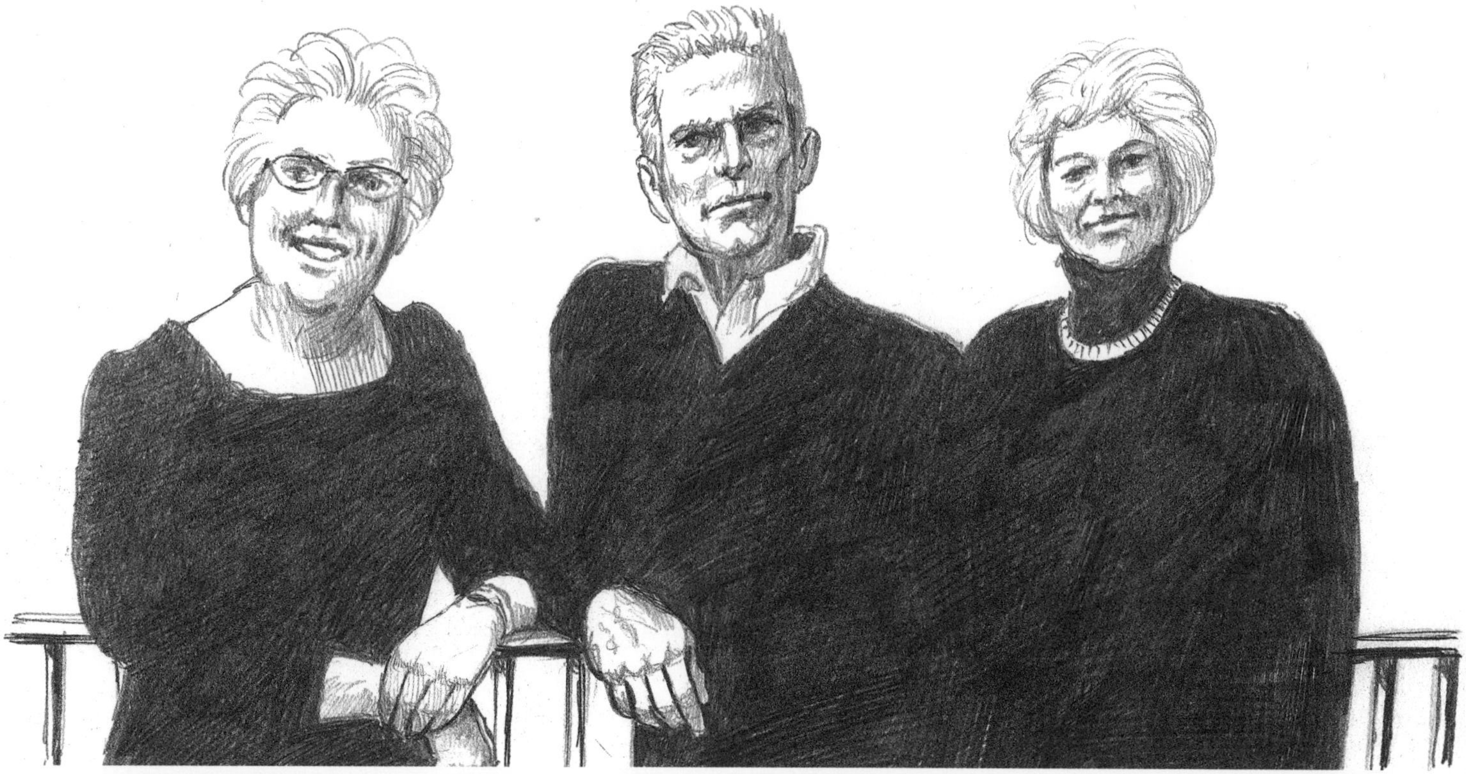

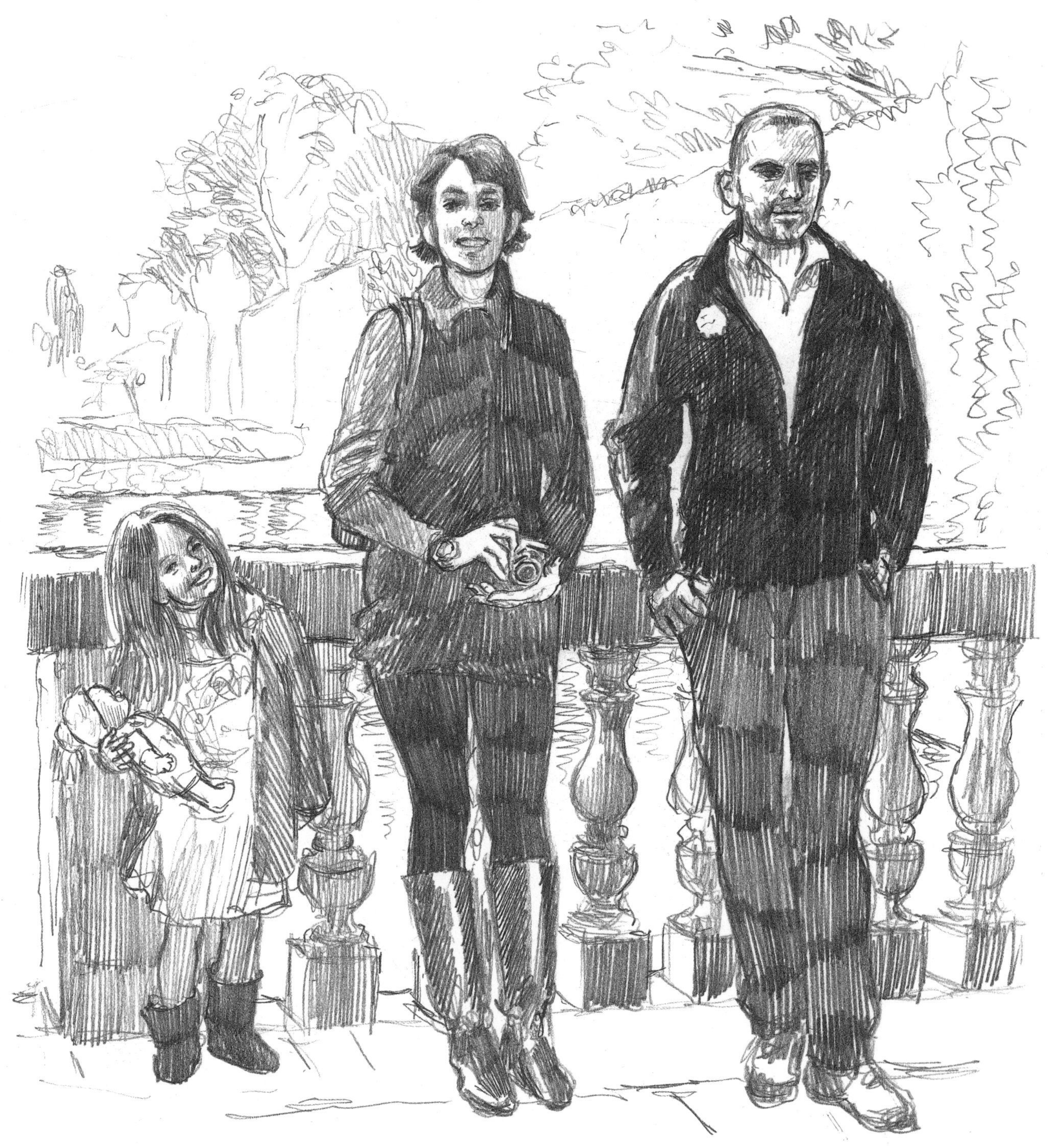

The next group is another trio with my youngest daughter, my son-in-law and their child all together. Again the actual pose was photographed and the drawings were all done separately later.

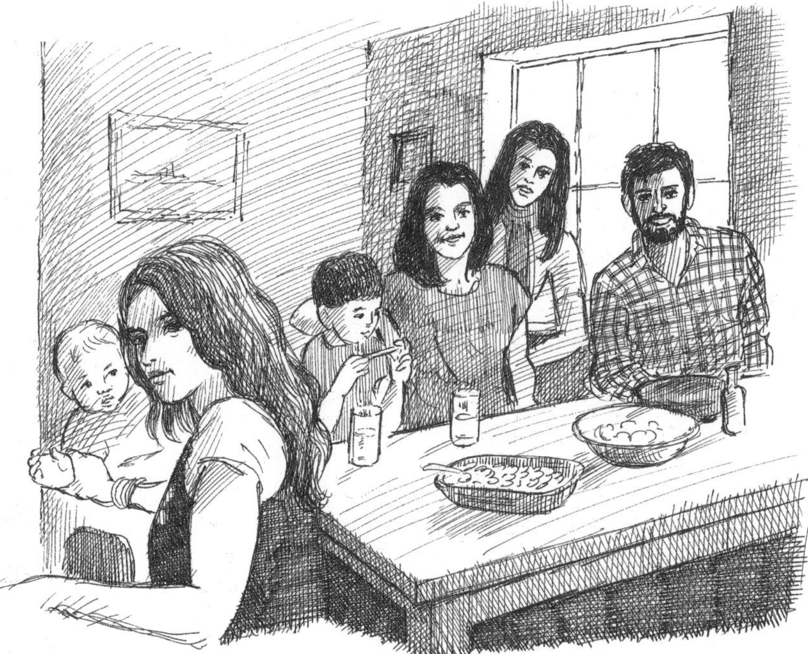

The next picture is based on a holiday photograph with a family group around a table where some lunch preparations were in progress. The looseness of the composition is typical of an informal photograph. The diagonal of the table and the turning movement of the nearest figure give a certain dynamic to the scene.

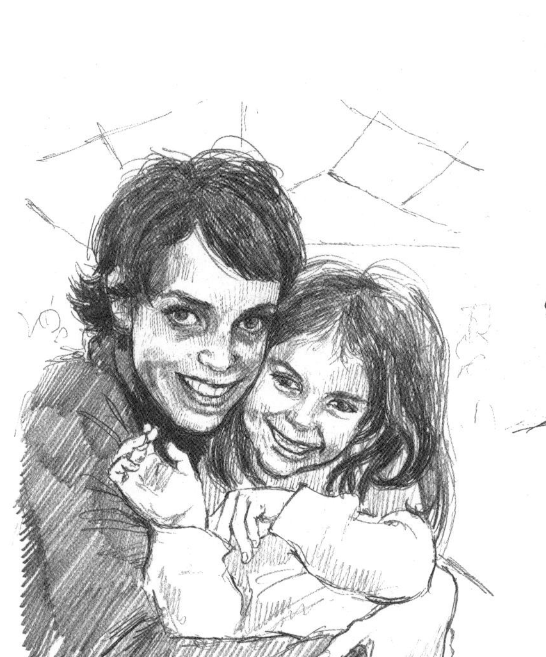

This drawing shows my daughter with her daughter, cuddling up together. I used a combination of photographic reference and sketches of them both.

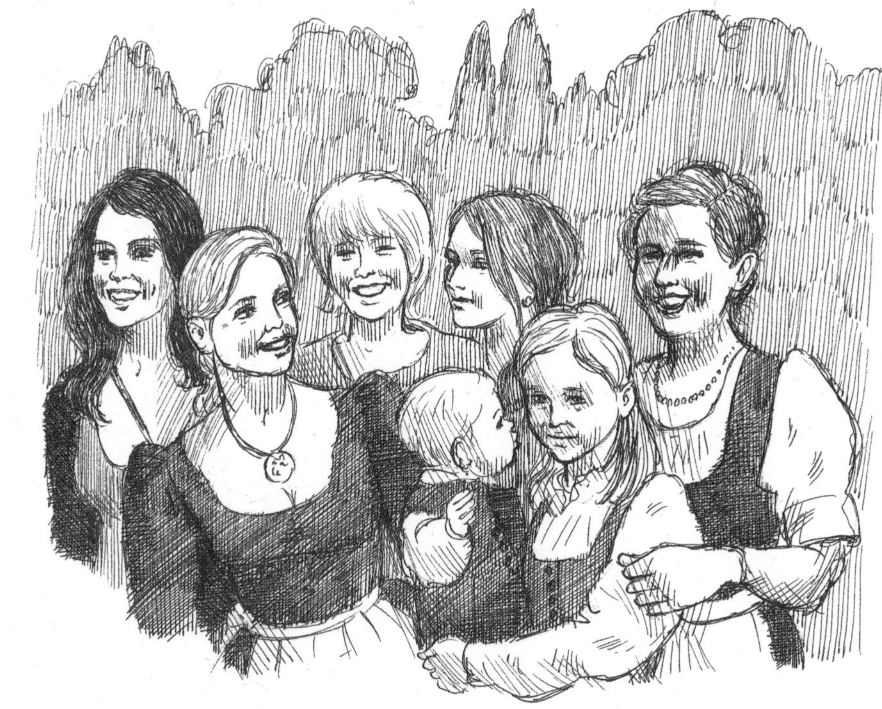

The last scene is of a time when we went to Bavaria to visit my daughter-in-law's family. At one point all the female members of the family were together with one grandson, closely gathered for a photograph. I later made drawings of each one individually.

A Portrait Composition

Once you have spent some time studying your subjects and sketching them in different arrangements, choose the composition you think works best and develop it in stages. Having decided that I would draw my youngest daughter and her family sitting close together on a sofa, I made a quick sketch of them in position. I also took photographs, as the little boy and the baby obviously weren't going to pose for long.

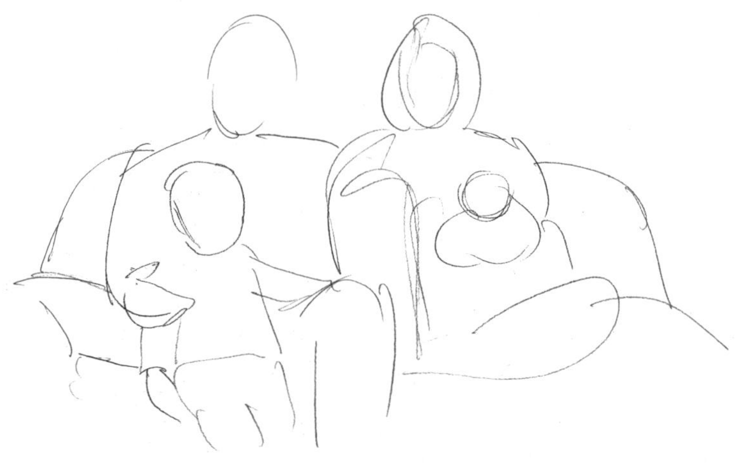

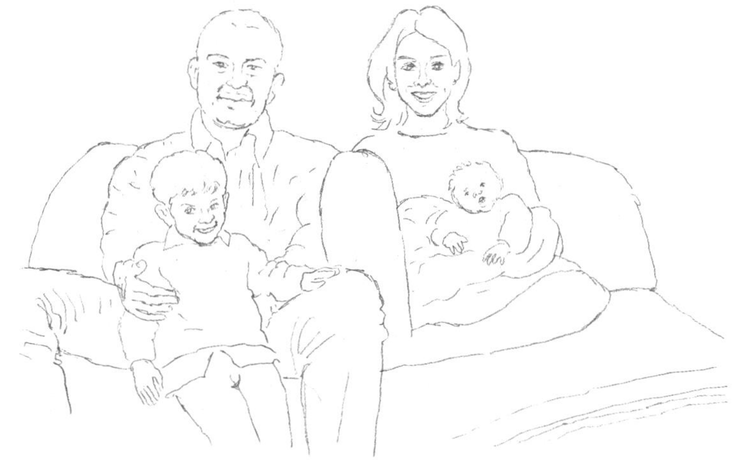

STEP 1

My first sketch shows the position of each figure within the composition. This is a basic outline of shapes and proportions.

STEP 2

Next I drew a more careful line drawing using my sketches and photographs to get the shapes and features correct. At this stage, any alterations can still be easily made, but you are trying to end up with a definitive drawing.

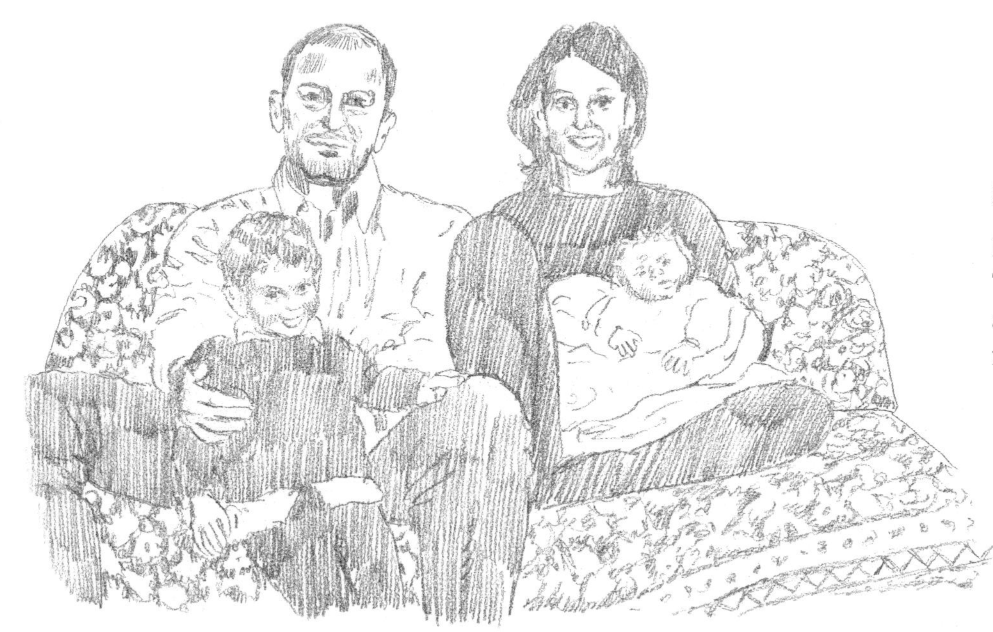

STEP 3

Next, I put in all the tone and texture. The texture of the flowery sofa that they are sitting on is important as well as the main tone of the clothing and features.

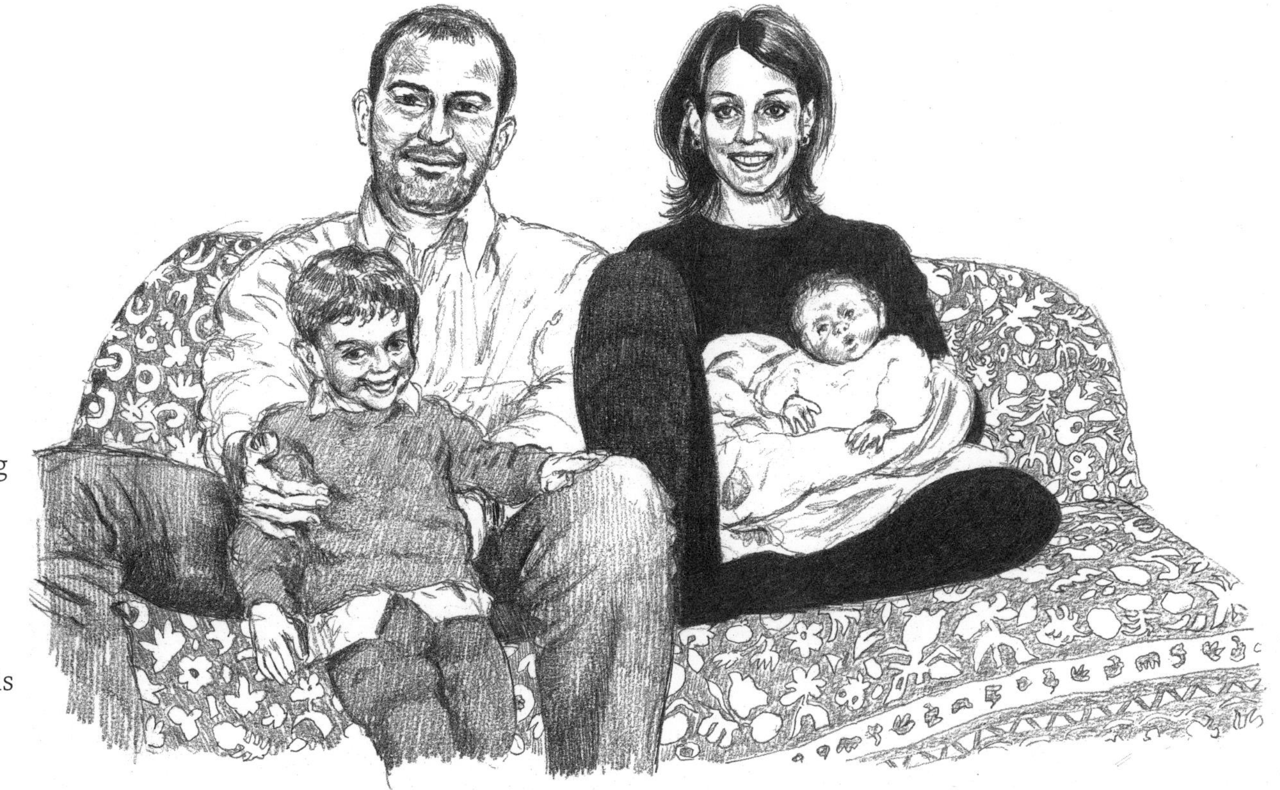

STEP 4

Then, with most of the drawing in place, it is time to build up the tone and texture and define everything for the final work. As you can see, there was no strongly angled light, everything being quite well-lit from in front. The pattern on the sofa is important as it is an attractive setting for the figures and helps to hold the composition together. Most of the stronger tones are based on the local colour of the clothes as there are no very strong shadows. The faces were all drawn separately, when the models could stay still for a while.

A Figure Composition

This next example is a less conventional choice of composition showing a group of figures on a beach. This is not a group portrait as such, because many of the faces are not visible; my aim here was to capture the feel of a family trip to the beach, as well as some interesting figure poses. There is depth from the view across the sea and complexity in the closer and further shapes of all the figures.

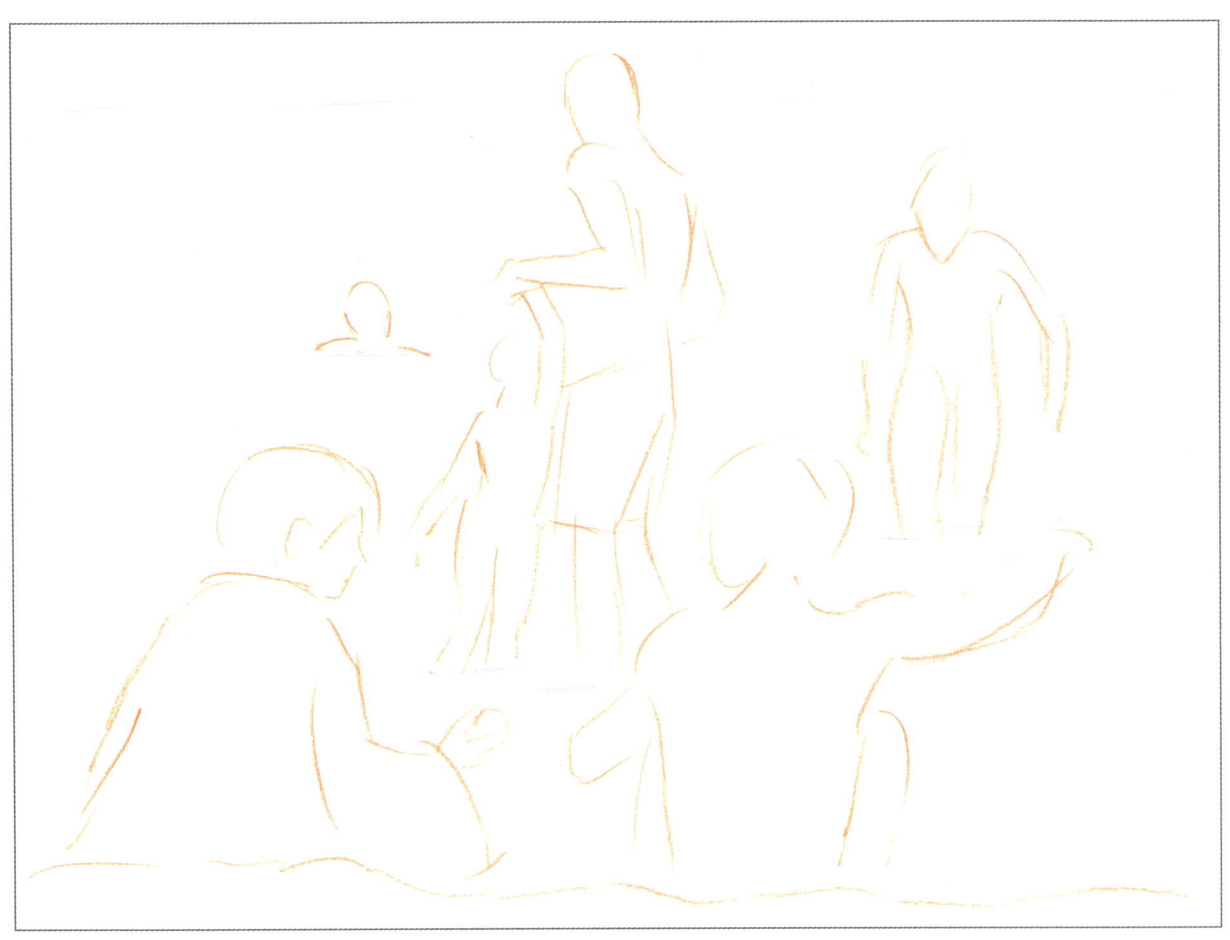

STEP 1

First, map out your scene, considering where the horizon line of the sea is and the beach in the near foreground. The two nearest seated figures frame the standing ones that are in varying depths of the sea. I've put in the tallest figure, a man holding his little daughter's hand up to keep her from stumbling. A young woman is walking towards us into the shallows on one side, while on the other side there is a young man up to his shoulders in deeper water. Keep the line light and sketchy.

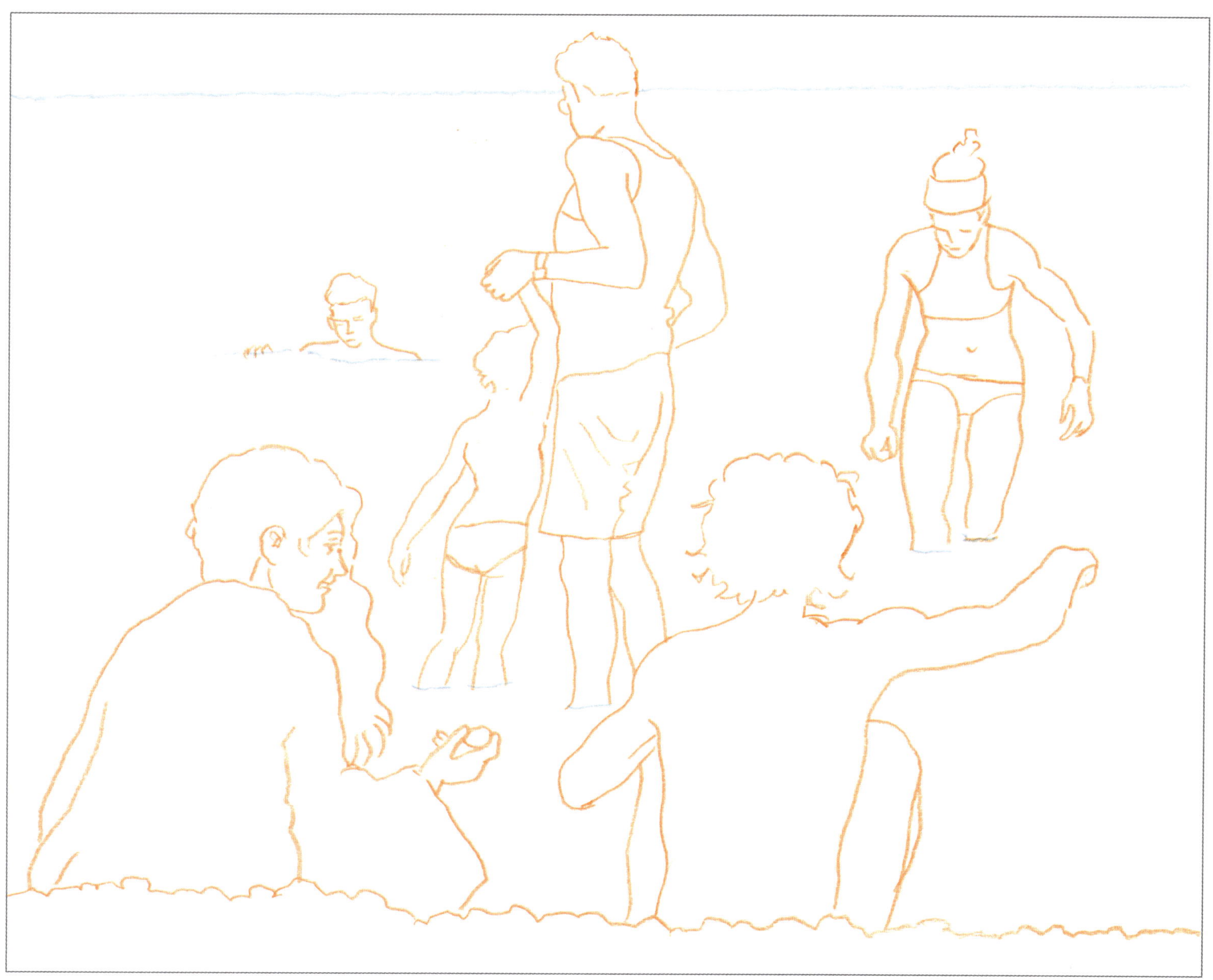

STEP 2

Now firm up the drawing, but still in outline. Make sure that your outlines show the proportions of each figure accurately, so that they relate to each other in the space. At this stage the drawing needs to be the best you are capable of doing.

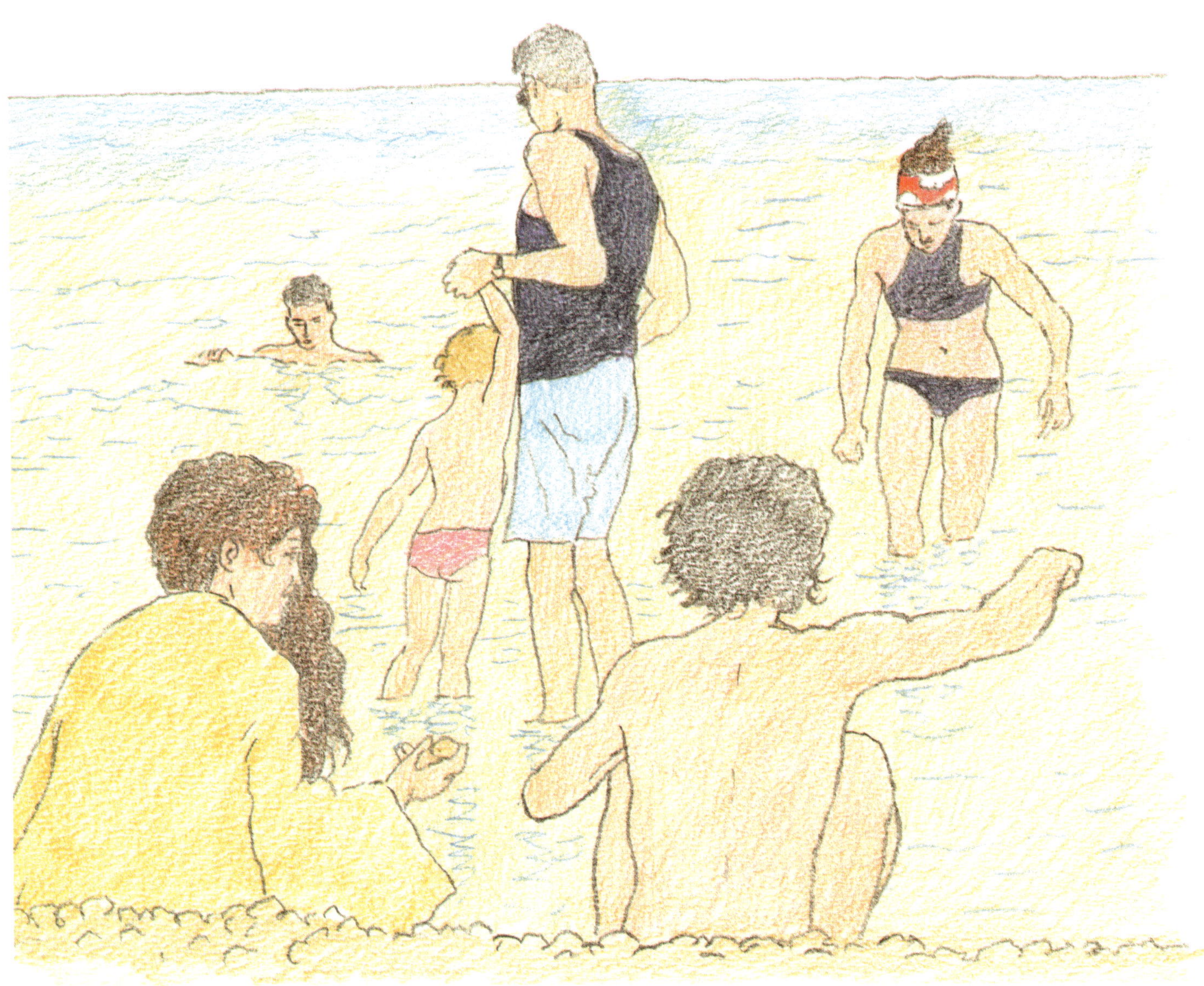

STEP 3

Now comes the application of colour to the scene. Keep it quite thin and light at this stage and don't concern yourself with tones yet – just smooth areas of the colours you want. At this stage I put in a few of the waves of the sea to give some idea of distance and depth. I also put more blue colour on the more distant sea and more green on the nearer part.

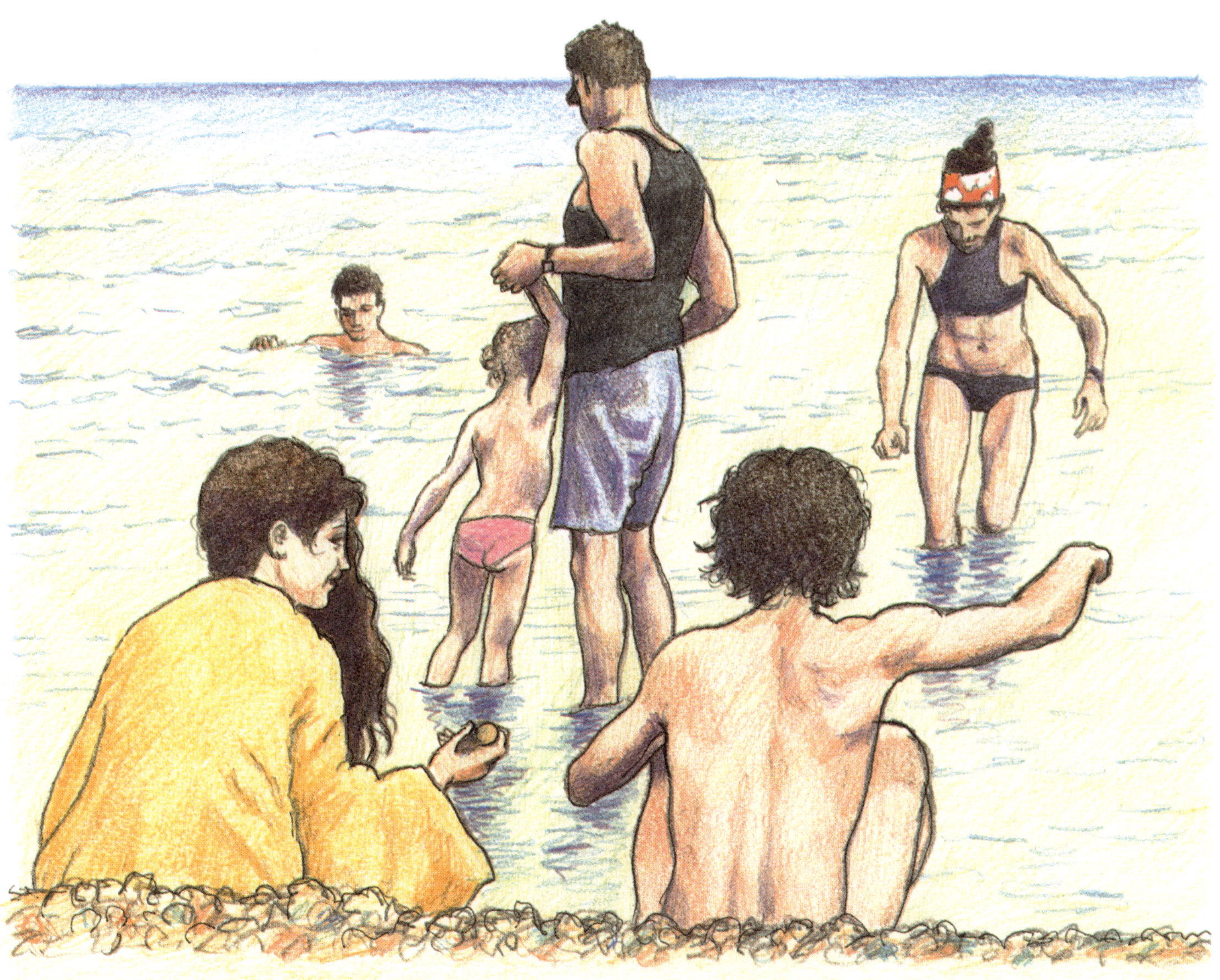

STEP 4

Now you can build up tone across the image. Darken certain colours such as the father's vest and the woman's swimming costume. Note how dark the hair looks and how the reflections below the figures in the sea give some idea of the water surface.

Clever Composition

On these pages we analyse various figure compositions by master artists. If you look carefully at the way the figures are placed in the overall frame and how they relate to each other, you can often detect an underlying geometry. Using a geometric structure in your compositions can help them to be successful.

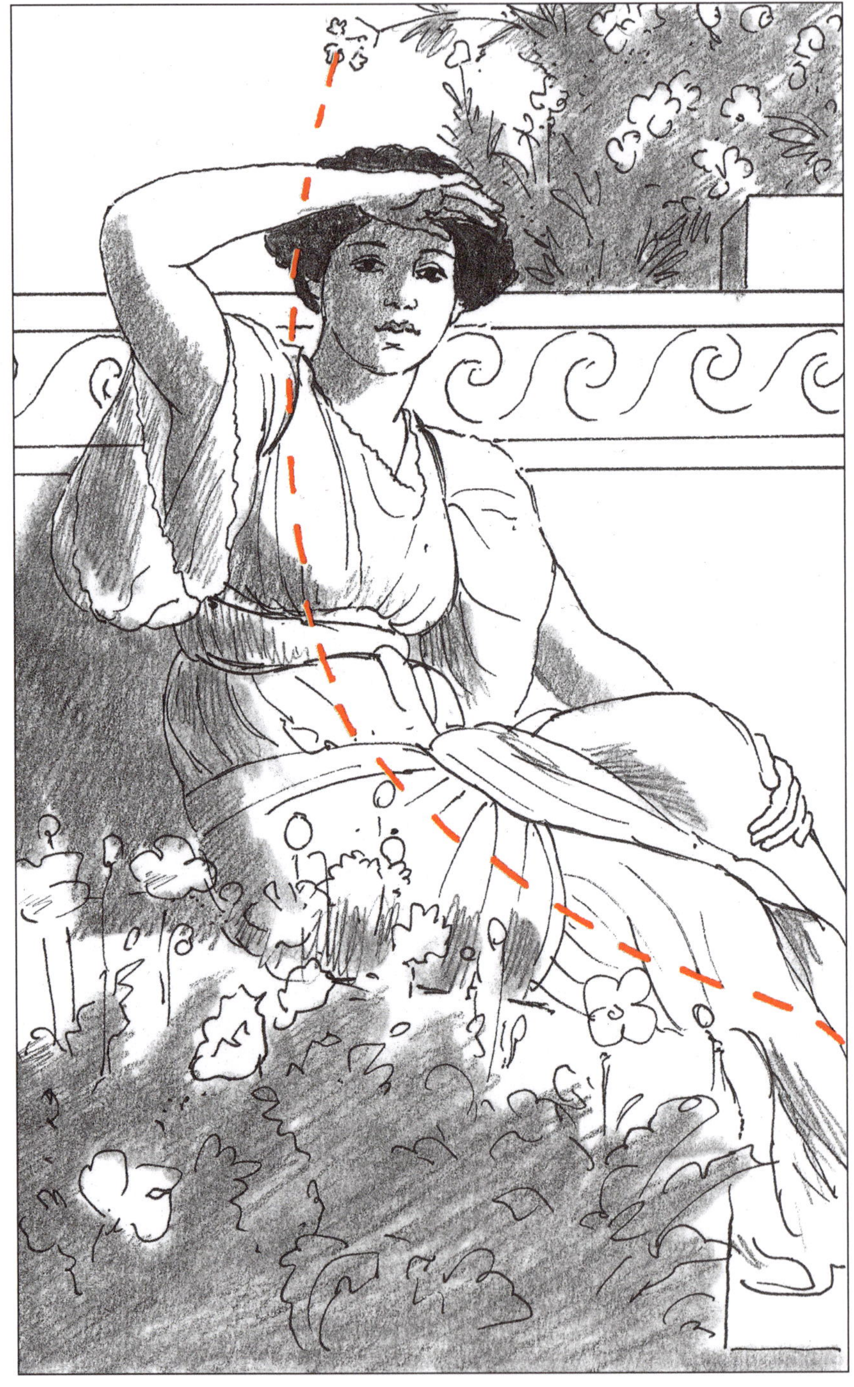

A Tryst (1912) is after the English Victorian painter John William Godward (1861–1922), who has posed a quasi-classical female figure against a wall, with flowers both behind and in front of her. The viewer's eye follows a smooth curve from the flowers in the top right corner, to the girl's head and raised arm, down through the line of her seated body, past the poppies growing below, and off to one side.

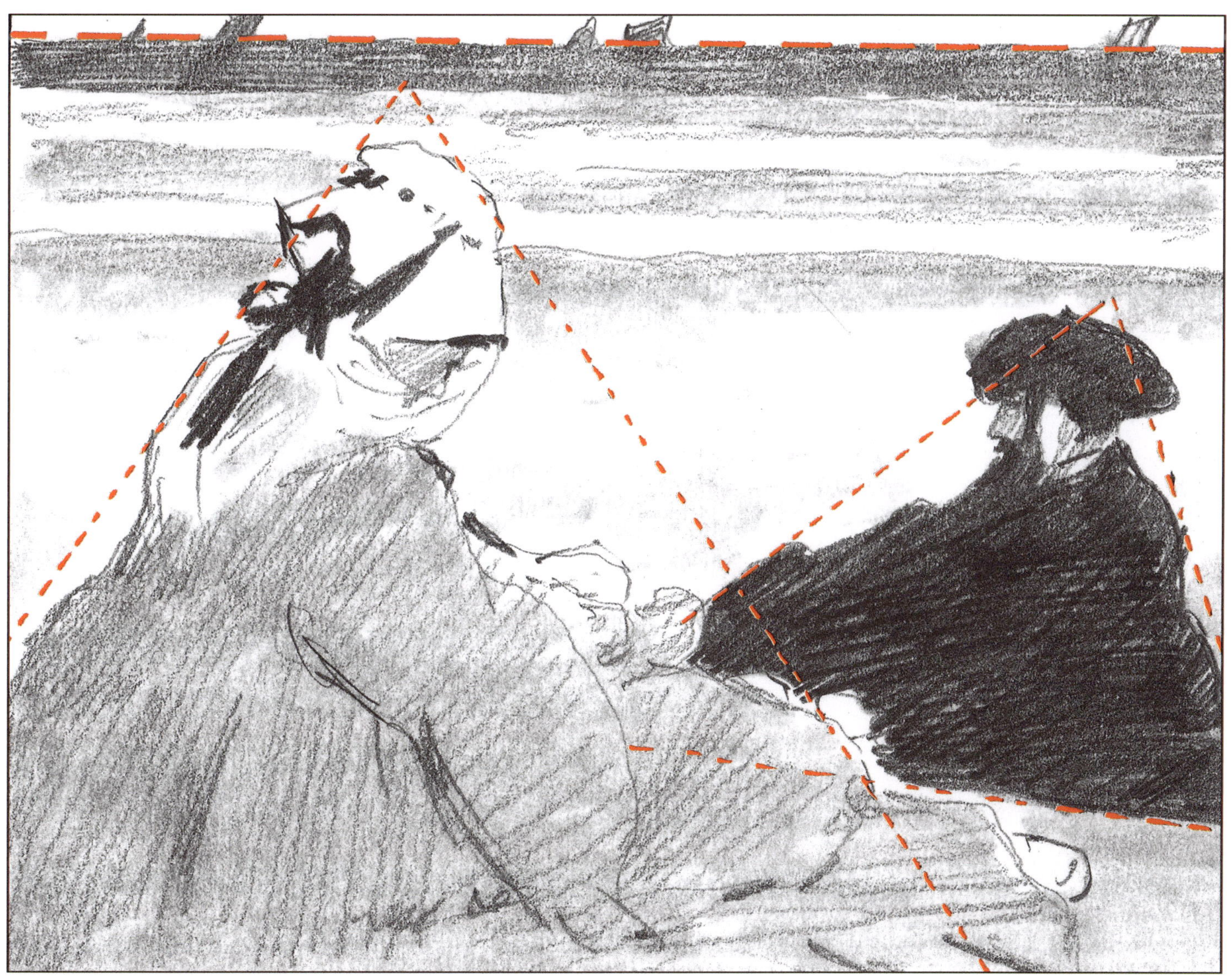

This composition by Edouard Manet (1832–83) of a beach scene at Berck-sur-Mer, northern France, features a high horizon line that places the area occupied by the sea in the top of the picture. The male and female figures are composed into larger and lesser triangles that 'answer' each other, with the female figure in the larger, more dominant triangle. They are both set below the level of the horizon, and the larger one sits firmly on the base of the picture.

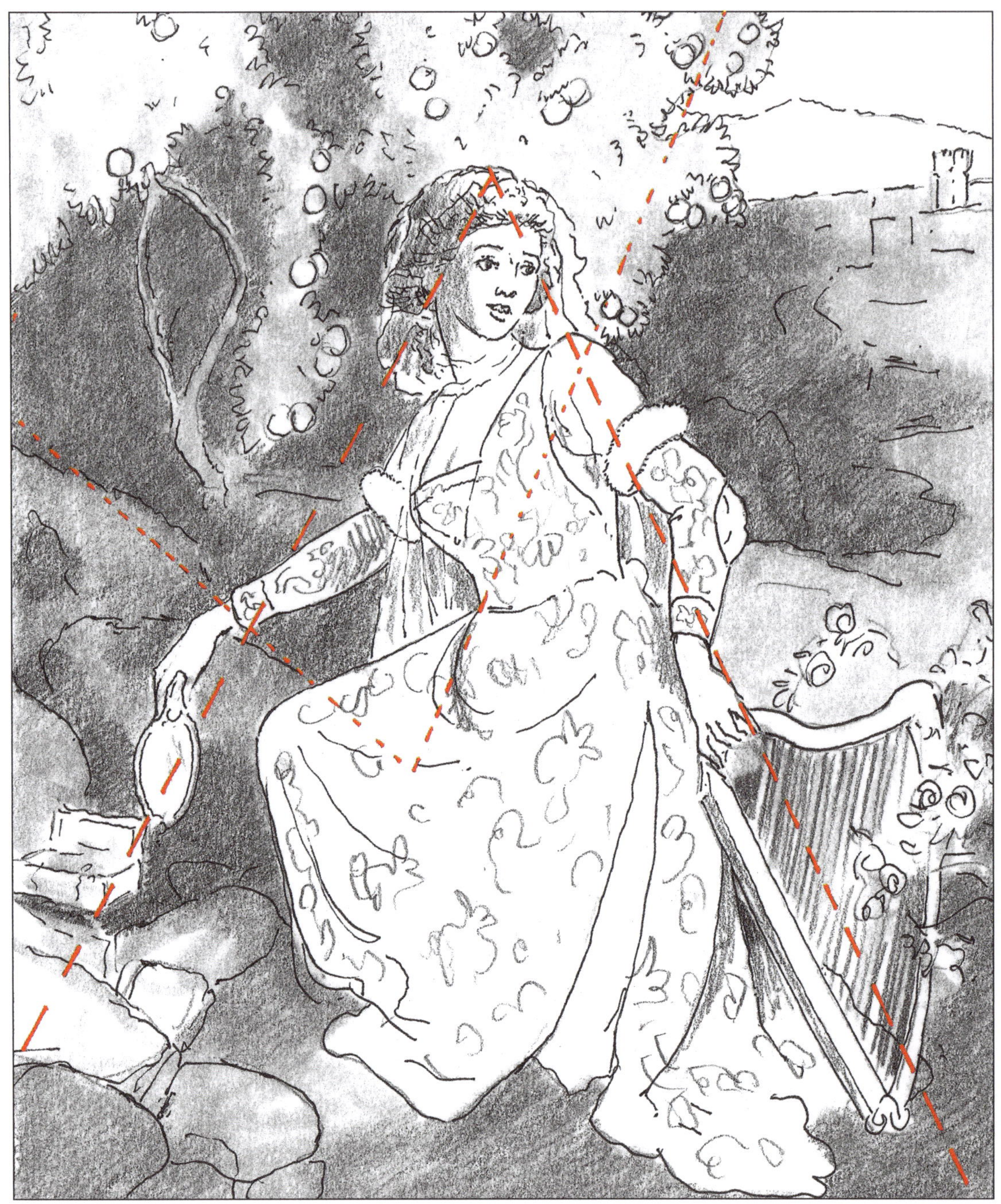

In my copy of *Bountiful Nature* (1897), by Talbot Hughes (1869–1942), the woman's figure forms a triangle rising from the base of the picture into the centre of the top half. All the surrounding 'props' serve to enhance the force of this dominant triangle. As you can see, I have indicated a smaller, inverted triangle intersecting the main one but this does not in any way detract from the power of the main shape.

Artist's Note

The triangle has been used time and time again to produce extremely stable and powerful compositions, and when you go around a traditional art gallery it is interesting to note how many of the artists have used a triangular or pyramidal framework for their pictures.

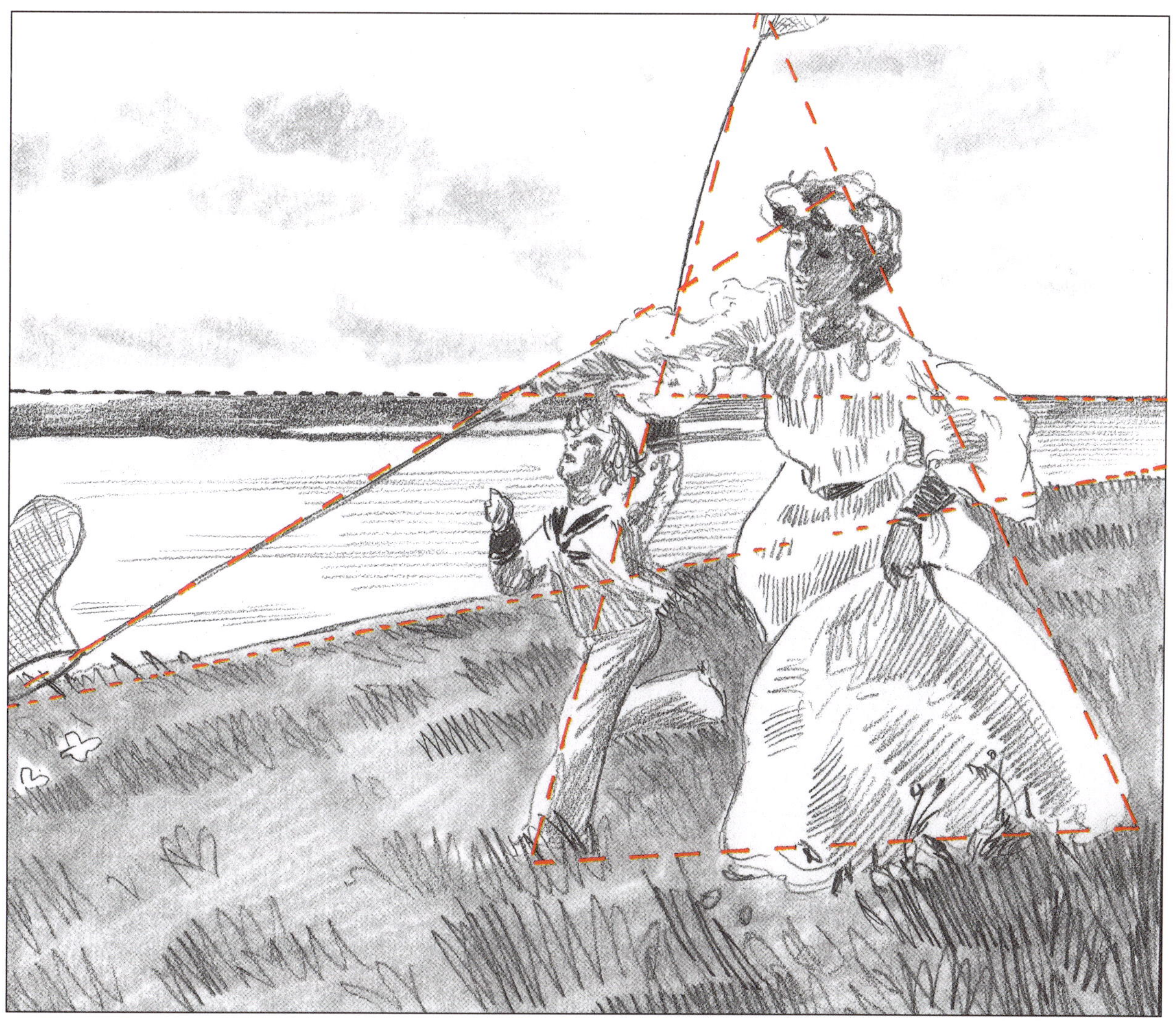

This example, after *Butterflies* (1904) by Charles Sims (1873–1928), is much more lively, despite using the stabilizing device of a triangle as its main figure position. With their careful positioning and angle, both the horizon and the slanting line of the cliff-edge produce a wide, open-air feel. The strong triangular combination of the young woman and the little boy doesn't detract from the activity of butterfly hunting. The outstretched arm of the woman cuts into the main triangle quite dramatically and effectively puts the dynamic into the scene.

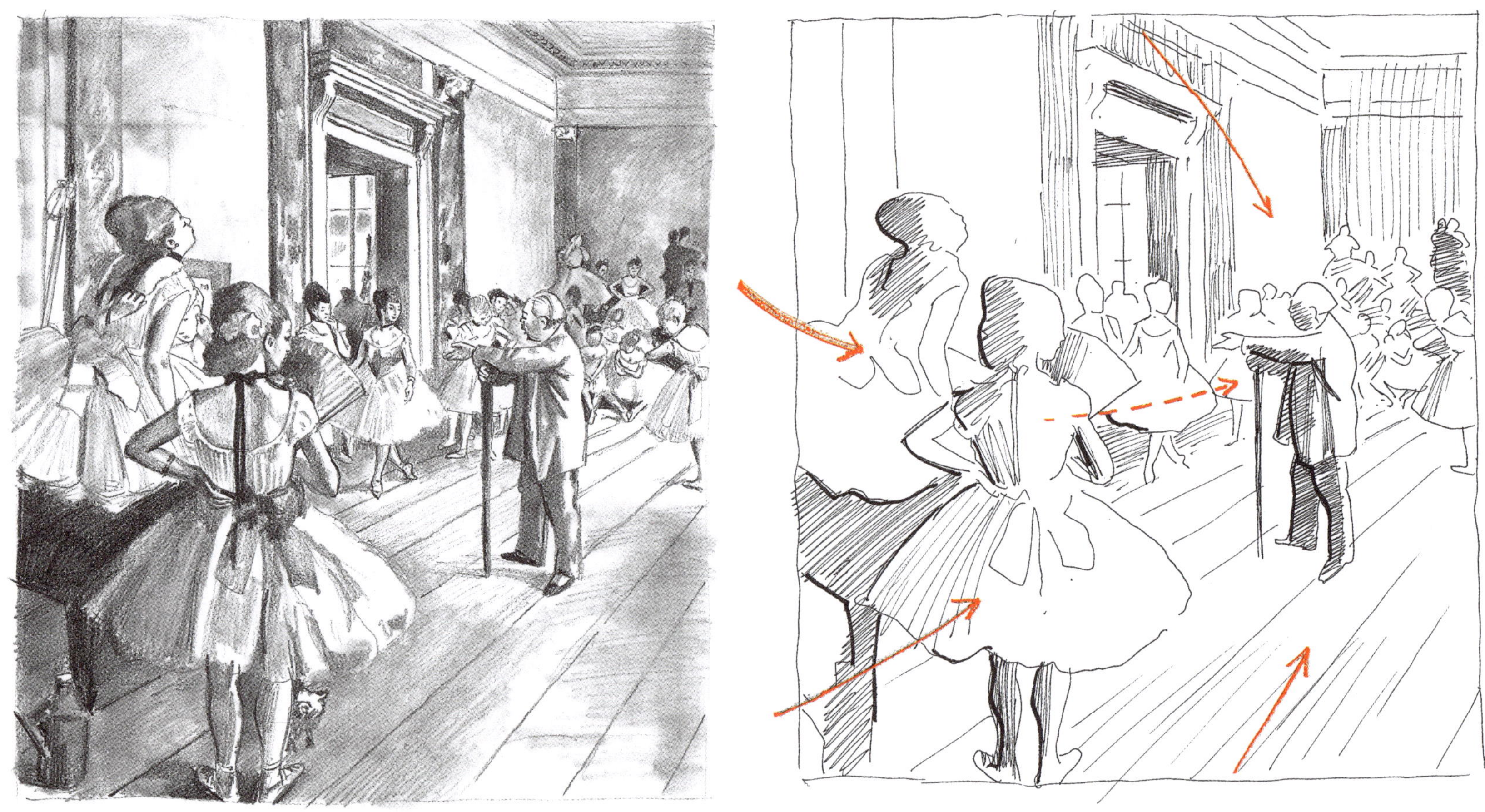

In this scene after Edgar Degas (1834–1917) we are in a 19th-century dance studio, with a master continuing to instruct his pupils as they rest. All the attention is on the master with his stick, which he uses to beat out the rhythm. The perspective takes you towards him. The way the girls are arranged further underlines his importance. The beautiful casual grouping of the dancers in their frothy tutus, starting with the nearest and swinging around the edge of the room to the other side, neatly frames the master's figure. He holds the stage.

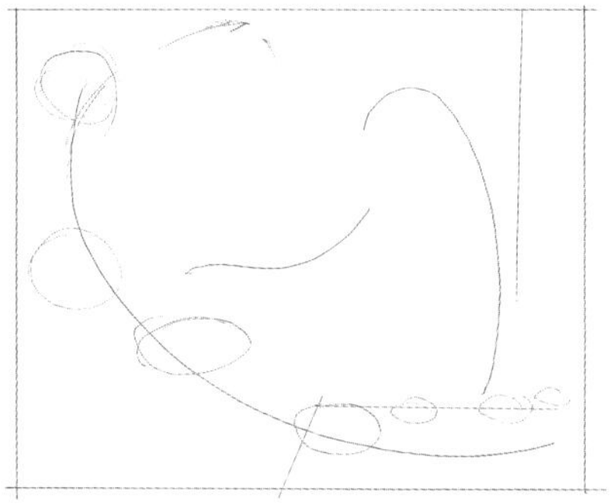

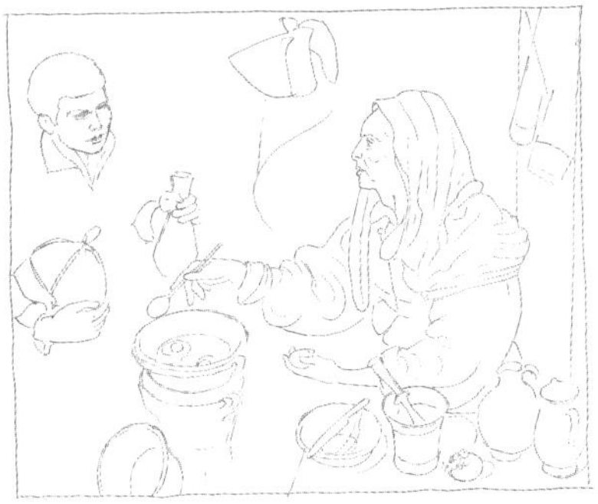

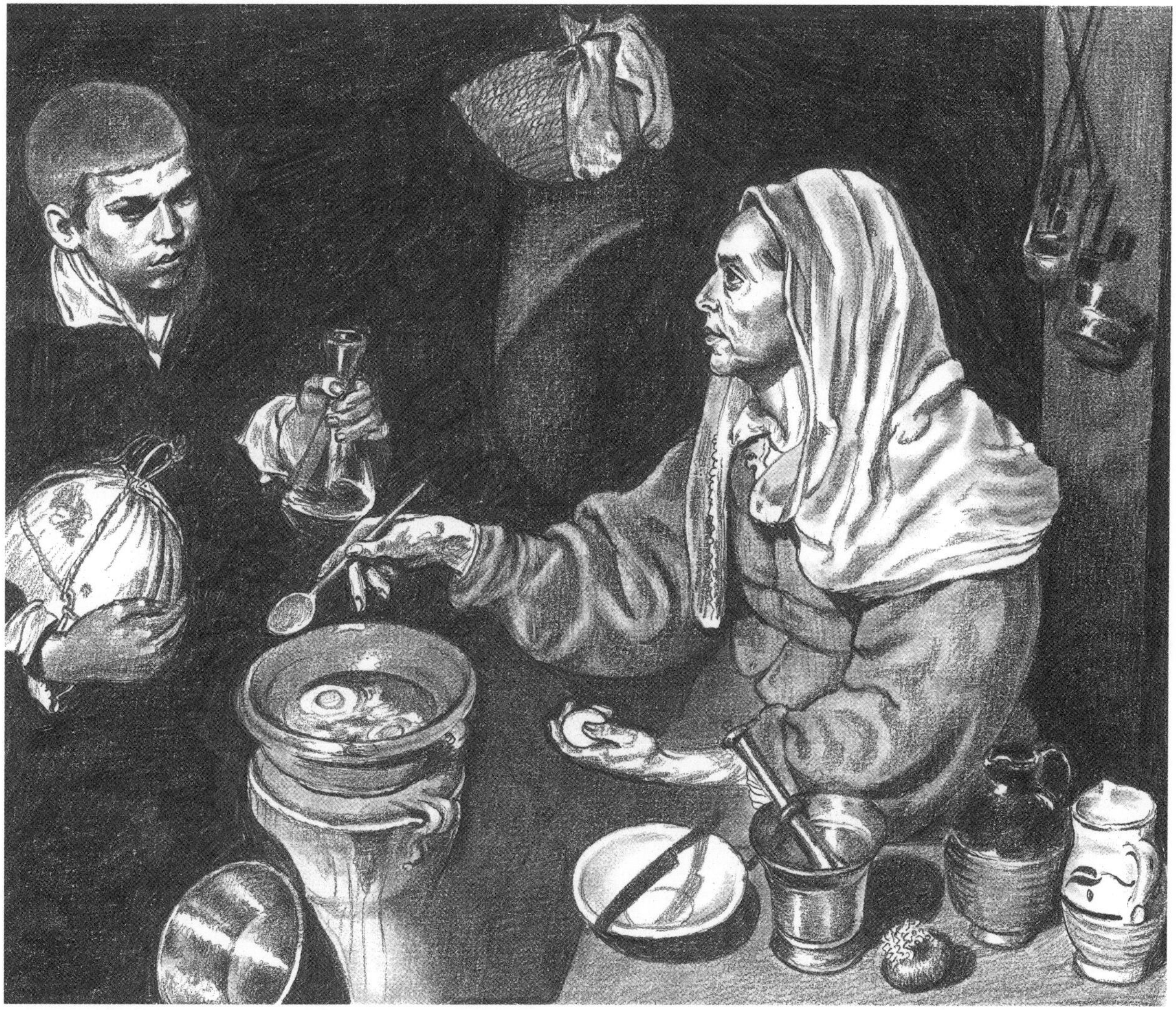

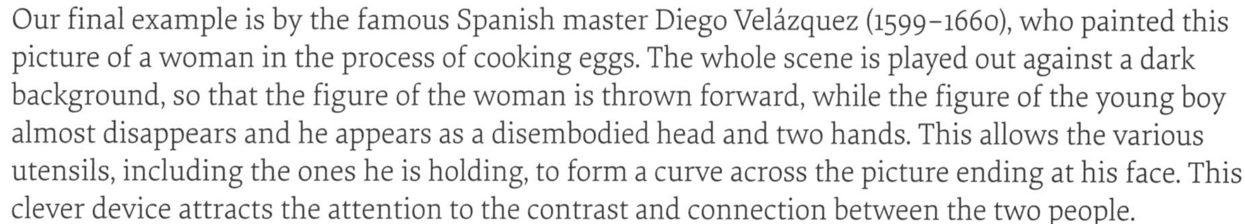

Our final example is by the famous Spanish master Diego Velázquez (1599–1660), who painted this picture of a woman in the process of cooking eggs. The whole scene is played out against a dark background, so that the figure of the woman is thrown forward, while the figure of the young boy almost disappears and he appears as a disembodied head and two hands. This allows the various utensils, including the ones he is holding, to form a curve across the picture ending at his face. This clever device attracts the attention to the contrast and connection between the two people.

Inspiration from a Great Artist

As we have seen, gaining inspiration from great master artists of history is a time-honoured way of working for all artists: it is often the attempt to realize the way a master painter designed his painting that increases the power of our own work. Here, take your study a step further and have a go at recreating a major work that you feel some affinity with.

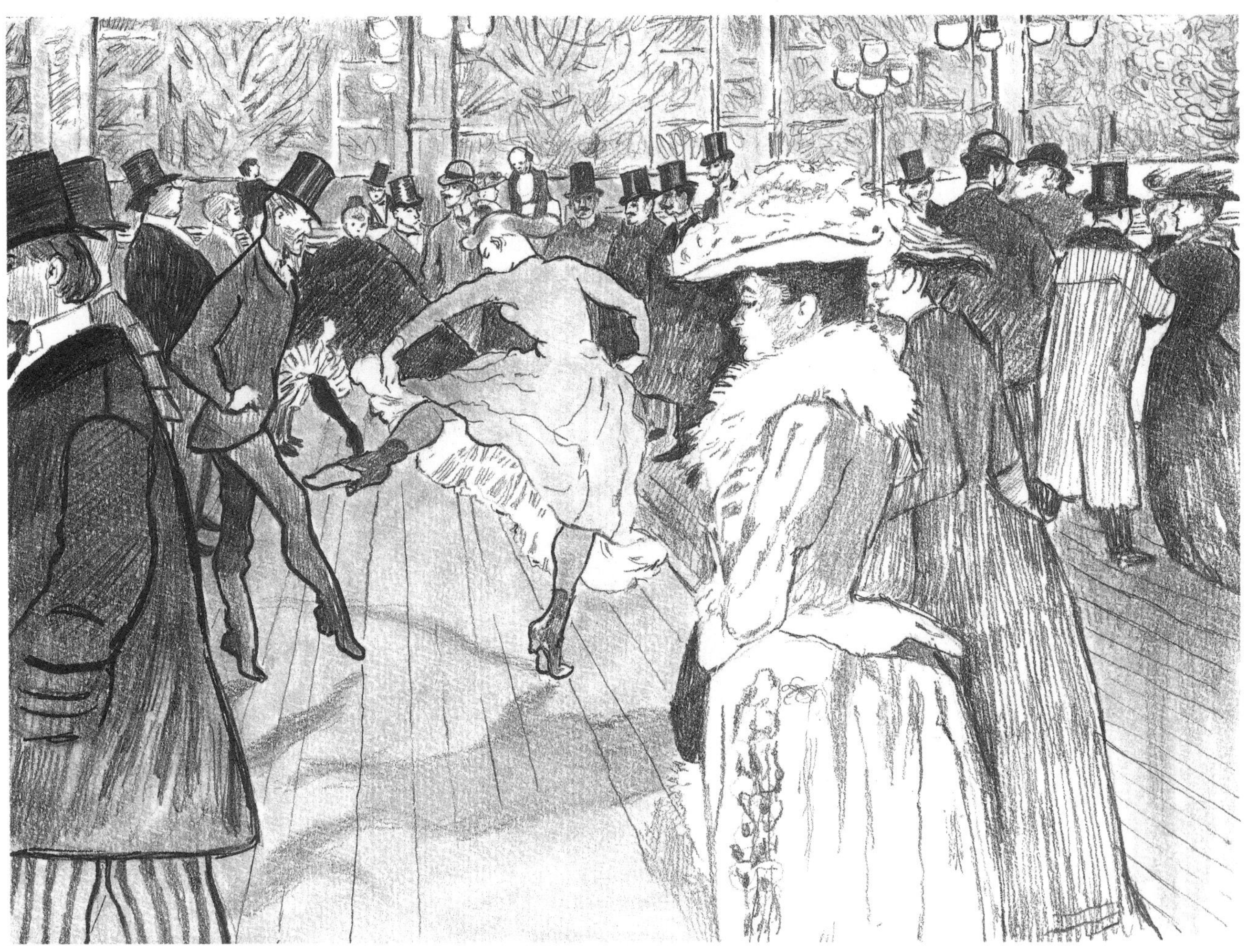

This drawing shows the disposition of the various figures in a painting by Henri de Toulouse-Lautrec (1864–1901). Set in the Moulin Rouge, the grouping of the two dancers in the centre among the strolling and drinking boulevardiers is a dynamic composition that is well-known among artists and art-lovers. The space around the figures is well realized, with all the characters placed in an interesting way in groups, meeting and greeting.

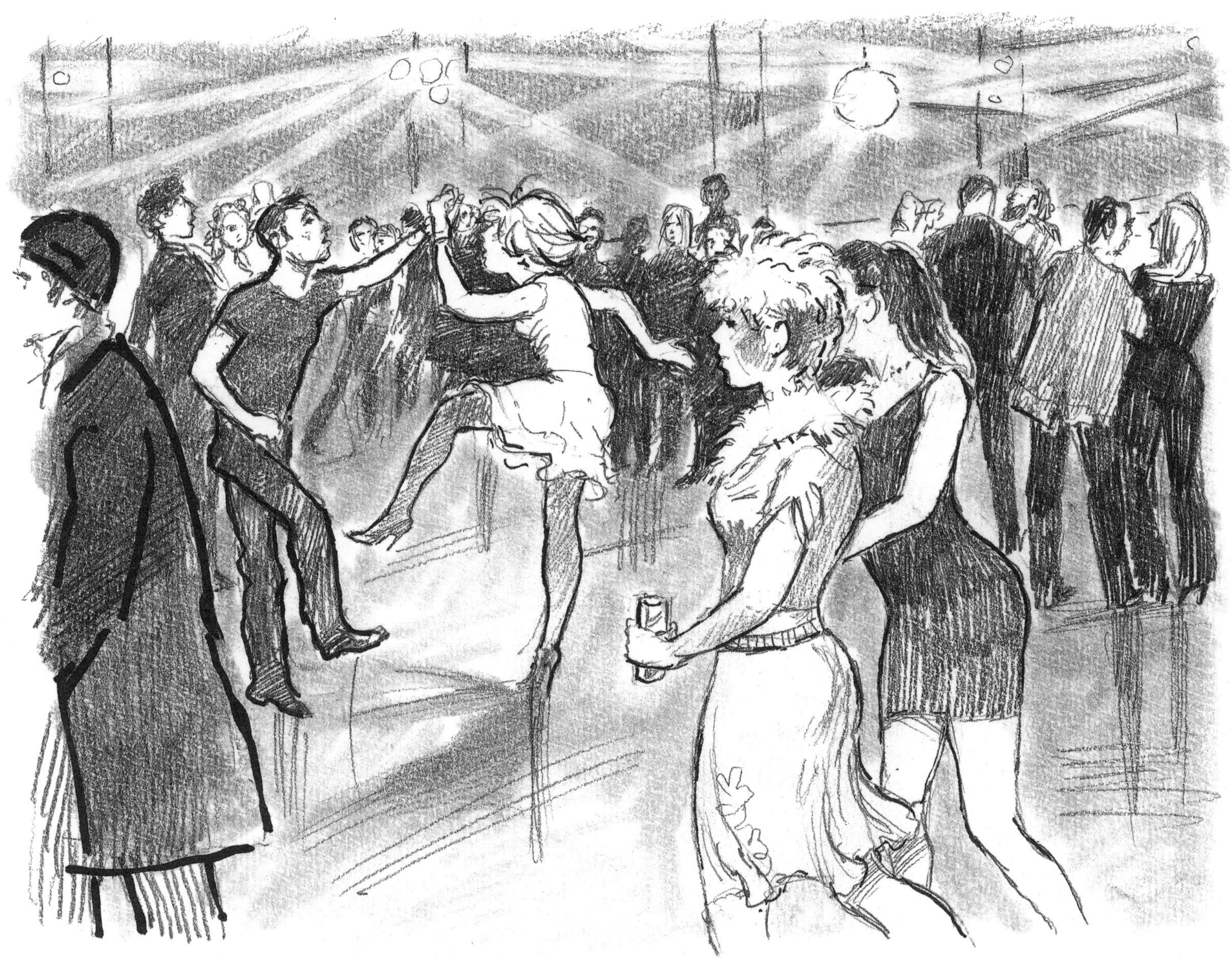

In my version of this painting of lively, late-night activity, I have grouped the figures in exactly the same way, but with references to a different era. The central couple are now two young people dancing to a jazz band. The other figures around are also similar in grouping but in modern dress, and the space above their heads is now filled with strobe lighting, as in a modern night-club. Once again, the composition makes for a very interesting picture, even though the occasion is very changed in time; so, basing your picture on a famous old master's work is not a bad way to learn how to compose a pleasing image.

Expressive Colour

The choice of colour always has a reason behind it, which dictates the kind of colour values used. Drama and colour often go hand-in-hand, as the power of colour to produce an active, dominant ingredient into the composition of the picture shows in these examples.

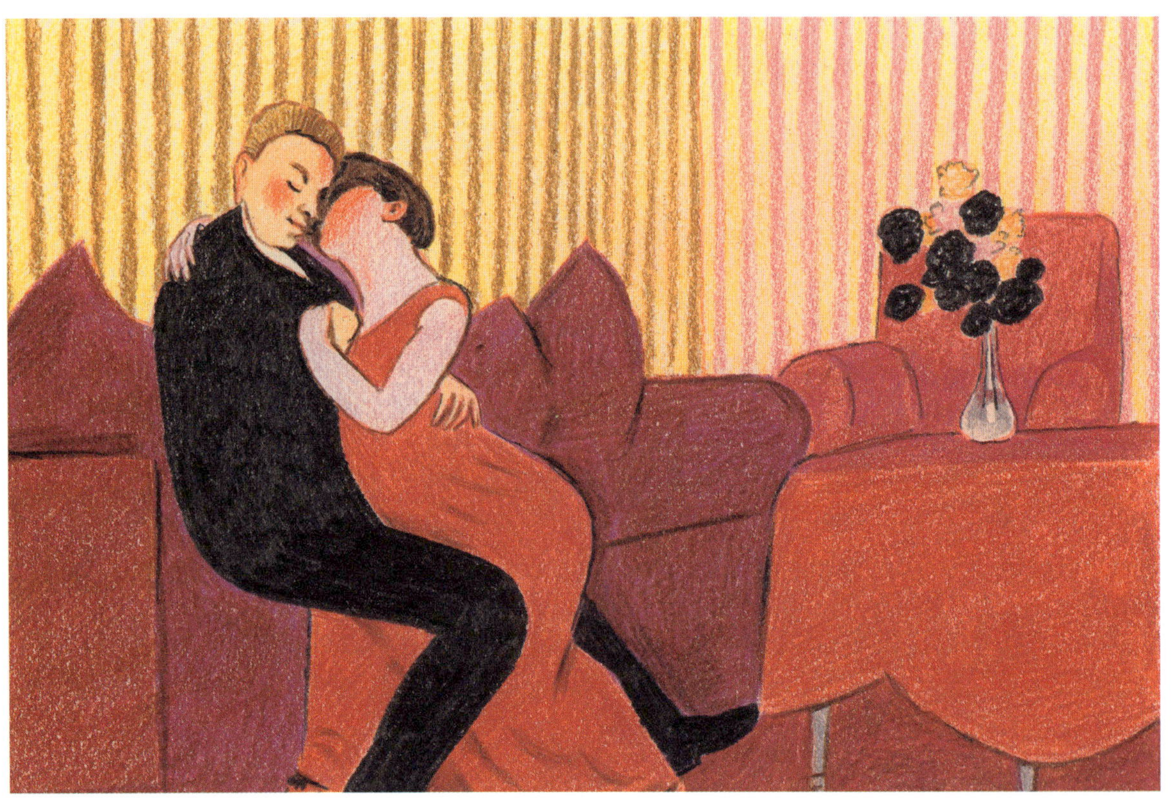

The Lie (1897) by Felix Vallotton (1865–1925) seems to be set in a scene full of deep red danger. The whole room is furnished in strong reds, with pink and yellow striped wallpaper and black and pink flowers in the vase. The embracing man and woman are wearing evening dress, him in deepest black and her in bright, hot red. Who is telling whom the lie? We don't know for sure, but no doubt we each have our own idea of the culprit. The quality of the dominant, obsessive red conveys both a sign of danger and the suggestion of liaisons less than innocent. The colour really does set the scene and we know that no good will come of it. But isn't it attractive, isn't it seductive? What deep waters we are getting into, and all because of a title and a suggestive colour scheme. Strong drama, of the psychological kind.

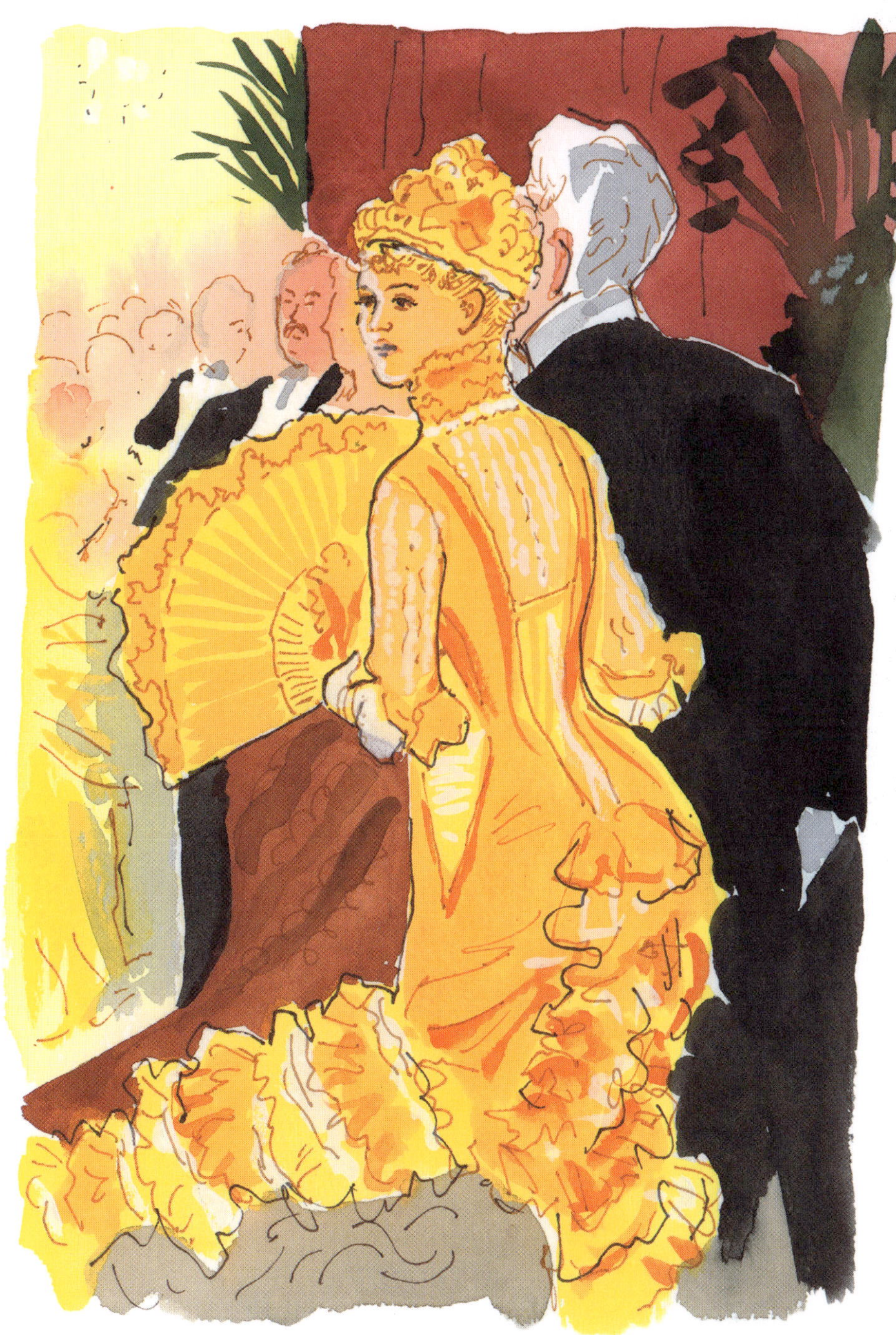

The next artist, James Tissot (1836–1902), was an Edwardian society painter who was in great demand for his ability to portray beautiful women and handsome men. At any rate, if you were painted by him, you usually came out looking much better than you had ever thought you could. When someone had a marvellous, fashionable dress to show off, it was reasonable to get Tissot to do a painting in which this elegant article was being given an airing. In this picture the brilliant yellow dress obscures everyone else at the ball and what the dress doesn't hide of the competition, the large fan does.

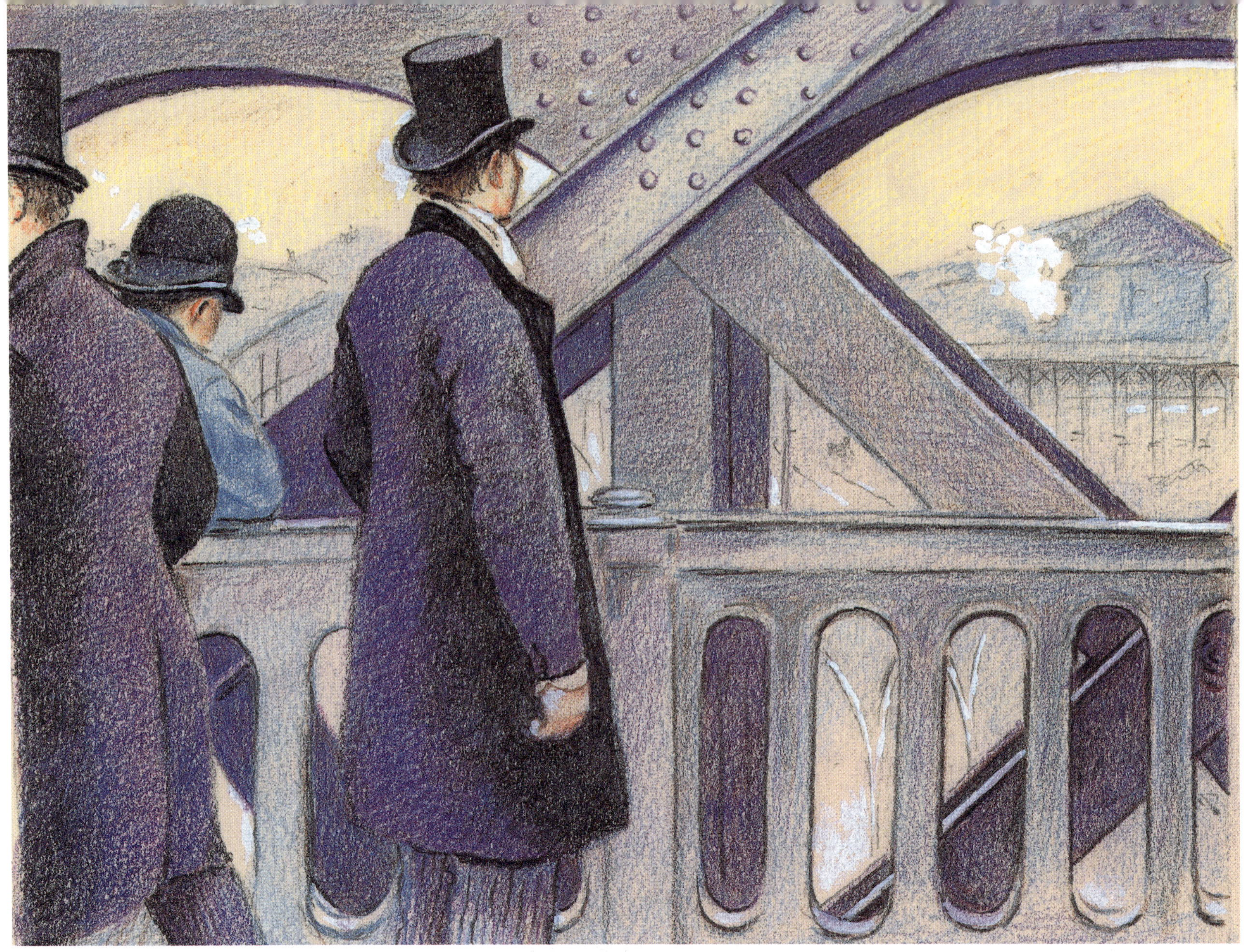

Gustave Caillebotte (1848–94) was a friend and artistic companion to several of the Impressionists but, although he was attracted to the same subject matter, he produced it in a very different manner. Most of his works seem to be in a very muted range of colours, with a very deliberate tonal harmony in his colour. This one, of the bridge over the railway in Paris, was painted several times by him and other artists of the time. This rather abstract arrangement of the girders of the bridge and the men looking on is typical of the way he saw his subject matter. Everything is in an industrial grey, including the men's coats, which look like a part of the same urban landscape.

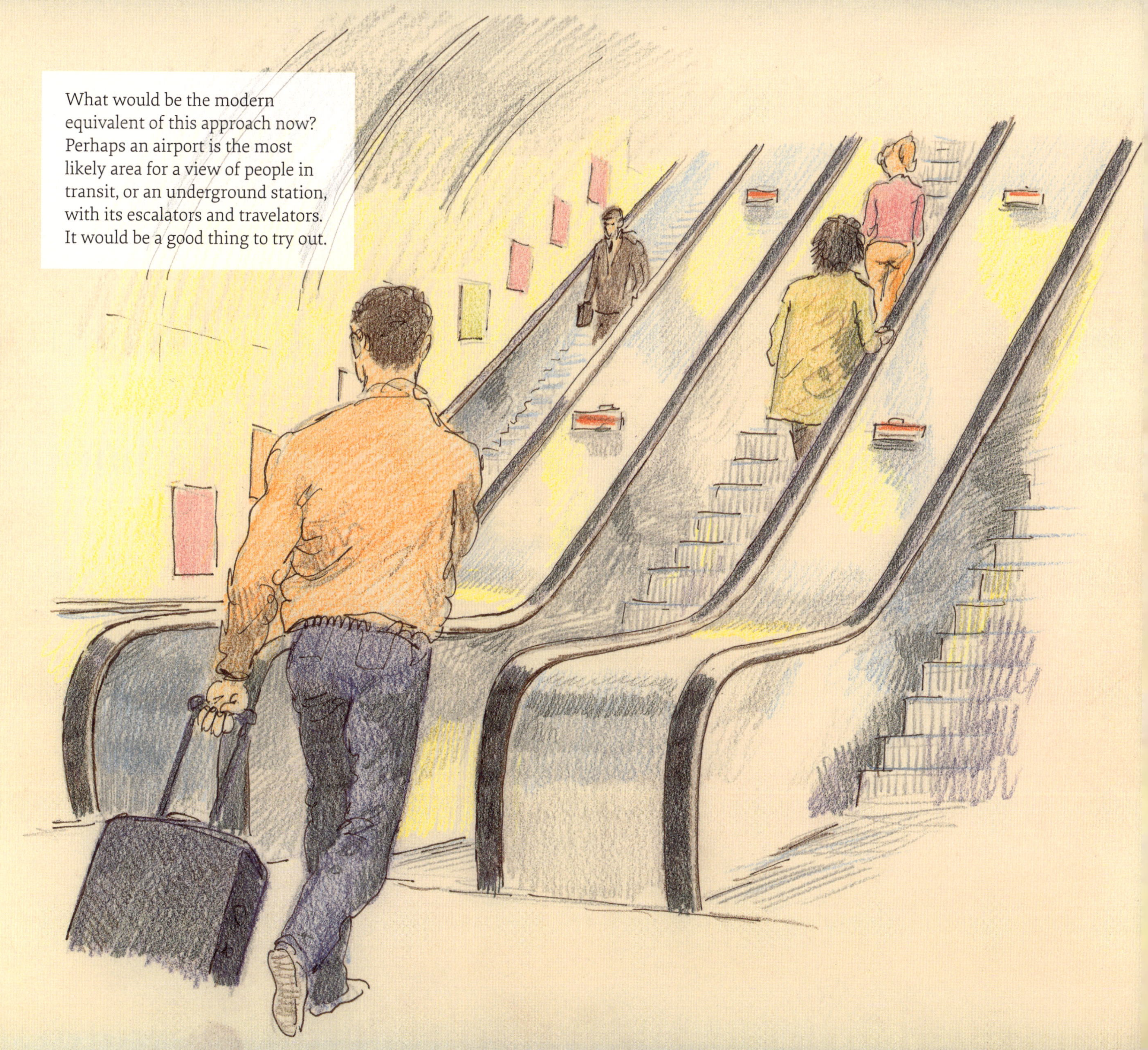

What would be the modern equivalent of this approach now? Perhaps an airport is the most likely area for a view of people in transit, or an underground station, with its escalators and travelators. It would be a good thing to try out.

Chapter Seven

CLOTHING AND HAIRSTYLES

At various times in history, fashions in clothing have tended to either reveal or disguise the shape of the figure. In the ancient civilizations of Greece and Rome, loose draped clothing was the norm: nowadays, there are so many variations of dress that you may find people showing off their figure one day and hiding it under heavy or loose garments the next.

Whatever the prevailing fashion, as artists we need to understand how clothing fits on the human figure and to use the sharpened perception that comes from constant practice at drawing both the clothing and the figure underneath.

When it comes to setting up a portrait, personal touches can provide unexpected opportunities for the artist. Notable items of clothing, jewellery, hair accessories and hats can all add something special. While capturing a likeness of your subject is undoubtedly the most important aspect of a portrait, their choice of clothing and hairstyle speaks volumes about their character and getting these right will contribute to the aesthetic quality of your drawing.

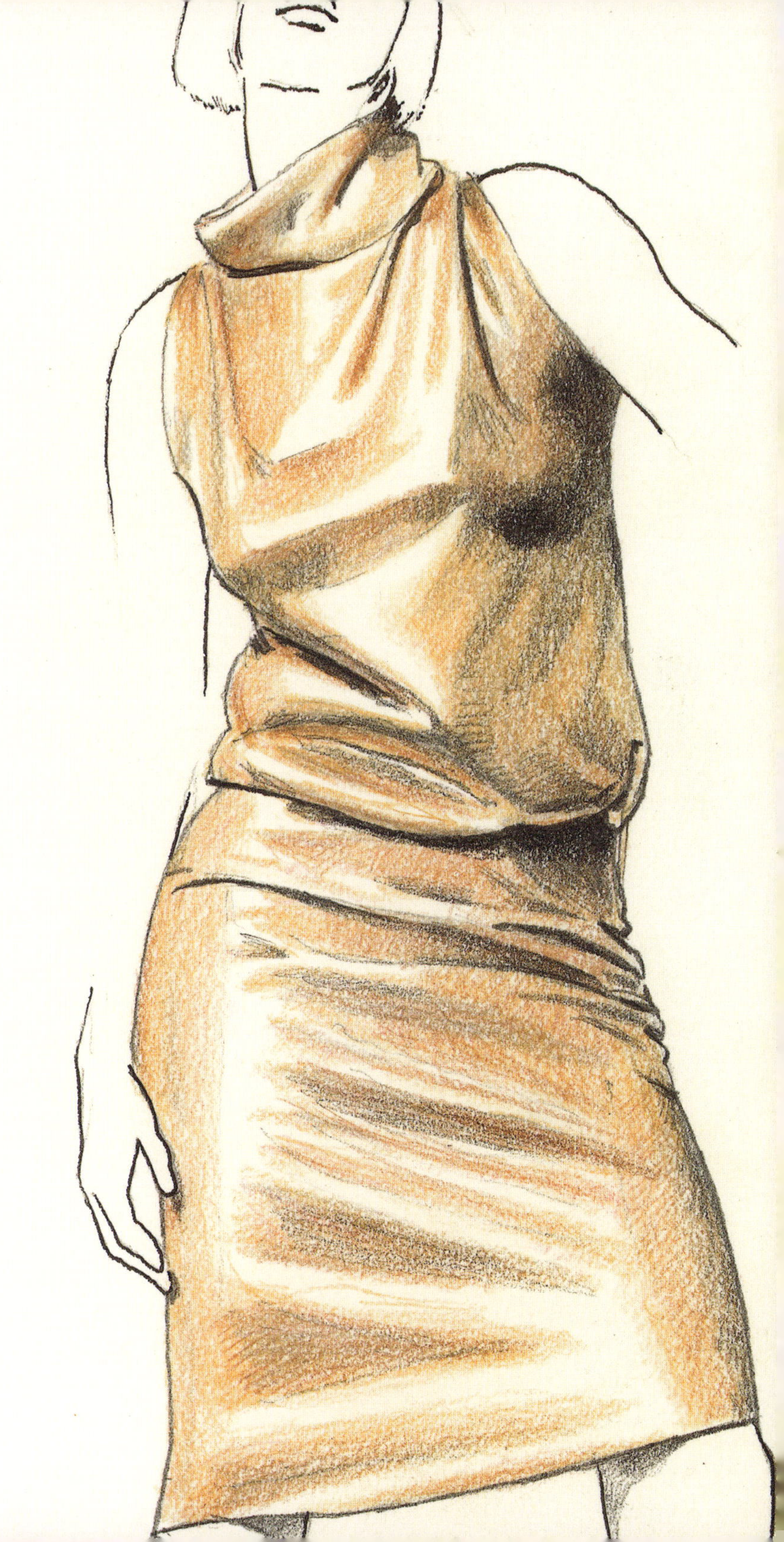

Clothing of the Past

The Ancient World

Among the earliest recorded clothes are the tunics, robes and togas of the ancient worlds of Greece, Rome and Egypt. Most early clothing was draped rather than tailored or cut to fit the body closely.

The first example shows an ancient Greek statue in a draped robe. On this funerary image from the fourth century BC, the material is draped around the woman's head and shoulders and gathered under her arms. It both reveals and hides the figure at the same time, depending on the action of the body under the drapery.

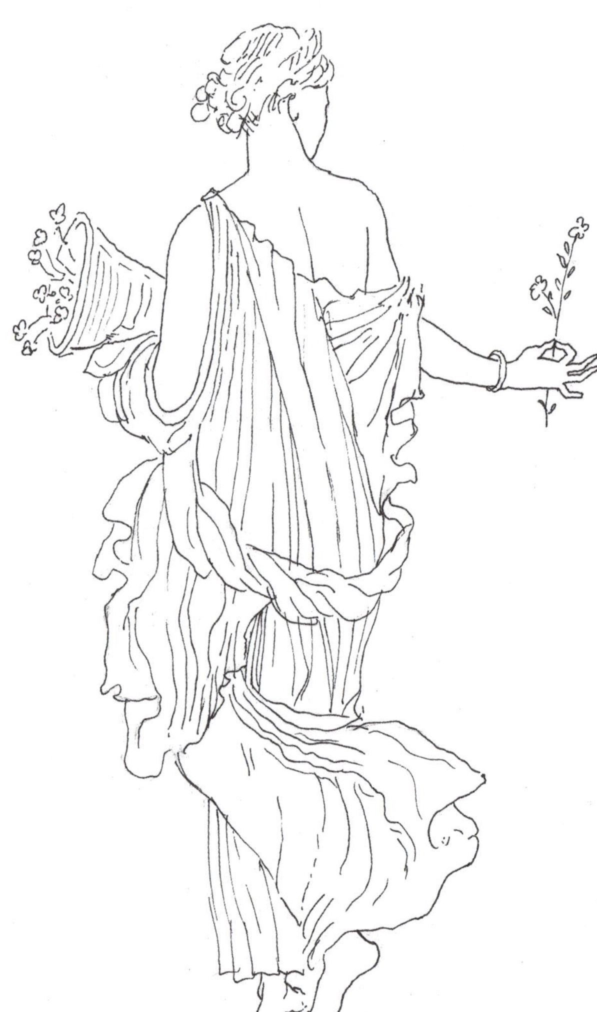

The second figure (left) is similar in some ways, but it originates from wall paintings near Naples in Italy, executed at about the same period as the previous example. This illustration gives a clearer idea of how the clothing draped the figure, and how part of the drapery was twisted around itself to act like a belt or girdle. People also wore brooches, which attached the robe to the shoulders, and could be adjusted to create the effect that the wearer wanted. As you can see from this example, it could be a very graceful form of dress, even though we might not consider it so practical now.

The Middle Ages and the Renaissance

The next drawing (right) is taken from a fresco by the Florentine painter Giotto di Bondone (1267–1337), showing two shepherds in contemporary dress. It is practical clothing for their line of work, consisting of hoods and hats to ward off the sun and rain, and short cloaks to keep them warm in cold weather. They also appear to have rather more robust footwear than people wore in earlier periods.

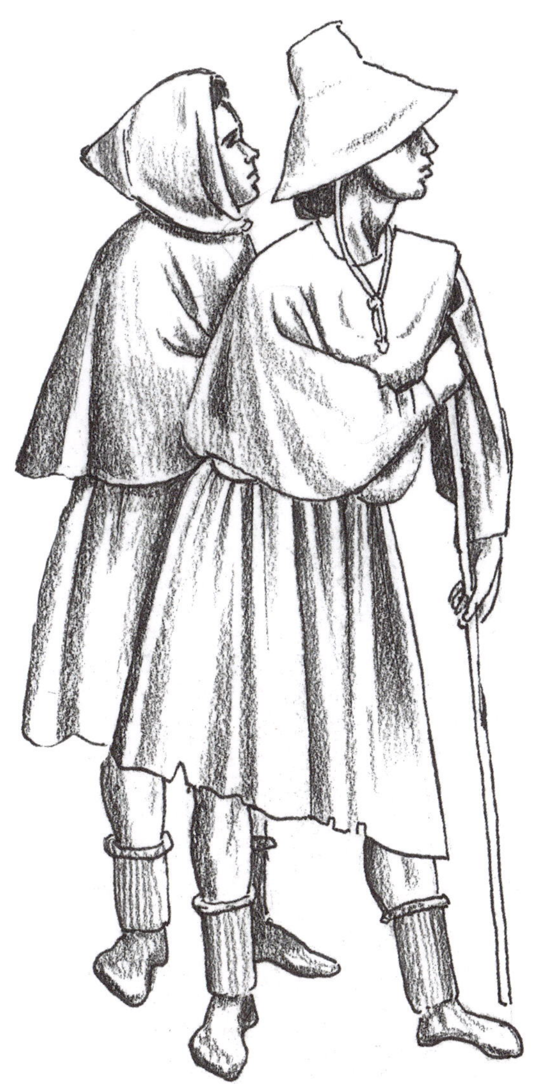

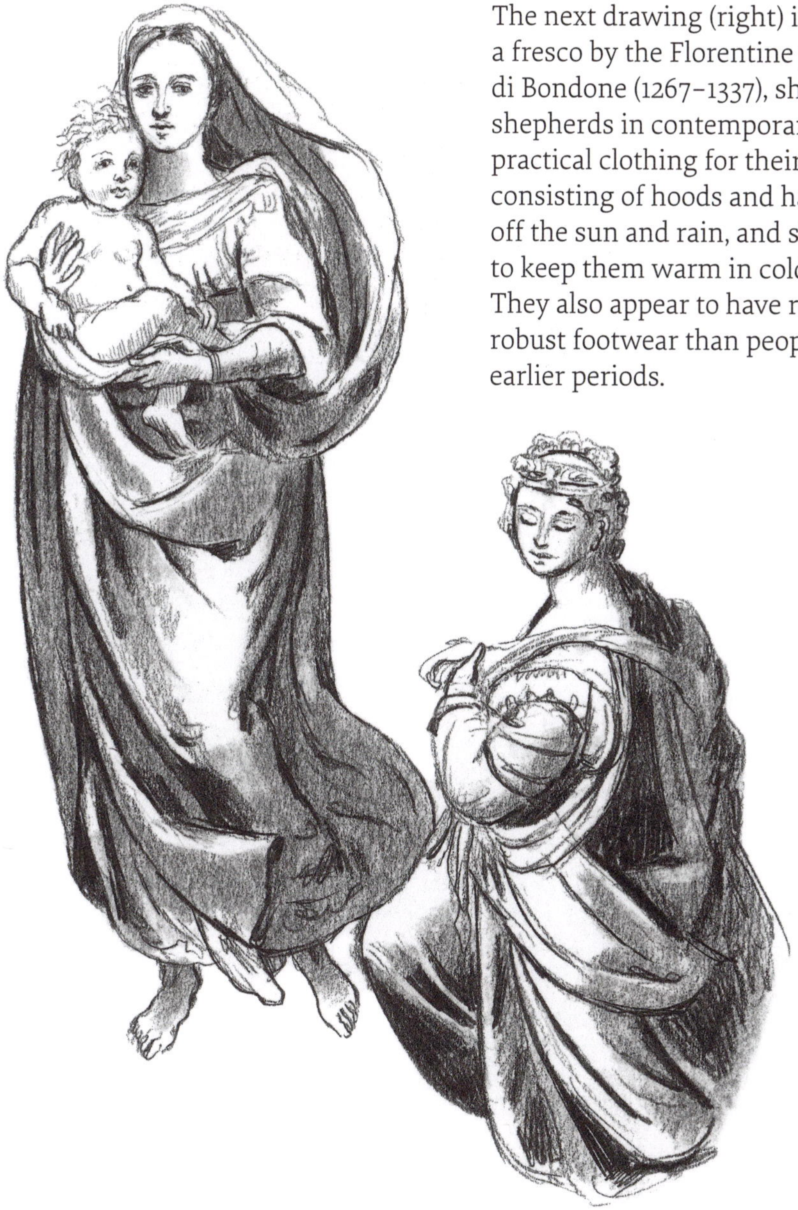

This example (left) comes from one to two hundred years later, showing some influence of the style of costume current during the Renaissance period. The draped cloaks and full skirts are very similar to the classical forms of dress shown on the facing page, but there are more tailored features, particularly the bodices and sleeves. Also, men of this period wore tight-fitting hose.

Drapery: Symbolic Colour

The examples of draped clothing shown here are taken from a range of contexts but each demonstrates a clear symbolic meaning behind their colours.

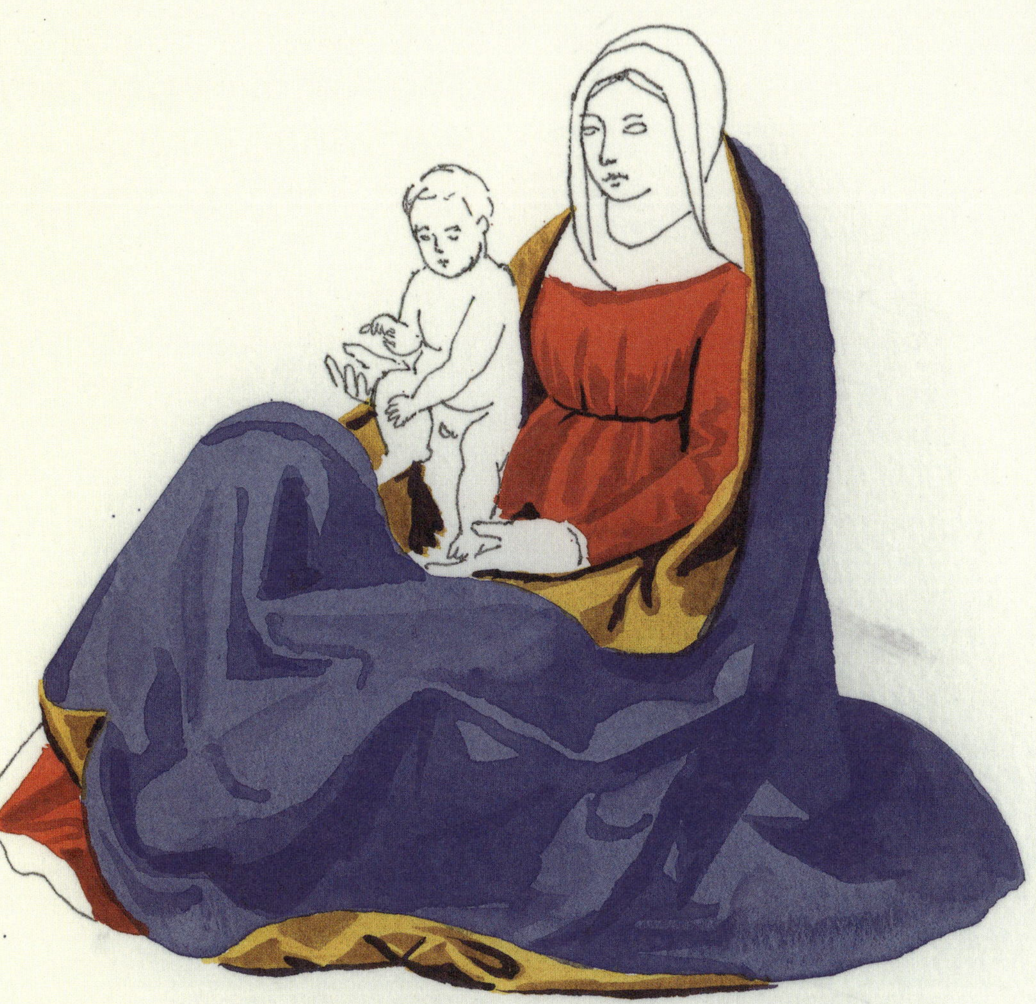

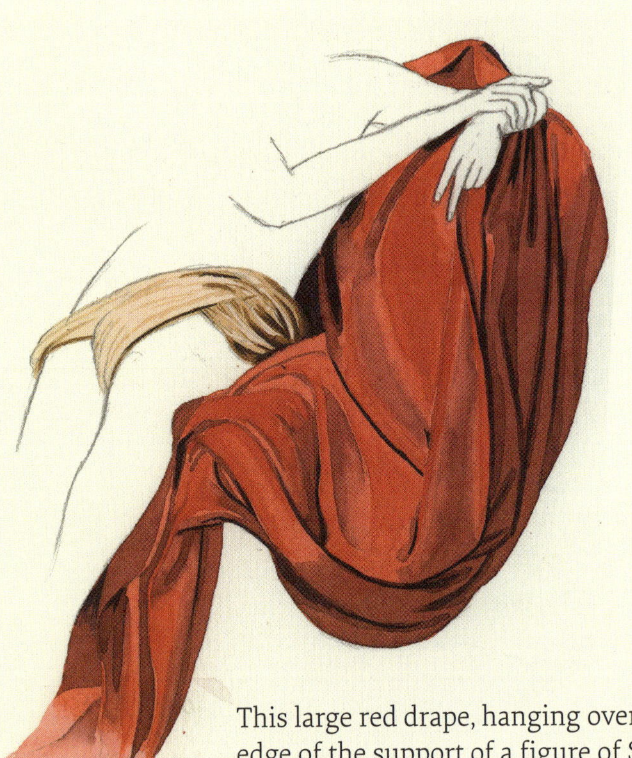

This large red drape, hanging over the edge of the support of a figure of St John, is emblematic of the martyrdom he will later endure, and hints at his passion and death.

The illustration of the Virgin Mary shows her wearing the typical medieval costume of a long dress with a heavy flowing cloak, in the powerful combination of red and blue. The red – representing Christ's Passion – is tonally particularly vibrant and the blue – associated with the Mother of God as the 'Stella Maris' or Star of the Sea – is a deep azure.

The colour chosen for the dominant figure in Delacroix's *Liberty Leading the People* (1830) – the female icon of the French revolutionary principle – suggests that she is a beacon for the people to follow through the smoke and fire of battle.

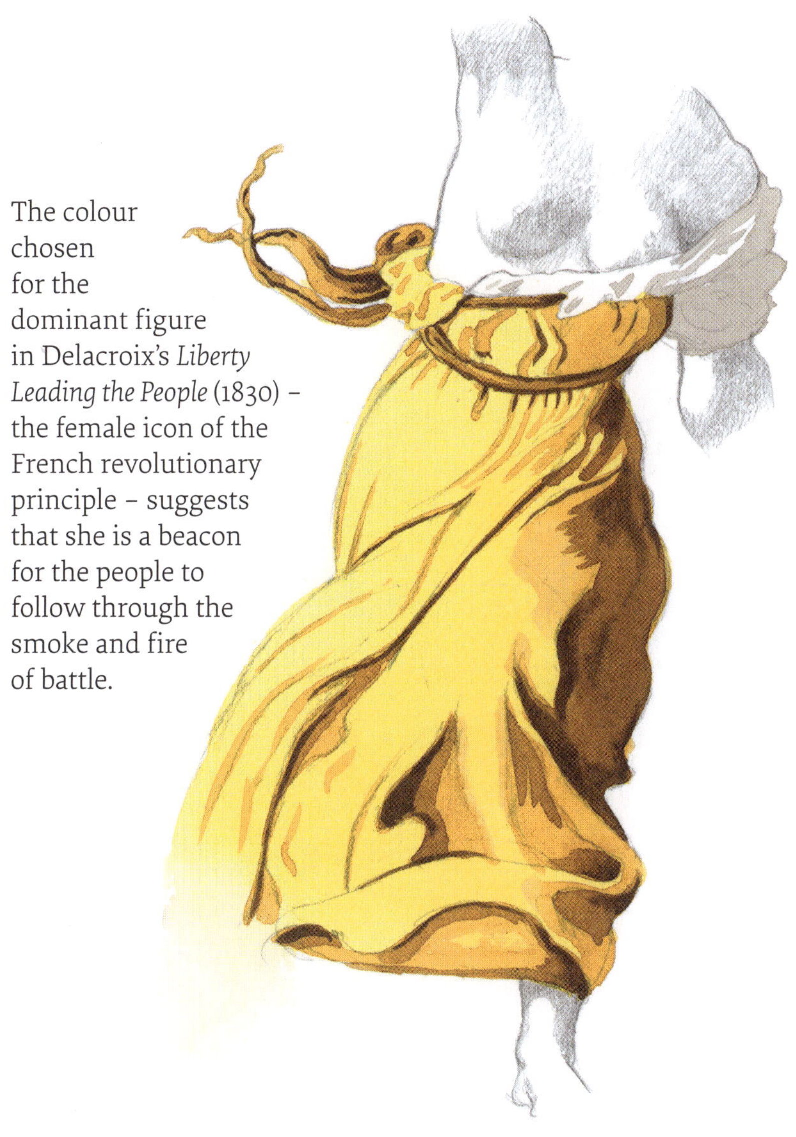

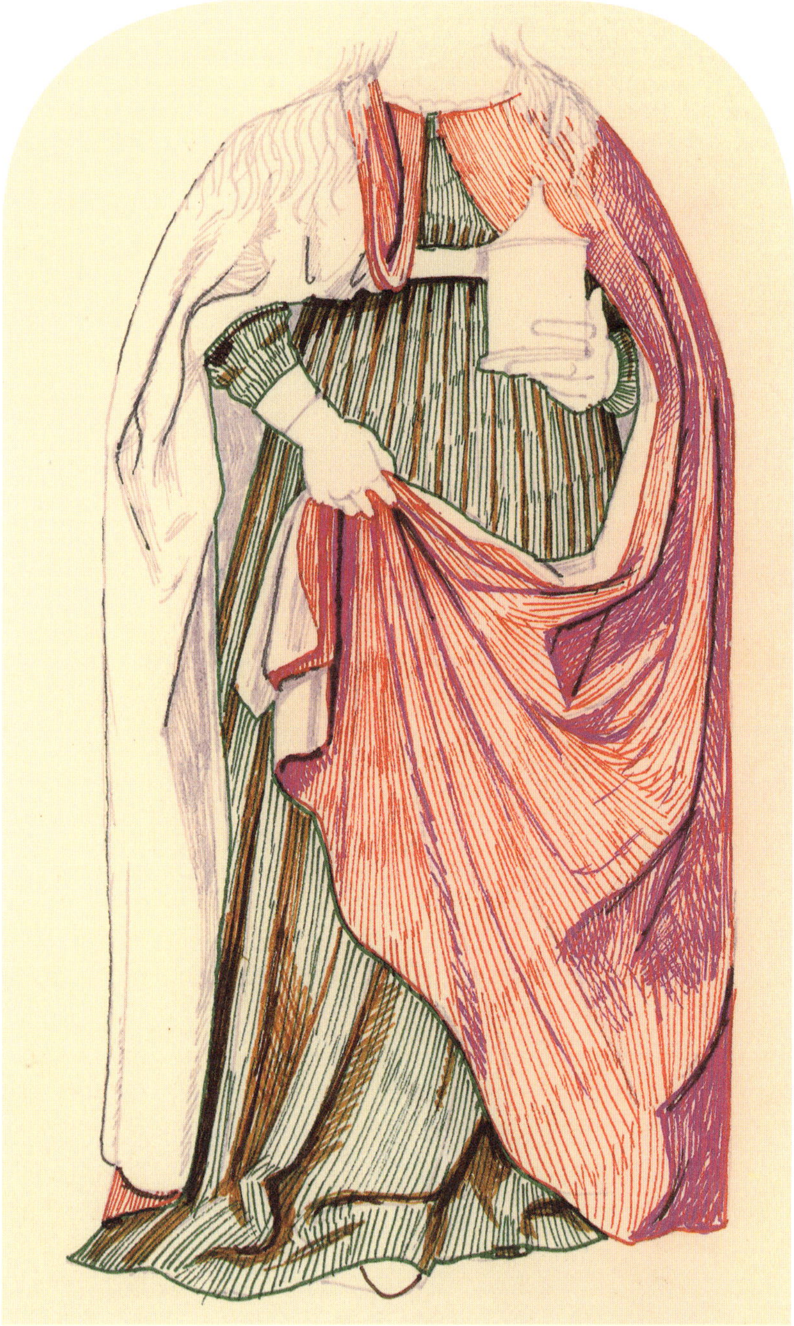

The dress of Mary Magdalene (after Piero della Francesca) signifies in both colour and style the penitence of the reformed courtesan who gave up her worldly life to follow one of sacrifice. The green signifies the rebirth of her soul and the red cloak (now worn as a badge of repentance) tells of her recent worldly career.

Clothing as Decoration

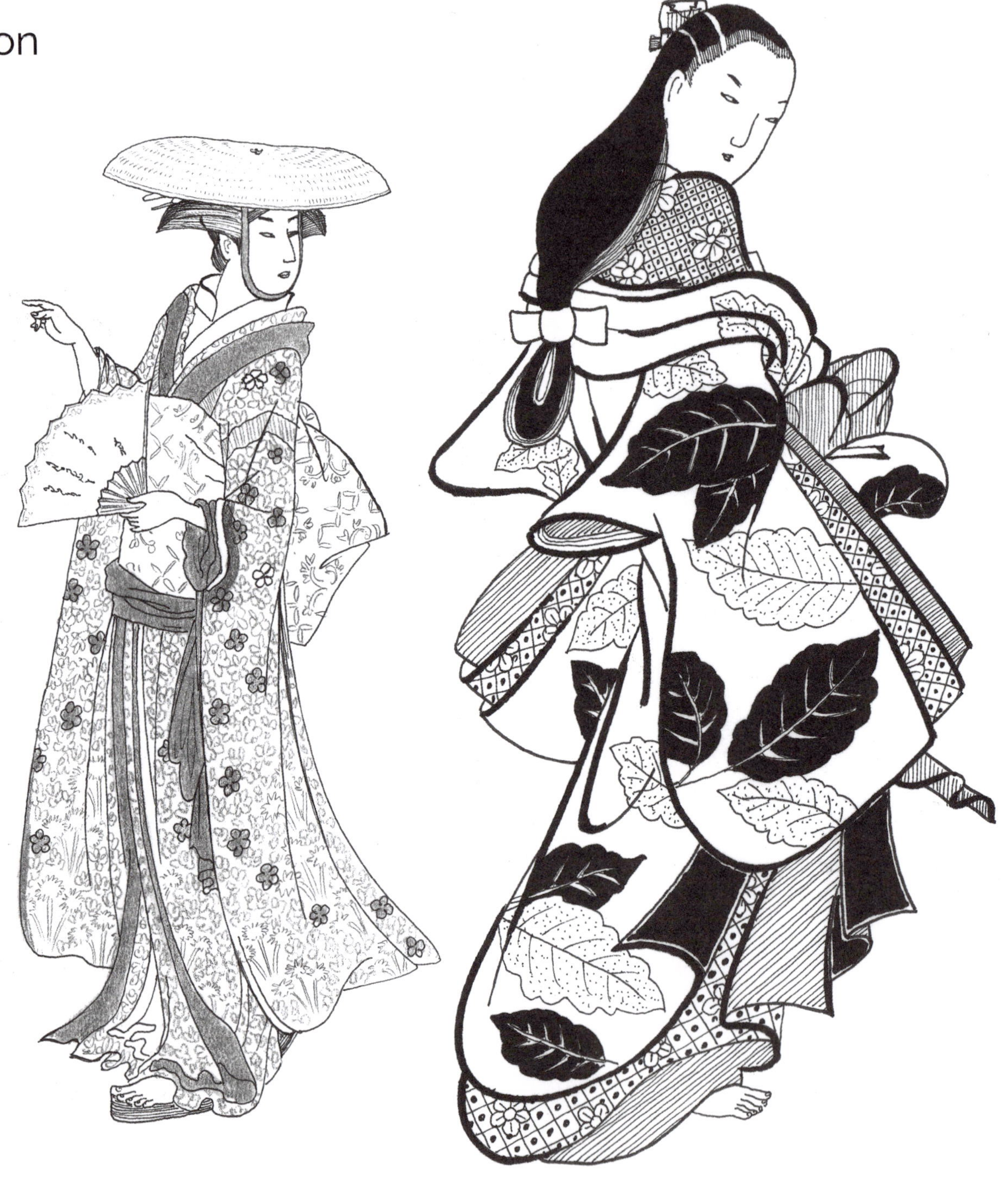

The Far East

The date is the eighteenth century, but the Japanese clothing shown here is more classical in form than the European styles of the day. This example does not so much show the evolution of costume as illustrate a different approach to the use of decorative elements. The patterns displayed on the surface of the fabric are drawn up in a manner that does not take any account of the folds in the material in any way that we might have expected. This is not through lack of ability on the part of the artist, but because the flat presentation of pattern on cloth was more attractive to the sensitivities of the time.

Regal decoration

The English Tudor dress of Queen Elizabeth I (1533–1603) has been drawn in a similar spirit to the two Japanese examples. The pattern of the brocade and the display of jewellery are equally as important to this picture as the impressive dress itself. Various parts of the gown were carefully tailored to mould the queen's body to a particular shape, but the decorative aspects have been taken just as seriously as her fashionable silhouette.

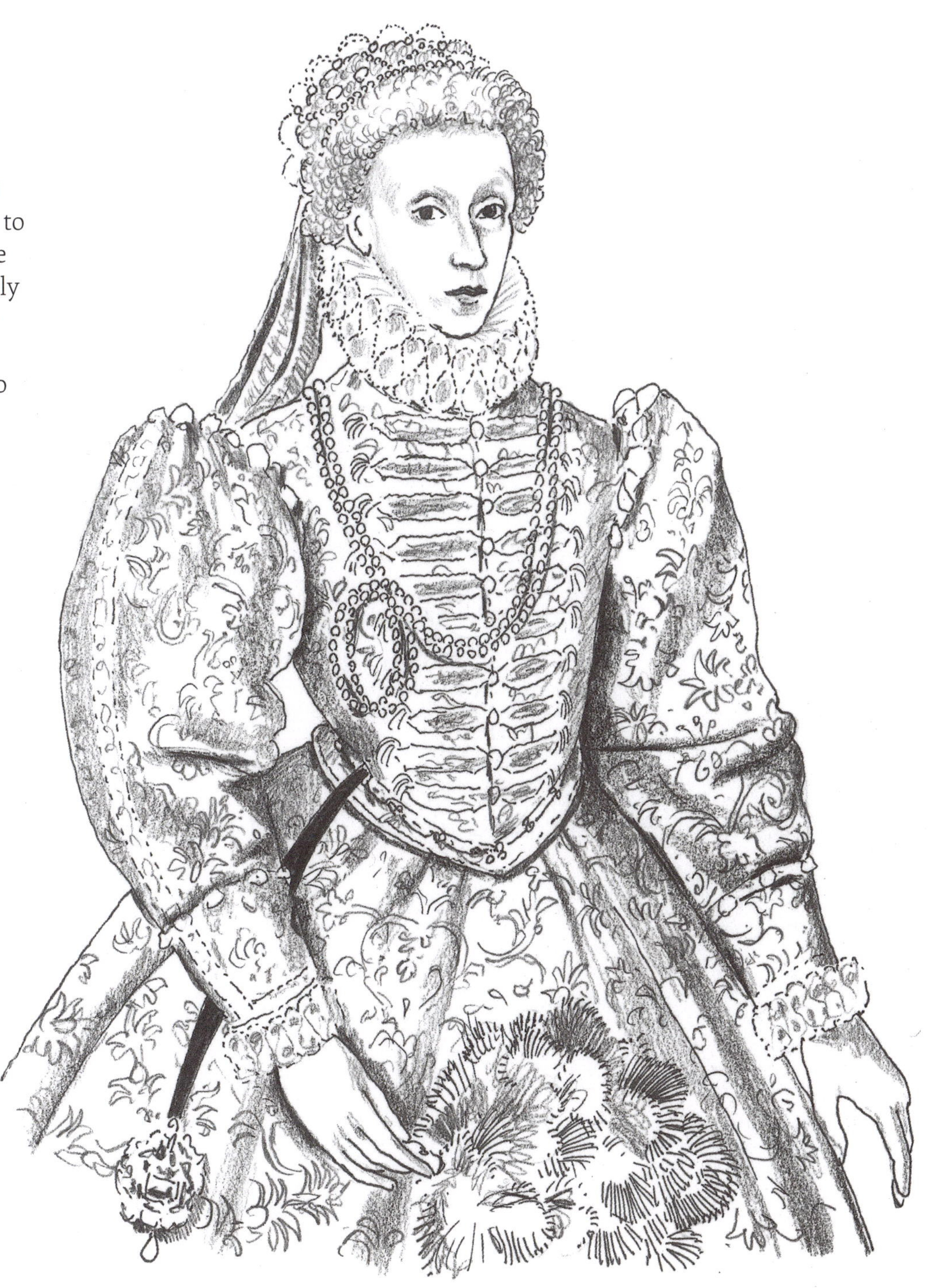

Clothing Made to Measure

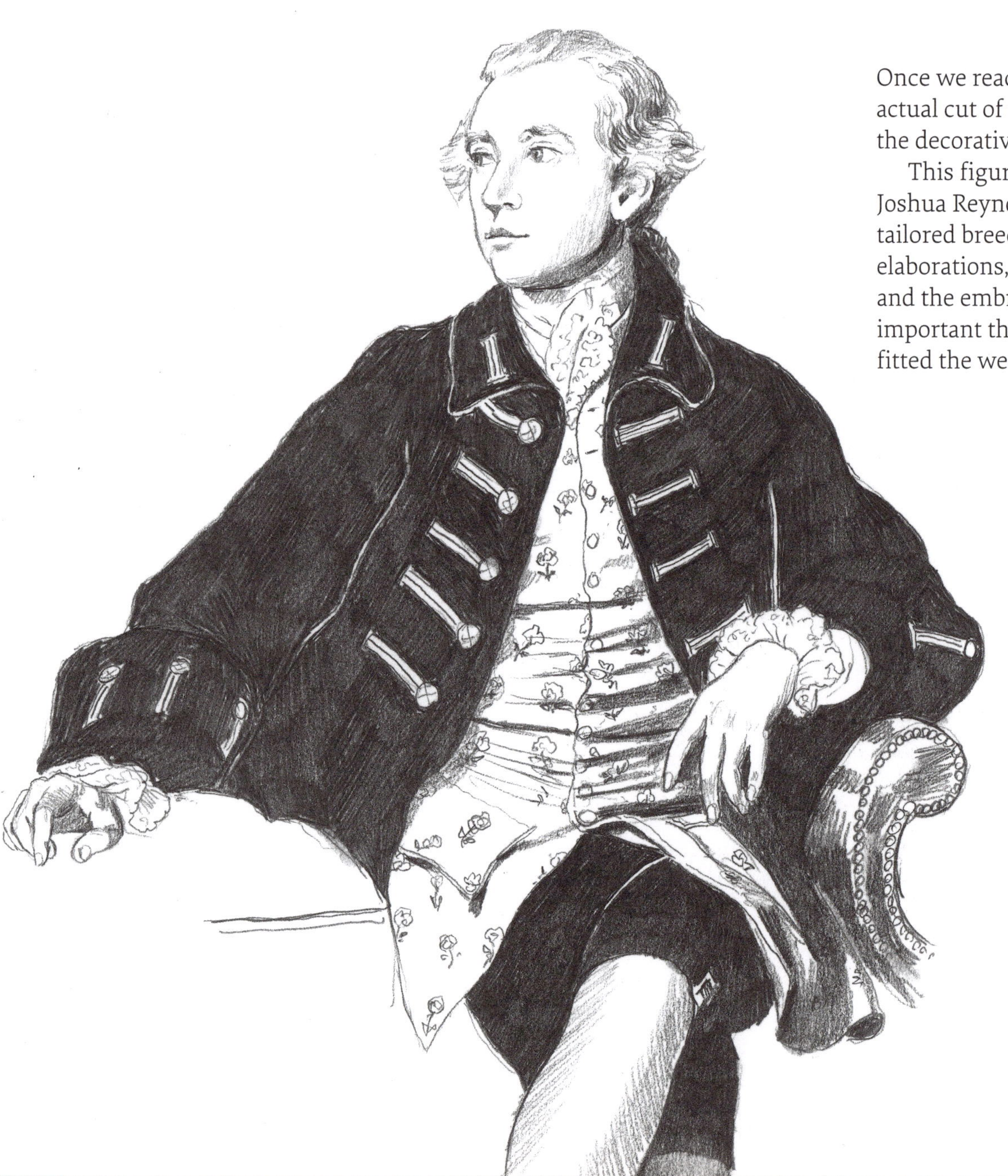

Once we reach the eighteenth century in Europe, the actual cut of the clothes becomes more important than the decorative elements.

This figure, from a picture of Warren Hastings by Sir Joshua Reynolds (1723–92), is fitted neatly into his closely tailored breeches and coat. Although there are still many elaborations, such as the lace at his throat and wrists and the embroidery on the coat and waistcoat, the most important thing about this sort of clothing was the way it fitted the wearer.

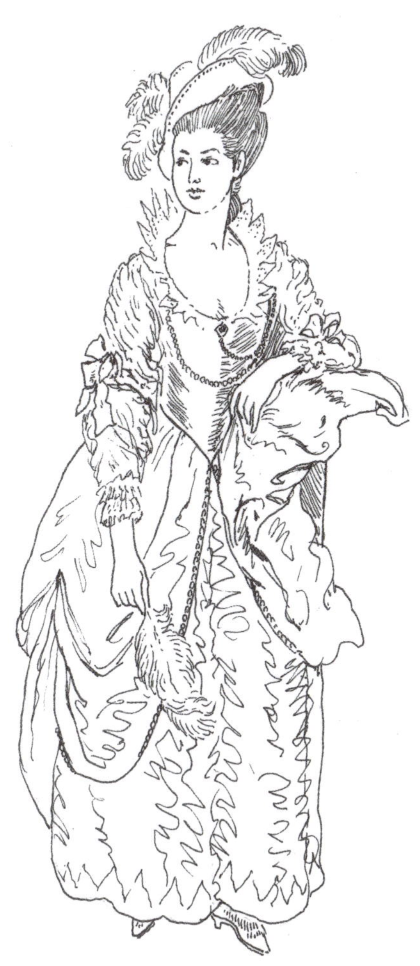

When we turn to a woman of the same period, the complex tailoring of her dress to make it look classical in some respects as well as form-fitting meant that the dressmaker's skills had to be of an extremely high standard. There are still many decorative features, but the main point of this sort of garment was that it had to fit well.

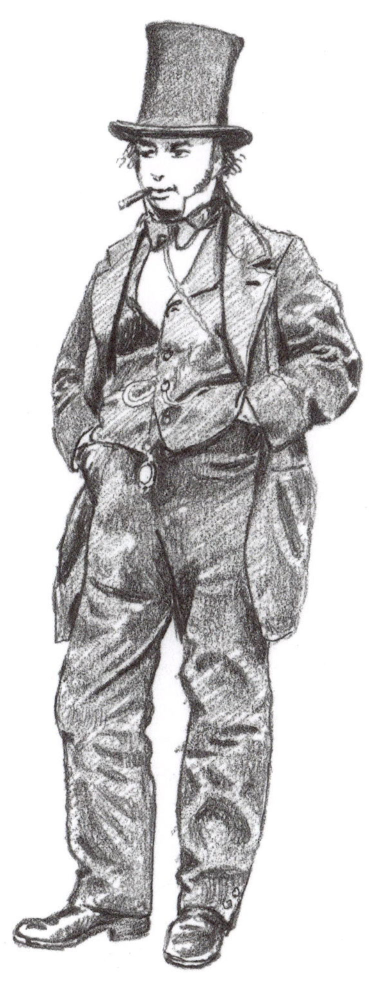

By the time we reach the nineteenth century, male attire was predominantly about tailoring and the fitting of well-made cloth to one's body and limbs. The more decorative elements of clothing were subordinated to the overall appearance of the cut. The British architect and engineer Isambard Kingdom Brunel (1806–59) is wearing a top hat, fitted jacket, waistcoat and trousers, which by this time was typical daywear for men.

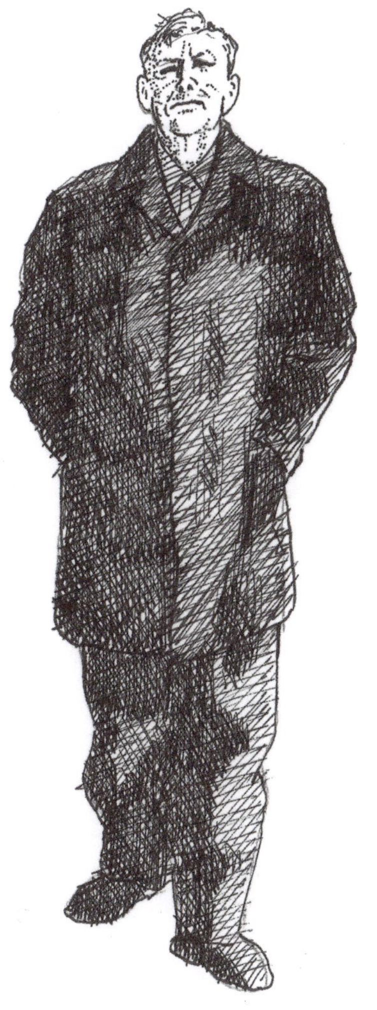

After the turn of the twentieth century, all over the world, the three- or two-piece suit became the male uniform that many businessmen still wear to this day. Here, the English poet and writer W. H. Auden (1907–73), is depicted wearing the typically box-shaped overcoat and wide, straight trousers that most men would wear in cold weather. Under the overcoat, no doubt he was wearing a fairly loose-fitting jacket that both covered and defined the limbs.

Modern Dress

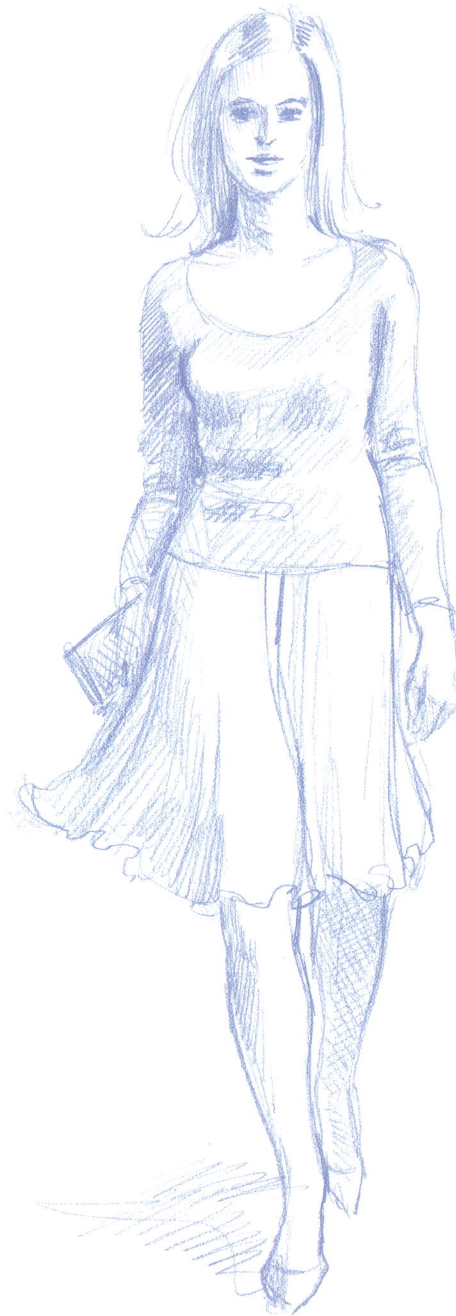

Worldwide, throughout the past century, clothing has settled into an easier, more casual version of the formal styles that originated in the Western world. Stiff collars, corsets and severe tailoring have now given way to softer, looser-looking garments. With synthetic fabrics, zip fasteners, Lycra and Velcro, most of our clothes incorporate comfort and convenience – factors undreamed of in past times.

These two examples of female attire show how much easier it is to live in modern dress than it would have been to wear the fashions of Victorian times.

The first woman has a skirt and jumper that fit her without being constricting, partly due to the materials they are made from.

The second woman wears a feminine-looking top but that is teamed with trousers, which until the twentieth century were worn only by men. These two young women are dressed both casually and comfortably, without loss of any decorative elements, now provided chiefly by cut and fabric.

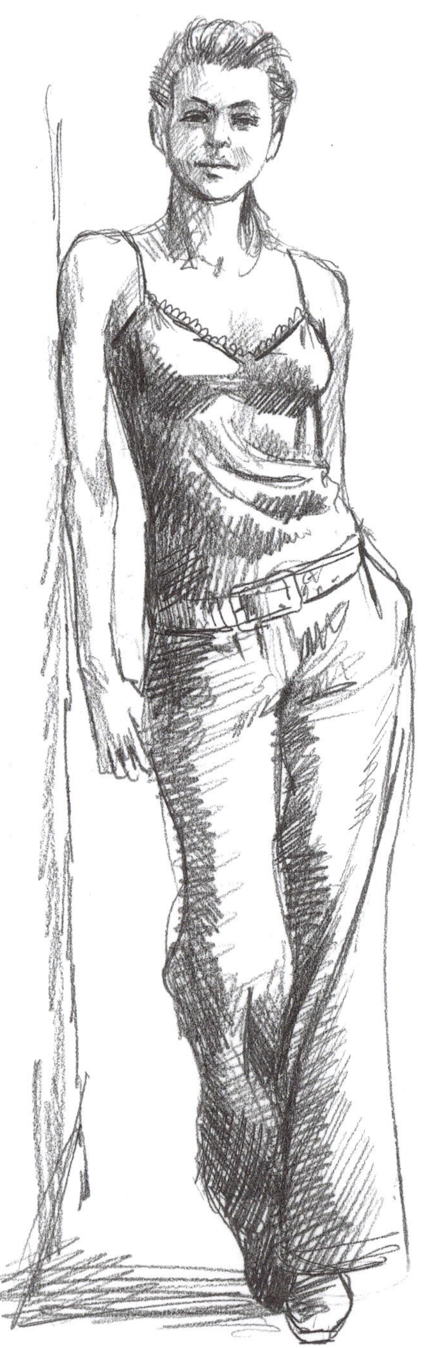

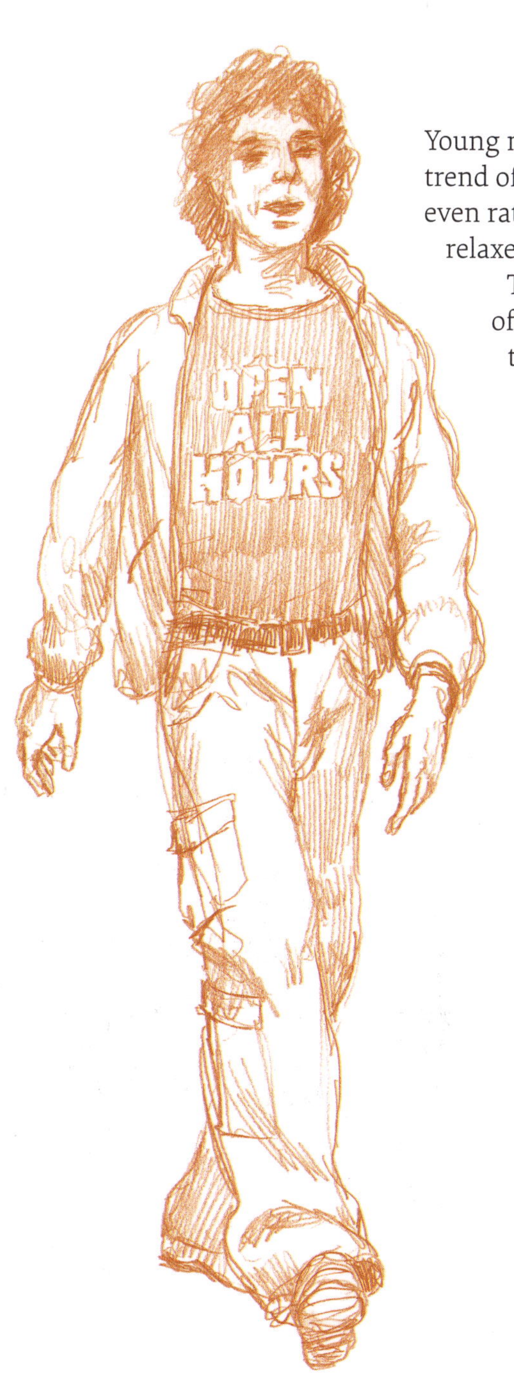

Young men also follow the modern trend of dressing for comfort, so that even rather more formal clothing is relaxed in style these days.

The first man wears a pair of loose-fitting, workman-like trousers, made from a light material, that resemble army khakis. He wears them with a printed T-shirt covered by a fleece for warmth. His shoes would probably be trainers.

The second man appears slightly more formal in that he is wearing a button-up shirt. His trousers are straight and narrow-legged. His shoes are more formal than trainers, but still fashionable, in a soft casual style.

Shapes under cloth

Because of the sophisticated tailoring and figure-hugging style of the dress, the next two examples could not really be from any time before the twentieth century.

The suit has dominated male attire for much of the past century and is probably the least compromising set of garments invented for the human form. It both describes the basic shape and yet hides its curves and bulges.

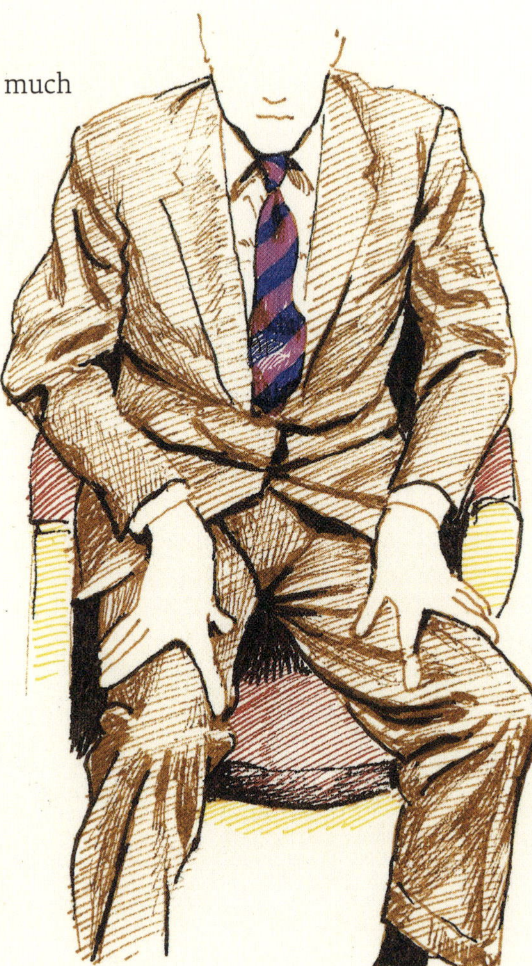

The woman's dress is designed to show off a fashionably slender figure. It is carefully cut and quite comfortable to wear.

Your main source of models will probably be figures clad in loose modern garments such as skirts, trousers and loose coats. These do not reveal the figure underneath, but nevertheless there are clues in the shapes. Unless the subject is rather stout, the characteristic shapes shown by clothing tend to be the bony parts of the figure.

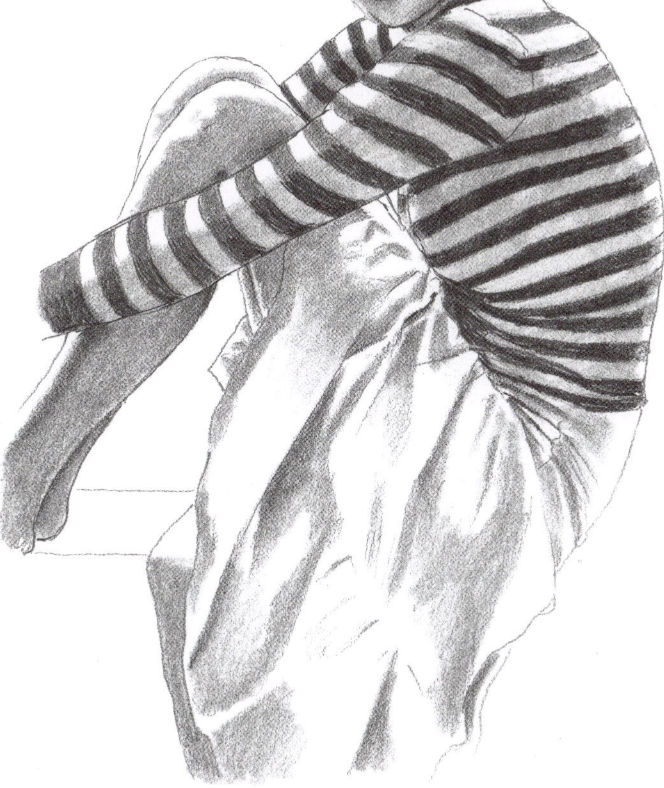

This drawing of a girl sitting on a window sill with her knees clasped up to her chest shows the effect of a loose lightweight skirt rucked up in small folds and then hanging in open undulations down over the wall. You can see how the legs join to the torso, but only by inference. The upper close-fitting garment is also very interesting in that the horizontal stripes curving round the arms and torso give a very clear idea of the shape of the body underneath.

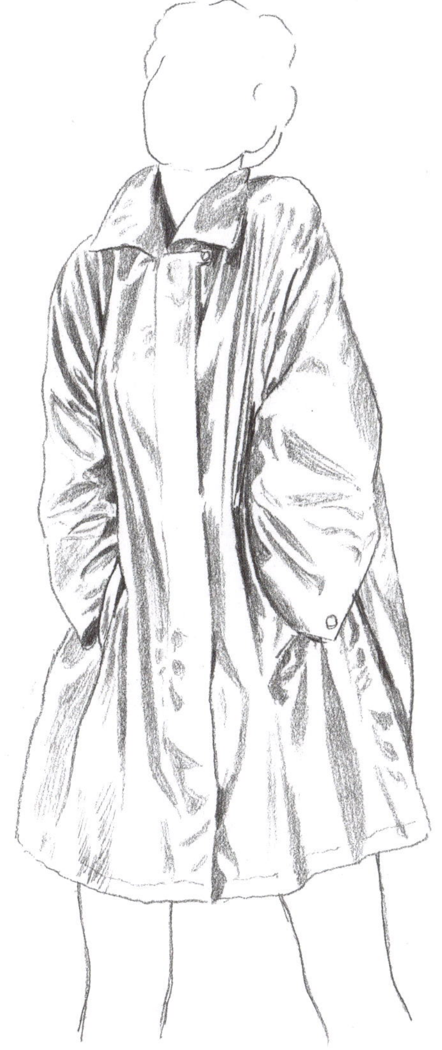

The loose lightweight coat hugged around the figure of the girl with her hands deep in her pockets creates a tent-like shape, with the sharp, narrow folds giving some indication of the shoulders, the bend of the arms and a slight curve indicating the chest.

The more masculine garments here are two very typical pieces of materiality, part-disguising and part-revealing the shape underneath. The T-shirt shape is loose and floppy, and the solidity of the shoulders and chest is obvious. The way the folds hang down round the lower part of the torso leaves very little to go on to discover the figure underneath. The only noticeable feature is the slight curve of the edge of the shirt around the hips.

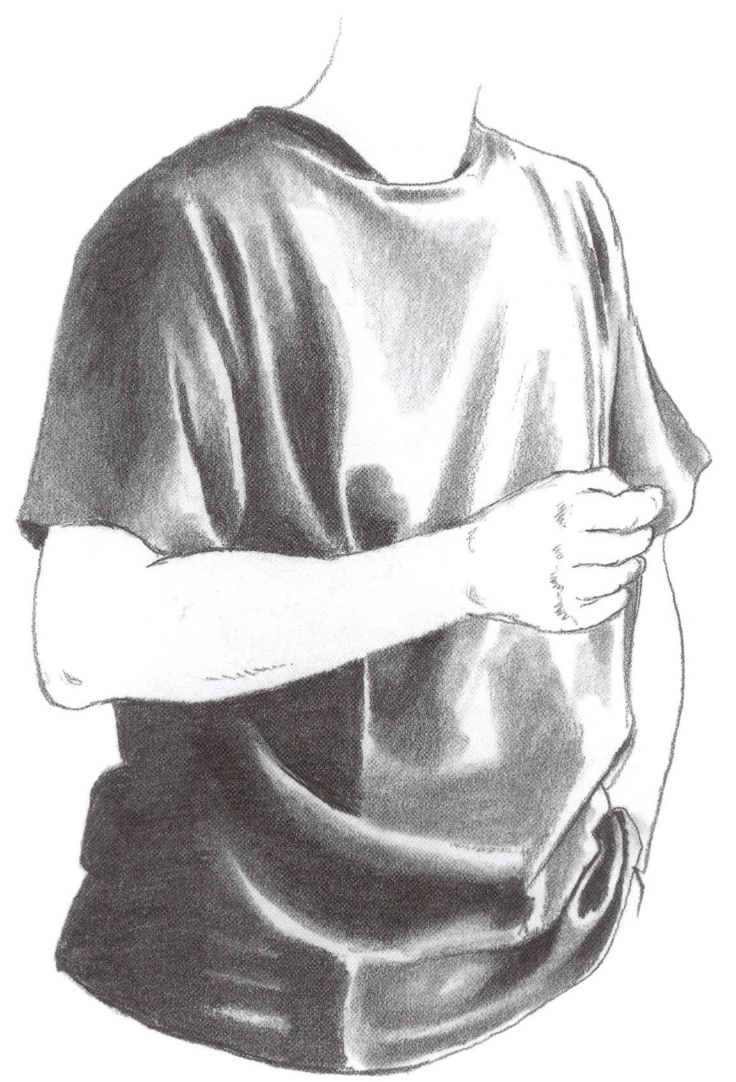

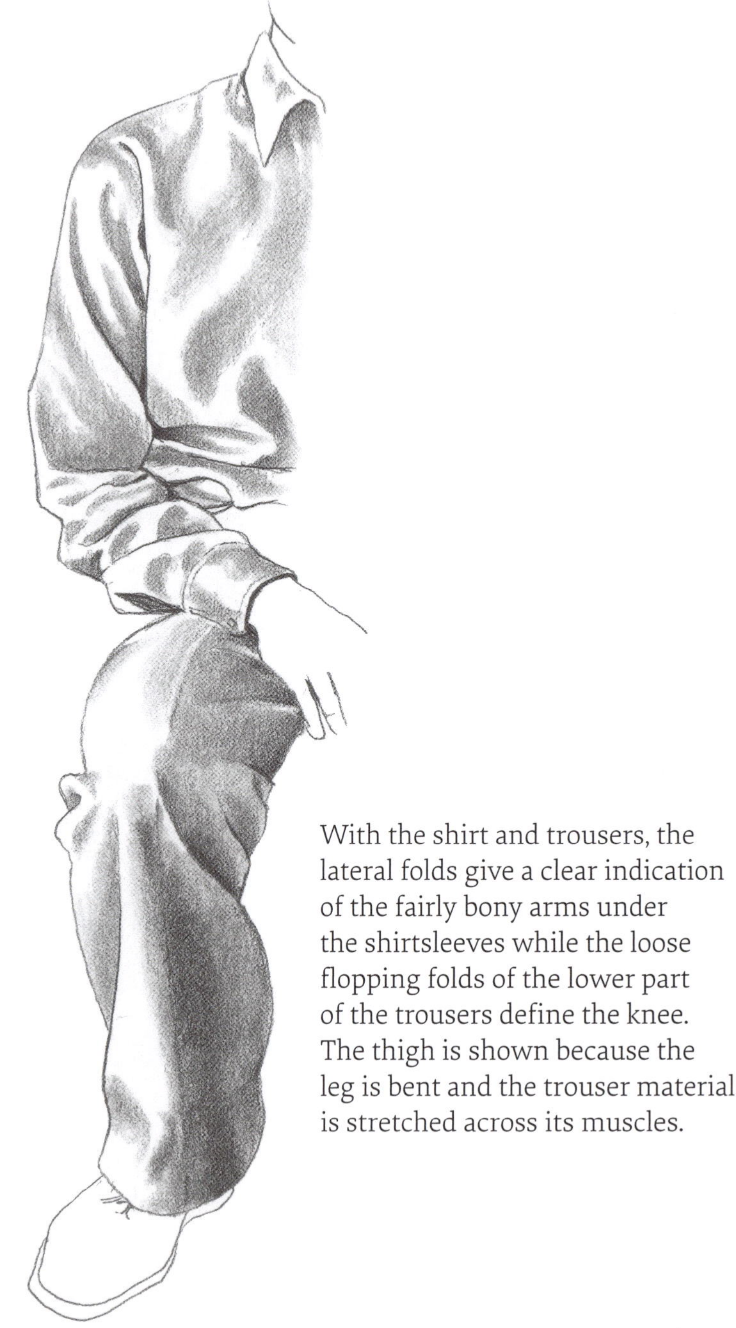

With the shirt and trousers, the lateral folds give a clear indication of the fairly bony arms under the shirtsleeves while the loose flopping folds of the lower part of the trousers define the knee. The thigh is shown because the leg is bent and the trouser material is stretched across its muscles.

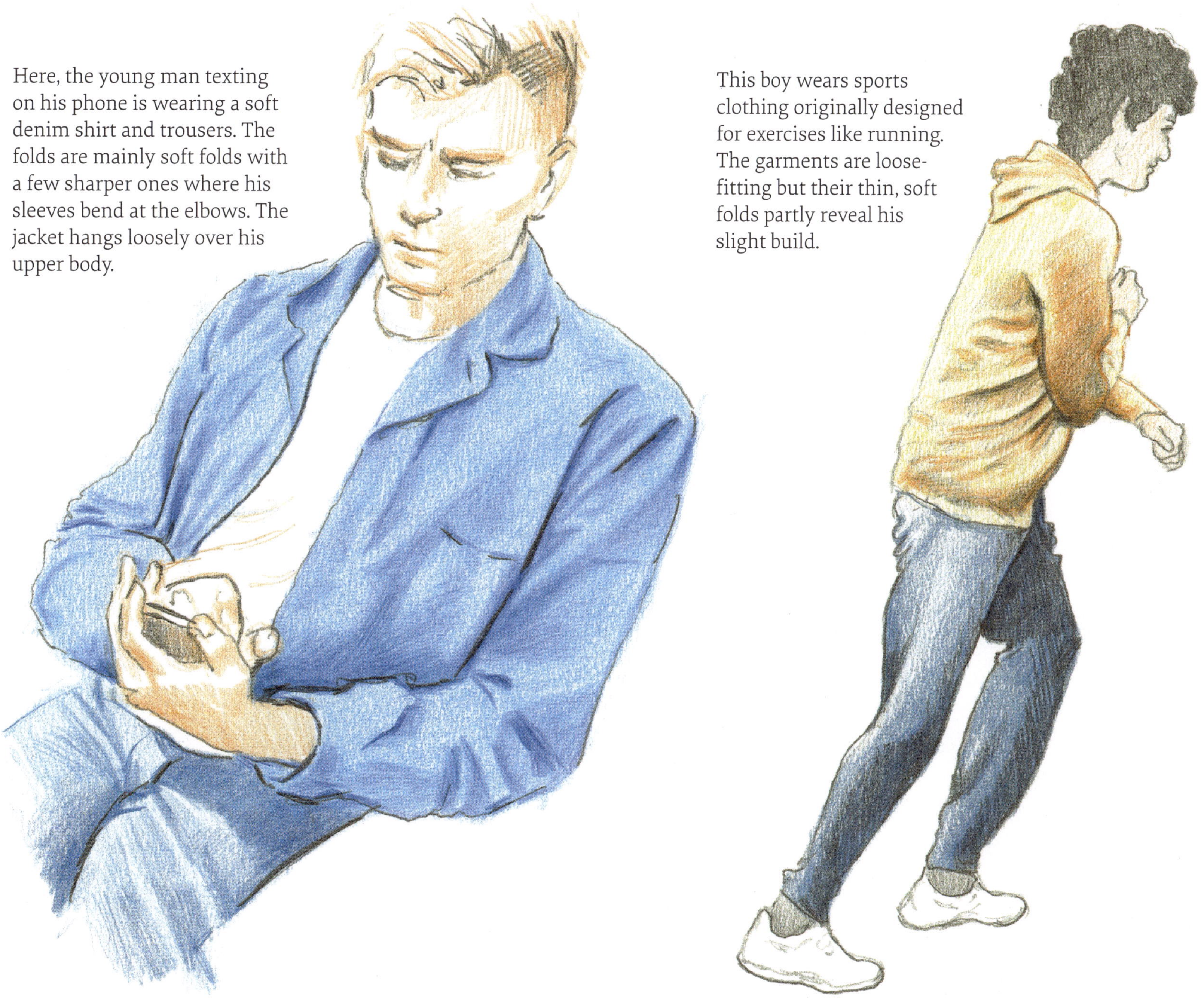

Here, the young man texting on his phone is wearing a soft denim shirt and trousers. The folds are mainly soft folds with a few sharper ones where his sleeves bend at the elbows. The jacket hangs loosely over his upper body.

This boy wears sports clothing originally designed for exercises like running. The garments are loose-fitting but their thin, soft folds partly reveal his slight build.

Hair

The look of the hair is a great asset in a portrait and should be considered when you arrange to draw someone. Although making it look realistic can be difficult, the texture it adds is worth it. Historically artists have used hair as a means of showing off their own talent as well as enhancing the charm of female sitters.

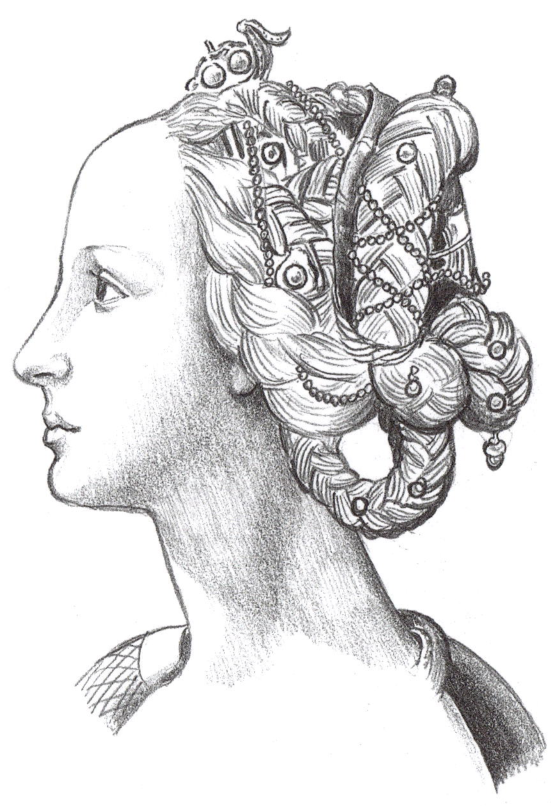

The famous Florentine beauty Simonetta Vespucci, niece of Amerigo Vespucci who gave his name to America, is given tremendous presence in this profile portrait (after Piero di Cosimo, 1462–1522), thanks largely to the fantastic jewel-studded plaits looped around her head.

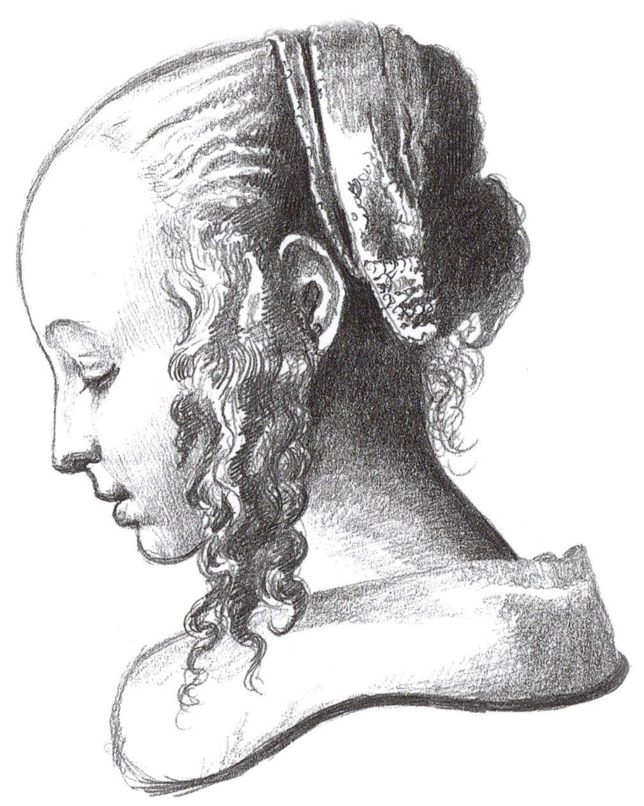

Johannes Vermeer (1632–75) used the ribbons and curled hairstyles of the 17th century with great skill to emphasize the femininity of his subjects, as this example shows.

By contrast modern hairstyles are less fussy and less structured than styles from earlier periods. Usually you need only to observe the direction of the combing or, in a more dishevelled look, just allow your pencil, brush or pen to move freely. The direction of the hair is important, but as there is usually less in the way of braiding or curling the problem is simpler.

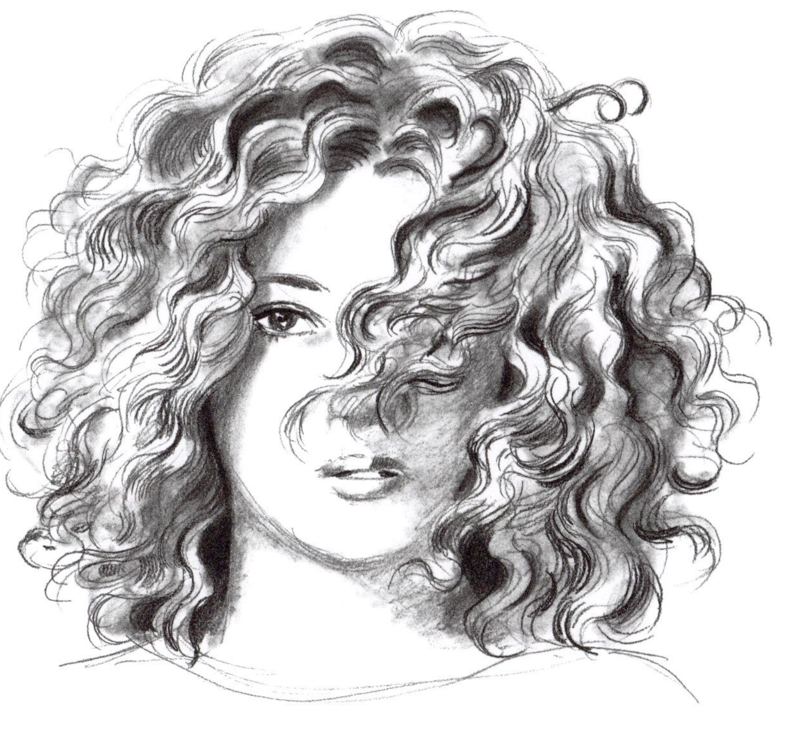

Here I show long straight hair with the ends curling a little. Follow the direction of the hair with long strokes of the pencil, making sure you leave some gaps for highlights.

A lot of effort has gone into this hairstyle, with every seemingly wayward strand beautifully arranged. Contrived it may be, but it does show to good effect how hair can wave and corkscrew in ringlets. Notice the many highlights on the bends of the curls and the darker, richer tones underneath. It's not easy to make this style look natural in a drawing.

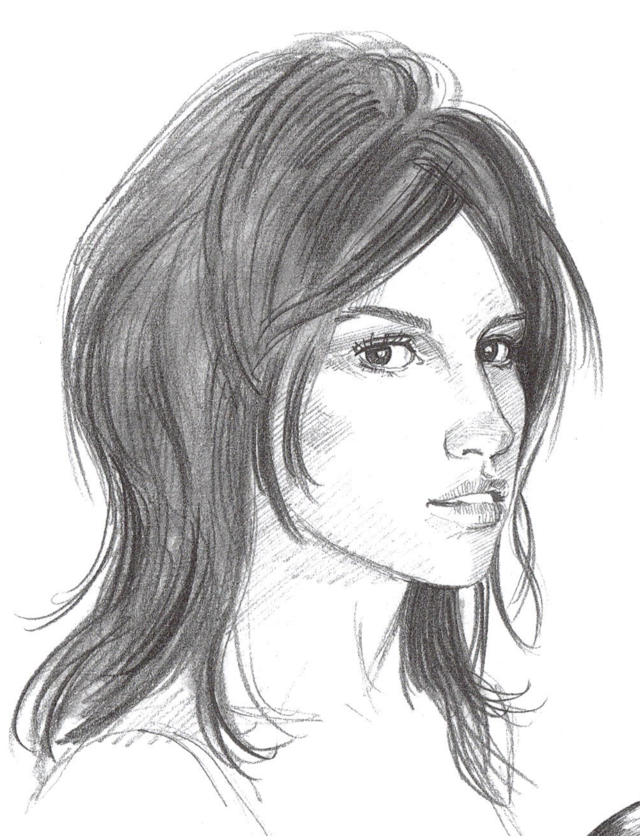

This example of a modern hairstyle, taken from a fashion magazine promoting hairdressing, gives a seemingly natural look, although this is sometimes attained at some effort and after a great deal of careful work.

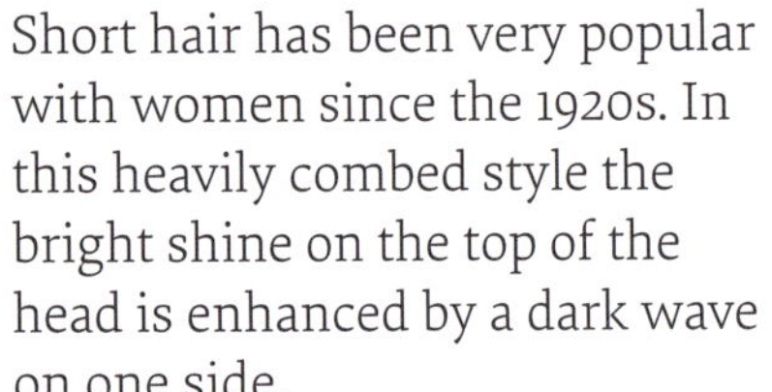

Short hair has been very popular with women since the 1920s. In this heavily combed style the bright shine on the top of the head is enhanced by a dark wave on one side.

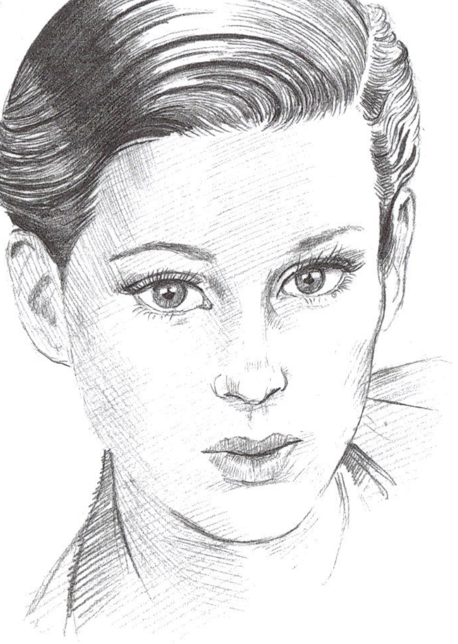

In this tight braid (above) the shine on the top of the head shows up strongly, despite the dark hair colour. There is also another slightly more subdued shine lower down, across the back of the head. Each pleat of the plait picks up the shine and accentuates the smooth, even strands of hair, none out of place.

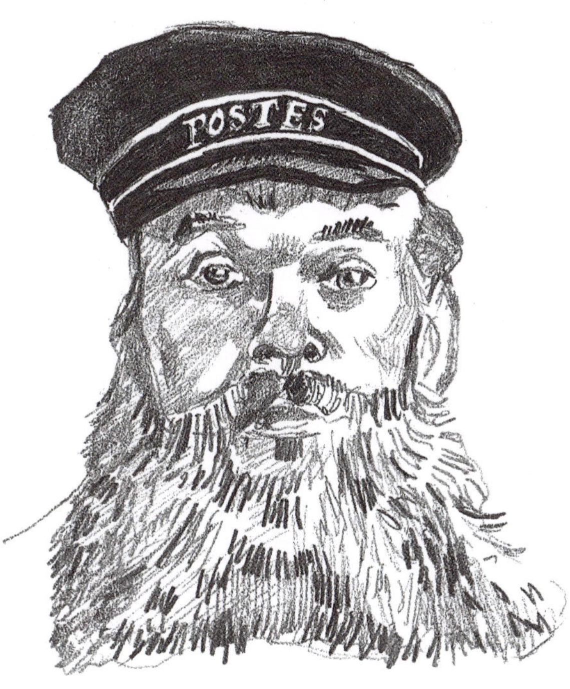

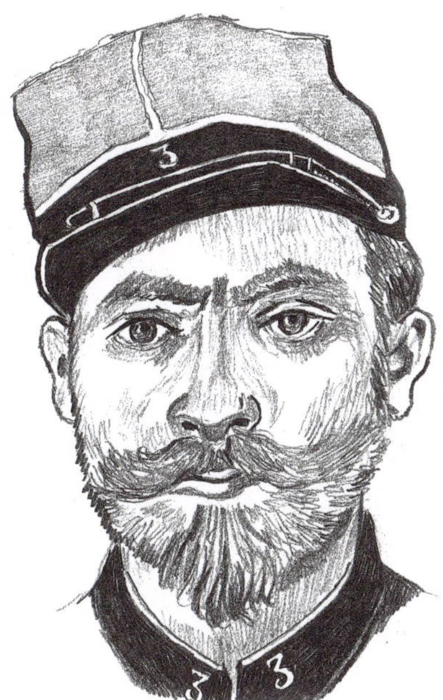

When Vincent Van Gogh (1853–90) was working in the South of France in the late 1880s, he painted a local postman and a young soldier who had befriended him. In both examples their hair is hidden under hats, but their characterful whiskers add drama to the portraits, depicting with vigorous strokes following the direction of growth.

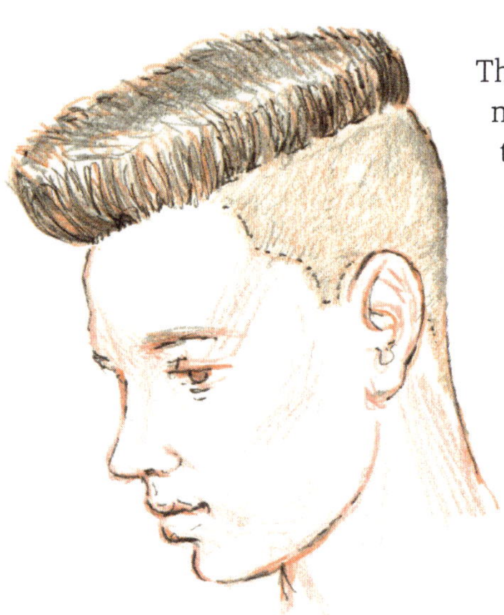

This is a fashionable cut that a young man might wear in a large modern town. The hair is cut very short with a razor up to the level of the top of the forehead all the way round the head, showing the lines of the skull above the ears and neck. Above this level it is quite luxuriant although carefully cut evenly across the top. The effect is of a trimmed hedge.

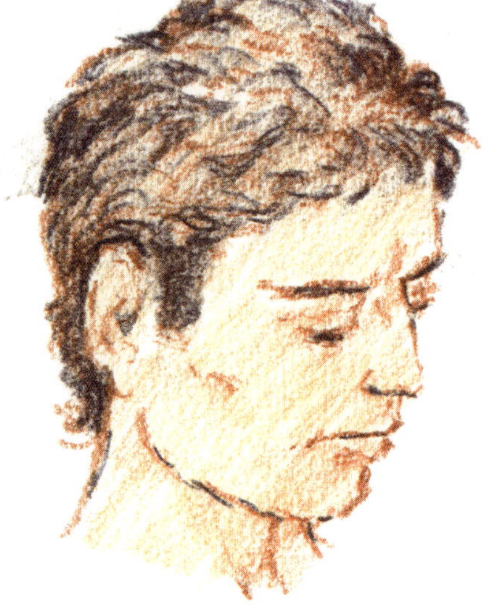

This man has an unremarkable haircut; neither very long nor very short. What is most noticeable about it is the way it hugs around the contours of his skull, coming down the neck a certain amount at the back and around the ears and along the top of the forehead in short tufts.

Chapter Eight

LEARNING FROM THE PAST

From the earliest cave art, human beings have striven to make drawings in their own image. Portraits and figure drawing have always taken pride of place in the spectrum of artistic subjects, and in the great art workshops (bottegas) of the Renaissance it was the master painter who would often be the only artisan to put in the figures, leaving the rest of the composition to be completed by his pupils. The evolution of artistic depictions of the human form is a fascinating topic in itself, and in this section I have shown just a small selection of masterpieces from the ancient world up to the 20th century.

For any student of drawing, it is especially useful to observe how other artists make their pictures. Luckily, the majority of countries now care for their artistic heritage and there are many galleries and museums that display great works of art for you to study. It is by getting out and discovering how other people see and communicate with the world that you learn to expand your own skills, away from the merely representative, to something much more interesting and alluring. Studying the works of other artists is never time wasted if you are serious about learning to draw people.

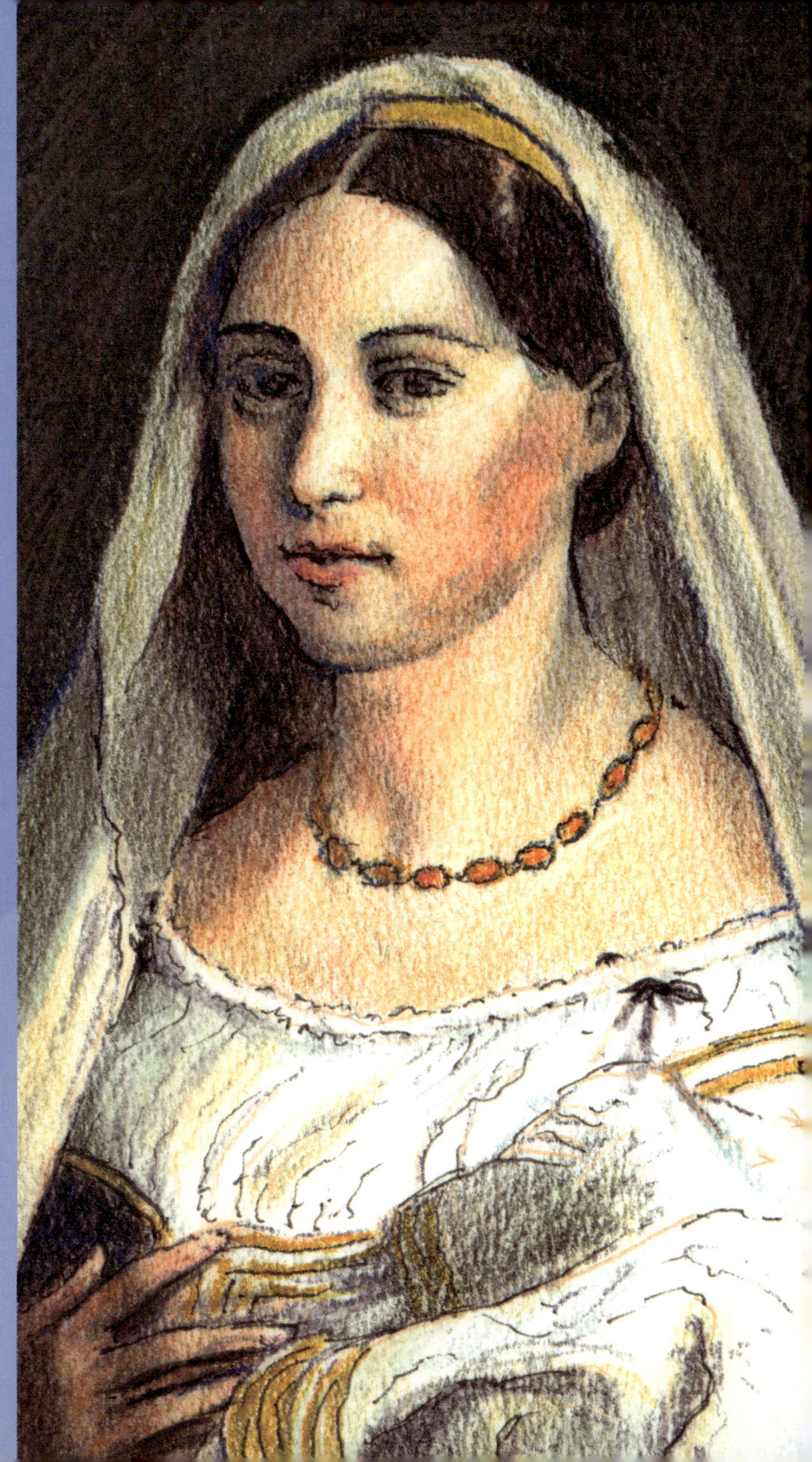

Ancient Art

Here are a few examples of the very oldest works available to us. Done in the earliest of times, they are still a marvel of close study, with evidence of an appreciation of perspective and close anatomical observation.

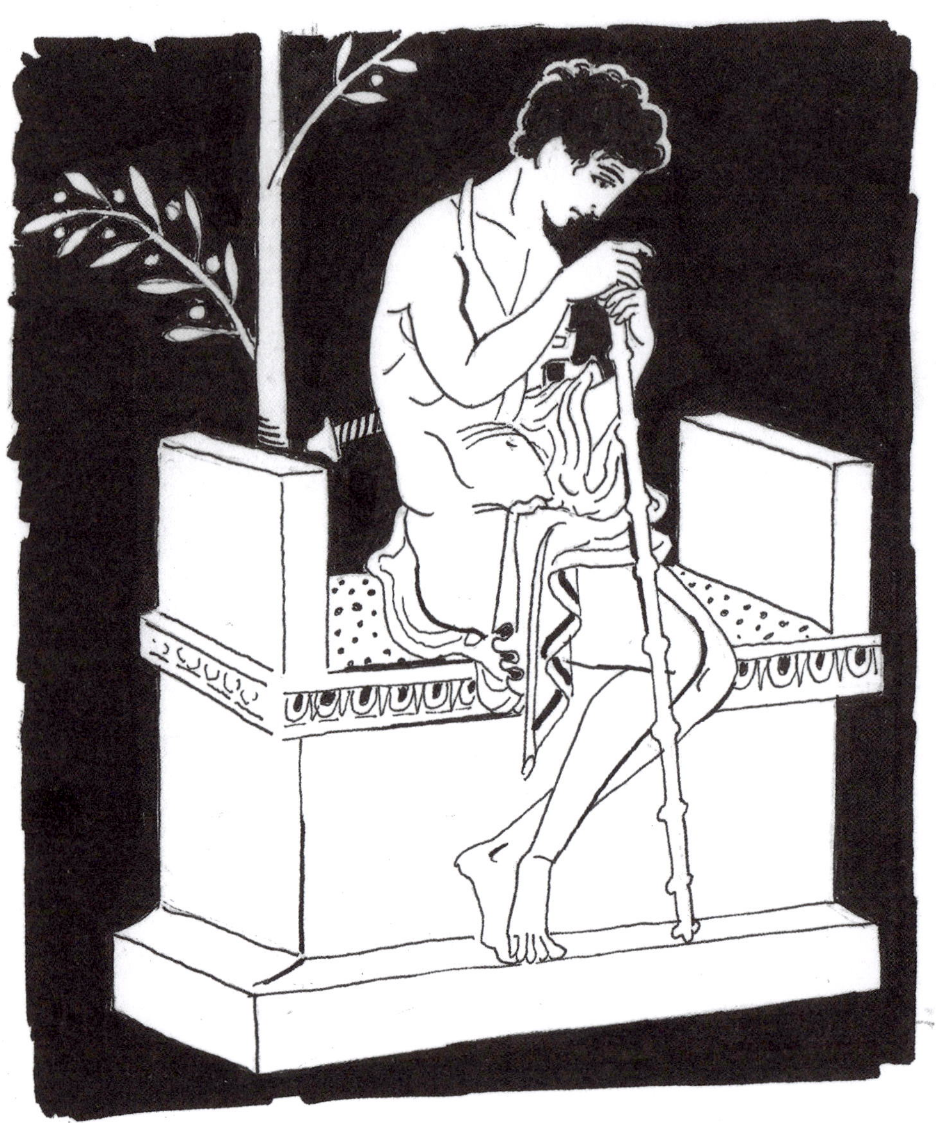

This image is from an Apulian krater (a bowl with a wide mouth, two handles and a foot or stand) painted in the fourth century BC. The drawing demonstrates the exceptional draughtsmanship of the Greek-inspired artists living in the 'heel' of Italy around that time, and although the perspective of the seat is a little suspect, the overall effect is quite modern. This was originally executed in paint on ceramic, so the artist probably had only one shot at it. The contrast of the line drawing with the dark surround is extremely elegant.

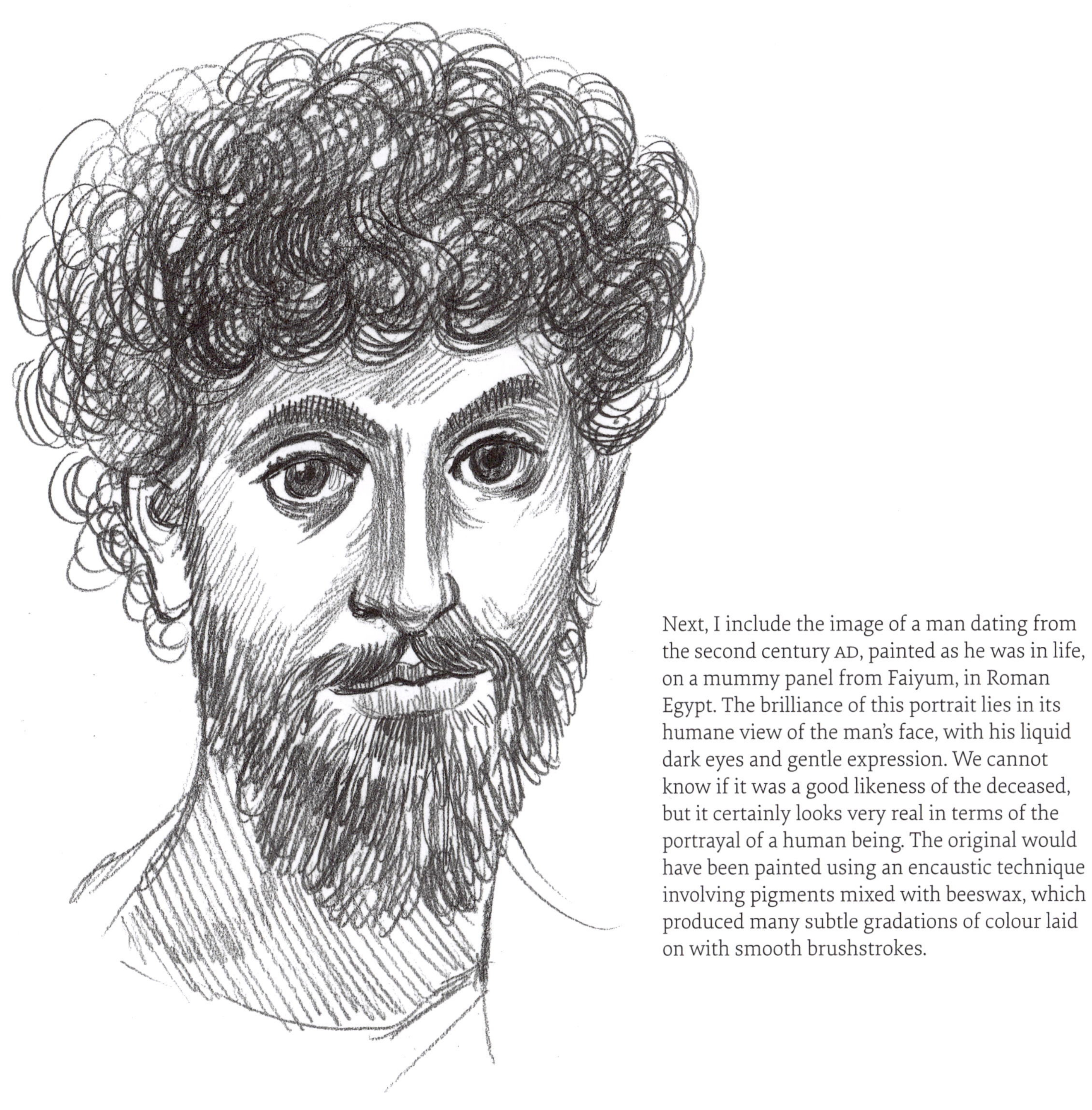

Next, I include the image of a man dating from the second century AD, painted as he was in life, on a mummy panel from Faiyum, in Roman Egypt. The brilliance of this portrait lies in its humane view of the man's face, with his liquid dark eyes and gentle expression. We cannot know if it was a good likeness of the deceased, but it certainly looks very real in terms of the portrayal of a human being. The original would have been painted using an encaustic technique involving pigments mixed with beeswax, which produced many subtle gradations of colour laid on with smooth brushstrokes.

Medieval Art

Produced at a time when art and religion were closely connected, these images suggest that it was to depict the glory of God that art and artists were pushed to new limits of experimentation and inventiveness.

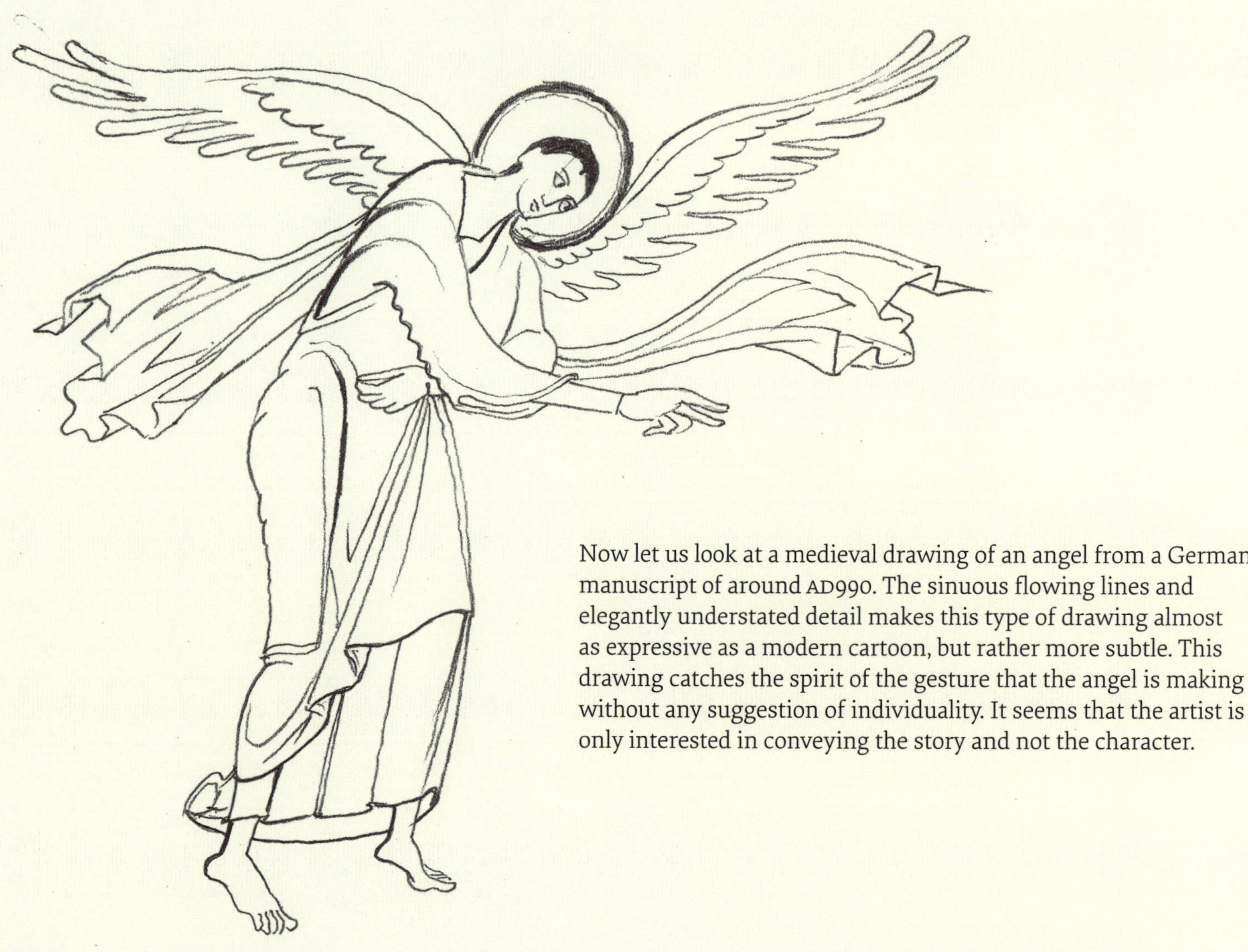

Now let us look at a medieval drawing of an angel from a German manuscript of around AD990. The sinuous flowing lines and elegantly understated detail makes this type of drawing almost as expressive as a modern cartoon, but rather more subtle. This drawing catches the spirit of the gesture that the angel is making without any suggestion of individuality. It seems that the artist is only interested in conveying the story and not the character.

The next example is a Byzantine Virgin and Child from the period AD1200. It typifies the style of work produced before Giotto (1267–1337) came upon the scene. The design is rigidly formal and follows the traditional methods of all the artists who had gone before. The positions of the hands, the tilt of the Virgin's head and the gesture of the Child were set stereotypes. Note also the stylized patterns on the robes of both figures. This in no way detracts from the value of the piece, but it is interesting to know that artists have often been expected to produce work to a specific structure. Highly formalized pictures like this one were no deterrent to the quality of a great artist, and the system also helped to support the lesser talents.

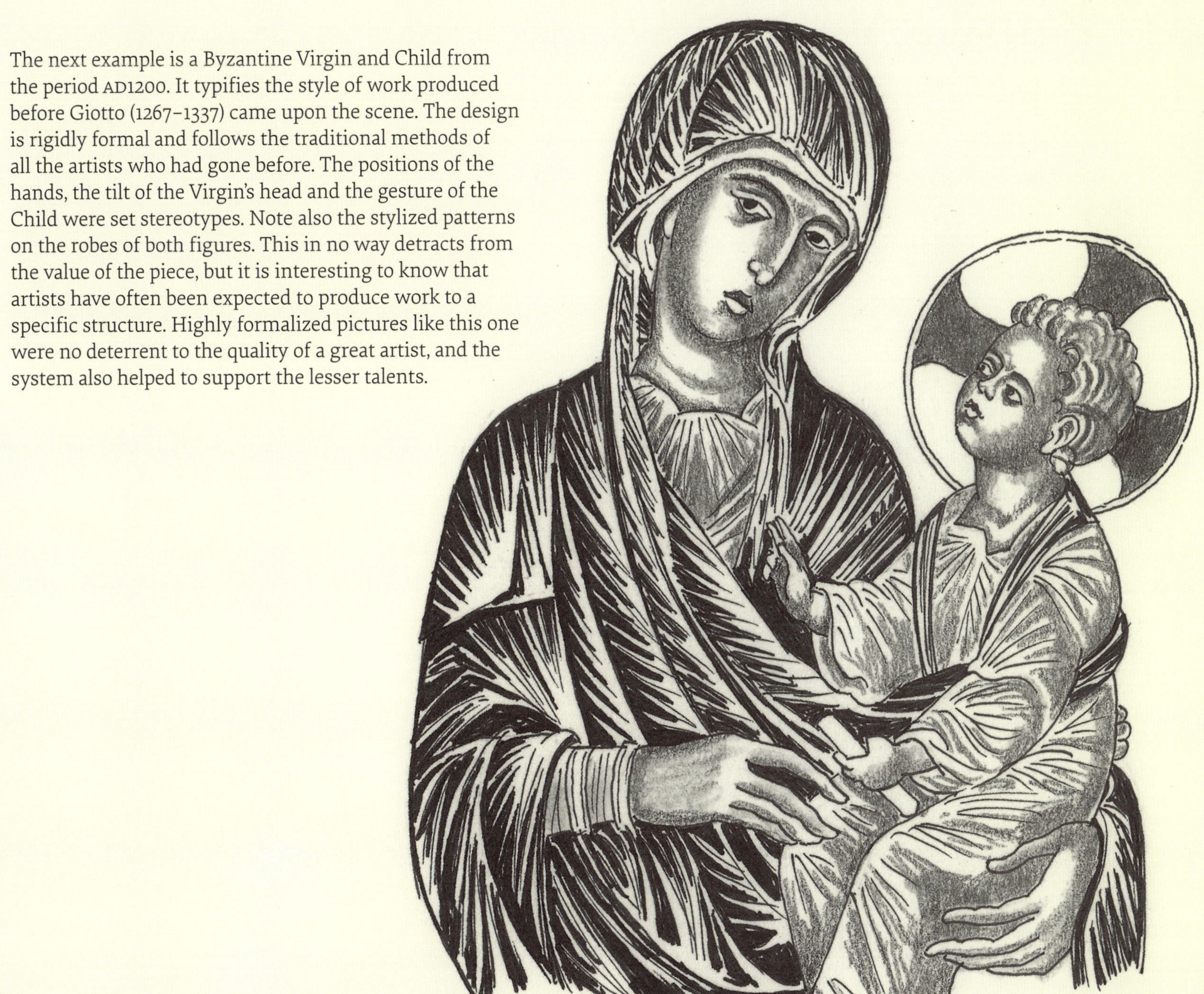

Master Artists of the Renaissance

The painters in Renaissance Italy and the rest of Europe (about 1400–1600) rejected the formal, stylized depictions of people in medieval religious imagery and produced works that we now regard as introducing humanism and realism to art.

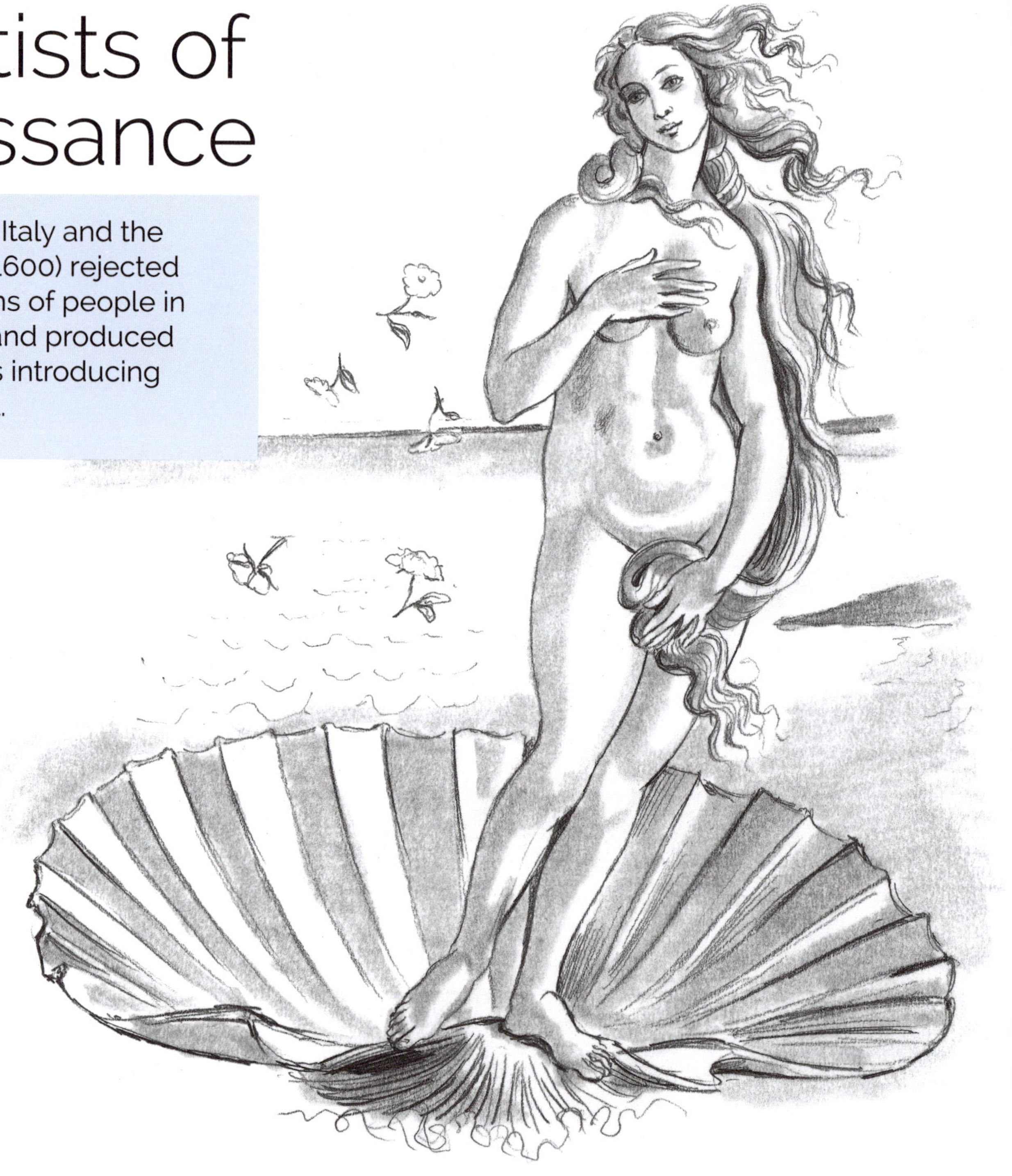

Sandro Botticelli

The Birth of Venus (1486) by Sandro Botticelli (1445–1510) is one of the most famous images in the history of art. The model for Venus was the legendary Florentine beauty Simonetta Vespucci, one of the favourites of the Medici family. Botticelli's drawing of the goddess arising from the sea is admired everywhere and reminds us that our ideals of beauty are still hugely influenced by the images that the Renaissance masters set before us. Venus' lissom body with elegant hands and feet is posed in an undulating fashion that we also recognize as the *contrapposto* copied from Ancient Greek sculpture. One of the guiding principles of Renaissance culture was to reconnect with classical antiquity.

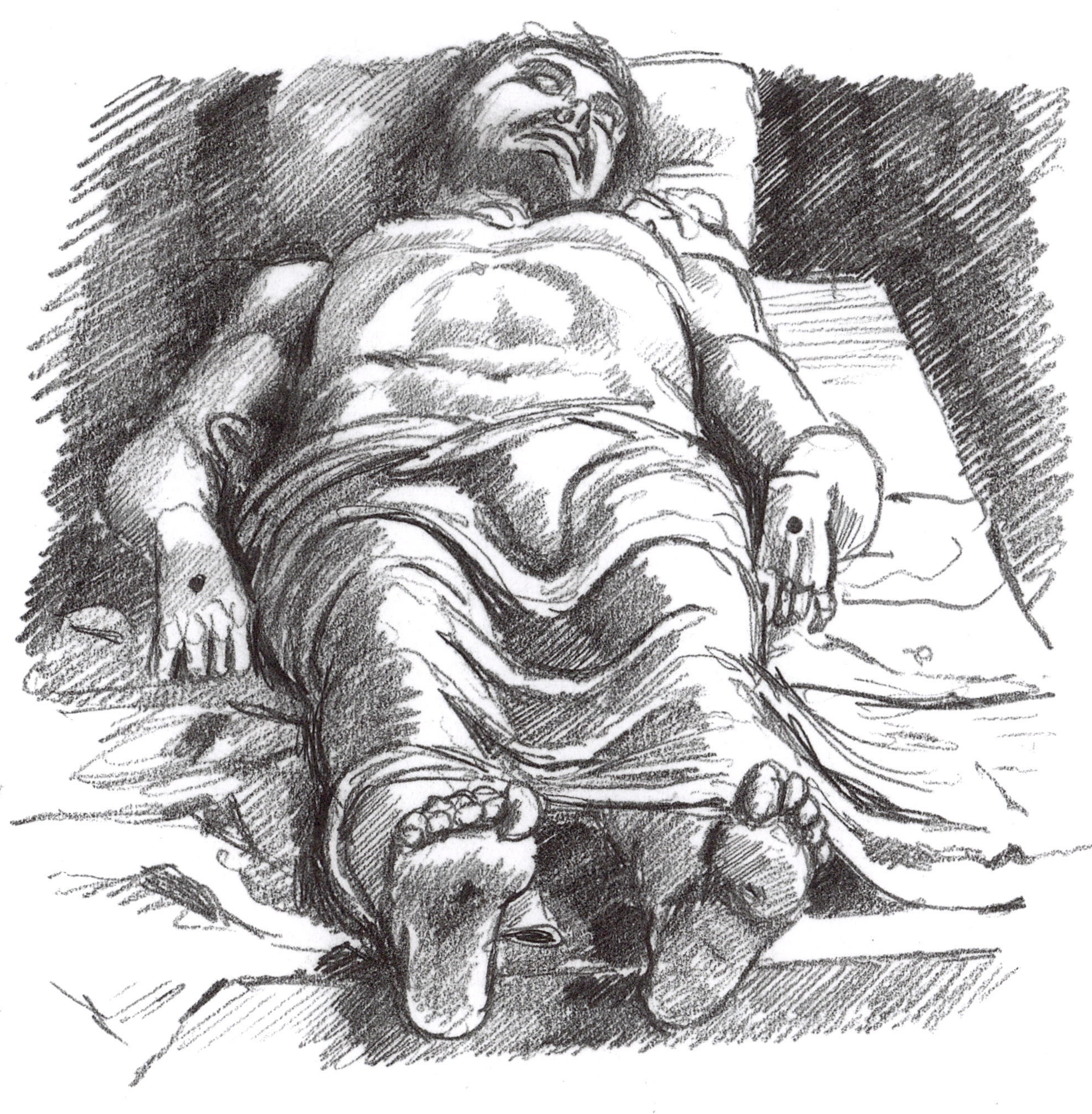

Andrea Mantegna

Andrea Mantegna (1430–1506) was another notable Renaissance figure, who worked mainly in the north of Italy. He knew many scholars involved in the study of Roman antiquities around Padua and used what he learned from them in his art. His extraordinary, austere view of Christ laid out after his death, *Lamentation over the Dead Christ* (c.1490), shows how far artists had progressed in the treatment of perspective, within about three generations. This could hardly be bettered by a photograph for accuracy of foreshortening. The original can be seen in the Pinacoteca di Brera, Milan.

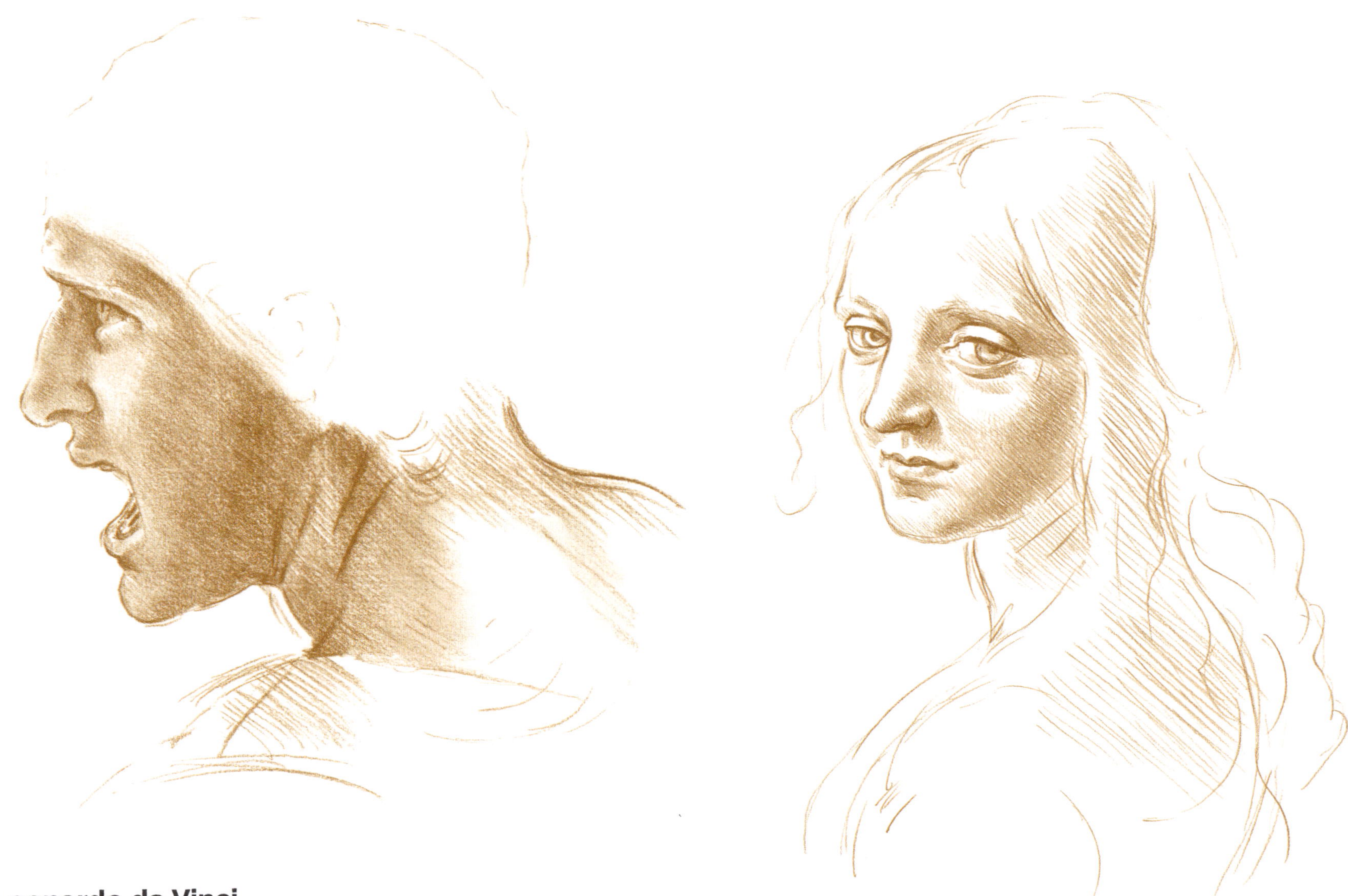

Leonardo da Vinci

When we look at a drawing by Leonardo da Vinci (1452–1519) we see the immense talent of an artist who could not only see more clearly than most of us, but also had the technical ability to express it on paper. We see the ease of the strokes of silverpoint or chalk outlining the various parts of the design, some sharply defined and others soft and in multiple marks that give the impression of the surface moving around the shape and disappearing from view.

Leonardo regulates light and shade by means of his famous *sfumato* method (Italian for 'evaporated'), a technique by which an effect of depth and volume is achieved by the use of dark, misty tones. The careful grading of the dark, smudgy marks helps us to see how the gradations of tone give the appearance of three dimensions.

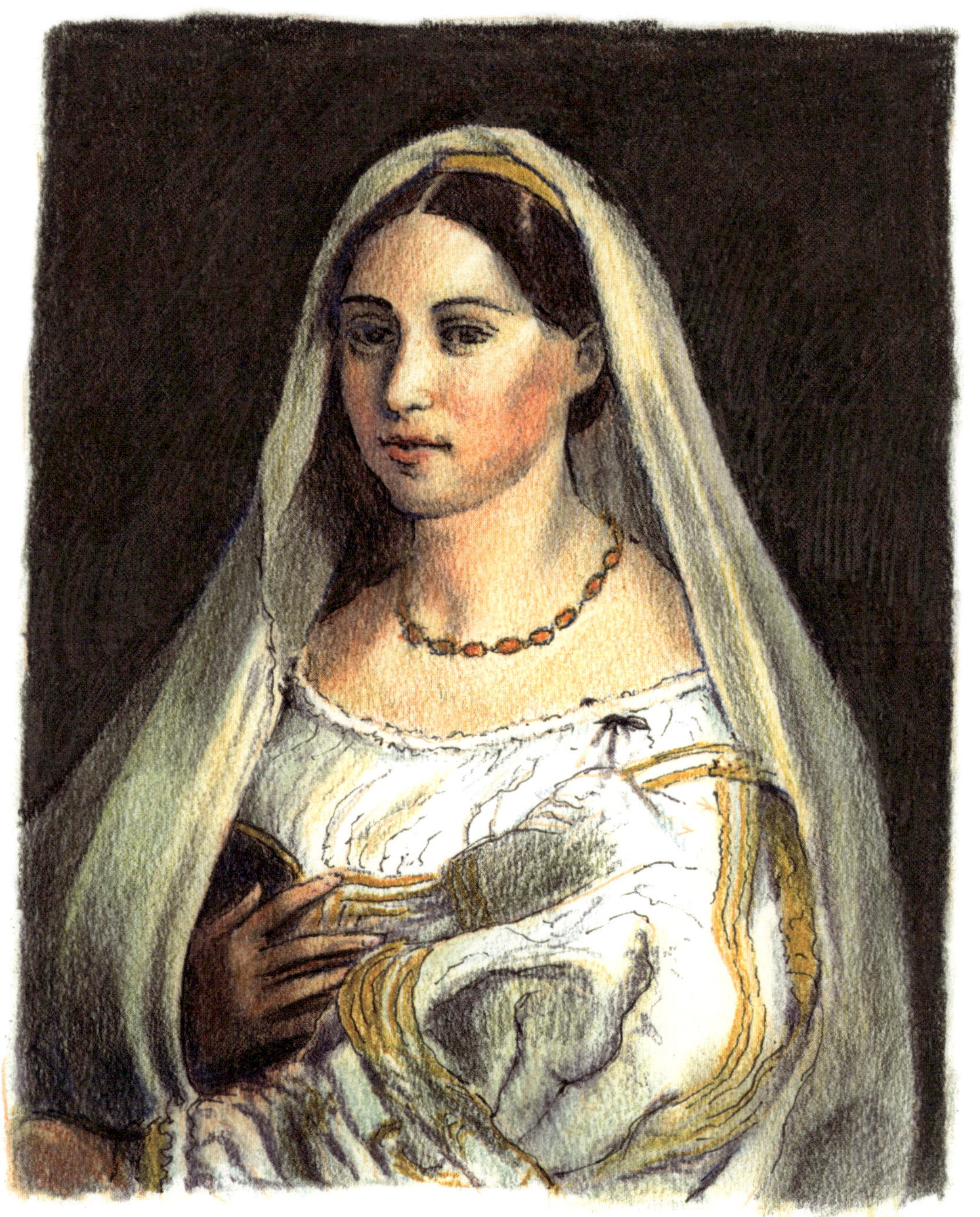

Raphael Sanzio

The perfection of the work of Raphael must have seemed quite extraordinary to his contemporaries, even though they had already seen the works of Filippo Lippi, Botticelli, Michelangelo and Leonardo. This portrait of *La Donna Velata* (The Woman with the Veil) was originally in oils, but my copy here is in coloured pastels. Raphael's painting of the subtleties of form give his subject a feeling of roundness and the flow of the draperies enclosing her figure and head lend a depth and sense of space to the picture that Raphael was famous for in his time. For many years this type of painting of form was the one most artists emulated: it is the classical version of portraiture.

Michelangelo

Michelangelo is arguably the most influential figure in the history of art. Study his drawings and then look at the work of his contemporaries and the artists who followed him and you will see how great was his influence. The copies shown here incorporate the original techniques he introduced. In the pen and ink drawing the style is very free and the shapes very basic, suggesting figures in motion; the second example is a very exact drawing, the careful *sfumato* in black chalk giving a clear definition of the arrangement of the flexing muscles under the skin. Michelangelo's deep knowledge of anatomy enabled him to produce an almost tactile effect in his life drawing. He shows clearly that there are no real hollows in the human form, merely dips between the mounds of muscles. This is worth noting by any student drawing from life and will give more conviction to your drawing.

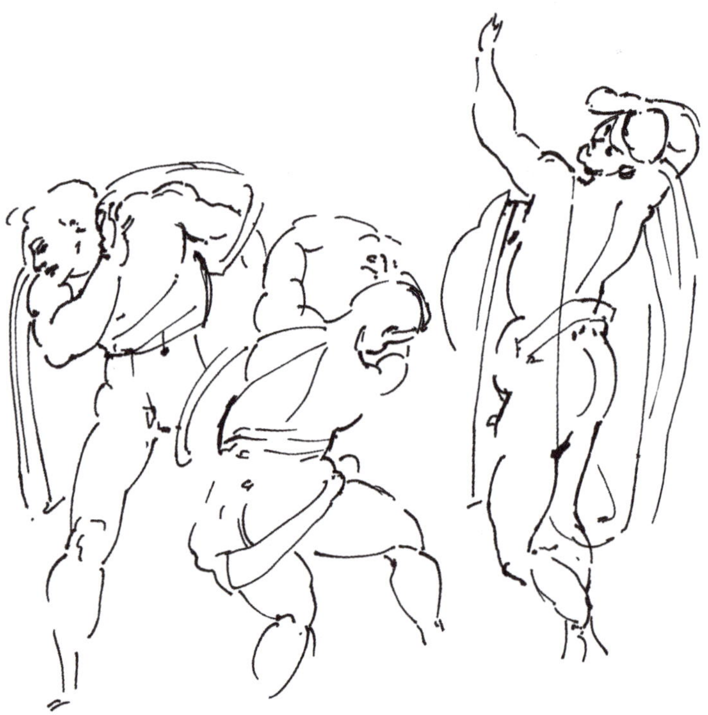

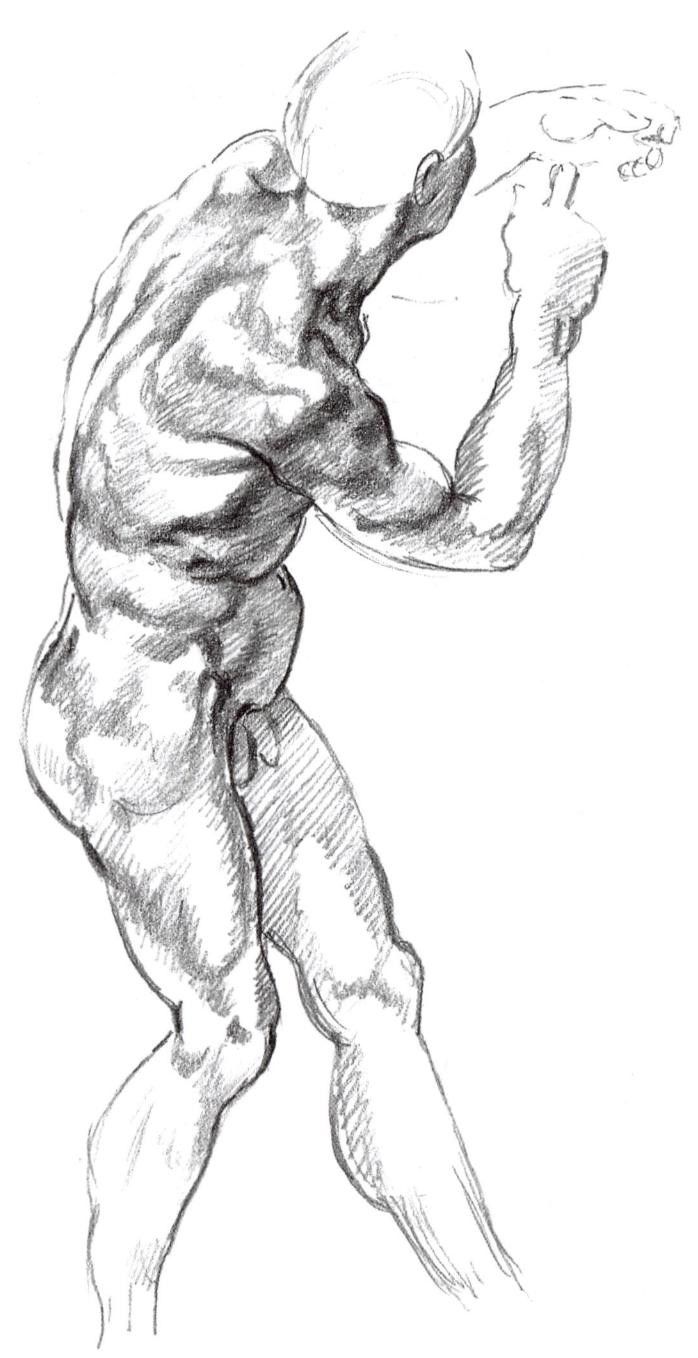

Giorgione

This picture, after one from the Accademia in Venice, is by the Venetian artist Giorgione (1477–1510). *Old Woman* (*c.*1505) is one of the best portraits of old age ever made. Possibly an allegorical work – the woman holds a piece of paper on which is written *col tempo* ('in time') while pointing to herself – it reminds the viewer that old age comes to everyone, beautiful or not. The quality of the skin and features has to be seen to be believed; Giorgione is a prime example of the Venetian genius for painted textures.

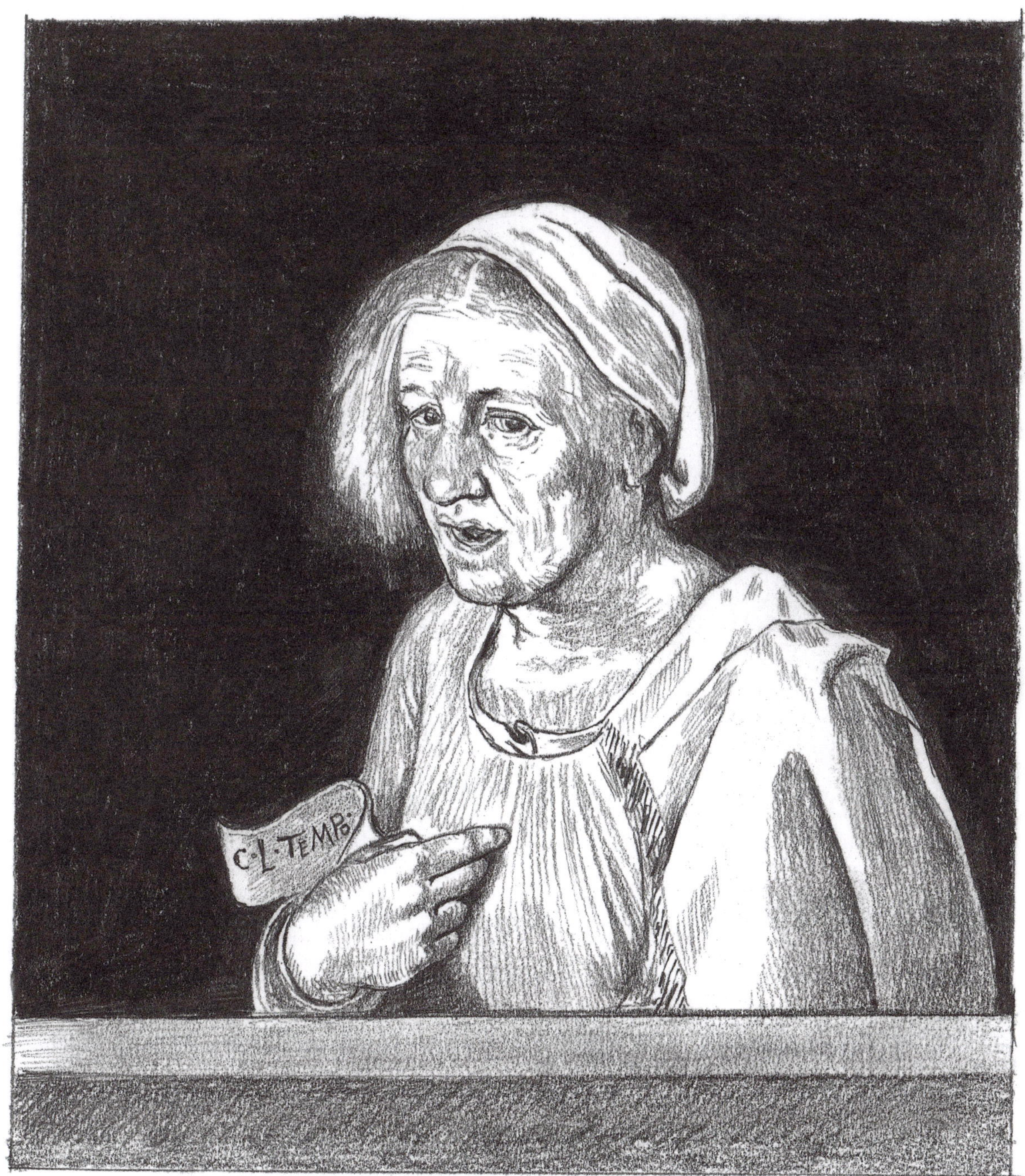

16th- and 17th-century Masters

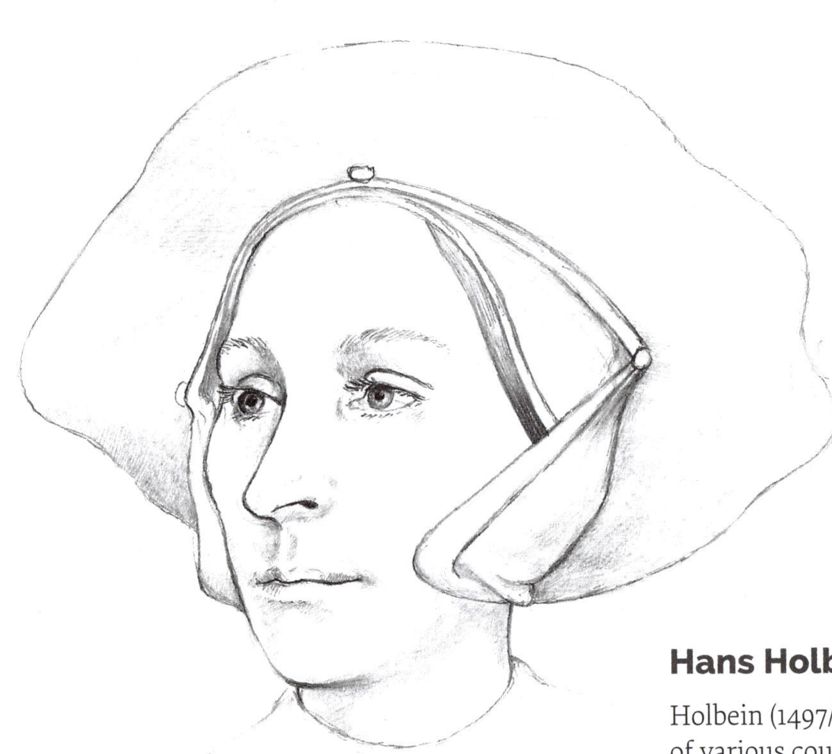

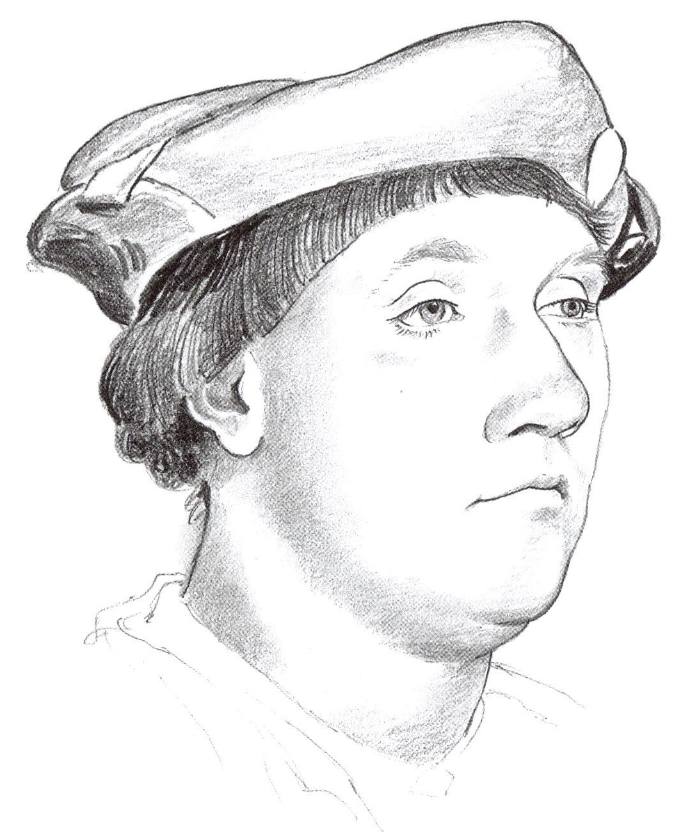

Hans Holbein the Younger

Holbein (1497/8–1543) left behind some extraordinarily subtle portrait drawings of various courtiers whom he painted during his time as court painter to Henry VIII. These works are now in the Queen's Collection (most of them at Windsor Castle, but some are in the Queen's Gallery at Buckingham Palace), and are worth studying for their brilliant subtle modelling. These subjects have no wrinkles to hang their character on, and their portraits are like those of children, with very little to show other than the shape of the head, the eyes, nostrils, mouth and hair. Holbein has achieved this quality by drastically reducing the modelling of the form and putting in just enough information to make the eye accept his untouched areas as the surfaces of the face. We tend to see what we expect to see. A good artist uses this to his or her advantage. So, less is more.

Peter Paul Rubens

Now let us look at a delicately executed chalk drawing by Rubens (1577–1640), who was referred to as a prince of painters. Before he produced his rich, flowing paintings, full of bravura and baroque asymmetry, he would make many informative sketches to clarify his composition. These sketches are soft and realistic, with the faintest of marks in some areas and precise modelling in others.

The rather gentle touch of the chalk belies the powerful composition of the figures. When completed the paintings were full and rich in form. His understanding of when to add emphasis and when to allow the slightest marks to do the work is masterly.

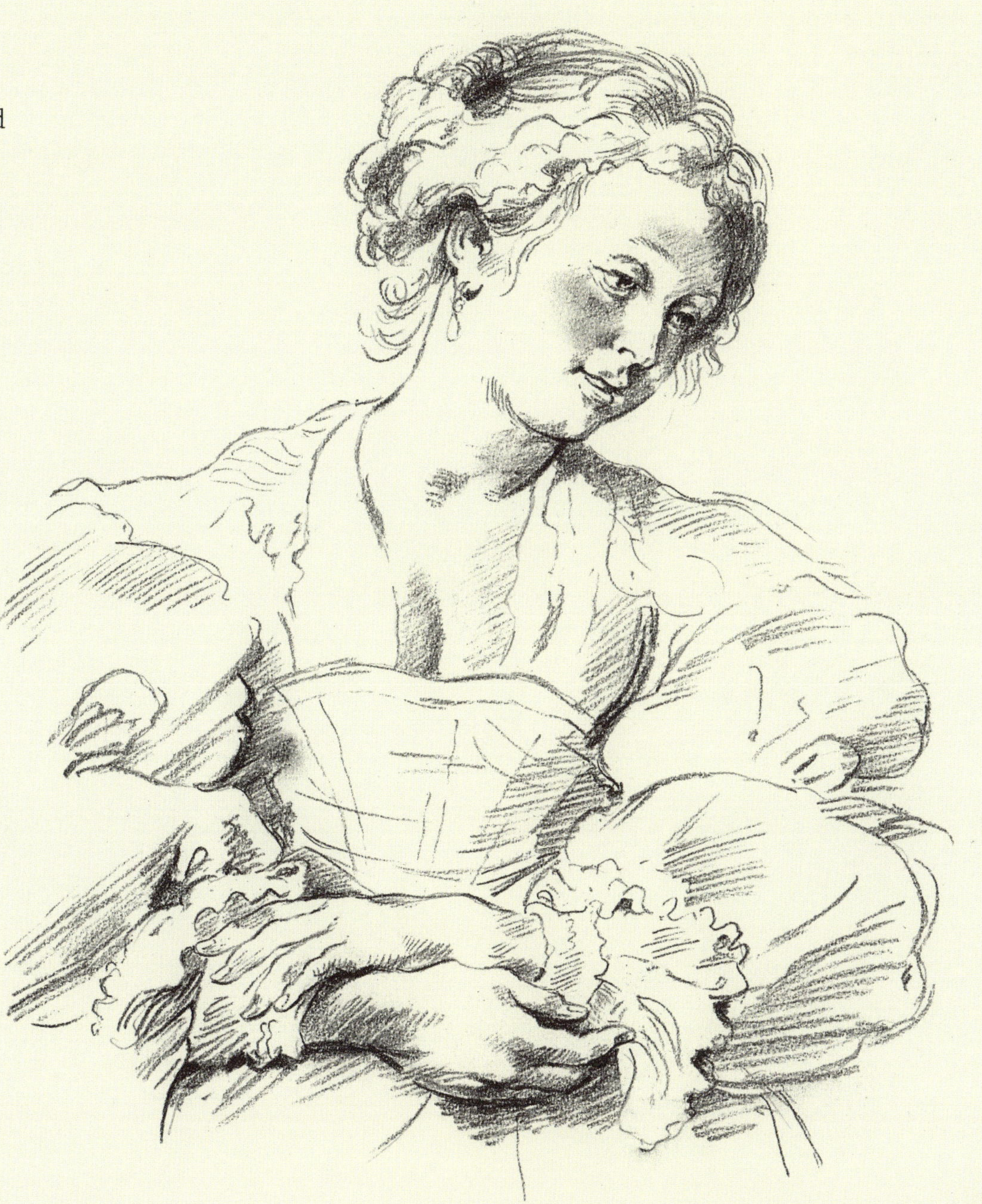

Rembrandt van Rijn

The drawings of Rembrandt (1606–69) probably embody all the qualities that any modern artist would wish to possess. His quick sketches are dashing, evocative and capture a fleeting action or emotion with enormous skill. His more careful drawings are like architecture, with every part of the structure clear and working one hundred per cent. Notice how his line varies with intention, sometimes putting in the least possible and at other times leaving nothing to chance. What tremendous skill!

To emulate Rembrandt we have to carefully consider how he has constructed his drawings. In some of his drawings the loose trailing line, with apparently vague markings to build up the form, are in fact the result of very clear and accurate observation. The dashing marks in some of his other, quicker sketches show exactly what is most necessary to get across the form and movement of the subject. Lots of practice is needed to achieve this level of draughtsmanship.

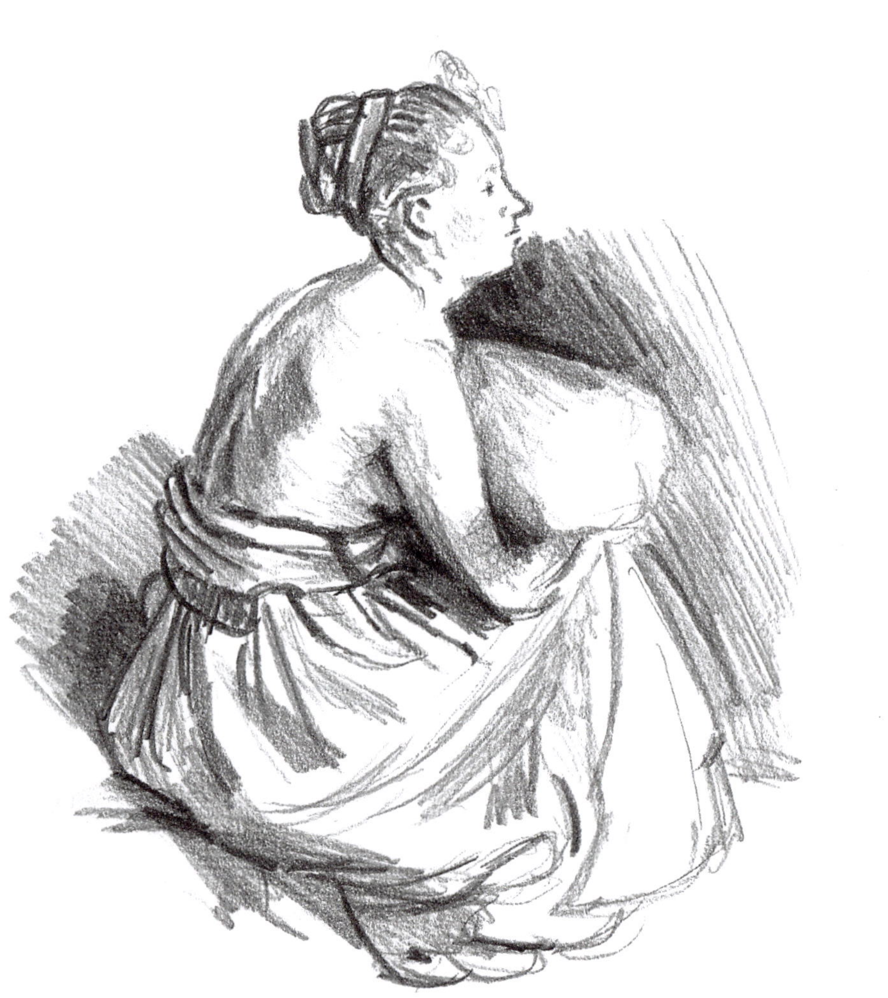

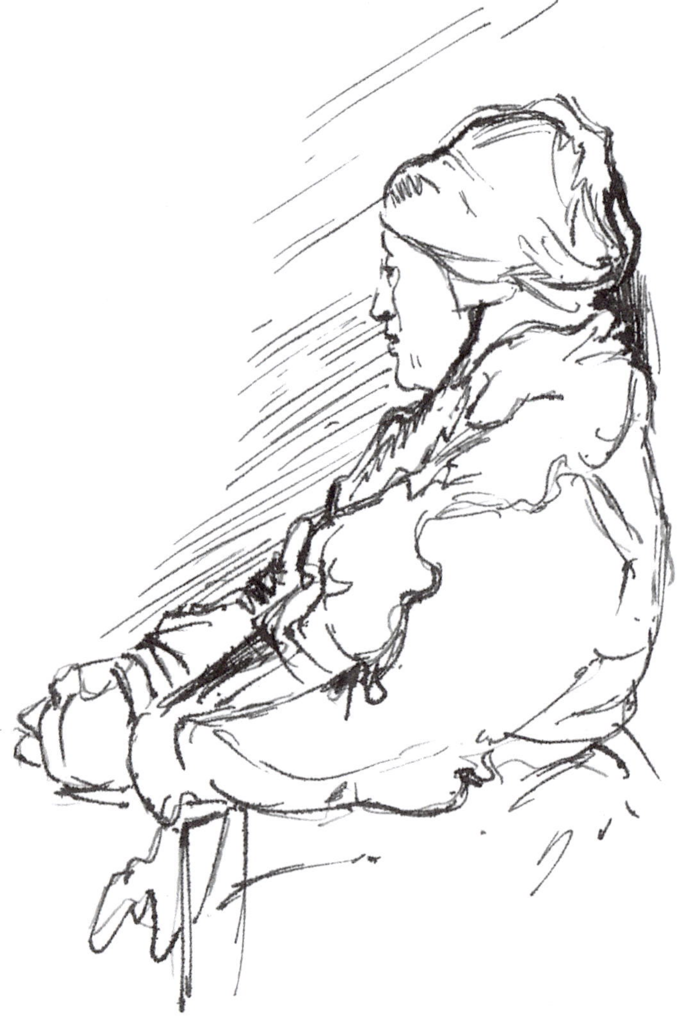

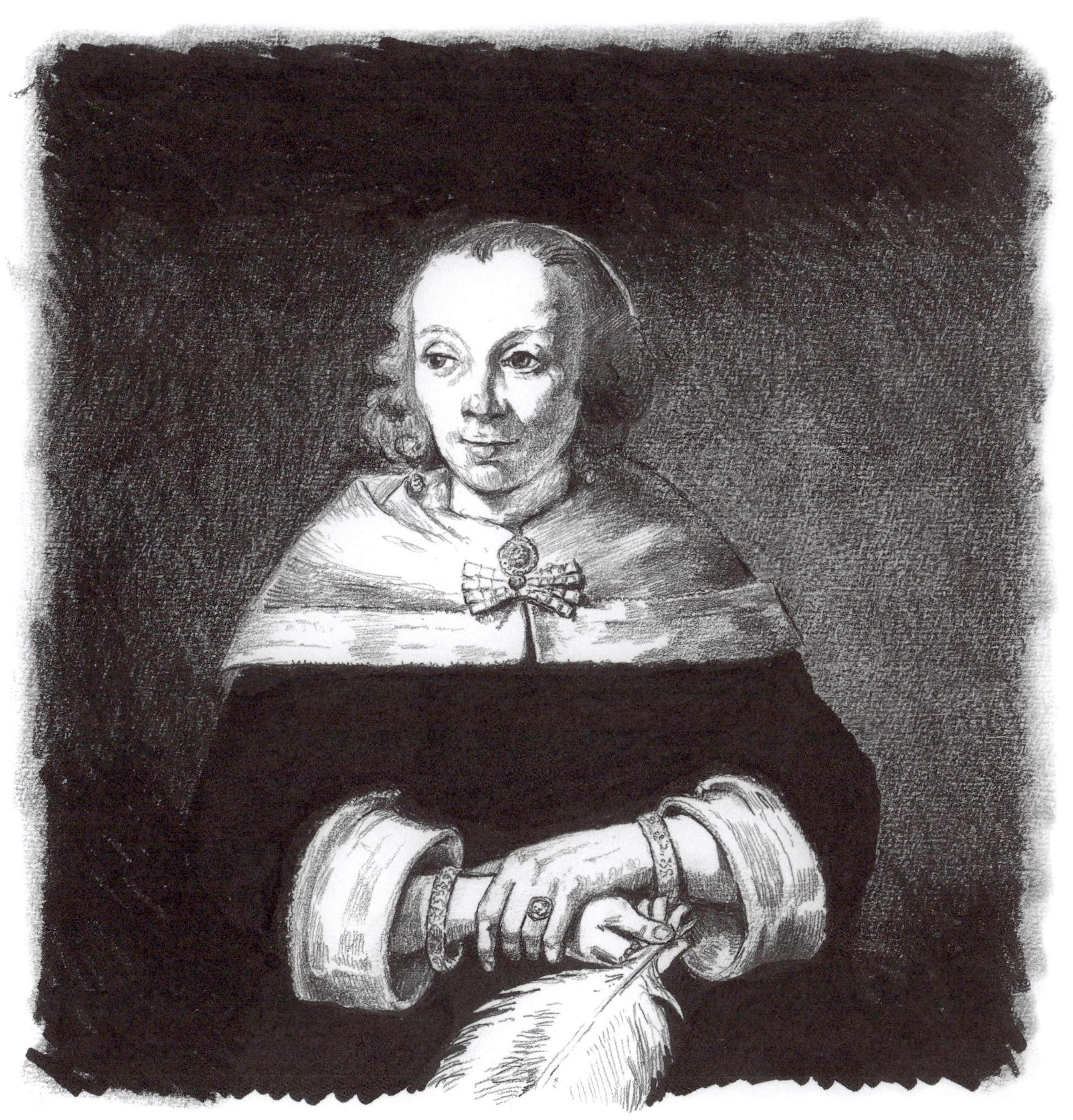

This painting, made in 1660, is called *Portrait of a Lady with an Ostrich-Feather Fan* and the sitter was probably the wife or daughter of some rich merchant.

Notice how strongly Rembrandt has lit the face and hands and reduced the rest of the composition to dark shapes in a shadowy space. The lighting gives strong modelling to the woman's features, and so the sense of a real person sitting before you is very compelling. The portrait is like a high-contrast black and white photograph in its intensity.

18th- and 19th-century Masters

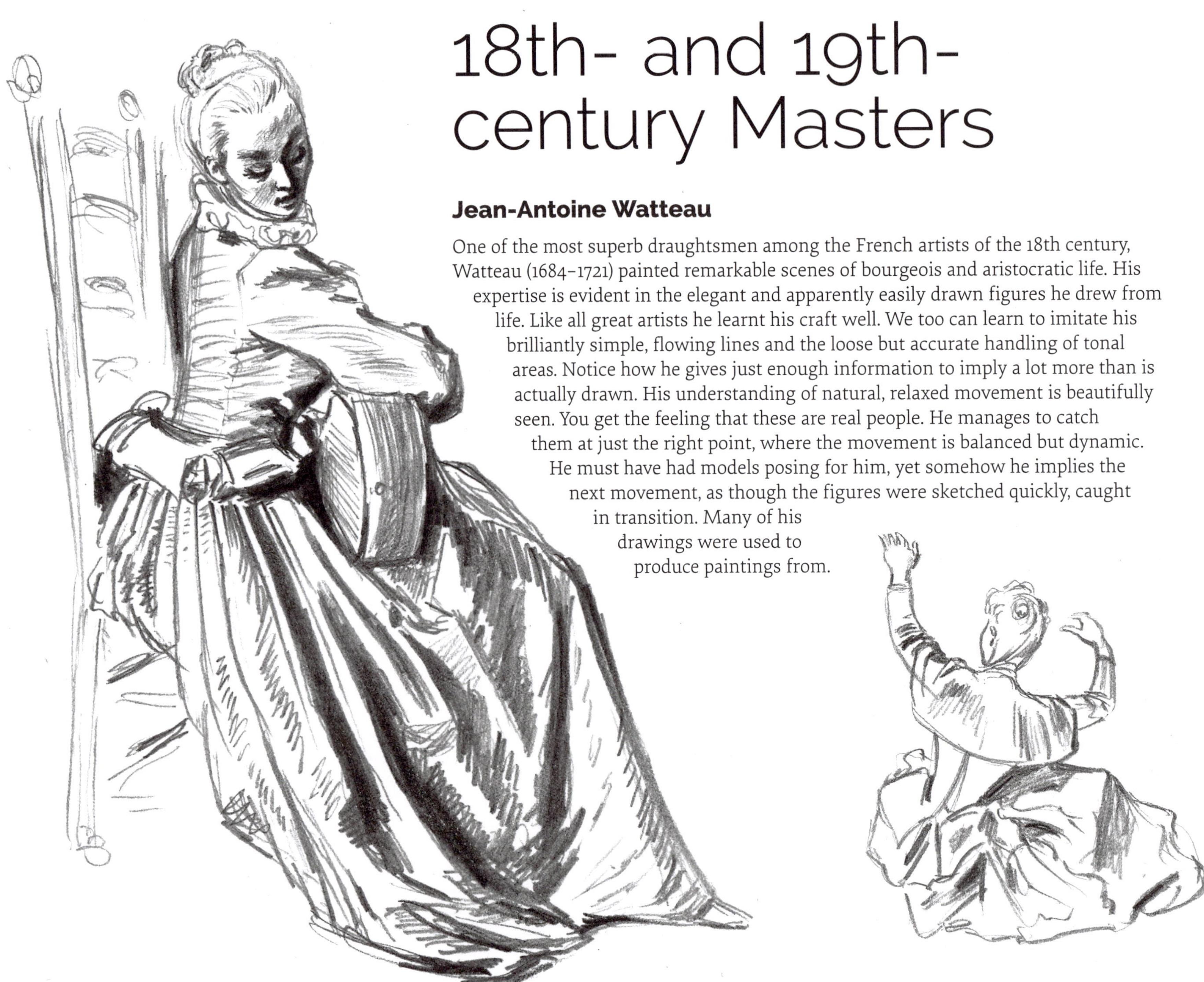

Jean-Antoine Watteau

One of the most superb draughtsmen among the French artists of the 18th century, Watteau (1684–1721) painted remarkable scenes of bourgeois and aristocratic life. His expertise is evident in the elegant and apparently easily drawn figures he drew from life. Like all great artists he learnt his craft well. We too can learn to imitate his brilliantly simple, flowing lines and the loose but accurate handling of tonal areas. Notice how he gives just enough information to imply a lot more than is actually drawn. His understanding of natural, relaxed movement is beautifully seen. You get the feeling that these are real people. He manages to catch them at just the right point, where the movement is balanced but dynamic. He must have had models posing for him, yet somehow he implies the next movement, as though the figures were sketched quickly, caught in transition. Many of his drawings were used to produce paintings from.

Giovanni Battista Tiepolo

Tiepolo (1696–1770) is noted for his painted walls and, particularly, ceilings. Although difficult to emulate, his methods of drawing are worth studying. Loose, scrawling lines are accompanied by splashes of wash to give them solidity. What appear to be little more than scribbles add up to wonderful examples of a master draughtsman's first thoughts on a painting. Compare his drawings closely with his elegant paintings and you will see premonitions of the latter in the former.

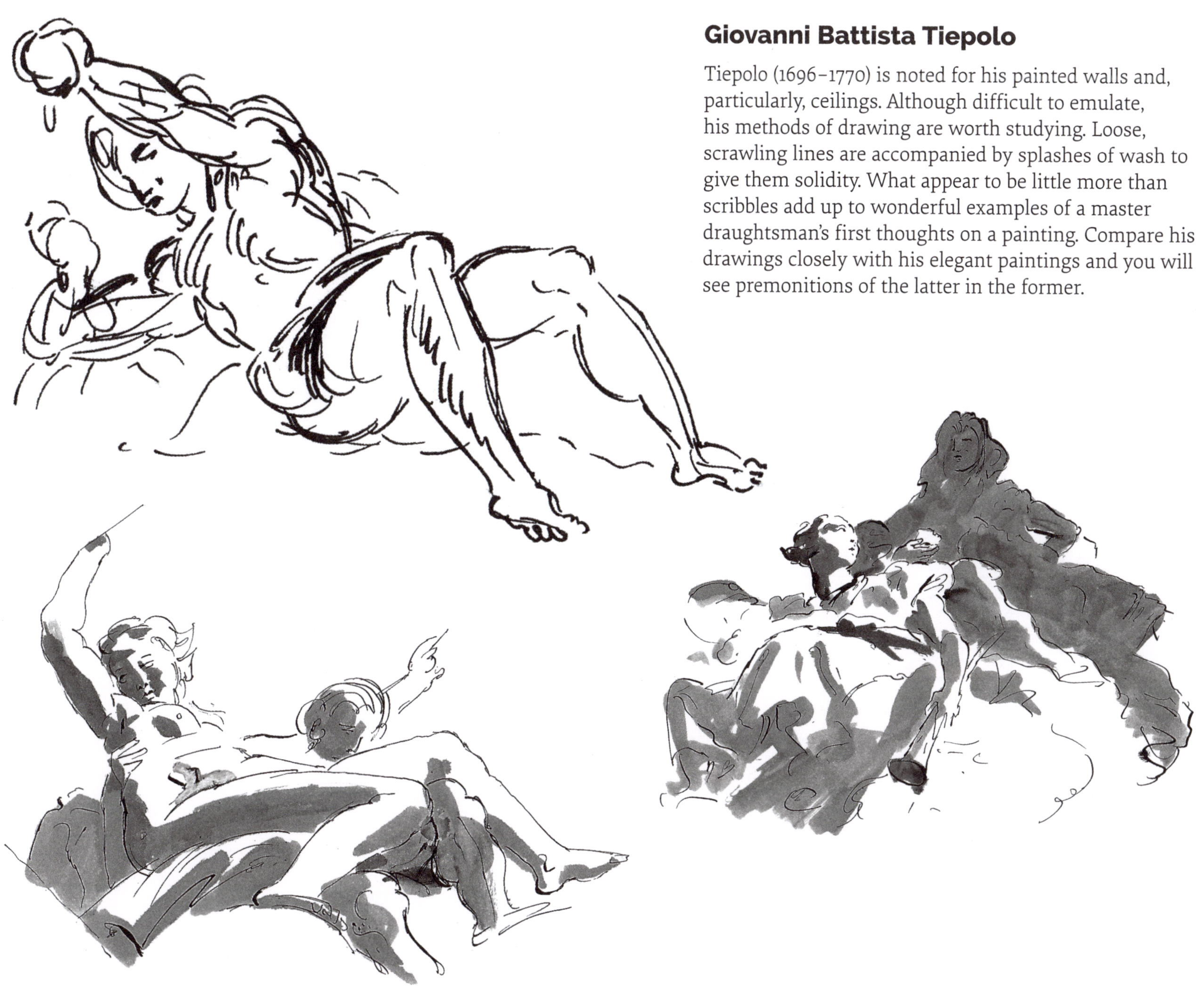

Jean-Auguste-Dominique Ingres

Ingres was noted for his draughtsmanship. His drawings are perfect even when unfinished, having a precision about them which is unusual. The incisive elegance of his line and the beautifully modulated tonal shading produce drawings that are as convincing as photographs. Unlike Watteau's, his figures never appear to be moving, but are held still and poised in an endless moment.

The student who would like to emulate this type of drawing could very well draw from photographs to start with, and when this practice has begun to produce a consistently convincing effect, then try using a live model. The model would have to be prepared to sit for a lengthy period, however, because this type of drawing can't be hurried. The elegance of Ingres was achieved by slow, careful drawing of outlines and shapes and subtle shading.

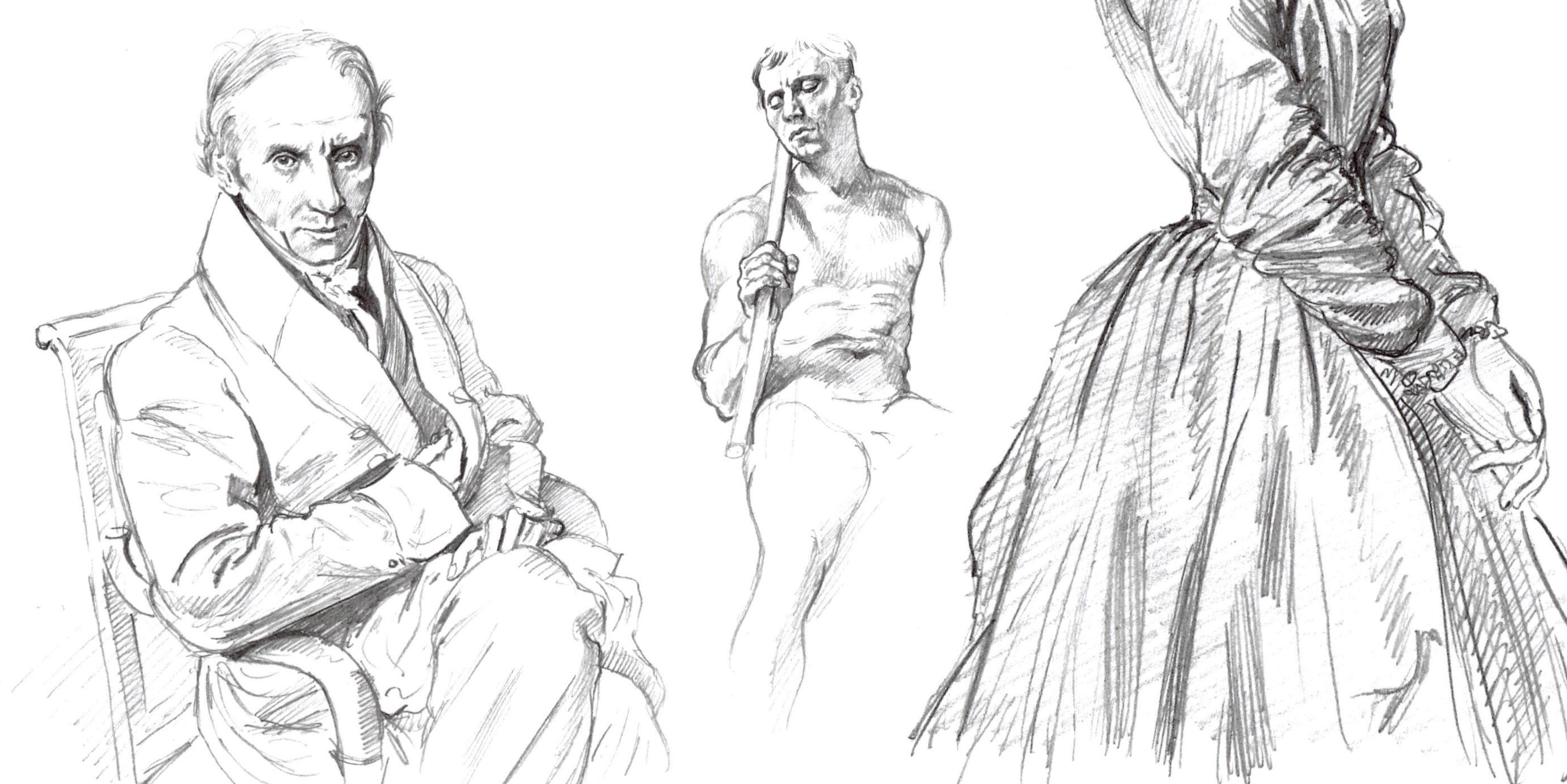

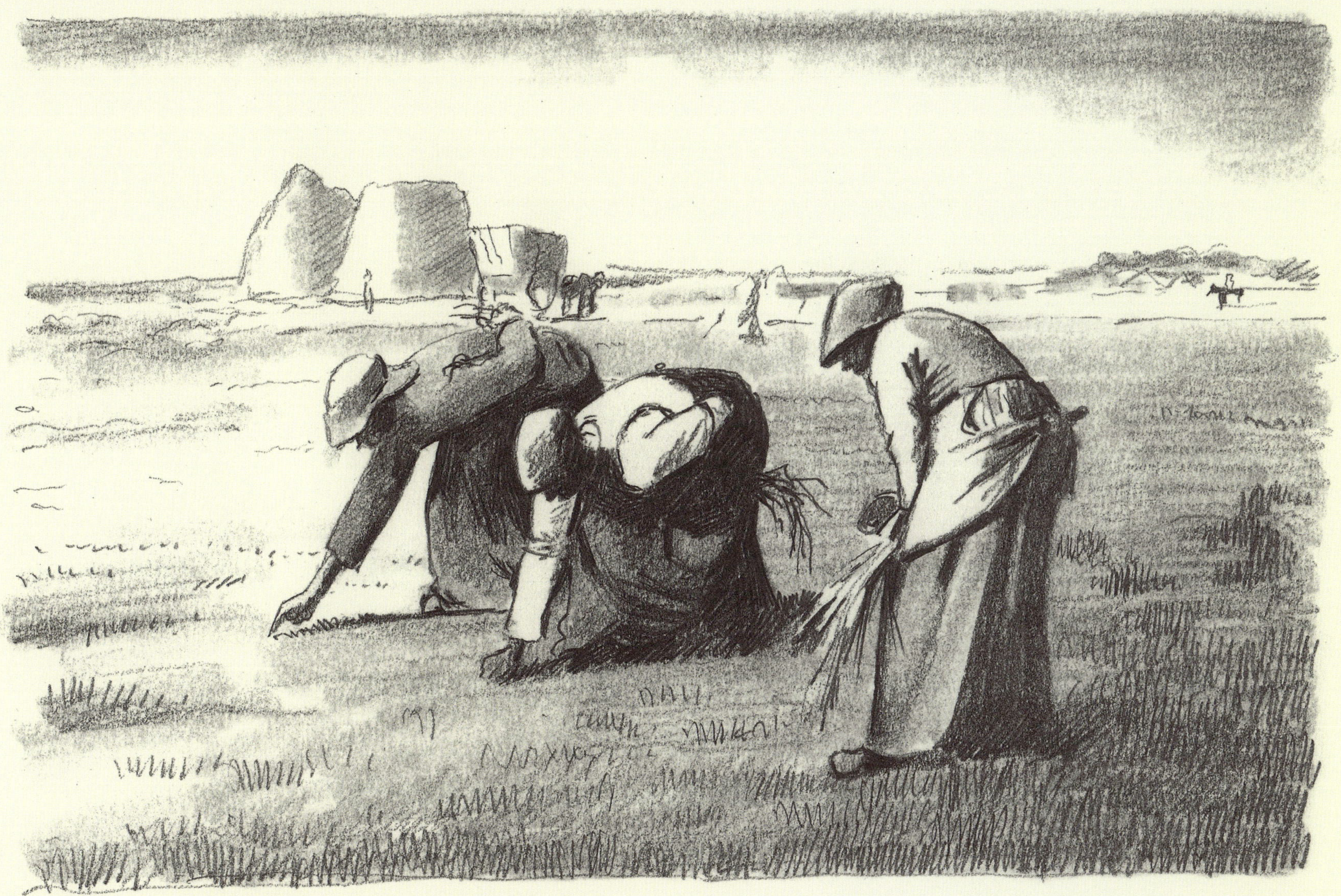

Jean-François Millet

The French artist Jean-François Millet (1814–75) was concerned with depicting peasant life and the dignity of manual labour. With Millet, realism had arrived; *The Gleaners* (1857) honoured the lowliest of rural dwellers – those who could only pick up the harvest leftovers. This master influenced Vincent van Gogh (see page 252) 30 years later, while the Dutchman drew and painted the peasants of northern Holland. Millet's three women have a monumental quality; the shapes they create as they bend to their task are echoed by the ample haystacks on the horizon.

Edouard Manet

Edouard Manet was one of the leading lights of the French Impressionist movement. His famous painting *Olympia* (1863), the portrait of a Parisian courtesan, shocked audiences when it was first exhibited. The style and pose pay tribute to earlier depictions of feminine beauty by artists such as Titian and Giorgione, but Manet came in for much criticism because he didn't try to conceal the girl's lifestyle under the guise of a goddess or nymph. This meant he was challenging the Parisian art critics to recognize that real life was as much the stuff of art as any mythological subject matter.

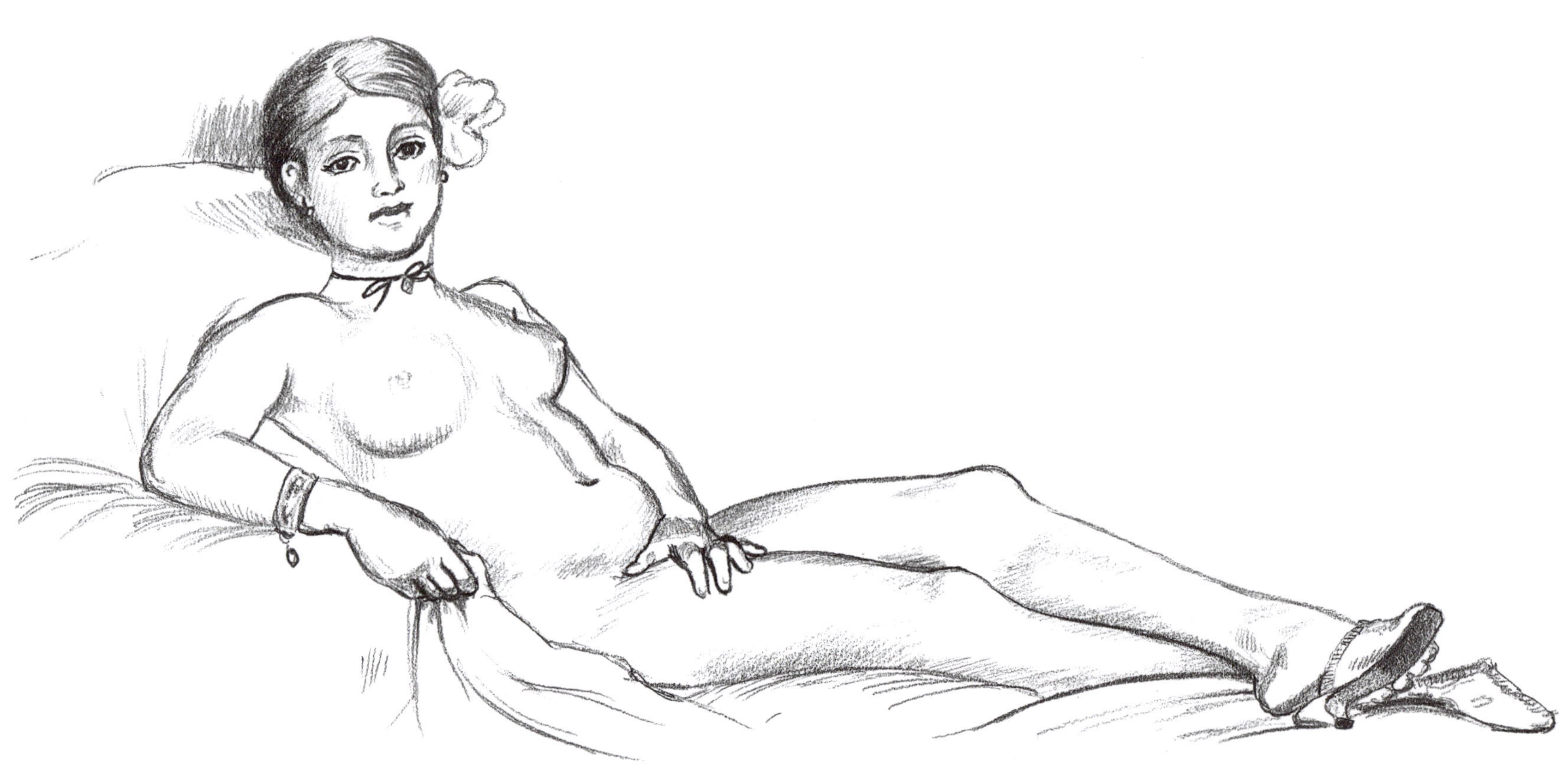

Edgar Degas

Degas was taught by a pupil of Ingres, and studied drawing in Italy and France until he was the most expert draughtsman of all the Impressionists. His loose flowing lines, often repeated several times to get the exact feel, look simple but are inordinately difficult to master. The skill evident in his paintings and drawings came out of continuous practice. He declared that his epitaph should be 'He greatly loved drawing'. He would often trace and retrace his own drawings in order to get the movement and grace he was after. Hard work and constant efforts to improve his methods honed his natural talent.

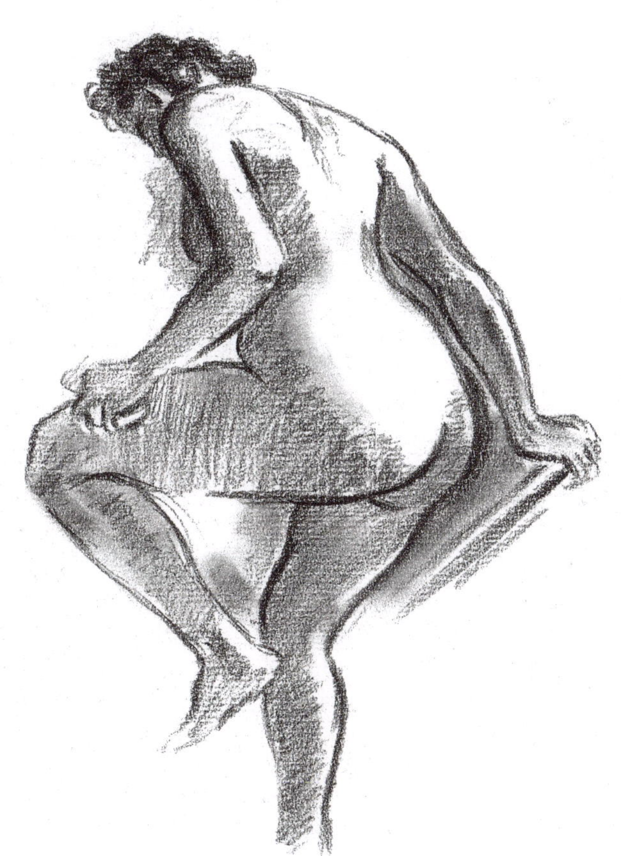

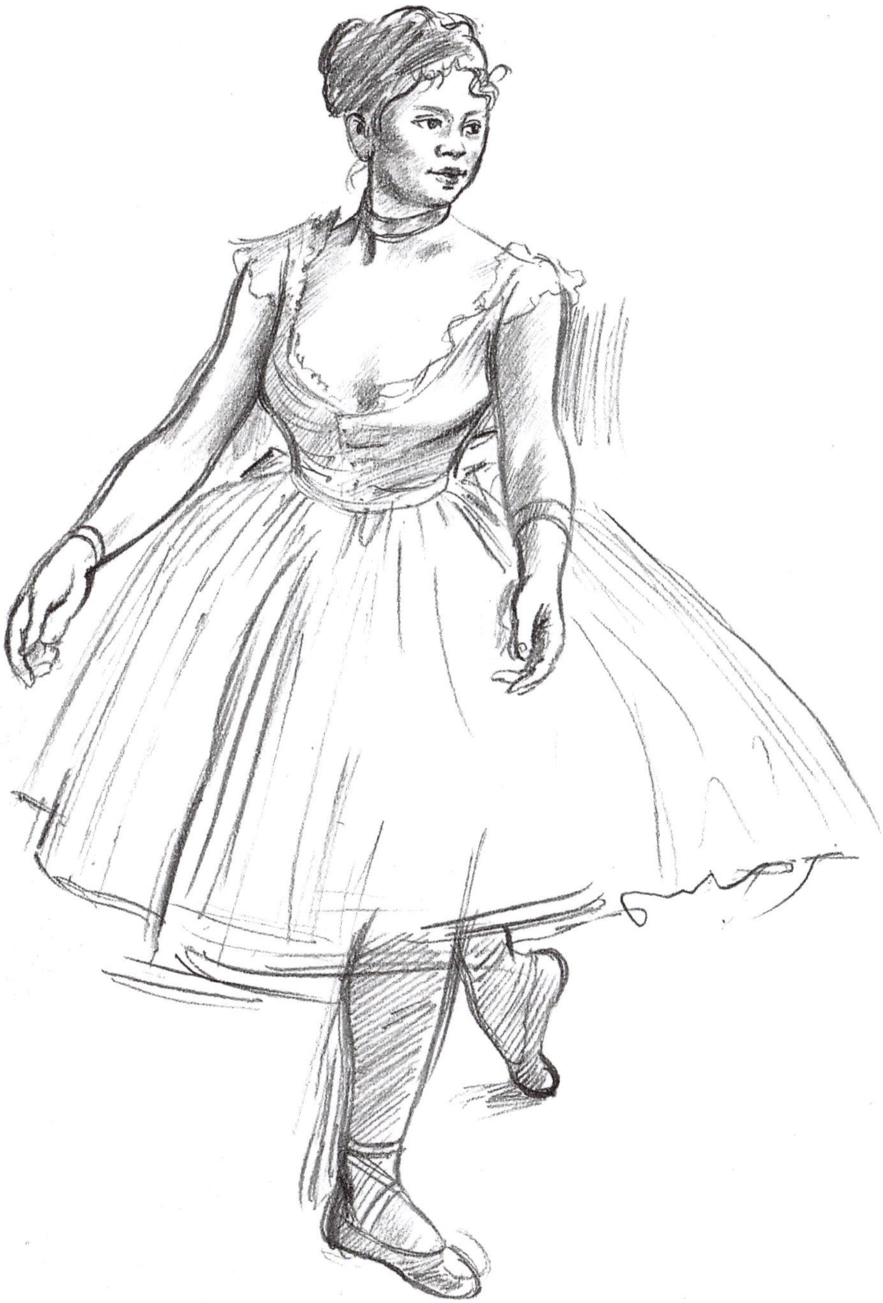

Vincent van Gogh

This portrait by the famous Post-Impressionist artist Vincent van Gogh shows a woman from Arles in the south of France. It is painted with great vigour and intense colour that was typical of van Gogh's later work. Van Gogh's paintings were more stylistic than realistic, the dramatic definition of the shape, and here, the quality of the colour, being more important than handling of depth or photographic realism.

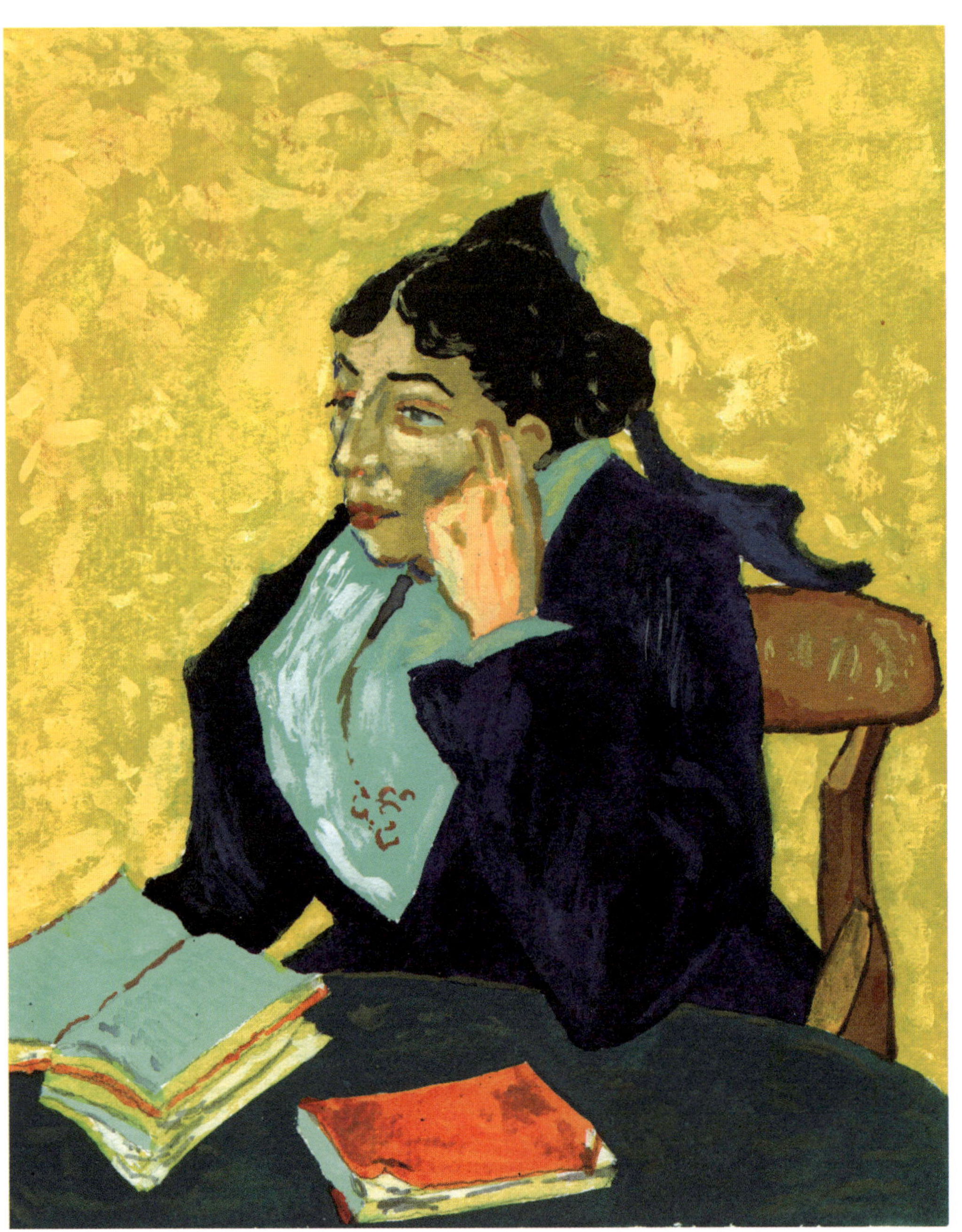

Artist's Note

The original of this painting is in oil paint; my copy is in gouache. Gouache is a water-based paint that can be painted quite densely, like oils. If you want to try your hand at painting, gouache is a good, easy-to-use alternative to oils.

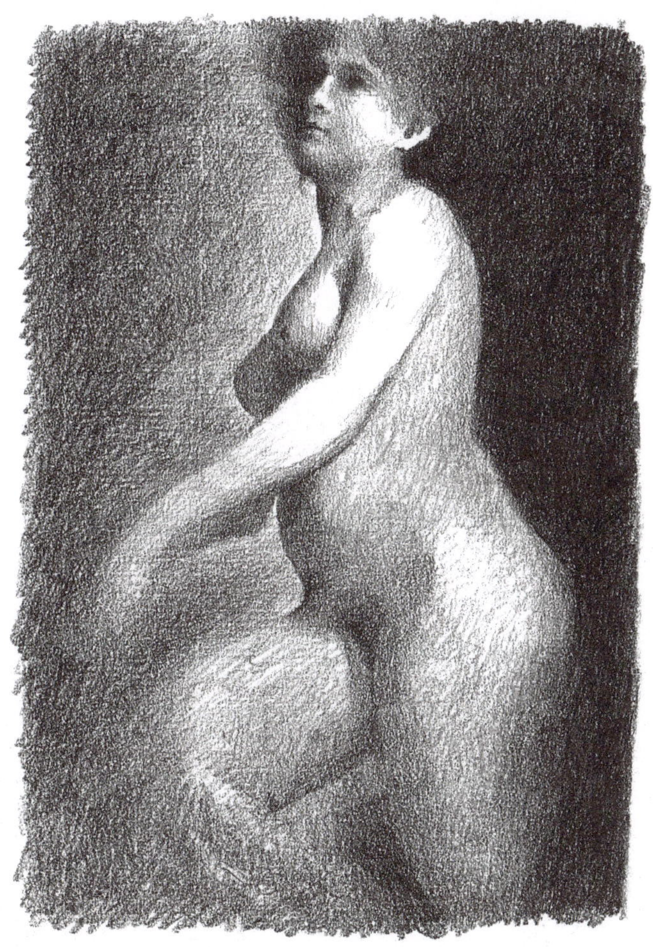

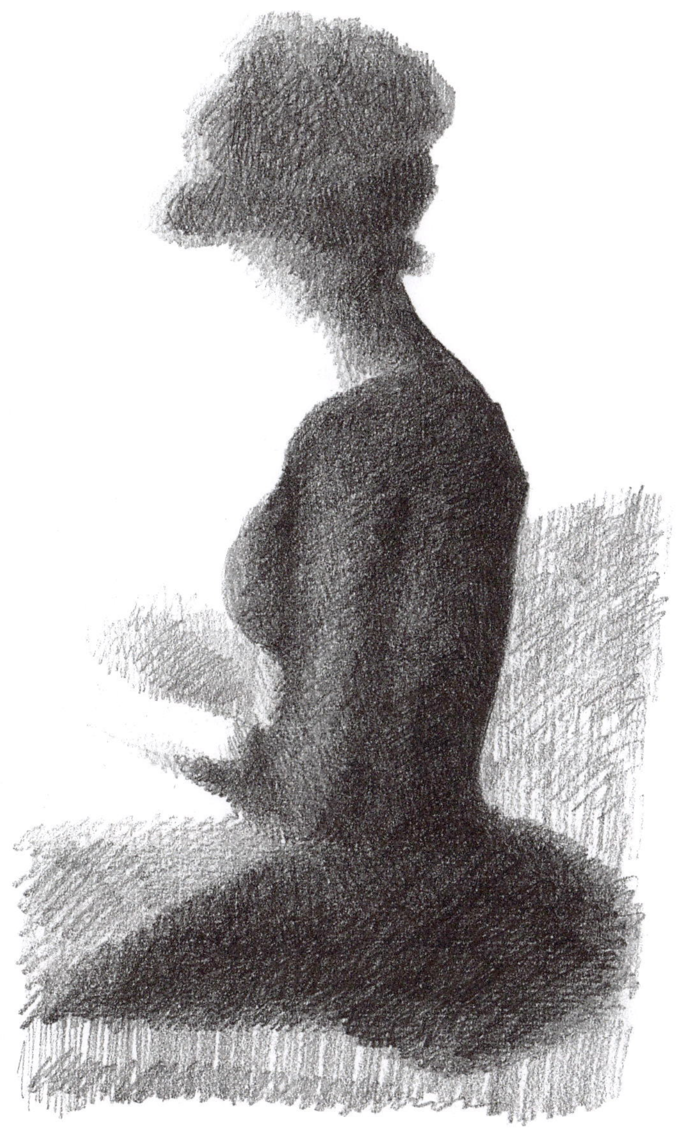

Georges Seurat

This style of drawing by Seurat (1859–91) is very different from what we have seen so far, mainly because he was so interested in producing a mass or area of shape that he reduced many of his drawings to tone alone. In these pictures there are no real lines but large areas of graduated tone rendered in charcoal, conté or thick pencil on faintly grainy textured paper. Their beauty is that they convey both substance and atmosphere while leaving a lot to the viewer's imagination. The careful grading of tone is instructive, as is how one mass can be made to work against a lighter area.

Henri de Toulouse-Lautrec

Next is a graphic representation of the singer Aristide Bruant, drawn by Toulouse-Lautrec for a lithographed poster in 1893. The elegance of the line contrasts with the solid mass of dark tones to produce a high-impact image. The flat expanses of colour were originally designed to be overprinted with poster lettering, depending on the venue at which Bruant was giving his performance.

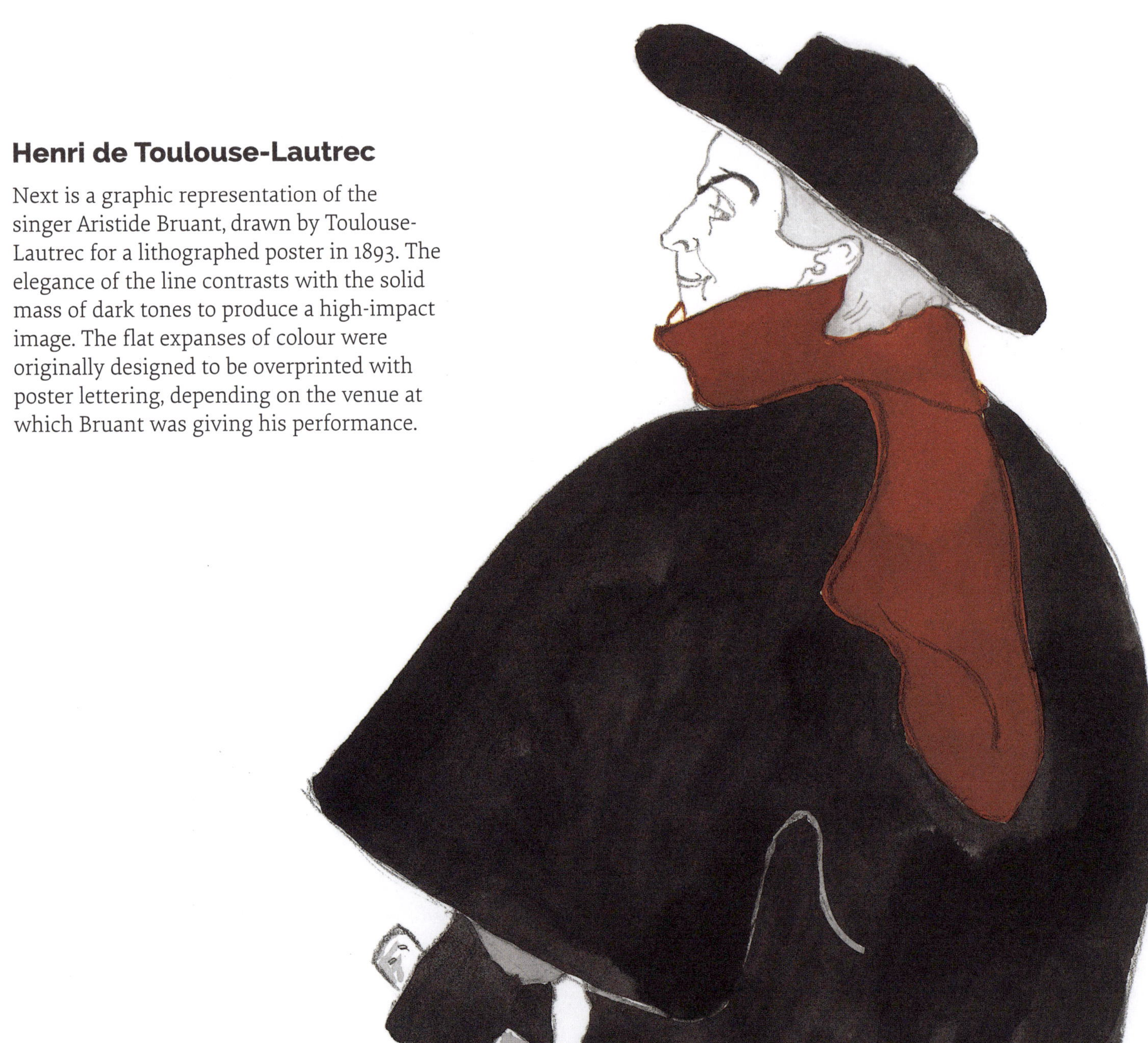

Gustav Klimt

Here I show a drawing based on *Expectation* by the Viennese Secessionist Gustav Klimt (1862–1918). It comes from the Stoclet Frieze (1905–11), a mural of mosaic decorations that Klimt designed for the Palais Stoclet in Brussels. Patterns abound both across and behind the female figure and set up a fascinating exchange between figure and ground. The stylized depiction of the figure in some ways harks back to images by artists working centuries earlier, but it also marks a departure into the modern era.

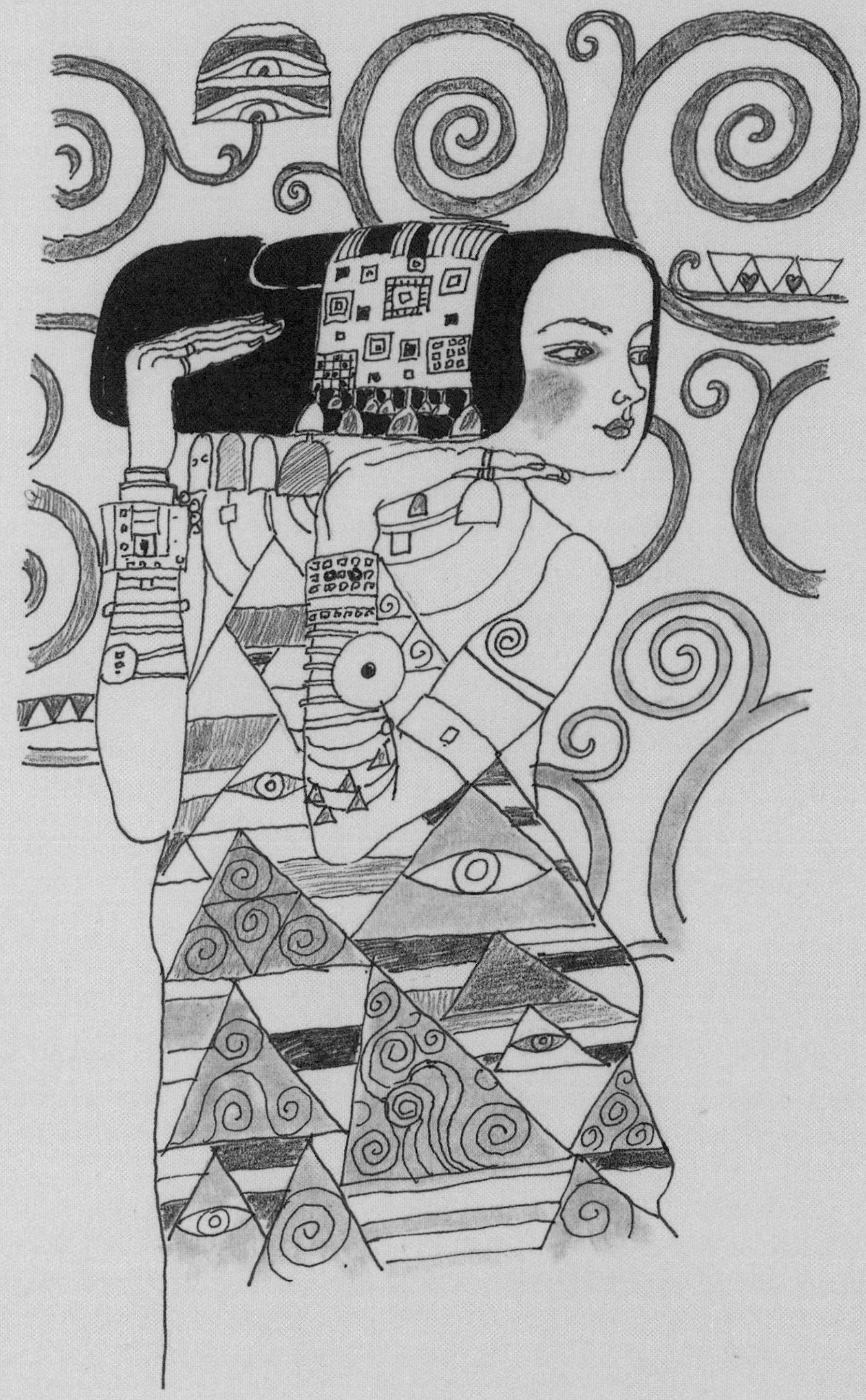

Index